Microsoft®

MCAD/MCSD
Self-Paced Training Kit

2
Second Edition

DEVELOPING
WEB APPLICATIONS
WITH MICROSOFT®
VISUAL BASIC® .NET
AND MICROSOFT
VISUAL C#® .NET

Exams
70-305 and 70-315

Microsoft®
.net™

Jeff Webb
with Microsoft Corporation

PUBLISHED BY
Microsoft Press
A Division of Microsoft Corporation
One Microsoft Way
Redmond, Washington 98052-6399

Library of Congress Cataloging-in-Publication Data
Webb, Jeff, 1961-
MCAD/MCSD Self-Paced Training Kit: Developing Web Applications with Microsoft
Visual Basic .NET and Microsoft Visual C# .NET/ Microsoft Corporation with Jeff
Webb--2nd ed.
     p. cm.
   Rev. ed of: MCAD/MCSD Self-Paced Training Kit: Developing Web Applications with
Microsoft Visual Basic .NET and Microsoft Visual C# .NET: Exams 70-305 and 70-315/
Microsoft. c2002.
    ISBN 0-7356-1927-1
     1. Electronic data processing personnel--Certification. 2.Microsoft
software--Examinations--Study guides. 3. Microsoft .NET Framework. 4. Microsoft
Windows (Computer file). I. Title: Developing Web applications with Microsoft Visual
Basic .NET and Microsoft Visual C# .NET. II. Microsoft Corporation. III.
MCAD/MCSD Self-Paced Training Kit. Developing Web Applications with Microsoft
Visual Basic .NET and Microsoft Visual C# .NET: Exams 70-305 and 70-315. IV. Title.

QA76.3.W462 2003
005.2'768--dc21   2003042220

Printed and bound in the United States of America.

2 3 4 5 6 7 8 9   QWT   8 7 6 5

Distributed in Canada by H.B. Fenn and Company Ltd.

A CIP catalogue record for this book is available from the British Library.

Microsoft Press books are available through booksellers and distributors worldwide. For further information about international editions, contact your local Microsoft Corporation office or contact Microsoft Press International directly at fax (425) 936-7329. Visit our Web site at www.microsoft.com/mspress. Send comments to *tkinput@microsoft.com*.

Acquisitions Editor: Kathy Harding
Project Editor: Aileen Wrothwell
Technical Editor: Jack Beaudry
Copy Editor: Jennifer Harris
Game Development: Michel Pahud
Body Part No. X09-46540

Contents

About This Book

Welcome to *MCAD/MCSD Self-Paced Training Kit: Developing Web Applications with Microsoft Visual Basic .NET and Microsoft Visual C# .NET*. By completing the lessons and exercises in this book, you will acquire the skills and knowledge necessary to develop Web-based applications in Microsoft Visual Basic .NET or Microsoft Visual C#.

This book is designed for developers interested in developing Web applications at an intermediate and advanced level. It includes developing server-based applications that use the .NET Framework to present HTML content and retrieve data from client browsers running over the Internet.

This book also addresses the objectives of the Microsoft Certified Professional Exam 70-305 and Exam 70-315. Programming is a conceptual skill that requires hands-on practice as well as familiarity with many facts. This training kit provides that practice in the form of labs at the end of each chapter. In order to be prepared for the Microsoft Certified Professional Exam 70-305 or 70-315 you must complete these labs. In some cases this will require use of additional materials—in particular the Visual Studio online Help.

Note For more information about becoming a Microsoft Certified Application Developer (MCAD) or a Microsoft Certified Solution Developer (MCSD), see the section titled "The Microsoft Certified Professional Program" later in this introduction.

The "Getting Started" section of this introduction provides important setup instructions that describe the hardware and software requirements to complete the exercises in this course. It also provides information about the networking configuration necessary to complete some of the hands-on exercises. Read through this section thoroughly before you start the lessons.

Intended Audience

This book was created for software developers who need to design, plan, implement and support Web applications or who plan to take the related Microsoft Certified Professional exams:

- *Developing and Implementing Web Applications with Microsoft Visual Basic .NET and Microsoft Visual Studio .NET* (Exam 70-305).
- *Developing and Implementing Web Applications with Microsoft Visual C# .NET and Microsoft Visual Studio .NET* (Exam 70-315).

Prerequisites

This course requires that students meet the prerequisites that follow.

- Be able to create Windows applications using Microsoft Visual Studio .NET in either the Visual Basic .NET or Visual C# .NET programming language.

- Have a basic understanding of the object-oriented programming concepts including classes, properties, methods, and events.
- Understand the fundamental elements in the Hypertext Markup Language (HTML) used to author Web content.
- Understand how Web content is stored and accessed over the Internet. This includes being able to explain the roles of Web servers, Internet protocols, and Web clients (such as browsers).

Reference Materials

You might find the following reference materials useful:

- The Visual Studio .NET online Help
- The World Wide Web Consortium Web site (*http://www.w3c.org*)
- The Microsoft ASP.NET public newsgroup (*news://msnews.microsoft.com /microsoft.public.dotnet.framework.aspnet*)

About the CD-ROM

The Supplemental Course Materials CD-ROM contains a variety of informational aids that may be used throughout this book:

- **eBook.**   A complete electronic version (eBook) of this training kit.
- **Lesson samples.**   Most lessons in this training kit include sample Web forms and other files that demonstrate the code shown in the training kit. These samples are organized into two Visual Studio solutions named MCSDWebAppsVB, for the Visual Basic .NET samples, and MCSDWebAppsCS, for the Visual C# samples.
- **Completed labs.**   Each chapter in this training kit concludes with a lab containing a series of exercises that reinforce the skills you learned. Completed versions of these applications are included in the chapter folders of the MCSD-WebAppsVB and MCSDWebAppsCS solutions so that you can compare your results. You can also use these completed applications as a reference if you get stuck while completing an exercise.
- **Required files.**   Practice files, such as sample databases, that are required to perform the hands-on procedures. You should use these files when indicated in the exercises.
- **Sample exam questions.**   To practice taking a certification exam, you can use the sample exam installed by the CD-ROM. The sample questions help you assess your understanding of the materials presented in this book.

About the DVD

The DVD contains a 60-day evaluation edition of Microsoft Visual Studio .NET Professional.

Caution   The 60-day Evaluation Edition provided with this training is not the full retail product and is provided only for the purposes of training and evaluation. Microsoft Technical Support does not support this evaluation edition.

For additional support information regarding this book and the CD-ROM and DVD (including answers to commonly asked questions about installation and use), visit the Microsoft Press Technical Support Web site at *http://www.microsoft.com /mspress/support/*. You can also email tkinput@microsoft.com, or send a letter to Microsoft Press, Attn: Microsoft Press Technical Support, One Microsoft Way, Redmond, WA 98502-6399.

Features of This Book

Each chapter contains sections that are designed to help you get the most educational value from the chapter.

- Each chapter opens with a "Before You Begin" section, which prepares you for completing the chapter.
- The chapters are then divided into lessons. Each lesson contains the reference and procedural information used for a specific skill.
- The "Summary" section identifies the key concepts from the lesson.
- The "Lab" section provides hands-on exercises that reinforce each of the skills taught in each of the chapter lessons. The exercises give you an opportunity to use the skills being presented or explore the part of the application being described. Wherever possible, the exercises in a lab build on each other to create a complete application by the end of that lab.
- The exercises offer step-by-step procedures that are identified with a bullet symbol like the one to the left of this paragraph.
- At the end of each chapter is the "Review" section that you can use to test what you have learned.

The appendix, "Questions and Answers," contains all of the questions asked in each chapter review and the corresponding answers.

Notes

Several types of Notes appear throughout the lessons.

- Notes marked **Tip** contain explanations of possible results or alternative methods for performing tasks.
- Notes marked **Important** contain information that is essential to completing a task.
- Notes marked **Note** contain supplemental information.
- Notes marked **Caution** contain warnings about possible loss of data.

Notational Conventions

The following notational conventions are used throughout this book.

- Characters or commands that you type appear in **bold** type. Bold type is also used for glossary terms the first time they are defined in text.
- *Italic* in syntax statements indicates placeholders for variable information. *Italic* is also used for book titles, elements from the .NET Framework, and programming language keywords.

- Names of files and folders appear in initial capital letters, except when you are to type them directly. Unless otherwise indicated, you can use lowercase letters when you type a file name in a dialog box or at a command prompt.
- Filename extensions, when they appear without a file name, are in lowercase letters.
- Acronyms appear in all uppercase letters.
- Monospace type represents code samples, examples of screen text, or entries that you might type at a command prompt or in initialization files.
- Icons represent specific sections in the book as follows:

Icon	Represents
	Supplemental course materials. You will find these materials on the Supplemental Course Materials CD-ROM.
	A hands-on exercise. You should perform the exercise to give yourself an opportunity to use the skills being presented in the lesson.

Chapter and Appendix Overview

This self-paced training kit combines notes, hands-on procedures, and review questions to teach you how to create Web applications with Visual Studio .NET. It is designed to be completed from beginning to end, but you can choose a customized track and complete only the sections that interest you. (See the next section, "Finding the Best Starting Point for You," for more information.) If you choose the customized track option, see the "Before You Begin" section in each chapter. Any hands-on procedures that require preliminary work from preceding chapters refer to the appropriate chapters.

The book is divided into the following sections and chapters:

- The "About This Book" section contains an overview and introduces the components of this training kit. Read this section thoroughly to get the greatest educational value from this training kit and to plan which lessons you will complete.
- Chapter 1, "Introduction to Web Programming," introduces you to the concepts and terms used throughout this book, including how Web applications work, the parts of a Web application, how the .NET Framework is organized, and how to use the Visual Studio programming environment. The sections in this chapter are intended to provide a high-level overview of concepts that are explained in greater detail in subsequent chapters.
- Chapter 2, "Creating Web Forms Applications," teaches how to create a Web application using Visual Studio .NET and ASP.NET. You learn how to start a new project, create a basic user interface, write code to respond to events, and preserve data within your application. Because ASP.NET is integrated with Microsoft Internet Information Services (IIS), you also learn about IIS and how to use it to organize your Web application.

- Chapter 3, "Working with Web Objects," explains creating and organizing objects in Visual Studio .NET, using the objects provided by ASP.NET, and saving objects and data between requests to Web forms. Visual Basic, Visual C#, and ASP.NET are based on a common framework, so the object-oriented programming techniques you learn in this chapter apply through all aspects of .NET programming.

- Chapter 4, "Creating a User Interface," demonstrates how to use ASP.NET controls to create a user interface for a multi-page Web forms application. This chapter teaches you about different styles of Web forms, how to choose controls based on the tasks you want to perform, how to validate data fields, and how to navigate between the Web forms in your application.

- Chapter 5, "Storing and Retrieving Data with ADO.NET," shows how to use ADO.NET to access and modify data stored in SQL, OLE, and Oracle databases from Web forms. You learn about the data tools included with Visual Studio and how to use them to create connections to, get records from, and perform commands on databases. You will also learn how to display data on a Web form using either data binding or code. Finally, you learn how to use transactions to maintain the integrity of a database.

- Chapter 6, "Catching and Correcting Errors," explains how to deal with problems that may occur in your application due to external circumstances. This chapter helps you identify, anticipate, and handle these types of problems effectively within your application.

- Chapter 7, "Advanced Web Forms Programming," teaches how to perform advanced programming tasks that don't fit neatly into any other category. Although you can successfully create Web applications without knowing the topics covered in this chapter, the lessons found here are an important part of mainstream Web programming and they help complete your skill set.

- Chapter 8, "Maintaining Security," covers how to control access to your Web application using the three different techniques that ASP.NET provides for identifying and authorizing users. You also learn how to secure data transmitted across the Internet so that it cannot be read by others.

- Chapter 9, "Building and Deploying Web Applications," describes how to publish your completed Web applications on a Web server for general use. You also learn how to monitor and maintain the application once it is in use so that it continues to perform well as the demands of your users change.

- Chapter 10, "Testing Web Applications," teaches how to systematically test your Web application during development. You learn how to plan, create, run, and correct problems found by tests.

- Chapter 11, "Creating Custom Web Controls," demonstrates how to create your own, custom user-interface components. This chapter explains the different types of controls you can create, describes the relative advantages of each, and shows you how to create each different type of control.

- Chapter 12, "Optimizing Web Applications with Caching," shows how to store Web forms, parts of Web forms, and application data in cache to speed application responses and reduce the amount of processing the server must perform. This chapter also demonstrates how to monitor cache performance to determine whether or not you are using caching effectively.

- Chapter 13, "Formatting Web Application Output," teaches you how to format the user interface of a Web application using cascading style sheets (CSS) and Extensible Stylesheet Language Transformations (XSLT). This chapter explains the best uses for each formatting technique and tells you how to combine the two techniques.

- Chapter 14, "Providing Help," discusses the different ways that you can display user assistance (Help) from within a Web application. You learn how to use the HTML Help Workshop to create compiled Help files, and how to display those files from a Web application interactively.

- Chapter 15, "Globalizing Web Applications," explains how to detect a user's culture and create appropriate responses, ranging from redirecting the user to a separate, localized Web application, to handling cultural differences within code and displaying a localized user interface.

- The appendix, "Questions and Answers," lists all of the review questions from the book, showing the page number for each question and the suggested answer.

- The glossary provides definitions for many of the terms and concepts presented in this training kit.

Finding the Best Starting Point for You

Because this book is self-paced, you can skip some lessons and revisit them later. Use the following table to find the best starting point for you:

If you	Follow this learning path
Are preparing to take the Microsoft Certified Professional exam 70-305 or 70-315	Read the "Getting Started" section. Then work through Chapters 1-4. Work through the remaining chapters in any order.
Want to review information about specific topics from the exam	Use the "Where to Find Specific Skills in This Book" section that follows this table.

Where to Find Specific Skills in This Book

The following tables provide a list of the skills measured on certification Exam 70-305, *Developing and Implementing Web Applications with Microsoft Visual Basic .NET and Microsoft Visual Studio .NET*, or Exam 70-315, *Developing and Implementing Web Applications with Microsoft Visual C# .NET and Microsoft Visual Studio .NET*. The table provides the skill, and where in this book you will find the lesson relating to that skill.

Note Exam skills are subject to change without prior notice and at the sole discretion of Microsoft.

Table A-1   Creating User Services

Skill Being Measured	Location in Book
Create ASP.NET pages:	Chapter 2, Lesson 1
■ Add and set directives on ASP.NET pages	■ Chapter 1, Lesson 3; Chapter 6, Lessons 2 and 3; Chapter 11, Lessons 1 and 2; and Chapter 12, Lesson 1
■ Separate user interface resources from business logic	■ Chapter 3, Lesson 1
Add Web server controls, HTML server controls, user controls, and HTML code to ASP.NET pages:	Chapter 4, Lessons 1 and 2
■ Set properties on controls	■ Chapter 4, Lesson 1
■ Load controls dynamically	■ Chapter 4, Lesson 1
■ Apply templates	■ Chapter 4, Lesson 1, and Chapter 5, Lesson 2
■ Set styles on ASP.NET pages by using cascading style sheets	■ Chapter 13, Lesson 1
■ Instantiate and invoke an ActiveX control	■ Chapter 14, Lesson 2
Implement navigation for the user interface:	Chapter 4, Lesson 3; Chapter 2, Lesson 2; and Chapter 3, Lesson 3
■ Manage the view state	■ Chapter 3, Lesson 3
■ Manage data during post-back events	■ Chapter 3, Lesson 3
■ Use session state to manage data across pages	■ Chapter 3, Lesson 3
Validate user input:	Chapter 4, Lesson 2
■ Validate non-Latin user input	■ Chapter 15, Lesson 3
Implement error handling in the user interface:	Chapter 6, Lessons 1, 2, and 3
■ Configure custom error pages	■ Chapter 6, Lesson 2
■ Implement Global.asax, application, page- level, and page event error handling	■ Chapter 6, Lesson 2
Implement online user assistance	Chapter 14, Lessons 1, 2, and 3
Incorporate existing code into ASP.NET pages	Chapter 1, Lesson 2; Chapter 7, Lessons 2 and 3
Display and update data:	Chapter 4, Lesson 1; Chapter 5, Lesson 2
■ Transform and filter data	■ Chapter 5, Lessons 1 and 2; Chapter 13, Lesson 2
■ Bind data to the user interface	■ Chapter 4, Lesson 1; Chapter 5, Lesson 2
■ Use controls to display data	■ Chapter 4, Lesson 1
Instantiate and invoke Web services or components:	Chapter 7, Lesson 5
■ Instantiate and invoke a Web service	■ Chapter 7, Lesson 5
■ Instantiate and invoke a COM or COM+ component	■ Chapter 7, Lesson 3

(continued)

Table A-1   Creating User Services   *(continued)*

Skill Being Measured	Location in Book
■ Instantiate and invoke a .NET component	■ Chapter 3, Lesson 1; Chapter 7, Lesson 3
Implement globalization:	Chapter 15, Lessons 1, 2, and 3
■ Implement localizability for the user interface	■ Chapter 15, Lesson 2
■ Convert existing encodings	■ Chapter 15, Lesson 3
■ Implement right-to-left and left-to-right mirroring	■ Chapter 15, Lesson 1
■ Prepare culture-specific formatting	■ Chapter 15, Lesson 1
Handle events:	Chapter 2, Lesson 2
■ Create event handlers	■ Chapter 2, Lesson 2; Chapter 3, Lesson 1
■ Raise events	■ Chapter 3, Lesson 1; Chapter 11, Lesson 2
Implement accessibility features	Chapter 13, Lesson 1
Use and edit intrinsic objects, including response, request, session, server, and application:	Chapter 3, Lesson 2
■ Retrieve values from the properties of intrinsic objects	
■ Set values on the properties of intrinsic objects	
■ Use intrinsic objects to perform operations	

Table A-2   Creating and Managing Components and .NET Assemblies

Skill Being Measured	Location in Book
Create and modify a .NET assembly:	Chapter 9, Lesson 1, and Chapter 11, Lesson 3
■ Create and implement satellite assemblies	■ Chapter 15, Lesson 2
■ Create resource-only assemblies	■ Chapter 15, Lesson 2

Table A-3   Consuming and Manipulating Data

Skill Being Measured	Location in Book
Access and manipulate data from a Microsoft SQL Server database by creating and using ad hoc queries and stored procedures	Chapter 5, Lessons 1, 2, and 3
Access and manipulate data from a data store. Data stores include relational databases, XML documents, and flat files. Methods include XML technique and ADO.NET.	Chapter 5, Lessons 1, 2, and 3; Chapter 7, Lesson 1
Handle data errors	Chapter 6, Lesson 1

Table A-4   Testing and Debugging

Skill Being Measured	Location in Book
Create a unit test plan	Chapter 10, Lesson 1
Implement tracing:	

Table A-4   Testing and Debugging

Skill Being Measured	Location in Book
▪ Add trace listeners and trace switches to an application	▪ Chapter 10, Lesson 3
▪ Display trace output	▪ Chapter 6, Lesson 3
Debug, rework, and resolve defects in code:	
▪ Configure the debugging environment	▪ Chapter 10, Lesson 3
▪ Create and apply debugging code to components, pages, and applications	▪ Chapter 10, Lesson 1
▪ Provide multicultural test data to components, pages, and applications	▪ Chapter 15, Lesson 2
▪ Execute tests	▪ Chapter 10, Lesson 2
▪ Resolve errors and rework code	▪ Chapter 10, Lesson 3

Table A-5   Deploying a Web Application

Skill Being Measured	Location in Book
Plan the deployment of a Web application:	Chapter 9, Lesson 2
▪ Plan the deployment of an application to a Web garden, a Web farm, or a cluster	▪ Chapter 9, Lesson 5
Deploy a Web application	Chapter 9, Lessons 2 and 3
Add assemblies to the global assembly cache	Chapter 9, Lessons 2 and 3

Table A-6   Maintaining and Supporting a Web Application

Skill Being Measured	Location in Book
Optimize the performance of a Web application	Chapter 9, Lesson 4; Chapter 12, Lessons 1, 2, 3, and 4
Diagnose and resolve errors and issues	Chapter 9, Lesson 4; Chapter 6, Lesson 3; and Chapter 10, Lesson 3

Table A-7   Configuring and Securing a Web Application

Skill Being Measured	Location in Book
Configure a Web application:	Chapter 9, Lesson 1
▪ Modify the Web.config file	▪ Chapter 9, Lesson 1; Chapter 8, Lesson 1; and Chapter 15, Lesson 3
▪ Modify the Machine.config file	▪ Chapter 9, Lesson 1
▪ Add and modify application settings	▪ Chapter 9, Lesson 1; Chapter 8, Lesson 1; and Chapter 15, Lessons 1 and 3
Configure security for a Web application:	Chapter 8, Lessons 1, 2, 3, 4, and 5

Table A-7   Configuring and Securing a Web Application

Skill Being Measured	Location in Book
■ Select and configure authentication type. Authentication types include Windows Authentication, None, forms-based, Microsoft Passport, Internet Information Services (IIS) authentication, and custom authentication.	■ Chapter 8, Lesson 1
Configure authorization. Authorization methods include file-based methods and URL-based methods:	Chapter 8, Lessons 1, 2, 3, and 4
■ Configure role-based authorization	■ Chapter 8, Lesson 2
■ Implement impersonation	■ Chapter 8, Lesson 1
Configure and implement caching. Caching types include output, fragment, and data:	Chapter 12, Lessons 1, 2, and 3
■ Use a cache object	■ Chapter 12, Lesson 3
■ Use cache directives	■ Chapter 12, Lessons 1 and 2
Configure and implement session state in various topologies such as a Web garden and a Web farm:	
■ Use session state within a process	■ Chapter 3, Lesson 3
■ Use session state with session state service	■ Chapter 9, Lesson 5
■ Use session state with Microsoft SQL server	■ Chapter 9, Lesson 5
Install and configure server services:	Chapter 2, Lesson 1
■ Install and configure a Web server	■ Chapter 2, Lessons 1 and 3; Chapter 6, Lesson 2; Chapter 8, Lessons 1 and 5; and Chapter 9, Lesson 2
■ Install and configure FrontPage Server Extensions	■ Chapter 2, Lesson 1

Getting Started

This self-paced training kit contains hands-on procedures to help you learn about developing Web applications.

To complete some of these procedures, you must have two networked computers or be connected to a larger network. Both computers must be capable of running Microsoft Windows XP Professional Edition, Windows 2000, or later.

Caution   Several exercises require you to make changes to your servers. This might cause undesirable results if you are connected to a larger network. Check with your network administrator before attempting these exercises.

Hardware Requirements

Each computer must have the following minimum configuration. All hardware should be on the Microsoft Windows XP or Microsoft Windows 2000 Hardware Compatibility List.

- Pentium II–class processor, 450 megahertz (MHz)
- 160 MB physical memory, 256 MB recommended

- CD-ROM or DVD drive, 12x or faster recommended

> **Note**   A DVD drive is required to install the Visual Studio .NET Professional Evaluation Edition software.

- 3.5 gigabytes (GB) on installation drive, which includes 500 megabytes (MB) on system drive.
- Super VGA (800 x 600) or higher-resolution monitor with 256 colors.
- Microsoft Mouse or compatible pointing device
- Internet connection and networking card (56K modem is the minimum acceptable Internet connection speed; higher speed connection is recommended)

Software Requirements

The following software is required to complete the procedures in this course.

- Microsoft Windows XP Professional Edition or Windows 2000.

> **Note**   The default installation configuration for these operating systems includes the Microsoft Internet Information Services (IIS) software required for developing Web applications.

- Microsoft Visual Studio .NET Professional Edition or Visual Studio .NET Enterprise Developer. Professional Edition is recommended, and Enterprise Developer Edition is ideal.

Setup Instructions

Set up your computer according to the manufacturer's instructions.

The Lesson Files

▶ **To install the lesson files and eBook to your hard disk drive**

1. Insert the Supplemental Course Materials CD-ROM into your CD-ROM drive.

> **Note**   If AutoRun is disabled on your machine, refer to the Readme file on the CD-ROM.

2. Run the Setup program included on the CD-ROM. Setup will automatically install the lesson files, support files, and eBook on your computer.
3. After Setup completes, it will display a Start page in your browser. You can use the Start page to view the lesson files, eBook, Readme, and additional information.

> **Note**   If you encounter problems installing any portion of this training kit, see the Readme included on the CD-ROM for Troubleshooting information and additional instructions.

▶ **To use the eBook**

You can view the eBook from a number of locations:

- From the Start page displayed at the end of Setup.
- From links within the default pages of the MCSDWebAppsVB and MCSD-WebAppsCS solutions installed by Setup.
- From the Windows Start menu using the eBook item installed in the Microsoft Press program group.
- From the Windows Explorer by opening the WebApp2.chm file.

Sample Exam Questions

▶ **To install the sample exam questions to your hard disk drive**

1. Insert the Supplemental Course Materials CD-ROM into your CD-ROM drive.

Note   If AutoRun is disabled on your machine, refer to the Readme.txt file on the CD-ROM.

---

2. Click Sample Exam Questions on the user interface menu and then select the exercise file you want to view.

The Microsoft Certified Professional Program

The Microsoft Certified Professional (MCP) program provides the best method to prove your command of current Microsoft products and technologies. Microsoft, an industry leader in certification, is on the forefront of testing methodology. Our exams and corresponding certifications are developed to validate your mastery of critical competencies as you design and develop, or implement and support, solutions with Microsoft products and technologies. Computer professionals who become Microsoft certified are recognized as experts and are sought after industry-wide.

The Microsoft Certified Professional program offers multiple certifications, based on specific areas of technical expertise, including:

- **Microsoft Certified Application Developer (MCAD) for Microsoft .NET.**   Qualified to develop and maintain department-level applications, components, Web or desktop clients, or back-end data services.
- **Microsoft Certified Solution Developer (MCSD).**   Qualified to design and develop custom business solutions with Microsoft development tools, technologies, and platforms and Microsoft Windows architecture.
- **Microsoft Certified Professional (MCP).**   Demonstrated in-depth knowledge of at least one Microsoft Windows operating system or architecturally significant platform. An MCP is qualified to implement a Microsoft product or technology as part of a business solution for an organization.
- **Microsoft Certified Systems Engineer (MCSE) on Windows 2000.**   Qualified to effectively analyze the business requirements and design and implement the infrastructure for business solutions based on the Microsoft Windows 2000 platform and Microsoft .NET Enterprise Servers.

- **Microsoft Certified Systems Administrator (MCSA) on Microsoft Windows 2000.** Individuals who implement, manage, and troubleshoot existing network and system environments based on the Microsoft Windows 2000 and Windows .NET Server operating systems.
- **Microsoft Certified Database Administrator (MCDBA) on Microsoft SQL Server 2000.** Individuals who derive physical database designs, develop logical data models, create physical databases, create data services by using Transact-SQL, manage and maintain databases, configure and manage security, monitor and optimize databases, and install and configure Microsoft SQL Server.
- **Microsoft Certified Trainer (MCT).** Instructionally and technically qualified to deliver Microsoft Official Curriculum through a Microsoft Certified Technical Education Center (CTEC).

Microsoft Certification Benefits

Microsoft certification, one of the most comprehensive certification programs available for assessing and maintaining software-related skills, is a valuable measure of an individual's knowledge and expertise. Microsoft certification is awarded to individuals who have successfully demonstrated their ability to perform specific tasks and implement solutions with Microsoft products. Not only does this provide an objective measure for employers to consider, it also provides guidance for what an individual should know to be proficient. And as with any skills-assessment and benchmarking measure, certification brings a variety of benefits: to the individual, and to employers and organizations.

Microsoft Certification Benefits for Individuals

As a Microsoft Certified Professional, you receive many benefits:

- Industry recognition of your knowledge and proficiency with Microsoft products and technologies.
- A Microsoft Developer Network subscription. MCPs receive rebates or discounts on a one-year subscription to the Microsoft Developer Network (*msdn.microsoft.com/subscriptions/*) during the first year of certification. (Fulfillment details will vary, depending on your location; please see your Welcome Kit.)
- Access to technical and product information direct from Microsoft through a secured area of the MCP Web site (go to *http://www.microsoft.com/traincert /mcp/mcpsecure.asp/*).
- Access to exclusive discounts on products and services from selected companies. Individuals who are currently certified can learn more about exclusive discounts by visiting the MCP secured Web site (go to *http://www.microsoft.com /traincert/mcp/mcpsecure.asp/* and select the "Other Benefits" link).
- MCP logo, certificate, transcript, wallet card, and lapel pin to identify you as a Microsoft Certified Professional (MCP) to colleagues and clients. Electronic files of logos and transcript may be downloaded from the MCP secured Web site (go to *http:// www.microsoft.com/traincert/mcp/mcpsecure.asp/*) upon certification.
- Invitations to Microsoft conferences, technical training sessions, and special events.

- Free access to Microsoft Certified Professional Magazine Online, a career and professional development magazine. Secured content on the Microsoft Certified Professional Magazine Online Web site includes the current issue (available only to MCPs), additional online-only content and columns, an MCP-only database, and regular chats with Microsoft and other technical experts.
- Discount on membership to PASS (for MCPs only), the Professional Association for SQL Server. In addition to playing a key role in the only worldwide, user-run SQL Server user group endorsed by Microsoft, members enjoy unique access to a world of educational opportunities (go to *http://www.microsoft.com /traincert/mcp/mcpsecure.asp/*).

An additional benefit is received by Microsoft Certified System Engineers (MCSEs):

- A 50-percent rebate or discount off the estimated retail price of a one-year subscription to TechNet or TechNet Plus during the first year of certification. (Fulfillment details will vary, depending on your location. Please see your Welcome Kit.) In addition, about 95 percent of the CD-ROM content is available free online at the TechNet Web site (*http://www.microsoft.com/technet/*).

An additional benefit is received by Microsoft Certified System Database Administrators (MCDBAs):

- A 50-percent rebate or discount off the estimated retail price of a one-year subscription to TechNet or TechNet Plus during the first year of certification. (Fulfillment details will vary, depending on your location. Please see your Welcome Kit.) In addition, about 95 percent of the CD-ROM content is available free online at the TechNet Web site (*http://www.microsoft.com/technet/*).
- A one-year subscription to SQL Server Magazine. Written by industry experts, the magazine contains technical and how-to tips and advice—a must for anyone working with SQL Server.

A list of benefits for Microsoft Certified Trainers (MCTs) can be found at *http: //www.microsoft.com/traincert/mcp/mct/benefits.asp.*

Microsoft Certification Benefits for Employers and Organizations

Through certification, computer professionals can maximize the return on investment in Microsoft technology. Research shows that Microsoft certification provides organizations with:

- Excellent return on training and certification investments by providing a standard method of determining training needs and measuring results.
- Increased customer satisfaction and decreased support costs through improved service, increased productivity, and greater technical self-sufficiency.
- Reliable benchmark for hiring, promoting, and career planning.
- Recognition and rewards for productive employees by validating their expertise.
- Retraining options for existing employees so they can work effectively with new technologies.
- Assurance of quality when outsourcing computer services.

Requirements for Becoming a Microsoft Certified Professional

The certification requirements differ for each certification and are specific to the products and job functions addressed by the certification.

To become a Microsoft Certified Professional, you must pass rigorous certification exams that provide a valid and reliable measure of technical proficiency and expertise. These exams are designed to test your expertise and ability to perform a role or task with a product, and are developed with the input of professionals in the industry. Questions in the exams reflect how Microsoft products are used in actual organizations, giving them "real-world" relevance.

- Microsoft Certified Product candidates are required to pass one operating system exam. Candidates may pass additional Microsoft certification exams to further qualify their skills with other Microsoft products, development tools, or desktop applications.
- Microsoft Certified Systems Engineers are required to pass five core exams and two elective exams.
- Microsoft Certified Systems Administrators are required to pass three core exams and one elective exam that provide a valid and reliable measure of technical proficiency and expertise.
- Microsoft Certified Database Administrators are required to pass three core exams and one elective exam that measure technical proficiency and expertise.
- Microsoft Certified Solution Developers are required to pass three core Microsoft Windows operating system technology exams and one BackOffice technology elective exam.
- Microsoft Certified Trainers are required to meet instructional and technical requirements specific to each Microsoft Official Curriculum course they are certified to deliver. The MCT program requires ongoing training to meet the requirements for the annual renewal of certification. For more information about becoming a Microsoft Certified Trainer, visit *http://www.microsoft.com /traincert/mcp/mct/* or contact a regional service center near you.

Technical Training for Computer Professionals

Technical training is available in a variety of ways, with instructor-led classes, online instruction, or self-paced training available at thousands of locations worldwide.

Self-Paced Training

For motivated learners who are ready for the challenge, self-paced instruction is the most flexible, cost-effective way to increase your knowledge and skills.

A full line of self-paced print and computer-based training materials is available direct from the source—Microsoft Press. Microsoft Official Curriculum courseware kits from Microsoft Press are designed for advanced computer system professionals and are available from Microsoft Press and the Microsoft Developer Division. Self-paced training kits from Microsoft Press feature print-based instructional materials, along with CD-ROM-based product software, multimedia presentations, lab exercises, and practice files. The Mastering Series provides in-depth, interactive training on CD-ROM for experienced developers. They're both great ways to prepare for Microsoft Certified Professional (MCP) exams.

Online Training

For a more flexible alternative to instructor-led classes, turn to online instruction. It's as near as the Internet and it's ready whenever you are. Learn at your own pace and on your own schedule in a virtual classroom, often with easy access to an online instructor. Without ever leaving your desk, you can gain the expertise you need. Online instruction covers a variety of Microsoft products and technologies. It includes options ranging from Microsoft Official Curriculum to choices available nowhere else. It's training on demand, with access to learning resources 24 hours a day. Online training is available through Microsoft Certified Technical Education Centers.

Microsoft Certified Technical Education Centers

Microsoft Certified Technical Education Centers (CTECs) are the best source for instructor-led training that can help you prepare to become a Microsoft Certified Professional. The Microsoft CTEC program is a worldwide network of qualified technical training organizations that provide authorized delivery of Microsoft Official Curriculum courses by Microsoft Certified Trainers to computer professionals.

For a listing of CTEC locations in the United States and Canada, visit the Web site at *http://www.microsoft.com/traincert/ctec/*.

Technical Support

Every effort has been made to ensure the accuracy of this book and the contents of the companion disc. If you have comments, questions, or ideas regarding this book or the companion disc, please send them to Microsoft Press using either of the following methods:

E-mail: TKINPUT@MICROSOFT.COM

Postal Mail: Microsoft Press
                 Attn: *MCAD/MCSD Self-Paced Training Kit: Developing Web Applications with Microsoft Visual Basic .NET and Microsoft Visual C# .NET*
                 Editor
                 One Microsoft Way
                 Redmond, WA 98052-6399

The Microsoft Press Web site (*http://www.microsoft.com/mspress/support/*) provides corrections for books. Please note that product support is not offered through this Web site. For further information regarding Microsoft software support options, please connect to *http://www.microsoft.com/support/* or call Microsoft Support Network Sales at (800) 936-3500.

For information about ordering the full version of any Microsoft software, please call Microsoft Sales at (800) 426-9400 or visit *http://www.microsoft.com*.

C H A P T E R 1

Introduction to Web Programming

About This Chapter

In this chapter, you will learn about Internet applications and the tools you use to create them. This chapter introduces you to the concepts and terms used throughout this book, including how ASP.NET Web applications work, the parts of a Web application, how the Microsoft .NET Framework is organized, and how to use the Microsoft Visual Studio .NET programming environment. The sections in this chapter will provide a high-level overview of concepts that are explained in greater detail in subsequent chapters.

Before You Begin

To complete the lessons in this chapter, you must have:

- Installed Visual Studio .NET on your computer
- Internet access through a local area network (LAN), broadband, or modem connection

Lesson 1: Types of Applications

Web applications are one of four types of Internet applications that you can create using Visual Studio .NET. In this lesson, you will learn a little about the different types of Internet applications and get an overview of how an ASP.NET Web application works.

After this lesson, you will be able to

- Describe four different types of Internet applications and know where to look for training on developing each type of application
- Explain how a Web application executes over the Internet and how that differs from a traditional, static Web site
- Understand the role that ASP.NET plays in creating Web applications
- List the parts that make up ASP.NET and describe some of its advantages over other Web application technologies, such as the Common Gateway Interface (CGI)

Estimated lesson time: 5 minutes

What Can You Create?

Strictly speaking, an Internet application is any application that uses the Internet in any way. That means applications that request that users register over the Internet or that provide Help through the Internet are, to some degree, Internet applications.

That definition is too broad for the subject of a single book. To narrow the focus a bit, let's identify four types of Internet applications:

- **Web applications**   These applications provide content from a server to client machines over the Internet. Users view the Web application through a Web browser.
- **Web services**   These components provide processing services from a server to other applications over the Internet.
- **Internet-enabled applications**   These are stand-alone applications that incorporate aspects of the Internet to provide online registration, Help, updates, or other services to the user over the Internet.
- **Peer-to-peer applications**   These are stand-alone applications that use the Internet to communicate with other users running their own instances of the application.

You can use Visual Studio .NET to create each of these types of applications. The first type, Web applications, is the subject of this book. Table 1-1 shows the Visual Studio .NET Help topics and the books in this series that deal with each type of Internet application.

Table 1-1   Sources of Information About Internet Applications

Application type	Use these topics in online Help	Prepare for the MCSD test using
Web applications	ASP.NET, Web forms, *System.Web* namespace	This book
Web services	ASP.NET, XML Web Services, *System.Web.Services* namespace	*MCAD/MCSD Self-Paced Training Kit: Developing XML Web Services and Server Components with Microsoft Visual Basic .NET and Microsoft Visual C# .NET*
Internet-enabled applications	Microsoft Windows forms, HTML Help, WebBrowser control, *System.Net* namespace	*MCAD/MCSD Self-Paced Training Kit: Developing Windows-Based Applications with Microsoft Visual Basic .NET and Microsoft Visual C# .NET*
Peer-to-peer applications	Accessing the Internet, pluggable protocols, *System.Net* and *System.Net.Sockets* namespaces	Online Help topics for these namespaces and MSDN articles on peer-to-peer and client/server applications with the .NET Framework

How Web Applications Work

Web applications use a client/server architecture. The Web application resides on a server and responds to requests from multiple clients over the Internet, as shown in Figure 1-1.

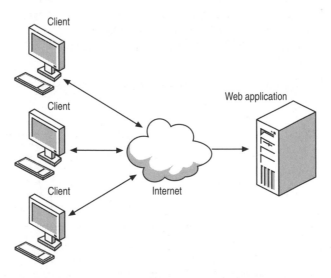

Figure 1-1   ASP.NET Web application architecture

On the client side, the Web application is hosted by a browser. The application's user interface takes the form of Hypertext Markup Language (HTML) pages that are interpreted and displayed by the client's browser.

On the server side, the Web application runs under Microsoft Internet Information Services (IIS). IIS manages the application, passes requests from clients to the application, and returns the application's responses to the client. These requests and responses are passed across the Internet using Hypertext Transport Protocol (HTTP). A *protocol* is a set of rules that describe how two or more items communicate over a medium, such as the Internet. Figure 1-2 shows how the client and server interact over the Internet.

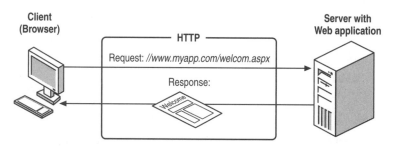

Figure 1-2   Client/server interaction in a Web application

The Web application composes responses to requests from resources found on the server. These resources include the executable code running on the server (what we traditionally think of as the "application" in Microsoft Windows programming), Web forms, HTML pages, image files, and other media that make up the content of the application.

Web applications are much like traditional Web sites, except that the content presented to the user is actually composed dynamically by executable, rather than being served from a static page stored on the server. Figure 1-3 shows how a Web application composes the HTML returned to a user.

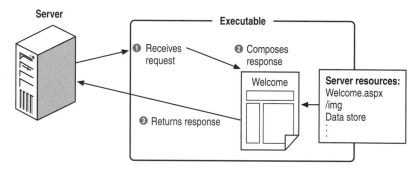

Figure 1-3   An ASP.NET Web application response from server resources

The executable portion of the Web application enables you to do many things that you can't do with a static Web site, such as:

■   Collect information from the user and store that information on the server

- Perform tasks for the user such as placing an order for a product, performing complex calculations, or retrieving information from a database
- Identify a specific user and present an interface that is customized for that user
- Present content that is highly volatile, such as inventory, pending order, and shipment information

This is only a partial list. Basically, you can do anything with a Web application that you can imagine doing with any client/server application. What makes a Web application special is that the client/server interaction takes place over the Internet.

What ASP.NET Provides

ASP.NET is the platform that you use to create Web applications and Web services that run under IIS. ASP.NET is not the only way to create a Web application. Other technologies, notably the CGI, also enable you to create Web applications. What makes ASP.NET special is how tightly it is integrated with the Microsoft server, programming, data access, and security tools.

ASP.NET provides a high level of consistency across Web application development. In a way, this consistency is similar to the level of consistency that Microsoft Office brought to desktop applications. ASP.NET is part of the .NET Framework and is made up of several components.

- **Visual Studio .NET Web development tools.**   These include visual tools for designing Web pages and application templates, project management, and deployment tools for Web applications.
- **The *System.Web* namespaces.**   These are part of the .NET Framework and include the programming classes that deal with Web-specific items such as HTTP requests and responses, browsers, and e-mail.
- **Server and HTML controls.**   These are the user-interface components that you use to gather information from and provide responses to users.

In addition to the preceding components, ASP.NET also uses the following, more general programming components and Windows tools. These items aren't part of ASP.NET. However, they are key to ASP.NET programming.

- **Microsoft Internet Information Services (IIS).**   As mentioned in the previous section, IIS hosts Web applications on the Windows server.
- **The Microsoft Visual Basic .NET, Microsoft Visual C#, and Microsoft Visual J# programming languages.**   These three languages have integrated support in Visual Studio .NET for creating Web applications.
- **The .NET Framework.**   This is the complete set of Windows programming classes, including the ASP.NET classes as well as classes for other programming tasks such as file access, data type conversion, array and string manipulation, and so on.

- **Microsoft ADO.NET database classes and tools.**   These components provide access to Microsoft SQL Server and ODBC databases. Data access is often a key component of Web applications.
- **Microsoft Application Center Test (ACT).**   This Visual Studio .NET component provides an automated way to stress-test Web applications.

ASP.NET is the most complete platform for developing Web applications that run under IIS. However, it is important to remember that ASP.NET is not platform-independent. Because it is hosted under IIS, ASP.NET must run on Windows servers. To create Web applications that run on non-Windows/IIS servers, such as Linux/Apache, you must use other tools—generally CGI.

Advantages of ASP.NET

ASP.NET has many advantages over other platforms when it comes to creating Web applications. Probably the most significant advantage is its integration with the Windows server and programming tools. Web applications created with ASP.NET are easier to create, debug, and deploy because those tasks can all be performed within a single development environment—Visual Studio .NET.

ASP.NET delivers the following other advantages to Web application developers:

- Executable portions of a Web application compiled so they execute more quickly than interpreted scripts
- On-the-fly updates of deployed Web applications without restarting the server
- Access to the .NET Framework, which simplifies many aspects of Windows programming
- Use of the widely known Visual Basic programming language, which has been enhanced to fully support object-oriented programming
- Introduction of the new Visual C# programming language, which provides a type-safe, object-oriented version of the C programming language
- Automatic state management for controls on a Web page (called **server controls**) so that they behave much more like Windows controls
- The ability to create new, customized server controls from existing controls
- Built-in security through the Windows server or through other authentication/ authorization methods
- Integration with ADO.NET to provide database access and database design tools from within Visual Studio .NET
- Full support for Extensible Markup Language (XML), cascading style sheets (CSS), and other new and established Web standards
- Built-in features for caching frequently requested Web pages on the server, localizing content for specific languages and cultures, and detecting browser capabilities

Lesson 2: Using ASP.NET

In this lesson, you will learn how ASP.NET organizes a Web application into parts, and you will learn the roles and names of those parts. You will be introduced to Web forms, which are the central user-interface element of Web applications.

ASP.NET is part of the larger .NET Framework, so this lesson will also discuss how the .NET Framework is organized and how .NET applications run differently from the traditional Windows applications you might be used to.

Finally, this lesson ends with a discussion of the programming languages you can use to create Web applications. ASP.NET is not bound to any one programming language, and the end of this lesson lists some of the other available languages and explains some of the major differences between the two languages (Visual Basic .NET and Visual C#) featured in this book.

After this lesson, you will be able to

- List the parts of a Web application and describe how they run on the server
- Explain how a Web form differs from and is similar to both an HTML page and a Windows form
- Describe some of the different components you can place on a Web form
- Explain the parts of the .NET Framework and how the common language runtime (CLR) executes .NET applications
- Understand how the .NET Framework is organized and know where to look for classes that handle common application programming tasks
- Compare the Visual Basic .NET and Visual C# programming languages

Estimated lesson time: 10 minutes

Parts of a Web Application

A Web application consists of three parts: content, program logic, and Web configuration information. Table 1-2 summarizes these parts and gives examples of where they reside in an ASP.NET Web application.

Table 1-2   Parts of an ASP.NET Web Application

Part	Types of files	Description
Content	Web forms, HTML, images, audio, video, other data	Content files determine the appearance of a Web application. They can contain static text and images as well as elements that are composed on the fly by the program logic (as in the case of a database query).
Program logic	Executable files, scripts	The program logic determines how the application responds to user actions. ASP.NET Web applications have a dynamic-link library (DLL) file that runs on the server, and they can also include scripts that run on the client machine.
Configuration	Web configuration file, style sheets, IIS settings	The configuration files and settings determine how the application runs on the server, who has access, how errors are handled, and other details.

The Web form is the key element of a Web application. A **Web form** is a cross between a regular HTML page and a Windows form. It has the same appearance as and similar behavior to an HTML page, but it also has controls that respond to events and run code, like a Windows form.

In a completed Web application, the executable portion of the Web form is stored in an assembly (.dll) that runs on the server under the control of the ASP.NET worker process (aspnet_wp.exe), which runs in conjunction with IIS. The content portion of the Web form resides in a content directory of the Web server, as shown in Figure 1-4.

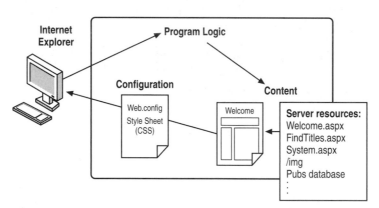

Figure 1-4   ASP.NET Web application parts on a Web server

When a user navigates to one of the Web forms from his or her browser, the following sequence occurs:

1. IIS starts the ASP.NET worker process if it is not already running. The ASP.NET worker process loads the assembly associated with the Web form.

2. The assembly composes a response to the user based on the content of the Web form that the user requested and any program logic that provides dynamic content.

3. IIS returns the response to the user in the form of HTML.

Once the user gets the requested Web form, he or she can enter data, select options, click buttons, and use any other controls that appear on the page. Some controls, such as buttons, cause the page to be posted back to the server for event processing, and the sequence repeats itself, as shown in Figure 1-5.

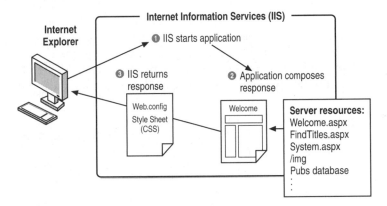

Figure 1-5   How the parts interact

This cycle of events is described in greater detail in Lesson 2 of Chapter 2, "Creating Web Forms Applications."

Web Form Components

Web forms can contain several different types of components, as summarized in Table 1-3.

Table 1-3   Components on a Web Form

Component	Examples	Description
Server controls	TextBox, Label, Button, ListBox, DropDownList, DataGrid	These controls respond to user events by running event procedures on the server. Server controls have built-in features for saving data that the user enters between page displays. You use server controls to define the user interface of a Web form.
HTML controls	Text Area, Table, Image, Submit Button, Reset Button	These represent the standard visual elements provided in HTML. HTML controls are useful when the more complete feature set provided by server controls is not needed.

Table 1-3   Components on a Web Form

Component	Examples	Description
Data controls	SqlConnection, SqlCommand, OleDbConnection, OleDbCommand, DataSet	Data controls provide a way to connect to, perform commands on, and retrieve data from SQL and OLE databases and XML data files.
System components	FileSystemWatcher, EventLog, MessageQueue	These components provide access to various system-level events that occur on the server.

You use the server and HTML controls to create the user interface on a Web form. The data controls and system components appear on the Web form only at design time to provide a visual way for you to set their properties and handle their events. At run-time, data controls and system components do not have a visual representation. Figure 1-6 shows a Web form containing components.

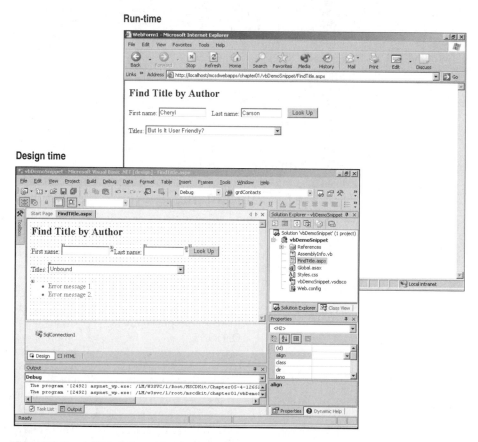

Figure 1-6   A Web form with components

Chapter 4, "Creating a User Interface," provides more detail about using server and HTML controls on a Web form.

The .NET Framework

ASP.NET is an important part of the .NET Framework, but it is just one part. Understanding what else the .NET Framework provides will help you program your ASP.NET application effectively and avoid writing new code to perform tasks that are already implemented within the .NET Framework.

First, a little background. The .NET Framework is the new Microsoft programming platform for developing Windows and Web software. It is made up of two parts:

- An execution engine called the common language runtime (CLR)
- A class library that provides core programming functions, such as those formerly available only through the Windows API, and application-level functions used for Web development (ASP.NET), data access (ADO.NET), security, and remote management

.NET applications aren't executed the same way as the traditional Windows applications you might be used to creating. Instead of being compiled into an executable containing native code, .NET application code is compiled into Microsoft intermediate language (MSIL) and stored in a file called an **assembly**. At run time, the assembly is compiled to its final state by the CLR. While running, the CLR provides memory management, type-safety checks, and other run-time tasks for the application. Figure 1-7 shows how this works.

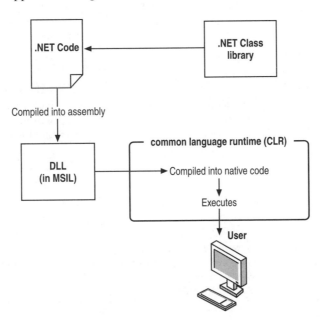

Figure 1-7   How a .NET application runs

Applications that run under the CLR are called **managed code** because the CLR takes care of many of the tasks that would have formerly been handled in the application's executable itself. Managed code solves the Windows programming problems of component registration and versioning (sometimes called DLL hell) because the assembly contains all the versioning and type information that the CLR needs to run the application. The CLR handles registration dynamically at run time, rather than statically through the system registry as is done with applications based on the Component Object Model (COM).

The .NET class library provides access to all the features of the CLR. The .NET class library is organized into namespaces. Each namespace contains a functionally related group of classes. Table 1-4 summarizes the .NET namespaces that are of the most interest to Web application programmers.

Table 1-4   Summary of the .NET Framework Class Library

Category	Namespaces	Provides classes for
Common types	*System*	All the common data types, including strings, arrays, and numeric types. These classes include methods for converting types, for manipulating strings and arrays, and for math and random number tasks.
Data access	*System.Data, System.Data.Common, System.Data.OleDb, System.Data.SqlClient, System.Data.SqlTypes*	Accessing databases. These classes include methods for connecting to databases, performing commands, retrieving data, and modifying data.
Debugging	*System.Diagnostics*	Debugging and tracing application execution.
File access	*System.IO, System.IO.IsolatedStorage, System.DirectoryServices*	Accessing the file system. These include methods for reading and writing files and getting paths and filenames.
Network communication	*System.Net, System.Net.Sockets*	Communicating over the Internet using low-level protocols such as TCP/IP. These classes are used when you're creating peer-to-peer applications.
Security	*System.Security, System.Security.Cryptography, System.Security.Permissions, System.Security.Policy, System.Web.Security*	Providing user authentication, user authorization, and data encrypting.

Table 1-4   Summary of the .NET Framework Class Library   *(continued)*

Category	Namespaces	Provides classes for
Web applications	*System.Web, System.Web.Caching, System.Web.Configuration, System.Web.Hosting, System.Web.Mail, System.Web.SessionState, System.Web.UI, System.Web.UI.Design, System.Web.UI.WebControls, System.Web.UI.HtmlControls*	Creating client/server applications that run over the Internet. These are the core classes used to create ASP.NET Web applications.
Web services	*System.Web.Services, System.Web.Services.Configuration, System.Web.Services.Description, System.Web.Services.Discovery, System.Web.Services.Protocols*	Creating and publishing components that can be used over the Internet. These are the core classes used to create ASP.NET Web services.
Windows applications	*System.Windows.Forms, System.Windows.Forms.Design*	Creating applications using Windows user interface components. These classes provide Windows forms and controls as well as the ability to create custom controls.
XML data	*System.Xml, System.Xml.Schema, System.Xml.Serialization, System.Xml.Xpath, System.Xml.Xsl*	Creating and accessing XML files.

Because the .NET namespaces organize classes by function, you can use them to help locate the classes and class members that provide the CLR features you want to use. For example, the *System* namespace is one of the most commonly used namespaces because it contains the classes for all the fundamental data types. Any time you declare a variable with a numeric, a string, or an array type, you are using the *System* namespace.

This approach allows the .NET Framework to provide built-in methods for converting data types and manipulating strings and arrays. For instance, the following lines of code use the built-in methods of the *String* and *Array* classes to sort a list.

Visual Basic .NET

```
' Declare and initialize a string.
Dim strFruit As String = "oranges apples peaches kumquats nectarines mangos"
' Declare an array.
Dim arrFruit As String()
' Place each word in an array element.
arrFruit = strFruit.Split(" ")
' Sort the array.
System.Array.Sort(arrFruit)
' Put the sorted data back in the string.
strFruit = String.Join(" ", arrFruit)
```

Visual C#

```
// Declare and initialize a string.
string strFruit = "oranges apples peaches kumquats nectarines mangos";
// Declare an array.
string[] arrFruit;
// Place each word in an array element.
arrFruit = strFruit.Split(" ".ToCharArray());
// Sort the array.
System.Array.Sort(arrFruit);
// Put the sorted array back in the string.
strFruit = System.String.Join(" ", arrFruit);
```

Many of the class methods in the *System* namespace can be used directly without first creating an object from the class. These are called **shared members** in Visual Basic .NET and **static members** in Visual C#. Shared and static members can be called from the class name itself, as in the *System.Array.Sort* line in the preceding code. Another example of a class with shared/static members is the *Math* class, as shown by the following *Pi* and *Pow* methods:

Visual Basic .NET

```
' Get the area of a circle.
dblCircArea = System.Math.Pi * System.Math.Pow(intRadius, 2)
```

Visual C#

```
// Get the area of a circle.
dblCircArea = System.Math.PI * System.Math.Pow(intRadius, 2) ;
```

The .NET Framework provides 124 different namespaces. Only about 40 of the most common ones are summarized in Table 1-4. For a list of the .NET Framework namespaces, see the topic titled "Class Library" in the Visual Studio .NET online Help.

Programming Languages

ASP.NET and, indeed, the whole .NET Framework are programming language–independent. This means that you can choose any language that has implemented a CLR-compliant compiler. In addition to developing its own programming languages, Microsoft has formed partnerships with many language vendors to provide .NET support for Perl, Pascal, Eiffel, Cobol, Python, Smalltalk, and other programming languages.

This book covers creating Web applications with the Visual Basic .NET and the Visual C# programming languages. These two languages are functionally equivalent, which means that they each provide equal capabilities to create Web applications. The differences between the two languages are syntactical and stylistic.

Most current programmers will choose the language they are most familiar with. Current Visual Basic programmers will be more comfortable developing Web applications in Visual Basic .NET; C or C++ programmers will be more comfortable developing with Visual C#.

If you are new to programming or if you are choosing to extend your programming skills to new languages, learning both Visual Basic .NET and Visual C# is a practical goal. This is especially true when you create Web applications, because most of the tasks are performed through the .NET Framework classes, which means Visual Basic .NET code and Visual C# code often look nearly identical.

Table 1-5 summarizes some significant differences between Visual Basic .NET and Visual C#. This information is useful to keep in mind if you are choosing a programming language for the first time or if you are planning to switch between languages.

Table 1-5   Visual Basic .NET and Visual C# Differences

Feature	Visual Basic .NET	Visual C# .NET

Case sensitive	Not case sensitive:
	`response.write("Yo") ' OK`
		Case sensitive:
		`response.write("Yo"); // Error!`
		`Response.Write("Yo"); // OK`

Functional blocks	Use beginning and ending statements to declare functional blocks of code:
	`Sub Show(strX as String)`
	`  Response.Write(strX)`
	`End Sub`
		Use braces to declare functional blocks of code:
		`void Show(string strX)`
		`{`
		`  Response.Write(strX);`
		`}`

Type conversion	Implicit type conversions are permitted by default:
	`Dim X As Integer`
	`X = 3.14  ' OK`
	
	You can limit conversions by including an *Option Strict On* statement at the beginning of modules.
		Implicit type conversions are limited to operations that are guaranteed not to lose information, such as converting from *int* to *float*:
		`int X = 0;`
		`float Y = X; // OK`
		
		Other type conversions are performed explicitly by casts:
		`Y = 3.14F;`
		`X = (int)Y; //Cast, OK.`
		
		Or, by using type conversion methods:
		`string Z;`
		`Z = Y.ToString();`

Table 1-5   Visual Basic .NET and Visual C# Differences   *(continued)*

Feature	Visual Basic .NET	Visual C# .NET

Comments	Comments always start with an apostrophe ('):
	
	`' This is a comment.`
		There are three different types of comments: block (/* */), inline (//), and documentation (///):
		
		`/* Block comments can`
		`span lines or be used`
		`to comment out code. */`
		
		`// Inline comments appear`
		`// to the right of code.`
		
		`/// <summary>Description`
		`/// of class.</summary>`
		
		For more information about documentation comments, see the "XML Documentation" topic in the Visual Studio online Help.

Arrays	Array elements are specified using parentheses: `arrFruit(1) = "Apple"`	Array elements are specified using square brackets: `arrFruit[1] = "Apple";`
Methods	You can omit parentheses after method names if arguments are omitted: `strX = objX.ToString`	You must include parentheses after all methods: `strX = objX.ToString();`
Statement termination	Statements are terminated by carriage return: `Response.Write("Hello")`	Statements are terminated by the semicolon (;): `Response.Write("Hello");`

Statement continuation	Statements are continued using the underscore (_):
	
	`intX = System.Math.PI * _`
	`    intRadius`
		Statements continue until the semicolon (;) and can span multiple lines if needed:
		
		`intX = System.Math.PI *`
		`    intRadius;`

String operator	Use the ampersand (&) or plus sign (+) to join strings:
	
	`strFruit = "Apples" & _`
	`    " Oranges"`
		Use the plus sign (+) to join strings:
		
		`strFruit = "Apples" +`
		`    " Oranges";`

Comparison operators	Use =, >, <, >=, <=, <> to compare values: `If intX >= 5 Then`	Use ==, >, <, >=, <=, != to compare values: `if (intX >= 5)`

Table 1-5   Visual Basic .NET and Visual C# Differences   *(continued)*

Feature	Visual Basic .NET	Visual C# .NET
Negation	Use the *Not* keyword to express logical negation: `If Not IsPostBack Then`	Use the *!* operator to express logical negation: `if (!IsPostBack)`
Object comparison	Use the *Is* keyword to compare object variables: `If objX Is objY   Then`	Use == to compare object variables: `if (objX == objY)`
Object existence	Use the *Nothing* keyword or the *IsNothing* function to check whether an object exists: `If IsNothing(objX) Then`	Use the *null* keyword to check whether an object exists: `if (objX == null)`

In addition to the differences shown in Table 1-5, there are significant keyword differences between the two languages. The code examples throughout this book illustrate those differences. The Visual Studio .NET Help topic "Language Equivalents" provides a complete comparison of Visual Basic .NET, Visual C#, and other Microsoft languages.

Lesson 3: Using Visual Studio .NET

The Visual Studio .NET programming environment presents new window types, new ways to manage those windows, and new integration with Internet content. This lesson offers a tour of these new features as well as an overview of some of the older Visual Studio .NET debugging and Help features presented from a Web application–programming viewpoint.

If you've programmed with earlier versions of Visual Studio and feel like skipping this lesson, be aware that you can no longer make changes to an application while debugging without restarting the application. That particular Visual Studio .NET feature, called edit-and-continue, is no longer available in Visual Basic .NET or Visual C#.

After this lesson, you will be able to

- Use the Start Page to open new or existing projects, get current product information, and set environment preferences
- List the two Visual Studio .NET window types and use the Auto Hide feature to make the most out of screen space for editing documents
- Cut and paste items using the Clipboard Ring in the Toolbox
- Edit Web forms and HTML pages visually or in HTML
- Write code using the Code Editor's automated features and modify Visual Studio .NET settings to turn those features on or off
- Build, run, and debug applications using Visual Studio .NET
- Get Help and set Help filters for your preferred programming language

Estimated lesson time: 30 minutes

The Start Page

When you start Visual Studio .NET, the first thing you see is the Start Page, shown in Figure 1-8. The Start Page contains various panes to make information easier to find and to help simplify some common tasks, such as opening a recent file.

The Projects pane, shown in Figure 1-8, displays the four most recently saved projects in the form of hyperlinks. To open one of these recent projects, click the project name. To create a new project or to open an existing project not displayed in the recent projects list, click the appropriate button on the Projects tab.

To the left of the Start Page is a list of other topics containing current information about Visual Studio .NET, other Microsoft products, programming, Web site hosting, and other information. If you click one of these topics, the Start Page displays the topic, as shown in Figure 1-9.

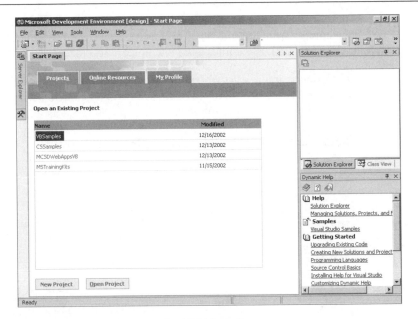

Figure 1-8   The Visual Studio .NET Start Page

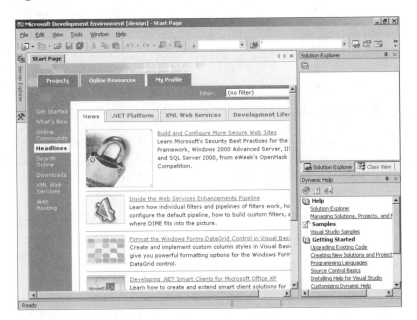

Figure 1-9   Current Visual Studio .NET headlines

The information displayed in the Start Page is dynamic, with much of the information coming from the Internet. This ensures that the information is current; it's a good idea to check the Headlines and Downloads panes occasionally to get the latest news.

Of particular interest to Web application developers is the Web Hosting pane, shown in Figure 1-10. This pane links to Web sites that will host your ASP.NET Web applications on the Internet.

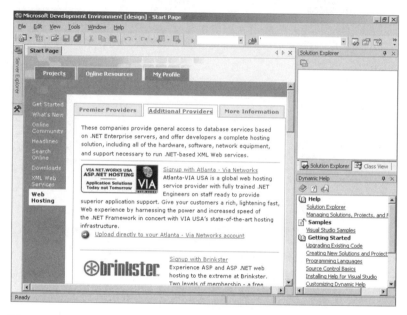

Figure 1-10   ASP.NET hosting services

Some of the sites, like Brinkster, offer limited free hosting. These hosting services are extremely useful when you're learning ASP.NET because they allow you to share your work with the world without the effort and expense of setting up your own Web server.

The My Profile pane of the Start Page lets you set your preferences for Visual Studio .NET, as shown in Figure 1-11.

These options let you change the default window layout for Visual Studio .NET, set the programming language you most commonly use, and specify whether Help is displayed in the Visual Studio .NET design panes or in a window as a separate application. The Help window can get a little cramped when displayed within Visual Studio .NET, so unless you have a 19-inch monitor, it's a good idea to select the External Help option.

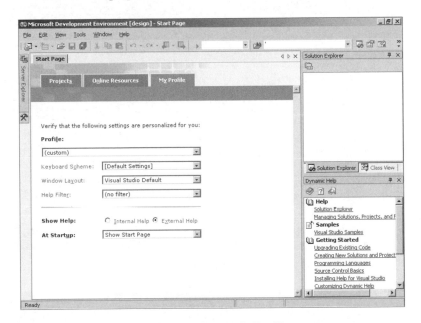

Figure 1-11   Set your preferences in the My Profile pane

Visual Studio .NET Windows

Visual Studio .NET has two types of windows: Document windows and Tool windows. Document windows display the content of your application: the forms, Web pages, and code all appear in Document windows. You can have multiple Document windows open at once, and you can choose between them by clicking their tabs near the top of the screen, as shown in Figure 1-12.

Tool windows display the components you use to create your application. These components include the controls, database connections, classes, and properties you use in the project. Tool windows are displayed to the left and right of the Document windows and they can be set to slide in or out of view by clicking their tabs, as shown in Figure 1-13.

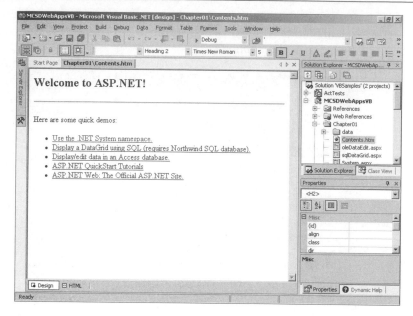

Figure 1-12   A Document window

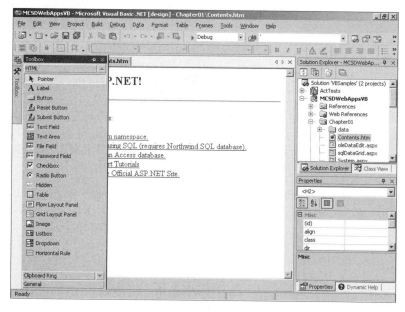

Figure 1-13   The Toolbox window

To cause a tabbed Tool window to remain on screen, toggle the Auto Hide button at the top right of the Tool window. The Auto Hide button looks like a tiny pushpin. Click the pushpin again to cause the Tool window to return to tabbed display. You can use the tabbed display to hide the Tool windows on both sides of the Document window and provide more space for editing your application's content, as shown in Figure 1-14.

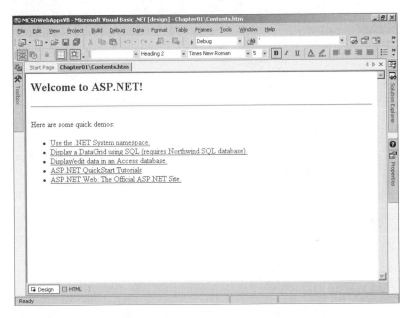

Figure 1-14   Tabbed Tool windows around the Document window

The tabbed display of the Document and Tool windows is the default setting for Visual Studio .NET. You can turn off this feature to use a more traditional windowed display by choosing Options from the Tools menu and then selecting your preferences from the dialog box shown in Figure 1-15.

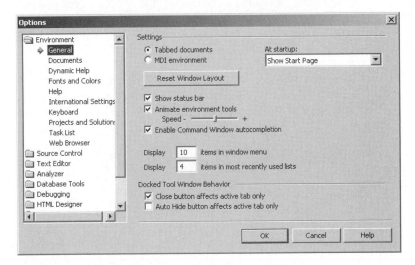

Figure 1-15   The Options dialog box

The Toolbox

The Visual Studio .NET Toolbox displays the controls and components you can add to a Document window. The contents of the Toolbox change depending on the type of document you are currently editing. When you are editing a Web form, for example, the Toolbox displays the server controls, HTML controls, data controls, and other components that you can add to a Web form, as shown in Figure 1-16.

Figure 1-16   The Toolbox window

The components in the Toolbox are categorized as shown in Figure 1-16. When you click one of the categories, the Toolbox displays the items in that category. You can scroll through the items in the Toolbox by clicking the up and down arrows at the top and the bottom of the component list.

When the current document is code, the Toolbox contains only the Clipboard Ring, as shown in Figure 1-17. The Clipboard Ring keeps track of the last 20 items you have copied (CTRL+C) or cut (CTRL+X) so that you can paste them back into a document.

To paste an item from the Clipboard Ring, click the item and drag it to where you want to insert it. When you move the mouse pointer over an item in the Clipboard Ring, Visual Studio expands that item to show you more of the text it contains.

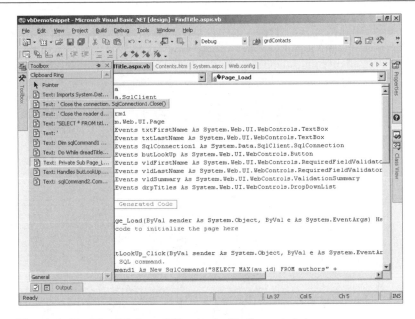

Figure 1-17   The Clipboard Ring in the Toolbox window

Editing Web Documents

You can edit Web forms and HTML documents visually by using the same drag-and-drop techniques that you use when editing Windows forms, or you can edit them as text files. To switch between edit modes, click the Design or HTML tabs at the bottom of the Document window, as shown in Figure 1-18.

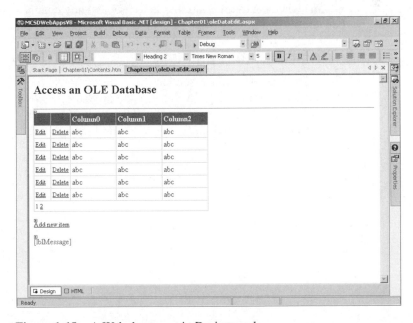

Figure 1-18   A Web document in Design mode

There is no way to do some tasks visually, so you will often need to edit Web documents as text. Using the HTML mode can also be more convenient than using the visual tools if you are already familiar with HTML. The IntelliSense technology in Visual Studio .NET provides help for completing HTML elements, as shown in Figure 1-19.

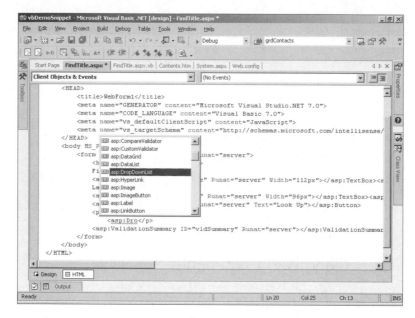

Figure 1-19   IntelliSense for HTML elements in Visual Studio .NET

You can switch back to Design mode to preview any changes you make in HTML mode simply by clicking on the Design tab at the bottom of the Document window.

Editing Code-Behind Files

Web forms have code files associated with them. These files are created automatically when you create a new Web form and are called *code-behind files*. Code-behind files have the same base name as the Web form with the .vb or .cs filename extension added, as shown in Figure 1-20 and Figure 1-21.

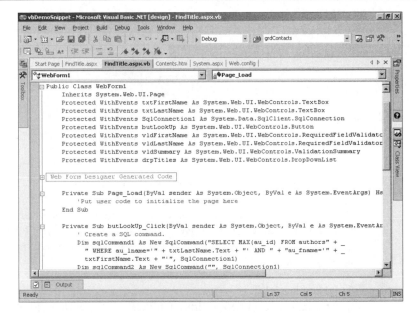

Figure 1-20   A Web form's code-behind file (Visual Basic .NET)

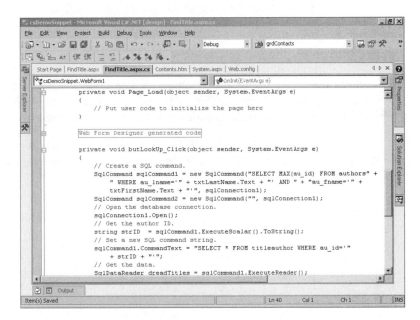

Figure 1-21   A Web form's code-behind file (Visual C#)

A Web form is associated with its code file by the *@Pagedirective* found in the Web form's HTML, as shown here:

Visual Basic .NET

```
<%@ Page Language="vb" AutoEventWireup="false" Codebehind="Form1.aspx.vb"
Inherits="WebApplication1.Webform1"%>
```

Visual C#

```
<%@ Page language="c#" Codebehind="WebForm1.aspx.cs" AutoEventWireup="false"
Inherits="WebApplication1.WebForm1" %>
```

Visual Studio automatically maintains the file information in this Page directive, so if you save the Web form with a different file name, the CodeBehind attribute is automatically updated. However, Visual Studio does not automatically maintain the information in the Page directive's Inherits attribute. If you change the root namespace of the project or class name of a Web form, you must manually update the information in the Web form's Page directive.

Visual Studio .NET generates a class definition, initialization procedure, and *Page_Load* event procedure for each Web form's code-behind file. You shouldn't change the code in the regions marked *Web Form Designer Generated Code*, because that code might later be modified by Visual Studio .NET and your changes could be overwritten.

You can hide the generated code by clicking the minus sign (–) to the left of the #Region directive. Clicking the minus sign collapses the region into a single line and changes the minus sign to a plus sign (+), which you can click to expand the region again. You can use this same outlining feature to collapse or expand other blocks of code, such as class definitions and procedures.

The Visual Studio .NET Code Editor also provides completion through IntelliSense for keywords and class members that you use in code, as shown in Figure 1-22.

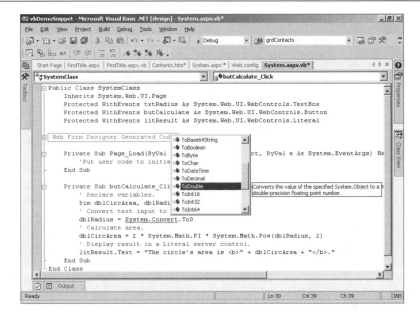

Figure 1-22   The autocomplete feature

If you are programming in Visual Basic, the autocomplete feature will also correct the capitalization of keywords and member names when you complete a line. If you are using Visual C#, however, Visual Studio .NET will not recognize a keyword or member name if it is not capitalized correctly. This is because Visual Basic .NET is not case sensitive, but Visual C# is.

The Visual Studio .NET Code Editor highlights syntax errors and undeclared variables as you complete each line. These errors are underlined with a squiggly line, and if you move the mouse pointer over the error, a description of the error is displayed, as shown in Figure 1-23.

You can turn most of the Code Editor's automatic features on or off by changing the settings in the Options dialog box shown in Figure 1-15. You can also use the Options dialog box to change automatic indentation, code block completion, and other language-specific settings.

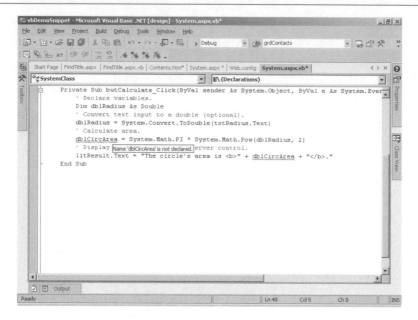

Figure 1-23   Error detection in the Code Editor

Editing Single-Source Web Forms

ASP.NET also supports single-source Web forms. As the name implies, a single-source Web form has its code and HTML stored in the same single file. Many of the ASP.NET code samples and tutorials posted on the Web use single-source files because they are easier to distribute and display. For example, the following single-source Web form calculates the area of a circle:

Visual Basic .NET

```vb
<%@ Page Language="VB" %>
<script runat="server">
    Private Sub butCalculate_Click(ByVal sender As System.Object, _
        ByVal e As System.EventArgs)
        ' Declare variables.
        Dim dblCircArea, dblRadius As Double
        ' Convert text input to a double (optional).
        If txtRadius.Text <> "" Then _
          dblRadius = System.Convert.ToDouble(txtRadius.Text)
        ' Calculate area.
        dblCircArea = System.Math.PI * System.Math.Pow(dblRadius, 2)
        ' Display result.
        ShowResult(dblCircArea)
    End Sub

    Sub ShowResult(ByVal Result As Double)
        litResult.Text = "<h3>Results</h3>"
        litResult.Text += "<p>The circle's area is: <b>"
```

```
        + Result.ToString() _
                    + "</b>"
        End Sub
</script>
<html>
<head>
    <title>Calculate Area</title>
</head>
<body>
    <form runat="server">
        <h2>Calculate Area
        </h2>
        <hr />
        Circle radius:
        <asp:TextBox id="txtRadius" Runat="server"></asp:TextBox>
        <asp:Button id="butCalculate" onclick="butCalculate_Click"
        Runat="server"
            Text="Calculate"></asp:Button>
        <p>
            <asp:Literal id="litResult" Runat="server"></asp:Literal>
        </p>
    </form>
</body>
</html>
```

Visual C#

```
<%@ Page Language="C#" %>
<script runat="server">
    private void butCalculate_Click(object sender, EventArgs e)
    {
        // Declare variables.
        double dblCircArea, dblRadius;
        // Convert text input to a double (optional).
        if (txtRadius.Text != "")
        {
            dblRadius = Convert.ToDouble(txtRadius.Text);
            // Calculate area.
            dblCircArea = 2 * Math.PI * Math.Pow(dblRadius, 2);
            // Display result.
            ShowResult(dblCircArea);
        }
    }

    void ShowResult(double Result)
    {
        litResult.Text = "<h3>Results</h3>";
        litResult.Text += "<p>The circle's area is: <b>"
        + Result.ToString() +
            "</b>";
    }
```

```
</script>
<html>
<head>
<title>Calculate Area</title>
</head>
<body>
    <form runat="server">
        <h2>Calculate Area
        </h2>
        <hr />
        Circle radius:
        <asp:TextBox id="txtRadius" Runat="server"></asp:TextBox>
        <asp:Button id="butCalculate" onclick="butCalculate_Click"
        Runat="server"
            Text="Calculate"></asp:Button>
        <p>
            <asp:Literal id="litResult" Runat="server"></asp:Literal>
        </p>
    </form>
</body>
</html>
```

Visual Studio can edit and even run these single-source Web forms; however, the advanced features like autocomplete are not enabled for any of the code entered between the *<script>* and *</script>* elements on the page. For this reason, the code samples in this book are shown as code-behind files.

Solution Explorer

Visual Studio .NET organizes applications into projects and solutions. A **project** is a collection of files that will ultimately make up a single executable. A **solution** is a group of projects that make up a single functional unit. You view the files in a solution by using the Solution Explorer, as shown in Figure 1-24.

Figure 1-24   The Solution Explorer

The project shown in bold is the start-up project. The **start-up project** is the project that runs when you click Start in Visual Studio .NET. When you're developing multiple projects as part of a single solution, the start-up project usually calls the other projects in the solution.

Information about a solution is stored in a solution file (.sln), which is placed in your My Documents folder by default. You can open the solution using this file, or you can open projects directly using their project files (.vbproj or .csproj), which are placed in the project folders. If you open a project file, Visual Studio .NET creates a new solution file when you save the project.

Running a Project

You can run a project within Visual Studio .NET by clicking Start on the toolbar, by choosing Start from the Debug menu, or by pressing F5. When you run a project, Visual Studio .NET builds the project files and displays any errors that occur in the Task List window, as shown in Figure 1-25.

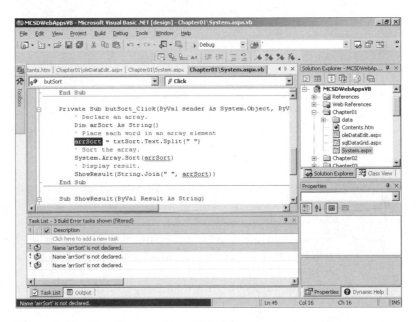

Figure 1-25   Running a project with build errors

Double-clicking the error description in the Task List selects the line with the error in the Document window so that you can correct the error. The Task List also displays comment tasks you have added to your code, such as 'TODO, //TODO, 'UNDONE, //UNDONE, 'HACK, or //HACK. You can add or modify the tokens you use to identify tasks by configuring the Environment settings in the Options dialog box of Visual Studio.

If no errors occur during the build, Visual Studio .NET starts the application in Debug mode and, in the case of a Web application, starts Internet Explorer and displays the application's start page. If an error occurs while the application is running in Debug mode, Visual Studio .NET displays the error in the browser, as shown in Figure 1-26.

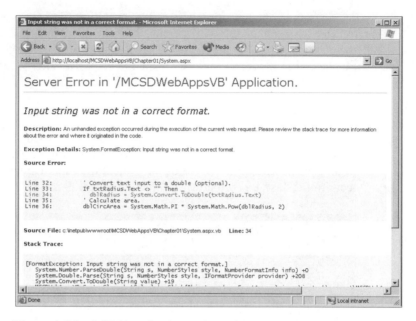

Figure 1-26   A Web application project with run-time errors

You have two choices at this point:

- If you know what caused the error, you can stop the application by closing the browser window to return to Visual Studio .NET and then correct the error shown.

- If you are unsure of what caused the error, you can click Back in the browser, switch to Visual Studio .NET to set a breakpoint at a position in the code before the error occurred, and then switch back to the browser to try the task again. Visual Studio .NET will stop the application at the breakpoint you set so that you can step through the code to locate the source of the error.

Once you locate the error, you must stop the application before you can correct it. In earlier versions of Visual Studio .NET, you could correct errors in Debug mode and continue running the application.

Setting Breakpoints and Watching Variables

You can stop a project at a particular line of code by setting a breakpoint. When Visual Studio .NET runs the project, it will stop the project and display the line with the breakpoint in the Code Editor before that line executes, as shown in Figure 1-27.

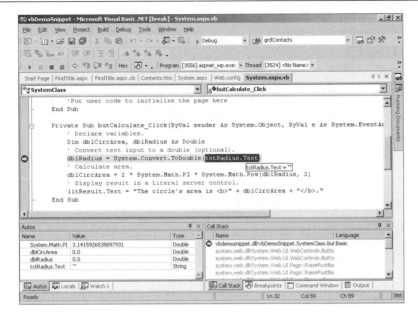

Figure 1-27   A project stopped at a breakpoint

To set a breakpoint, click the gray margin to the left of the line you want to break at, or select the line and press F9. Figure 1-28 shows a breakpoint that has been set.

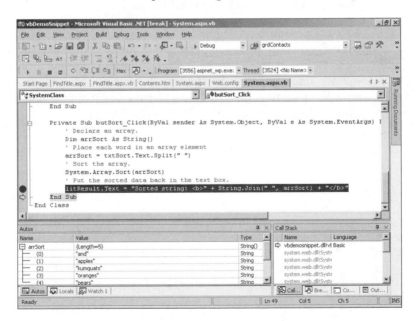

Figure 1-28   Setting a breakpoint

Once Visual Studio .NET stops at a breakpoint, you can view the value of active variables by moving the mouse pointer over the variable. If the variable is a complex type, such as an object or an array, you can view its data by adding it to the Watch window, as shown in Figure 1-29.

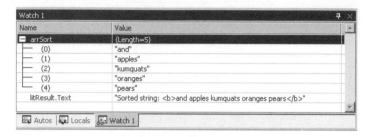

Figure 1-29   The Watch window

To add an item to the Watch window, select the item and drag it to the Watch window. Click the plus sign (+) next to the item in the Watch window to view subitems, such as array elements or object properties.

Executing Statements

After you have stopped at a breakpoint, you can continue running your application by clicking Continue on the toolbar or by pressing F5. Alternatively, you can execute one line at a time by pressing F10 or F11.

F10 executes each procedure call as a single statement. In other words, F10 **steps over** a procedure by executing it and stopping at the next line in the current procedure. F11 executes procedure calls by **stepping in** to the procedure and stopping at the first line in the called procedure. To execute a single line of code outside of the context of the project, type the code in the Command window. Figure 1-30 shows these different techniques.

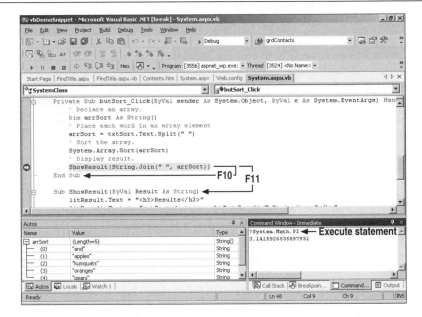

Figure 1-30   Ways to execute statements

The results of statements entered in the Command window are directed to the next line of the command window. For example, the statement *?System.Math.PI* displays 3.1415926535897931 on the next line.

Getting Help

Visual Studio .NET includes a combined collection of Help for the programming environment, languages, .NET Framework, technical support, and developer's network articles. The Help is displayed either within a Document window or outside Visual Studio .NET in a separate window, depending on the preferences you set on the Start Page or in the Options dialog box.

The Help system includes three ways to find topics: the Contents window, the Index window, and the Search window. These windows act like the Tool windows in Visual Studio .NET: they can be "docked" and then hidden or displayed using tabs, as shown in Figure 1-31.

Each of the navigation windows provides a Filter drop-down list that lets you choose a particular programming language or subject to look in. This feature is especially useful in the Search and Index windows because the combined Help collection is large. The Visual Basic And Related filter and the Visual C# And Related filter include most of the topics you need for this book.

Topics that include syntax or code samples have a language filter icon at the top of each page that looks like a funnel. Click the filter icon to change the programming language displayed in the topic or to view all language samples, as shown in Figure 1-32.

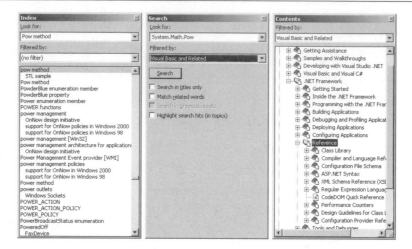

Figure 1-31   The Help navigation windows

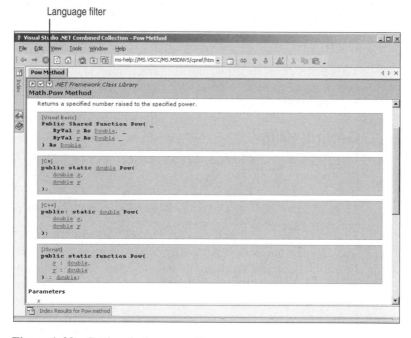

Figure 1-32   Setting the language filter

In addition to the Help included with Visual Studio .NET, Microsoft hosts the Got-DotNet Web site, at *www.gotdotnet.com*. That Web site includes tutorials on using ASP.NET and contains links to many other related Web sites.

Summary

- There are four types of Internet applications: Web applications, Web services, Internet-enabled applications, and peer-to-peer applications.
- Web applications run on a server, processing user requests for pages and composing those pages using executable code and static resources on the server.
- Web applications can provide dynamic content based on dynamic server resources, such as a database, and based on user inputs, such as creating a mortgage payoff table from user loan information.
- ASP.NET is a platform for creating Web applications that run on Windows servers using IIS and the .NET Framework.
- Web applications are made up of content, an executable, and configuration files.
- The content of a Web application is presented through Web forms. Web forms use HTML components like conventional HTML pages; like Windows forms, however, they can also respond to user events such as mouse clicks.
- The Web application's executable is stored in a .dll file called an assembly. Assemblies are compiled to an intermediate state, and the final compilation is done by the CLR just before running the application.
- The .NET Framework is made up of the CLR and the .NET class library. The .NET class library makes the CLR run-time tasks available to programmers.
- The .NET classes are grouped by programming task into namespaces. These groupings help you locate the class, method, or property you need to accomplish a task.
- Use the Visual Studio .NET Start Page to view current product information, to open new or existing projects, to set user environment preferences, and to sign up for Web hosting services.
- Edit Web forms and HTML pages visually by using the Document window's Design mode; edit them as text by using the Document window's HTML mode.
- Set the Help language filter to view code samples in a single programming language or in multiple languages.
- Modify the Visual Studio .NET environment features using the Options dialog box.

Lab: Getting Started with Visual Studio .NET

In this lab, you will familiarize yourself with the Visual Studio .NET programming environment, sign up for Web application hosting, and view the ASP.NET Quick-Start Tutorials. These exercises establish a foundation for the specific programming skills you will learn in later chapters.

Estimated lesson time: 30 minutes

Exercise 1: Customize the Visual Studio .NET Environment

In this exercise, you will customize the window display in Visual Studio .NET to maximize the design area. You will also change your Visual Studio .NET settings to display Help in a separate, external window and specify a language filter within Help. When complete, the Visual Studio .NET environment will appear as shown in Figure 1-33.

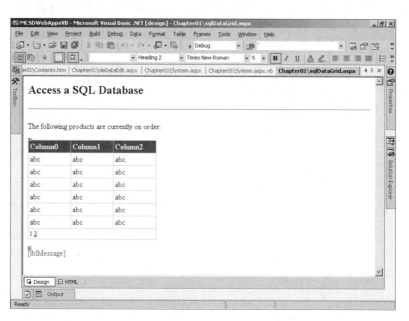

Figure 1-33   The customized Visual Studio .NET environment

When you start Visual Studio .NET for the first time, the default window layout displays the Server Explorer and Toolbox windows as tabs on the left side of the screen and the Solution Explorer and Properties windows on the right side of the screen.

► **To maximize the screen space for editing Web documents and code**

■ From the Window menu, choose Auto Hide All.

Or

■ Click Auto Hide in the upper right corner of the Solution Explorer and the Properties windows. The Auto Hide button looks like a pushpin.

When the Auto Hide feature is on, the window disappears when the mouse pointer moves off it. The window reappears when the mouse pointer moves over the window's tab at the edge of the screen.

Another Visual Studio .NET default setting is to display Help within a Visual Studio .NET Document window. Help itself has quite a few windows, so this window-within-window display can become crowded.

► **To display Help in its own window**

1. From the Tools menu, choose Options. Visual Studio .NET displays the Options dialog box.

2. In the Options dialog box, click Help under the Environment folder. Visual Studio .NET displays the Help options, as shown in Figure 1-34.

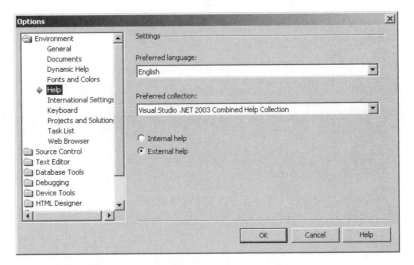

Figure 1-34   Setting Help options

3. Click the External Help option, and then click OK. Visual Studio displays a message stating that the changes will not take effect until the environment is restarted.

If you experiment with the Visual Studio .NET window layout and don't like the results, you can restore the default window settings.

▶ **To restore the default window settings**

1. From the Tools menu, choose Options. Visual Studio .NET displays the Options dialog box.

2. In the Options dialog box, under the Environment folder, select General.

3. Click the Reset Window Layout button. Visual Studio .NET displays a warning asking you to confirm that you want to reset the window layout to the default.

4. Click OK to clear the warning, and then click OK again to close the Options dialog box. Visual Studio .NET restores the default window layout.

Exercise 2: Set Up a Web Hosting Account

In this exercise, you will set up a Web hosting account that will allow you to deploy Web applications for public testing and evaluation over the Internet. You don't have to have a Web hosting account to complete the lessons in this book, because you can run and debug Web applications locally on your workstation. However, having a Web hosting account enables you to test how your Web application handles multiple simultaneous users, and it also allows you to share your programming achievements with others, which is just plain fun.

▶ **To set up Web hosting**

1. Choose a hosting service provider.

2. Register with the service.

3. Sign on to the service and upload your application.

4. To display the Web Hosting pane in Visual Studio .NET, select the Start Page Document window, click Web Hosting, and then click the Hosting Services tab. The Web Hosting pane appears, as shown in Figure 1-35.

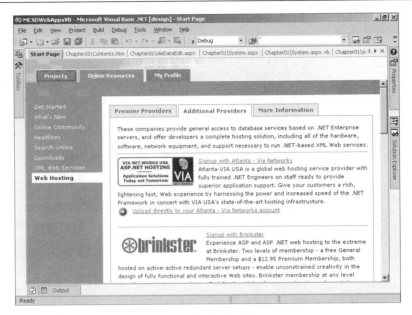

Figure 1-35   ASP.NET Web application hosting services

The following sections describe the steps for setting up a Web hosting account in greater detail.

Exercise 3: Choose a Service Provider

The Web Hosting pane lists a number of Web hosting service providers that support ASP.NET Web applications. Each of these providers offers a different combination of free and fee-based services. To evaluate which hosting service is right for you, visit the hosting service Web sites by clicking on their links on the Visual Studio Start Page. In addition to cost, you should consider the following:

- **Level of support**   Does the hosting service provide a users' forum or other area where your questions can be answered? If it does, check it out to see what other users are saying.

- **Ability to migrate**   Will you be able to easily move applications from a testing stage to full deployment? Does the hosting service provide the storage and performance you will need?

- **Database support**   Most services provide SQL database hosting, but each service charges differently for this feature.

▶ **To register with a service provider**

1. In the Web Hosting pane, click the Sign Up With link for the service provider you have chosen. Visual Studio .NET displays the service provider's registration procedure in a Document window, as shown in Figure 1-36.

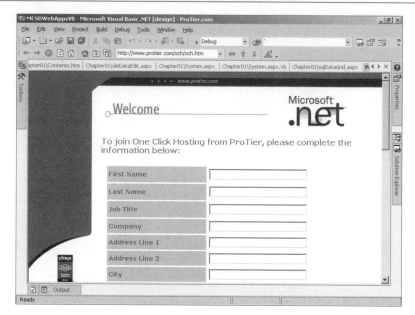

Figure 1-36   ProTier Welcome page

2. Follow the service provider's instructions, which usually involve providing name, address, and e-mail information. When the information is complete, the service provider will e-mail you a user name and password to provide access to your new account.

Note   Register with the service to create your own account. The exact procedure varies for each service provider, but they all follow these basic steps.

The service providers shown in the Web Hosting pane all provide **One-Click Hosting**, which means that you can upload your completed Web applications directly from the Visual Studio .NET Web Hosting pane.

▶ **To upload an application to the hosting service**

1. From the Visual Studio .NET Web Hosting pane, click the Upload Directly To Your Account link for the service provider you signed up for. Visual Studio .NET displays the service's logon page in a Document window, as shown in Figure 1-37.

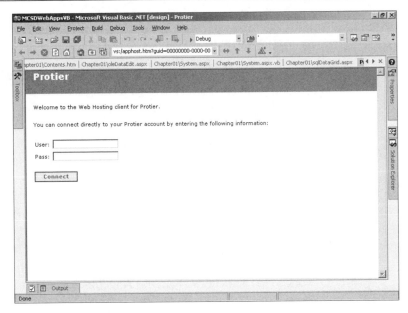

Figure 1-37   ProTier logon page

2. On the logon page, enter the user name and password provided for your account. (Usually this is sent to you in e-mail after you sign up for the account.) After you sign on, the service provider displays an upload page in a Document window, as shown in Figure 1-38.

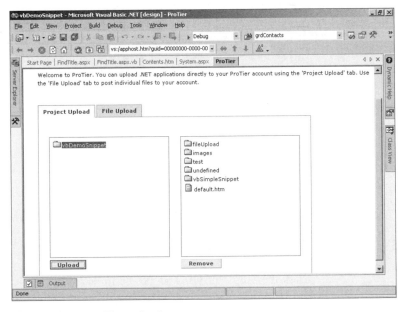

Figure 1-38   ProTier upload page

3. From the list on the left, select the folder containing the application to upload. From the list on the right, select a folder on the server to upload the application to. Click Upload to upload the project to the hosting service.

After you've uploaded an application, you and others can view it by navigating to its location on the Internet. The Web hosting service providers don't require users to sign on to view applications, just to upload them.

Exercise 4: Explore the ASP.NET QuickStart Tutorials

In this exercise, you will install the .NET SDK Samples QuickStart Tutorials and view the QuickStart Tutorials for ASP.NET. The QuickStart Tutorials contain a host of information about the different aspects of the .NET Framework and are one of the best resources for learning how to program using ASP.NET.

▶   **To install and view the QuickStart Tutorial for ASP.NET**

1. From the Windows Start menu, point to All Programs, Microsoft .NET Framework SDK, and choose Samples And QuickStart Tutorials. Windows displays the Microsoft .NET Framework SDK QuickStarts, Tutorials And Samples install page, as shown in Figure 1-39.

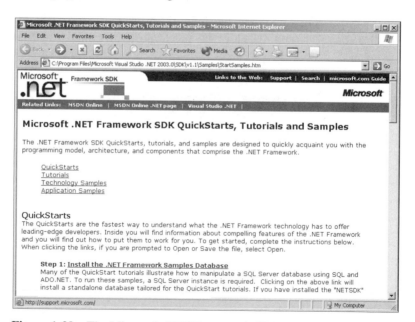

Figure 1-39   The Microsoft .NET Framework SDK QuickStarts, Tutorials And Samples install page

2. Click the Step 1 Install The .NET Framework Samples Database link to install and configure the SQL database used by the QuickStart samples.

3. Click the Step 2 Set Up The QuickStarts hyperlink to install and configure the Web sites used by the QuickStart samples.

4. The next time you access the Microsoft .NET Framework QuickStart Tutorials from the Start menu, Internet Explorer skips the install page and takes you directly to the Microsoft .NET Framework SDK QuickStarts, Tutorials And Samples page, as shown in Figure 1-40.

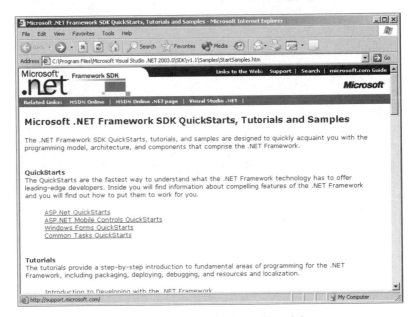

Figure 1-40   The .NET Framework QuickStart Tutorials page

5. Click the ASP.NET QuickStarts link to view the tutorial page, as shown in Figure 1-41.

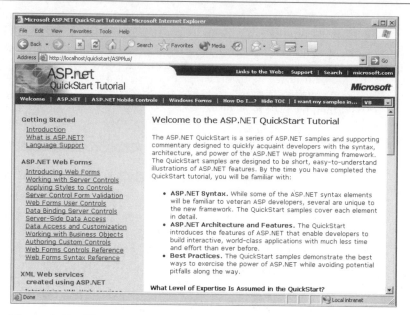

Figure 1-41   The ASP.NET QuickStart Tutorials page

The ASP.NET QuickStart Tutorials demonstrate how to perform various ASP.NET programming tasks in Visual Basic .NET, Visual C#, and JScript. Most of the samples in the QuickStart Tutorials place server code within script blocks, rather than using code-behind files as is done in this book. In general, it is preferable to use code-behind files because it separates the user interface from the program logic.

Review

The following questions are intended to reinforce key information presented in this chapter. If you are unable to answer a question, review the appropriate lesson and then try the question again. Answers to the questions can be found in the appendix.

1. Give two examples of how an ASP.NET Web application is different from a traditional Windows application.

2. What are the two main parts of the .NET Framework?

3. How do you restore the default window settings in Visual Studio .NET?

4. Why doesn't the Visual Studio .NET Code Editor automatically complete the following partial line of code (Visual C# users only)?

   ```
   int intX = system.math
   ```

5. When can't you use ASP.NET to create a Web application?

C H A P T E R   2

Creating Web Forms Applications

About This Chapter

In this chapter, you'll learn how to create an ASP.NET Web application using Microsoft Visual Studio .NET and ASP.NET. You'll learn how to start a new project, create a basic user interface, write code to respond to events, and preserve data within your application. Because ASP.NET is integrated with Microsoft Internet Information Services (IIS), you'll also learn about IIS and how to use it to organize your Web application.

Before You Begin

To complete the lessons in this chapter, you must:

- Have installed Visual Studio .NET, IIS, and the Microsoft FrontPage Server Extensions on your computer.
- Be familiar with the basics of using Visual Studio .NET, including how to add controls to a Microsoft Windows form, how to add code to controls, and how to run an application within Visual Studio .NET. See the QuickStart tutorials included with Visual Studio .NET for instructions on these tasks.

Lesson 1: Creating an ASP.NET Web Application Project

Web forms are the application objects that define the user interface of your Web application. The text and controls you place on a Web form determine what a user sees when he or she runs your application. In this way, Web forms are similar to Windows forms in a Windows application.

Unlike Windows applications, however, Web applications run on a server and are distributed to clients through the Internet. Therefore, how you create and organize a Web application project has significant differences from working with Windows applications in Visual Studio .NET. These differences are explained in the following sections.

After this lesson, you will be able to

- Start a Web Forms project in Visual Studio .NET
- Set the physical location where your projects will be stored
- Add server controls to a Web form and write code to respond to events on those controls
- Run the Web application in the programming environment
- Identify the purpose of the files in a Web Forms project

Estimated lesson time: 30 minutes

Creating a New Web Application

The first step in creating an ASP.NET Web application is to start a new project in Visual Studio .NET. Visual Studio .NET provides templates for each type of application you can create. The template for a Web application is named ASP.NET Web Application. When you create a new project using this template, Visual Studio .NET creates a project file; a new, blank Web form; and other supporting files used by your application.

To create a Web application project from Visual Studio .NET, follow these steps:

1. On the Visual Studio .NET Start Page, click New Project. Visual Studio .NET displays the New Project dialog box, as shown in Figure 2-1. Visual Studio .NET puts Web applications in the localhost virtual directory.

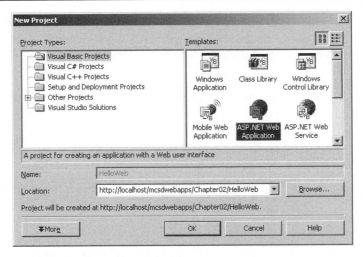

Figure 2-1   The New Project dialog box

2. In the New Project dialog box, select the ASP.NET Web Application template, type the name of the new project in the Location text box, and click OK.

When you create a Web application project in Visual Studio .NET, the programming environment creates a new folder and generates a set of files for the project. Visual Studio .NET gives the folder the same name as the project and puts the folder in the root folder of the default Web site that IIS hosts on your computer. This location is shown in the Location box of the New Project dialog box as http://localhost/projectname.

Organizing Your Projects with IIS

It's important to realize that Web applications can exist only in a location that has been published by IIS as a **virtual folder**. A virtual folder is a shared resource identified by an alias that represents a physical location on a server. If you try to select a physical folder from the New Project dialog box, such as C:\MyFiles, Visual Studio .NET disables the OK button. It's *not* OK—you can't create a Web application there!

The virtual folder named //localhost is the Web root folder on your computer. IIS determines the physical location of your Web root folder. By default, IIS installs the folder on your boot drive at \Inetpub\wwwroot. Instead of using the //localhost default and letting it get cluttered with sample projects, production code, and other stuff, organize your projects by creating separate folders for samples, tests, and production code. Then share those folders with the Web *before* you create new projects. Remember that Visual Studio .NET creates a new folder for each new project, so create only the folders you need to organize the types of projects you create.

Creating Virtual Folders to Organize Web Applications

Use IIS to create new virtual folders and to manage Web sites hosted on your computer. Creating a virtual folder for use with Visual Studio .NET requires two major tasks:

- **Creating the virtual folder.**   Virtual folders specify where your Web application projects are physically stored, so you use them to help organize your projects during development.
- **Adding the FrontPage Server Extensions to the virtual folder to create a subweb.**   A **subweb** is simply a virtual folder that contains a Web site. Adding the FrontPage Server Extensions to a virtual folder enables Visual Studio .NET to create and maintain Web applications in that folder.

Creating a Virtual Folder

To create a new virtual folder in IIS, follow these steps:

1. Open the IIS management console by clicking Start, pointing to All Programs, Administrative Tools, and clicking Internet Information Services.
2. In the console tree, expand the local computer and Web sites. Right-click Default Web Site, point to New, and click Virtual Directory on the shortcut menu, as shown in Figure 2-2. The Virtual Directory Creation Wizard opens.

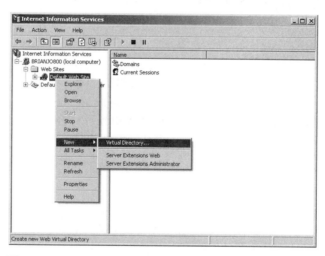

Figure 2-2   Creating a new virtual folder

3. IIS starts the Virtual Directory Creation Wizard to walk you through creating a new virtual folder. Click Next on the wizard title page to display the Virtual Directory Alias page, as shown in Figure 2-3.

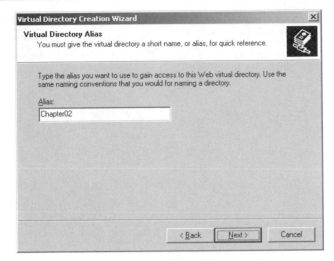

Figure 2-3   The Virtual Directory Alias page

4. Type an alias for the folder. The **alias** is the name you will use to identify the resource in this folder. In Visual Studio .NET, this is the name you will use to specify the location of your project. Click Next. The wizard displays the Web Site Content Directory page, as shown in Figure 2-4.

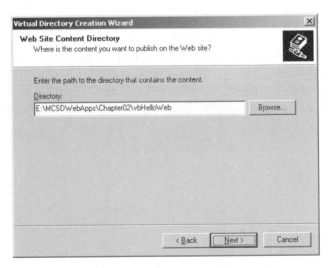

Figure 2-4   The Web Site Content Directory page

5. In the Directory box, type the path specification of the physical folder to associate with the virtual folder. This is the base folder where your project folders will be stored. Click Next. The wizard displays the Access Permissions page, as shown in Figure 2-5.

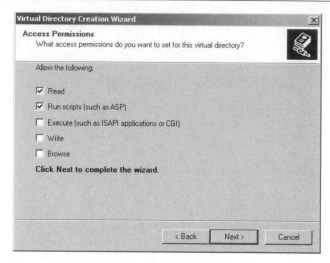

Figure 2-5   The Access Permissions page

6. Keep the default permissions shown in Figure 2-5. Click Next and then click Finish to create the virtual folder and complete the wizard.

Creating a Subweb

To add the FrontPage Server Extensions to a virtual folder, follow these steps:

1. Right-click the Default Web Site icon in the IIS management console, point to New, and click Server Extensions Web on the shortcut menu.

2. IIS starts the New Subweb Wizard to walk you through adding the FrontPage Server Extensions to your virtual folder. Click Next on the wizard title page to display the Subweb Name page, as shown in Figure 2-6.

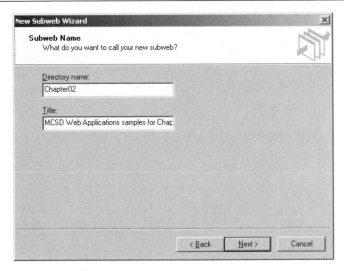

Figure 2-6 The Subweb Name page

3. Type the name of the virtual folder in the Directory Name box. This name corresponds to the alias you entered in step 4 of the previous procedure. Type a description of the folder in the Title box or leave it blank. Click Next. The wizard displays the Access Control page, as shown in Figure 2-7.

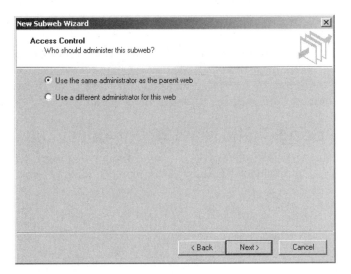

Figure 2-7 The Access Control page

4. Accept the default access control settings by clicking Next, and then click Finish to create the subweb.

Creating a New Project in the Virtual Folder

After you create a new virtual folder and add the server extensions to it, you can use it within Visual Studio .NET to create new projects. To create a Web application project in your new virtual folder, choose New Project from the Visual Studio .NET File menu, and specify the name of the virtual folder in the New Project dialog box, as shown in Figure 2-8.

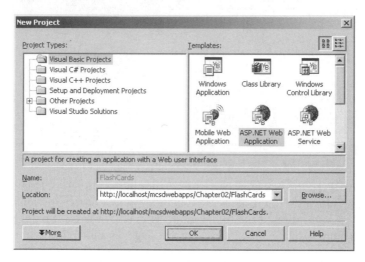

Figure 2-8   Create a Project in the new virtual folder

The location you specify in the New Project dialog box takes the form http://*servername*/*virtualfolder*. The server name localhost indicates that the server is running on your development machine. The name *virtualfolder* is the alias you created for the virtual folder in the preceding tasks.

Adding Controls and Writing Code

When Visual Studio .NET creates a Web application, it displays a new Web form in the center window, as shown in Figure 2-9. Drag controls from the Toolbox to the Web form as you would with a Windows form.

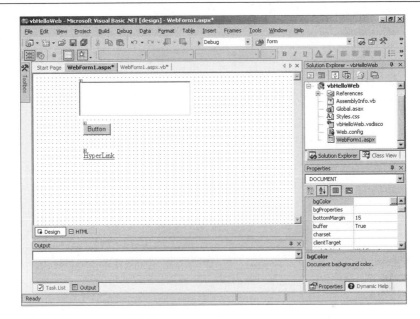

Figure 2-9   A new Web form

To add code to respond to events on the Web form, double-click the control. Visual Studio .NET displays the Code window. Add your code to the event procedure provided for the control. For example, the following code displays *Hello, Web!* in Internet Explorer when you click the *Button1* command button:

Visual Basic .NET

```
Private Sub Button1_Click(ByVal sender As System.Object, _
    ByVal e As System.EventArgs) Handles Button1.Click
    Response.Write("Hello, Web!<br>")
End Sub
```

Visual C#

```
private void Button1_Click(object sender, System.EventArgs e)
{
    Response.Write("Hello, Web!<br>");
}
```

Visual Studio automatically creates the event procedures for an object's default event when you double-click the control in the Design window. The *Button1_Click* event procedure shown above responds, or handles, the *Click* event for the Button control. In Microsoft Visual Basic .NET, the *Handles* clause at the end of the procedure declaration makes the connection between the *Click* event and this event procedure.

In Microsoft Visual C#, this connection is hidden in the code generated by the Web Forms Designer. To view this code, click the plus sign next to the *Web Form Designer Generated Code* region in the Code window. The following code shows the generated code connecting the *Form Load* event and *Button Click* events to event procedures.

Visual C#

```
#region Web Form Designer generated code
override protected void OnInit(EventArgs e)
{
    //
    // CODEGEN: This call is required by the ASP.NET Web Form Designer.
    //
    InitializeComponent();
    base.OnInit(e);
}


/// <summary>
/// Required method for Designer support - do not modify
/// the contents of this method with the code editor.
/// </summary>
private void InitializeComponent()
{
    this.Button1.Click += new System.EventHandler(this.Button1_Click);
    this.Load += new System.EventHandler(this.Page_Load);
}
#endregion
```

Creating this connection between an object's event and the event procedure that responds to the event is called **wiring the event**. Visual Basic .NET automatically creates this connection through the *Handles* clause, but Visual C# requires you to wire the event manually by adding code to the *InitializeComponent* procedure for any of the nondefault events you want to use.

To run the application, press F5. Visual Studio .NET builds the application, starts the browser, and then displays the page in the browser. When you click Button1, the browser displays *Hello, Web!* as shown in Figure 2-10. Closing the browser ends the Web application.

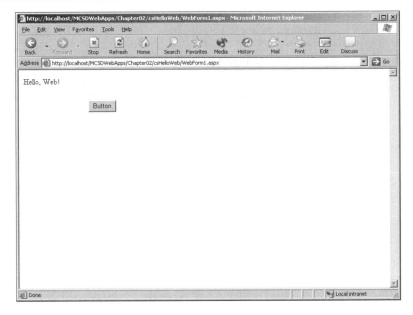

Figure 2-10   The Web form

As you can see from this example, Web Forms applications are similar to Windows Forms applications. However, Web Forms applications have the following significant differences:

- **Tools.**   Web forms can't use the standard Windows controls. Instead, they use server controls, HTML controls, user controls, or custom controls created specially for Web forms.

- **User interface.**   The appearance of a Web form is determined by the browser that displays it. Your Web application can appear in Internet Explorer, Netscape Communicator, or any other HTML-compliant browser. Different browsers (and different versions within browsers) support different HTML features, which can change the appearance and behavior of your Web forms. Don't get too alarmed, though. Server controls handle most of these differences gracefully, as you'll see in Chapter 4, "Creating a User Interface."

- **Lifetime.**   Windows forms are instantiated, exist for as long as needed, and are destroyed. Web forms *appear* to behave this way, but in fact they are instantiated, sent to the browser, and then usually thrown away. This means that all of the variables and objects declared in a Web form are usually not available after the Web form is displayed! (It is possible to keep these variables and objects around after a Web form is displayed, but that is not the standard programming practice. More on this topic later.) To get anything interesting done, you need to save information in special state objects provided by ASP.NET. There's more on state objects in Chapter 3, "Working with Web Objects."

- **Execution.**   The executable portions of a Web application live on the Web server. In this way, Web applications are sort of the ultimate client/server application: the browser is the only software installed on the client side, and all of the user interface and business logic runs on the server. All communication between the client and the server occurs through HTML. This means that even sophisticated Web applications pose little security risk to clients and therefore pass through firewalls undisturbed. The physical structure of a Web application and where processing occurs are explained in more depth in Lesson 3.

The Files in a Web Forms Project

The Web form is only one of 11 files Visual Studio .NET generates when it creates a new Web forms project. Table 2-1 describes the purpose of each of these project files. Visual Studio .NET creates these different files for each new Web application project. Only the files shown in bold are displayed in the Visual Studio .NET Solution Explorer.

Table 2-1   Web Forms Project Files

File name	Contains
AssemblyInfo.vb **AssemblyInfo.cs**	All of the attributes that are written into the compiled assembly, including version, company name, GUID, and so on.
Global.asax	The global events that occur in your Web application, such as when the application starts or ends. You can have only one Global.asax file per project, and it exists in the root folder of the project.
Global.asax.vb Global.asax.cs	The code used in Global.asax. This file is not shown in Solution Explorer.
Styles.css	The style definitions to use for the HTML generated by your project. This file appears only in Visual Basic .NET projects. For Visual C# projects, you can add it manually.
Web.config	The settings your Web server uses when processing this project. These settings specify how errors are reported, what type of user authentication to use, and so on.
Projectname.vsdisco	Descriptions of the Web Services that this project provides. This file is used for dynamic discovery of Web services (.asmx files) included in a Web application. This file is not shown in Solution Explorer.
WebForm1.aspx	The visual description of a Web form.
WebForm1.aspx.vb WebForm1.aspx.cs	The code that responds to events on the Web form. By default, this file is not shown in Solution Explorer.

Table 2-1   Web Forms Project Files

File name	Contains
WebForm1.aspx.resx	The Extensible Markup Language (XML) resources used by the Web form. This file is not shown in Solution Explorer.
Projectname.vbproj *Projectname*.csproj	The project file listing the files and settings used at design time. This file is not shown in Solution Explorer.
Projectname.vbproj.webinfo *Projectname*.csproj.webinfo	This file tracks the root virtual folder for the Web application. This file is not shown in Solution Explorer.

In addition to the files listed in Table 2-1, Web application projects can contain any number of other file types. The primary types of files that you'll add to a Web application project are shown in Table 2-2. Web application projects will often include these different types of source files.

Table 2-2   File Types for Web Forms Projects

File extension	Project item	Description
.aspx	Web form	Each Web form constitutes an ASP.NET Web page in your application. Applications can have one or many Web forms. Web forms have code files associated with them with the file extension .aspx.vb. Visual C# forms have associated .aspx.cs files.
.htm	HTML page	Web pages that don't have server code can appear as HTML pages in your project.
.vb or .cs	Class or module	Code that defines objects in your application is stored in classes.
.ascx	Web user control	User controls that are built from other Web forms and server controls in Visual Studio .NET.
.asmx	Web service	Web services that expose classes for remote execution over a network, such as the Internet.
.xml	XML file	Data files that store information used by your application.
.xsd	XML Schema	Schema files that describe the format and constraints to apply to stored data.
.xslt	XML Style Sheet	Formatting rules to apply when displaying XML data.

The Files in a Web Application

When you build a Web Forms project, Visual Studio .NET compiles all of the source code into an executable assembly (DLL) and places that file in a /bin directory. The appearance portion of your application remains as .aspx and .html files. Figure 2-11 shows the files you deploy after you build your Web application.

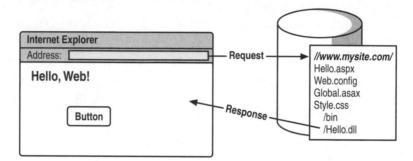

Figure 2-11   Files in a Web application

As shown in Figure 2-11, when a browser requests a page from the application, IIS starts the application's executable (Hello.dll) and generates a response. In this case, the response is to display the page defined in Hello.aspx. If an event, such as a button click, occurs on the page, it is sent back to the server, where it is handled by the application's DLL.

The following two lessons cover the details of how events are handled and where processing occurs.

Lesson 2: Responding to Events

In this lesson, you will learn about events in the life cycle of a Web application and how this life cycle is different from the life cycle of a Windows application. Web application events occur at the application, page, and server control levels. The sequence of these events and how they are executed affect how you respond to them in code.

After this lesson, you will be able to

■ Understand the sequence of events in an application's lifetime

■ Explain how the events in an application interact

■ List the events for each of the major objects in a Web application

■ Identify the three different types of server control events

■ Use state variables to preserve information in a Web application

Estimated lesson time: 35 minutes

Events in the Life Cycle of a Web Application

A Web application lives as long as it has active sessions, whereas Web forms live for barely a moment. The life of a Web application begins when a browser requests the start page of the application. (See Figure 2-12.) At that point, the Web server swings into action, starting the assembly (DLL) that responds to that request. The executable creates an instance of the requested Web form, generates the HTML to respond to the request, and posts that response to the browser. It then destroys the instance of the Web form.

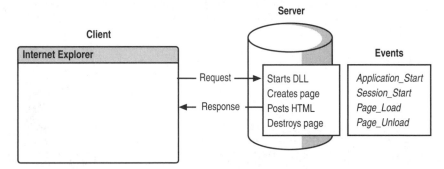

Figure 2-12   Life begins!

When the browser has the generated HTML, the user can type text in boxes, select options, and perform other tasks until triggering a postback event, such as a button click. Postback events cause the browser to send the page's data (view state) back to the server for event processing. When the server receives the view state, it creates a new instance of the Web form, fills in the data from the view state, and processes any events that occurred. (See Figure 2-13.) As soon as the server has finished, it posts the resulting HTML back to the browser and destroys the instance of the Web form.

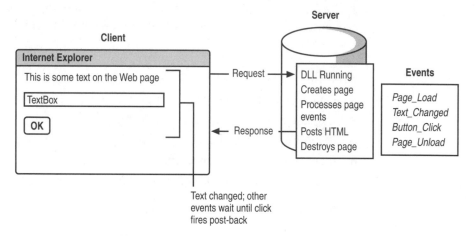

Figure 2-13   Life goes on.

When the user stops using the Web application for a period of time (the default is 20 minutes), the user's session times out and ends. (See Figure 2-14.) If there are no other sessions from other users, the application ends. This doesn't always happen right away. The common language runtime (CLR) manages memory using garbage collection rather than reference counting, as OLE did. Garbage collection means that the server periodically traces through the references between objects. When the runtime finds an object that is no longer used, it throws the object away and recovers the memory. This means that you don't know exactly when an *Application_End* event will occur.

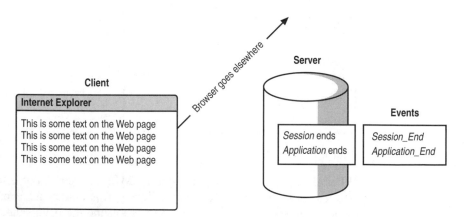

Figure 2-14   This is the end.

Preserving Data on a Web Form

Because Web forms have very short lifetimes, ASP.NET takes special steps to preserve the data entered in the controls on a Web form, as shown in Figure 2-15. Data entered in controls is sent with each request and restored to controls in *Page_Init*. The data in these controls is then available in the *Page_Load* event.

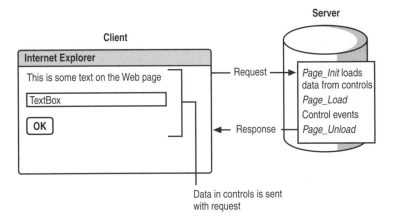

Figure 2-15   ASP.NET preserves Web form data.

The data that ASP.NET preserves between requests is called the Web form's **view state**. By default, a Web form's view state is available only within that Web form. To make data entered on a Web form available to other Web forms in an application, you need to save the data in a state variable in the *Application* or *Session* objects. These objects provide two levels of scope:

- *Application* **state variables**   These are available to all users of an application. You can think of *Application* state as multiple-user global data. All sessions can read or write these variables.

- *Session* **state variables**   These are available only to a single session (user). *Session* state is like global data in a standard Windows application. Only the current session has access to its *Session* state.

Application and *Session* state variables aren't declared the way you declare regular variables. Instead, they are created on the fly in code. For example, the following code saves the number of button clicks in *Session* state:

Visual Basic .NET

```
Private Sub Button1_Click(ByVal sender As System.Object, _
    ByVal e As System.EventArgs) Handles Button1.Click
    ' Save the number of clicks in Session state.
    Session("Clicks") = Session("Clicks") + 1
    ' Display the number of clicks.
    Response.Write("Number of clicks: " & Session("Clicks"))
End Sub
```

Visual C#

```
// From Global.asax.cs
protected void Session_Start(Object sender, EventArgs e)
{
    // Initialize Clicks Session state variable.
    Session["Clicks"] = 0;
}

// From StateNEvents.asax.cs
private void Button1_Click(object sender, System.EventArgs e)
{
    // Increment click count.
    Session["Clicks"] = (int)Session["Clicks"] + 1;
    // Display the number of clicks.
    Response.Write("Number of clicks: " + Session["Clicks"] + "<br>");
}
```

You can save any type of data in a state variable, from a simple integer to whole objects. Because state variables are global data, you need to develop strategies for working with them in your application. Managing state variables in your code is explained in depth in Chapter 3, "Working with Web Objects."

Important   *Application* state variables must be initialized in Visual C# before you perform most operations on them. For example, you need to assign a value to the *Clicks* state variable before performing the cast *(int)Session["Clicks"]*. Otherwise, you will receive the error "Value null was found where an instance of an object was required" at run time.

Application and Session Events

You can write code to respond to *Application* and *Session* events in the Global.asax file. Use *Application* events to initialize objects and data that you want to make available to all the current sessions of your Web application. Use *Session* events to initialize data that you want to keep throughout individual sessions, but that you don't want to share between sessions. Table 2-3 lists each of the *Application* event handlers and describes when they occur.

Table 2-3   Application Event Handlers

Event handler name	Occurs when
Application_Start	The first user visits a page within your Web application.
Application_End	There are no more users of the application.
Application_BeginRequest	At the beginning of each request to the server. A request happens every time a browser navigates to any of the pages in the application.

Table 2-3   Application Event Handlers

Event handler name	Occurs when
Application_EndRequest	At the end of each request to the server.
Session_Start	A new user visits a page within your application.
Session_End	A user stops requesting pages from the Web application and their session times out. Sessions time out after a period specified in the Web.config file.

In Web forms, a **session** is a unique instance of the browser. A single user can have multiple instances of the browser running on his or her machine. If each instance visits your Web application, each instance has a unique session.

To see how *Application* and *Session* events occur, add the following code to the Global.asax file in a Web forms project:

Visual Basic .NET
```
Sub Application_Start(ByVal Sender As Object, ByVal E As  EventArgs)
    ' Record application start.
    Application("AppCount") = Application("AppCount") +  1
End Sub

Sub Session_Start(ByVal Sender As Object, ByVal E As EventArgs)
    ' Count sessions.
    Application("SessCount") = Application("SessCount")  + 1
    ' Display Application count.
    Response.Write("Number of applications: " & _
        Application("AppCount") & "<br>")
    ' Display session count.
    Response.Write("Number of sessions: " & _
        Application("SessCount") & "<br>")
End Sub

Sub Session_End(ByVal Sender As Object, ByVal E As EventArgs)
    ' Decrement sessions.
    Application("SessCount") = Application("SessCount")  - 1
End Sub
```

Visual C#
```
protected void Application_Start(Object sender, EventArgs e)
{
    // Create Application state variables.
    Application["AppCount"] = 0;
    Application["SessCount"] = 0;
    // Record application start.
    Application["AppCount"] = (int)Application["AppCount"] + 1;
}
```

```
protected void Session_Start(Object sender, EventArgs e)
{
    // Count sessions.
    Application["SessCount"] = (int)Application["SessCount"] + 1;
    // Display Application count.
    Response.Write("Number of applications: " +
        Application["AppCount"] + "<br>");
    // Display session count.
    Response.Write("Number of sessions: " +
        Application["SessCount"] + "<br>");
}

protected void Session_End(Object sender, EventArgs e)
{
    // Decrement sessions.
    Application["SessCount"] = (int)Application["SessCount"] - 1;
}
```

To demonstrate the events, run the preceding code, and then start a new instance of the browser and navigate to the address. Each new instance of the browser increments the session count, but the application count stays at 1.

It's important to realize that intrinsic objects such as *Session* and *Response* are not available at *Application_Start*. To use these objects, you have to wait until their creation event occurs.

Web Form Events

You use Web form events to process and maintain data used on a Web page, to respond to data binding, and to handle exceptions on the Web page. Table 2-4 lists the events that occur on a Web form; the first five events are shown in order of occurrence.

Table 2-4   Web Form Events

Event handler name	Occurs when
Page_Init	The server controls are loaded and initialized from the Web form's view state. This is the first step in a Web form's life cycle.
Page_Load	The server controls are loaded in the *Page* object. View state information is available at this point, so this is where you put code to change control settings or display text on the page.
Page_PreRender	The application is about to render the *Page* object.
Page_Unload	The page is unloaded from memory.
Page_Disposed	The *Page* object is released from memory. This is the last event in the life of a *Page* object.

Table 2-4   Web Form Events

Event handler name	Occurs when
Page_Error	An unhandled exception occurs.
Page_AbortTransaction	A transaction is aborted.
Page_CommitTransaction	A transaction is accepted.
Page_DataBinding	A server control on the page binds to a data source.

You can couple the *Page_Load* event with the *IsPostback* property to initialize data the first time a user visits a Web form. This is similar to a *Session_Start* event; however, it occurs at the page level rather than the application level. The following code initializes an object and stores it in the *Session* state the first time a page is viewed:

Visual Basic .NET

```
' Declare a new object.
Dim FlashCard As New FlashCardClass()

Private Sub Page_Load(ByVal sender As System.Object, _
    ByVal e As System.EventArgs) Handles MyBase.Load
    ' If this is the first time the page is viewed...
    If Not (Page.IsPostBack) Then
        ' Shuffle the FlashCards.
        FlashCard.Shuffle()
        ' Store the object in a Session variable.
        Session("FlashCard") = FlashCard
    End If
    ' Get the Session FlashCard variable.
    FlashCard = Session("FlashCard")
    RefreshDisplay()
End Sub
```

Visual C#

```
// From the Web Form Designer generated code region.
private void InitializeComponent()
{
    this.Load += new System.EventHandler(this.Page_Load);
}


// Declare a new object.
FlashCardClass FlashCard = new FlashCardClass();

private void Page_Load(object sender, System.EventArgs e)
{
    if(!IsPostBack)
    {
        // Shuffle the FlashCards.
        FlashCard.Shuffle();
        // Store the object in a Session variable.
```

```
            Session["FlashCard"] = FlashCard;
        }
        // Get the Session FlashCard variable.
        FlashCard = (FlashCardClass)Session["FlashCard"];
        RefreshDisplay();
    }
```

The other page events let you customize the appearance of the page and respond to data events. Data binding, transaction processing, and rendering are covered in greater detail in subsequent chapters.

Server Control Events

Server controls, such as a Button, TextBox, and DropDownList, each have their own sets of events that occur in response to user actions. However, not all server control events are created equal. There are three types of server control events:

- **Postback events**   These events cause the Web page to be sent back to the server for immediate processing. Postback events affect perceived performance because they trigger a round-trip to the server.
- **Cached events**   These events are saved in the page's view state to be processed when a postback event occurs.
- **Validation events**   These events are handled on the page without posting back or caching. The validation server controls use these types of events.

Figure 2-16 shows the sequence of server control events on a Web form. The validations controls are evaluated before the page is posted back to the server. When the page is posted back, the *Page_Init* and *Page_Load* events are handled, then cached events are handled, and finally the event that caused the postback is processed. Among cached events, the event order is determined by the order of the controls on the Web form.

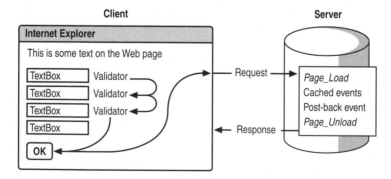

Figure 2-16   A Web form's sequence of events

The Button, Link Button, and Image Button controls all cause postback events. The TextBox, DropDownList, ListBox, RadioButton, and CheckBox controls provide cached events; however, you can override this behavior by setting the *AutoPostBack* property to *True*.

To see how validation, cached, and postback events interact, create a Web form with a TextBox control, a RequiredFieldValidator control, and a Button control. Set the *ControlToValidate* property of the validator control to *TextBox1*, and then add the following code to the TextBox and Button event handlers:

Visual Basic .NET

```
Private Sub Button1_Click(ByVal sender As System.Object, _
    ByVal e As System.EventArgs) Handles Button1.Click
    Response.Write("Button Clicked!<br>")
End Sub

Private Sub TextBox1_TextChanged(ByVal sender As Object, _
    ByVal e As System.EventArgs) Handles TextBox1.TextChanged
    Response.Write("Text has changed!<br>")
End Sub
```

Visual C#

```
private void Button1_Click(object sender, System.EventArgs e)
{
    Response.Write("Button Clicked!<br>");
}

private void TextBox1_TextChanged(object sender, System.EventArgs e)
{
    Response.Write("Text has changed!<br>");
}

// From the Web Form Designer generated code region.
private void InitializeComponent()
{
    this.Button1.Click += new System.EventHandler(this.Button1_Click);
    this.TextBox1.TextChanged += new EventHandler(this.TextBox1_TextChanged);
    this.Load += new System.EventHandler(this.Page_Load);
}
```

If you leave the TextBox control blank and click OK, the RequiredFieldValidator control is displayed—no other events are processed and the page is not posted back to the server. If you type text in the TextBox control and click OK, the page is posted back and the *TextChanged* event occurs before the *Click* event.

Lesson 3: Where Does Processing Occur?

As you know from the previous lesson, Web applications run on a server. But Web applications aren't like Windows applications, which start when the user invokes an executable file and end when the user closes the application. Instead, Web applications start when a browser requests a Web page and end when no more requests are made.

After this lesson, you will be able to

- Use folder structure to define the boundaries of an application
- Set a start page for your application in Visual Studio and set a default document for your application in IIS
- Explain how ASP.NET manages application processes
- Set the time-out value that indirectly determines when an application ends

Estimated lesson time: 15 minutes

Application Boundaries and Start Pages

IIS defines a Web application as any file that is executed within a set of folders on your Web site. The boundaries of a Web application are determined by its folder structure. The application boundary starts in the root application folder, which contains the application's start page, its Web.config file, and the /bin folder containing the application's assembly. The application ends at the last subordinate folder or when another root application folder is encountered. Figure 2-17 shows several separate applications.

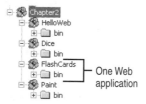

Figure 2-17   Web application boundaries in IIS

When Visual Studio .NET creates a new Web application project, it creates a new folder for the project and identifies the first Web form in the project (Webform1.aspx) as the start page. A **start page** is a page designated by Visual Studio as the first page to display in your application. All of the subordinate folders, such as /bin, are part of that application.

If your application design changes during development, or if you just want to quickly run the current page during debugging, you might want to change the start page of your application.

To set a different Web form or HTML page as the start page, do the following:

- In Solution Explorer, right-click the Web form or HTML page you want to specify as the start page of your application, and choose Set As Start Page on the shortcut menu.

When you are ready to deploy your Web application, you will usually want to set the application's start page as its default document in IIS. The IIS **default document** is the page that IIS displays if the user omits the document name as part of his or her requested address. By default, IIS specifies these default document file names: Default.htm, Default.asp, Index.htm, and Iisstart.asp.

To set your application's start page as the default document in IIS, either rename the start page to one of the file names in the preceding list, or add the start page's file name to the IIS default document list by following these steps:

1. In the IIS management console, select the Web application in the console tree, and the choose Properties from the Action menu. The Web site's Properties dialog box opens.

2. On the Documents tab of the Properties window, click Add. The Add Default Document dialog box opens and allows you to add the name of your application's start page to the default document list, as shown in Figure 2-18.

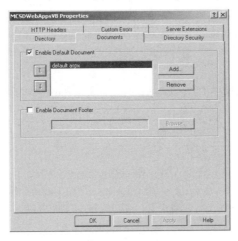

Figure 2-18   The Add Default Document dialog box

3. In the Add Default Document dialog box, type the name of your document and click OK. Click OK to close the Web site's Properties window.

The order of the file names shown in Figure 2-18 determines the precedence of default documents. IIS checks for these documents in the order shown and displays the first document that matches.

How IIS and ASP.NET Manage Processes

Understanding application boundaries is important because ASP.NET uses these boundaries to determine how your application is run on the server. When IIS receives a request for a resource within a Web application, IIS uses aspnet_isapi.dll to call the ASP.NET worker process (aspnet_wp.exe). The ASP.NET worker process loads the Web application's assembly, allocating one process space, called the **application domain**, for each application.

In this way, ASP.NET maintains process isolation for each Web application. This is different from the way IIS provided different isolation levels for older Active Server Pages (ASP) applications running under DLLHost.exe. The isolation level settings in IIS have no effect on ASP.NET applications.

In IIS version 6.0, you will be able to configure multiple application pools, each of which can be served by one or more process instances (w3wp.exe). In addition, ASP.NET is integrated with the IIS version 6.0 kernel mode HTTP listener, which will allow requests to pass directly from the operating system to the ASP.NET worker process. For more information about IIS version 6.0, see the TechNet article *http://www.microsoft.com/technet/prodtechnol/iis/evaluate/iis6ovw.asp*.

Determining When an Application Ends

When a user requests a page from a Web application for the first time, IIS starts the Web application, if it is not already running, and creates a session for that user. All of the subsequent requests made by that user are part of the same session. Sessions are important for two reasons:

- They allow ASP.NET to keep user-specific data called the *Session* state. *Session* state and *Application* state are explained in Lesson 2.
- They determine when the application ends. When the last session ends, IIS ends the application.

How long a session lasts is determined by a time-out value set in your project's Web.config file. The default is 20 minutes. That means that 20 minutes after a user makes his or her last request to an application, the user's session ends. When there are no more sessions, the application ends.

Remember that IIS defines a Web application as any file that is executed within a set of folders on your Web site. So if a user requests any of the .aspx files in that application's set of folders within 20 minutes, that user's session is maintained.

> **Note**   You have only indirect control over when an application ends through the session time-out. It is important to understand this because the session timeout controls the life cycle of the application on the server.

Reducing the session time-out value can free up resources on the server because session data expires more quickly. However, setting the value too low can cause sessions to time out while they are still being used.

To change the session time-out value, follow these steps:

1. Open the project in Visual Studio .NET.
2. Open the Web.config file by double-clicking it in the Solution Explorer window.
3. Edit the time-out value (shown in boldface) in the following line in the file:

   ```
   <sessionState mode="InProc" stateConnectionString="tcpip=127 .0.0.1:42424"
   sqlConnectionString="data source=127.0.0.1;use r id=sa;password="
   cookieless="false" timeout="20" />
   ```

4. Save the file.

Any changes to the Web.config file automatically restart the Web application. If you change the Web.config file on a deployed Web application, *Application* state and *Session* state variables are lost for any current users.

Summary

- Web applications use Web forms to create a user interface that is presented through an Internet browser on the user's computer.
- The code and resources that respond to events and perform useful tasks reside and run on the Web server hosting the application.
- Because Web applications are distributed between a client and a server, there are five significant differences between programming for the Web and programming for Windows:

    - Web applications use server controls and HTML controls rather than Windows controls.
    - Web applications are displayed in a Web browser rather than in their own window.
    - Web forms are not persistent while displayed. You must preserve persistent data in a state variable during page and control events.
    - Processing occurs on the server, and data is exchanged through a cycle of requests and responses.
    - Web applications are event-driven, and events occur at the application, page, and server control levels.

- Server control events have three types, which occur in the following order:

    - Validation events occur before the page is returned to the server.
    - Cached events are collected while the page is displayed and then processed once the page sends a request to the server.
    - Postback events cause the page to send a request to the server, but their event procedure is processed last in order of events handled.

- The boundaries of a Web application are determined by its folder structure.
- Application boundaries affect the scope of data stored in *Application* state.
- You use IIS to create root folders for your applications, set application boundaries, and determine the process in which IIS runs your application.

Lab: Building a Simple Web Application

In this lab, you will create the FlashCards application. FlashCards is a simple, one-form Web application that displays math problems and evaluates the entered result—just like the flash cards used in an elementary-school math class.

To complete the FlashCards application, you will create a Web form, add server controls to the form, and control those server controls from the *Page_Load* event procedure. The completed Web form will look like Figure 2-19.

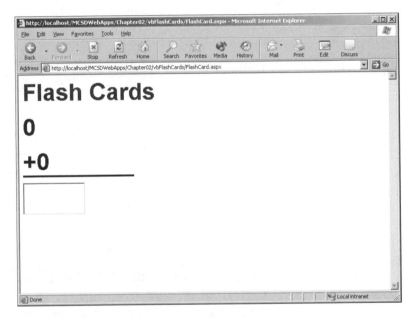

Figure 2-19   The completed FlashCard Web form

Estimated lesson time: 20 minutes

Exercise 1: Create the User Interface

In this exercise, you will start the FlashCards project and create the user interface by adding server controls to the FlashCard Web form.

▶ **To create a new Web application project**

1. On the File menu of Visual Studio .NET, point to New and choose Project. In the New Project dialog box, select ASP.NET Web Application, change the path in the Location box to end with **FlashCards**, and click OK.

2. In the Properties window, change the name of the WebForm1.aspx file to Flash-Card.aspx.

▶   **To add the controls to the user interface**

Add server controls to the Web form, as shown in Figure 2-19, and define the following properties:

Control	Control type	Property	Value
Label1	Label	ID	lblFeedback
		Font	Arial, Bold, XXL
		Text	Flash Cards
Label2	Label	ID	lblFirst
		Font	Arial, Bold, XXL
Label3	Label	ID	lblSecond
		Font	Arial, Bold, XXL
<HR>	Horizontal Rule	Size	4
		Color	#000000
TextBox1	Text Box	ID	txtAnswer
		AutoPostBack	True
		Font	Arial, Bold, XXL

Tip   If you want to create several controls with similar properties, create the first control, set its properties as desired, and then copy and paste to create new controls with the same properties. In Web forms, this does not create a control array as it does in Windows forms.

Exercise 2: Create a Class Named *FlashCardClass*

In this exercise, you will create a class to contain the logic and data that the Flash-Cards application uses. A **class** is a definition of an object used to perform a task in a program. Chapter 3, "Working with Web Objects," has more information about object-oriented programming.

The *FlashCardClass* class created here generates random math problems to display on the Web form. This is the logic that the application uses. In this application, and in most Web form applications, the logic (*FlashCardClass*) is separated from the user interface (the Web form).

▶   **To create a class**

1. From the Project menu, choose Add Class. Visual Studio .NET displays the Add New Item dialog box. Name the class **FlashCardClass**, and click Open.

2. In the Code window, add the following code:

Visual Basic .NET

```
Public Class FlashCardClass

    Dim mintFirstNumber, mintSecondNumber As Integer
    Dim mstrOp As String = "+"
    Dim mrndNumber As Random

    Public Sub New()
        ' Initialize the random number generator object.
        mrndNumber = New Random()
    End Sub

    Public Sub Shuffle(Optional ByVal Min As Integer = 1, _
            Optional ByVal Max As Integer = 12)
        ' Get random numbers.
        mintFirstNumber = mrndNumber.Next(Min, Max)
        mintSecondNumber = mrndNumber.Next(Min, Max)
    End Sub

    Public ReadOnly Property FirstNumber()
        Get
            FirstNumber = mintFirstNumber
        End Get
    End Property

    Public ReadOnly Property SecondNumber()
        Get
            SecondNumber = mintSecondNumber
        End Get
    End Property

    Public Property Operation() As String
        Get
            Operation = mstrOp
        End Get
        Set(ByVal Value As String)
            mstrOp = Value
        End Set
    End Property

      ' Calculates answer based on current operation.
    Public Function Answer() As Integer
        Select Case mstrOp
            Case "+"
                Answer = mintFirstNumber + mintSecondNumber
            Case "x", "*"
                Answer = mintFirstNumber * mintSecondNumber
            Case "-"
                Answer = mintFirstNumber - mintSecondNumber
```

```
            End Select
        End Function

End Class
```

Visual C#

```csharp
public class FlashCardClass
{
    int mintFirstNumber, mintSecondNumber;
    string mstrOp = "+";
    Random mrndNumber;

    public FlashCardClass()
    {
        // Initialize the random number generator object.
    mrndNumber = new Random();
    }

    public void Shuffle(int Min, int Max)
    {
        // Get random numbers.
        mintFirstNumber = mrndNumber.Next(Min, Max);
        mintSecondNumber = mrndNumber.Next(Min, Max);
    }

    // Shuffle with no parameters defaults to Min = 0, Max = 12.
    public void Shuffle()
    {
        // Get random numbers.
        mintFirstNumber = mrndNumber.Next(0, 12);
        mintSecondNumber = mrndNumber.Next(0, 12);
    }

    public int FirstNumber
    {
        get
        {
            return mintFirstNumber;
        }
    }

    public int SecondNumber
    {
        get
        {
            return mintSecondNumber;
        }
    }
```

```
        public string Operation
        {
            get
            {
                return mstrOp;
            }
            set
            {
                mstrOp = value;
            }
        }

        // Calculates answer based on current operation.
public int Answer()
        {
            switch(mstrOp)
            {
                case "+":
                    return mintFirstNumber + mintSecondNumber;
                case "x":
                    return mintFirstNumber * mintSecondNumber;
                case "*":
                    return mintFirstNumber * mintSecondNumber;
                case "-":
                    return mintFirstNumber - mintSecondNumber;
                default :
                    return 0;
            }
        }
    }

}
```

Exercise 3: Store a *FlashCardClass* Object in *Session* State

In this exercise, you will add code to initialize a *Session* state variable containing the *FlashCardClass* object that your Web form will use. The *FlashCardClass* is stored in a *Session* variable, so it is retained during the user's session.

▶ **To create a *Session* state variable**

■   In the Code View window for the Web form FlashCard.aspx, add the following code to the *Page_Load* event procedure:

Visual Basic .NET

```
' FlashCard.aspx.vb
Dim FlashCard As FlashCardClass

Private Sub Page_Load(ByVal sender As System.Object, _
    ByVal e As System.EventArgs) Handles MyBase.Load
```

```
' Create a Session FlashCard object the first time page displays.
If Not IsPostBack Then
    ' Create a new FlashCard object
    FlashCard = New FlashCardClass
    ' Store the object in a Session variable.
    Session("FlashCard") = FlashCard
Else
    ' Get the Session FlashCard object.
    FlashCard = Session("FlashCard")
End If
RefreshDisplay()
End Sub
```

Visual C#

```csharp
// FlashCard.aspx.cs
FlashCardClass FlashCard;

private void Page_Load(object sender, System.EventArgs e)
    {
        // Run the following code the first time the page is displayed.
        if(!IsPostBack)
        {
            FlashCard = new FlashCardClass();
            Session["FlashCard"] = FlashCard;
        }
        else
        {
            // Get the Session FlashCard object.
            FlashCard = (FlashCardClass)Session["FlashCard"];
        }
        RefreshDisplay();
    }
```

Exercise 4: Use the *FlashCardClass* Object from Web Form Events

In this exercise, you will add code to the Web form to use the *FlashCardClass* object stored in the *Session* state variable. This links the logic (*FlashCardClass*) to the user interface (FlashCard.aspx).

▶ **To use the *FlashCardClass* object from event procedures in the Web form**

1. In the Design window, double-click the TextBox control to automatically create the event procedure and wire the TextChanged event. Add the following code to the *Text_Changed* event procedure:

Visual Basic .NET

```
Private Sub txtAnswer_TextChanged(ByVal sender As System.Object, _
    ByVal e As System.EventArgs) Handles txtAnswer.TextChanged
    If txtAnswer.Text = FlashCard.Answer Then
        lblFeedback.Text = "Correct!"
        ' Get another set of numbers.
        FlashCard.Shuffle()
        ' Refresh display to show new numbers.
        RefreshDisplay()
        ' Clear answer
        txtAnswer.Text = ""
    Else
        lblFeedback.Text = "Oops! Try Again."
    End If
End Sub
```

Visual C#

```
private void txtAnswer_TextChanged(object sender, System .EventArgs e)
{
    if(txtAnswer.Text == FlashCard.Answer().ToString())
    {
        lblFeedback.Text = "Correct!";
        // Get another set of numbers.
        FlashCard.Shuffle();
        // Refresh display to show new numbers.
        RefreshDisplay();
        // Clear answer
        txtAnswer.Text = "";
    }
    else
    {
        lblFeedback.Text = "Oops! Try Again.";
    }
}


// From the Web Form designer generated code region (create automatically
// when you double-click the TextBox control.
private void InitializeComponent()
{
    this.txtAnswer.TextChanged += new
        System.EventHandler(this.txtAnswer_TextChanged);
    this.Load += new System.EventHandler(this.Page_Load);
}
```

2. In the *WebForm1* class, add the following helper procedure to refresh the labels on the display:

Visual Basic .NET

```
Private Sub RefreshDisplay()
    lblFirst.Text = FlashCard.FirstNumber
    lblSecond.Text = FlashCard.Operation & _
      FlashCard.SecondNumber
End Sub
```

Visual C#

```
private void RefreshDisplay()
{
    lblFirst.Text = FlashCard.FirstNumber.ToString();
    lblSecond.Text = FlashCard.Operation +
        FlashCard.SecondNumber.ToString();
}
```

3. Run and test the application.

Tip   Using a form-level variable to hold data stored in *Session* or *Application* state variables, as shown in steps 2 and 3, helps you catch errors. Visual Studio .NET does not require you to declare state variables. Misspelling a state variable name simply creates a new, empty state variable.

Review

The following questions are intended to reinforce key information presented in this chapter. If you are unable to answer a question, review the appropriate lesson and then try the question again. Answers to the questions can be found in the appendix.

1. Explain where Visual Studio .NET stores Web application projects.

2. List the four major differences between Web and Windows applications.

3. Describe the life cycle of a Web application: When are Web forms instantiated and how long do they exist?

4. How do you preserve persistent data, such as simple variables, in a Web application?

5. What determines the boundaries of a Web application?

C H A P T E R 3

Working with Web Objects

About This Chapter

In this chapter, you'll learn how to create and organize objects in Microsoft Visual Studio .NET, use the objects provided by Microsoft ASP.NET, and save objects and data between requests to Web forms. Microsoft Visual Basic .NET, Microsoft Visual C#, and ASP.NET share a common framework, so all of the object-oriented programming techniques you learn here apply to all aspects of Web Forms application programming.

Before You Begin

To complete the lessons in this chapter, you must:

- Be familiar with the basics of the Visual Basic, C#, or C++ programming language. This should include familiarity with the concepts of variables, procedures, decision structures, and scope. See the "Language Changes in Visual Basic" or "C# Language Tour" Help topics included with Visual Studio for introductions to these languages.
- Understand events in the life cycle of a Web application as discussed in Lesson 2 of Chapter 2, "Creating Web Forms Applications."

Lesson 1: Namespace Fundamentals

Visual Basic .NET and Visual C# provide a full set of object-oriented programming concepts, including abstract classes, interfaces, and overloading or overriding class members. These features are fundamental to the language and are used throughout the Microsoft .NET Framework. By learning how to use these features yourself, you will understand how the .NET Framework is implemented and you'll be better able to use it in your applications.

After this lesson, you will be able to

- Organize your code using namespaces
- Create classes and control access to those classes
- Create abstract and base classes and derive new classes from them
- Understand how the members of an inherited class can be overloaded, overridden, or shadowed
- Create interfaces for classes and explain how they are different from abstract classes

Estimated lesson time: 40 minutes

Understanding Namespaces

At the beginning of the code for each Web form, you'll see some generated code that looks like this:

Visual Basic .NET

```
Imports System
Imports System.Web
```

Visual C#

```
using System;
using System.Web;
```

These statements permit you to use code from the ASP.NET namespaces *System* and *System.Web* without specifying their full names. Without these statements, a call to a simple method from the *System* namespace, for example, would look like this:

Visual Basic .NET

```
System.Array.Sort(strArray)
```

Visual C#

```
System.Array.Sort(strArray);
```

By including the *System* namespace at the beginning of the code, that *Array* method can be shortened to:

Visual Basic .NET

```
Array.Sort(strArray)
```

Visual C#

```
Array.Sort(strArray);
```

Namespaces are a way of organizing code. They provide protection from conflicting names, sometimes called **namespace collisions**. This protection is especially necessary in large projects in which it is very easy for two items to accidentally have the same name. By organizing your code into namespaces, you reduce the chance of these conflicts.To create a namespace, enclose a *Class* or *Module* in a *Namespace…End Namespace* block.

To add more than one class or module to a namespace, specify the same namespace for each.

The following code (in boldface) creates a namespace for the *Strings* module:

Visual Basic .NET

```
' Project name: MCSDWebAppsVB
Namespace Utils
    Public Module Strings
        Public Function Sort(ByVal strText As String, _
            Optional ByVal bAlphaOrder As Boolean = True) As String
            ' Declare and initialize a string array.
            Dim strArray As String() = {""}
            ' Convert the string to an array using System.String.
            strArray = strText.Split(" ")
            ' Use System.Array to sort.
            System.Array.Sort(strArray)
            ' If it's not alphabetic order, reverse the array.
            If Not bAlphaOrder Then
                ' Use System.Array to reverse.
                System.Array.Reverse(strArray)
            End If
            ' Return the a string.
            Sort = System.String.Join(" ", strArray)
        End Function
    End Module
End Namespace
```

Visual C#

```
// Project name: MCSDWebAppsCS
namespace Utils
{
    class Strings
```

```
    {
        // Takes a string, sorts it, and returns a string.
        public static string Sort(string strText , bool bAlphaOrder)
        {
            // Declare and initialize a string array.
            string[] strArray = {""};
            char[] strSep = {' '};
            //  Convert the string to an array using System.String.
            strArray = strText.Split(strSep);
            // Use System.Array to sort.
            System.Array.Sort(strArray);
            //  If it's not alphabetic order, reverse the array.
            if (!bAlphaOrder)
            {
                // Use System.Array to reverse.
                System.Array.Reverse(strArray);
            }
            // Return the string.
            return System.String.Join(" ", strArray);
        }

        // Same method with one parameter.
        public static string Sort(string strText)
        {
            return Sort(strText, true);
        }

    }
}
```

Important   The preceding example also *uses* two .NET namespaces: *System.Array* and *System.String*. The *System* namespaces are the new way to access functions you used to access in the Microsoft Windows API through *Declare* statements. This is even easier now because Visual Basic .NET, Visual C#, and the .NET Framework use the same fundamental types and default parameter passing conventions. Unlike the Windows API, the *System* namespaces provide an object-oriented interface to the Windows functions. This might take some getting used to if you are already familiar with the Windows API. However, the benefits of the common language runtime and managed code are enormous.

Because namespaces are an organization tool for code you want to use elsewhere, they are public by definition. When used in code, the reference takes the form:

ProjectName.NameSpace.ModuleName.MemberName

You can use code from a namespace in your application in one of two ways:

- Use the fully qualified name of the member. The following code (in boldface) calls the *Sort* function from the MCSDWebAppsVB or MCSDWebAppsCS project's *Utils* namespace:

Visual Basic .NET

```
Private Sub Button1_Click(ByVal sender As System.Object, _
    ByVal e As System.EventArgs) Handles Button1.Click
    ' Sort the text.
    txtValue.Text = MCSDWebAppsVB.Utils.Strings.Sort(txtValue.Text)
  End Sub
End Class
```

Visual C#

```
private void Button1_Click(object sender, System.EventArgs e )
    {
    txtValue.Text = MCSDWebAppsCS.Utils.Strings.Sort(txtValue.Text);
    }
```

- Add a Visual Basic .NET *Imports* or Visual C# *using* statement at the beginning of a class or module. The *Imports* or *using* statement provides a shortcut to the member name—you no longer have to use the full name in code. The following code (in boldface) uses the namespace in the MCSDWebAppsVB or MCSD-WebAppsCS project's *Utils* namespace:

Visual Basic .NET

```
' Import the Utils namespace from the MCSDWebAppsVB project.
Imports MCSDWebAppsVB.Utils

Public Class Namespaces
    ' Declarations and initialization code omitted…

    Private Sub butSort_Click(ByVal sender As System.Object, _
      ByVal e As System.EventArgs) Handles Button1.Click
        ' Call a helper function
        txtValue.Text = Strings.Sort(txtValue.Text)
    End Sub
End Class
```

Visual C#

```
// Import the Utils namespace from the MCSDWebAppsCS project.
using MCSDWebAppsCS.Utils;
namespace csNamespaces
{
    public class Namespaces : System.Web.UI.Page
    {
        // Declarations and initialization code omitted...

        private void butSort_Click(object sender, EventArgs  e)
```

```
            {
                txtValue.Text = Strings.Sort(txtValue.Text);

            }
        }
    }
```

Namespaces use dot notation (.) to specify hierarchy. Consider the following namespace declaration:

Visual Basic .NET

```
' Project name: MCSDWebAppsVB
Namespace Utils
    Namespace Types
        Class Digits
            Public Enum Numeric
                Zero
                One
                Two
                Three
                Four
                Five
                Six
                Seven
                Eight
                Nine
            End Enum
        End Class
    End Namespace
End Namespace
```

Visual C#

```
// Project name: MCSDWebAppsCS
namespace Utils
{
    namespace Types
    {
        class Digits
        {
            public enum Numeric
            {
                Zero, One, Two, Three, Four, Five,
                Six, Seven, Eight, Nine
            }
        }
    }
}
```

This declaration is equivalent to the following code:

Visual Basic .NET

```
' Project name: MCSDWebAppsVB
Namespace Utils.Types
    Class Digits
                Public Enum Numeric
                Zero
                One
                Two
                Three
                Four
                Five
                Six
                Seven
                Eight
                Nine
            End Enum
    End Class
End Namespace
```

Visual C#

```
// Project name: MCSDWebAppsCS
namespace Utils.Types
{
    class Digits
    {
        public enum Numeric
        {
            Zero, One, Two, Three, Four, Five,
            Six, Seven, Eight, Nine
        }
    }
}
```

To use either of the preceding namespace declarations, you can use the fully quali-fied name, as shown here:

Visual Basic .NET

```
Dim numVar As MCSDWebAppsVB.Utils.Types.Digits.Numeric
```

Visual C#

```
MCSDWebAppsCS.Utils.Types.Digits.Numeric numVar;
```

Or you can use an *Imports* or *using* statement, as shown here:

Visual Basic .NET

```
Imports MCSDWebAppsVB.Utils.Types
Dim numVar As Digits.Numeric
```

Visual C#

```
using MCSDWebAppsCS.Utils.Types;
Digits.Numeric numVar;
```

References vs. Imports

You add project references to use namespaces outside of the current project. Use the *Imports* statement to provide a shortcut to that namespace. The *Imports* statement simply provides an abbreviated way to refer to a namespace in code.

To add a reference to a project:

1. From the Project menu, choose Add Reference. Visual Studio .NET displays the Add Reference dialog box, as shown in Figure 3-1.

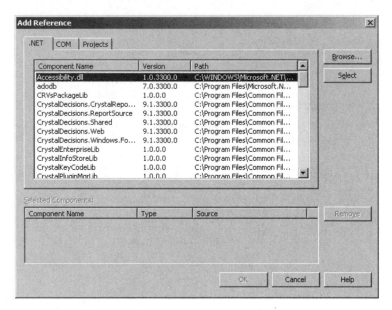

Figure 3-1   Adding a project reference

2. Select the reference to add from within the .NET, COM, or Project component lists. Click OK.

Visual Studio adds references to the project in the Solution Explorer.

Classes and Modules

Visual Studio projects store code in classes and modules. Earlier versions of Visual Basic introduced the concept of classes and how classes are unique from code modules. This concept is the same in Visual Basic .NET: you use classes for items that define their own storage, and you use modules for code that does not have persistent data. Also, you instantiate classes to create objects before you use them, whereas you can simply call code modules directly.

In Visual C#, however, all code is contained in a class. If you want to create methods or properties that can be called without first creating an object, declare those items as static. The *Utils* class's *Sort* method created in the preceding section demonstrates the Visual C# equivalent of a Visual Basic .NET module.

Visual Basic .NET and Visual C# use six key concepts for working with modules and classes. These concepts are new to Visual Basic and, of course, Visual C#, because that is an entirely new language. However, C++ programmers should already be familiar with these concepts. Table 3-1 describes these key concepts in both languages.

Table 3-1 Key Object-Oriented Concepts

Concept	In Visual Basic .NET	In Visual C#
Definition	You define whether something is a class or a module by using *Class...End Class* or *Module...End Module* blocks. In earlier versions, this was implicit with the file type and you could have only one *Class* or *Module* per file.	You define classes using the *class* keyword. All executable code is part of a class.
Access	There are five levels of access to classes, modules, and their members: *Public*, *Protected*, *Friend*, *Protected Friend*, and *Private*. Access is also explicit in the item's definition, rather than hidden in file properties.	There are five levels of access to classes and their members: *public*, *protected*, *internal*, *protected internal*, and *private*.
Inheritance	Classes can inherit members from each other and override, shadow, or overload members of the inherited class.	Classes can inherit members from base classes and override or overload members of the inherited class.
Constructors and destructors	Classes have *New* and *Finalize* methods that are called when an object based on the class is created or destroyed.	Classes have constructors and destructors that are called when an object based on the class is created or destroyed. Constructor methods have the same name as their class, and destructor methods use the class name preceded by a tilde (~).

Table 3-1   Key Object-Oriented Concepts

Concept	In Visual Basic .NET	In Visual C#
Delegates	The *Delegates* statement provides a safe way to call methods by their address rather than by their name. This is the .NET equivalent of a callback. Delegates are commonly used with events and asynchronous procedures.	The *delegates* keyword provides a safe way to call methods by their address rather than by their name. This is the .NET equivalent of a callback. Delegates are commonly used with events and asynchronous procedures.
Abstract classes and interfaces	You can create interfaces and abstract classes. Interfaces define the member names and member parameter lists for classes that use the interface. Abstract classes provide the members to be inherited by classes derived from them.	You can create interfaces and abstract classes. Interfaces define the member names and member parameter lists for classes that use the interface. Abstract classes provide the members to be inherited by classes derived from them.

Creating Classes/Modules and Providing Access

In Visual Basic .NET, use *Class...End Class* and *Module...End Module* blocks to define classes and modules. In Visual C#, use the *class* keyword to define classes. You can have one or more classes and/or modules per file. Use one of the access keywords described in Table 3-2 to define which other classes and modules can use the members of the current class or module.

Table 3-2   Levels of Access for Classes and Modules

Visual Basic	Visual C#	Available to
Public	*public*	All members in all classes and projects.
Friend	*internal*	All members in the current project.
Protected	*protected*	All members in the current class and in classes derived from this member's class. Can be used only in member definitions, not for class or module definitions.
Protected Friend	*protected internal*	All members in the current project and all members in classes derived from this member's class. Can be used only in member definitions, not for class or module definitions.
Private	*private*	Members of the current class only.

For example, the following class is available only in the current project:

Visual Basic .NET

```vbnet
Friend Class Translator
    Private mstrText As String

    ' Controls access to the class-level
    ' variables.
    Public Property Text() As String
        Get
            Text = mstrText
        End Get
        Set(ByVal Value As String)
            mstrText = Value
        End Set
    End Property

    ' Translates the value in the Text property.
    Public Sub Translate()
        Dim strWord As String, intCount As Integer
        Dim arrWords() As String
        Dim bCaps As Boolean
        ' Convert the string to an array using System.String.
        arrWords = mstrText.Split(" ")
        For intCount = 0 To UBound(arrWords)
            ' Check if word is capitalized.
            If LCase(arrWords(intCount)) <> arrWords(intCount) Then
                bCaps = True
                arrWords(intCount) = LCase(arrWords(intCount))
            End If
            strWord = arrWords(intCount)
            ' Do translation.
            If strWord <> "" Then
                strWord = Right(strWord, Len(strWord) - 1) & _
                    Left(strWord, 1) & "ay"
                ' Recapitalize if necessary
                If bCaps Then
                    strWord = UCase(Left(strWord, 1)) & _
                        Right(strWord, Len(strWord) - 1)
                End If
            End If
            ' Store back in the array.
            arrWords(intCount) = strWord
            ' Reset caps flag.
            bCaps = False
        Next
        ' Rebuild string from array.
        mstrText = String.Join(" ", arrWords)
    End Sub
End Class
```

Visual C#

```csharp
internal class Translator
    {
        string mstrText;

        // Controls access to class-level variables.
        public string Text
        {
            get
            {
                return mstrText;
            }
            set
            {
                mstrText = value;
            }
        }

        // Translates the value in the Text property.
        public void Translate()
        {
            string strWord;
            string[] arrWords;
            bool bCaps = false;

            //  Convert the string into an array using System.String.
            arrWords = mstrText.Split(' ');
            for(int intCount = 0; intCount <= arrWords.GetUpperBound(0);
                intCount++)
            {
                // Change to lowercase.
                strWord = arrWords[intCount].ToLower();
                // Check if word is capitalized.
                if(!arrWords[intCount].Equals(strWord))
                    bCaps = true;
                // Do translation.
                if(strWord != "")
                {
                    strWord = strWord.Substring(1,strWord.Length - 1) +
                        strWord.Substring(0,1) + "ay";
                    // Recapitalize if necessary.
                    if(bCaps)
                        strWord = strWord.Substring(0,1).ToUpper() +
                            strWord.Substring(1, strWord.Length - 1);
                }
                // Store the word back in the array.
                arrWords[intCount] = strWord;
                // Reset the caps flag.
                bCaps = false;
```

```
        }
        // Rebuild the string from the array.
        mstrText = String.Join(" ", arrWords);
    }
}
```

You can access the *Text* property and *Translate* method of the preceding *Translator* class from within the project where it is included, but not from other projects. The following code (in boldface) shows using the *Text* and *Translate* members from a Web form:

Visual Basic .NET

```
Private Sub butTranslate_Click(ByVal sender As System.Object , _
  ByVal e As System.EventArgs) Handles butTranslate.Click
    ' Create a new Translator object.

    Dim TranslateText As New Translator()
    ' Put the source text into the translator.
    TranslateText.Text = txtInput.Text
    ' Turn the crank.
    TranslateText.Translate()
    ' Display result.
    txtOutput.Text = TranslateText.Text
End Sub
```

Visual C#

```
private void butTranslate_Click(object sender, System.EventArgs e)
{
    // Create a new Translator object.
    Translator TranslateText = new Translator();
    // Put the source text into translator.
    TranslateText.Text = txtInput.Text;
    // Turn the crank.
    TranslateText.Translate();
    // Display the result.
    txtOutput.Text = TranslateText.Text;
}
```

When you look at the code Visual Studio generates for a Web form, notice that the server controls on the Web form are declared as *Protected*:

Visual Basic .NET

```
Protected System.Web.UI.WebControls.TextBox txtInput
Protected System.Web.UI.WebControls.Button butTranslate
```

Visual C#

```
protected System.Web.UI.WebControls.TextBox txtInput;
protected System.Web.UI.WebControls.Button butTranslate;
```

By default, server control objects are set to be available only in the current Web form and in Web forms derived from that Web form.

Inheritance: Who's Deriving?

Inheritance is the process of basing one class on another. In this process, a **base class** provides methods, properties, and other members to a **derived class**. The advantage of inheritance is that you can write and maintain code once it is in the base class and reuse it over and over in the derived classes. How familiar you are with inheritance usually depends on which programming language you have been using.

- Visual Basic .NET introduces inheritance to Visual Basic programming. This is a huge step forward for the language and is the reason that many things had to change between all earlier versions of Visual Basic. Windows Forms and data types are now derived from the .NET Framework, rather than being implemented through the "Ruby" engine that powered earlier versions of Visual Basic. You'll now find a lot more agreement and consistency between Visual Basic and Windows.

- C# programmers who are familiar with C++ are probably very familiar with the concept of inheritance. However, Visual C# adds refinements not found in C++ syntax, including the *interface* and *abstract* keywords.

How you specify inheritance also depends on your programming language. In Visual Basic .NET, you use the *Inherits* statement to base a new class on an existing one. In Visual C#, no keyword is needed; instead, you use the class definition. The following lines show the different syntaxes for each language:

Visual Basic .NET

```
Public Class DerivedClass
    Inherits BaseClass
End Class
```

Visual C#

```
public class DerivedClass : BaseClass
{
}
```

Visual Studio uses the keywords described in Table 3-3 for creating base classes and deriving new classes from them. The sections that follow explain how to use each of these keywords.

Table 3-3   Overview of the Inheritance Keywords

Visual Basic	Visual C#	Use to
Inherits	*derivedclass : baseclass*	Base one class on another, inheriting members from the base class.
Overridable	*virtual*	Declare that a member of the base class can be overridden in a derived class.

Table 3-3   Overview of the Inheritance Keywords

Visual Basic	Visual C#	Use to
Overrides	*override*	Declare that a member of a derived class overrides the member of the same name in the base class.
Shadows	*new*	Declare that a member of a derived class hides the member of the same name in the base class.
MustInherit	*abstract*	Declare that a class provides a template for derived classes. This type of class is called an **abstract class**, and it can't be instantiated.
MustOverride	*abstract*	Declare that a member of a class provides a template for derived members. This type of member is called an **abstract member**, and it can't be invoked.
MyBase	*base*	Call a base class member from within the derived class.
Me	*this*	Call a member of the current instance of a class.
Interface	*interface*	Create an interface that defines the members a class must provide.
Implements	*classname : interfacename*	Use an interface definition in a class.

Before we look at inheritance in more detail, you should understand the two things you *can't* do with inheritance:

- You can't inherit from more than one base class in a single derived class definition. The concept of **multiple inheritance** exists in many object-oriented programming languages, but as a practical matter, it is not widely used.
- Derived Web forms inherit the code from their base Web form, but not the base form's HTML or server controls. That is because the Web form's class (.vb or .cs) is separate from its appearance (.aspx).

Overriding, Overloading, and Shadowing Members

A derived class inherits the members of its base class. If the derived class defines a member with the same signature, the derived member **overrides** the base member. A member's **signature** includes its name, parameter list, parameter types, and return type.

If a derived class defines a member with the same name but a different parameter list, parameter type, or return type than the base member, the derived member either overloads or shadows the base member. A member **overloads** another member if the base member is still available. A member **shadows** another member if the derived member replaces the base member.

In the following example, the class *Sphere* is based on the class *Circle*. In Visual Basic .NET, members that can be overridden must be declared as *Overridable (1)*. In Visual C#, members that can be overridden must be declared as *virtual (1)*. The *Circle* class is shown here:

Visual Basic .NET

```vb
Public Class Circle
    Private sxCenter, syCenter As Single
    Private sRadius As Single

    Public Property Top() As Single
        Get
            Top = sxCenter - sRadius
        End Get
        Set(ByVal Value As Single)
            sxCenter = Value + sRadius
        End Set
    End Property

    Public Property Left() As Single
        Get
            Left = syCenter - sRadius
        End Get
        Set(ByVal Value As Single)
            syCenter = Value + sRadius
        End Set
    End Property

    Public Overridable Function Area() As Single        ' (1)
        Area = System.Math.PI * (sRadius ^ 2)
    End Function

    Public Function Perimeter() As Single
        Perimeter = 2 * sRadius * System.Math.PI
    End Function

    Public Property Radius() As Single
        Get
            Radius = sRadius
        End Get
        Set(ByVal Value As Single)
            sRadius = Value
        End Set
    End Property
```

```
        Public Overridable Sub Center(ByVal X As Single, _
          ByVal Y As Single) ' (1)
            sxCenter = X
            syCenter = Y
        End Sub
    End Class
```

Visual C#

```
public class Circle
{
    float fxCenter, fyCenter, fRadius;
    // Constructor
    public Circle()
    {
        // Initialize internal variables.
        fxCenter = 0;
        fyCenter = 0;
        fRadius = 0;
    }
    public float Top
    {
        get
        {
            return fyCenter - fRadius;
        }
        set
        {
            fyCenter = value + fRadius;
        }
    }
    public float Left
    {
        get
        {
            return fyCenter - fRadius;
        }
        set
        {
            fyCenter = value + fRadius;
        }
    }

    public virtual float Area()              // (1)
    {
        return (float)(System.Math.PI * Math.Pow((double)fRadius, 2));
    }

    public float Perimeter()
    {
        return 2 * fRadius * (float)System.Math.PI;
    }
```

```
public float Radius
{
    get
    {
        return fRadius;
    }
    set
    {
        fRadius = value;
    }
}

public virtual void Center(float X, float Y)          // (1)
{
        fxCenter = X;
        fyCenter = Y;
}
}
```

In the following example, *Sphere* class inherits all of the methods and properties defined in *Circle (1)*. *Sphere* overrides the method for *Area (2)* because spheres use a different formula for this calculation. *Sphere* shadows the *Center* method *(3)* because spheres have an additional coordinate (z) and you wouldn't want users to accidentally set xy-coordinates without setting a z-coordinate. Notice that *Sphere* uses the Visual Basic .NET *MyBase* or the Visual C# *base* keyword *(4)* to call the base class's *Center* method within the shadowed method.

Visual Basic .NET

```
Public Class Sphere
    Inherits Circle                                      ' (1)
    Private sCenter As Single

    Public Overrides Function Area() As Single           ' (2)
        Area = 4 * System.Math.PI * (MyBase.Radius ^ 2)
    End Function

    Public Shadows Sub Center(ByVal X As Single, _
      ByVal Y As Single, ByVal Z As Single)             ' (3)
        MyBase.Center(X, Y)                              ' (4)
        sCenter = Z
    End Sub

    Public Function Volume() As Single
        Volume = (4 / 3) * System.Math.PI * (Radius ^ 3)
    End Function

    Public Property Front() As Single
        Get
            Front = sCenter - Radius
        End Get
```

```
        Set(ByVal Value As Single)
            sCenter = Value + MyBase.Radius
        End Set
    End Property
End Class
```

Visual C#

```csharp
public class Sphere : Circle                        // (1)
{
    float fzCenter;

    // Constructor.
    public Sphere()
    {
        // Initialize internal variable.
        fzCenter = 0;
    }

    public override float Area()                     // (2)
    {
        return (float)(4 * System.Math.PI * Math.Pow((double)base.Radius, 2));
    }

    public new void Center(float X, float Y)         //  (3)
    {
        this.Center(X, Y, 0);
    }

    public void Center(float X, float Y, float Z)
    {
        base.Center(X, Y);                           //  (4)
        fzCenter = Z;
    }

    public float Volume()
    {
        return (float)((4 / 3) * System.Math.PI *
            Math.Pow((double)base.Radius, 3));
    }

    public float Front
    {
        get
        {
            return fzCenter - base.Radius;
        }
        set
        {
            fzCenter = value + base.Radius;
        }
    }
}
```

To see how inheritance works, create a new object of each type and call each object's properties and methods. The following code demonstrates the *Circle* and *Sphere* classes by displaying calculated values on a Web form:

Visual Basic .NET

```
Private Sub Page_Load(ByVal sender As System.Object, _
  ByVal e As System.EventArgs) Handles MyBase.Load
    Dim MyCircle As New Circle()
    MyCircle.Radius = 2
    MyCircle.Center(10, 2)
    Response.Write("Circle area: " & MyCircle.Area & "<br>")
    Response.Write("Circle circumference: " & MyCircle.Perimeter _
      & "<br>")
    Dim MySphere As New Sphere()
    MySphere.Radius = 10
    MySphere.Center(10, 20, 25)
    Response.Write("Sphere top: " & MySphere.Top & "<br>")
    Response.Write("Sphere left: " & MySphere.Left & "<br>")
    Response.Write("Sphere front: " & MySphere.Front & "<br> ")
    Response.Write("Sphere volume: " & MySphere.Volume & "<b r>")
    Response.Write("Sphere surface area: " & MySphere.Area &  _
      "<br>")
    Response.Write("Sphere circumference: " & _
      MySphere.Perimeter & "<br>")
End Sub
```

Visual C#

```
private void Page_Load(object sender, System.EventArgs e)
{
    Circle MyCircle = new Circle();
    MyCircle.Radius = 2;
    MyCircle.Center(10, 2);
    Response.Write("Circle area: " + MyCircle.Area() + " <br>");
    Response.Write("Circle circumference: " + MyCircle.Perimeter() +
      "<br>");
    Sphere MySphere = new Sphere();
    MySphere.Radius = 10;
    MySphere.Center(10,20,25);
    Response.Write("Sphere top: " + MySphere.Top + "<br> ");
    Response.Write("Sphere left: " + MySphere.Left + "<b r>");
    Response.Write("Sphere front: " + MySphere.Front + " <br>");
    Response.Write("Sphere volume: " + MySphere.Volume()  + "<br>");
    Response.Write("Sphere surface area: " + MySphere.Area() + "<br>");
    Response.Write("Sphere circumference: " + MySphere.Perimeter() +
      "<br>");
}
```

In the Abstract

Visual Studio also lets you define abstract classes. An **abstract class** is a class that defines an interface for derived classes. An abstract class is essentially a contract saying that all classes based on it will provide certain methods and properties. You can't create objects from abstract classes—you can only derive new classes from them.

Abstract classes are declared with the Visual Basic .NET *MustInherit* or the Visual C# *abstract* keyword. Methods and properties that base classes must provide are declared as *MustOverride* in Visual Basic .NET or as *abstract* in Visual C#. The following *Shape* class demonstrates an abstract class:

Visual Basic .NET

```
' Definition of abstract class.
Public MustInherit Class Shape
    Public MustOverride Property Top() As Single
    Public MustOverride Property Left() As Single
    Public MustOverride Function Area() As Single
    Public MustOverride Function Perimeter() As Single
End Class
```

Visual C#

```
// Definition of abstract class.
public abstract class Shape
{
    public Shape()
    {
    }
    public abstract float Top
    {
        get;
        set;
    }
    public abstract float Left
    {
        get;
        set;
    }
    public abstract float Area();

    public abstract float Perimeter();

}
```

Notice that the Visual Basic .NET *MustOverride* and Visual C# *abstract* members are just definitions—there is no procedure body statement because these members will be defined (overridden) in the derived class.

The following *Circle* class demonstrates how an abstract class is inherited. In Visual Basic .NET, the *Inherits* statement *(1)* declares that this class is based on the abstract class *Shape*. The *Overrides* keywords *(2)* are required in each of the member definitions that override members of the abstract class. In Visual C#, the class definition *(1)* declares that this class is based on the abstract class *Shape*. The *override* keywords *(2)* are required in each of the member definitions that override members of the abstract class.

Visual Basic .NET

```vb
Public Class Circle
    Inherits Shape                              ' (1)
    Private sxCenter, syCenter As Single
    Private sRadius As Single

    Public Overrides Property Top() As Single   ' (2)
        Get
            Top = sxCenter - sRadius
        End Get
        Set(ByVal Value As Single)
            sxCenter = Value + sRadius
        End Set
    End Property

    Public Overrides Property Left() As Single
        Get
            Left = syCenter - sRadius
        End Get
        Set(ByVal Value As Single)
            syCenter = Value + sRadius
        End Set
    End Property

    Public Overrides Function Area() As Single
        Area = 2 * System.Math.PI * (sRadius ^ 2)
    End Function

    Public Overrides Function Perimeter() As Single
        Perimeter = 2 * sRadius * System.Math.PI
    End Function

    Public Property Radius() As Single
        Get
            Radius = sRadius
        End Get
        Set(ByVal Value As Single)
            sRadius = Value
        End Set
    End Property

    Public Overridable Sub Center(ByVal X As Single, ByVal Y  As Single)
```

```
                sxCenter = X
                syCenter = Y
        End Sub
End Class
```

Visual C#

```
public class Circle : Shape                    // (1)
{
    float fxCenter, fyCenter, fRadius;

    // Constructor.
    public Circle()
    {
        // Initialize internal variables.
        fxCenter = 0;
        fyCenter = 0;
        fRadius = 0;
    }
    public override float Top                  // (2)
    {
        get
        {
            return fxCenter - fRadius;
        }
        set
        {
            fxCenter = value + fRadius;
        }
    }

    public override float Left
    {
        get
        {
            return fyCenter - fRadius;
        }
        set
        {
            fyCenter = value + fRadius;
        }
    }

    public override float Area()
    {
        return (float)(Math.PI * Math.Pow((double)fRadius, 2));
    }
        public override float Perimeter()
    {
        return 2 * fRadius * (float)System.Math.PI;
    }
```

```
        public float Radius
    {
        get
        {
            return fRadius;
        }
        set
        {
            fRadius = value;
        }
    }

    public virtual void Center(float X, float Y)
    {
            fxCenter = X;
            fyCenter = Y;
    }
}
```

Delegates and Events

Delegates are types used to invoke one or more methods where the actual method invoked is determined at run time. This provides a safe way for derived objects to subscribe to events provided by their base class. Delegates also provide a way for programs to respond to asynchronous procedures.

Simply put, delegates provide a way to invoke methods by their address rather than by their name. For example, the following Web form code declares a delegate named *MathDelegate* and then invokes two different methods through the delegate from the *AboutNumber* procedure. When run, this code displays the message *The number 42 is even and is not prime.*

Visual Basic

```
Public Class SimpleDelegate
    Inherits System.Web.UI.Page

    ' Declare a delegate.
    Delegate Function MathDelegate(ByVal x As Integer) As Boolean

    Private Sub Page_Load(ByVal sender As System.Object, _
    ByVal e As System.EventArgs) Handles MyBase.Load
        Dim MyNumber As Integer = 42
        Response.Write("<h2>Using Delegates</h2><hr />")
        Response.Write("The number " & MyNumber.ToString())
        ' Call AboutNumber to invoke IsEven.
        AboutNumber(AddressOf IsEven, MyNumber)
        Response.Write(" even and it ")
        ' Call AboutNumber to invoke IsPrime.
        AboutNumber(AddressOf IsPrime, MyNumber)
```

```
            Response.Write(" prime.")
    End Sub


    ' Invoke the delegate.
    Sub AboutNumber(ByVal Func As MathDelegate, ByVal x As Integer)
        If Func.Invoke(x) Then
            Response.Write(" is ")
        Else
            Response.Write(" is not ")
        End If
    End Sub


    ' These procedures may be invoked through MathDelegate.
    Function IsEven(ByVal x As Integer) As Boolean
        If x Mod 2 Then
            Return False
        Else
            Return True
        End If
    End Function


    Function IsPrime(ByVal x As Integer) As Boolean
        Dim i As Integer
        For i = 2 To x \ 2
            If (x Mod i = 0) Then
                Return False
            End If
        Next
        Return True
    End Function
End Class
```

Visual C#

```csharp
public class SimpleDelegate : System.Web.UI.Page
{
    delegate bool MathDelegate(int x);
    private void Page_Load(object sender, System.EventArgs e)
    {
        int MyNumber = 42;
        Response.Write("<h2>Using Delegates</h2><hr />");
        Response.Write("The number " + MyNumber.ToString());
        // Call AboutNumber to invoke IsEven.
        AboutNumber(new MathDelegate(IsEven), MyNumber);
        Response.Write(" even and it ");
        // Call AboutNumber to invoke IsPrime.
        AboutNumber(new MathDelegate(IsPrime), MyNumber);
        Response.Write(" prime.");
    }


    // Invoke the delegate.
```

```
void AboutNumber(MathDelegate Func, int x)
{
    if (Func(x))
        Response.Write(" is ");
    else
        Response.Write(" is not ");
}

// These procedures may be invoked through MathDelegate.
bool IsEven(int x )
{
    if (x % 2 == 0)
        return true;
    else
        return false;
}

bool IsPrime(int x )
{
    for(int i = 2; i > (x /2); i++)
        if (x % i == 0)
            return false;
    return true;
}
}
```

Note   The delegate's declaration must match the signature of the methods invoked. This rule ensures that delegation is type-safe.

But why provide an alternative way to invoke methods? Perhaps the most important reason is that delegates provide the flexibility required for responding to events and asynchronous tasks running in separate threads.

For example, the following class finds factors of a given seed number. Because such calculations may take a while, the class launches the calculations in a separate thread. The class declares an event and raises the event when a factor is found, returning the factor in the event arguments. The delegate that appears above the event declaration allows Web forms (or other code) to subscribe to the event.

Visual Basic

```
' MathClass exposes an event that fires every time a new factor is found.
Public Class MathClass
    ' Declares the signature of the procedures that handle this event.
    Delegate Sub OnFactorHandler(ByVal sender As Object, _
        ByVal e As MathEventArgs)
    ' Exposes the event.
    Public Event OnGotFactor As OnFactorHandler
    ' Internal variable used by this class.
```

```
    Protected Seed As Double
    ' This class uses a delegate from the System.Threading namespace to
    ' invoke the CalcFactors procedure in asynchronously in as separate
    ' thread.
    Protected Thread As New System.Threading.Thread(AddressOf CalcFactors)

    ' Class constructor sets the seed value and launches the thread.
    Public Sub New(ByVal X As Integer)
        Seed = X
        ' Launch the thread to begin calculating factors.
        Thread.Start()
    End Sub

    ' Provides a way to stop the asynchronous processing.
    Public Sub StopCalc()
        Thread.Abort()
    End Sub

    ' Finds the positive factors of the seed value and raises an event each
    ' time one is found.
    Protected Sub CalcFactors()
        ' Create a MathEventArgs object as a means to return the factors.
        Dim e As New MathEventArgs
        ' Declare a counter.
        Dim i As Integer
        For i = 2 To Math.Abs(Seed \ 2)
            ' If the number is evenly divisible by the counter, return the
            ' counter in the event arguments.
            If (Seed Mod i = 0) Then
                e.Factor = i
                RaiseEvent OnGotFactor(Me, e)
            End If
        Next
    End Sub

End Class

' This class provides a way to return values from the event.
Public Class MathEventArgs
    Inherits System.EventArgs
    Public Factor As Integer
End Class
```

Visual C#

```
// MathClass exposes an event that fires every time a new factor is found.
public class MathClass
{
    // Declares the signature of the procedures that handle this event.
    public delegate void OnFactorHandler(Object sender, MathEventArgs e);
    // Exposes the event.
```

```csharp
        public event OnFactorHandler OnGotFactor;
        // Internal variable used by this class.
        protected long Seed;
        // This class uses a delegate from the System.Threading namespace to
        // invoke the CalcFactors procedure asynchronously in a
        // separate thread.
        System.Threading.Thread CalcThread;

        // Class constructor sets the seed value and launches the thread.
        public MathClass(int X)
        {
            Seed = X;
            // Create a new thread for the calculations.
            CalcThread = new System.Threading.Thread(new
                    System.Threading.ThreadStart(CalcFactors));
            // Launch the thread to begin calculating factors.
            CalcThread.Start();
        }


        // Provides a way to stop the asynchronous processing.
        public void StopCalc()
        {
            CalcThread.Abort();
        }


        // Finds the positive factors of the seed value and raises an event each
        // time one is found.
        public void CalcFactors()
        {
            // Create a MathEventArgs object as a means to return the factors.
            MathEventArgs e = new MathEventArgs();
            // Declare a counter.
            for (int i = 2; i < Math.Abs(Seed / 2); i++)
            {
                // If there is a listener for the OnGotFactor event
                // and if the number is evenly divisible by the
                // counter, return the counter in the event
                // arguments.
                if ((OnGotFactor != null) && (Seed % i == 0))
                {
                    e.Factor = i;
                    // Raise the event.
                    OnGotFactor(this, e);
                }
            }
        }
    }


    // This class provides a way to return values from the event.
    public class MathEventArgs : System.EventArgs
```

```
{
    public int Factor;
}
```

To subscribe to the event, a Web form can declare an instance of the class using the
WithEvents keyword in Visual Basic or using the event += new delegate (handler)
event handler syntax in Visual C#, as shown in the following Web form code.
Notice that both the *ShowFactor* and *StopCalc* event handler procedures respond to
the *MathClass* class's *OnGotFactor* event—that's a key part of the flexibility
afforded by delegates.

Visual Basic

```
Public Class EventDelegate
    Inherits System.Web.UI.Page

    ' Create an object and subscribe to it's events.
    WithEvents MyMath As MathClass

    Private Sub Page_Load(ByVal sender As System.Object, _
      ByVal e As System.EventArgs) Handles MyBase.Load
        If Not IsPostBack Then
            ' Create a new instance of MathClass with a very large
            ' seed value.
            MyMath = New MathClass(Integer.MaxValue - 1)
            ' Store the class in a Session variable
            Session("MyMath") = MyMath
        Else
            ' Get the stored Session variable
            MyMath = Session("MyMath")
        End If
    End Sub

    ' This procedure subscribes to the MathClass OnGotFactor event.
    Sub ShowFactor(ByVal sender As Object, ByVal e As MathEventArgs) _
        Handles MyMath.OnGotFactor
        ' Save Factor in Session object for retrieval in
        ' PreRender page event.
        Session("Factor") = e.Factor
    End Sub

    ' This procedure also subscribes to the MathClass OnGotFactor event.
    Sub StopCalc(ByVal sender As Object, ByVal e As MathEventArgs) _
        Handles MyMath.OnGotFactor
        ' After the limit, stop the calculations.
        If e.Factor > CType(txtLimit.Text, Integer) Then
            ' Stop the MathClass thread.
            MyMath.StopCalc()
        End If
    End Sub
```

```vb
' This procedure handles the Page's PreRender event.
' It's required to display the asynchronously calculated Factor.
Private Sub Page_PreRender(ByVal sender As Object, _
  ByVal e As System.EventArgs) Handles MyBase.PreRender
    ' Get the Factor that was calculated asynchronously.
    If Not IsNothing(Session("Factor")) Then
        lblFactor.Text = Session("Factor")
    End If
End Sub

End Class
```

Visual C#

```csharp
public class EventDelegate : System.Web.UI.Page
{
    protected System.Web.UI.WebControls.Label lblFactor;
    protected System.Web.UI.WebControls.TextBox txtLimit;
    protected System.Web.UI.WebControls.RangeValidator RangeValidator1;
    protected System.Web.UI.WebControls.Button butUpdate;

    // Declare an object.
    MathClass MyMath;

    private void Page_Load(object sender, System.EventArgs e)
    {
        if (!IsPostBack)
        {
            // Create a new instance of MathClass with a
            // very large seed value.
            MyMath = new MathClass(Int32.MaxValue - 1);
            // Store the class in a Session variable
            Session["MyMath"] = MyMath;
        }
        else
            // Get the stored Session variable
            MyMath = (MathClass)Session["MyMath"];
        // Subscribe to the OnGotFactor event.
        MyMath.OnGotFactor += new
            MathClass.OnFactorHandler(this.ShowFactor);
        MyMath.OnGotFactor += new MathClass.OnFactorHandler(this.StopCalc);
    }

    // This procedure subscribes to the MathClass OnGotFactor event.
    private void ShowFactor(Object sender, MathEventArgs e )
    {
        // Save the factor as the event is raised.
        Session["Factor"] = e.Factor.ToString();
    }
```

```csharp
    // This procedure also subscribes to the MathClass OnGotFactor event.
    private void StopCalc(Object sender, MathEventArgs e )
    {
        // After the limit, stop the calculations.
        if (e.Factor > Convert.ToInt32(txtLimit.Text))
            // Stop the MathClass thread.
            MyMath.StopCalc();
    }


    // This procedure handles the Page's PreRender event.
    // It's required to display the asynchronously calculated Factor.
    private void Page_PreRender(object sender, EventArgs e)
    {
        // Display the current Factor.
        if (Session["Factor"] != null)
            lblFactor.Text = Session["Factor"].ToString();
    }
}
```

At run time, the preceding Web form code displays the largest factor found by the time the Web form has finished processing. Clicking the Update button refreshes that number from the *MathClass* object as it calculates factors in a separate thread.

Visual Basic .NET provides two ways to use a delegate. The first is shown in the preceding example using the *WithEvents* and *Handles* keywords. The second way uses the Visual Basic .NET *AddHandler* and *RemoveHandler* statements, and it looks a lot more like C# syntax. For example, the following code associates the *ShowFactor* and *StopCalc* methods with the *OnGotFactor* event:

Visual Basic

```vb
AddHandler MyMath.OnGotFactor, AddressOf this.ShowFactor
AddHandler MyMath.OnGotFactor, AddressOf this.StopCalc
```

The advantage of this syntax is that you can also disassociate a method from the event using the *RemoveHandler* statement.

Interface-to-Face

Interfaces are similar to abstract classes in that they both provide a template that you can use to create new classes. The difference is that interfaces don't provide any implementation of class members, whereas abstract classes can implement members that then become common to all the classes derived from them.

When you implement a particular interface in a class, instances of that class can be used for any argument or variable declared as that interface. For example, the following code declares an interface for the shape objects created earlier in this lesson:

Visual Basic .NET

```
' Interface for all shapes.
Public Interface IFigure
    Property Top() As Single
    Property Left() As Single
    Function Area() As Single
    Function Perimeter() As Single
End Interface
```

Visual C#

```
// Interface for all shapes.
public interface IFigure
{
    float Top
    {
        get;
        set;
    }
        float Left
    {
        get;
        set;
    }
        float Area();
        float Perimeter();
}
```

To use the interface, implement it in a class, as shown here in boldface:

Visual Basic .NET

```
' Definition of abstract class.
Public MustInherit Class Shape
    Implements IFigure
    Public MustOverride Property Top() As Single Implements IFigure.Top
    Public MustOverride Property Left() As Single Implements  IFigure.Left
    Public MustOverride Function Area() As Single Implements  IFigure.Area
    Public MustOverride Function Perimeter() As Single Implements _
        IFigure.Perimeter
End Class
```

Visual C#

```
public abstract class Shape : IFigure
{
    // Constructor
    public Shape()
    {
    }

    public abstract float Top
```

```
    {
        get;
        set;
    }
        public abstract float Left
    {
        get;
        set;
    }

    public abstract float Area();

    public abstract float Perimeter();

}
```

Because the *Shape* abstract class in this example implements the *IFigure* interface, all classes derived from *Shape* inherit the implementation of *IFigure* as well. This means that objects of the type *Circle* and *Sphere*, which derive from *Shape*, can be used as the arguments of the type *IFigure*, as shown in the following procedure calls:

Visual Basic .NET

```
Private Sub Page_Load(ByVal sender As System.Object, _
    ByVal e As System.EventArgs) Handles MyBase.Load
        ' Show header.
        Response.Write("<h2>Using Inheritance</h2><hr />")
        ' Create a circle.
        Dim MyCircle As New Circle()
        MyCircle.Radius = 2
        MyCircle.Center(10, 2)
        ' Create a sphere.
        Dim MySphere As New Sphere()
        MySphere.Radius = 10
        MySphere.Center(10, 20, 25)
        ' Show info about the shapes.
        ShowShapeInfo(MySphere)
        ShowShapeInfo(MyCircle)
End Sub


' Display the shape info on the Web form.
Sub ShowShapeInfo(ByVal Shape As IFigure)
        Response.Write("Shape top: " & Shape.Top & "<br>")
        Response.Write("Shape left: " & Shape.Left & "<br>")
        Response.Write("Shape perimeter: " & Shape.Perimeter & "<br>")
        Response.Write("Shape surface area: " & Shape.Area & _
            "<br>")
        Response.Write("Shape perimeter: " & _
            Shape.Perimeter & "<br>")
End Sub
```

Visual C#

```csharp
private void Page_Load(object sender, System.EventArgs e)
{
    // Show header.
    Response.Write("<h2>Using Inheritance</h2><hr />");
    // Create a circle.
    Circle MyCircle = new Circle();
    MyCircle.Radius = 2;
    MyCircle.Center(10, 2);
    // Create a sphere.
    Sphere MySphere = new Sphere();
    MySphere.Radius = 10;
    MySphere.Center(10,20,25);
    // Show info about each shape.
    ShowShapeInfo(MySphere);
    ShowShapeInfo(MyCircle);
}

// Display the shape info on the Web form.
private void ShowShapeInfo(IFigure Shape)
{
    //  Since Shape argument is IFigure, we know it has these membe rs.
    Response.Write(String.Format("Shape top: {0} <br>", Shape.Top));
    Response.Write(String.Format("Shape left: {0} <br>", Shape.Left));
    Response.Write(String.Format("Shape perimeter: {0} <br>",
    Shape.Perimeter()));
    Response.Write(String.Format("Shape area: {0} <br>",
    Shape.Area()));
}
```

The key here is that all items defined in the interface must exist in any class that implements the interface. If you omit any member, you get an error when you compile the code.

Lesson 2: Namespaces in a Web Application

In this lesson, you'll learn how to navigate the ASP.NET namespaces to find the objects you use to create a Web application. You will also see how to use the *Application*, *Page*, *Request*, and *Response* objects in code. These four objects form the core of Web application programming.

After this lesson, you will be able to

- Navigate the .NET Framework to find objects for Web applications
- Explain how objects relate to each other in the ASP.NET architecture
- Get at the ASP.NET objects and control them in code
- Navigate the object hierarchy to get subordinate ASP.NET objects such as the *Browser* and *Cookies* objects.

Estimated lesson time: 30 minutes

Overview of Web Namespaces

The class definitions for objects used in Web applications reside in the *System.Web* namespace. Table 3-4 shows the namespace hierarchy and describes the kinds of class definitions you will find in each namespace. Use this table as a guide to finding objects that perform specific tasks.

Table 3-4   Namespace Hierarchy

Namespace	Contains classes for
System.Web	The *Application*, *Browser*, *Cache*, *Cookies*, *Exception*, *Request*, *Response*, *Server*, and *Trace* objects. Use these classes in most Web programming tasks. The *Application* object defined in Global.asax is based on the *Application* class.
System.Web.SessionState	The *Session* object. Use these classes to save and retrieve items saved in the *Session* state.
System.Web.Services	The *WebService* object. Use these classes to create and use Web services.
System.Web.UI	The *Page* and *Control* objects. Use these classes within a Web form to create and control an application's user interface. Web forms are based on the *Page* class.
System.Web.UI.WebControls	All server control objects. Use these classes within Web forms.
System.Web.UI.HTMLControls	All HTML control objects. Use these classes within Web forms.

Table 3-4   Namespace Hierarchy

Namespace	Contains classes for
System.Web.Caching	The *Cache* object. Use these classes to control server-side caching to improve application performance.
System.Web.Mail	The *MailMessage*, *MailAttachment*, and *SmtpMail* objects. Use these classes to send mail messages from your application.
System.Web.Security	Authentication objects and modules. Use these classes to authenticate users and provide security within your application.

When programming a Web application, you deal directly with two types of objects derived from classes in the Web namespaces:

- **The *Application* object**   Derived from the *HttpApplication* class. In your application, this definition resides in the Global.asax file.
- **Web Form objects**   Derived from the *Page* class. In your application, this definition resides in Web Form modules.

The following code shows the declarations that Visual Studio generates for the *Global* and *WebForm1* classes. These classes are instantiated automatically by the ASP.NET run time.

Visual Basic .NET

```
Public Class Global
    Inherits System.Web.HttpApplication
End Class

Public Class WebForm1
    Inherits System.Web.UI.Page
End Class
```

Visual C#

```
public class Global : System.Web.HttpApplication
{
}

public class WebForm1 : System.Web.UI.Page
{
}
```

These *Global* and *WebForm1* objects are the entry points you use to get at other Web objects in an application. Those objects, along with *Request* and *Response*, are the objects you will most commonly work with in code. The following sections explain how to use the *Application*, *Page*, *Request*, and *Response* objects to navigate among other objects.

Using the *Application* Object

The *Application* object is a top-level object in your Web application's object hierarchy. Use the *Application* object to configure your application, to save state information, and to respond to application-wide events. The *Application* object has properties and methods that provide access to other objects in your application, as shown in Figure 3-2.

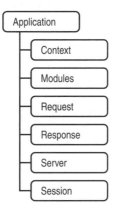

Figure 3-2   The *Application* object

When ASP.NET starts your application, it automatically instantiates the *Global* object defined in Global.asax. Use the events in the *Global* object to configure your application and to initialize application-level state variables.

The *HttpApplication* base class provides the properties and methods to access the subordinate objects for the *Global* object. These properties and methods are described in Table 3-5. Use these properties and methods to get at other objects from the *Application* object.

Table 3-5   Properties and Methods of the *Application* Object

Property/method	Use to
Application	Save data items in the *Application* state.
Context	Get *Handler*, *Trace*, *Cache*, *Error*, and other objects for the current context.
Modules	Access HTTP modules.
Request	Read a request and get *Browser*, *ClientCertificates*, *Cookies*, and *Files* objects from the current request.
Response	Write text or data to a response and get *Cache*, *Cookies*, and *Output* objects from the current response.
Server	Process requests and responses. The *Server* object provides helper methods for URL encoding and decoding.

Table 3-5   Properties and Methods of the *Application* Object   *(continued)*

Property/method	Use to
Session	Save data items in the *Session* state.
User	Get authentication information about the user making the current request. By default, Web applications allow anonymous access.

The following code uses the *Request* and *Browser* objects available from within the *Application* object to determine whether a browser making a request is version 4.0 or later:

Visual Basic .NET

```
Sub Application_BeginRequest(ByVal sender As Object, _
  ByVal e As EventArgs)
    ' Fires at the beginning of each request
    If Request.Browser.MajorVersion < 4 Then
        ' Disable advanced features.
    End If
End Sub
```

Visual C#

```
protected void Application_BeginRequest(Object sender, EventArgs e)
{
    // Fires at the beginning of each request.
    if (Request.Browser.MajorVersion < 4)
    {
        // Disable advanced features.
    }
}
```

Using the *Page* Object

The *Page* object controls your application's user interface. The *Page* object has properties and methods that provide access to other objects in the user interface, as shown in Figure 3-3.

Chapter 3   Working with Web Objects   127

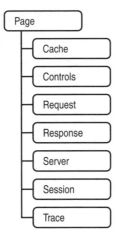

Figure 3-3   The *Page* object

When a user requests a page from your application, ASP.NET automatically instantiates the Web form and displays the page. You add event procedures to the form to control the user interface and to interact with the user.

The *Page* base class provides the core methods and properties that you use most frequently when programming Web forms. These properties and methods are shown in Table 3-6.

Table 3-6   Properties and Methods of the *Page* Object

Property/method	Use to
Application	Save data items in the *Application* state.
Cache	Control how responses are cached on the server.
Controls	Get at controls on the page.
Request	Read a request and get *Browser*, *ClientCertificates*, *Cookies*, and *Files* objects from the current request.
Response	Write text or data to a response and get *Cache*, *Cookies*, and *Output* objects from the current response.
Server	Process requests and responses. The *Server* object provides helper methods for URL encoding and decoding.
Session	Save data items in the *Session* state.
Trace	Turn tracing on or off and write to the trace log.

The following code adds a new control to the Web form at run time:

Visual Basic

```
Private Sub Page_Load(ByVal sender As System.Object, _
    ByVal e As System.EventArgs) Handles MyBase.Load
    ' Create a new control.
    Dim txtNew As New TextBox()
    ' Set some text to display in the control.
    txtNew.Text = "Some new text"
    ' Add the control between the <form> </ form> elements
    ' as the second control on the page.
    FindControl("Form1").Controls.AddAt(2, txtNew)
End Sub
```

Visual C#

```
private void Page_Load(object sender, System.EventArgs e)
{
    // Create a new control.
    TextBox txtNew = new TextBox();
    // Set some text to display in the control.
    txtNew.Text = "Some new text";
    // Add the control between the <form> </ form> elements
    // as the second control on the page.
    FindControl["Form1"].Controls.AddAt(2, txtNew);
}
```

Using the *Request* Object

The *Request* object contains the information sent by the client browser when a page is requested from the application. The *Request* object has properties and methods that provide access to other objects that make up the request, as shown in Figure 3-4.

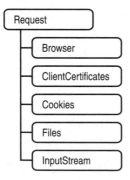

Figure 3-4   The *Request* object

The *Request* object provides the methods and properties to access the subordinate objects described in Table 3-7.

Table 3-7   Properties and Methods of the *Request* Object

Property/method	Use to
Browser	Determine the capabilities of the browser making the request. Browser properties provide the browser version number, determine whether it is the AOL browser, determine whether the browser supports cookies, and supply other information.
ClientCertificates	Authenticate the client.
Cookies	Get information from the client in the form of cookies.
Files	Get files that are uploaded by the client.
InputStream	Read and write to the raw data sent in the request.

The following code uses the *Request* object to check whether the browser supports cookies and whether a particular cookie exists before saving the value of a cookie in the *Session* state:

Visual Basic .NET

```
Private Sub Page_Load(ByVal sender As System.Object, _
    ByVal e As System.EventArgs) Handles MyBase.Load
    ' Run first time page is displayed.
    If Not IsPostBack Then
        ' Check if Browser supports cookies.
        If Request.Browser.Cookies Then
            ' Check if the UName cookie exists.
            If Not IsNothing(Request.Cookies("UName")) Then
                ' Save the value of the cookie.
                Session("User") = Request.Cookies("UName").Value
            End If
        End If
    End If
End Sub
```

Visual C#

```
private void Page_Load(object sender, System.EventArgs e)
{
    // Run first time page is displayed.
    if(!IsPostBack)
        // Check if Browser supports cookies.
        if(Request.Browser.Cookies)
            // Check if the UName cookie exists.
            if(Request.Cookies["UName"] != null)
                // Get the value of the cookie.
                Session["User"] = Request.Cookies["UName"].Value;
}
```

Using the *Response* Object

Use the *Response* object to form the response sent from the server to the client browser. The *Response* object has properties and methods that provide access to other objects that make up the request, as shown in Figure 3-5.

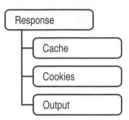

Figure 3-5   The *Response* object

The *Response* object provides methods and properties to access the subordinate objects, as described in Table 3-8.

Table 3-8   Properties and Methods of the *Response* Object

Property/method	Use to
Cache	Determine how the server caches responses before they are sent to the client
Cookies	Set the content of cookies to send to the client
Output	Get or set the raw data returned to the client as the response

The following code creates a cookie and sends it to the client as part of the response:

Visual Basic .NET

```
Private Sub Page_Load(ByVal sender As System.Object, _
    ByVal e As System.EventArgs) Handles MyBase.Load
    ' Run the first time this page is displayed.
    If Not IsPostBack Then
        ' If the browser supports cookies
        If Request.Browser.Cookies Then
            ' Create a cookie.
            Dim cookUname As New HttpCookie("UName")
            cookUname.Value = "Wombat"
            ' Add the cookie.
            Response.Cookies.Add(cookUname)
        End If
    End If
End Sub
```

Visual C#

```csharp
private void Page_Load(object sender, System.EventArgs e)
{
    if(!IsPostBack)
        // If the browser supports cookies
        if (Request.Browser.Cookies)
        {
            // Create a cookie.
            HttpCookie cookUname = new HttpCookie("UName");
            cookUname.Value = "Wombat";
            // Add the cookie.
            Response.Cookies.Add(cookUname);
        }
}
```

Lesson 3: Maintaining State Information

In this lesson, you'll learn how to retain data on a Web form between requests. ASP.NET provides different mechanisms for saving form data, depending on the nature and scope of the information.

After this lesson, you will be able to

- Choose from the different ways to save data on a Web form based on your needs
- Transfer data between Web forms with query strings
- Save items on the client as cookies
- Store page data in a Web form's *ViewState* property
- Keep application-wide variables in *Application* and *Session* state
- Structure access to *Application* and *Session* state variables to avoid programming errors

Estimated lesson time: 30 minutes

Overview of Levels of State

As explained in Chapter 2, "Creating Web Forms Applications," Web forms are created and destroyed each time a client browser makes a request. Because of this characteristic, variables declared within a Web form do not retain their value after a page is displayed. To solve this problem, ASP.NET provides the following ways to retain variables between requests:

- **Context.Handler object**   Use this object to retrieve public members of one Web form's class from a subsequently displayed Web form.
- **Query strings**   Use these strings to pass information between requests and responses as part of the Web address. Query strings are visible to the user, so they should not contain secure information such as passwords.
- **Cookies**   Use cookies to store small amounts of information on a client. Clients might refuse cookies, so your code has to anticipate that possibility.
- **View state**   ASP.NET stores items added to a page's *ViewState* property as hidden fields on the page.
- **Session state**   Use *Session* state variables to store items that you want keep local to the current session (single user).
- **Application state**   Use *Application* state variables to store items that you want be available to all users of the application.

Using *Context.Handler*

Ordinarily the members of one Web form are unavailable from a subsequently displayed Web form. However, when navigating between Web forms using the *Transfer* or *Execute* method, you can retrieve read-only properties from the previous Web form the first time a subsequent Web form is displayed.

For example, the following code declares a public property named *Value* that returns the data entered in a text box on the *Context1* Web form:

Visual Basic .NET

```
Public Class Context1
    Inherits System.Web.UI.Page

    ' Create a property to return the value of a text box.
    Friend ReadOnly Property Value() As String
        Get
            Return txtValue.Text
        End Get
    End Property

    Private Sub butNext_Click(ByVal sender As System.Object, _
      ByVal e As System.EventArgs) Handles butNext.Click
        ' Transfer to the next page.
        Server.Transfer("Context2.aspx")
    End Sub
End Class
```

Visual C#

```
public class Context1 : System.Web.UI.Page
{
    // Create a property to return the value of a text box.
    internal string Value
    {
        get
        {
            return txtValue.Text;
        }
    }

    private void butNext_Click(object sender, System.EventArgs e)
    {
        // Transfer to the next page.
        Server.Transfer("Context2.aspx");
    }
}
```

When the user clicks the Button control, he or she is transferred to the Context2 Web form, which retrieves the previous Web form's *Context.Handler* object, coerces that object to the previous Web form's type, and then accesses the Context1 *Value* property, as shown here:

Visual Basic

```
Public Class Context2
    Inherits System.Web.UI.Page

    Private Sub Page_Load(ByVal sender As System.Object, _
        ByVal e As System.EventArgs) Handles MyBase.Load
        ' The first time this page is displayed
        If Not IsPostBack Then
            ' Declare an object with the previous page's type.
            Dim LastPage As Context1
            ' Convert the context handler to the previous page's type.
            LastPage = CType(Context.Handler, Context1)
            ' Display the value from the page's Value property.
            lblValue.Text = LastPage.Value
        End If
    End Sub
End Class
```

Visual C#

```
public class Context2 : System.Web.UI.Page
{
    private void Page_Load(object sender, System.EventArgs e)
    {
        if (!IsPostBack)
        {
            // Declare an object using the previous page's type.
            Context1 LastPage;
            // Coerce the Context.Handler object to the page's type.
            LastPage = (Context1)Context.Handler;
            // Display the Value property.
            lblValue.Text = LastPage.Value;
        }
    }

    private void butBack_Click(object sender, System.EventArgs e)
    {
        // Transfer back to the preceding page.
        Server.Transfer("Context1.aspx");
    }
}
```

You can transfer complex types from one Web form to another in this way, but remember that the *Context.Handler* object reflects only the immediately previous Web form—on postback events, it will reflect the currently displayed Web form. Also remember that the *Transfer* method does not notify the user's browser that the page address has changed. If the user clicks Refresh on his or her browser, the user receives a warning that the page can't be refreshed without resending information.

Using Query Strings

Query strings allow you to send additional information along with an address. In HTML, query strings appear after a question mark in a hyperlink, as shown here:

```
<A HREF= "WebForm1.aspx?UName=Wombat">Query string sample.</ A>
```

To send a query string in code, add it to the address of a *Redirect* method. The following *Click* event procedure is equivalent to the preceding HTML:

Visual Basic .NET

```
Private Sub butSend_Click(ByVal sender As System.Object, _
   ByVal e As System.EventArgs) Handles Button1.Click
        ' Redisplay this page with a QueryString.
        Response.Redirect(Request.FilePath & "?UName=Wombat")
End Sub
```

Visual C#

```
private void butSend_Click(object sender, System.EventArgs e)
{
    // Redisplay this page with a QueryString
    Response.Redirect(Request.FilePath + "?UName=Wombat");
}
```

To retrieve a query string in code, use the *QueryString* method of the *Request* object. The following code displays the *UName* item from the query string created in the preceding examples:

Visual Basic .NET

```
Private Sub Page_Load(ByVal sender As System.Object, _
    ByVal e As System.EventArgs) Handles MyBase.Load
    ' Check for QueryString
    If Not IsNothing(Request.QueryString("UName")) Then
        ' Display message.
        lblQstring.Text = "QueryString UName="
        ' Display QueryString
        lblQstring.Text += Request.QueryString("UName")
    End If
End Sub
```

Visual C#

```
private void Page_Load(object sender, System.EventArgs e)
{
    // Check for QueryString
    if (Request.QueryString["UName"] != null)
    {
```

```
        // Display message.
        lblQstring.Text = "QueryString UName=";
        // Display QueryString
        lblQstring.Text += Request.QueryString["UName"];
    }
}
```

Using Cookies

Use cookies to store small amounts of information on the client's machine. Web sites often use cookies to store user preferences or other information that is client-specific. Because cookies can be refused, it is important to check whether the browser allows them before you try to create them.

The following code checks whether a browser allows cookies and then saves user preferences if it does:

Visual Basic .NET

```
Private Sub Page_Load(ByVal sender As System.Object, _
    ByVal e As System.EventArgs) Handles MyBase.Load
    ' Run the first time this page is displayed.
    If Not IsPostBack Then
        ' If the browser supports cookies
        If Request.Browser.Cookies Then
            ' Create a cookie.
            Dim cookUPrefs As New HttpCookie("UPrefs")
            cookUPrefs.Value = "English"
            ' Add the cookie.
            Response.Cookies.Add(cookUPrefs)
        End If
    End If
End Sub
```

Visual C#

```
private void Page_Load(object sender, System.EventArgs e)
{
    // Run the first time this page is displayed.
    if(!IsPostBack)
        // If the browser supports cookies.
        if(Request.Browser.Cookies)
        {
            // Create a cookie.
            HttpCookie cookUPrefs = new HttpCookie("UPrefs");
            cookUPrefs.Value = "English";
            // Add the cookie.
            Response.Cookies.Add(cookUPrefs);
        }
}
```

The following code checks for a cookie and then gets the cookie if it is available:

Visual Basic .NET

```
Private Sub Page_Load(ByVal sender As System.Object, _
    ByVal e As System.EventArgs) Handles MyBase.Load
    ' Run first time page is displayed.
    If Not IsPostBack Then
        ' Check if Browser supports cookies.
        If Request.Browser.Cookies Then
            ' Check if the UPrefs cookie exists.
            If Not IsNothing(Request.Cookies("UPrefs")) Then
                ' Save the value of the cookie.
                Session("Lang") = Request.Cookies("UPrefs").Value
            End If
        End If
    End If
End Sub
```

Visual C#

```
private void Page_Load(object sender, System.EventArgs e)
{
    // Run the first time this page is displayed.
    if(!IsPostBack)
        // If the browser supports cookies.
        if(Request.Browser.Cookies)
            // Check if the UPrefs cookie exists
            if(Request.Cookies["UPrefs"] != null)
                // Save the value of the cookie.
                Session["Lang"] = Request.Cookies["UPrefs"]. Value;
}
```

Using *ViewState*

Use the *ViewState* property to save data in a hidden field on a page. Because *View-State* stores data on the page, it is limited to items that can be serialized. If you want to store more complex items in *ViewState*, you must convert the items to and from a string.

For example, the following code adds text from a text box to cells in a table on the page. Because you can't store objects directly in *ViewState*, you must store the strings in the *butAdd_Click* procedure and then create the table row controls from the strings, as shown in the *Page_PreRender* procedure.

Visual Basic .NET

```
Private Sub butAdd_Click(ByVal sender As System.Object, _
    ByVal e As System.EventArgs) Handles butAdd.Click
    ' Add text to ViewState
```

```vbnet
        ViewState.Add(ViewState.Count, txtValue.Text)
    End Sub


    ' This executes just before the page is displayed,
    ' so it exhibits the affects of the button clicks.
    Private Sub Page_Prerender(ByVal sender As System.Object, _
        ByVal e As System.EventArgs) Handles MyBase.PreRender
        ' Create a new row object.
        Dim rowNew As New TableRow
        ' Add row to the table.
        tblViewState.Rows.Add(rowNew)
        ' Variable used to enumerate ViewState collection.
        Dim Item As StateItem
        ' For each item in the ViewState
        For Each Item In ViewState.Values()
            ' Create a new table cell
            Dim celNew As New TableCell
            ' Set cell text.
            celNew.Text = Item.Value
            ' Add cell to row.
            rowNew.Cells.Add(celNew)
            ' Create a new row every four cells.
            If rowNew.Cells.Count > 3 Then
                rowNew = New TableRow
                tblViewState.Rows.Add(rowNew)
            End If
        Next
    End Sub
```

Visual C#

```csharp
// This executes just before the page is displayed,
// so it exhibits the affects of the button clicks.
private void Page_PreRender(object sender, EventArgs e)
{
    // Create a new row object.
    TableRow rowNew = new TableRow();
    // Add row to the table
    tblViewState.Rows.Add(rowNew);
    // For each item in the ViewState
    foreach (StateItem Item in ViewState.Values)
    {
        // Create a new table cell
        TableCell celNew = new TableCell();
        // Set cell text.
        celNew.Text = Item.Value.ToString();
        // Add cell to row.
        rowNew.Cells.Add(celNew);
        // Create a new row every four cells.
        if (rowNew.Cells.Count > 3)
        {
            rowNew = new TableRow();
            tblViewState.Rows.Add(rowNew);
```

```
        }
      }
    }
```

ASP.NET hashes the hidden data stored on the page so that it is not intelligible to users. If you add a few items to the table using the preceding code and then choose View Source from the browser, the HTML for the hidden field looks something like this:

```
</HEAD>
<body MS_POSITIONING="GridLayout">
<form name="Form1" method="post" action="WebForm1.aspx" id=" Form1">
<input type="hidden" name="__VIEWSTATE"
value="dDwtMTMwNzIzM zU0Mzt0PHA8bDwwOzE7Mjsz0zQ7PjtsPFxlO1RoaXMgaXMgc29tZSB0Z
Xh
001RoaXMgaXMgc29tZSB0ZXh001RoaXMgaXMgc29tZSB0ZXh001RoaXMgaXM gc29tZSB0ZXh00z4
+0zs+0z4=" />
```

This hashing prevents malicious users from manipulating *ViewState* data between requests to corrupt data on the server and also makes the *ViewState* information from one Web form unreadable from other Web forms.

Using *Application* and *Session* States

Use the *Application* and *Session* states to store data that you want to keep for the lifetime of an application or for the lifetime of a session. You can store any type of data in the *Application* or *Session* state, including objects. However, you should consider the following issues before using the *Application* and *Session* states:

- *Application* and *Session* state variables are created on the fly, without variable name or type checking. You should limit your access points to these variables.

- Maintaining *Session* state affects performance. *Session* state can be turned off at the application and page levels.

- *Application* state variables are available throughout the current process, but not across processes. If an application is scaled to run on multiple servers or on multiple processors within a server, each process has its own *Application* state.

- The Web application's boundaries determine the scope of the *Application* state.

Structuring Access to State Variables

Application and *Session* state variables are powerful and therefore scary things. It is easy to introduce some old-style Basic errors in your code if you use these variables in an unstructured manner. For instance, the following code references two different *Application* state variables:

Visual Basic .NET

```
Application("Uname") = "Wombat"
Response.Write(Application("Unamme"))
```

Visual C#

```
Application["Uname"] = "Wombat";
Response.Write(Application["Unamme"]);
```

The first line creates a variable and stores some text in it. The second line retrieves a new, empty variable and displays nothing, simply because the variable name is misspelled. The problem is obvious here, but if it occurred deep in a decision structure, it would be very hard to find.

To ameliorate this problem, structure your access to *Application* and *Session* state variables. The easiest way to do this is to declare a page-level variable for each item you need, retrieve the *Application* or *Session* state value in the *Page_Load* event procedure, and save the page-level variables back to state in the *Page_Unload* event procedure. You might want to make retrieving and saving state variables from a consistent location part of your coding conventions.

The following code demonstrates structuring access to state variables:

Visual Basic .NET

```
Public Class AppSessState
    Inherits System.Web.UI.Page

    ' Variable for controlling state access
    Dim strAppState, strSessState As String

    Private Sub Page_Load(ByVal sender As System.Object, _
      ByVal e As System.EventArgs) Handles MyBase.Load
        ' Get Application and session variables here.
        ' Check if they exist.
        If Not IsNothing(Application("AppState")) Then _
          strAppState = Application("AppState")
        If Not IsNothing(Session("SessState")) Then _
          strSessState = Session("SessState")
    End Sub

    Private Sub butApp_Click(ByVal sender As System.Object, _
      ByVal e As System.EventArgs) Handles butApp.Click
        strAppState = txtValue.Text
    End Sub

    Private Sub butSess_Click(ByVal sender As System.Object, _
      ByVal e As System.EventArgs) Handles butSess.Click
        strSessState = txtValue.Text
    End Sub

    Private Sub Page_PreRender(ByVal sender As Object, _
      ByVal e As System.EventArgs) Handles MyBase.PreRender
        ' Display values.
        lblValue.Text = "Application state is: "
        lblValue.Text += strAppState
```

```
              lblValue.Text += " Session state is: "
              lblValue.Text += strSessState
       End Sub

       Private Sub Page_Unload(ByVal sender As Object, _
          ByVal e As System.EventArgs) Handles MyBase.Unload
             ' Store values before unloading page.
             Application("AppState") = strAppState
             Session("SessState") = strSessState
       End Sub
End Class
```

Visual C#

```csharp
public class AppSessState : System.Web.UI.Page
{

    // Variable for controlling state access
    string strAppState = "", strSessState = "";

    private void Page_Load(object sender, System.EventArgs e)
    {
        // Get Application and session variables here.
        // Check if they exist.
        if (Application["AppState"] != null)
            strAppState = Application["AppState"].ToString();
        if (Session["SessState"] != null)
            strSessState = Session["SessState"].ToString();
    }

    private void butApp_Click(object sender, System.EventArgs e)
    {
        strAppState = txtValue.Text;
    }

    private void butSess_Click(object sender, System.EventArgs e)
    {
        strSessState = txtValue.Text;
    }

    private void AppSessState_PreRender(object sender,
        EventArgs e)
    {
        // Display values.
        lblValue.Text = "Application state is: ";
        lblValue.Text += strAppState;
        lblValue.Text += " Session state is: ";
        lblValue.Text += strSessState;
    }

    private void AppSessState_Unload(object sender, EventArgs e)
    {
```

```
        // Store values before unloading page.
        Application["AppState"] = strAppState;
        Session["SessState"] = strSessState;
    }
}
```

Important   In Visual C#, be sure to test whether a state variable is *null* before invoking any of its methods, such as *ToString*. Otherwise, you will receive a run-time error if the state variable does not contain a value.

Turning Off *Session* State

ASP.NET maintains *Session* state for each page in your application by default. If a page does not require state information at the session level, you can turn this off to achieve better performance.

To turn *Session* state off for a Web form:

- From the Web Form Properties window, set *EnableSessionState* to *False*.

To turn *Session* state off for an entire application:

- In the Web.config file, set the *<sessionstate mode=>* tag to *False*, as shown here:

```
<sessionstate mode="False"/>
```

Summary

- Namespaces organize your code and provide access to code in the .NET Framework. To use a namespace from outside your project, establish a reference to the namespace using the References dialog box from the Project menu. Add an *Imports* (Visual Basic .NET) or *using* (Visual C#) statement to the source file to provide a shortcut for referring to members of the namespace in code.

- Classes define objects within a namespace. You can base one class on another using inheritance. When using inheritance, the base class provides its members to the derived class, where they can be overridden, overloaded, or hidden.

- Web applications use the *System.Web* and *System.Web.UI* namespaces. These namespaces define most of the objects used in a Web application, including the *Application*, *Page*, *Request*, and *Response* objects. These four objects provide access to most of the subordinate objects in a Web application.

- Because ordinary variables defined in a Web form are not persistent, you need to save volatile data between requests. ASP.NET lets you save data items as query strings, cookies, *ViewState*, *Session* state, or *Application* state.

Lab: Using Objects and Saving Data

In this lab, you'll create the Translator application. containing a Web form and a Class module. You'll create an instance of an object, save that instance in *Session* state, and use *Session* state and *ViewState* from the Web form. When complete, the application will look like Figure 3-6.

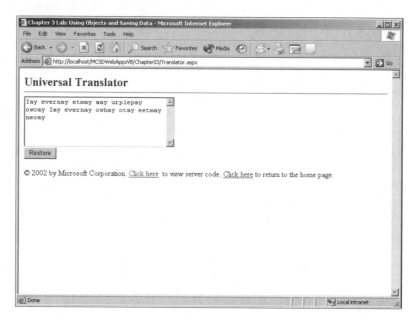

Figure 3-6   The completed Translator application

Estimated lesson time: 20 minutes

Exercise 1: Create the User Interface

In this exercise, you'll create the user interface by adding server controls to the Web form.

▶ **To create a new Web application project**

1. Open a new ASP.NET Web application project. In the New Project dialog box, enter the name **Translator** and click OK.

2. In the Properties window, change the name of the WebForm1.aspx file to **Translator.aspx**.

► **To add the controls to the user interface**

Add server controls to the Web form, as shown in Figure 3-6, and define the following properties:

Control	Control type	Property	Value
LabeOl 1	Label	*Text*	*Universal Translator*
		Font	*Bold, Large*
TextBox1	Text Box	*ID*	*txtSource*
		TextMode	*MultiLine*
Button1	Button	*ID*	*butTranslate*
		Text	*Translate*

Exercise 2: Create a Translator Class

In this exercise, you'll create a *Friend* class to contain the logic and data that the Translator application uses.

► **To create a class**

1. From the Project menu, choose Add Class. Visual Studio displays the Add New Item dialog box. Name the class **TranslatorClass.vb** and click Open.

2. In the Code window, add the following code:

Visual Basic .NET

```
Friend Class TranslatorClass
    Private mstrText As String
    Private mstrOriginal As String

    ' Controls access to the module-level
    ' variables.
    Public Property Text() As String
        Get
            Text = mstrText
        End Get
        Set(ByVal Value As String)
            mstrText = Value
            ' Keep a copy of the original for Restore.
            mstrOriginal = Value
        End Set
    End Property

    ' Restores translated text back to the original.
    Public Sub Restore()
        mstrText = mstrOriginal
    End Sub
```

```vb
' Translates the value in the Text property.
Public Sub Translate()
    Dim strWord As String, intCount As Integer
    Dim arrWords() As String
    Dim bCaps As Boolean
    ' Convert the string to an array using System.String .
    arrWords = mstrText.Split(" ")
    For intCount = 0 To UBound(arrWords)
        ' Check if word is capitalized.
        If LCase(arrWords(intCount)) <> arrWords(intCount) Then
            bCaps = True
            arrWords(intCount) = LCase(arrWords(intCount))
        End If
        strWord = arrWords(intCount)
        ' Do translation.
        If strWord <> "" Then
            strWord = Right(strWord, Len(strWord) -  1) & _
                Left(strWord, 1) & "ay"
            ' Recapitalize if necessary
            If bCaps Then
                strWord = UCase(Left(strWord, 1)) & _
                    Right(strWord, Len(strWord) - 1)
            End If
        End If
        ' Store back in the array.
        arrWords(intCount) = strWord
        ' Reset caps flag.
        bCaps = False
    Next
    ' Rebuild string from array.
    mstrText = String.Join(" ", arrWords)
End Sub

End Class
```

Visual C#

```csharp
internal class TranslatorClass
{

    string mstrText, mstrOriginal;

    // Controls access to class-level variables.
    public string Text
    {
        get
        {
            return mstrText;
        }
        set
```

```
            {
                mstrText = value;
                    // Keep a copy of the original for Restore.
                mstrOriginal = value;
            }
        }


        // Restores translated text back to the original.
        public void Restore()
        {
            mstrText = mstrOriginal;
        }


        // Translates the value in the Text property.
        public void Translate()
        {
            string strWord;
            string[] arrWords;
            bool bCaps = false;
            //  Convert the string into an array using System.String.
            arrWords = mstrText.Split(' ');
            for(int intCount = 0; intCount <= arrWords.GetUpperBound(0);
                intCount++)
            {
                // Change to lowercase.
                strWord = arrWords[intCount].ToLower();
                // Check if word is capitalized.
                if(!arrWords[intCount].Equals(strWord))
                    bCaps = true;
                  // Do translation.
                if(strWord != "")
                {
                    strWord = strWord.Substring(1,strWord.Length  - 1) +
                        strWord.Substring(0,1) + "ay";
                    // Recapitalize if necessary.
                    if(bCaps)
                        strWord = strWord.Substring(0,1).ToUpper () +
                        strWord.Substring(1, strWord.Length -  1);
                }
                // Store the word back in the array.
                arrWords[intCount] = strWord;
                // Reset the caps flag.
                bCaps = false;
            }
            // Rebuild the string from the array.
            mstrText = String.Join(" ", arrWords);
        }
    }
```

Exercise 3: Store a *Translator* Object in *Session* State

In this exercise, you'll add code to the Web form's *Page_Load* event procedure to initialize a *Session* state variable containing the *TranslatorClass* object that your Web form will use.

▶ **To create a *Session* state variable**

In the Code window for the Web form, add the following *Page_Load* event procedure:

Visual Basic .NET

```
Dim TransClass As TranslatorClass

Private Sub Page_Load(ByVal sender As System.Object, _
    ByVal e As System.EventArgs) Handles MyBase.Load
    ' The first time this page is displayed
    If Not IsPostBack Then
        ' Create a new Translator object.
        TransClass = New TranslatorClass
        ' Store the object in a Session state variable.
        Session("TransClass") = TransClass
    Else
        ' Get the Session TransClass variable.
        TransClass = Session("TransClass")
    End If
End Sub
```

Visual C#

```
// Declare an object.
TranslatorClass TransClass;

private void Page_Load(object sender, System.EventArgs e)
{
    // The first time this page is displayed
    if (!IsPostBack)
    {
        // Create a new Translator object.
        TransClass = new TranslatorClass();
        // Store the object in a Session state variable.
        Session["TransClass"] = TransClass;
    }
    else
        // Get the Session TransClass variable.
        TransClass = (TranslatorClass)Session["TransClass"];
}
```

Exercise 4: Use the *TransClass* Object from Web Form Events

In this exercise, you'll add code to the Web form to use the *TransClass* object stored in the *Session* state variable. You'll also use a Boolean variable stored in the page's *ViewState* property to switch the function of the command button from *Translate* to *Restore*.

▶ **To use the *TransClass* object from event procedures in the Web form**

1. Open the Web form's code module in the Code window.
2. Add the following code to the *butTranslate_Click* event procedure:

Visual Basic .NET

```
Private Sub butTranslate_Click(ByVal sender As System.Object, _
    ByVal e As System.EventArgs) Handles butTranslate.Click
    ' Declare a boolean switch.
    Dim bSwitch As Boolean
    ' Get the value from ViewState and switch it.
    bSwitch = Not Viewstate("bSwitch")
    ' Save the new value in ViewState.
    ViewState("bSwitch") = bSwitch
    ' Use the switch to either translate or restore
    ' the text in TextBox1.
    If bSwitch Then
        ' Get the text.
        TransClass.Text = txtSource.Text
        ' Translate it.
        TransClass.Translate()
        ' Display the text.
        txtSource.Text = TransClass.Text
        ' Change the Button text.
        butTranslate.Text = "Restore"
    Else
        ' Restore the original text.
        TransClass.Restore()
        ' Display the text.
        txtSource.Text = TransClass.Text
        ' Change the Button text.
        butTranslate.Text = "Translate"
    End If
End Sub
```

Visual C#

```
private void butTranslate_Click(object sender, System.EventArgs e)
{
    // Declare a boolean switch.
    bool bSwitch;
    // Check if ViewState variable exists.
```

```
        if(ViewState["bSwitch"] != null)
            // Get the value from ViewState and switch it.
            bSwitch = !(bool)ViewState["bSwitch"];
        else
            // Set the switch.
            bSwitch = true;
        // Save the new value in ViewState.
        ViewState["bSwitch"] = bSwitch;
        // Use the switch to either translate or restore
        // the text in txtSource.
        if (bSwitch)
        {
            // Get the text.
            TransClass.Text = txtSource.Text;
            // Translate it.
            TransClass.Translate();
            // Display the text.
            txtSource.Text = TransClass.Text;
            // Change the Button text.
            butTranslate.Text = "Restore";
        }
        else
        {
            // Restore the original text.
            TransClass.Restore();
            // Display the text.
            txtSource.Text = TransClass.Text;
            // Change the Button text.
            butTranslate.Text = "Translate";
        }
    }
```

3. Run and test the application.

Review

The following questions are intended to reinforce key information presented in this chapter. If you are unable to answer a question, review the appropriate lesson and then try the question again. Answers to the questions can be found in the appendix.

1. How does the .NET Framework organize its classes?

2. In Visual Basic .NET, what is the difference between a class module and a code module?

3. In Visual C#, how do you declare a method to make it available without having to first instantiate an object from the class?

4. How do you call a member of a base class from within a derived class?

5. Where would you save the following data items so that they persist between requests to a Web form?
    - A control created at run time
    - An object that provides services to all users
    - User preferences

C H A P T E R   4

Creating a User Interface

About This Chapter

In this chapter, you'll learn how to use Microsoft ASP.NET controls to create a user interface for a multipage Web forms application. You'll learn about different styles of Web forms, how to choose controls based on the tasks you want to perform, how to validate data fields, and how to navigate between the Web forms in your application.

Before You Begin

To complete the lessons in this chapter, you must:

- Be familiar with the basic elements of HTML
- Understand the life cycle of Web forms, as discussed in Chapter 2, "Creating Web Forms Applications"

Lesson 1: Using Controls

Controls are the tools for all of the tasks you perform on a Web form. They define the appearance of the form and provide a way to get information and perform tasks on behalf of the user.

Microsoft Visual Studio .NET includes two types of controls that you can use on a Web form and two ways to position those controls on the form. In this lesson, you'll learn about these differences and how they relate to major programming tasks.

After this lesson, you will be able to

- Select a layout style for your Web form based on the type of application you are creating
- Explain the differences between server controls and HTML controls and select the appropriate type of control for a particular programming task
- Bind control values to data items, such as variables, in your application
- Create templates for controls that contain repeating items
- Write code to respond to user events on controls
- Receive files uploaded from a client and store them on the server

Estimated lesson time: 60 minutes

Selecting a Layout

When you draw controls on a Web form, you have two options for how those controls are arranged:

- **Grid layout**   This is the default. Controls are placed exactly where you draw them, and they have absolute positions on the page. Use grid layout for Microsoft Windows–style applications, in which controls are not mixed with large amounts of text. Pages using grid layout will not always display correctly in non-Microsoft browsers.
- **Flow layout**   This layout positions controls relative to other elements on the page. If you add elements at run time, the controls that appear after the new element move down. Use flow layout for document-style applications, in which text and controls are intermingled.

To set how controls are placed on a page:

1. In the Design window, select the Web form.
2. In the Properties window, select the *DOCUMENT* object.
3. Set the *DOCUMENT* object's *pageLayout* property to *FlowLayout* or *GridLayout*.

Figure 4-1 shows the difference between *GridLayout* and *FlowLayout* on a Web form. You use *GridLayout* for Web forms that have a fixed appearance. You use *FlowLayout* for Web forms that incorporate text and controls.

Figure 4-1   Selecting a layout

When you create controls with *GridLayout*, Visual Studio adds style attributes to each control that set the position of the control, as shown in boldface in the following form definition:

```
<form action="webform1.aspx" method="post"
    enctype="multipart/form-data" runat="server" ID="Form1">
<h2>
Upload and View Files on Server
</h2>
<INPUT id="filUpload" style="Z-INDEX: 101; LEFT: 86px; WIDTH: 347px;
    POSITION: absolute; TOP: 20px; HEIGHT: 27px" runat="server"
    type="file" size="38">
```

```
<asp:Button id="butUpload" style="Z-INDEX: 102; LEFT: 357px;
 POSITION: absolute; TOP: 60px" runat="server" Text="Upload"
 Width="74px" Height="31px"></asp:Button>
<asp:ListBox id="lstServerFiles" style="Z-INDEX: 103; LEFT: 86px;
 POSITION: absolute; TOP: 79px" runat="server" Height="140px"
 Width="168px"></asp:ListBox>
<asp:Button id="butView" style="Z-INDEX: 104; LEFT: 268px;
 POSITION: absolute; TOP: 178px" runat="server" Height="31px"
 Width="76px" Text="View"></asp:Button>
<asp:Image id="imgView" style="Z-INDEX: 106; LEFT: 441px;
    POSITION: absolute; TOP: 24px" runat="server"
    Height="132px" Width="162px"></asp:Image>
</form>
```

When you create controls with *FlowLayout*, Visual Studio omits the style attribute. You can also create controls by double-clicking the control in the Toolbox, instead of using the drag-and-drop operation. Using *FlowLayout* makes it easier to mix controls and text on a Web form, especially when you're editing the form's HTML source, as shown in following form definition:

```
<form id="Form1" method="post" runat="server">
    <h2>
        File Manager
    </h2>
    <p>
    To create a new file, type the name of the file below and click New.
    </p>
    <asp:Literal id="litNoFile" runat="server"></asp:Literal>
    <asp:TextBox id="txtNewFile" runat="server" width="191px"> </asp:TextBox>
    <asp:Button id="butNew" runat="server" Width="62px" Height="29px"
        Text="New"></asp:Button>
    <p>
        To edit a file, select the file from the list below and click  Edit.
        Click Delete to delete the selected file.
    </p>
    <asp:Literal id="litNoneSelected" runat="server"></asp:Literal>
    <asp:ListBox id="lstFiles" runat="server" Width="252px"
        Height="161px"></asp:ListBox>
    <br>
    <asp:Button id="butEdit" runat="server" Width="62" Height="29"
        Text="Edit"></asp:Button>
      
    <asp:Button id="butDelete" runat="server" Width="62px" Height="29px"
        Text="Delete"></asp:Button>
</form>
```

Choosing the Right Control

You can use server controls or HTML controls on a Web form. What's the difference? Basically, server controls are a superset of HTML controls and offer the advantages described in Table 4-1.

Table 4-1   Server Controls vs. HTML Controls

Feature	Server controls	HTML controls
Server events	Trigger control-specific events on the server.	Can trigger only page- level events on server (postback).
State management	Data entered in a control is maintained across requests.	Data is not maintained; must be saved and restored using page-level scripts.
Adaptation	Automatically detect browser and adapt display as appropriate.	No automatic adaptation; must detect browser in code or write for least common denominator.
Properties	The Microsoft .NET Framework provides a set of properties for each control. Properties allow you to change the control's appearance and behavior within server-side code.	HTML attributes only.

So why use anything other than server controls? Because HTML controls have a one-to-one correspondence with standard HTML elements, they provide more direct control over what appears on a page. You use HTML controls for the following reasons:

- **Migration from earlier versions of Active Server Pages (ASP).**   You can load an ASP application into Visual Studio and revise it gradually, rather than rewrite it completely. Earlier versions of ASP supported only HTML elements, and these elements become HTML controls when you load the project in Visual Studio .NET.

- **Not all controls require server-side events or state management.**   This is particularly true when you're doing data binding. Bound items are usually refreshed from the data source with each request, so it's more efficient not to maintain state information for bound controls. This means that you can use HTML controls or turn off state management for bound server controls.

- **You have complete control over what is rendered with HTML controls.**   ASP.NET adjusts the appearance of server controls based on the browser making the request. HTML controls are not adjusted, so you have direct control over their appearance.

Server and HTML controls provide overlapping functionality. In general, it is easier to work with server controls. Table 4-2 lists the server controls and HTML controls by programming task.

Table 4-2   Server and HTML Controls by Programming Task

Task	Server controls	HTML controls
Display text	Label, TextBox, Literal	Label, Text Field, Text Area, Password Field
Display tables	Table, DataGrid	Table
Select from list	DropDownList, ListBox, DataList, Repeater	List Box, Dropdown
Perform commands	Button, LinkButton, ImageButton	Button, Reset Button, Submit Button
Set values	CheckBox, CheckBoxList, RadioButton, RadioButtonList	Checkbox, Radio Button
Display images	Image, ImageButton	Image
Navigation	Hyperlink	none (use <a> tags in text)
Group controls	Panel, Placeholder	Flow Layout, Grid Layout
Work with dates	Calendar	none
Display ads	AdRotator	none
Display horizontal rules	Literal	Horizontal Rule
Get filenames from client	none	File Field
Store data on page	(provided by state management)	Input Hidden
Validate data	RequiredFieldValidator, CompareValidator, RangeValidator, RegularExpressionValidator, CustomValidator, ValidationSummary	none (use page- level scripts)

The following sections describe the major programming tasks you perform with controls to create a user interface.

Working with Text

There are a lot of ways to display text on a page. For read-only text, you can write directly to the *Response* object, as in `Response.Write("Some text")`; you can use a Label control; you can use a TextBox control and set its *ReadOnly* property to *True*; or you can use a Literal control and compose the text in HTML as you would with the *Response.Write* method.

To display editable text, however, you want to use a TextBox server control. The TextBox control has the key properties listed in Table 4-3.

Table 4-3   TextBox Control Properties

Property	Use to
Text	Get or set the data in the TextBox control.
TextMode	Display *SingleLine*, *MultiLine* (scrollable), or *Password* text. When set to *Password*, the text box displays dots in place of the characters typed.
ReadOnly	Prevent the user from changing the text.
AutoPostBack	When set to *True*, causes the TextBox control to fire a *TextChanged* postback event when the user leaves the TextBox control after changing the contents. By default, this property is set to *False* and the *TextChanged* event is cached until some other postback event occurs.

To see the text controls in action, perform the following steps to create a logon page:

1. Start a new Web application with two Web forms named Webform1 and Webform2.
2. On Webform1, draw Label, TextBox, and Button controls, and set their properties to the values shown in the following table:

Control	Property	Setting
Label1	*Text*	*Username:*
Label2	*Text*	*Password:*
TextBox1	*ID*	*txtUser*
TextBox2	*ID*	*txtPassword*
	TextMode	*Password*
Button1	*ID*	*butOK*
	Text	*OK*

3. Add the following code to the *butOK_Click* event procedure:

Visual Basic .NET

```
Private Sub butOK_Click(ByVal sender As System.Object, _
    ByVal e As System.EventArgs) Handles butOK.Click
    If txtUser.Text = "Guest" And txtPassWord.Text = "Moondog" Then
        Response.Redirect("Text2.aspx")
    Else
        txtPassword.Text = ""
    End If
End Sub
```

Visual C#

```
private void butOK_Click(object sender, System.EventArgs e)
{
    if ((txtUser.Text == "Guest") &&
        (txtPassword.Text == "Moondog"))
        Response.Redirect("Text2.aspx");
    else
        txtPassword.Text = "";
}
```

4. Run the application. When you enter the username and password specified in the code, Text2 is displayed, as shown in Figure 4-2. Notice that setting the *TextMode* property to *Password* causes each character entered to be replaced with a symbol.

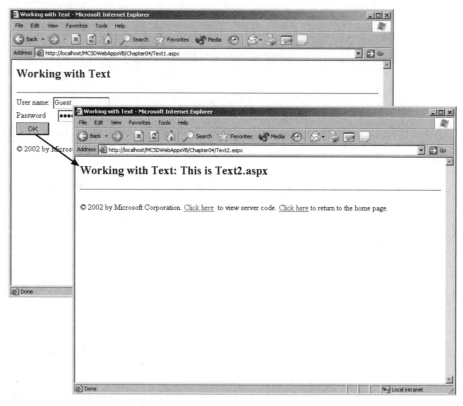

Figure 4.2.   Web forms Text1 and Text2

Of course, it's usually not a good idea to put passwords and usernames in code. Instructions on how to save and retrieve passwords from a secure file on the server are included in Chapter 8, "Maintaining Security."

Working with Tables and Lists

Text displayed in Label and TextBox controls is arranged in a single block. To arrange text in rows and columns, you need to use one of the list or table controls described in Table 4-4. Use the ListBox, DropDownList, and Table controls for simple dynamic tables and lists. Use the DataGrid, DataList, and Repeater controls for complex tables and lists that contain other controls or are bound to data.

Table 4-4   ASP.NET List and Table Controls

Control	Use to
ListBox	Display read-only text in a simple scrollable list format.
DropDownList	Display read-only text in a simple drop-down list format.
Table	Display text and controls in columns and rows. Table controls allow you to dynamically build tables in code using *TableRows* and *TableCells* collections.
DataGrid	Display text and controls in columns and rows using a template to control appearance. DataGrid controls have built-in formatting, sorting, and paging capabilities.
DataList	Display rows of text and controls using a template to control appearance. DataList controls have built-in formatting and selection capabilities.
Repeater	Display rows of other controls using a template to control appearance. Repeater controls do not include the built-in capabilities found in the DataGrid and DataList controls.

Adding Items to a List or Table at Design Time

The ListBox, DropDownList, and Table controls allow you to add static items at design time using the Collection Editor dialog box, as shown in Figure 4-3.

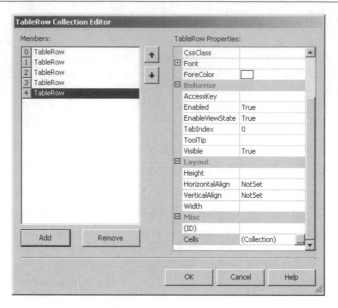

Figure 4-3   The Collection Editor

You use the Collection Editor to add static items to a ListBox, DropDownList, or Table control, as follows:

- To add static items to a ListBox or DropDownList control, select the *Items* property in the Properties window and click the button next to (Collection).

- To add static items to a Table control, select the *Rows* property in the Properties window and click (Collection).

Adding Items to a List or Table at Run Time

To add items to a list at run time, use the *Add* method of the control's *Items* collection. For example, the following code adds items entered in a TextBox control to ListBox and DropDownList controls:

Visual Basic .NET

```
Private Sub butAdd_Click(ByVal sender As System.Object, _
    ByVal e As System.EventArgs) Handles butAdd.Click
    ListBox1.Items.Add(txtSource.Text)
    DropDownList1.Items.Add(txtSource.Text)
End Sub
```

Visual C#

```
private void butAdd_Click(object sender, System.EventArgs e)
{
    ListBox1.Items.Add(txtSource.Text);
    DropDownList1.Items.Add(txtSource.Text);
}
```

Both the ListBox control and the DropDownList control automatically store the items you add to them at run time. The Table control, however, will automatically store data only for the table cells created at design time in the Collection Editor. To create additional table rows and cells at run time, you need to rebuild the table from information stored in a state variable. For example, the following code displays comma-delimited items entered in a text box as cells in a table, adding rows to the table each time the user clicks the Add button:

Visual Basic .NET

```
Private Sub butAdd_Click(ByVal sender As System.Object, _
    ByVal e As System.EventArgs) Handles butAdd.Click
    ' Add text to the page's ViewState.
    ViewState.Add(Viewstate.Count, txtSource.Text)
    ' Rebuild the table.
    RebuildTable()
End Sub

Private Sub RebuildTable()
    Dim iCount1, iCount2 As Integer
    Dim arrWords As String()
    Dim strWords As String
    ' For each string saved in ViewState...
    For iCount1 = 0 To ViewState.Count - 1
        ' Create a new table row.
        Dim rowNew As New TableRow()
        ' Get the string from ViewState.
        strWords = ViewState(iCount1)
        ' Break item list into an array.
        arrWords = Split(strWords, ",")
        ' For each item in the array.
        For iCount2 = 0 To UBound(arrWords)
            ' Create a new table cell.
            Dim celNew As New TableCell()
            ' Set the text to display in the cell.
            celNew.Text = arrWords(iCount2)
            ' Add the cell to the table row.
            rowNew.Cells.Add(celNew)
        Next
        ' Add the row to the table.
        Table1.Rows.Add(rowNew)
    Next
End Sub
```

Visual C#

```
private void butAdd_Click(object sender, System.EventArgs e)
{
    ListBox1.Items.Add(txtSource.Text);
    DropDownList1.Items.Add(txtSource.Text);
    // Add text to the page's ViewState.
```

```csharp
            ViewState.Add(ViewState.Count.ToString(), txtSource.Text);
            RebuildTable();
        }

        private void RebuildTable()
        {
            string[] arrWords;
            string strWords;
            TableRow rowNew;
            TableCell celNew;
            // For each string saved in ViewState.
            for (int iCount1 = 0; iCount1 < ViewState.Count; iCount1++)
            {
                char[] strSep = {','};
                // Create a new table row.
                rowNew = new TableRow();
                // Get the string from ViewState.
                strWords = ViewState[iCount1.ToString()].ToString();
                // Break the item list into an array.
                arrWords = strWords.Split(strSep);
                // For each item in the array.
                for (int iCount2 = 0;
                        iCount2 <= arrWords.GetUpperBound(0); iCount2++)
                {
                    // Create a new table cell.
                    celNew = new TableCell();
                    // Set the text to display in the cell.
                    celNew.Text = arrWords[iCount2];
                    // Add the cell to the table row.
                    rowNew.Cells.Add(celNew);
                }
                // Add the row to the table.
                Table1.Rows.Add(rowNew);
            }
        }
```

Getting the Selected Item from a List

Use the *SelectedItem* property to get the current selection from a list. For example, the following code displays the items selected from a list box in a label on a Web form:

Visual Basic .NET

```vbnet
Private Sub Page_Load(ByVal sender As System.Object, _
    ByVal e As System.EventArgs) Handles MyBase.Load
    ' Test if there is a selected item.
    If Not IsNothing(ListBox1.SelectedItem) Then
        ' Display the selected item.
        Label1.Text = "The selected item is: " _
          & ListBox1.SelectedItem.Text
```

```
    Else
        Label1.Text = "No item is selected."
    End If
End Sub
```

Visual C#

```
private void Page_Load(object sender, System.EventArgs e)
{
    // Test if an item is selected.
    if (ListBox1.SelectedItem == null)
        Label1.Text = "No item is selected.";
    else
        // Display the selected item.
        Label1.Text = "The selected item is: " +
            ListBox1.SelectedItem.Text;
}
```

If an item is selected, the *SelectedItem* property returns a *ListItem* object; otherwise, *SelectedItem* returns *Nothing* or *null*. Therefore, you should always check the value of *SelectedItem* before using the returned object's properties.

Using Simple Data Binding with Lists

Controls can get their values from any data source in your application. Data sources can be any public data—whether the data is a database table, an array, a property of an object, or an expression combining several items. At its simplest level, data binding provides an easy way to initialize the values of ListBox and DropDownList controls on a Web form.

To see how simple data binding works, follow these steps:

1. Create a Web form with a DropDownList control and the following code:

   ### Visual Basic .NET

   ```
   ' Public data item for DropDownList.
   Public arrData As String() = {"This", "that", "and", _
       "the", "other"}

   Private Sub Page_Load(ByVal sender As System.Object, _
       ByVal e As System.EventArgs) Handles MyBase.Load
       ' Bind data to controls on this page.
       Page.DataBind()
   End Sub
   ```

   ### Visual C#

   ```
   // Public data item for DropDownList
   public string[] arrData= {"This", "that", "and", "the",  "other"};

   private void Page_Load(object sender, System.EventArgs e)
   ```

```
{
    Page.DataBind();
}
```

2. Select the DropDownList control, and click the button in the *DataBindings* property in the Properties window. Visual Studio displays the DataBindings dialog box, as shown in Figure 4-4. You use the DataBindings dialog box to load items from any public data source to list or table controls.

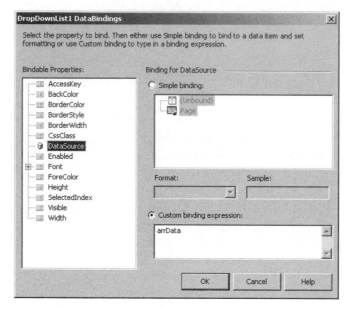

Figure 4.4.   The DataBindings dialog box

3. Select the *DataSource* property in the Bindable Properties list, and then select the Custom Binding Expression option button, type **arrData** in the expression box, and click OK. When you run the application, the items in the *arrData* array are displayed in the DropDownList control, as shown in Figure 4-5.

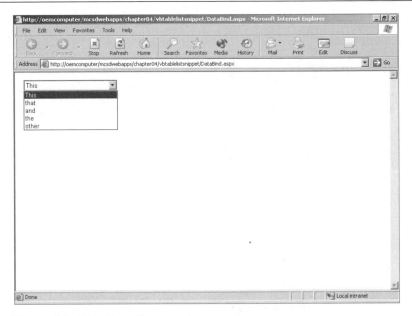

Figure 4.5.   Binding a list control to an array

When you use data binding with a server control, you can turn off state management for that control. This improves performance because the *DataBind* method replaces the automatic view state management provided by ASP.NET.

To turn off state management for a server control, set the control's *EnableViewState* property to *False*.

Adding Items to DataGrid, DataList, and Repeater Controls

Use data binding to add items to the DataGrid, DataList, and Repeater controls. These three controls use templates to define their appearance at run time. A **template** is a set of HTML elements or server controls, or both, that will be repeated for each data item in the control.

To add items to a DataGrid, DataList, or Repeater control, follow these steps:

1. Define the data source.
2. Draw the DataGrid, DataList, or Repeater control and bind to the data source.
3. Edit the templates in the control to add HTML elements or server controls that will be repeated within the list or grid.
4. Set the properties of the server controls contained in the list or grid to bind to data items in the container's data source.

The following example shows how to add template columns to a DataGrid control and how to bind the controls in those columns to a simple data source:

1. Create a public data source in your application as you did in the previous procedure. For example, the following code creates an array to demonstrate a simple
   data source:

Visual Basic .NET

```
' Public data item for DataGrid.
   Public arrData As String() = {"This", "that", "and", _
       "the", "other"}
```

Visual C#

```
// Public data item for DataGrid.
   public string[] arrData = new string[] {"This", "that",
       "and", "the", "other"};
```

2. Draw a DataGrid control on a Web form.

3. Add template columns to the control by selecting the DataGrid control and then
   clicking the Property Builder link at the bottom of the Properties window.
   Visual Studio displays the Properties dialog box, as shown in Figure 4-6.

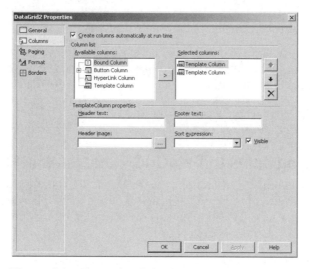

Figure 4.6. Properties dialog box

4. In the Properties dialog box, select Columns, and then select Template Column
   in the Columns list and click the Add (>) button to add a template column to the
   DataGrid control. For this example, add two template columns and click OK.

5. In the Properties window, select the *DataSource* property and specify the data
   source for the control. For this example, type **arrData**, the array created in step 1.

6. Create the template used to display data in the control: right-click the DataGrid
   control, point to Edit Template, and select Columns[0] from the shortcut menu.
   The control's appearance changes to Edit mode, as shown in Figure 4-7.

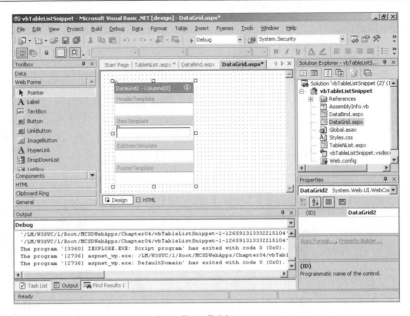

Figure 4.7.   Adding controls to DataGrid

7. Draw other controls on the Web form, and then drag them onto the template to add them to the DataGrid control. For this example, draw a TextBox control and drag it on to the template for column 0.

8. In the Properties window, select the *DataBindings* property of the control you just added to the template, and click the button that appears. Visual Studio displays the DataBindings dialog box, as shown in Figure 4-8.

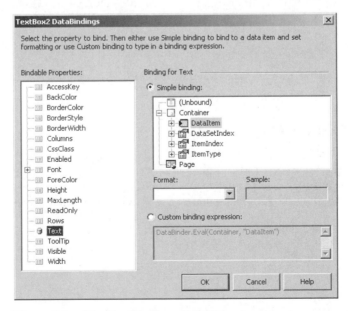

Figure 4.8.   The DataBindings dialog box

9. In the Bindable Properties list, select the property to receive the data item. For this example, select *Text*. Select Simple Binding, and then expand Container and select DataItem to specify which data item to put into the selected property. Click OK to close the dialog box.

10. Edit the second template column. To do this, right-click the DataGrid control, select Edit Template, and then select Columns[1] from the shortcut menu.

11. Repeat steps 4 through 7 for Column(1). For this example, draw a Button control and drag it onto the Column(1) template in the DataGrid control.

12. Close the template when you've finished. To do this, right-click the template and select End Template Editing from the shortcut menu. Visual Studio displays the contained controls, as shown in Figure 4-9. To change any of the contained control's properties, edit the template as we did in the preceding steps.

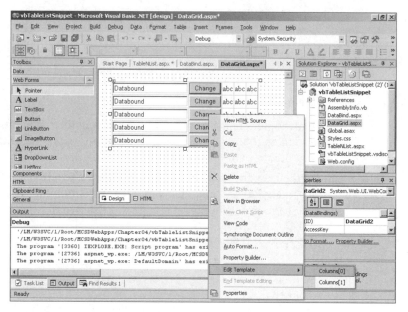

Figure 4.9.   The bound controls

Performing Commands

The Button, LinkButton, and ImageButton server controls all trigger postback events to perform commands. A postback event begins a request from the browser, causing the server to process the page's events. The *Click* event procedure for a button control is processed after any validation or cached events on a page.

To see the order of page events, place a TextBox control, a ListBox control, and a Button control on a Web form and add the following code:

Visual Basic .NET

```vb
Private Sub Page_Load(ByVal sender As System.Object, _
    ByVal e As System.EventArgs) Handles MyBase.Load
    Response.Write("Page load.<br>")
    ' Add items to list box the first time the page loads.
    If Not IsPostBack Then
        ListBox1.Items.Add("This")
        ListBox1.Items.Add("That")
        ListBox1.Items.Add("The other")
    End If
End Sub

Private Sub TextBox1_TextChanged(ByVal sender As System.Object, _
    ByVal e As System.EventArgs) Handles TextBox1.TextChanged
    Response.Write("Text changed.<br>")
End Sub

Private Sub ListBox1_SelectedIndexChanged(ByVal sender As System.Object, _
    ByVal e As System.EventArgs) Handles ListBox1.SelectedIndexChanged
    Response.Write("Item selected.<br>")
End Sub

Private Sub Button1_Click(ByVal sender As System.Object, _
    ByVal e As System.EventArgs) Handles Button1.Click
    Response.Write("Button clicked.<br>")
End Sub
```

Visual C#

```csharp
private void Page_Load(object sender, System.EventArgs e)
{
    Response.Write("Page load.<br>");
    // Add items to list box the first time the page loads.
    if (!IsPostBack)
    {
        ListBox1.Items.Add("This");
        ListBox1.Items.Add("That");
        ListBox1.Items.Add("The other");
    }
}

private void TextBox1_TextChanged(object sender,
    System.EventArgs e)
{
    Response.Write("Text changed.<br>");
}

private void ListBox1_SelectedIndexChanged(object sender,
    System.EventArgs e)
{
```

```
    Response.Write("Item selected.<br>");
}
private void Button1_Click(object sender, System.EventArgs e)
{
    Response.Write("Page load.<br>");
}
```

When you run the preceding code, the page displays the event order, as shown in
Figure 4-10. The *Click* event procedure is the last control event processed on a
page.

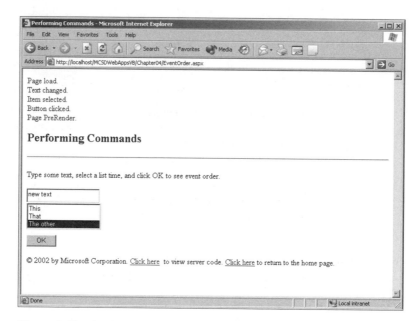

Figure 4-10   Event order

Using the Button and LinkButton controls' *Click* event procedure is straightforward. The ImageButton control provides an additional capability. The *Click* event
argument for the ImageButton control includes the xy-coordinates for where the
user clicked on the control. The image response depends on where it was clicked,
as shown in Figure 4-11. Images that respond to clicks in this way are called **image
maps**.

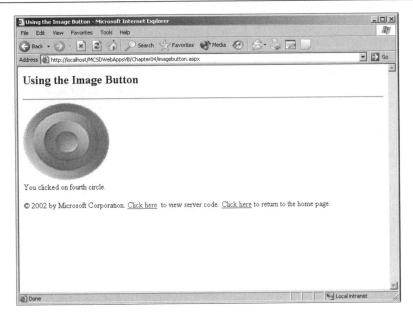

Figure 4-11   ImageButton control

The following code uses the ImageButton control's *e.X* and *e.Y* arguments to calculate which circle was clicked in Figure 4-11:

Visual Basic .NET

```
Private Sub ImageButton1_Click(ByVal sender As System.Object, _
    ByVal e As System.Web.UI.ImageClickEventArgs) Handles ImageButton1.Click
    Dim xOffset, yOffset, X, Y, Radius As Single
    Dim strMessage As String
    ' Calculate the radius of the click from X, Y.
    xOffset = CSng(sender.width.value) / 2
    yOffset = CSng(sender.height.value) / 2
    X = System.Math.Abs(CSng(e.X) - xOffset)
    Y = System.Math.Abs(CSng(e.Y) - yOffset)
    Radius = System.Math.Sqrt((X ^ 2) + (Y ^ 2))
    ' Set the message to display.
    Select Case CInt(Radius)
        Case 0 To 21
            strMessage = "on center circle."
        Case 22 To 42
            strMessage = "on second circle."
        Case 43 To 64
            strMessage = "on third circle."
        Case 65 To 86
            strMessage = "on fourth circle."
        Case Else
            strMessage = "outside of circle."
    End Select
```

```
    ' Display the message.
    Label1.Text = "You clicked " & strMessage
End Sub
```

Visual C#

```csharp
private void ImageButton1_Click(System.Object sender,
    System.Web.UI.ImageClickEventArgs e)
{
    double xOffset, yOffset, X, Y, Radius;
    string strMessage;
    // Calculate the radius of the click from X, Y.
    xOffset = Convert.ToDouble(ImageButton1.Width.Value) / 2;
    yOffset = Convert.ToDouble(ImageButton1.Height.Value) / 2;
    X = Math.Abs(Convert.ToDouble(e.X) - xOffset);
    Y = Math.Abs(Convert.ToDouble(e.Y) - yOffset);
    Radius = Math.Sqrt(Math.Pow(X, 2) + Math.Pow(Y, 2));
    if (Radius < 22)
    {
        strMessage = "on center circle.";
    }
    else if ((Radius >= 22) && (Radius <= 42))
    {
        strMessage = "on second circle.";
    }
    else if ((Radius > 42) && (Radius <= 64))
    {
        strMessage = "on third circle.";
    }
    else if ((Radius > 64) && (Radius <= 86))
    {
        strMessage = "on fourth circle.";
    }
    else
    {
        strMessage = "outside of circle.";
    }
    // Display the message.
    Label1.Text = "You clicked " + strMessage;
}
```

Getting and Setting Values

Use the RadioButton, RadioButtonList, CheckBox, or CheckBoxList controls to
get *Boolean* value settings from the user. As with the ListBox and DropDownList
controls, use the Collection Editor to add items to a RadioButtonList or a Check-
BoxList control. Click the control's *Items* property to display the Collection Editor
for that control.

Use the *Checked* property to get the setting from a CheckBox or a RadioButton control. For example, the following code displays whether or not the CheckBox1 control is selected:

Visual Basic .NET

```
Private Sub Button1_Click(ByVal sender As System.Object, _
    ByVal e As System.EventArgs) Handles Button1.Click
    Response.Write("Checkbox1 is " & CheckBox1.Checked.ToString)
End Sub
```

Visual C#

```
private void Button1_Click(object sender, System.EventArgs e)
{
    Response.Write("Checkbox1 is " + CheckBox1.Checked.ToString());
}
```

When you first draw a RadioButton control on a Web form, it doesn't automatically interact with the other RadioButton controls on the form the way OptionButton controls do on a Windows form. To get the controls to interact, you need to set the *GroupName* property for each RadioButton. Figure 4-12 shows three RadioButton controls with the same *GroupName*. Because these RadioButton controls have the same *GroupName*, selecting one clears any other selected control.

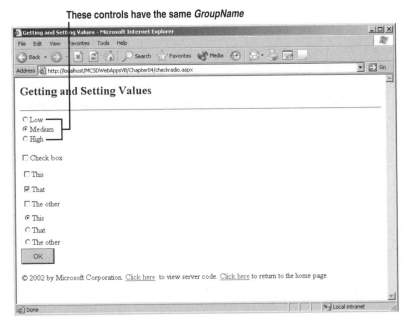

Figure 4-12   Grouped RadioButton controls

To get or set the values from a CheckBoxList or RadioButtonList control, use a *For Each* loop to check each control in the list. The controls contained in a CheckBox-List control are not CheckBox controls, as you might expect. Instead, the Check-BoxList and RadioButtonList controls contain ListControls. To determine the setting of a ListControl control, use the *Selected* property, as shown in the following code:

Visual Basic .NET

```
Private Sub Button1_Click(ByVal sender As System.Object, _
    ByVal e As System.EventArgs) Handles Button1.Click
    Dim lstItem As ListItem
    For Each lstItem In RadioButtonList1.Items
        If lstItem.Selected Then
            Response.Write(lstItem.Text & " is selected.<br>")
        End If
    Next
End Sub
```

Visual C#

```
private void Button1_Click(object sender, System.EventArgs e)
{
    foreach (ListItem lstItem in RadioButtonList1.Items)
    {
        if (lstItem.Selected)
            Response.Write(lstItem.Text +
                " is selected.<br>");
    }
}
```

Displaying Graphics and Advertisements

There are many ways to display graphics on a Web form:

- **As a background**   Use the *Background* property of the Web form to display an image on the entire page. Use the *BackImageUrl* property of the Panel control to display a background image in one region of a page, rather than over the entire page.

- **As a foreground**   Use the Image control to display images in the foreground.

- **As a button**   Use the ImageButton control to display images that respond to user events. See the section "Performing Commands," earlier in this lesson, for an example of responding to click events on an image.

- **As an ad**   Use the AdRotator control to display images from a list of ads. Ads displayed in the AdRotator control contain hyperlinks to the advertiser's Web site.

The Image control does not respond to user events, but it allows you to display graphics dynamically based on input from other controls. To display an image in an

Image control at run time, use the *ImageUrl* property. For example, the following code displays a picture of Venice, Italy, when the user clicks a button:

Visual Basic .NET

```
Private Sub Button1_Click(ByVal sender As System.Object, _
    ByVal e As System.EventArgs) Handles Button1.Click
    Image1.ImageUrl = "gondola.jpg"
End Sub
```

Visual C#

```
private void Button1_Click(object sender, System.EventArgs e)
{
    Image1.ImageUrl = "gondola.jpg";
}
```

A common use of graphics is for advertisements—most Internet ads are stored as .gif files. Visual Studio includes the AdRotator control to handle the tasks associated with displaying these types of ads. The AdRotator control uses an XML file to schedule the ads that are displayed. The XML file stores the URL of the advertisement's image, the URL of the page to display if the user clicks the ad, the priority of the ad, and other properties of the ad. At run time, the AdRotator control selects one of the ads listed in its XML file and displays it on the page.

To use the AdRotator control, follow these steps:

1. Draw an AdRotator control on a Web form.
2. Add an XML file to the current project and open it.
3. In the Properties window, select the *TargetSchema* property, and then select AdRotator Schedule File from the drop-down list of property settings. Visual Studio adds the following lines to the XML file:

```
<Advertisements xmlns=
    "http://schemas.microsoft.com/AspNet/AdRotator-Schedule-File">

</Advertisements>
```

4. Add *<Ad>* tags to the *<Advertisements>* section of the XML file for each ad you want to display.
5. Save the XML file, and switch back to the Web form in Design view.
6. Select the AdRotator control, and set the *AdvertisementsFile* property to the XML file you just created.

Now edit the XML file to display the desired information. For example, the following XML file displays two different ads:

```
<?xml version="1.0" encoding="utf-8" ?>
<Advertisements xmlns=
    "http://schemas.microsoft.com/AspNet/AdRotator-Schedule-File">
```

```
<Ad>
    <ImageUrl>../ads/sponsorad.gif</ImageUrl>
    <NavigateUrl>/ads/sponsorad.htm</NavigateUrl>
    <AlternateText>Click here to visit our sponsor.</AlternateText>
    <Keyword></Keyword>
    <Impressions>1</Impressions>
</Ad>
<Ad>
    <ImageUrl>../ads/net.gif</ImageUrl>
    <NavigateUrl>//www.gotdotnet.com</NavigateUrl>
    <AlternateText> ASP.NET tutorials and more.</AlternateText>
    <Keyword>ASP</Keyword>
    <Keyword>.NET</Keyword>
    <Impressions>5</Impressions>
</Ad>
</Advertisements>
```

The tags in the AdRotator XML schema are defined in Table 4-5.

Table 4-5   The AdRotator XML Schema

Tag	Meaning
<Ad>	Begins an ad.
<ImageUrl>	The address of the ad to display.
<NavigateUrl>	The address to navigate to if the user clicks the ad.
<AlternateText>	The text to display in a ToolTip if the user pauses the mouse over the ad. Also, if the ad at the *ImageUrl* address can't be displayed, this text appears in its place.
<Keyword>	A category name to use for filtering the ads to display.
<Impressions>	A number representing the likelihood that an ad will be displayed. Ads with higher numbers are more likely to be displayed.

Grouping Controls

Place controls in a group when you want to manipulate a particular region of your Web form in code. For example, you might want to allow users to log on to a system from a region of a page and then hide or disable that region once they are logged on.

Use the Panel control to group controls on a Web form. Using the Panel control on a Web form is different from using the Panel control on a Windows form. For one thing, you can't draw controls on a Panel control. You must first draw your controls on the Web form, and then drag them onto the Panel control. For another thing, the Web Forms Panel control uses flow layout rather than grid layout. This means that you can't drag a control to an exact position on a panel.

> **Note**   You don't have to place RadioButton controls in a panel to get them to work together. Instead, you enter a name in their *GroupName* property. See the section "Getting and Setting Values," earlier in this lesson, for more information.

To position controls on a Panel control, follow these steps:

1. Draw the controls on the Web form.
2. Drag the controls onto the Panel control in the order in which you want them displayed. Visual Studio will place each control immediately after the next in sequence.
3. Use carriage returns and spaces to place the controls where you want them to appear.

Figure 4-13 shows a group of controls that allow you to log on to a Web site. After the user logs on, the panel is hidden and a welcome message is displayed.

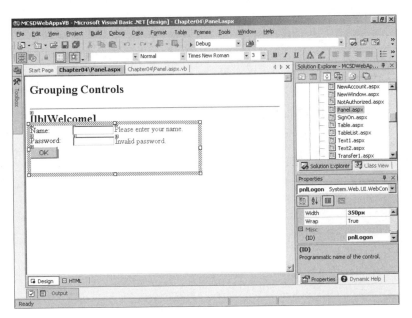

Figure 4-13   Positioning controls in a panel

The following code hides the panel after the user is logged on:

Visual Basic .NET

```
Private Sub butOK_Click(ByVal sender As System.Object, _
    ByVal e As System.EventArgs) Handles butOK.Click
    ' If name/password match, hide logon panel and show message.
    If txtName.Text = "Guest" And txtPassword.Text = "Wombat" Then
        pnlLogon.Visible = False
        lblWelcome.Text = "Welcome " & txtName.Text
    Else
```

```
        txtPassword.Text = ""
        vldPassword.Validate()
    End If
End Sub
```

Visual C#

```
private void butOK_Click(object sender, System.EventArgs e)
{
    // If name/password match, hide the logon panel
    // and show message.
    if ((txtName.Text == "Guest") &&
            (txtPassword.Text == "Wombat"))
    {
        pnlLogon.Visible = False;
        lblWelcome.Text = "Welcome " + txtName.Text;

    }
    else
    {
        txtPassword.Text = "";
        vldPassword.Validate();
    }
}
```

Getting Dates

Use the Calendar control to get or display date information. The Calendar control provides properties to control the appearance of elements on the calendar, as shown in Figure 4-14.

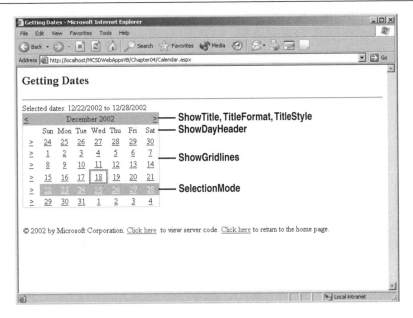

Figure 4-14   Calendar control properties

To get or set dates selected on the Calendar control, use the *SelectionChanged* event procedure and the *SelectedDate* or *SelectedDates* properties. *Selection-Changed* is a postback event, so the following code displays the selected date or dates as soon as the selection changes:

Visual Basic .NET

```
Private Sub Page_Load(ByVal sender As System.Object, _
    ByVal e As System.EventArgs) Handles MyBase.Load
    ' Display current date in the label to start.
    lblDate.Text = "Current date: " & Date.Now.Date
End Sub

Private Sub calSource_SelectionChanged(ByVal sender As System.Object, _
    ByVal e As System.EventArgs) Handles calSource.SelectionChanged
    If calSource.SelectedDates.Count = 1 Then
        ' If one date is selected, display it in a label.
        lblDate.Text = "Selected date: " & calSource.SelectedDate
    Else
        ' If multiple dates are selected, display them.
        lblDate.Text = "Selected dates: " & calSource.SelectedDates(0) & _
        " to " & _
        calSource.SelectedDates(calSource.SelectedDates.Count - 1)
    End If
End Sub
```

Visual C#

```csharp
private void Page_Load(object sender,  System.EventArgs e)
{
    // Display the current date.
    lblDate.Text = "Current date: " +
            calSource.TodaysDate;
}

private void calSource_SelectionChanged(object sender,
    System.EventArgs e)
{
    // Display the current date.
    lblDate.Text = "Current date: " +
        calSource.TodaysDate;
    if (calSource.SelectedDates.Count == 1)
        // If one date is selected, display it.
        lblDate.Text = "Selected date: " +
            calSource.SelectedDate;
    else
        // If multiple dates are selected, display them.
        lblDate.Text = "Selected dates: " +
            calSource.SelectedDates[0] + " to " +
            calSource.SelectedDates
            [calSource.SelectedDates.Count - 1];
}
```

Getting Files from the Client

Use the File Field HTML control to upload files from the client to the server. The File Field HTML control is actually a Text Field HTML control and a Submit Button HTML control bound together. Clicking the Browse button runs a built-in script that displays the Windows Choose File dialog box on the client's computer, as shown in Figure 4-15.

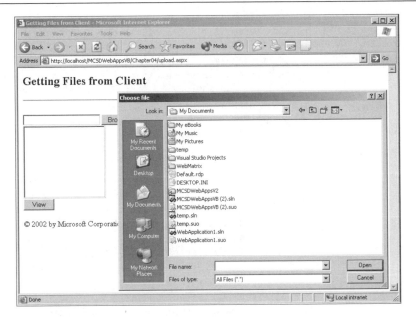

Figure 4-15   The Windows Choose File dialog box

To receive the selected client file on the server, follow these steps:

1. Draw a File Field HTML control on a Web form.
2. Right-click the control, and select Run As Server Control from the shortcut menu.
3. Right-click the Web form, and select View HTML Source. Visual Studio displays the HTML code for the Web form.
4. Add an *enctype* attribute to the *<form>* tag in the Web form's HTML. The *enctype* attribute sets the MIME type of the form, and uploading a file requires both a MIME type of *multipart/form-data* and a form method of *post*, as shown here in boldface:

```
<form action="webform1.aspx" method="post" enctype="multipart/form-data"
runat="server" ID="Form1">
```

5. Right-click the Web form, and select View Design from the shortcut menu. Visual Studio displays the Web Forms Designer.
6. Add a Button control and a *Click* event procedure to the Web form to get and save the selected file. For example, the following event procedure saves the file to the server:

Visual Basic .NET

```
Private Sub butUpload_Click(ByVal sender As System.Object, _
    ByVal e As System.EventArgs) Handles butUpload.Click
    Dim strFilename As String
    Try
```

```vb
        ' Get the file name.
        strFilename = filUpload.PostedFile.FileName
        ' Exit if no file name was entered.
        If strFilename = "" Then Return
        ' If file has zero length (did not exist on client)
        If filUpload.PostedFile.ContentLength = 0 Then
            ' Display message.
            lblMsg.Text = "File not found on client or contains no data."
            ' Exit.
            Return
        End If
        ' Get the base name for the file (exclude path).
        strFilename = System.IO.Path.GetFileName(strFilename)
        ' Save uploaded file to server.
        filUpload.PostedFile.SaveAs(Request.MapPath("./uploadfiles") & _
            "\" & strFilename)
        ' Add file to list of server files.
        lstServerFiles.Items.Add(strFilename)
        ' Select an item in the list.
        lstServerFiles.SelectedIndex = 0
    Catch ex As System.UnauthorizedAccessException
        lblMsg.Text = "You must set the permissions on the server " & _
            "to allow the ASPNET user to write to the destination folder."
    Catch ex As Exception
        lblMsg.Text = "An unexpected error occurred: " & ex.Message
    Finally
    End Try
End Sub
```

Visual C#

```csharp
private void butUpload_Click(object sender, System.EventArgs e)
{
    string strFilename;
    try
    {
        // Get the file name.
        strFilename = filUpload.PostedFile.FileName;
        // Exit if no file name was entered.
        if (strFilename == "") return;
        // if file is zero length, it is empty or doesn't exist.
        if (filUpload.PostedFile.ContentLength == 0)
        {
            lblMsg.Text = "File was not found on client
or file contains no data.";
            return;
        }
        // Get the base name for the file (exclude path).
        strFilename = System.IO.Path.GetFileName(strFilename);
        // Save uploaded file to server.
```

```
        filUpload.PostedFile.SaveAs(Request.MapPath("./uploadfiles")
            +  "\\" + strFilename);
        // Add file to list of server files.
        lstServerFiles.Items.Add(strFilename);
        // Select an item in the list.
        lstServerFiles.SelectedIndex = 0;
    }
    catch (System.UnauthorizedAccessException ex)
    {
        lblMsg.Text = "You must set the permissions on the server
to allow the ASPNET user to write to the destination folder.";
    }
    catch (Exception ex)
    {
        lblMsg.Text = "An unexpected error occurred: "
            + ex.Message;
    }
    finally {}
}
```

The *PostedFile* method of the File Field HTML control represents the file being uploaded. You can use the *FileName* property and *SaveAs* method of the returned object to save the file on the server, as shown in the preceding code. The following code shows one way to retrieve the file from the server. In this case, the file is displayed in the browser.

Visual Basic .NET

```
Private Sub butView_Click(ByVal sender As System.Object, _
    ByVal e As System.EventArgs) Handles butView.Click
    Dim strFilename As String
    ' Get selected file name.
    strFilename = lstServerFiles.SelectedItem.ToString
    ' Display as Web page.
    Response.Redirect("./uploadfiles/" & "/" & strFilename)
End Sub
```

Visual C#

```
private void butView_Click(object sender, System.EventArgs e)
{
    // Get selected file name.
    string strFilename =
        lstServerFiles.SelectedItem.ToString();
    // Display as web page.
    Request.MapPath(".\\uploadfiles\\") + strFilename);
}
```

Lesson 2: Validating Data

One of the most important steps in getting data entries from a user is ensuring that the data is valid. Validity is determined by a number of criteria: Did the user enter anything? Is the entry the appropriate kind of data (a telephone number, for example)? Is the data within a required range?

ASP.NET provides validation controls to help you check Web form data entries against these and other criteria before the data items are accepted. This lesson teaches you how to use the validation controls to catch invalid data and direct the user to fix the problems that occur.

After this lesson, you will be able to

- Explain how ASP.NET checks validity, including why it checks validity both on the client side and on the server side
- Validate data entries in a TextBox control using one or more criteria
- Display error messages to help users correct data validation problems on a Web form
- Cancel validation to allow the user to exit from a Web form that has validation errors
- Create custom validation criteria to be evaluated on the server or client, or both

Estimated lesson time: 40 minutes

Using Validation

The validation controls check the validity of data entered in associated server controls on the client before the page is posted back to the server. This is an important improvement to previous validation schemes—most validity problems can be caught and corrected by the user without a round-trip to the server.

Client-side validation is provided by a JScript library named WebUIValidation.js, which is downloaded separately to the client. Although JScript is widely supported, the Document Object Model (DOM) that the library relies on is available only in Microsoft Internet Explorer version 4.0 and later. Therefore, validation controls also automatically provide server-side validation. Server-side validation is always performed, whether or not client-side validation has occurred. This double-checking ensures that custom validations are performed correctly and that client-side validation has not been circumvented.

The validation controls check the value of the server control specified in their *ControlToValidate* property. Table 4-6 describes the six validation controls.

Table 4-6   ASP.NET Validation Controls

Validation control	Use to
RequiredFieldValidator	Check whether a control contains data
CompareValidator	Check whether an entered item matches an entry in another control
RangeValidator	Check whether an entered item is between two values
RegularExpressionValidator	Check whether an entered item matches a specified format
CustomValidator	Check the validity of an entered item using a client-side script or a server-side code, or both
ValidationSummary	Display validation errors in a central location or display a general validation error description

To use the validation controls, follow these steps:

1. Draw a validation control on a Web form and set its *ControlToValidate* property to the control you want to validate. If you're using the CompareValidator control, you also need to specify the *ControlToCompare* property.

2. Set the validation control's *ErrorMessage* property to the error message you want displayed if the control's data is not valid.

3. Set the validation control's *Text* property if you want the validation control to display a message other than the message in the *ErrorMessage* property when an error occurs. Setting the *Text* property lets you briefly indicate where the error occurred on the form and display the longer *ErrorMessage* property in a ValidationSummary control.

4. Draw a ValidationSummary control on the Web form to display the error messages from the validation controls in one place.

5. Provide a control that triggers a postback event. Although validation occurs on the client side, validation doesn't start until a postback is requested.

Figure 4-16 shows simple validation being performed on a Web form.

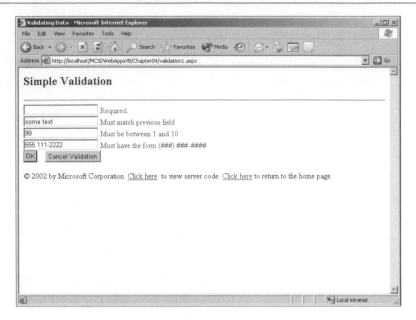

Figure 4-16   Validation on a Web form

Figure 4-17 shows validation using a ValidationSummary control. Notice that the individual validators display their *Text* properties, whereas the longer *ErrorMessage* property is displayed in the ValidationSummary control.

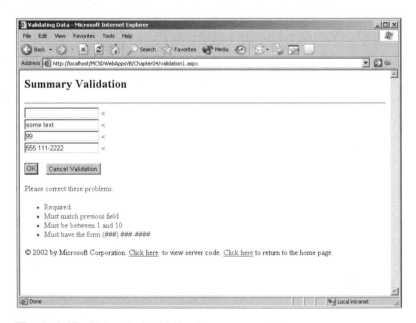

Figure 4-17   Using the ValidationSummary control

To display validation errors as a dialog box, set the ValidationSummary control's *ShowMessage* property to *True.* You can see the result in Figure 4-18.

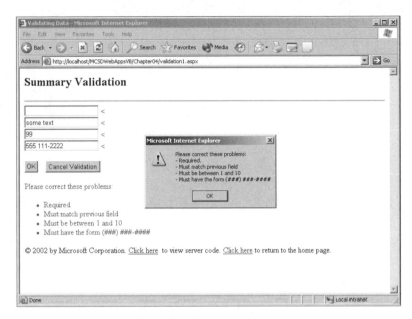

Figure 4-18   The validation errors dialog box

Tip   Use the RequiredFieldValidator control's *InitialValue* property to ignore instructions included in the control to validate. For example, if the control to validate is a DropDownList that includes an item in with the text *Select an item*, enter **Select an item** in the RequiredFieldValidator control's *InitialValue* property to make that selection invalid.

Combining Validations

A server control can have multiple validators. For instance, a TextBox control for a telephone number might be both a required field and a regular expression, so the TextBox would be checked by two validation controls, as shown in Figure 4-19.

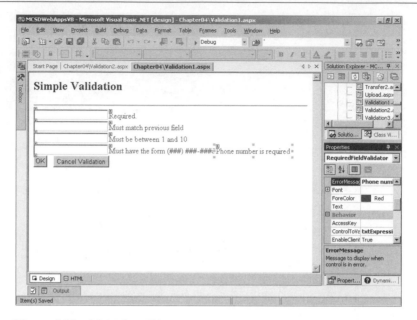

Figure 4-19   Multiple validators

To write meaningful error messages when more than one validation control checks a single control, you need to understand the ASP.NET validation rules. These rules might not make obvious sense, but they make it possible to write error messages that address specific problems.

For example, all validation controls except the RequireFieldValidator control are considered valid if they are blank. This makes it possible to provide one error message if the control is blank, using the RequiredFieldValidator control, and a different error message if the control is out of range or not in the appropriate format, as shown in the telephone number example in Figure 4-19.

The rules listed in Table 4-7 apply to data conversion for the CompareValidator control.

Table 4-7   CompareValidator Validation Rules

If the value from the control	The result is
Specified in the *ControlToValidate* property can't be converted to the appropriate data type	Invalid
Specified in the *ControlToCompare* property can't be converted to the appropriate data type	Valid

In the second case in Table 4-7, you should provide a separate validation control for the control specified in the *ControlToCompare* property to make sure value entered in the control is the appropriate data type.

Canceling Validation

Because validation occurs before the server processes the page, a user can become trapped by validation unless you provide a way to cancel validation without posting back.

To let the user cancel validation, provide a Submit HTML control that sets the *Page_ValidationActive* attribute, as shown in boldface in the following HTML code:

```
<INPUT id="butCancel" onclick="Page_ValidationActive=false;"
style="Z INDEX :
114; LEFT: 386px; WIDTH: 62px; POSITION: absolute; TOP: 130px; HEIGHT:  30px"
type="submit" value="Cancel">
```

The preceding button definition cancels validation and posts the page back to the server. You can determine whether the user has cancelled the operation by checking the *Page* object's *IsValid* property in the *Page_Load* event procedure. You have to revalidate the page because canceling validation sets *IsValid* to *True*. The following code shows how to check whether the user cancelled validation:

Visual Basic .NET

```
Private Sub Page_Load(ByVal sender As System.Object, _
    ByVal e As System.EventArgs) Handles MyBase.Load
    ' Validate in case user cancelled validation.
    If Page.IsPostBack Then Page.Validate()
    ' Check if page is valid.
    If Not Page.IsValid Then
        ' User cancelled operation, return home.
        Response.Redirect("default.htm")
    End If
End Sub
```

Visual C#

```
private void Page_Load(object sender, System.EventArgs e)
{
    // Validate in case user cancelled validation.
    if (Page.IsPostBack)
    {
        Page.Validate();
        if (!Page.IsValid)
            // User cancelled validation.
            Response.Redirect("default.htm");
    }
}
```

Customizing Validation

To perform complex types of validation not provided by the standard validation control, use a CustomValidator control and write code to perform the validation on the server side and (optionally) on the client side.

On the server side, place your validation code in the *ServerValidate* event procedure. The arguments to this procedure provide access to the control to validate. The following event procedure validates that an entered number is prime:

Visual Basic .NET

```vb
' Validate a prime number.
Private Sub CustomValidator1_ServerValidate _
    (ByVal source As System.Object, ByVal args As _
    System.Web.UI.WebControls.ServerValidateEventArgs) _
    Handles CustomValidator1.ServerValidate
    Try
        Dim iPrime, iCount As Integer
        ' Get value from ControlToValidate (passed as args)
        iPrime = Integer.Parse(args.Value)
        For iCount = 2 To iPrime \ 2
            ' If number is evenly divisible, it's
            ' not prime, return False.
            If iPrime Mod iCount = 0 Then
                args.IsValid = False
                Return
            End If
        Next
        ' Number is Prime, return True.
        args.IsValid = True
        Return
    Catch ex As Exception
        ' If there was an error parsing, return False.
        args.IsValid = False
        Return
    End Try
End Sub
```

Visual C#

```csharp
private void vldtxtPrime_ServerValidate(object source,
    System.Web.UI.WebControls.ServerValidateEventArgs args)
{
    try
    {
        // Get value from ControlToValidate (passed as args).
        int iPrime = Int32.Parse(args.Value);
        for (int iCount = 2; iCount <= (iPrime / 2);  iCount++)
        {
            // If number is evenly divisible, it's
```

```
                    // not prime,return False.
                    if((iPrime % iCount) == 0)
                    {
                        args.IsValid = false;
                        return;
                    }
                    // Number is prime, return True.
                    args.IsValid = true;
                    return;
                }
            }
            catch(Exception e)
            {
                // If there was an error parsing, return False.
                args.IsValid = false;
                return;
            }
        }
```

To provide client-side validation, specify a validation script in the CustomValidator control's *ClientValidationFunction* property. Client-side validation is optional, and if you provide it, you should maintain similar validation code in both places. The following script provides a client-side version of the prime number validation performed on the server:

VBScript

```
<script language="vbscript">
    Sub ClientValidate(source, arguments)
        For iCount = 2 To arguments.Value \ 2
            ' If number is evenly divisible, it's
            ' not prime, return False.
            If arguments.Value Mod iCount = 0 Then
                arguments.IsValid = False
                Exit Sub
            End If
        Next
        arguments.IsValid = True
    End Sub
</script>
```

JScript

```
<script language="jscript">
    function ClientValidate(source, arguments)
    {
        for (var iCount = 2; iCount <= arguments.Value / 2; iCount++)
        {
            // If number is evenly divisible,
            // it's not prime. Return false.
```

```
            if ((arguments.Value % iCount) == 0)
            {
                arguments.IsValid = false;
                return false;
            }
        }
        // Number is prime, return True.
        arguments.IsValid = true;
        return true;
    }
</script>
```

Lesson 3: Navigating Between Forms

Linking information is the essence of the Web. In a Web Forms application, hyperlinks and the navigation methods are what link multiple Web forms together into a cohesive application. ASP.NET provides several ways to navigate between pages in your application, and each of these techniques yields different effects in terms of how the page is displayed and how data is exchanged between pages.

In this lesson, you'll learn how to use each of the different navigation techniques in code and in HTML.

After this lesson, you will be able to

- List different ways to navigate between pages in a Web forms application
- Choose the appropriate navigation technique based on your programming needs
- Retain form *ViewState* data across a request
- Process a second Web form without leaving the current Web form
- Display a page in a new browser window and control that window from server code

Estimated lesson time: 35 minutes

Ways to Navigate

ASP.NET provides five distinct ways to navigate between pages in your application, as shown in Table 4-8.

Table 4-8   Navigating Between Pages

Navigation method	Use to
Hyperlink control	Navigate to another page.
Response.Redirect method	Navigate to another page from code. This is equivalent to clicking a hyperlink.
Server.Transfer method	End the current Web form and begin executing a new Web form. This method works only when navigating to a Web Forms page (.aspx).
Server.Execute method	Begin executing a new Web form while still displaying the current Web form. The contents of both forms are combined. This method works only when navigating to a Web Forms page (.aspx).
Window.Open script method	Display a page in a new browser window on the client.

Using Hyperlinks and Redirection

Hyperlink server controls respond to user click events by displaying the page specified in the control's *NavigateURL* property. The Hyperlink control does not expose any server-side user events; if you want to intercept a click event in code, use the LinkButton control or the ImageButton server control.

To navigate from a LinkButton or ImageButton control, use the *Response* object's *Redirect* method, as shown here:

Visual Basic .NET

```
Private Sub LinkButton1_Click(ByVal sender As System.Object, _
    ByVal e As System.EventArgs) Handles LinkButton1.Click
    ' Display next page.
    Response.Redirect("NextPage.aspx")
End Sub
```

Visual C#

```
private void LinkButton1_Click(object sender, System.EventArgs e)
{
    // Display next page.
    Response.Redirect("NextPage.aspx");
}
```

Using the *Transfer* Method

Using the *Transfer* method is similar to executing a hyperlink or using the *Redirect* method, with one difference: *Transfer* can retain some information from the source page across requests. Setting the *Transfer* method's *preserveForm* argument to *True* makes the form's *QueryString*, *ViewState*, and event procedure information available in the destination form.

To be able to read one Web form's ViewState from another, you must first set the *EnableViewStateMac* attribute in the Web form's *Page* directive to *False*. By default, ASP.NET hashes *ViewState* information, and setting this attribute to *False* disables that hashing so that the information can be read on the subsequent Web form. The following line shows how to disable hashing so that a page's *ViewState* can be used from another page:

Visual Basic .NET

```
<%@ Page language="vb" EnableViewStateMac="false"
Codebehind="RedirectNTransfer.aspx.vb"
Inherits="MCSDWebAppsVB.Transfer1" %>
```

Visual C#

```
<%@ Page language="c#" EnableViewStateMac="false"
Codebehind="RedirectNTransfer.aspx.cs" AutoEventWireup="false"
Inherits=" MCSDWebAppsVB.Transfer2" %>
```

The following event procedure for an ImageButton control shows how information can be passed between forms with the *Transfer* method:

Visual Basic .NET

```
' Transfer1.aspx
Private Sub imgTransfer_Click(ByVal sender As System.Object, _
    ByVal e As System.Web.UI.ImageClickEventArgs) _
    Handles imgTransfer.Click
    ' Transfer to another form, retaining ViewState.
    Server.Transfer("Transfer2.aspx", True)
End Sub
```

Visual C#

```
// Transfer1.aspx
private void ImageButton1_Click(object sender,
    System.Web.UI.ImageClickEventArgs e)
{
    // Transfer to another form, retaining ViewState.
    Server.Transfer("Transfer2.aspx", true);
}
```

Warning   ASP.NET hashes ViewState information to prevent malicious users from manually changing the information passed back to the server and thus somehow corrupting data stored there. Disabling this hashing decreases the security of your Web application.

Use the *Request* object's *Form* method to retrieve the *ViewState* information from the source Web form. The following code displays the values of two controls from the Transfer1.aspx Web form after the preceding *Transfer* method executes:

Visual Basic .NET

```
' Transfer2.aspx
Private Sub Page_Load(ByVal sender As System.Object, _
  ByVal e As System.EventArgs) Handles MyBase.Load
    Dim colForm As _
      System.Collections.Specialized.NameValueCollection
    ' Get data from source Web form.
    colForm = Request.Form
    ' Display the value from Webform1's TextBox.
    Response.Write("TextBox1.Text: " & _
      colForm.Item("TextBox1") & "<br>")
    ' Display the x, y coordinates of where the click occurr ed.
    Response.Write("ImageButton X, Y coords: " & _
      colForm.Item("imgTransfer.x") & ", " & _
      colForm.Item("imgTransfer.y") & "<br>")
End Sub
```

Visual C#

```
// Transfer2.aspx
    private void Page_Load(object sender, System.EventArgs e )
    {
        System.Collections.Specialized.NameValueCollection c olForm;
        // Get data from the source Web form.
        colForm = Request.Form;
        // Display the value from Webform1's TextBox.
        Response.Write("TextBox1.Text: " + colForm["TextBox1"]
            + "<br>");
        //  Display the X, Y coordinated of where the click occurred.
        Response.Write("ImageButton X, Y coords: " +
            colForm["imgTransfer.x"] + ", " + colForm["imgTransfer.y"]
            + "<br>");
    }
```

You can use the *Server* object's *Transfer* method to link control values across requests, as shown in Figure 4-20.

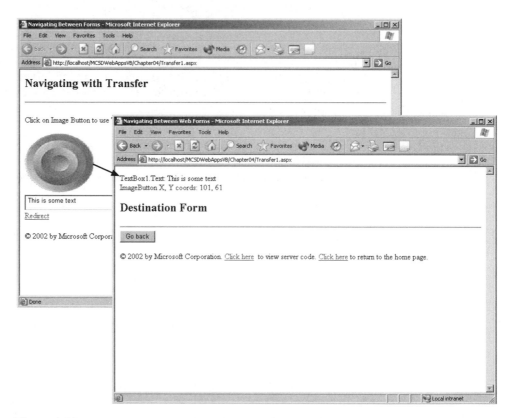

Figure 4-20   The *Server* object's *Transfer* method

> **Note**   The *Server* object's *Transfer* and *Execute* methods work exclusively with Web forms. Trying to navigate to an HTML page using one of these methods results in a run-time error.

Using the *Execute* Method

Use the *Server* object's *Execute* method to process a second Web form without leaving the first Web form. This technique lets you direct the results from a Web form to a region on the current page. As with the *Transfer* method, *Execute* requires that the Web form's *EnableViewStateMac* attribute be set to *False* to disable *ViewState* hashing.

For example, the following code executes the Table.aspx Web form and displays it in a Literal control on the current page:

Visual Basic .NET

```
Private Sub butExecute_Click(ByVal sender As System.Object, _
    ByVal e As System.EventArgs) Handles butExecute.Click
    Dim swrTarget As New System.IO.StringWriter()
    ' Execute a Web form, store the results.
    Server.Execute("Table.aspx", swrTarget)
    ' Display the result in a Literal control.
    litTable.Text = "<h2>Table Results</h2>" & swrTarget.ToString
End Sub
```

Visual C#

```
private void butExecute_Click(object sender, System.EventArg s e)
{
    System.IO.StringWriter swrTarget = new System.IO.StringWriter();
    // Execute a Web form, store the results.
    Server.Execute("Table.aspx", swrTarget);
    // Display the result in a literal control.
    litTarget.Text = "<h2>Table Results</h2>" + swrTarget.ToString();
}
```

The *Execute* method's second argument is optional. If you omit it, the result is written to the current page. The result is additive—the content of both pages is displayed at the same time and server controls on both pages can respond to user events, as shown in Figure 4-21.

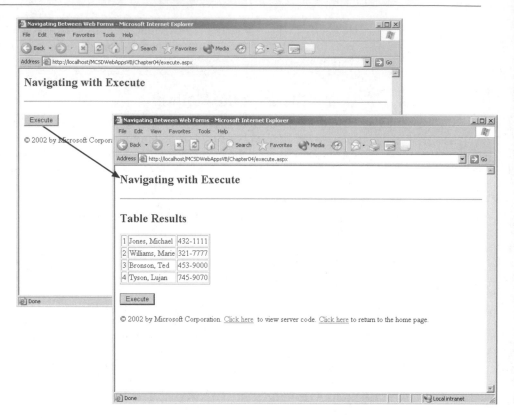

Figure 4-21   The *Server* object's *Execute* method

When you combine Web forms using the *Execute* method, be aware that any post-back events occurring on the second Web form will clear the first Web form. For this reason, combining Web forms is mainly useful when the second Web form does not contain controls that trigger postback events.

Displaying a Page in a New Browser Window

To start a new instance of the browser, use the client-side *Window* object's *Open* method. You can do this only as part of a client script because the new window is created on the client. However, there are ways to control the content and appearance of the new browser window from the server.

In its simplest form, the *Window.Open* method takes the form shown in boldface for the following Button HTML control definition:

```
<INPUT style="Z-
 INDEX: 102; LEFT: 55px; WIDTH: 81px; POSITION: absolute; TOP: 156px; H EIGHT
: 24px" onclick="window.open('transfer2.aspx')" type="submit"
value="New Window">
```

To use a variable as the target URL, replace `webform2.aspx` with a data tag:

```
<INPUT style="Z-
 INDEX: 102; LEFT: 55px; WIDTH: 81px; POSITION: absolute; TOP: 156px; H EIGHT
: 24px" onclick="window.open('<%# urlTarget %>')" type="submit"
value="New Window">
```

To update the target URL from server code, use a *Public* variable and data binding. The following *Page_Load* event procedure sets the target URL and updates it with data binding when the page loads:

Visual Basic .NET

```
Public urlTarget As String
Private Sub Page_Load(ByVal sender As System.Object, _
    ByVal e As System.EventArgs) Handles MyBase.Load
    urlTarget = "transfer2.aspx"
    Page.DataBind()
End Sub
```

Visual C#

```
public string urlTarget;
private void Page_Load(object sender, System.EventArgs e)
{
    urlTarget = "transfer2.aspx";
        Page.DataBind();
}
```

Because the *Window.Open* method takes many different arguments to control the various aspects of the new browser window, you might want to create a class to handle all the various settings. Classes allow you to encapsulate all the possible settings so that they can be used in an object-oriented manner. The following *Page_Load* event procedure and class definition demonstrate how to control the size, location, and URL of the new window from server-side code using a class named *BrowserWindow*:

Visual Basic .NET

```
Public urlTarget As New BrowserWindow()

Private Sub Page_Load(ByVal sender As System.Object, _
    ByVal e As System.EventArgs) Handles MyBase.Load
    With urlTarget
        ' Set URL for new window
        .URL = "execute.htm"
        .Top = 100
        .Left = 100
        .Width = 400
        .Height = 400
    End With
    ' Update HTML Button.
```

```
        Page.DataBind()
End Sub


' Class to control new browser windows created in scripts.
' Default settings shown here are the same as browser defaul ts.
Public Class BrowserWindow
    ' String settings: default is blank.
    Public URL As String = "about:blank"
    ' Integer settings: 0 invokes default.
    Public Height As Integer = 0
    Public Width As Integer = 0
    Public Top As Integer = 0
    Public Left As Integer = 0
    ' Boolean-like settings: 0 is "no" 1, is "yes"
    Public ChannelMode As Integer = 0
    Public Directories As Integer = 1
    Public FullScreen As Integer = 0
    Public Location As Integer = 1
    Public Resizable As Integer = 1
    Public ScrollBars As Integer = 1
    Public Status As Integer = 1
    Public TitleBar As Integer = 1
    Public ToolBar As Integer = 1
    Public MenuBar As Integer = 1
End Class
```

Visual C#

```
public BrowserWindow urlTarget = new BrowserWindow();

private void Page_Load(object sender, System.EventArgs e)
{
    urlTarget.URL = "Execute.aspx";
    urlTarget.Top = 100;
    urlTarget.Left = 100;
    urlTarget.Width = 400;
    urlTarget.Height = 400;
    // Update HTML Button.
    Page.DataBind();
}


// Class to control new browser window create in scripts.
//  Default settings shown here are the same as browser default s.
public class BrowserWindow
{
    // String settings: default is blank.
    public string URL = "about:blank";
    // Integer settings: 0 invoked default.
    public int Height = 0;
    public int Width = 0;
    public int Top = 0;
```

```
    public int Left = 0;
    // Boolean-like settings: 0 is "no", 1 is "yes".
    public int ChannelMode = 0;
    public int Directories = 1;
    public int FullScreen = 0;
    public int Location = 1;
    public int Resizable = 1;
    public int ScrollBars = 1;
    public int Status = 1;
    public int TitleBar = 1;
    public int ToolBar = 1;
    public int MenuBar = 1;
}
```

The HTML code for a button that uses these settings would look like the following example. (The server-supplied variable is shown in boldface.)

```
<INPUT style="Z-
INDEX: 103; LEFT: 25px; WIDTH: 126px; POSITION: absolute; TOP: 60px; H
EIGHT: 33px" type="button" value="Show New Window"
onclick="window.open('<%# urlTarget.URL %>', null,
'height=<%# urlTarget. Height %>,
width-<%# urlTarget.Width %>,
top=<%# urlTarget.Top %>,
left=<%# urlTarget.Left %>,
channelmode=<%# urlTarget.ChannelMode %>,
directories=<%# urlTarget.Directories %>,
fullscreen=<%# urlTarget.FullScreen %>,
location=<%# urlTarget.Location %>,
menubar=<%# urlTarget.MenuBar %>,
resizable=<%# urlTarg et.Resizable %>,
scrollbars=<%# urlTarget.ScrollBars %>,
status=<%# urlTarget.Status %>,
titlebar=<%# urlTarget.TitleBar %>,
toolbar=<%# urlTarget.ToolBar %>')">
```

Summary

- Server controls provide properties, methods, and events that can be used in server code.

- HTML controls provide attributes and events that can be used in scripts that run on the client. To access properties of an HTML control in server code, add a *runat=server* attribute to the control's HTML definition.

- ASP.NET performs control validation on the client side immediately before posting the Web form back to the server. Once client-side validation succeeds, the Web form is validated again on the server side before the *Page_Load* event occurs. This ensures that the Web form has not been modified on the client to bypass validation, and it also guarantees that validation will work with a wide variety of browsers.

- Use multiple validation controls to check multiple conditions on a single data field. For example, a TextBox control that requires a telephone number should be validated by both a RequiredFieldValidator and a RegularExpressionValidator control.

- To navigate between pages in a Web forms application, use one of the following techniques. (The two *Server* object methods work only with Web forms.)

  - Hyperlinks
  - The *Response.Redirect* method
  - The *Server.Transfer* method
  - The *Server.Execute* method
  - Client script procedures

- To perform an action in the client browser, you must use a client script. For example, to open a page in a new window, you would use a Button HTML control with an *onclick="window.open()"* attribute. This is because client scripts are the only executable code in a Web forms application that runs on the client.

Lab: Building a Web-Based Text Editor

In this lab, you will create a multipage Web forms application that allows users to create and edit text files stored on a server. The application uses the user's sign-on name to determine where files are stored. It does not do rigorous password checking—in fact, the password is always *Guest*. Password authentication is covered in Chapter 8, "Maintaining Security."

Estimated lesson time: 45 minutes

Important   To create and delete files, the ASPNET user account must have write and modify privileges in the application's root folder. By default, the ASPNET user account has only read and execute privileges. See Chapter 9, "Building and Deploying Web Applications," for information about how to assign security privileges in the application folder.

Exercise 1: Create the Sign-On Form

In this exercise, you'll create the Web form that allows users to sign on to the text editor. The Web form created here uses validation, flow layout, navigation to other pages, and the System.IO namespace for directory services. When you have finished creating the Web form, it will appear as shown in Figure 4-22.

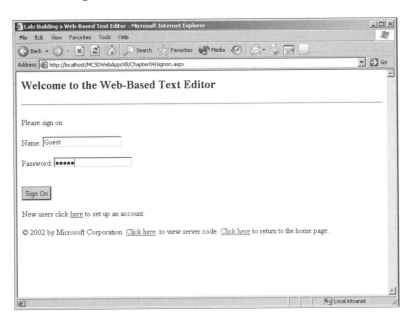

Figure 4-22   The SignOn.aspx Web form

▶ **To start the application and create the SignOn Web form**

1. Open a new ASP.NET Web application project. In the New Project dialog box, enter the name **WebTextEditor**.

2. In the Properties window, change the name of the Webform1.aspx file to SignOn.aspx.

3. In the Properties window, select the *DOCUMENT* object and set the *pageLayout* property to *FlowLayout*.

After you've set *pageLayout* to *FlowLayout*, you can add controls to the page by double-clicking the controls in the Toolbox. If you create the controls in the order they appear on the page, this process goes quickly. The following table shows the controls you should create in the order in which you create them, along with their property settings.

Control	Property	Value
Literal	*ID*	*litNoAccount*
TextBox	*ID*	*txtName*
RequiredFieldValidator	*ID*	*vldtxtName*
	ControlToValidate	*txtName*
	ErrorMessage	*Please enter a name.*
TextBox	*ID*	*txtPassword*
RequiredFieldValidator	*ID*	*vldtxtPassword*
	ControlToValidate	*txtPassword*
	ErrorMessage	*Please enter the password.*
RangeValidator	*ID*	*vldtxtPasswordGuest*
	ControlToValidate	*txtPassword*
	ErrorMessage	*The password is "Guest".*
	MinimumValue	*Guest*
	MaximumValue	*Guest*
Button	*ID*	*butSignOn*
	Text	*Sign On*

After you create the controls and set their properties, switch to HTML view, and edit the HTML elements directly.

▶ **To edit the Web form in HTML mode**

1. Right-click the Web form, and select View HTML Source from the shortcut menu.

2. Edit the Web form by adding the following text and HTML tags shown in boldface:

```
<form id="Form1" method="post" runat="server">
<h2>
Welcome to the Web-Based Text Editor
</h2>
<asp:Literal id="litNoAccount" runat="server"></asp:Literal>
<p>
Please sign on:
</p>
Name:
<asp:TextBox id="txtName" runat="server" Width="165px"></asp:TextBox>
<asp:RequiredFieldValidator id="vldtxtName" runat="server"
ErrorMessage="Please enter a name."
ControlToValidate="txtName"></asp:RequiredFieldValidator>
<br>
<br>
Password:
<asp:TextBox id="txtPassword" runat="server" Width="163px" Height="21p x"
TextMode="Password"></asp:TextBox>
<asp:RequiredFieldValidator id="vldtxtPassword" runat="server"
ErrorMessage="Please enter a password."
ControlToValidate="txtPassword"></asp:RequiredFieldValidator>
<br>
<asp:RangeValidator id="vldtxtPasswordGuest" runat="server"
ControlToValidate="txtPassword" ErrorMessage='The password is "Guest".'
MaximumValue="Guest" MinimumValue="Guest"></asp:RangeValidator>
<br>
<br>
<asp:Button id="butSignOn" runat="server" Text="Sign On" Width="61px"
Height="28px"></asp:Button>
<p>
New users click <a href="NewAccount.aspx">here</a> to set up an account.
</p>
</form>
```

3. To view the results of the changes, right-click the Web form, and select View Design from the shortcut menu.

When you have finished editing the Web form, switch to Design view and double-click Sign On to display the Code window. Place the following *Imports* or *using* statement before the Web form's class definition:

Visual Basic .NET

```
Imports System.IO
```

Visual C#

```
using System.IO;
```

Add the following code to the *butClick* event procedure:

Visual Basic .NET

```
Private Sub butSignOn_Click(ByVal sender As System.Object, _
    ByVal e As System.EventArgs) Handles butSignOn.Click
    Dim strPath As String
    'If the user exists, there is a directory of the same name.
    strPath = Server.MapPath(Request.ApplicationPath) & "\" & txtName. Text
    If Directory.Exists(strPath) Then
        ' Set session variables.
        Session("Path") = strPath
        Server.Transfer("FileManager.aspx")
    Else
        ' Otherwise, report that user wasn't found.
        litNoAccount.Text = ("<p>The name " & txtName.Text & _
        " wasn't found." & _
        "Check the name, or click <A href='NewAccount.aspx'>here</ A>" & _
        " if you are a new user.</p>")
    End If
End Sub
```

Visual C#

```
private void butSignOn_Click(object sender, System.EventArgs e)
{
    string strPath;
    // If the user exists, there is a directory of the same name.
    strPath = Server.MapPath(Request.ApplicationPath) + "\\"
        + txtName.Text;
    if(Directory.Exists(strPath))
    {
        // Set session variables.
        Session["Path"] = strPath;
        Server.Transfer("FileManager.aspx");
    }
    else
        // Otherwise, report that user wasn't found.
        litNoAccount.Text = "<p>The name " + txtName.Text +
            " wasn't found. Check the name, or click " +
            "<A href='NewAccount.aspx'>here</A> if you " +
            "are a new user.</p>";
}
```

Exercise 2: Create the NewAccount Form

In this exercise, you'll create the Web form that creates an account for new users. In this application, an account consists of a directory in the application's root that bears the user's name. Again, there is no security provided in this exercise; security is covered in Chapter 8, "Maintaining Security."

The Web form created here uses validation, flow layout, navigation, HTML controls, and the *System.IO* namespace for directory services. The form uses the username to create a directory for the user's files in the application's server root. When you have finished creating the Web form, it will appear as shown in Figure 4-23.

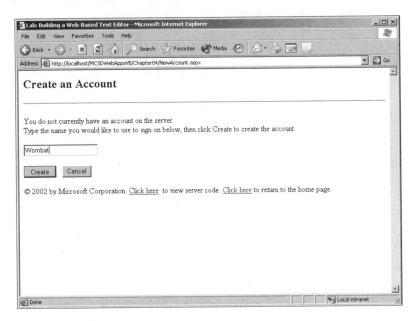

Figure 4-23   The NewAccount.aspx Web form

▶ **To create the NewAccount Web form**

1. Create a new Web form named NewAccount.aspx.
2. In the Properties window, select the *DOCUMENT* object and set its *pageLayout* property to *FlowLayout*.
3. Add controls and set their properties as shown in the following table:

Control	Property	Value
Literal	ID	litNameExists
TextBox	ID	txtName
RequiredFieldValidator	ID	vldtxtName
	ControlToValidate	txtName
	ErrorMessage	Please enter a name.
Button	ID	butCreate
	Text	Create
Button HTML control	id	butCancel
	value	Cancel

4. Switch the Web form to HTML view, and add the following text and HTML tags shown in boldface:

```
<form id="Form1" method="post" runat="server">
<h2>
Create an Account
</h2>
<asp:Literal id="litNameExists" runat="server"></asp:Literal>
<p>
You do not currently have an account on the server.
<br>
Type the name you would like to use to sign on below, then click Create to
create the account.
</p>
<asp:TextBox id="txtName" runat="server" Width="153px"
Height="24px"></asp:TextBox>
<asp:RequiredFieldValidator id="vldtxtName" runat="server"
ErrorMessage="Please enter a name."
ControlToValidate="txtName"></asp:RequiredFieldValidator>
<p>
</p>
<asp:Button id="butCreate" runat="server" Text="Create" Width="67"
Height="24"></asp:Button>
   <INPUT type="button" onclick="history.back()"
value="Cancel"></BUTTON>
</form>
```

The last edit in the preceding HTML code, *onclick="history.back()"*, enables the user to cancel the operation without causing validation. Using an HTML control here is important because you don't want server-side processing—you just want to go back to the SignOn Web form.

When you have finished editing the Web form, switch back to Design view and double-click Create to display the Code window. Place the following *Imports* or *using* statement before the Web form's class definition:

Visual Basic .NET

```
Imports System.IO
```

Visual C#

```
using System.IO;
```

Add the following code to the *butCreate_Click* event procedure:

Visual Basic .NET

```
Private Sub butCreate_Click(ByVal sender As System.Object, _
    ByVal e As System.EventArgs) Handles butCreate.Click
    Dim strPath As String
    'Check if directory exists.
    strPath = Server.MapPath(Request.ApplicationPath) & "\" & txtName. Text
```

```
    If Directory.Exists(strPath) Then
        ' Tell the user to choose another name.
        litNameExists.Text = "<p>The name " & txtName.Text & _
            " already exists. Please choose a different one.</p>"
        Return
    Else
        Try
            ' Create the directory.
            Directory.CreateDirectory(strPath)
            ' Set the session variable.
            Session("Path") = strPath
            ' Go to file manager.
            Server.Transfer("FileManager.aspx")
        Catch ex As System.UnauthorizedAccessException
            Server.Transfer("NotAuthorized.aspx")
        End Try
    End If
End Sub
```

Visual C#

```csharp
private void butCreate_Click(object sender, System.EventArgs e)
{
    string strPath;
    //Check if directory exists.
    strPath = Server.MapPath(Request.ApplicationPath) + "\\"
        + txtName.Text;
    if (Directory.Exists(strPath))
    {
        // Tell the user to choose another name.
        litNameExists.Text = "<p>The name " + txtName.Text +
            " already exists. Please choose a different one.</p>";
        return;
    }
    else
    {
        try
        {
            // Create the directory.
            Directory.CreateDirectory(strPath);
            // Set the session variable.
            Session["Path"] = strPath;
            // Go to file manager.
            Server.Transfer("FileManager.aspx");
        }
        catch (System.UnauthorizedAccessException ex)
        {
            Server.Transfer("NotAuthorized.aspx");
        }
    }
}
```

Exercise 3: Create the File Manager Form

In this exercise, you'll create the Web form that lets users create, open, and delete files in their accounts on the server. The Web form created here uses data binding, flow layout, navigation, QueryStrings, and the System.IO namespace for file access. When you have finished creating the Web form, it will appear as shown in Figure 4-24.

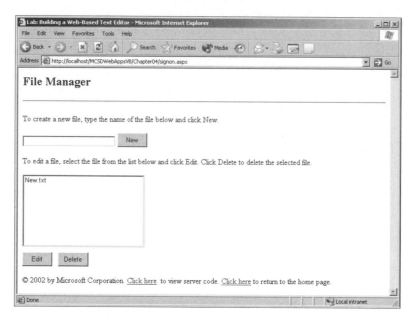

Figure 4-24   The FileManager.aspx Web form

▶ **To create the FileManager Web form**

1. Create a new Web form named FileManager.aspx.
2. In the Properties window, select the *DOCUMENT* object and set its *pageLayout* property to *FlowLayout*.
3. Add controls and set their properties as shown in the following table:

Control	Property	Value
Literal	*ID*	*litNoFile*
TextBox	*ID*	*txtNewFile*
Button	*ID*	*butNew*
	Text	*New*
Literal	*ID*	*litNoneSelected*
ListBox	*ID*	*lstFiles*
	DataSource	*strFiles*

Control	Property	Value
Button	*ID*	*butEdit*
	Text	*Edit*
Button	*ID*	*butDelete*
	Text	*Delete*

4. Switch the Web form to HTML view, and add the following text and HTML tags shown in boldface:

```
<form id="Form1" method="post" runat="server">
<h2>
File Manager
</h2>
<p>
To create a new file, type the name of the file below and click New.
</p>
<asp:Literal id="litNoFile" runat="server"></asp:Literal>
<asp:TextBox id="txtNewFile" runat="server" Width="191px"></asp:TextBox>
<asp:Button id="butNew" runat="server" Width="62px" Height="29px"
Text="New"></asp:Button>
<p>
To edit a file, select the file from the list below and click Edit. Click
Delete to delete the selected file.
</p>
<asp:Literal id="litNoneSelected" runat="server"></asp:Literal>
<asp:listbox id="lstFiles" runat="server" Width="252px" Height="161px"
DataSource="<%# strFiles %>"></asp:listbox>
<br>
<asp:Button id="butEdit" runat="server" Width="62" Height="29"
Text="Edit"></asp:Button>
  
<asp:Button id="butDelete" runat="server" Width="62px" Height="29px"
Text="Delete"></asp:Button>
</form>
```

5. When you have finished editing the Web form, switch back to Design view and double-click New to display the Code window. Place the following *Imports* or *using* statement before the Web form's class definition:

Visual Basic .NET

```
Imports System.IO
```

Visual C#

```
using System.IO;
```

6. Add the following code to the form event procedures:

Visual Basic .NET

```
Public strPath As String, strFiles As String()
Private Sub Page_Load(ByVal sender As System.Object, _
    ByVal e As System.EventArgs) Handles MyBase.Load
    ' Get path.
    strPath = Session("Path")
    ' If this is not a post-back event.
    If Not IsPostBack Then
        Dim iCount As Integer
        'Get list of files in the current directory.
        strFiles = Directory.GetFiles(strPath)
        ' Get the short names for the files.
        For iCount = 0 To UBound(strFiles)
            strFiles(iCount) = Path.GetFileName(strFiles(iCount))
        Next
    End If
    ' Bind lstFiles to file array.
    lstFiles.DataBind()
End Sub

Private Sub butNew_Click(ByVal sender As System.Object, _
    ByVal e As System.EventArgs) Handles butNew.Click
    ' If there is a file name, then start the editor.
    If txtNewFile.Text <> "" Then
        Response.Redirect("EditFile.aspx?file=" & txtNewFile.Text)
    Else
        ' Otherwise, display a message.
        litNoFile.Text = "<p>You must enter the name of a file" & _
                         " to create.<p>"
    End If
End Sub

Private Sub butEdit_Click(ByVal sender As System.Object, _
    ByVal e As System.EventArgs) Handles butEdit.Click
    ' If there is a file name, then start the editor.
    If Not IsNothing(lstFiles.SelectedItem) Then
        Response.Redirect("EditFile.aspx?file=" & _
            lstFiles.SelectedItem.ToString)
    Else
        ' Otherwise, display a message.
        litNoneSelected.Text = "<p>You must select a file.<p>"
    End If
End Sub
Private Sub butDelete_Click(ByVal sender As System.Object, _
    ByVal e As System.EventArgs) Handles butDelete.Click
    ' If there is a file name, then start the editor.
    If Not IsNothing(lstFiles.SelectedItem) Then
```

```
            Try
                Dim filToDelete As File
                filToDelete.Delete(strPath & "\" & _
                    lstFiles.SelectedItem.ToString)
                lstFiles.Items.Remove(lstFiles.SelectedItem)
            Catch ex As System.Security.SecurityException
                Server.Transfer("NotAuthorized.aspx")
            End Try
        Else
            ' Otherwise, display a message.
            litNoneSelected.Text = "<p>You must select a file.<p>"
        End If
End Sub
```

Visual C#

```
string strPath;
public string[] strFiles;

private void Page_Load(object sender, System.EventArgs e)
{
    // Get path.
    strPath = Session["Path"].ToString();
    // If this is not a post-back event.
    if(!Page.IsPostBack)
    {
        // Get list of files in the current directory.
        strFiles = Directory.GetFiles(strPath);
        // Get the short names for the files.
        for (int iCount = 0; iCount <= strFiles.GetUpperBound(0);
            iCount++)
            strFiles[iCount] =
                    Path.GetFileName(strFiles[iCount]);
    }
    // Bind lstFiles to file array.
    lstFiles.DataBind();
}

private void butNew_Click(object sender, System.EventArgs e)
{
    //If there is a file name, then start the editor.
    if (!(txtNewFile.Text == ""))
        Response.Redirect("EditFile.aspx?file=" +
                txtNewFile.Text);
    else
    // Otherwise, display a message.
    litNoFile.Text = "<p>You must enter the name of a file " +
        " to create.<p>";
}
```

```
private void butEdit_Click(object sender, System.EventArgs e)
{
    // If there is a file name, then start the editor.
    if (lstFiles.SelectedItem != null)
        Response.Redirect("EditFile.aspx?file=" +
            lstFiles.SelectedItem.ToString());
    else
        // Otherwise, display a message.
        litNoneSelected.Text = "<p>You must select a file.<p>";
}


private void butDelete_Click(object sender, System.EventArgs e)
{
    // If there is a file name, then start the editor.
    if (lstFiles.SelectedItem != null)
        try
        {
            File.Delete(strPath + "\\" +
                lstFiles.SelectedItem.ToString());
            lstFiles.Items.Remove(lstFiles.SelectedItem);
        }
        catch(System.UnauthorizedAccessException ex)
        {
            Server.Transfer("NotAuthorized.aspx");
        }
    else
        // Otherwise, display a message.
        litNoneSelected.Text = "<p>You must select a file.<p>";
}
```

Exercise 4: Create the File Editor Form

In this exercise, you'll create the Web form that edits files stored on the server in the user's account. The Web form created here uses the same layout and programming techniques as the Web form example in Exercise 3. When you have finished creating the Web form, it will appear as shown in Figure 4-25.

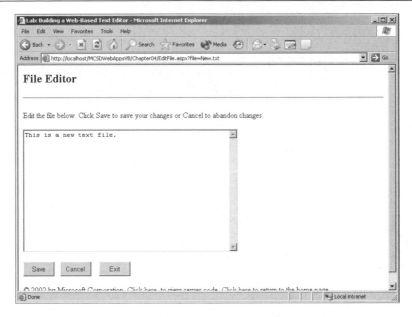

Figure 4-25   The EditFile.aspx Web form

▶ **To create the File Editor Web form**

1. Create a new Web form named EditFile.aspx.
2. In the Properties window, select the *DOCUMENT* object and set its *pageLayout* property to *FlowLayout*.
3. Add controls and set their properties as shown in the following table:

Control	Property	Value
TextBox	*ID*	*txtEditFile*
	TextMode	*Multiline*
Button	*ID*	*butSave*
	Text	*Save*
HTML Button	*id*	*butCancel*
	value	*Cancel*
Button	*ID*	*butExit*
	Text	*Exit*

4. Switch the Web form to HTML view, and add the following text and HTML tags shown in boldface:

```
<form id="Form1" method="post" runat="server">
<h2>
File Editor
</h2>
```

```
<p>
Edit the file below. Click Save to save your changes or Cancel to abandon
changes.
</p>
<asp:TextBox id="txtEditFile" runat="server" Width="448px" Height="253px"
TextMode="MultiLine"></asp:TextBox>
<p>
</p>
<asp:Button id="butSave" runat="server" Width="65" Height="30"
Text="Save"></asp:Button>
   <INPUT id="butCancel" onclick="history.back()" type="button"
value="Cancel" style="WIDTH: 65px; HEIGHT: 30px">
  
<asp:Button id="butExit" runat="server" Width="65" Height="30"
Text="Exit"></asp:Button>
</form>
```

5. When you have finished editing the Web form, switch back to Design view and double-click New to display the Code window. Place the following *Imports* or *using* statement before the Web form's class definition:

Visual Basic .NET

```
Imports System.IO
```

Visual C#

```
using System.IO;
```

6. Add the following code to the form event procedures:

Visual Basic .NET

```
Dim strPath, strFile As String
Private Sub Page_Load(ByVal sender As System.Object, _
    ByVal e As System.EventArgs) Handles MyBase.Load
    ' Get the path and file names.
    strPath = Session("Path")
    strFile = Request.QueryString("file")
    ' If this is not a post-back event.
    If Not IsPostBack Then
        Dim strmEditFile As StreamReader
        Try
            ' Open the file.
            strmEditFile = File.OpenText(strPath & "\" & _
                strFile)
            ' Read its text.
            txtEditFile.Text = strmEditFile.ReadToEnd.ToString
            ' Close the file.
            strmEditFile.Close()
        Catch ex As System.IO.FileNotFoundException
            ' If it doesn't exist, create it.
            File.CreateText(strPath + "\\" + strFile).Close()
```

```
                ' Clear text box.
                txtEditFile.Text = ""
            Catch ex As System.UnauthorizedAccessException
                Server.Transfer("NotAuthorized.aspx")
            End Try
        End If
End Sub

Private Sub butExit_Click(ByVal sender As System.Object, _
    ByVal e As System.EventArgs) Handles butExit.Click
    If ViewState("changed") Then
        SaveFile()
    End If
    ' Return to File Manager.
    Server.Transfer("FileManager.aspx")
End Sub

Private Sub txtEditFile_TextChanged(ByVal sender As System.Object, _
    ByVal e As System.EventArgs) Handles txtEditFile.TextChanged
    ' Set changed flag.
    ViewState("changed") = True
End Sub

Private Sub butSave_Click(ByVal sender As System.Object, _
    ByVal e As System.EventArgs) Handles butSave.Click
    SaveFile()
End Sub

Private Sub SaveFile()
    Dim strmEditWrite As StreamWriter
    ' Delete the file.
    File.Delete(strPath & strFile)
    ' Create the file with new text.
    strmEditWrite = File.CreateText(strPath & "\" & strFile)
    strmEditWrite.Write(txtEditFile.Text)
    strmEditWrite.Close()
    ' Reset changed flag.
    ViewState("changed") = False
End Sub
```

Visual C#

```
string strPath;
string strFile;

private void Page_Load(object sender, System.EventArgs e)
{
    // Get the path and file names.
    strPath = Session["Path"].ToString();
    strFile = Request.QueryString["file"];
```

```
// If this is not a post-back event.
if (! Page.IsPostBack)
{
    StreamReader strmEditFile;
    try
    {
        // Open the file.
        strmEditFile = File.OpenText(strPath + "\\" +
          strFile);
        // Read its text.
        txtEditFile.Text =
          strmEditFile.ReadToEnd().ToString();
        // Close the file.
        strmEditFile.Close();
    }
    catch(FileNotFoundException ex)
    {
        // If it doesn't exist, create it.
        File.CreateText(strPath + "\\" +
          strFile).Close();
        // Clear text box.
        txtEditFile.Text = "";
    }
    catch(System.UnauthorizedAccessException ex)
    {
        Server.Transfer("NotAuthorized.aspx");
    }
}
}

private void butExit_Click(object sender, System.EventArgs e)
{
    if ((ViewState["Changed"] != null) &&
      (ViewState["Changed"].ToString() == "true"))
        SaveFile();
    // Return to File Manager.
    Server.Transfer("FileManager.aspx");
}

private void txtEditFile_TextChanged(object sender, System.EventArgs e)
{
    // Set changed flag.
    ViewState["Changed"] = "true";
}

private void butSave_Click(object sender, System.EventArgs e)
{
    SaveFile();
}
```

```
void SaveFile()
{
    StreamWriter strmEditWrite;
    // Delete the file.
    File.Delete(strPath + strFile);
    // Create the file with new text.
    strmEditWrite = File.CreateText(strPath + "\\" + strFile);
    strmEditWrite.Write(txtEditFile.Text);
    strmEditWrite.Close();
    // Reset changed flag.
    ViewState["Changed"] = "false";
}
```

Exercise 5: Create the Not Authorized Web Form

As mentioned at the beginning of this lab, you must authorize the ASPNET user account to create and delete files in the application's root folder. If you don't grant these permissions, all attempts to create, save, or delete files result in a *System.UnauthorizedAccessException* error.

The code in the preceding exercises handles this error by using *Try...Catch/ try...catch* exception handling blocks. If the error occurs, the Web-Based Text Editor displays a Web form with instructions for how to fix the error, as shown in Figure 4-26.

Figure 4-26   The NotAuthorized.aspx Web form

► **To create the Not Authorized Web form**

1. Add a new Web form to the project, and name it NotAuthorized.aspx.

2. Switch to HTML mode, and add the following HTML to the Web form:

```
<h2>You are not authorized for this request.</h2>
<p>
This error occurs when ASPNET user account is not authorized to access ,
create, or modify a folder or file on the server. Use Windows
Explorer to set the permissions for the project folder to allow the AS PNE
Tuser account to modify, read, and write files to that folder.
</p>
<a href="SignOn.aspx">Return to sign-on.</a>
```

Review

The following questions are intended to reinforce key information presented in this chapter. If you are unable to answer a question, review the appropriate lesson and then try the question again. Answers to the questions can be found in the appendix.

1. What is the main difference between the Button server control and the Button HTML control?

2. How do you get several RadioButton controls to interoperate on a Web form so that only one of the RadioButton controls can have a value of *True/true* at any given time?

3. Why does ASP.NET perform validation on both the client and the server?

4. What types of validation would you use to verify that a user entered a valid customer number?

5. What is wrong with the following line of code?

Visual Basic .NET

```
Server.Transfer("Default.htm")
```

Visual C#

```
Server.Transfer("Default.htm");
```

6. Why can't you open a new browser window from within server code?

CHAPTER 5

Storing and Retrieving Data with ADO.NET

About This Chapter

In this chapter, you'll learn how to use Microsoft ADO.NET to access and modify data stored in SQL and OLE databases from Web forms. You'll learn about the data tools included with Microsoft Visual Studio .NET and how to use them to create connections to, get records from, and perform commands on databases. You'll also learn how to display data on a Web form using either data binding or code. Finally, you'll learn how to use transactions to maintain the integrity of a database.

Before You Begin

To complete the lessons in this chapter, you must:

- Have Microsoft Data Engine (MSDE) or Microsoft SQL Server installed on your computer. The .NET Framework installs MSDE as part of the default setup.
- Install the Contacts SQL database (Contacts.mdf) from this book's companion CD onto your computer. This sample SQL database is used throughout the examples in this chapter. This database can be installed using the Setup program found on this book's companion CD.
- Be familiar with the basic elements of the Transact-SQL language. To find information about the SQL language, see the "Transact-SQL Language Reference" Help topic in Microsoft SQL Server Books Online.

Lesson 1: Accessing Data with ADO.NET

Visual Studio .NET provides access to databases through the set of tools and namespaces collectively referred to as *Microsoft ADO.NET*. Data access in ADO.NET is standardized to be mostly independent of the source of the data— once you've established a connection to a database, you use a consistent set of objects, properties, and methods, regardless of the type of database you are using.

In this lesson, you'll learn how to use ADO.NET to connect to a database and how to read, modify, and delete records from that database. The lessons in this chapter use the Contacts database (Contacts.mdf) included on the companion CD for all the examples. Be sure to install that database before trying to work with the examples.

After this lesson, you will be able to

- Understand the structure and steps involved in accessing data through ADO.NET
- Connect to a database and create a data set at design time
- Explain how ADO.NET refers to data items using type information
- Add, delete, and modify records in a data set
- Update a database from a data set
- Connect to a database and create a data set at run time

Estimated lesson time: 35 minutes

Understanding ADO.NET

There are four layers to data access in ADO.NET:

- **The physical data store**   This can be a SQL, an OLE, or an Oracle database or an Extensible Markup Language (XML) file.
- **The data provider**   This consists of the *Connection* object and command objects that create the in-memory representation of the data.
- **The data set**   This is the in-memory representation of the tables and relationships that you work with in your application.
- **The data view**   This determines the presentation of a table in the data set. You typically use data views to filter or sort data to present to the user. Each data set has a default data view matching the row order used to create the data set.

The data provider layer provides abstraction between the physical data store and the data set you work with in code. After you've created the data set, it doesn't matter where the data set comes from or where it is stored. This architecture is referred to as *disconnected* because the data set is independent of the data store.

Figure 5-1 shows the ADO.NET object model in action.

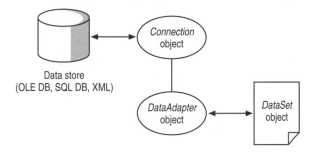

Figure 5-1   The *Connection* and *DataAdapter* objects

There are currently three types of database connection in ADO.NET:

- **Use an *OleDbConnection* object to connect to a Microsoft Access or third-party database, such as MySQL.**   OLE database connections use the *OleDb-DataAdapter* object to perform commands and return data.
- **Use a *SqlConnection* object to connect to a Microsoft SQL Server database.**   SQL database connections use the *SqlDbDataAdapter* object to perform commands and return data.
- **Use an *OracleConnection* object to connect to Oracle databases.**   Oracle database connections use the *OracleDataAdapter* object to perform commands and return data. This connection object was introduced in Microsoft .NET Framework version 1.1.

In addition to these database connections, you can access XML files directly from data sets using the *DataSet* object's *ReadXML* and *WriteXML* methods. XML files are static representations of data sets. ADO.NET uses XML for all data transfer across the Internet.

ADO.NET provides its objects, properties, and methods through the three namespaces described in Table 5-1. The *System.Data.SqlClient*, *System.Data.Oracle-Client*, and *System.Data.OleDb* namespaces listed in the table provide equivalent features for Microsoft SQL Server and other databases, respectively.

Table 5-1   ADO.NET Namespaces

Namespace	Provides
System.Data	Classes, types, and services for creating and accessing data sets and their subordinate objects
System.Data.SqlClient	Classes and types for accessing Microsoft SQL Server databases
System.Data.OracleClient	Classes and types for accessing Oracle databases (Microsoft .NET Framework version 1.1 and later)
System.Data.OleDb	Classes and types for accessing other databases

When working with databases in code, you need to add the following *Imports* or *using* declarations at the top of your code module:

Visual Basic .NET

```
Imports System.Data
' For Microsoft SQL Server database connections.
Imports System.Data.SqlClient
' For Oracle database connections.
Imports System.Data.OracleClient
' For other database connections.
Imports System.Data.OleDb
```

Visual C#

```
using System.Data;
// For Microsoft SQL Server database connections.
using System.Data.SqlClient;
// For Oracle database connections.
using System.Data.OracleClient;
// For other database connections.
using System.Data.OleDb;
```

To access a database through ADO.NET, follow these steps:

1. Create a connection to the database using a connection object.
2. Invoke a command to create a *DataSet* object using an adapter object.
3. Use the *DataSet* object in code to display data or to change items in the database.
4. Invoke a command to update the database from the *DataSet* object using an adapter object.
5. Close the database connection if you explicitly opened it in step 2 using the *Open* method. Invoking commands without first invoking the *Open* method implicitly opens and closes the connection with each request.

The following sections discuss each of these steps in more detail.

Connecting to a Database

Use the Server Explorer to connect to a database in Visual Studio.

To connect to a database in the Visual Studio design environment, follow these steps:

1. From the View menu, choose Server Explorer. Visual Studio displays the Server Explorer window.
2. In the Server Explorer, click Connect To Database on the toolbar. Visual Studio .NET displays the DataLink Properties dialog box shown in Figure 5-2.

Figure 5-2   The DataLink Properties dialog box

3. Click the Provider tab to select the type of database for the connection. By default, the database provider is Microsoft OLE DB Provider For SQL Server. That is the correct selection if your database is running under Microsoft SQL Server. To access a different type of database, select the appropriate provider. For instance, to access a Microsoft Access database directly, select Microsoft Jet 4.0 OLE DB Provider.

4. Click the Connection tab to specify the database to connect to. Changing the database provider in step 3 changes the connection settings, as shown in Figure 5-3.

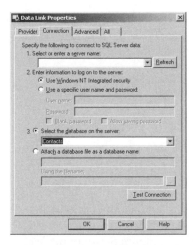

Figure 5-3   The Connection tab

5. Enter the connection settings and click Test Connection to make sure your settings are correct. Click OK when the connection succeeds. Visual Studio adds the data connection to the Server Explorer, as shown in Figure 5-4.

Figure 5-4   The Server Explorer

6. Clicking the plus signs in the Server Explorer expands items. To view the tables in a data connection, expand the items under the data connection, and then expand the items under Tables. Visual Studio displays the tables, as shown in Figure 5-5.

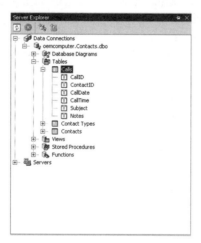

Figure 5-5   Expanded items in the Server Explorer

7. To add a data item to your application, drag the item from the Server Explorer onto your Web form. For instance, create a new Web Forms project, and drag the Contacts table shown in Figure 5-5 onto the Web form. When you drop the table onto the Web form, Visual Studio creates connection and adapter objects with the appropriate settings, as shown in Figure 5-6.

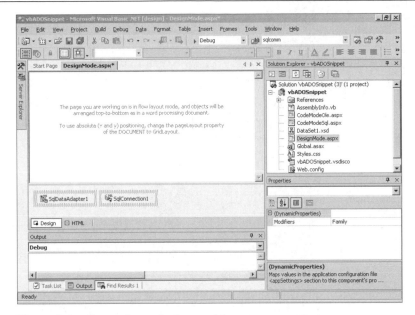

Figure 5-6   Connection and adapter objects

Important   Web applications run using the ASPNET user account. The SQL database administrator will have to set up this account and grant it permissions before your Web application will have access to a SQL database. For file-based databases, such as Microsoft Access, you must grant permissions on the database file to the ASPNET user account using Windows file security settings.

Creating a Data Set

Use the data connection and adapter objects created in step 7 in the preceding section to create a data set.

To create a data set in Design mode, follow these steps:

1. Right-click the data adapter object, and select Generate Dataset from the shortcut menu. Visual Studio displays the Generate Dataset dialog box, as shown in Figure 5-7.

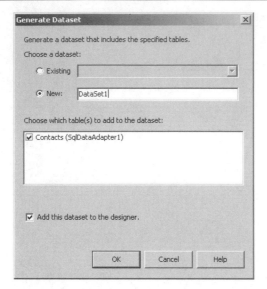

Figure 5-7   The Generate Dataset dialog box

2. Select the Contacts table to add to the data set, and click OK. Visual Studio creates a new *DataSet* object and adds it to the Web form.

To view the data in the data set in Design mode, right-click the *DataSet* object, and then select View Schema from the shortcut menu. Visual Studio displays the data set in the XML Designer window, as shown in Figure 5-8.

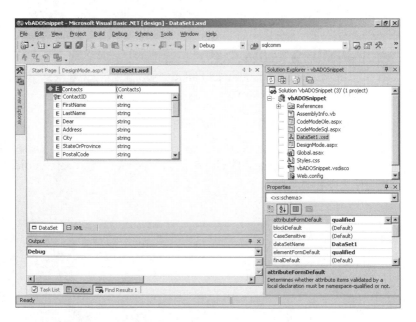

Figure 5-8   Data set schema in Design mode

Displaying a Data Set

To display the data set on the Web form at run time, follow these steps:

1. Add a control to the Web form to display the data. For instance, add a DataGrid control to the Web form.

2. Set the data set as the data source for the control. For instance, for the DataGrid control, click the Property Builder link in the Properties window, set the *Data-Source* property to the *DataSet* object, and set the *DataMember* property to a table in the data set, as shown in Figure 5-9.

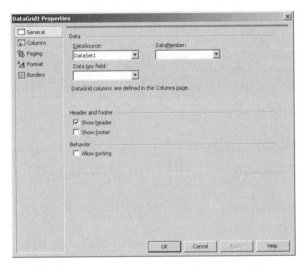

Figure 5-9   Data binding on a DataGrid control

3. Set the columns to display in the control. For the DataGrid control, click the Columns item in the Properties dialog box, clear the Create Columns Automatically At Run Time check box, and then add the columns to display from the Available Columns list, as shown in Figure 5-10. Click OK when you have finished.

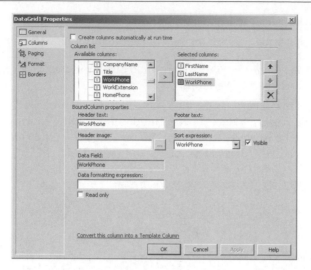

Figure 5-10   Adding columns to display in the DataGrid control

4. Add code to the Web form's *Page_Load* event procedure to fill the data set from
    the data adapter and to bind the data from the *DataSet* object to the control. For
    example, the following code displays the data in the DataGrid control created in
    the preceding steps:

Visual Basic .NET

```
Private Sub Page_Load(ByVal sender As System.Object, _
    ByVal e As System.EventArgs) Handles MyBase.Load
    ' Fill the data set.
    SqlDataAdapter1.Fill(DataSet1)
    ' Update the DataGrid.
    DataGrid1.DataBind()
End Sub
```

Visual C#

```
private void Page_Load(object sender, System.EventArgs e)
{
    // Fill the data set.
    sqlDataAdapter1.Fill(DataSet1);
    // Update the DataGrid.
    dataGrid1.DataBind();
}
```

5. Run the application. When the page loads, the data set is displayed, as shown in
    Figure 5-11.

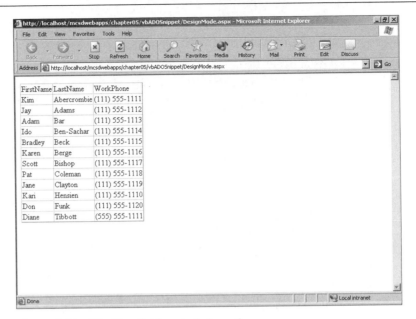

Figure 5-11   The DataGrid control at run time

Tip   Because you are filling the data set and binding the data to the DataGrid control in the *Page_Load* event procedure, you don't need to maintain state information for the DataGrid control. Turning off state information improves performance because the data in the DataGrid control does not have to be saved to the page's ViewState between requests. Set the DataGrid control's *EnableViewState* property to *False* to turn off state maintenance for the control.

Creating a Custom Data View

The preceding section displays the default view of the data set in a DataGrid control, which is the quickest way to display data. However, you'll often want to sort and filter data within the DataGrid control. To do that, you'll need to bind the DataGrid to the *DataSet* object's *DataView* property.

To create and display a data view in Design mode:

1. Drag a DataView control from the Data Controls tab of the Toolbox to the Web form's Design window.

2. Set the *Table* property of the DataView control to one of the tables in a *DataSet* object.

3. Add a DataGrid control to the form and set its *DataSource* property to the DataView control created in step 1.

After you've created a data view in Design mode, you can use the data view to change the sort order or apply filters to data displayed in a DataGrid control. For example, the following procedures change the sort order and apply a filter to a data view displayed in a DataGrid control:.

Visual Basic .NET

```
Private Sub Page_Load(ByVal sender As System.Object, _
    ByVal e As System.EventArgs) Handles MyBase.Load
    ' Fill data set.
    SqlDataAdapter1.Fill(DataSet11)
    ' Bind to data grid.
    DataGrid1.DataBind()
End Sub

Private Sub DataGrid1_SortCommand(ByVal source As Object, _
    ByVal e As System.Web.UI.WebControls.DataGridSortCommandEventArgs) _
    Handles DataGrid1.SortCommand
    ' Change the sorting in the data view.
    DataView1.Sort = e.SortExpression
    ' Bind to display the new view.
    DataGrid1.DataBind()
End Sub

Private Sub butFilter_Click(ByVal sender As System.Object, _
    ByVal e As System.EventArgs) Handles butFilter.Click
    ' Apply a filter.
    DataView1.RowFilter = "FirstName = 'New'"
End Sub
```

Visual C#

```
// From Web Form Designer generated region.
private void InitializeComponent()
{
    // generated statements omitted here...
    this.Load += new System.EventHandler(this.Page_Load);
    this.butFilter.Click += new
        System.EventHandler(this.butFilter_Click);
    this.dataGrid1.SortCommand += new
        DataGridSortCommandEventHandler(dataGrid1_SortCommand);
}

private void Page_Load(object sender, System.EventArgs e)
{
    // Fill data set.
    SqlDataAdapter1.Fill(DataSet11);
    // Bind to data grid.
    DataGrid1.DataBind();
}

private void dataGrid1_SortCommand(object source,
    DataGridSortCommandEventArgs e)
```

```
{
    // Change the sorting in the data view.
    dataView1.Sort = e.SortExpression;
}

private void butFilter_Click(object sender, System.EventArgs e)
{
    // Apply a filter.
    dataView1.RowFilter = "FirstName = 'New'";
}
```

Changing Records in a Database

The *DataSet* object is the central object in ADO.NET. Any additions, deletions, or changes to records in a database are generally done through a *DataSet* object.

To change records through a *DataSet* object, follow these steps:

1. Get a *DataSet* object as described in the preceding sections.
2. Modify the *DataSet* object.
3. Update the database from the *DataSet* object by calling the data adapter's *Update* method.

You use the *Tables*, *Rows*, and *Columns* collections to get to data items in a *DataSet* object, as shown in Figure 5-12.

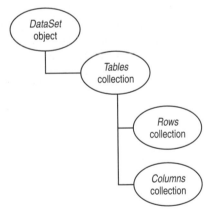

Figure 5-12   *DataSet* collections

How ADO.NET Refers to Objects

When you create connection, adapter, and data set objects in Design mode, you enable data typing for those objects. This means that you can use the specific names from the database schema to identify tables, rows, and fields. This is a big change from Microsoft ActiveX Data Objects (ADO), which provided only untyped references to data objects.

The following equivalent lines of code show a typed reference vs. an untyped reference to an object from a database:

Visual Basic .NET

```
' Typed reference to the Contacts table's HomePhone column.
DataSet1.Contacts.HomePhoneColumn.Caption = "@Home"
' Untyped reference to the Contacts table's HomePhone column.
DataSet1.Tables("Contacts").Columns("HomePhone").Caption = "@Home"
```

Visual C#

```
// Typed reference to the Contacts table's HomePhone column.
dataSet1.Contacts.HomePhoneColumn.Caption = "@Home";
// Untyped reference to the Contacts table's HomePhone column.
dataSet1.Tables["Contacts"].Columns["HomePhone"].Caption = "@Home";
```

The first line in the preceding code is not only easier to type and to read, but also much less error prone, because Visual Studio checks data types as you work, flagging any typos as unrecognized references.

In general, you should use typed references when working with data objects. The exception to this rule occurs when you don't know the specific object you are working with. Usually, this situation arises when the data source is supplied at run time rather than at design time.

Type information for data objects comes from the XML Schema that Visual Studio generates when you create a data set in Design mode.

To view type information for a data set, right-click the data set in the Design window and select View Schema from the shortcut menu. Visual Studio displays the data set in the XML Designer, as shown in Figure 5-13.

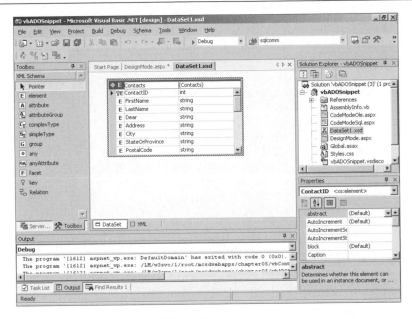

Figure 5-13   Viewing type information

You can use the XML Designer to add elements, specify unique keys, and view or change the data types of elements in a data set.

Adding, Changing, and Deleting Rows

Use the *Rows* collection to add, change, or delete rows in the *DataSet* object's *Table* object. To add a record to a data set, create a new *Row* object and add it to the *DataSet* object's *Rows* collection, as shown in the following code:

Visual Basic .NET

```
' Uses connection, adapter, and data set created in Design mode.
Private Sub butAddRow_Click(ByVal sender As System.Object, _
    ByVal e As System.EventArgs) Handles butAddRow.Click
    ' Create a new row object for the Contacts table.
    Dim rowNew As DataSet1.ContactsRow = DataSet1.Contacts.NewRow
    ' Add data to the columns in the row.
    rowNew.ContactID = m_NextID
    rowNew.FirstName = "New"
    rowNew.LastName = "User " + m_NextID.ToString()
    rowNew.WorkPhone = "(111) 555-1212"
    ' Add the row to the data set.
    DataSet1.Contacts.Rows.Add(rowNew)
End Sub
```

Visual C#

```csharp
// Uses connection, adapter, and data set created in Design mode.
private void butAdd_Click(object sender, System.EventArgs e)
{
    // Create a new row object for the Contacts table.
    DataSet1.ContactsRow rowNew =
        dataSet1.Contacts.NewContactsRow();
    // Add data to the columns in the row.
    rowNew.ContactID = m_NextID;
    rowNew.FirstName = "New";
    rowNew.LastName = "User " + m_NextID.ToString();
    rowNew.WorkPhone = "(111) 555-1212";
    // Add the row to the data set.
    dataSet1.Contacts.AddContactsRow(rowNew);
}
```

To change a row in a data set, get a *Row* object from the table using the *FindBy* method, and then make changes to the fields in the row, as shown in the following code:

Visual Basic .NET

```vb
' Uses connection, adapter, and data set created in Design mode.
Private Sub butChangeRow_Click(ByVal sender As System.Object, _
    ByVal e As System.EventArgs) Handles butChangeRow.Click
    ' Declare a row object.
    Dim rowChange As DataSet1.ContactsRow
    ' Get the last row using the primary key.
    rowChange = DataSet1.Contacts.FindByContactID(m_NextID - 1)
    ' Change a field in the row.
    rowChange.WorkPhone = "(111) 555-9000"
End Sub
```

Visual C#

```csharp
// Uses connection, adapter, and data set created in Design mode.
private void butChange_Click(object sender, System.EventArgs e)
{
    // Declare a row object.
    DataSet1.ContactsRow rowChange;
    // Get the row to change using the primary key.
    rowChange = dataSet1.Contacts.FindByContactID(m_NextID - 1);
    // Change a field in the row.
    rowChange.WorkPhone = "(555) 222-9000";
}
```

To delete a row in a data set, get a *Row* object from the table using the *FindBy* method, and then delete the row using the *Row* object's *Delete* method, as shown here:

Visual Basic .NET

```
' Uses connection, adapter, and data set created in Design mode.
Private Sub butDeleteRow_Click(ByVal sender As System.Object, _
    ByVal e As System.EventArgs) Handles butDeleteRow.Click
    ' Declare a row object.
    Dim rowDelete As DataSet1.ContactsRow
    ' Get the last row
    rowDelete = DataSet1.Contacts.FindByContactID(m_NextID - 1)
    ' Delete the row.
    rowDelete.Delete()
End Sub
```

Visual C#

```
// Uses connection, adapter, and data set created in Design mode.
private void butDelete_Click(object sender, System.EventArgs e)
{
    // Declare a row object.
    MCSDWebAppsCS.Chapter05.DataSet1.ContactsRow rowDelete;
    // Get the row to delete
    rowDelete = dataSet1.Contacts.FindByContactID(m_NextID - 1);
    // Delete the row.
    rowDelete.Delete();
}
```

Updating the Database from the *DataSet*

Use the data adapter's *Update* method to update the database with changes from a *DataSet* object. You will usually want to do this after all of the control events on a page have been processed; therefore, the *Update* method is usually called from the *Page_PreRender* event procedure, as shown here:

Visual Basic .NET

```
' Uses connection, adapter, and data set created in Design mode.
Private Sub Page_PreRender(ByVal sender As Object, _
    ByVal e As System.EventArgs) Handles MyBase.PreRender
    ' Update the database with changes from the data set.
    SqlDataAdapter1.Update(DataSet1)
    ' Rebind to reflect the data set changes in the DataGrid
    DataGrid1.Bind()
End Sub
```

Visual C#

```
// From Web Designer generated code region.
private void InitializeComponent()
{
    // generated code omitted...
    this.PreRender += new EventHandler(Page_PreRender);
}
```

```
// Uses connection, adapter, and data set created in Design mode.
private void Page_PreRender(object sender, EventArgs e)
{
    // Update the database with changes from the data set.
    sqlDataAdapter1.Update(dataSet1);
    // Refresh data grid just before the page is displayed.
    DataGrid1.DataBind();
}
```

When you update a database from a data set, ADO.NET follows these steps:

1. Determines the changes to the data set by checking each *DataRow* object's *RowState* property. Possible values are *Added*, *Deleted*, *Modified*, *Unchanged*, or *Detached*.

2. Invokes the adapter object's *InsertCommand*, *DeleteCommand*, or *UpdateCommand* properties to make the required changes in the database. These operations automatically open the database connection and close it when finished.

3. Resets the updated *DataRow* objects' *RowState* properties to *Unchanged*.

The adapter object's *InsertCommand*, *DeleteCommand*, and *UpdateCommand* properties are generated automatically from the adapter object's *SelectCommand* when you create a data set from a data adapter in Design mode. Each of these properties represents an *OleCommand* or *SqlCommand* object. Command objects have the following properties that determine how the command is executed:

- The *CommandText* property contains the SQL statement or the stored procedure name to perform the command.

- The *CommandType* property determines how the command is performed by the following possible settings:

    - The *StoredProcedure* setting executes the command as a procedure stored in the database.

    - The *Text* setting executes the command as a SQL statement. (This is the default.)

    - The *TableDirect* setting returns the entire table. This setting applies only to OLE DB .NET data providers.

You can change the contents of the data set and how the data set is updated by changing the SQL statements used by these command objects.

To view or modify these commands, follow these steps:

1. In the Properties window, double-click the command property you want to change. This expands the list of properties that apply to the command object, as shown in Figure 5-14.

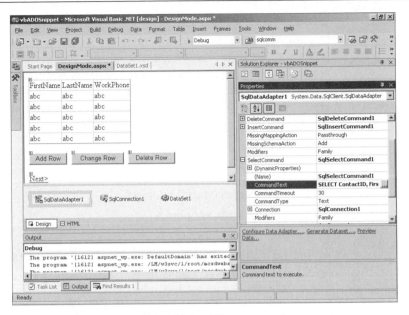

Figure 5-14   Viewing and modifying SQL commands

2. Select the *CommandText* property for the command, and then click the ellipsis button to the right of the property setting. Visual Studio displays the Query Builder dialog box, as shown in Figure 5-15.

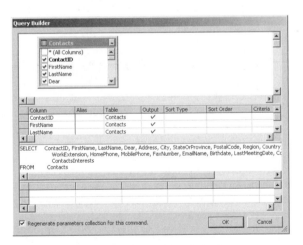

Figure 5-15   The Query Builder dialog box

3. Select the columns to include in the command by selecting the check boxes next to the data field names in the table pane of the Query Builder dialog box, or type the SQL statement directly in the command pane of the Query Builder. When you have finished, click OK to close the dialog box.

Creating a Database Connection at Run Time

Creating data objects in Design mode is a great way to learn about data access in ADO.NET because Visual Studio generates the connection and adapter object property settings for you. Some of the property settings, such as *ConnectionString*, can be difficult and confusing to construct without the help of Design mode. After you've created a connection in Design mode, you can cut and paste the property settings to create similar connections in code.

Using data-access objects in code follows the same sequence of events as it does in Design mode:

1. Create the data connection object.
2. Create a data adapter object.
3. Create a data set object.
4. Invoke methods on the adapter object to fill or update the data set.
5. Use data binding or another technique to display the data from the data set.

For example, the following code creates data objects and displays data from a Microsoft SQL data provider:

Visual Basic .NET

```
Dim m_adptContactMgmt As SqlDataAdapter

Private Sub Page_Load(ByVal sender As System.Object, _
    ByVal e As System.EventArgs) Handles MyBase.Load
    ' (1) Create the data connection.
    Dim ContactMgmt As New SqlConnection _
        ("server=(local);database=Contacts;Trusted_Connection=yes")
    ' (2) Create a data adapter.
    m_adptContactMgmt = New _
        SqlDataAdapter("select * from Contacts", ContactMgmt)
    ' (3) Create a data set.
    Dim dsContacts As New DataSet
    ' (4) Fill the data set.
    m_adptContactMgmt.Fill(dsContacts, "Contacts")
    ' (5) Display the table in a data grid using data binding.
    DataGrid1.DataSource = dsContacts.Tables("Contacts").DefaultView
    DataGrid1.DataBind()
End Sub
```

Visual C#

```
SqlDataAdapter m_adptContactMgmt;

private void Page_Load(object sender, System.EventArgs e)
{
    // (1) Create the data connection.
    SqlConnection ContactMgmt = new SqlConnection("server=(local);" +
```

```
        "database=Contacts;Trusted_Connection=yes");
    // (2) Create a data adapter.
    m_adptContactMgmt = new SqlDataAdapter("select * from Contacts",
        ContactMgmt);
    // (3) Create a data set.
    DataSet dsContacts = new DataSet();
    // (4) Fill the data set.
    m_adptContactMgmt.Fill(dsContacts, "Contacts");
    // (5) Display the table in a data grid using data binding.
    DataGrid1.DataSource = dsContacts.Tables["Contacts"].DefaultView;
    DataGrid1.DataBind();
}
```

Updating a Run-Time Database Connection

As mentioned earlier in this section, ADO.NET uses the adapter object's *Insert-Command*, *DeleteCommand*, and *UpdateCommand* properties to update the database from the data set. When you create a data adapter at run time, you need to generate these properties before you can call the adapter object's *Update* method.

To generate *InsertCommand*, *DeleteCommand*, and *UpdateCommand* properties at run time, follow these steps:

1. Set the adapter object's *SelectCommand*. The *SelectCommand* is set by the data adapter's constructor, or it can be set using the *SelectCommand* property. ADO.NET uses the *SelectCommand*'s *CommandText* property to generate the settings for the *InsertCommand*, *DeleteCommand*, and *UpdateCommand* properties.

2. Create a command builder object for the adapter object. The command builder object is dependent on the data provider, so it has three forms: *SqlCommand-Builder*, *OracleCommandBuilder*, and *OleDbCommandBuilder*.

The following code creates a database connection, data adapter, and data set in code and then displays that data set in a DataGrid (1 through 5). Next the code adds a row to the data set (6), creates a command builder for the adapter object (7), and then uses the dynamically created commands to update the database in the *Page_PreRender* event procedure (8):

Visual Basic .NET

```
Dim m_NextID As Integer
Dim m_dtContacts As DataTable
Dim m_adptContactMgmt As SqlDataAdapter

Private Sub Page_Load(ByVal sender As System.Object, _
    ByVal e As System.EventArgs) Handles MyBase.Load
    ' (1) Create the data connection.
    Dim ContactMgmt As New SqlConnection _
        ("server=(local);database=Contacts;Trusted_Connection=yes")
```

```
               ' (2) Create a data adapter.
               m_adptContactMgmt = New _
                   SqlDataAdapter("select * from Contacts", ContactMgmt)
               ' (3) Create a data set.
               Dim dsContacts As New DataSet
               ' (4) Fill the data set.
               m_adptContactMgmt.Fill(dsContacts, "Contacts")
               ' Get the data table
               m_dtContacts = dsContacts.Tables("Contacts")
               ' Create a primary key on data table.
               m_dtContacts.PrimaryKey = New _
                   DataColumn() {m_dtContacts.Columns("ContactID")}
               ' Get a new, unique row ID.
               m_NextID = GetNewID(m_dtContacts)
               ' (5) Display the table in a data grid using data binding.
               DataGrid1.DataSource = m_dtContacts.DefaultView
           End Sub

           Private Sub butAdd_Click(ByVal sender As System.Object, _
               ByVal e As System.EventArgs) Handles butAdd.Click
               ' (6) Create and add a new row.
               ' Create a new row object.
               Dim rowInsert As DataRow = m_dtContacts.NewRow
               ' Add data to fields in the row.
               rowInsert("ContactID") = m_NextID
               rowInsert("FirstName") = "New"
               rowInsert("LastName") = "User " + m_NextID.ToString()
               rowInsert("WorkPhone") = "(555) 555-1212"
               ' Add the row to the data set.
               m_dtContacts.Rows.Add(rowInsert)
           End Sub

           Private Sub Page_PreRender(ByVal sender As Object, _
               ByVal e As System.EventArgs) Handles MyBase.PreRender
               ' (7) Create insert, delete, and update commands automatically.
               Dim cmdContactMgmt As SqlCommandBuilder = New _
                   SqlCommandBuilder(m_adptContactMgmt)
               ' (8) Update the database.
               m_adptContactMgmt.Update(m_dtContacts)
               ' Bind data to DataGrid to update the display.
               DataGrid1.DataBind()
           End Sub

           ' Helper function to get a new, valid row ID.
           Function GetNewID(ByVal dt As DataTable) As Integer
               ' Get a new row number.
               Dim NextID As Integer = dt.Rows.Count + 1
               ' If it isn't found in the table, return it.
               If IsNothing(dt.Rows.Find(NextID)) Then Return NextID
               ' Otherwis, check for free IDs between 1 and the row count.
```

```
    For NextID = 1 To dt.Rows.Count
        ' Check if this ID already exists.
        If IsNothing(dt.Rows.Find(NextID)) Then
            Return NextID
        End If
    Next
    ' Failed, return zero.
    Return 0
End Function
```

Visual C#

```csharp
int m_NextID;
DataTable m_dtContacts;
SqlDataAdapter m_adptContactMgmt;

private void Page_Load(object sender, System.EventArgs e)
{
    // (1) Create the data connection.
    SqlConnection ContactMgmt = new SqlConnection("server=(local);" +
        "database=Contacts;Trusted_Connection=yes");
    // (2) Create a data adapter.
    m_adptContactMgmt = new SqlDataAdapter("select * from Contacts",
        ContactMgmt);
    // (3) Create a data set.
    DataSet dsContacts = new DataSet();
    // (4) Fill the data set.
    m_adptContactMgmt.Fill(dsContacts, "Contacts");
    // Get the data table
    m_dtContacts = dsContacts.Tables["Contacts"];
    // Create a primary key on data table.
    m_dtContacts.PrimaryKey = new DataColumn[]
        {m_dtContacts.Columns["ContactID"]};
    // Get a new, unique row ID.
    m_NextID = GetNewID(m_dtContacts);
    // (5) Display the table in a data grid using data binding.
    DataGrid1.DataSource = m_dtContacts.DefaultView;
}

private void butAdd_Click(object sender, System.EventArgs e)
{
    // (6) Create a new row object for the Contacts table.
    DataRow rowNew  = m_dtContacts.NewRow();
    // Add data to the columns in the row.
    rowNew["ContactID"] = m_NextID;
    rowNew["FirstName"] = "New";
    rowNew["LastName"] = "User " + m_NextID.ToString();
    rowNew["WorkPhone"] = "(111) 555-1212";
    // Add the row to the data set.
    m_dtContacts.Rows.Add(rowNew);
}
```

```
private void Page_PreRender(object sender, EventArgs e)
{
    // (7) Create insert, delete, and update commands automatically.
    SqlCommandBuilder cmdContactMgmt = new
        SqlCommandBuilder(m_adptContactMgmt);
    // (8) Update the database.
    m_adptContactMgmt.Update(m_dtContacts);
    // Bind data to DataGrid to update the display.
    DataGrid1.DataBind();
}

// Helper function to get a new, valid row ID.
int GetNewID(DataTable dt)
{
    // Get a new row number.
    int NextID  = dt.Rows.Count + 1;
    // If it isn't found in the table, return it.
    if (dt.Rows.Find(NextID) == null)  return NextID;
    // Otherwis, check for free IDs between 1 and the row count.
    for(NextID = 1; NextID <= dt.Rows.Count; NextID++)
    {
        // Check if this ID already exists.
        if (dt.Rows.Find(NextID) == null) return NextID;
    }
    // Failed, return zero.
    return 0;
}
```

The *Update* method in the preceding code requires that you create the *SqlCommandBuilder* object first. Creating that object provides the settings for the *InsertCommand* property that the adapter object uses to add the new row. The *Update* method automatically opens the database connection before making changes and closes it when finished.

Storing Multiple Tables and Caching Data Sets

So far, we've used data sets to store a single data table. This is convenient because Visual Studio can automatically generate the appropriate *Select*, *Update*, *Delete*, and *Insert* command objects for data adapter objects that create a data set containing one data table. However, data sets can just as easily contain multiple tables, relations between tables, and constraints.

Use the *Add* method to add tables to a data set. Remember that ASP.NET throws away Web form variables after the form is displayed, so you'll usually want to save data sets as *Application*, *Session*, or *Cache* variables so that you don't have to re-create them each time the form is displayed.

The *Cache* object is uniquely useful when you're working with data sets because it allows you to specify an expiration for the data it contains. Data sets can be large, and you usually don't want to leave them in memory indefinitely. As with *Application* state, all code within the application has access to data in the *Cache* object.

For example, the following code creates a data set containing two data tables, establishes a relationship between the tables, and stores the data set in the application cache:

Visual Basic .NET

```
' Data adapter, combines SQL command and connection string.
Dim adptDB As New SqlDataAdapter("SELECT * FROM Contacts", _
    "server=(local);database=Contacts;Trusted_Connection=yes")
' Data set to contain two data tables
Public dsBoth As New DataSet

Private Sub Page_Load(ByVal sender As System.Object, _
    ByVal e As System.EventArgs) Handles MyBase.Load
    ' Create Cache if this is the first time the page is displayed
    ' or if the Cache object doesn't yet exist.
    If Not (IsPostBack) Or IsNothing(Cache.Get("dsBoth")) Then
        ' Create the Contacts table.
        Dim Contacts As New DataTable("Contacts")
        adptDB.Fill(Contacts)
        ' Change the adapter's SELECT command.
        adptDB.SelectCommand.CommandText = "SELECT * FROM Calls"
        ' Create the Calls table.
        Dim Calls As New DataTable("Calls")
        adptDB.Fill(Calls)

        ' Add both tables to a single dataset.
        dsBoth.Tables.Add(Calls)
        dsBoth.Tables.Add(Contacts)

        ' Cache data set for 20 minutes.
        Cache.Add("dsBoth", dsBoth, Nothing, DateTime.MaxValue, _
            System.TimeSpan.FromMinutes(20), _
        Caching.CacheItemPriority.Default, Nothing)
        ' Bind the drop-down list to display data.
        drpContacts.DataBind()
    Else
        ' If this is post-back get the Cached data set.
        dsBoth = Cache("dsBoth")
    End If
End Sub

Private Sub drpContacts_SelectedIndexChanged(ByVal sender As _
    System.Object, ByVal e As System.EventArgs) _
    Handles drpContacts.SelectedIndexChanged
```

```
        ' Set a filter on the view of the Calls table.
        dsBoth.Tables("Calls").DefaultView.RowFilter = "ContactID=" + _
            drpContacts.SelectedItem.Value
        ' Bind to the data grid.
        grdCalls.DataBind()
End Sub
```

Visual C#

```csharp
// Data adapter, combines SQL command and connection string.
SqlDataAdapter adptDB =new SqlDataAdapter("SELECT * FROM Contacts",
    "server=(local);database=Contacts;Trusted_Connection=yes");
// Data set to contain two data tables
public DataSet dsBoth = new DataSet("Both");

private void Page_Load(object sender, System.EventArgs e)
{
    // Create Cache if this is the first time the page is displayed
    // or if the Cache object doesn't yet exist.
    if  ((!IsPostBack) || (Cache.Get("dsBoth") == null))
    {
        // Create the Contacts table.
        DataTable Contacts = new DataTable("Contacts");
        adptDB.Fill(Contacts);

        // Change the adapter's SELECT command.
        adptDB.SelectCommand.CommandText = "SELECT * FROM Calls";
        // Create the Calls table.
        DataTable Calls = new DataTable("Calls");
        adptDB.Fill(Calls);

        // Add both tables to a single dataset.
        dsBoth.Tables.Add(Calls);
        dsBoth.Tables.Add(Contacts);

        // Cache data set for 20 minutes.
        Cache.Add("dsBoth", dsBoth, null, DateTime.MaxValue,
            System.TimeSpan.FromMinutes(20),
            System.Web.Caching.CacheItemPriority.Default, null);
        // Bind the drop-down list to display data.
        drpContacts.DataBind();
    }
    else
        // If this is post-back get the Cached data set.
        dsBoth = (DataSet) Cache["dsBoth"];
}

private void drpContacts_SelectedIndexChanged(object sender,
    System.EventArgs e)
{
    // Set a filter on the view of the Calls table.
```

```
        dsBoth.Tables["Calls"].DefaultView.RowFilter = "ContactID=" +
        drpContacts.SelectedItem.Value.ToString();
        // Bind to the data grid.
        grdCalls.DataBind();
}
```

The preceding code creates the data set once, the first time anyone visits the page. The data set is then maintained in memory for 20 minutes after it was last accessed—at which time, it is discarded. This produces very quick response time for most requests but doesn't tie up the server memory with unused data.

Also, by combining both data tables in a single data set, you ensure that both items exist in the *Cache* object. If you store the data tables separately, it's possible that one item might be discarded before the other.

Lesson 2: Using Data Sets on Web Forms

Most ASP.NET server controls support **data binding**, which is a way to link data in your application, such as data sets, to properties of a control. In particular, the DataGrid and DataList server controls are specifically designed to make displaying data sets on a Web form easy and efficient.

In this lesson, you'll learn how to display a data set on a Web form using the Data-Grid, DataList, and other server controls. You'll learn how to select records from a data set on a Web form and how to perform SQL commands on a database from control event procedures.

After this lesson, you will be able to

- Quickly display a data set on a Web form through data binding
- Format the data displayed in a DataGrid, DataList, or other data-bound server control
- Display data from a data set in a server control using code rather than data binding
- Get records from a data set displayed on a Web form
- Perform SQL commands on a database to return values or to modify data directly

Estimated lesson time: 30 minutes

Displaying a Data Set in a DataGrid Control

The simplest way to display a data set on a Web form is through a DataGrid control using data binding.

To display a data set in this way, follow these steps:

1. Create the database connection, adapter, and data set objects as described in the previous lesson.
2. Add a DataGrid control to the Web form.
3. Set the *DataSource* property of the DataGrid control to the name of the data set.
4. Add code to the Web form's *Page_Load* event procedure to fill the data set from the adapter and to bind the data from the data set to the DataGrid control.

For example, the following event procedure creates a data set from the Contacts database's Contacts table and then displays the data in a DataGrid control:

Visual Basic .NET

```
Private Sub Page_Load(ByVal sender As System.Object, _
    ByVal e As System.EventArgs) Handles MyBase.Load
    ' Fill the data set.
    adptContacts.Fill(dsContacts1)
    ' Bind the data to the DataGrid control.
    grdContacts.DataBind()
End Sub
```

Visual C#

```
private void Page_Load(object sender, System.EventArgs e)
{
    // Fill the data set.
    adptContacts.Fill(dsContacts1);
    // Bind the data to the DataGrid control.
    grdContacts.DataBind();
}
```

This procedure and code displays all of the columns in the data set without formatting, as shown in Figure 5-16.

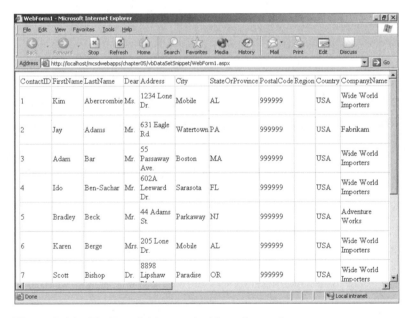

Figure 5-16   The DataGrid control without formatting

This is generally not what you want. For instance, the Birthdate column (not shown in Figure 5-16) includes a time as well as the date.

To select the columns you want to display and to format the data in the DataGrid control, follow these steps:

1. Click the Property Builder link in the Properties window. Visual Studio displays the Properties dialog box for the DataGrid control.

2. Select the Columns item on the left side of the Properties dialog box to select and format the columns of data displayed from the data set. Visual Studio displays the columns' properties, as shown in Figure 5-17.

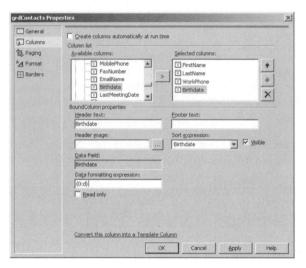

Figure 5-17   Specifying columns and formatting for a DataGrid control

To display specific columns from the data set, follow these steps:

1. Clear the Create Columns Automatically At Run Time check box. This limits the columns in the DataGrid control to only the ones you select.

2. Select the column in the Available Columns list, and click the Add (>) button to add the column to the Selected Columns list.

To format data in a column, follow these steps:

1. Select the column to format in the Selected Columns list.

2. Type the format expression in the Data Formatting Expression box. Data formatting expressions take the form:

{0:formattingexpression}

where formattingexpression is one of the predefined Microsoft .NET Framework format expressions, as described in the "Date and Time Format Strings," "Numeric Format Strings," and "Custom Format Strings" topics in the Visual Studio online Help.

You use the DataGrid Properties dialog box to specify all aspects of the appearance and behavior of the DataGrid, including formatting the column headings, specifying how the grid scrolls (pages) through records, specifying whether borders or rules are displayed, and much more.

Figure 5-18 shows the Contacts data set displayed in a DataGrid control with formatting applied. The DataGrid control displays only four columns from the data set and formats the Birthdate column as a short date (*{0:d}*).

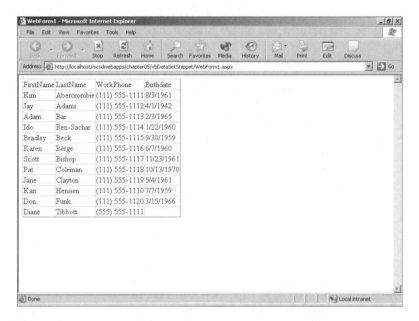

Figure 5-18   Selected columns from a data set with formatting applied

Displaying a Data Set in a DataList Control

Use the DataList control to display information from a data set as a list of rows, rather than rows and columns as in a DataGrid control.

To display a data set in a DataList control, follow these steps:

1. Create the database connection, adapter, and data set objects as described in the previous lesson.
2. Add a DataList control to the Web form.
3. Set the *DataSource* property of the DataGrid control to the name of the data set.
4. Add code to the Web form's *Page_Load* event procedure to fill the data set from the adapter and to bind the data from the data set to the DataGrid control.
5. Edit the DataList control's header, item, and separator templates to create the appearance of the DataList.

The DataList control uses templates to determine the content of its headers, footers, and rows. You edit these templates to add literals and controls that bind to items in the data set. The DataList control provides three different categories of templates to control the different aspects of its appearance:

- **Header and footer templates**   These include the title and rule lines that appear at the top and the bottom of the DataList control.

- **Items templates**   These determine the contents of the rows in the data list and allow you to alternate the appearance of odd, even, selected, or edited rows.

- **Separator templates**   These add rule lines or other separators between rows.

To edit a DataList template:

1. Right-click the DataList control, point to Edit Template, and then select the template to edit from the shortcut menu.

2. The DataList control changes its appearance when it is in Edit mode, as shown in Figure 5-19. Type the text you want to appear in the template and add controls as desired.

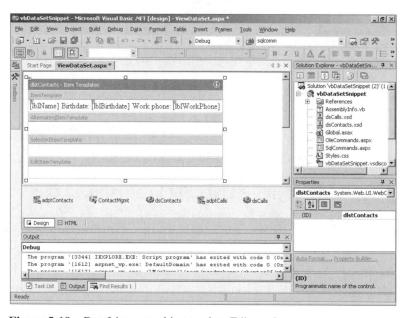

Figure 5-19   DataList control in template Edit mode

3. To display an item from the data set in the template, add a control to the template, and then click the *DataBindings* property for the control. Click the ellipsis button to the right of the *DataBindings* property. Visual Studio displays the DataBindings dialog box for the control, as shown in Figure 5-20.

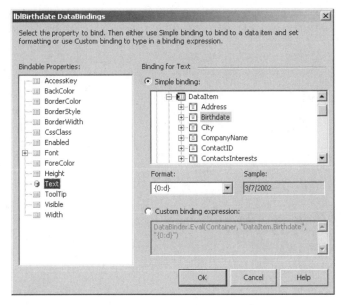

Figure 5-20   DataBindings dialog box

4. When you have finished editing the DataList control's templates, right-click the DataList control and select End Template Editing from the shortcut menu.

Data binding for controls in the DataList control's Items template can be a simple binding to an item from the container, as shown in Figure 5-20, or it can be a more complex expression using the *Eval* method. For example, the following custom binding expression combines first name and last name information in a single control:

Visual Basic .NET

```
DataBinder.Eval(Container, "DataItem.FirstName") & " " & _
    DataBinder.Eval(Container, "DataItem.LastName")
```

Visual C#

```
DataBinder.Eval(Container, "DataItem.FirstName") + " " +
  DataBinder.Eval(Container, "DataItem.LastName");
```

The *DataBinder* object's *Eval* method is actually what is generated by Visual Studio in the Web form's HTML when you create a DataList control template with data binding. It is sometimes easier to edit templates directly in HTML than through the edit template procedure described previously.

To edit a DataList template directly in HTML, right-click the Web form and select View HTML Source from the shortcut menu. Visual Studio displays the Web form in HTML mode.

For example, the following HTML displays a DataList control that contains name, birthday, and telephone information from the Contacts data set:

```
<asp:DataList id="dlstContacts" runat="server"
DataSource="<%# dsContacts1 %>">
<HeaderTemplate>
<h2>
    Contact Information
    <HR width="100%" SIZE="1">
</h2>
</HeaderTemplate>

<FooterTemplate>
<HR>
</FooterTemplate>

<ItemTemplate>
    <asp:Label id="lblName" runat="server"
        Text='<%# DataBinder.Eval(Container, "DataItem.FirstName") + " "
        + DataBinder.Eval(Container,"DataItem.LastName") %>'>
    </asp:Label>
     Birthdate:
    <asp:Label id="lblBirthdate" runat="server"
        Text='<%# DataBinder.Eval(Container, "DataItem.Birthdate",
    "{0:d}") %>'>
    </asp:Label>
     Work phone:
    <asp:Label id="lblWorkPhone" runat="server"
        Text='<%# DataBinder.Eval(Container, "DataItem.WorkPhone") %>'>
    </asp:Label>
</ItemTemplate>

<SeparatorTemplate>
    <HR>
</SeparatorTemplate>
</asp:DataList>
```

To display the data set in the preceding control, fill the data set from the data adapter and bind to the DataList control, as shown by the following *Page_Load* event procedure:

Visual Basic .NET

```
Private Sub Page_Load(ByVal sender As System.Object, _
    ByVal e As System.EventArgs) Handles MyBase.Load
    ' Fill the data set.
    adptContacts.Fill(dsContacts1)
    ' Bind the data to the DataList control
    dlstContacts.DataBind()
End Sub
```

Visual C#

```
private void Page_Load(object sender, System.EventArgs e)
{
    // Fill the data set.
    adptContacts.Fill(dsContacts1);
    // Bind the data to the DataList control.
    dlstContacts.DataBind();
}
```

At run time, the preceding DataList control displays the header, items, and separators, as shown in Figure 5-21.

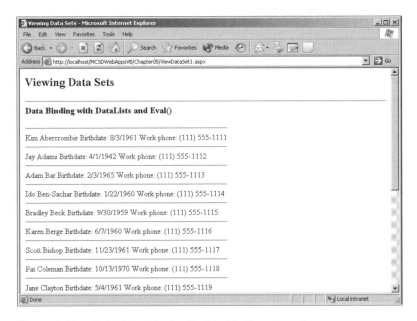

Figure 5-21   DataList control with data binding at run time

Displaying Data Items in Other List Controls

Of course, you can bind the items from a data set to any list control on a Web form. The DataGrid and DataList controls are just two of the most versatile ways to display a data set.

To display items from a data set in a ListBox, DropDownList, CheckBoxList, or RadioButtonList control, follow these steps:

1. Set the control's *DataSource* property to the name of the data set.
2. Set the control's *DataText* property to the data set member to display as the *Text* property of the list item.
3. Set the control's *DataValue* property to the data set member to return as the *Value* property of the list item.

4. In code, fill the data set from data adapter and bind to the control.

The following HTML shows the property settings for a DropDownList control that is bound to the Contacts data set:

```
<asp:DropDownList id="drpContacts" runat="server" Width="384px" Height="22px"
DataSource="<%# dsContacts1 %>"
DataTextField='LastName' DataValueField="ContactID"></asp:DropDownList>
```

The following code fills the data set and binds the data to the DropDownList control:

Visual Basic .NET

```
Private Sub Page_Load(ByVal sender As System.Object, _
    ByVal e As System.EventArgs) Handles MyBase.Load
    If Not IsPostBack Then
        ' Fill the data set.
        adptContacts.Fill(dsContacts1)
        ' Bind the data to the control.
        drpContacts.DataBind()
    End If
End Sub
```

Visual C#

```
private void Page_Load(object sender, System.EventArgs e)
{
    if (!IsPostBack)
    {
        // Fill the data set.
        adptContacts.Fill(dsContacts1);
        // Bind the data to the DataList control.
        drpContacts.DataBind();
    }
}
```

At run time, the DropDownList control displays a list of the last names from the Contacts table, and the *SelectedItem.Value* property returns the ContactID, which is useful for looking up other information about the individual.

The limitation here is that you can include only one value for the list control's *DataText* and *DataValue* properties. If you want to include the first and last names of the contact in the DropDownList control, you have to do it from code. The following *Page_Load* event procedure adds the first and last names to the DropDown-List control and includes the ContactID as the *Value* property for each list item:

Visual Basic .NET

```
Private Sub Page_Load(ByVal sender As System.Object, _
    ByVal e As System.EventArgs) Handles MyBase.Load
    ' Run first time page is displayed.
    If Not IsPostBack Then
```

```
                ' Fill the Contacts data set.
                adptContacts.Fill(dsContacts1)
                ' For each row in the table...
                Dim drowItem As dsContacts.ContactsRow
                For Each drowItem In dsContacts1.Contacts
                    ' Create a new list item.
                    Dim lstNew As New ListItem
                    lstNew.Text = drowItem.FirstName & " " & drowItem.LastName
                    lstNew.Value = drowItem.ContactID
                    ' Add the list item to the drop-down list.
                    drpContacts.Items.Add(lstNew)
                Next
            End If
    End Sub
```

Visual C#

```
private void Page_Load(object sender, System.EventArgs e)
{
    // Run first time page is displayed.
    if (!IsPostBack)
    {
        // Fill the Contacts data set.
        adptContacts.Fill(dsContacts1);
        // For each row in the table...
        foreach (dsContacts.ContactsRow drowItem in dsContacts.Contacts)
        {
            // Create a new list item.
            ListItem lstNew = new ListItem();
            lstNew.Text = drowItem.FirstName + " " +
                drowItem.LastName;
            lstNew.Value = drowItem.ContactID.ToString();
            // Add the list item to the drop-down list.
            drpContacts.Items.Add(lstNew);
        }
    }
}
```

Selecting Specific Records

The DropDownList control created in the preceding section is useful for selecting items from the Calls table in the Contacts database. Because ContactID is a unique key in the database, you can use it to select the Call records for a specific contact. The following code builds a data set containing the calls for the contact selected from the DropDownList control:

Visual Basic .NET

```
Private Sub drpContacts_SelectedIndexChanged(ByVal sender As System.Object, _
    ByVal e As System.EventArgs) Handles drpContacts.SelectedIndexChanged
    ' When a contact is selected, display the contact's calls.
    adptCalls.SelectCommand.CommandText = "SELECT * FROM Calls" & _
```

```
        " WHERE ContactID =" & drpContacts.SelectedItem.Value
    adptCalls.Fill(dsCalls1)
    If dsCalls1.Tables("Calls").Rows.Count > 0 Then
        ' Display the results in a data grid.
        grdCalls.DataBind()
        grdCalls.Visible = True
        lblMsg.Text = ""
    Else
        grdCalls.Visible = False
        lblMsg.Text = drpContacts.SelectedItem.Text + " has no calls."
    End If
End Sub
```

Visual C#

```csharp
private void drpContacts_SelectedIndexChanged(object sender, EventArgs e)
{
    // When a contact is selected, display the contact's calls.
    adptCalls.SelectCommand.CommandText = "SELECT * FROM Calls" +
        " WHERE ContactID =" + drpContacts.SelectedItem.Value.ToString();
    adptCalls.Fill(dsCalls1);
    if (dsCalls1.Tables["Calls"].Rows.Count > 0)
    {
        // Display the results in a data grid.
        grdCalls.DataBind();
        grdCalls.Visible = true;
        lblMsg.Text = "";
    }
    else
    {
        grdCalls.Visible = false;
        lblMsg.Text = drpContacts.SelectedItem.Text + " has no calls.";
    }
}
```

At run time, the Web form displays a list of the calls for the contact selected in the DropDownList control, as shown in Figure 5-22.

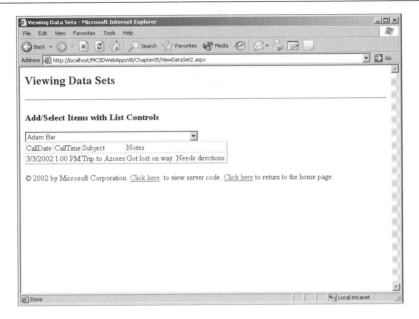

Figure 5-22 Selecting Records with a DropDownList control

Executing Commands on a Database

In addition to working with data sets, you can perform commands directly on a database connection. The database connection object provides these three command methods:

- *ExecuteScalar* Performs query commands that return a single value, such as counting the number of records in a table.
- *ExecuteNonQuery* Performs commands that change the database but do not return a specific value, including adding and deleting items from a database. The *ExecuteNonQuery* method returns the number of rows affected by the command.
- *ExecuteReader* Reads records sequentially from the database.

To use these methods, follow these steps:

1. Create a connection to the database.
2. Open the connection.
3. Create a command object containing the SQL command or stored procedure to execute.
4. Execute the method on the command object.
5. Close the database connection.

Because any command that executes on a database has at least some potential to fail, you should always use exception handling to ensure that the database connection is closed whether or not the command succeeds. Calling the connection's *Close* method from a *Finally/finally* exception-handling clause ensures that the database connection is closed before the code continues.

Returning a Value from a Database

Use the *ExecuteScalar* method to execute a command that returns a single value from a database. For example, the following code executes a SQL MAX function to retrieve the highest number used for ContactID and then uses that value as the seed value for adding a new row to the Contacts table:

Visual Basic .NET

```
' Create a database connection.
Dim connContacts As New SqlConnection("integrated security=SSPI;" + _
    "data source=(local);initial catalog=Contacts")

Private Sub butAdd_Click(ByVal sender As System.Object, _
    ByVal e As System.EventArgs) Handles butAdd.Click
    Try
        ' Create a SQL command to get a unique ContactID.
        Dim cmdNewID As New SqlCommand("SELECT MAX(ContactID)" & _
            " FROM Contacts", connContacts)
        ' Open the database connection.
        connContacts.Open()
        ' Execute the SQL command.
        Dim intNextID As Integer = CInt(cmdNewID.ExecuteScalar()) + 1
        ' Create a command to add a new row.
        Dim cmdAddRow As New SqlCommand(String.Format("INSERT INTO " + _
        "Contacts(ContactID, FirstName, LastName, WorkPhone) " + _
        "VALUES({0}, '{1}', '{2}', '{3}')", intNextID, txtFirstName.Text, _
        txtLastName.Text, txtPhone.Text), connContacts)
        ' Execute the command.
        If cmdAddRow.ExecuteNonQuery Then
            lblMsg.Text = "Record added."
        Else
            lblMsg.Text = "Couldn't add record."
        End If
    Catch ex As Exception
        lblMsg.Text = "Couldn't access database due to this error: " + _
        ex.Message
    Finally
        ' Close connection
        connContacts.Close()
    End Try
End Sub
```

Visual C#

```csharp
SqlConnection connContacts = new SqlConnection("integrated security=SSPI;" +
    "data source=(local);initial catalog=Contacts");

private void butAdd_Click(object sender, System.EventArgs e)
{
    try
    {
        // Create a SQL command to get a unique ContactID.
        SqlCommand cmdNewID =new SqlCommand("SELECT MAX(ContactID)" +
            " FROM Contacts", connContacts);
        // Open the database connection.
        connContacts.Open();
        // Execute the SQL command.
        int intNextID  = (int)cmdNewID.ExecuteScalar() + 1;
        // Create a command to add a new row.
        SqlCommand cmdAddRow = new SqlCommand(String.Format("INSERT " +
            "INTO Contacts(ContactID, FirstName, LastName, WorkPhone) " +
            "VALUES({0}, '{1}', '{2}', '{3}')", intNextID,
            txtFirstName.Text, txtLastName.Text,
            txtPhone.Text), connContacts);
        // Execute the command.
        if (cmdAddRow.ExecuteNonQuery() > 0)
        {
            lblMsg.Text = "Record added.";
            // Database changed, so refresh list.
            RefreshList();
            // Clear text boxes.
            ClearText();
        }
        else
        {
            lblMsg.Text = "Couldn't add record.";
        }
    }
    catch (Exception ex)
    {
        lblMsg.Text = "Couldn't access database due to this error: " +
            ex.Message;
    }
    finally
    {
        // Close connection
        connContacts.Close();
    }
}
```

The *ExecuteScalar* method can be used with any SQL statement that returns a single value. To execute other types of SQL statements, use the *ExecuteNonQuery* or *ExecuteReader* method.

Changing Records Directly in a Database

The *ExecuteNonQuery* method performs commands that do not return a data set, such as SQL INSERT, DELETE, or UPDATE. For example, the following code uses *ExecuteNonQuery* to delete a row directly from the database:

Visual Basic .NET

```
' Create a database connection.
Dim connContacts As New SqlConnection("integrated security=SSPI;" + _
    "data source=(local);initial catalog=Contacts")

Private Sub butDelete_Click(ByVal sender As System.Object, _
    ByVal e As System.EventArgs) Handles butDelete.Click
    Try
        ' Create a SQL command to delete record.
        Dim sqlDelete As New _
            SqlCommand("DELETE FROM Contacts WHERE ContactID=" + _
            lblContactID.Text, connContacts)
        ' Open the database connection
        connContacts.Open()
        ' Execute the command.
        If sqlDelete.ExecuteNonQuery Then
            lblMsg.Text = "Record deleted."
        Else
            lblMsg.Text = "Couldn't find record to delete."
        End If
    Catch ex As Exception
        lblMsg.Text = "Couldn't access database due to this error: " + _
        ex.Message
    Finally
        ' Close connection
        connContacts.Close()
    End Try
End Sub
```

Visual C#

```
SqlConnection connContacts = new SqlConnection("integrated security=SSPI;" +
    "data source=(local);initial catalog=Contacts");

private void butDelete_Click(object sender, System.EventArgs e)
{
    try
    {
        // Create a SQL command to delete record.
        SqlCommand sqlDelete = new SqlCommand("DELETE FROM Contacts " +
```

```
                    "WHERE ContactID=" + lblContactID.Text, connContacts);
        // Open the database connection
        connContacts.Open();
        // Execute the command.
        if (sqlDelete.ExecuteNonQuery() > 0)
        {
            lblMsg.Text = "Record deleted.";
            // Database changed, so refresh list.
            RefreshList();
            // Clear text boxes
            ClearText();
        }
        else
        {
            lblMsg.Text = "Couldn't find record to delete.";
        }
    }
    catch (Exception ex)
    {
        lblMsg.Text = "Couldn't access database due to this error: " +
            ex.Message;
    }
    finally
    {
        // Close connection
        connContacts.Close();
    }
}
```

The *ExecuteNonQuery* method acts directly on the database connection—it does not go through a data adapter or a data set. If you make changes to a table in the database through *ExecuteNonQuery*, you must update any data sets affected by those changes by calling the *Fill* method on the data adapter.

Retrieving Records Directly from the Database

The *ExecuteReader* method performs commands that return records, such as SQL SELECT. Each record is returned as a data reader object, which is sort of a read-only version of a data set. Because the *ExecuteReader* method acts directly on the database connection, there are two versions of the data reader object: *OleDbDataReader* and *SqlDataReader*.

Using *ExecuteReader* to create data reader objects provides better performance than creating a data set from a data adapter object, but it doesn't provide you with much flexibility. Data reader objects are read-only and they only read forward, one record at a time. Data sets allow you to get records in any order and, more important, allow you to write changes back to the database.

The following code gets all the contacts and displays their names in a drop-down list using a data reader object and the *Execute* reader command:

Visual Basic .NET

```vbnet
' Create a database connection.
Dim connContacts As New SqlConnection("integrated security=SSPI;" + _
    "data source=(local);initial catalog=Contacts")

Private Sub Page_Load(ByVal sender As System.Object, _
    ByVal e As System.EventArgs) Handles MyBase.Load
    ' Get values for drop-down list the first time
    ' the page is displayed.
    If Not IsPostBack Then
        RefreshList()
    End If
End Sub


' Loads values from database into a drop-down list.
Sub RefreshList()
    Try
        ' Clear the list
        drpContacts.Items.Clear()
        ' Create SQL command to get table.
        Dim cmdGetContacts As New SqlCommand("Select * From Contacts", _
            connContacts)
        ' Open database connection if it is closed.
        If connContacts.State = ConnectionState.Closed Then _
            connContacts.Open()
        ' Execute command.
        Dim readContacts As SqlDataReader = cmdGetContacts.ExecuteReader()
        ' Read the names and contact IDs into a drop-down list
        Do While readContacts.Read()
            ' Create a new list item.
            Dim NewItem As New ListItem
            ' Set the item's values.
            NewItem.Text = readContacts.GetString(1) + " " _
                + readContacts.GetString(2)
            NewItem.Value = readContacts.GetValue(0)
            ' Add the new item to the list.
            drpContacts.Items.Add(NewItem)
        Loop
    Catch ex As Exception
        lblMsg.Text = "Couldn't access data due to this error: " + _
            ex.Message
    Finally
        ' Close the connection.
        connContacts.Close()
    End Try
End Sub
```

Visual C#

```csharp
SqlConnection connContacts = new SqlConnection("integrated security=SSPI;" +
    "data source=(local);initial catalog=Contacts");

private void Page_Load(object sender, System.EventArgs e)
{
    // Get values for drop-down list the first time
    // the page is changed.
    if (!IsPostBack)
    {
        RefreshList();
    }
}

private void RefreshList()
{
    try
    {
        // Clear the list
        drpContacts.Items.Clear();
        // Create SQL command to get table.
        SqlCommand cmdGetContacts = new SqlCommand("Select * " +
            "From Contacts", connContacts);
        // Open database connection if it is closed.
        if (connContacts.State == ConnectionState.Closed)
            connContacts.Open();
        // Execute command.
        SqlDataReader readContacts = cmdGetContacts.ExecuteReader();
        // Read the names and contact IDs into a drop-down list
        while (readContacts.Read())
        {
            // Create a new list item.
            ListItem NewItem = new ListItem();
            // Set the item's values.
            NewItem.Text = readContacts.GetString(1) + " "
                + readContacts.GetString(2);
            NewItem.Value = readContacts.GetValue(0).ToString();
            // Add the new item to the list.
            drpContacts.Items.Add(NewItem);
        }
    }
    catch (Exception ex)
    {
        lblMsg.Text = "Couldn't access data due to this error: " +
            ex.Message;
    }
    finally
    {
```

```
        // Always close the connection.
        connContacts.Close();
    }
}
```

The data reader object is a read-forward set of records, so the *Read* method reads each subsequent line until it reaches the end of the record set. A reader object locks the database connection while it is executing, so you should call the reader object's *Close* method when you have finished getting records, as shown in the preceding code.

Executing Stored Procedures

One well-known performance tip when you're working with databases is to move frequently used tasks into stored procedures. Stored procedures execute within the context of the database manager and therefore can be optimized for ideal performance.

Use the *ExecuteScalar*, *ExecuteNonQuery*, or *ExecuteReader* method to run stored procedures. For example, the following code executes a stored procedure that returns the ten most expensive products in the Northwind Traders database.

Visual Basic .NET

```
Private Sub butExecute_Click(ByVal sender As System.Object, _
    ByVal e As System.EventArgs) Handles butExecute.Click
    ' Create a connection for NorthWind Traders database.
    Dim connNWind As New SqlConnection("integrated security=SSPI;" + _
        "data source=(local);initial catalog=Northwind")
    ' Create a command object to execute.
    Dim cmdTopTen As New SqlCommand("Ten Most Expensive Products", _
        connNWind)
    ' Set the command properties.
    cmdTopTen.CommandType = CommandType.StoredProcedure
    ' Create a data reader object to get the results.
    Dim drdTopTen As SqlDataReader
    ' Open the connection.
    connNWind.Open()
    Try
        ' Excecute the stored procedure.
        drdTopTen = cmdTopTen.ExecuteReader()
        ' Display a header.
        litData.Text = "<h3>Ten Most Expensive Products:</h3>"
        ' Display the results on the page.
        Do While drdTopTen.Read()
            ' Create an array to receive data.
            Dim items() As Object = {"", "", "", "", "", ""}
            ' If the row contains items.
            If drdTopTen.GetValues(items) > 0 Then
                Dim item As Object
```

```
                        ' Get each row item and add it to the literal control.
                        For Each item In items
                            litData.Text += item.ToString + " "
                        Next
                        ' Add a break between rows.
                        litData.Text += "<br>"
                    End If
                Loop
            Catch ex As Exception
                litData.Text = "The following error occurred: <br>"
                litData.Text += ex.Message
            Finally
                ' Close the connection.
                connNWind.Close()
            End Try
        End Sub
```

Visual C#

```
private void butExecute_Click(object sender, System.EventArgs e)
{
    // Create a connection for NorthWind Traders database.
    SqlConnection connNWind = new SqlConnection("integrated " +
        "security=SSPI;data source=(local);initial catalog=Northwind");
    // Create a command object to execute.
    SqlCommand cmdTopTen = new SqlCommand("Ten Most Expensive Products",
        connNWind);
    // Set the command properties.
    cmdTopTen.CommandType = CommandType.StoredProcedure;
    // Create a data reader object to get the results.
    SqlDataReader drdTopTen;
    // Open the connection.
    connNWind.Open();
    try
    {
        // Excecute the stored procedure.
        drdTopTen = cmdTopTen.ExecuteReader();
        // Display a header.
        litData.Text = "<h3>Ten Most Expensive Products:</h3>";
        // Display the results on the page.
        while (drdTopTen.Read())
        {
            // Create an array to receive data.
            object[] items  = {"", "", "", "", "", ""};
            // If the row contains items.
            if (drdTopTen.GetValues(items) > 0)
            {
                // Add each row item to the literal control.
                foreach(object item in items)
                    litData.Text += item.ToString() + " ";
                // Add a break between rows.
```

```
                    litData.Text += "<br>";
                }
            }
        }
        catch (Exception ex)
        {
            litData.Text = "The following error occurred: <br>";
            litData.Text += ex.Message;
        }
        finally
        {
            // Close the connection.
            connNWind.Close();
        }
}
```

Lesson 3: Processing Transactions

ADO.NET lets you group database operations into transactions. A **transaction** is a group of commands that change the data stored in a database. The transaction, which is treated as a single unit, assures that the commands are handled in an all-or-nothing fashion—if one of the commands fails, all of the commands fail, and any data that was written to the database by the commands is backed out. In this way, transactions maintain the integrity of data in a database.

In this lesson, you'll learn how to implement transaction processing in a Web application for data sets and for databases.

After this lesson, you will be able to

- Understand the importance of transaction processing for Web applications that use data access
- Explain the levels of transaction processing that ADO.NET supports
- Manage changes to a data set as a transaction
- Create transaction objects for a database
- Track commands performed on a database through a transaction object
- Commit or roll back (undo) changes to a database using the transaction object

Estimated lesson time: 30 minutes

Understanding Transactions

As stated earlier, a transaction is a group of database commands that are treated as a single unit. Database programmers determine what database commands belong in a transaction by using the ACID test: commands must be *atomic*, *consistent*, *isolated*, and *durable*. Commands belong in a transaction if they are:

- **Atomic**   In other words, they make up a single unit of work. For example, if a customer moves, you want your data entry operator to change all of the customer's address fields as a single unit, rather than changing street, then city, then state, and so on.
- **Consistent**   All the relationships between data in a database are maintained correctly. For example, if customer information uses a tax rate from a state tax table, the state entered for the customer must exist in the state tax table.
- **Isolated**   Changes made by other clients can't affect the current changes. For example, if two data entry operators try to make a change to the same customer at the same time, one of two things occurs: either one operator's changes are accepted and the other is notified that the changes weren't made, or both operators are notified that their changes were not made. In either case, the customer data is not left in an indeterminate state.

- **Durable**   Once a change is made, it is permanent. If a system error or power failure occurs before a set of commands is complete, those commands are undone and the data is restored to its original state once the system begins running again.

Transaction processing is particularly important for Web applications that use data access, because Web applications are distributed among many different clients. In a Web application, databases are a shared resource, and having many different clients distributed over a wide area can present these key problems:

- **Contention for resources**   Several clients might try to change the same record at the same time. This problem gets worse the more clients you have.

- **Unexpected failures**   The Internet is not the most reliable network around, even if your Web application and Web server are 100 percent reliable. Clients can be unexpectedly disconnected by their service providers, by their modems, or by power failures.

- **Web application life cycle**   Web applications don't follow the same life cycle as Windows applications—Web forms live for only an instant, and a client can leave your application at any point by simply typing a new address in his or her browser.

Transaction processing follows these steps:

1. Begin a transaction.
2. Process database commands.
3. Check for errors.
4. If errors occurred, restore the database to its state at the beginning of the transaction. If no errors occurred, commit the transaction to the database.

In ADO.NET, transactions are handled in different ways, depending on the level you're working at:

- **Data sets provide transaction processing through the *RejectChanges* and *Update* methods.**   Data sets also provide an *AcceptChanges* method that resets the state of records in a data set to *Unchanged*.

- **Database connection objects provide transaction processing through the Transaction object.**   Transaction objects track commands performed on a database and provide the *Rollback*, *Commit*, and *Save* methods to restore database state, commit changes, or create a save point within a transaction, respectively.

- **The *System.EnterpriseServices* namespace provides enterprise-level transactions through the *ContextUtil* class.**   Enterprise-level transactions use the Microsoft Distributed Transaction Coordinator (MS DTC) provided with Microsoft SQL Server 2000 to track transactions across multiple Web forms and across multiple COM+ components.

Data Set Transactions

Data sets provide implicit transaction processing, because changes to a data set are not made in the database until you invoke the *Update* method on the data adapter object. This lets you perform a set of commands on the data and then choose a point at which to make the changes permanent in the database.

If an error occurs during the *Update* method, none of the changes from the data set is made in the database. At that point, you can either attempt to correct the error and try the *Update* method again or undo the changes pending in the data set using the data set's *RejectChanges* method. For example, the following code displays the Contacts list in a DataGrid control and allows the user to delete rows by clicking Delete in the DataGrid:

Visual Basic .NET

```vbnet
Private Sub Page_Load(ByVal sender As System.Object, _
    ByVal e As System.EventArgs) Handles MyBase.Load
    ' Check if this is the first time page is displayed.
    If Not IsPostBack Then
        ' On first display:
        '   Fill the data set.
        adptContacts.Fill(dsContacts)
        '   Save data set as state variable.
        Session("dsContacts") = dsContacts
    Else
        ' On subsequent displays:
        '   Get the data set from the state variable.
        dsContacts = Session("dsContacts")
    End If
    ' Bind to data set.
    grdContacts.DataBind()
End Sub


Private Sub grdContacts_ItemCommand(ByVal source As Object, _
    ByVal e As System.Web.UI.WebControls.DataGridCommandEventArgs) _
    Handles grdContacts.ItemCommand
    ' If the Delete button was clicked.
    If e.CommandName = "Delete" Then
        Dim intContactID
        ' Get selected row's ContactID.
        intContactID = _
            CInt(grdContacts.Items(e.Item.ItemIndex).Cells(3).Text)
        Dim rowDelete As dsContacts.ContactsRow
        ' Get the row to delete from the data set.
        rowDelete = dsContacts.Contacts.FindByContactID(intContactID)
        ' Delete the row.
        rowDelete.Delete()
        ' Refresh the data grid.
        grdContacts.DataBind()
    End If
End Sub
```

Visual C#

```csharp
private void Page_Load(object sender, System.EventArgs e)
{
    // Check if this is the first time page is displayed.
    if (!IsPostBack)
    {
        // On first display:
        //    Fill the data set.
        adptContacts.Fill(dsContacts);
        //    Save data set as state variable.
        Session["dsContacts"] = dsContacts;
    }
    else
        // On subsequent displays:
        //    Get the data set from the state variable.
        dsContacts = (dsContacts)Session["dsContacts"];
    // Bind to data set.
    grdContacts.DataBind();
}

private void grdContacts_ItemCommand(object sender,
    System.Web.UI.WebControls.DataGridCommandEventArgs e)
{
    // If the Delete button was clicked.
    if (e.CommandName == "Delete")
    {
        int intContactID;
        // Get selected row's ContactID.
            intContactID = Convert.ToInt16
            (grdContacts.Items[e.Item.ItemIndex].Cells[3].Text);
        dsContacts.ContactsRow rowDelete;
        // Get the row to delete from the data set.
        rowDelete = dsContacts.Contacts.FindByContactID(intContactID);
        // Delete the row.
        rowDelete.Delete();
        // Refresh the data grid.
        grdContacts.DataBind();
    }
}
```

The following event procedures for the Restore and Commit buttons let the user restore the data set to its previous state or, alternatively, update the database with the deletions made in the preceding code:

Visual Basic .NET

```vbnet
Private Sub butRestore_Click(ByVal sender As System.Object, _
    ByVal e As System.EventArgs) Handles butRestore.Click
    ' Restore the data set to its original state.
    dsContacts.RejectChanges()
```

```
                        ' Refresh the data grid.
                        grdContacts.DataBind()
End Sub

Private Sub butCommit_Click(ByVal sender As System.Object, _
        ByVal e As System.EventArgs) Handles butCommit.Click
                        ' Update the database from the data set.
                        adptContacts.Update(dsContacts)
                        ' Save changes to state variable.
                        Session("dsContacts") = dsContacts
                        ' Refresh the data grid.
                        grdContacts.DataBind()
End Sub
```

Visual C#

```
private void butRestore_Click(object sender, System.EventArgs e)
{
        // Restore the data set to its original state.
        dsContacts.RejectChanges();
        // Refresh the data grid.
        grdContacts.DataBind();
}

private void butCommit_Click(object sender, System.EventArgs e)
{
        int intRows;
        // Update the database from the data set.
        intRows = adptContacts.Update(dsContacts);
        // Save changes to state variable.
        Session["dsContacts"] = dsContacts;
        // Refresh the data grid.
        grdContacts.DataBind();
}
```

The *RejectChanges* method in the preceding *butRestore_Click* event procedure returns the data set to its state before the row was deleted. The data set's *AcceptChanges* method is the inverse of *RejectChanges*—it resets the *DataRowState* property for all the changed rows in a data set to *Unchanged* and removes any deleted rows.

The *AcceptChanges* method prevents the *Update* method from making those changes in the database, however, because *Update* uses the rows' *DataRowState* property to determine which rows to modify in the database. For this reason, the *AcceptChanges* method is useful only when you do not intend to update a database from the data set.

Database Transactions

You can manage transactions at the database level through a transaction object. Since there are three types of database connections in ADO.NET, there are also three types of transaction object: *SqlTransaction*, *OracleTransaction*, and *OleDbTransaction*.

To use either type of transaction object, follow these steps:

1. Open a database connection.
2. Create the transaction object using the database connection object's *BeginTransaction* method.
3. Create command objects to track with this transaction, assigning the *Transaction* property of each command object to the name of the transaction object created in step 2.
4. Execute the commands. Because the purpose of transaction processing is to detect and correct errors before data is written to the database, this is usually done as part of an error-handling structure.
5. Commit the changes to the database or restore the database state, depending on the success of the commands.
6. Close the database connection.

The following code uses a DataGrid control to display a list of contacts from the Contacts database. The DataGrid control includes a column of buttons that allow the user to delete contacts. The *DeleteContact* function uses a transaction to ensure that a contact's calls are deleted if the contact is deleted. This helps ensure the integrity of the database.

Visual Basic .NET

```
Private Sub Page_Load(ByVal sender As System.Object, _
    ByVal e As System.EventArgs) Handles MyBase.Load
    ' Fill the data set.
    adptContacts.Fill(dsContacts)
    ' Bind to data set.
    grdContacts.DataBind()
End Sub

Private Sub grdContacts_ItemCommand(ByVal source As Object, _
    ByVal e As System.Web.UI.WebControls.DataGridCommandEventArgs) _
    Handles grdContacts.ItemCommand
    ' If the Delete button was clicked.
    If e.CommandName = "Delete" Then
        Dim intContactID
        ' Get selected row's ContactID.
        intContactID = _
            CInt(grdContacts.Items(e.Item.ItemIndex).Cells(3).Text)
        ' Delete the contact information.
```

```vbnet
                    lblStatus.Text = DeleteContact(intContactID)
            End If
            ' Refresh the data set.
            adptContacts.Fill(dsContacts)
            ' Refresh the DataGrid.
            grdContacts.DataBind()
    End Sub

    Function DeleteContact(ByVal intContactID As Integer) As String
        ' Open the database connection.
        ContactMgmt.Open()
        ' Declare a transaction object.
        Dim transDelete As SqlTransaction
        ' Create the tranasction.
        transDelete = ContactMgmt.BeginTransaction _
         (IsolationLevel.ReadCommitted)
        ' Create the command to delete from Contacts table.
        Dim cmdDelete As New SqlCommand("DELETE FROM Contacts" & _
            " WHERE ContactID=" & intContactID, _
              ContactMgmt, transDelete)
        ' Execute the commands
        Try
            Dim intRows As Integer
            ' Delete row from Contacts table.
            intRows = cmdDelete.ExecuteNonQuery()
            ' Delete Calls for this ContactID.
            cmdDelete.CommandText = "DELETE FROM Calls WHERE " & _
                " ContactID=" & intContactID
            intRows = intRows + cmdDelete.ExecuteNonQuery()
            ' Commit the transaction.
            transDelete.Commit()
            ' Return success message.
            Return intRows & " deleted."
        Catch
            ' Restore the database state if there was an error.
            transDelete.Rollback()
            ' Return error message.
            Return "Contact could not be deleted."
        Finally
            ' Close the database.
            ContactMgmt.Close()
        End Try
    End Function
```

Visual C#

```csharp
private void Page_Load(object sender, System.EventArgs e)
{
    // Fill the data set.
    adptContacts.Fill(dsContacts);
        // Bind to the data set.
        grdContacts.DataBind();
}
```

```csharp
private void grdContacts_ItemCommand(object sender,
    System.Web.UI.WebControls.DataGridCommandEventArgs e)
{
    // If the Delete button was clicked.
    if (e.CommandName == "Delete")
    {
        int intContactID;
        // Get selected row's ContactID.
        intContactID = Convert.ToInt16(grdContacts.Items
            [e.Item.ItemIndex].Cells[3].Text);
        // Delete the contact information.
        lblStatus.Text = DeleteContact(intContactID);
    }
    // Refresh the data set.
    adptContacts.Fill(dsContacts);
    // Refresh the data grid.
    grdContacts.DataBind();
}

string DeleteContact(int intContactID)
{
    // Open the database connection.
    ContactMgmt.Open();
    // Declare a transaction object.
    SqlTransaction transDelete;
    // Create the tranasction.
    transDelete = ContactMgmt.BeginTransaction
        (IsolationLevel.ReadCommitted);
    // Create the command to delete from Contacts table.
    SqlCommand cmdDelete = new SqlCommand("DELETE FROM Contacts" +
        " WHERE ContactID=" + intContactID.ToString(),
        ContactMgmt, transDelete);
    // Execute the commands
    try
    {
        int intRows;
        // Delete row from Contacts table.
        intRows = cmdDelete.ExecuteNonQuery();
        // Delete Calls for this ContactID.
        cmdDelete.CommandText = "DELETE FROM Calls WHERE " +
            " ContactID=" + intContactID.ToString();
            intRows = intRows + cmdDelete.ExecuteNonQuery();
        // Commit the transaction.
        transDelete.Commit();
        // Return success message.
        return intRows.ToString() + " deleted.";
    }
    catch
    {
```

```
        // Restore the database state if there was an error.
        transDelete.Rollback();
        // Return error message.
        return "Contact could not be deleted.";
    }
    finally
    {
        // Close the database.
        ContactMgmt.Close();
    }
}
```

The transaction object determines how concurrent changes to a database are handled through the *IsolationLevel* property. The level of protection varies, as specified by the settings described in Table 5-2.

Table 5-2   Isolation Level Settings

Isolation level	Behavior
ReadUncommitted	Does not lock the records being read. This means that an uncommitted change can be read and then rolled back by another client, resulting in a local copy of a record that is not consistent with what is stored in the database. This is called a **dirty read** because the data is inconsistent.
Chaos	Behaves the same way as *ReadUncommitted*, but checks the isolation level of other pending transactions during a write operation so that transactions with more restrictive isolation levels are not overwritten.
ReadCommitted	Locks the records being read and immediately frees the lock as soon as the records have been read. This prevents any changes from being read before they are committed, but it does not prevent records from being added, deleted, or changed by other clients during the transaction. This is the default isolation level.
RepeatableRead	Locks the records being read and keeps the lock until the transaction completes. This ensures that the data being read does not change during the transaction.
Serializable	Locks the entire data set being read and keeps the lock until the transaction completes. This ensures that the data and its order within the database do not change during the transaction.

SQL database connections provide one transaction capability that is unavailable for OLE database connections: the ability to create **save points** within a transaction. Save points let you restore the database state to a specific position within the current transaction. To set a save point within a SQL transaction, use the *Save* method:

Visual Basic .NET

```
transDelete.Save("FirstStep")
```

Visual C#

```
transDelete.Save("FirstStep");
```

To restore a SQL transaction to a save point, specify the name of the save point in the *Rollback* method:

Visual Basic .NET

```
transDelete.Rollback("FirstStep")
```

Visual C#

```
transDelete.Rollback("FirstStep");
```

Enterprise Transactions

Because transactions can span multiple Web forms, or even multiple components within a distributed application, ASP.NET provides a way for Web forms to work with MS DTC.

To use MS DTC from a Web form, follow these steps:

1. Start a new transaction or continue an existing transaction by setting the document element's *Transaction* attribute. For example, the following @ *Page* directive starts a new transaction:

   ```
   <%@ Page Language="vb" AutoEventWireup="false"
     Codebehind="Transaction3.aspx.vb"
     Inherits="MCSDWebAppsVB.Transaction3"
   Transaction="RequiresNew"%>
   ```

2. Add a reference to the *System.EnterpriseServices* namespace to your project.
3. Use the *ContextUtil* class's *SetAbort* and *SetComplete* methods to change the status of the transaction as required.
4. Use the Page class's *CommitTransaction* and *AbortTransaction* events to respond to changes in the transaction's status.

See the Visual Studio .NET online Help for more information about MS DTC.

Summary

- ADO.NET includes five key components used for most data access: database connection, data adapter, data set, data table, and data view.
- ADO.NET provides typed data sets. Typed data sets use explicit names and data types that help prevent errors during programming.
- Use data binding to quickly display data sets on Web forms through the Data-Grid, DataList, or other list controls.
- Create command objects to execute SQL commands directly on a database. Command objects can return a single value (*ExecuteScalar*), modify the database (*ExecuteNonQuery*), or return data (*ExecuteReader*).
- Transactions group database commands so that they succeed or fail in an all-or-nothing fashion. This ensures that changes are not partially made, thus preserving the integrity of the database.
- To determine which commands should be included in a transaction, use the ACID test. A transaction must be *atomic*, *consistent*, *isolated*, and *durable*.
- To use a transaction, follow these steps:

  1. Begin the transaction.
  2. Perform commands and make changes that are part of the transaction.
  3. Check for errors.
  4. If errors occurred, undo (roll back) the changes. If no errors occurred, commit the changes. This ends the transaction.

- Manage data set transactions using the *Update* method to commit changes and the *RejectChanges* method to undo (or roll back) changes.
- Manage database transactions using the transaction object's *Commit* and *Rollback* methods.

Lab: Building the Contact Management Application

In this lab, you'll create a multipage Web application that uses a database to store contact and call information. The application lets you add contacts, view and add calls made by a contact, and add new contact types. This application uses the Contacts SQL database installed by Setup on the companion CD.

The Contact Management application demonstrates these key concepts:

- **Navigation**   Users navigate from a central switchboard page to specific task pages. After users have finished a task, they navigate back to the switchboard page.
- **Central data connection**   The database connection, data adapter, and data set components reside in the Switchboard Web form. These objects are shared between Web forms using the application's *Cache* object.
- **Data set transactions**   All changes to the database are processed through data sets, and all updates are contained within error-handling structures. If an update fails, the user can try again or cancel the operation without damaging the integrity of the database.
- **Bound and unbound controls**   Calls are displayed using a DataList control containing data-bound label controls. Contacts are displayed in a DropDownList control using code rather than data binding.

Estimated lesson time: 60 minutes

Exercise 1: Start a Project and Create the SwitchBoard Form

In this exercise, you start a new project and create the Web form used to navigate to the other Web forms in the application.

When you have finished creating the SwitchBoard form, it will appear as shown in Figure 5-23.

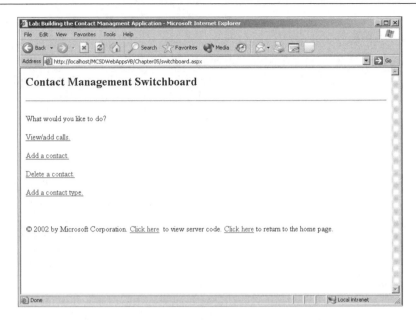

Figure 5-23   The SwitchBoard form

▶ **To start the new application and create the SwitchBoard Web form**

1. Create a new ASP.NET Web application project named **ContactManagement**.

2. Change the name of the Webform1.aspx file to **SwitchBoard.aspx**, and display the Web form in HTML mode.

3. Type the following HTML between the *<form>* and *</form>* tags:

```
<h2>Contact Management Switchboard</h2>
    <P>What would you like to do? </P>
    <P><a href="Calls.aspx">View/add calls.</a></P>
    <P><a href="AddContact.aspx">Add a contact.</a></P>
    <P><a href="DeleteContact.aspx">Delete a contact.</a></P>
    <P><a href="ContactTypes.aspx">Add a contact type.</a></P>
```

Exercise 2: Add Database Components

The Contact Management application performs data access from several different Web forms. The database connection, adapter, and data set components are added to the SwitchBoard Web form and saved as *Cache* variables so that they can be accessed from the other Web forms.

All the Web forms, and all users of the application, share a single database connection. This improves performance and makes it easier to maintain connection and adapter settings while developing the application because the database components are all located in one place: the SwitchBoard.aspx file.

▶ **To add the database components for the Contact Management application**

1. Open the SwitchBoard Web form in the Design window and click the Server Explorer link. Visual Studio displays the Server Explorer.

2. Click the Connect To A Database button in the Server Explorer window. Visual Studio displays the Data Link Properties dialog box.

3. Select the name of the SQL server where the Contacts sample database is installed, choose the Use Windows NT integrated security option, and then type **Contacts** in the Select The Database On The Server box. Click Test Connection to verify your settings, and then click OK when you have finished. Visual Studio adds the database connection to the Server Explorer.

4. In the Server Explorer window, expand the items under the data connection you created by clicking the plus signs to the left of the Contacts.dbo data connection, and then do the same to the Tables subitem. Drag the Calls, ContactTypes, and Contacts tables from the Server Explorer to the SwitchBoard Web form. Visual Studio adds a database connection component and data adapter components for each of the tables.

5. Each data adapter represents one of the tables you dragged onto the page. Right-click one of the data adapters and select Generate Data Set from the shortcut menu. Visual Studio displays the Generate DataSet dialog box.

6. Type the name of the data set to create in the New text box. Name the data set after the table it represents (for example, **dsCalls** for the Calls table), and then select the Add This Dataset To The Designer check box and click OK. Visual Studio adds the data set to the SwitchBoard Web form.

Note   When Visual Studio adds a data set, it appends a number to the name you provide.

---

7. Repeat steps 5 and 6 for each of the data adapters.

8. Double-click the SwitchBoard Web form in the Design window to display the code for the page. Add the following *Page_Load* event procedure to create the *Cache* variables that you'll use from subsequent Web forms to access the database components:

Visual Basic .NET

```
Private Sub Page_Load(ByVal sender As System.Object, _
    ByVal e As System.EventArgs) Handles MyBase.Load
    ' The first time this page is displayed...
    If Not IsPostBack Then
        AddToCache("adptCalls", SqlDataAdapter1)
        AddToCache("adptContactTypes", SqlDataAdapter2)
        AddToCache("adptContacts", SqlDataAdapter3)
        ' Fill data sets and add them to Cache.
        SqlDataAdapter1.Fill(DsCalls1)
        AddToCache("dsCalls", DsCalls1)
```

```
            SqlDataAdapter2.Fill(DsContactTypes1)
            AddToCache("dsContactTypes", DsContactTypes1)
            SqlDataAdapter3.Fill(DsContacts1)
            AddToCache("dsContacts", DsContacts1)
        End If
    End Sub

    Sub AddToCache(ByVal Name As String, ByVal Item As Object)
        ' If item is already in cache, simply return.
        If Not IsNothing(Cache(Name)) Then Return
        ' Otherwise, cache the item for 20 minutes with sliding expiration.
        Cache.Add(Name, Item, Nothing, DateTime.MaxValue, _
        System.TimeSpan.FromMinutes(20), _
            Caching.CacheItemPriority.Default, Nothing)
    End Sub
```

Visual C#

```
private void Page_Load(object sender, System.EventArgs e)
{
    // The first time this page is displayed...
    if (!IsPostBack)
    {
        AddToCache("adptCalls", sqlDataAdapter1);
        AddToCache("adptContactTypes", sqlDataAdapter2);
        AddToCache("adptContacts", sqlDataAdapter3);
        // Fill data sets and add them to Cache.
        sqlDataAdapter1.Fill(dsCalls1);
        AddToCache("dsCalls", dsCalls1);
        sqlDataAdapter2.Fill(dsContactTypes1);
        AddToCache("dsContactTypes", dsContactTypes1);
        sqlDataAdapter3.Fill(dsContacts1);
        AddToCache("dsContacts", dsContacts1);
    }
}

void AddToCache(string Name, object Item)
{
    // If item is already in cache, simply return.
    if (Cache[Name] != null) return;
    // Otherwise, cache the item for 20 minutes with sliding expiration.
    Cache.Add(Name, Item, null, DateTime.MaxValue,
        System.TimeSpan.FromMinutes(20),
            System.Web.Caching.CacheItemPriority.Default, null);
}
```

The preceding code adds the database connection, adapters, and data sets to the
application's cached data. The *Cache* object is just like the *Application* state object;
however, *Cache* allows you to set expiration rules for the data. The *AddToCache*
procedure checks whether the items are already cached (perhaps because another

session started the application previously) and adds the items if they are not found. If the cached item is not accessed for more than 20 minutes, it is unloaded from memory.

Exercise 3: Create the AddContact Form

The Contact Management application allows users to add information about new contacts through the AddContact Web form. The AddContact Web form is a straightforward data entry form with text boxes for each of the data items in a Contacts table record. When complete, the AddContact Web form will appear as shown in Figure 5-24.

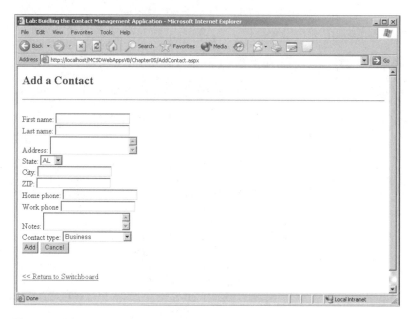

Figure 5-24   The AddContact Web form

▶ **To create the AddContact data entry Web form**

1. Add a new Web form to the project named **AddContact.aspx**.

2. In the Properties window, select the *DOCUMENT* object and set the *pageLayout* property to *FlowLayout*.

3. Add controls to the Web form with the property settings shown in the following table:

Control	Property	Setting
TextBox	*ID*	*txtFirstName*
TextBox	*ID*	*txtLastName*
TextBox	*ID*	*txtAddress*

Control	Property	Setting
	TextMode	*MultiLine*
TextBox	*ID*	*txtCity*
DropDownList	*ID*	*drpStates*
	DataSource	*arrState*
TextBox	*ID*	*txtZIP*
TextBox	*ID*	*txtHomePhone*
TextBox	*ID*	*txtWorkPhone*
TextBox	*ID*	*txtNotes*
DropDownList	*ID*	*drpContactTypes*
	DataSource	*dsContactTypes*
	DataTextField	*ContactType*
	DataValueField	*ContactTypeID*
Button	*ID*	*butAdd*
	Text	Add
Button	*ID*	*butCancel*
	Text	Cancel
Literal	*ID*	*litStatus*
Hyperlink	*Text*	Return to SwitchBoard
	NavigateUrl	SwitchBoard.aspx

4. Type text to identify the fields directly on the Web form. Use carriage returns to start new lines.

5. Double-click the Web form to display the Code window, and then add the following *Imports* or *using* statement to the top of the module:

Visual Basic .NET

```
Imports System.Data.SqlClient
```

Visual C#

```
using System.Data.SqlClient;
```

6. The AddContact Web form uses the database components created in Exercise 2 in the SwitchBoard Web form. To use these components in this Web form, declare class-level variables, and then retrieve the references to the components from the state variables where they are stored. The following code demonstrates how to do this:

Visual Basic .NET

```
Dim adptContacts As SqlDataAdapter
Dim dsContacts As  dsContacts
' These variables are public for data binding.
Public dsContactTypes As dsContactTypes
```

```vb
Public arrState As String() = {"AL", "AK", "AR", "AZ", _
    "CA", "CO", "CT", "DE", "FL", "GA", "HI", "ID", "IL", _
    "IN", "IA", "KS", "KY", "LA", "MA", "ME", "MD", "MI", _
    "MN", "MO", "MS", "MT", "NC", "ND", "NE", "NH", "NJ", _
    "NM", "NV", "NY", "OH", "OK", "OR", "PA", "RI", "SC", _
    "SD", "TN", "TX", "UT", "VA", "VT", "WA", "WI", "WY"}

Private Sub Page_Load(ByVal sender As System.Object, _
    ByVal e As System.EventArgs) Handles MyBase.Load
    ' Get the Cached variables.
    adptContacts = Cache("adptContacts")
    dsContacts = Cache("dsContacts")
    dsContactTypes = Cache("dsContactTypes")
    If Not IsPostBack Then
        ' Bind to data --
 populates the drpContactTypes and drpState lists.
        drpContactTypes.DataBind()
        drpStates.DataBind()
    End If
End Sub
```

Visual C#

```csharp
SqlDataAdapter adptContacts;
MCSDWebAppsCS.Chapter05.dsContacts dsContacts;
// These variables are public for data binding.
public MCSDWebAppsCS.Chapter05.dsContactTypes dsContactTypes;
public string[] arrState = {"AL", "AK", "AR", "AZ",
    "CA", "CO", "CT", "DE", "FL", "GA", "HI", "ID", "IL",
    "IN", "IA", "KS", "KY", "LA", "MA", "ME", "MD", "MI",
    "MN", "MO", "MS", "MT", "NC", "ND", "NE", "NH", "NJ",
    "NM", "NV", "NY", "OH", "OK", "OR", "PA", "RI", "SC",
    "SD", "TN", "TX", "UT", "VA", "VT", "WA", "WI", "WY"};

private void Page_Load(object sender, System.EventArgs e)
{
    // Get the Cached variables.
    adptContacts = (SqlDataAdapter) Cache["adptContacts"];
    dsContacts = (dsContacts) Cache["dsContacts"];
    dsContactTypes = (dsContactTypes) Cache["dsContactTypes"];
    if (!IsPostBack)
    {
        // Bind to data -- populates drpContactTypes and drpState lists.
        drpContactTypes.DataBind();
        drpStates.DataBind();
    }
}
```

7. Each contact in the Contacts table is identified by a ContactID. This is the primary key for the table, so it must be unique for each contact. Therefore, before you can add a contact to the Contacts data set, you must obtain a new, unique ContactID from the database. Add the following helper function to the Web form class to get this unique ID before adding the contact:

Visual Basic .NET

```
' Helper function to get a new, valid row ID.
Function GetNewID(ByVal dt As DataTable) As Integer
    ' Get a new row number.
    Dim NextID As Integer = dt.Rows.Count + 1
    ' If it isn't found in the table, return it.
    If IsNothing(dt.Rows.Find(NextID)) Then Return NextID
    ' Otherwise, check for free IDs between 1 and the row count.
    For NextID = 1 To dt.Rows.Count
        ' Check if this ID already exists.
        If IsNothing(dt.Rows.Find(NextID)) Then
            Return NextID
        End If
    Next
    ' Failed, return zero.
    Return 0
End Function
```

Visual C#

```
// Helper function to get a new, valid row ID.
int GetNewID(DataTable dt)
{
    // Get a new row number.
    int NextID  = dt.Rows.Count + 1;
    // If it isn't found in the table, return it.
    if (dt.Rows.Find(NextID) == null)  return NextID;
    // Otherwise, check for free IDs between 1 and the row count.
    for(NextID = 1; NextID <= dt.Rows.Count; NextID++)
    {
        // Check if this ID already exists.
        if (dt.Rows.Find(NextID) == null) return NextID;
    }
    // Failed, return zero.
    return 0;
}
```

8. Add the following *butAdd_Click* event procedure to add the new contact information to the database:

Visual Basic .NET

```
Private Sub butAdd_Click(ByVal sender As System.Object, _
    ByVal e As System.EventArgs) Handles butAdd.Click
    ' Create a new row for the data set.
```

```
                    Dim rowNew As dsContacts.ContactsRow
                    rowNew = dsContacts.Contacts.NewContactsRow()
                    ' Add data to the row.
                    rowNew.ContactID = GetNewID(dsContacts.Tables("Contacts"))
                    rowNew.FirstName = txtFirstName.Text
                    rowNew.LastName = txtLastName.Text
                    rowNew.Address = txtAddress.Text
                    rowNew.City = txtCity.Text
                    rowNew.StateOrProvince = drpStates.SelectedItem.Text
                    rowNew.PostalCode = txtZip.Text
                    rowNew.HomePhone = txtHomePhone.Text
                    rowNew.WorkPhone = txtWorkPhone.Text
                    rowNew.Notes = txtNotes.Text
                    rowNew.ContactTypeID = drpContactTypes.SelectedItem.Value
                    ' Add the row to the data set.
                    dsContacts.Contacts.AddContactsRow(rowNew)
                   'dsContacts.Contacts.Rows(0).Table.Columns(0).ToString()
                    Try
                        ' Modify the database.
                        adptContacts.Update(dsContacts)
                        ' Show success.
                        litStatus.Text = rowNew.FirstName & " " & rowNew.LastName & _
                            " added successfully.<br>"
                        ' Clear fields.
                        ClearTextBoxes()
                        ' Occurs if ContactID is not unique.
                    Catch ex As Exception
                        litStatus.Text = "The following database error occurred:<br>" & _
                            ex.Message & "<br>" & _
                            "Correct the error and click Add to add the contact " & _
                            "or click Cancel to abort.<br>"
                    End Try
                End Sub
```

Visual C#

```
private void butAdd_Click(object sender, System.EventArgs e)
{
    // Create a new row for the data set.
    dsContacts.ContactsRow rowNew;
    rowNew = dsContacts.Contacts.NewContactsRow();
    // Add data to the row.
    rowNew.ContactID = GetNewID(dsContacts.Tables["Contacts"]);
    rowNew.FirstName = txtFirstName.Text;
    rowNew.LastName = txtLastName.Text;
    rowNew.Address = txtAddress.Text;
    rowNew.City = txtCity.Text;
    rowNew.StateOrProvince = drpStates.SelectedItem.Text;
    rowNew.PostalCode = txtZip.Text;
    rowNew.HomePhone = txtHomePhone.Text;
```

```
rowNew.WorkPhone = txtWorkPhone.Text;
rowNew.Notes = txtNotes.Text;
rowNew.ContactTypeID =
  Convert.ToInt16(drpContactTypes.SelectedItem.Value);
// Add the row to the data set.
dsContacts.Contacts.AddContactsRow(rowNew);
try
{
    // Modify the database.
    adptContacts.Update(dsContacts);
    // Show success.
    litStatus.Text = rowNew.FirstName + " " + rowNew.LastName +
        " added successfully.<br>";
    // Redisplay page to clear fields.
    ClearTextBoxes();
}
// General data exception, so report it.
catch(Exception)
{
    litStatus.Text = "The following database error occurred:<br>" +
        ex.Message + "<br>" +
        "Correct the error and click Add to add the contact " +
        "or click Cancel to abort.<br>";
}
}
```

9. Add the *butCancel_Click* event procedure to allow the user to cancel the operation and clear the text boxes on the form:

Visual Basic .NET

```
Private Sub butCancel_Click(ByVal sender As System.Object, _
    ByVal e As System.EventArgs) Handles butCancel.Click
    ' Clear text fields on this page.
    ClearTextBoxes()
End Sub

' Helper function to clear all the text boxes on this page.
Sub ClearTextBoxes()
    Dim ctrl As Control
    For Each ctrl In Page.Controls
        If TypeOf ctrl Is HtmlForm Then
            Dim subctrl As Control
            For Each subctrl In ctrl.Controls
                If TypeOf subctrl Is System.Web.UI.WebControls.TextBox _
                    Then CType(subctrl, TextBox).Text = ""
            Next
        End If
    Next
End Sub
```

Visual C#

```csharp
private void butCancel_Click(object sender, System.EventArgs e)
{
    ClearTextBoxes();
}

void ClearTextBoxes()
{
    foreach(object ctrl in Page.Controls)
    {
        if (ctrl is System.Web.UI.HtmlControls.HtmlForm)
        {
            System.Web.UI.HtmlControls.HtmlForm form =
                (System.Web.UI.HtmlControls.HtmlForm)ctrl;
            foreach(object subctrl in form.Controls)
            {
                if (subctrl is System.Web.UI.WebControls.TextBox)
                {
                    TextBox textctrl = (TextBox)subctrl;
                    textctrl.Text = "";
                }
            }
        }
    }
}
```

Exercise 4: Create the Calls Form

The Calls Web form lets users enter and view telephone calls from a contact. It uses a DataList control to view the telephone calls for a contact selected in a Drop-DownList control and contains the controls that add a call in a Panel control so that they can be hidden and displayed when the user clicks Add.

When completed, the Calls Web form appears as shown in Figure 5-25.

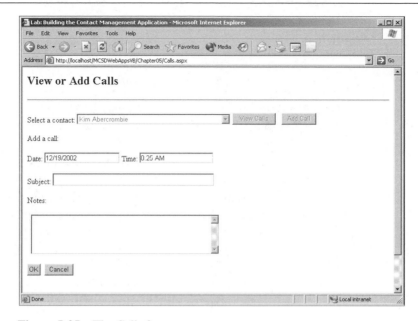

Figure 5-25   The Calls form

▶ **To create the Calls Web form**

1. Add a new Web form to the project named **Calls.aspx**.
2. Add controls to the Web form with the property settings shown in the following table. Place the controls shown after the Panel control inside the panel so that you can easily control their display at run time.

Control	Property	Setting
DropDownList	*ID*	*drpContacts*
Button	*ID*	*butView*
	Text	*View Call*
Button	*ID*	*butAddCall*
	Text	*Add Call*
Panel	*ID*	*pnlAdd*
TextBox	*ID*	*txtDate*
TextBox	*ID*	*txtTime*
TextBox	*ID*	*txtSubject*
TextBox	*ID*	*txtNotes*
	TextMode	*Multiline*
Button	*ID*	*butOKAdd*
	Text	*OK*

Control	Property	Setting
Button	*ID*	*butCancelAdd*
	Text	*Cancel*
Literal	*ID*	*litError*

3. Open the Data tab in the Toolbox, and drag a *DataSet* onto the Web form. Visual Studio displays the Add Dataset dialog box with the Typed Dataset option selected.

4. In the Name drop-down list, select the typed data set named ContactManagement.dsCalls, and click OK. Visual Studio adds the data set to the Web form.

5. From the Web Forms tab in the Toolbox, add a DataList control to the Web form below the panel. Set its properties and edit its templates as shown in the following table:

Control	Property	Setting
DataList	*ID*	*dlstCalls*
	DataSource	*dsCalls.Tables("Calls").DefaultView (VB)*
		dsCalls.Tables["Calls"].DefaultView (C#)
DataList Header Template		
Regular text	*None*	*Calls*
HTML rule	*None*	*<HR>*
DataList Footer Template		
HTML rule	*None*	*<HR>*
DataList Item Template		
Label	*ID*	*lblDate*
	(DataBindings)	Using the DataBindings dialog box, select the *Text* property, and enter this custom binding expression: *DataBinder.Eval(Container, "DataItem.CallDate", "{0:d}")*.
Label	*ID*	*lblTime*
	(DataBindings)	Using the DataBindings dialog box, select the *Text* property and enter this custom binding expression: *DataBinder.Eval(Container, "DataItem.CallTime", "{0:t}")*.
Regular text	*None*	*Subject:*

Control	Property	Setting
Label	*ID*	*lblSubject*
	(DataBindings)	Using the DataBindings dialog box, select the *Text* property and enter the following custom binding expression: *DataBinder.Eval(Container, "DataItem.Subject")*.
Regular text	*None*	*Notes:*
Label	*ID*	*lblNotes*
	(DataBindings)	Using the DataBindings dialog box, select the *Text* property and enter the following custom binding expression: *DataBinder.Eval(Container, "DataItem.Notes")*.
Separator Template		
HTML rule	*None*	*<HR>*

6. Copy the Hyperlink control from the bottom of the AddContact form to the bottom of the Calls form. To copy the control, select the control and press CTRL+C. To paste the copy onto the Calls form, click the form in Design mode and press CTRL+V.

7. Double-click the Calls Web form to display the Code window, and add the following *Imports* or *using* statements to the top of the module:

Visual Basic .NET

```
Imports System.Data.SqlClient
```

Visual C#

```
using System.Data.SqlClient;
```

8. The Calls Web form uses the data components from the cache, so you need to retrieve references to those components from the *Cache* variables created in Exercise 2. The following declarations and *Page_Load* event procedure retrieve references to the data components and make them available to the form code:

Visual Basic .NET

```
Dim adptCalls As SqlDataAdapter
Dim dsCalls As dsCalls
Dim dsContacts As dsContacts

Private Sub Page_Load(ByVal sender As System.Object, _
  ByVal e As System.EventArgs) Handles MyBase.Load
    ' Get cached variables.
    adptCalls = Cache("adptCalls")
    dsCalls = Cache("dsCalls")
    dsContacts = Cache("dsContacts")
    ' Run the first time page is displayed.
```

```
        If Not IsPostBack Then
            ' For each row in the table...
            Dim rowNext As dsContacts.ContactsRow
            For Each rowNext In dsContacts.Contacts
                ' Create a new list item.
                Dim lstNew As New ListItem()
                lstNew.Text = rowNext.FirstName & " " & rowNext.LastName
                lstNew.Value = rowNext.ContactID
                ' Add the list item to the drop-down list.
                drpContacts.Items.Add(lstNew)
            Next
            ' Select the first item in the list.
            drpContacts.SelectedIndex = 0
        End If
    End Sub
```

Visual C#

```
SqlDataAdapter adptCalls;
dsContacts dsContacts;
public dsCalls dsCalls;

private void Page_Load(object sender, System.EventArgs e)
{
    // Get cached variables.
    adptCalls = (SqlDataAdapter) Cache["adptCalls"];
    dsCalls = (dsCalls)Cache["dsCalls"];
    dsContacts = (dsContacts)Cache["dsContacts"];
    // Run the first time page is displayed.
    if (!IsPostBack)
    {
        // For each row in the table...
        foreach (dsContacts.ContactsRow rowNext in dsContacts.Contacts)
        {
            // Create a new list item.
            ListItem lstNew = new ListItem();
            lstNew.Text = rowNext.FirstName + " " + rowNext.LastName;
            lstNew.Value = rowNext.ContactID.ToString();
            // Add the list item to the drop-down list.
            drpContacts.Items.Add(lstNew);
        }
    // Select the first item in the list.
    drpContacts.SelectedIndex = 0;
    }
```

9. Add the following code for the View Call and Add Call button Click event procedures:

Visual Basic .NET

```
Private Sub butView_Click(ByVal sender As System.Object, _
    ByVal e As System.EventArgs) Handles butView.Click
```

```
        ' Set the filter for the view to display.
        dsCalls.Tables("Calls").DefaultView.RowFilter = "ContactID=" + _
            drpContacts.SelectedItem.Value.ToString()
        ' Bind to the DataList control
        dlstCalls.DataBind()
End Sub


Private Sub butAddCall_Click(ByVal sender As System.Object, _
        ByVal e As System.EventArgs) Handles butAddCall.Click
        ' Set the initial date and time values.
        txtDate.Text = Now.ToShortDateString()
        txtTime.Text = Now.ToShortTimeString()
        ' Make add call panel visible
        pnlAdd.Visible = True
        ' Disable buttons/DropDown list.
        butView.Enabled = False
        butAddCall.Enabled = False
        drpContacts.Enabled = False
End
Sub
```

Visual C#

```
private void butView_Click(object sender, System.EventArgs e)
{
    // Set the filter for the view to display.
    dsCalls.Tables["Calls"].DefaultView.RowFilter = "ContactID=" +
    drpContacts.SelectedItem.Value.ToString();
    // Bind to the DataList control
    dlstCalls.DataBind();
}


private void butAddCall_Click(object sender, System.EventArgs e)
{
    // Set the initial date and time values.
    txtDate.Text = System.DateTime.Now.ToShortDateString();
    txtTime.Text = System.DateTime.Now.ToShortTimeString();
    // Make add call panel visible
    pnlAdd.Visible = true;
    // Disable buttons/DropDown list.
    butView.Enabled = false;
    butAddCall.Enabled = false;
    drpContacts.Enabled = false;
}
```

10. Add the following helper function to get a new CallID value. Because CallID is the primary key in the Calls table, you need a value that is unique within the database. This code is the same as used in the AddContact Web form and can, alternatively, be placed in a class module of helper functions and used from there.

Visual Basic .NET

```vb
' Helper function to get a new, valid row ID.
Function GetNewID(ByVal dt As DataTable) As Integer
    ' Get a new row number.
    Dim NextID As Integer = dt.Rows.Count + 1
    ' If it isn't found in the table, return it.
    If IsNothing(dt.Rows.Find(NextID)) Then Return NextID
    ' Otherwis, check for free IDs between 1 and the row count.
    For NextID = 1 To dt.Rows.Count
        ' Check if this ID already exists.
        If IsNothing(dt.Rows.Find(NextID)) Then
            Return NextID
        End If
    Next
    ' Failed, return zero.
    Return 0
End Function
```

Visual C#

```csharp
// Helper function to get a new, valid row ID.
int GetNewID(DataTable dt)
{
    // Get a new row number.
    int NextID  = dt.Rows.Count + 1;
    // If it isn't found in the table, return it.
    if (dt.Rows.Find(NextID) == null)  return NextID;
    // Otherwis, check for free IDs between 1 and the row count.
    for(NextID = 1; NextID <= dt.Rows.Count; NextID++)
    {
        // Check if this ID already exists.
        if (dt.Rows.Find(NextID) == null) return NextID;
    }
    // Failed, return zero.
    return 0;
}
```

11. Add the following code to the OK and Cancel button event procedures. These event procedures are very similar to the ones used to add or cancel the adding of records in the Contacts table in Exercise 3.

Visual Basic .NET

```vb
Private Sub butOKAdd_Click(ByVal sender As System.Object, _
    ByVal e As System.EventArgs) Handles butOKAdd.Click
    Dim rowNew As dsCalls.CallsRow
    rowNew = dsCalls.Calls.NewCallsRow
    rowNew.ContactID = drpContacts.SelectedItem.Value
    rowNew.CallID = GetNewID(dsCalls.Tables("Calls"))
    rowNew.CallDate = txtDate.Text
    rowNew.CallTime = txtDate.Text & " " + txtTime.Text
```

```
        rowNew.Subject = txtSubject.Text
        rowNew.Notes = txtNotes.Text
        ' Add row to calls data set.
        dsCalls.Calls.AddCallsRow(rowNew)
        Try
            adptCalls.Update(dsCalls)
            ' Hide the add call panel.
            pnlAdd.Visible = False
            ' Clear the fields.
            txtSubject.Text = ""
            txtNotes.Text = ""
            ' Enable the other controls.
            butView.Enabled = True
            butAddCall.Enabled = True
            drpContacts.Enabled = True
        Catch ex As Exception
            ' Display error.
            litError.Text = "The following error occurred while adding " + _
                "the call:<br>" + ex.Message & "<br>" + _
"Correct the error and try again, "+_
"or click Cancel to abort.<br>"
        End Try
End Sub

Private Sub butCancelAdd_Click(ByVal sender As System.Object, _
    ByVal e As System.EventArgs) Handles butCancelAdd.Click
    ' Hide the add call panel.
    pnlAdd.Visible = False
    ' Clear the fields.
    txtSubject.Text = ""
    txtNotes.Text = ""
    ' Enable the other controls.
    butAddCall.Enabled = True
    drpContacts.Enabled = True
End Sub
```

Visual C#

```
private void butOKAdd_Click(object sender, System.EventArgs e)
{
    MCSDWebAppsCS.Chapter05.dsCalls.CallsRow rowNew;
    rowNew = dsCalls.Calls.NewCallsRow();
    rowNew.ContactID = Convert.ToInt16(drpContacts.SelectedItem.Value);
    rowNew.CallID = GetNewID(dsCalls.Calls);
    rowNew.CallDate = Convert.ToDateTime(txtDate.Text);
    rowNew.CallTime = Convert.ToDateTime(txtTime.Text);
    rowNew.Subject = txtSubject.Text;
    rowNew.Notes = txtNotes.Text;
    // Add row to calls data set.
    dsCalls.Calls.AddCallsRow(rowNew);
```

```
    try
    {
        adptCalls.Update(dsCalls);
        // Hide the add call panel.
        pnlAdd.Visible = false;
        // Clear the fields.
        txtSubject.Text = "";
        txtNotes.Text = "";
        // Enable the other controls.
        butView.Enabled = true;
        butAddCall.Enabled = true;
        drpContacts.Enabled = true;
    }
    catch (Exception ex)
    {
        // Display error.
        litError.Text = "The following error occurred while adding " +
        "the call:<br>" +
        ex.Message + "<br>" +
        "Correct the error and try again, or click Cancel to " +
        "abort.<br>";
    }
}

private void butCancelAdd_Click(object sender, System.EventArgs e)
{
    // Hide the add call panel.
    pnlAdd.Visible = false;
    // Clear the fields.
    txtSubject.Text = "";
    txtNotes.Text = "";
    // Enable the other controls.
    butAddCall.Enabled = true;
    drpContacts.Enabled = true;
}
}
```

Exercise 5: Create the DeleteContact and ContactTypes Forms

So far, this lab has shown you how to create Web forms in a step-by-step fashion. Now it's time to strike out on your own! Create the DeleteContact and Contact-Types Web forms by yourself.

These Web forms should perform the following tasks:

- Use the data components from the cache.
- Perform operations on the database. The DeleteContact form should allow users to delete contacts from the database. The ContactTypes form should allow users to view and add new contact types.
- Use data set transactions, as demonstrated by the AddContact and Calls forms.
- Provide navigation back to the SwitchBoard form.

When you have finished, compare your results to the Contact Management sample included on the companion CD. Good luck!

Review

The following questions are intended to reinforce key information presented in this chapter. If you are unable to answer a question, review the appropriate lesson and then try the question again. Answers to the questions can be found in the appendix.

1. What steps would you follow and what objects would you use to quickly find the number of records in a database table?

2. How do typed data sets differ from untyped data sets, and what are the advantages of typed data sets?

3. How do you call a stored procedure?

4. Explain the difference between handling transactions at the data set level and at the database level.

C H A P T E R   6

Catching and Correcting Errors

About This Chapter

In this chapter, you'll learn how to deal with problems that can occur in your application as a result of external circumstances. This chapter will help you anticipate, identify, and handle these types of problems effectively within your application.

Lessons 1 and 2 cover the two major techniques for dealing with these types of programming problems within ASP.NET Web applications. Lesson 3 explains how to monitor an application during testing or after it is deployed to ensure that problems are being handled effectively.

Before You Begin

To complete the lessons in this chapter, you must:

- Be familiar with the basics of the Microsoft Visual Basic or Microsoft Visual C# programming language. This should include familiarity with the concepts of variables, procedures, decision structures, and scope. See the Help topics "Language Changes in Visual Basic" and "C# Language Tour" included with Microsoft Visual Studio .NET for introductions to these languages.

- Understand how to create a basic Web application using the Web forms, server controls, and event procedures that were introduced in Chapter 2, "Creating Web Forms Applications."

- Have completed the Contact Management application discussed in Chapter 5, "Storing and Retrieving Data with ADO.NET." The lab at the end of this chapter extends the exception handling in that sample.

Lesson 1: Using Exception Handling

Exceptions are unusual occurrences that happen within the logic of an application. The terms *exception* and *error* are often used interchangeably in the Visual Studio .NET documentation because you use the same programming techniques to handle either situation.

In this lesson, you'll learn the different programming techniques that you can use to handle exceptions in a Web application. This lesson discusses only the modern techniques provided by Visual Studio .NET and Microsoft ASP.NET. It does not cover earlier exception-handling syntax, such as *On Error*, which is still supported by Visual Basic .NET.

After this lesson, you will be able to

- Explain the two main exception-handling techniques used in Web applications
- Create an exception-handling structure to catch and handle exceptions within a procedure
- Cause exceptions to occur in response to unexpected occurrences
- Define new exceptions that your application can use to describe exception conditions
- Handle exceptions from within error events

Estimated lesson time: 30 minutes

Exception-Handling Techniques

When an unanticipated problem occurs in a Web application, it is immediately apparent to the user. Figure 6-1 shows what the user sees if a Web application tries to open a file that doesn't exist on the server.

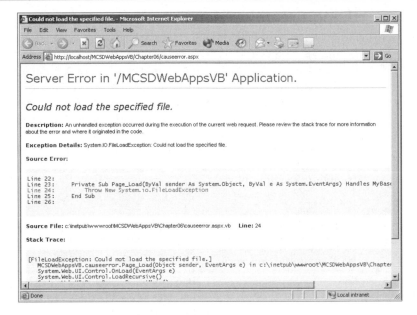

Figure 6-1   An unhandled exception

When this happens, the user is stuck—he or she can only click Back on the browser and try again. As a programmer, you are responsible for anticipating and dealing with these situations in your code before they occur. The process of dealing with these types of situations is called **exception handling**. Errors that are not dealt with in code are called **unhandled exceptions**, and they appear to the user as shown in Figure 6-1.

There are three approaches to handling exceptions in a Web application:

- Use exception-handling structures to deal with exceptions within the scope of a procedure. This technique is called **structured exception handling (SEH)** in the Visual Studio .NET documentation.
- Use error events to deal with exceptions within the scope of an object.
- Use custom error pages to display informational messages for unhandled exceptions within the scope of a Web application.

You can combine approaches to effectively handle all possible exceptions within your application, as explained in the following sections.

Using Exception-Handling Structures

Use exception-handling structures to enclose statements that access nonmemory resources, such as files and database connections. Access to these types of resources might fail because of external conditions. A common situation where you need exception handling is accessing files. When you try to read a file from disk, a variety of problems can occur: the file might not be found, the file might be locked because it is already open, or access might be denied because of security settings.

To deal with these potential problems, enclose the file access statements in an exception-handling structure. Table 6-1 describes the keywords used to create an exception-handling block.

Table 6-1   Exception-Handling Keywords

Visual Basic .NET keyword	Visual C# keyword	Use to
Try	*try*	Begin an error-handling structure. If a statement that follows this keyword causes an exception, control flow passes immediately to the next *Catch/catch* statement.
Catch	*catch*	Retrieve any exceptions that occurred and handle them. When control flow passes to a *Catch/catch* block, the statements contained in the block are processed to correct the error or otherwise handle the exception.
Finally	*finally*	Free resources used within the *Try/try* section and process any other statements that must run, whether or not an exception has occurred.
End Try	N/A	End an exception-handling structure.
Throw	*throw*	Cause an exception to occur. Use this keyword within your exception-handling structure to immediately pass control flow to the *Catch/catch* statement.

The easiest way to demonstrate how to use these keywords together is with an example. Figure 6-2 shows a Web form that allows the user to select a file from his or her machine to upload to the server. When the file is uploaded, it is added to the list box.

Figure 6-2   File upload sample

When the user enters a file name on the Web form and clicks Upload, a number of exception conditions can occur:

- The file might not exist on the client's computer.
- The file might already exist on the server.
- The file might be too large to transfer over the Internet.
- The server might not have enough available disk space for the file.

To handle these and other unforeseen conditions, enclose the statements that might cause these conditions in an exception-handling structure, as shown in the following code:

Visual Basic .NET

```
Dim strPath As String = Server.MapPath("./uploadfiles/")

Private Sub butUpload_Click(ByVal sender As System.Object, _
    ByVal e As System.EventArgs) Handles butUpload.Click
    Dim strFilename As String = filUpload.PostedFile.FileName
    ' Get the file name from the uploaded file spec.
    strFilename = Path.GetFileName(strFilename)
```

```
        Try
            ' (1) Check if file is zero-length (file does not exist).
            If filUpload.PostedFile.ContentLength = 0 Then _
                Throw New FileNotFoundException
            ' (2) Save uploaded file to server using the file base name.
            filUpload.PostedFile.SaveAs(strPath + strFilename)
            ' Set the file a ReadOnly so it can't be overwritten.
            File.SetAttributes(strPath + strFilename, FileAttributes.ReadOnly)
            ' Add file to list of server files.
            lstFiles.Items.Add(strFilename)
            ' Display success if no errors.
            litError.Text = strFilename + " uploaded successfully."
            ' (3) Handle possible exceptions.
        Catch ex As System.IO.FileNotFoundException
            litError.Text = "The file does not exist or is zero-length."
        Catch ex As System.UnauthorizedAccessException
            litError.Text = "You must delete the file from the server " + _
                "before uploading a new version."
            ' Enable the delete button
            butDelete.Visible = True
            ' Select the existing file in the list box.
            lstFiles.Items.FindByText(strFilename).Selected = True
        Catch ex As Exception
            litError.Text = "The following error occurred:<br>"
            litError.Text += ex.Message
        End Try
    End Sub
```

Visual C#

```csharp
private void butUpload_Click(object sender, System.EventArgs e)
{
    strPath=Server.MapPath("./uploadfiles/");
    // Hide delete button if it was displayed.
    butDelete.Visible = false;
    // Get the uploaded file spec.
    string strFilename = filUpload.PostedFile.FileName;
    // Get the filename from the file spec.
    strFilename = Path.GetFileName(strFilename);
    try
    {
        // (1) Check if file is zero-length (file does not exist).
        if (filUpload.PostedFile.ContentLength == 0)
            throw new System.IO.FileNotFoundException();
        // (2) Save uploaded file to server using the file base name.
        filUpload.PostedFile.SaveAs(strPath + "\\" + strFilename);
        // Set the file a ReadOnly so it can't be overwritten.
        File.SetAttributes(strPath + strFilename, FileAttributes.ReadOnly);
        // Add file to list of server files.
        lstFiles.Items.Add(strFilename);
        // Select the first item in the list box.
```

```
            lstFiles.SelectedIndex = 0;
            // Display success if no errors.
            litError.Text = strFilename + " uploaded successfully.";
        }
        // (3) Handle possible exceptions.
        catch (System.IO.FileNotFoundException)
        {
            litError.Text = "The file does not exist.";
        }
        catch ( System.UnauthorizedAccessException)
        {
            litError.Text = "You must delete the file from the server ";
            litError.Text += "before uploading a new version.";
            // Enable the delete button.
            butDelete.Visible = true;
            // Select the existing file in the list box.
            lstFiles.Items.FindByText(strFilename).Selected = true;
        }
        catch (Exception ex)
        {
            litError.Text = "The following error occurred:<br>";
            litError.Text += ex.Message;
        }
    }
}
```

As the preceding code executes, it follows these steps:

1. Checks whether the file exists on the client machine. If the entered file has zero length, the file does not exist, so the code throws the *System.IO.FileNotFound-Exception*, and control flow passes immediately to step 3.

2. Saves the file to the server. If saving succeeds, control flow continues by adding the file name to the ListBox control and displaying success. If saving fails, control flow passes to step 3.

3. Handles exceptions. In this case, exceptions are handled by displaying a message on the Web form. If no exceptions occurred, control flow skips to the end of the exception-handling structure. *Catch* blocks are evaluated in the order in which they appear in code. The exception declaration of each catch block determines which type of exception the catch block handles. Always order catch blocks from most specific to most general. So, in the preceding sample, *FileNotFoundException* and *UnAuthorizedAccessException* catch blocks are placed before the general *Exception* catch block.

Use the *Finally/finally* block to include statements that are *always executed* before leaving the exception-handling structure. For example, in the following code, the *Return/return* statement in the catch block causes execution to skip the rest of the procedure when an exception occurs; however, the finally block is always executed whether or not an exception occurred.

Visual Basic .NET

```vbnet
Private Sub butDelete_Click(ByVal sender As System.Object, _
ByVal e As System.EventArgs) Handles butDelete.Click
Try
    ' Set the file attributes to allow deletion.
    File.SetAttributes(strPath + lstFiles.SelectedItem.Text, _
        FileAttributes.Normal)
    ' Delete the file.
    File.Delete(strPath + lstFiles.SelectedItem.Text)
    ' Remove the file from the list.
    lstFiles.Items.Remove(lstFiles.SelectedItem)
Catch ex As Exception
    litError.Text = "Could not delete the file due to this error: "
    litError.Text += ex.Message
    Return
Finally
    ' Hide this button.
    butDelete.Visible = False
End Try
' Show success.
litError.Text = "File deleted."
End Sub
```

Visual C#

```csharp
private void butDelete_Click(object sender, System.EventArgs e)
{
    try
    {
        // Set the file attributes to allow deletion.
        File.SetAttributes(strPath + lstFiles.SelectedItem.Text,
            FileAttributes.Normal);
        // Delete the file.
        File.Delete(strPath + lstFiles.SelectedItem.Text);
        // Remove the file from the list.
        lstFiles.Items.Remove(lstFiles.SelectedItem);
    }
    catch (Exception ex )
    {
        litError.Text = "Could not delete the file due to this error: ";
        litError.Text += ex.Message;
        return;
    }
    finally
    {
        // Hide this button.
        butDelete.Visible = false;
    }
    // Show success.
    litError.Text = "File deleted.";
}
```

The Microsoft .NET Framework includes specific exception types with the individual .NET Framework classes. This means that there is no single, comprehensive list of exception types in the .NET documentation. Instead, you must use the Visual Studio .NET Exceptions dialog box to view specific exception types, as described in the following procedure.

To view the exception types that the .NET Framework provides, follow these steps:

1. From the Debug menu, choose Exceptions. Visual Studio .NET displays the Exceptions dialog box, as shown in Figure 6-3.

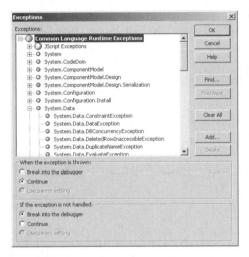

Figure 6-3   The Exceptions dialog box

2. Click the plus signs to the left of items in the Exceptions list to see the exceptions each item provides.

Causing Exceptions

As you saw in the preceding section, you use the *Throw/throw* keyword to cause specific exceptions to occur. This technique is useful to illustrate how exception handling works, but it begs the question, "Why would you *want* to cause an exception in a real-world application?"

Exception handling is a way to implement a certain kind of logic in your application. You are simply specifying a set of occurrences that are not normally part of the application's course of events and then saying, "These are the exceptions." That lets you set aside the complexity of dealing with those exceptions, thereby simplifying the main logic of your application.

For example, in the preceding File Upload sample, it's reasonable to cause the *File-NotFoundException* exception if the uploaded file has a length of 0. Otherwise, it's very difficult to determine whether a file exists on a client's machine before uploading. *FileNotFoundException* is a standard exception in the *System.IO* namespace, and it is descriptive of what happened.

Defining New Exceptions

In some cases, you'll want to cause an exception in your application that doesn't have an effective, descriptive equivalent in the .NET Framework. In those cases, you should create a new exception of the type *ApplicationException*. For example, the following code fragment causes an exception indicating that the user is already logged on:

Visual Basic .NET
```
Throw New ApplicationException("User is already logged on.")
```

Visual C#
```
throw new ApplicationException("User is already logged on.");
```

To handle this exception, use the following *Catch/catch* statement:

Visual Basic .NET
```
Catch ex As ApplicationException
```

Visual C#
```
catch (ApplicationException ex)
```

The *ApplicationException* class provides the same features as the standard *Exception* class. It simply provides a way to differentiate between those exceptions defined in the .NET Framework and those defined in your application.

If you are creating a large application or creating components that are used by other applications, you might want to define your own exception classes based on the *ApplicationException* class. For example, the following code defines a class for the *UserLoggedOnException*:

Visual Basic .NET
```
Public Class UserLoggedOnException
    Inherits ApplicationException

    ' Exception constructor.
    Sub New(Optional ByVal Message As String = "The user is already " & _
        "logged on to the server.", _
        Optional ByVal Inner As Exception = Nothing)
        MyBase.New(Message, Inner)
    End Sub

End Class
```

Visual C#

```
public class UserLoggedOnException : System.ApplicationException
{
    // Exception constructor (overloaded).
    public UserLoggedOnException() :
    this("The user is already logged on to the server", null)
    {
    }

    public UserLoggedOnException(string message) : this(message, null)
    {
    }

    public UserLoggedOnException(string message, Exception inner) :
    base(message, inner)
    {
    }

}
```

The preceding *UserLoggedOnException* class inherits its properties and methods from the *ApplicationException* base class. The new exception class provides only its own constructor to set the default message to display. This is a standard practice.

Using Error Events

Another way to handle exceptions is through the Web objects' built-in error events. When an unhandled exception occurs in a Web application, ASP.NET fires the error events described in Table 6-2.

Table 6-2   Exception-Handling Events

Event procedure	Occurs when
Page_Error	An unhandled exception occurs on the page. This event procedure resides in the Web form.
Global_Error	An unhandled exception occurs in the application. This event procedure resides in the Global.asax file.
Application_Error	An unhandled exception occurs in the application. This event procedure resides in the Global.asax file.

Error events let you handle exceptions for an entire object in a single, centralized location—the error event procedure. This is different from using exception-handling structures, in which exceptions are handled within the procedure where they occurred. You can use error events in the following ways:

- **As a substitute for exception-handling structures**   Because error events occur outside the scope of the procedure in which the error occurred, you have less information about the steps leading up to the exception and therefore less ability to correct the exception condition for the user. However, using exception-handling events is fine for tasks where you might not be able to correct the exception in code.

- **As an adjunct to exception-handling structures.**   Error events can provide a centralized "backstop" against exceptions that were not foreseen or handled elsewhere. Using the two exception-handling techniques together lets you catch all exceptions before the user sees them, display a reasonable message, and even record the exception in a log as part of an ongoing effort to improve your application.

When handling exceptions in error events, use the *Server* object to get information about the exception that occurred. The *Server* object provides the methods described in Table 6-3 for working with exceptions.

Table 6-3   The *Server* Object's Exception-Handling Events

Server method	Use to
GetLastError	Get the last exception that occurred on the server.
ClearError	Clear the last exception that occurred on the server. Invoking *ClearError* handles the exception so that it doesn't trigger subsequent error events or appear to the user in the browser.

To handle an exception in an error event, follow these steps:

1. In the *Page_Error*, *Global_Error*, or *Application_Error* event procedure, get the exception that occurred using the *GetLastError* method.
2. Do something with the exception, such as display a message to the user, take steps to correct the problem, or write to an error log.
3. Clear the exception using the *ClearError* method.
4. Redisplay the page. Web form processing stops immediately when an exception occurs, so server controls and other items on the page might not be displayed after the exception is cleared.

The following code demonstrates these steps:

Visual Basic .NET

```
Private Sub Page_Error(ByVal sender As Object, _
    ByVal e As System.EventArgs) Handles MyBase.Error
    ' Get error.
    Dim ex As Exception = Server.GetLastError()
    ' Store the error message.
    Session("Error") = ex.Message()
    ' Clear error.
    Server.ClearError()
```

```
' Transfer back to this page.
    Server.Transfer ("ErrorEvents.aspx")
End Sub
```

Visual C#

```csharp
private void Page_Error(object sender, System.EventArgs e)
{
    // Get the error.
    Exception ex = Server.GetLastError();
    // Store the message.
    Session["Error"] = ex.Message;
    // Clear the error.
    Server.ClearError();
    // Redisplay this page.
    Server.Transfer("ErrorEvents.aspx");
}
```

The preceding code stores the exception message as a *Session* state variable before clearing the exception so that the message can be displayed when the page is reloaded by the *Transfer* method. The following code displays the saved exception message when the page is redisplayed:

Visual Basic .NET

```vbnet
Private Sub Page_Load(ByVal sender As System.Object, _
    ByVal e As System.EventArgs) Handles MyBase.Load
    ' Display error. if any.
    If Session("Error") <> Nothing Then
        litError.Text = "The following error occurred:<br>" + _
            Session("Error")
        ' Clear the Session state variable.
        Session("Error") = Nothing
    End If
End Sub
```

Visual C#

```csharp
private void Page_Load(object sender, System.EventArgs e)
{
    // Display error. if any.
    if(Session["Error"] != null)
    {
        litError.Text = "The following error occurred:<br>" +
            Session["Error"].ToString();
        // Clear the Session state variable.
        Session["Error"] = null;
    }
}
```

Lesson 2: Using Error Pages

Lesson 1 provided techniques for handling exceptions that occur on the server running your Web application. However, because Web applications run over the Internet, there's a whole class of exceptions that can't be detected from within code. To intercept these errors and provide the best possible response, you need to use error pages.

In this lesson, you'll learn how to use error pages in ASP.NET to intercept and respond to HTTP errors at the application and page levels.

After this lesson, you will be able to

- Identify types of exceptions that can't be detected from within application code
- Respond to HTTP exceptions at the application and page levels
- Specify error pages for specific HTTP errors using the Web.config file

Estimated lesson time: 15 minutes

Handling Internet-Related Exceptions

When a user runs a Web application from his or her browser, a variety of exceptions can occur outside the scope of the actual application. For example, server errors can occur when a server times out waiting for a response from a user or when the page requested by a user isn't found on the server.

When these types of events happen, ASP.NET displays an error page like the one shown in Figure 6-4.

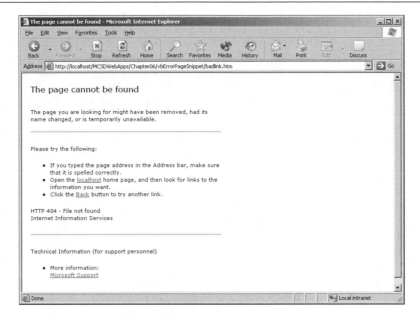

Figure 6-4   Page not found error page

Error pages are .htm or .aspx pages on the server that the user is redirected to if an unhandled exception occurs. ASP.NET lets you define error pages at two levels:

- **Specify application-wide error page settings in the *customErrors* section of the Web.config file.**   These settings determine the page to display for specific IITTP errors.

- **Specify an error page for a specific Web form in the *ErrorPage* attribute of the Web form's @ *Page* directive.**   This setting determines the error page to display if the Web form encounters an unhandled exception.

The following sections describe these levels in more detail.

Using Application-Wide Error Pages

Microsoft Internet Information Services (IIS) defines the error pages that are displayed by default for specific HTTP responses. To see or change the error page settings for an application in IIS, follow these steps:

1. Right-click the Web application folder, and select Properties from the shortcut menu. IIS displays the application's Properties dialog box.
2. Click the Custom Errors tab in the Properties dialog box. IIS displays the error page settings for specific HTTP response codes, as shown in Figure 6-5.

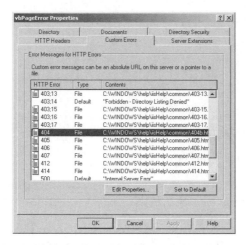

Figure 6-5   IIS Custom Errors settings

3. Select the response code you want to change the error page for in the Error Messages For HTTP Errors list, and then click Edit Properties to change the setting. IIS displays the Error Mapping Properties dialog box, as shown in Figure 6-6.

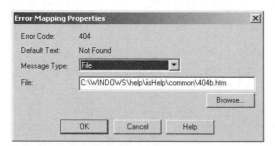

Figure 6-6   IIS Error Mapping Properties dialog box

4. Click Browse to replace the default error page with a page from your own application folder. Click OK in each dialog box when you have finished.

Using IIS to change application-wide error pages makes the changes on the server where the application is deployed. If you redeploy your application, you will have to repeat those changes for the new server using IIS. Alternatively, you can make application-wide error page settings part of your application using the project's Web.config file.

Use the *customErrors* section in the Web.config file to specify pages to display if specific, unhandled HTTP errors occur in a Web application. HTTP errors are identified by status codes defined in the HTTP 1.1 specification. ASP.NET lists these status codes in the *HTTPStatusCode* enumeration. Some of the common status codes are listed in Table 6-4.

Table 6-4   Common HTTP Status Codes

Status code value	*HTTPStatusCode* **member**	**Indicates**
200	*OK*	The request succeeded.
204	*NoContent*	The request succeeded, but the response is intentionally blank.
301	*Moved, MovedPermanently*	The request is being redirected to another address.
302	*Found, Redirect*	The request is being redirected to another address.
400	*BadRequest*	The request could not be understood by the server.
401	*Unauthorized*	The requested resource requires authorization, which was not provided with the request.
403	*Forbidden*	The server refuses to fulfill the request.
404	*NotFound*	The requested resource does not exist on the server.
408	*RequestTimeOut*	The client did not send a request before the server's request time-out occurred.
500	*InternalServerError*	A generic error occurred on the server. This error code represents any unhandled exception that occurs within the application.
503	*ServiceUnavailable*	The server is temporarily unavailable.
505	*HttpVersionNotSupported*	The requested HTTP version is not supported by the server.

To display a specific page in response to one or more of these status codes, include an *<error>* tag in the *customErrors* section of your application's Web.config file. For example, the following *customErrors* section specifies a default error page to display, along with three different error pages for specific HTTP response codes that indicate errors:

```
<customErrors mode="On" defaultRedirect="ErrDefault.aspx">
    <error statusCode="401" redirect="ErrUnauthorized.aspx" />
    <error statusCode="404" redirect="ErrPageNotFound.aspx" />
    <error statusCode="500" redirect="ErrServer.htm" />
</customErrors>
```

The *customErrors mode* attribute must equal *On* to view the error pages while debugging the application on your local machine. Setting the *mode* to *RemoteOnly* (the default) will display the designated error pages when the application is accessed from client computers, but not when the application is accessed locally.

The *customErrors* settings in Web.config apply only to resource types that ASP.NET considers to be part of the Web application. For example, the custom error page for Page Not Found (status code *404*) will not be displayed when redirecting to a page with the .htm or .html file type. To intercept those cases, use the IIS settings.

Note   The HTTP status code *500* represents an unhandled exception in the Web application. This status code can be used to present a "friendly" message to users or to automatically notify the development team when users are encountering unhandled exceptions.

Using Page-Level Error Pages

Use the *Page* object's *ErrorPage* attribute to display a specific page when an unhandled exception occurs on a Web form. The page-level setting supersedes the application-level settings in the Web.config file.

For example, the following HTML sets the *ErrorPage* attribute for a Web form:

Visual Basic .NET

```
<%@ Page Language="vb" AutoEventWireup="false"
Codebehind="ErrorPages.aspx.vb"
    Inherits="MCSDWebAppsVB.ErrorPages" errorPage="ErrDefault.aspx"%>
```

Visual C#

```
<%@ Page language="c#" Codebehind="ErrorPages.aspx.cs"
    AutoEventWireup="false" Inherits="MCSDWebAppsCS.ErrorPages"
    errorPage="ErrDefault.aspx"%>
```

The following code then causes an exception when the user clicks *butError*:

Visual Basic .NET

```
Private Sub butError_Click(ByVal sender As System.Object, _
    ByVal e As System.EventArgs) Handles butError.Click
    ' Cause exception.
    Throw New System.Net.WebException()
End Sub
```

Visual C#

```
private void butError_Click(object sender, System.EventArgs e)
{
    // Cause exception.
    throw new System.Net.WebException();
}
```

When the exception occurs, the user is redirected to the ErrDefault.aspx page. Because ErrDefault.aspx is displayed through redirection, the context for the error is lost and *Server.GetLastError* returns nothing from the target error page.

Lesson 3: Logging Exceptions

As you develop your application, it's a good idea to use exception logging to provide a means to track exceptions. An **exception log** is a list of handled exceptions that occur while your application is running. Reviewing the exception log periodically helps you verify that exceptions are being handled correctly, are not occurring too frequently, and are not preventing users from accomplishing tasks with your application.

In this lesson, you'll learn how to use the ASP.NET tracing features to implement exception logging in your Web application.

After this lesson, you will be able to

- List the advantages of tracing as a way to record exceptions
- Turn tracing on or off for an application or a Web form
- Write messages to the trace log
- View the trace log
- Clear the trace log and get a new set of tracing information

Estimated lesson time: 20 minutes

Using Tracing to Log Errors

Tracing is a technique for recording events, such as exceptions, in an application. There have always been ways to record errors in an application—usually by opening a file and writing error messages to it—but tracing offers these significant advantages:

- **Standardization**   Building tracing into the .NET Framework ensures that programming techniques are the same across all the applications you develop with the .NET Framework.
- **Built-in Web support**   ASP.NET extends the .NET Framework tools by including information related to the performance and behavior of Web requests.
- **Configuration**   You can turn tracing on and off using settings in your application's configuration file. You don't have to recompile your application to enable or disable tracing.
- **Performance**   While disabled, tracing statements do not affect application performance.

To use tracing in a Web application, follow these steps:

1. Turn tracing on.
2. Write to the trace log.

3. Read the trace log.

The following sections provide details on these three steps.

Turning Tracing On and Off

Tracing can be turned on or off for an entire Web application or for an individual page in the application:

- To turn tracing on for an entire application, in the application's Web.config file, set the *<trace>* element's *Enabled* attribute to *True*.
- To turn tracing on for a single page, set the DOCUMENT object's *Trace* property to *True* in the Visual Studio .NET Properties window. This sets the @ *Page* directive's *Trace* attribute to True in the Web form's HTML.

By default, trace output is displayed at the end of each Web page, as shown in Figure 6-7.

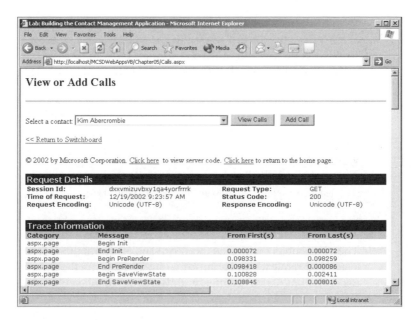

Figure 6-7   Tracing output

While this is fine for debugging purposes, you'll generally want to write trace output to a log file when you start testing your completed application. To write trace messages to a log file for an entire application, in the application's Web.config file, set the *<trace>* element's *PageOutput* attribute to *False*. ASP.NET then writes trace output to the Trace.axd file in your application's root folder.

The *<trace>* element also includes a *RequestLimit* attribute to specify how many page requests to write to the trace log. For example, the following line from a

Web.config file turns on tracing for the application and writes the first 20 requests to the Trace.axd file:

```
<trace enabled="true" requestLimit="20" pageOutput="false"
traceMode="SortByTime" localOnly="true" />
```

Writing trace messages to a log file does not affect tracing set at the page level. When the @ *Page* directive's *Trace* attribute is set to *True*, all trace messages for that page are displayed on the page.

To write trace messages to a log file for only selected pages in an application, follow these steps:

1. In the application's Web.config file, set the <*trace*> element's *Enabled* attribute to *True* and *PageOutput* attribute to *False*.
2. For each Web page you want to exclude from tracing, set the @ *Page* directive's *Trace* attribute to *False*.

When you have set the @ *Page* directive's *Trace* attribute to *True* or *False*, you can't restore the default setting from the Properties window in Visual Studio .NET. Instead, you must edit the Web form's HTML to remove the *trace* attribute from the @ *Page* directive. The following HTML shows the text to delete (in boldface):

Visual Basic .NET

```
<%@ Page Language="vb" AutoEventWireup="false" Codebehind="Trace.aspx.vb"
      Inherits="MCSDWebAppsVB.Trace" trace="True" %>
```

Visual C#

```
<%@ Page language="c#" Codebehind="WebForm1.aspx.cs" AutoEventWireup="false"
      Inherits="MCSDWebAppsVB.Trace" trace="True"%>
```

Writing Messages to the Trace Log

The *Trace* object provides the *Write* and *Warn* methods to allow you to write messages to a request's trace information. The two methods are identical with one exception: messages written with *Write* are displayed in black, whereas messages written with *Warn* are displayed in red.

For example, the following code writes information about unhandled exceptions to the trace log using the *Warn* method, so they are displayed in red:

Visual Basic .NET

```
Private Sub Page_Error(ByVal sender As Object, _
    ByVal e As System.EventArgs) Handles MyBase.Error
    ' Write a message to the trace log.
    Trace.Warn("Error", "", Server.GetLastError())
    ' Clear the error so the application can continue.
    Server.ClearError()
```

```
    ' Redisplay the page.
    Response.Redirect("Trace.aspx")
End Sub
```

Visual C#

```
private void Page_Error(object sender, System.EventArgs e)
{
    // Write a message to the trace log.
    Trace.Warn("Error", "", Server.GetLastError());
    // Clear the error so the application can continue.
    Server.ClearError();
    // Redisplay the page.
    Response.Redirect("Trace.aspx");
}
```

The following code causes an unhandled exception when the user clicks *butError*:

Visual Basic .NET

```
Private Sub butError_Click(ByVal sender As System.Object, _
    ByVal e As System.EventArgs) Handles butError.Click
    Throw New System.IO.FileNotFoundException()
End Sub
```

Visual C#

```
private void butError_Click(object sender, System.EventArgs e)
{
    throw new System.IO.FileNotFoundException();
}
```

In some cases, you might want to take additional actions while tracing is enabled. For example, you might want to get specific user information to add to the trace message. The *Trace* object's *IsEnabled* property lets you run this code conditionally, so that it does not affect performance while tracing is disabled. For example, the following code adds browser information to the trace message if tracing is enabled:

Visual Basic .NET

```
Private Sub Page_Error(ByVal sender As Object, _
    ByVal e As System.EventArgs) Handles MyBase.Error
    If Trace.IsEnabled Then
        Dim strMessage As String
        If Request.Browser.AOL Then
            strMessage = "AOL Browser"
        Else
            strMessage = "Non-AOL Browser"
        End If
        Trace.Warn("Error", strMessage, Server.GetLastError())
    End If
    Server.ClearError()
```

```
        Response.Redirect("Trace.aspx")
End Sub
```

Visual C#

```
private void Page_Error(object sender, System.EventArgs e)
{
    if (Trace.IsEnabled)
    {
        string strMessage;
        if (Request.Browser.AOL)
            strMessage = "AOL Browser";
        else
            strMessage = "Non-AOL Browser";
        // Write a message to the trace log.
        Trace.Warn("Error", strMessage, Server.GetLastError());
    }
    // Clear the error so the application can continue.
    Server.ClearError();
    // Redisplay the page.
    Response.Redirect("Trace.aspx");
}
```

Reading the Trace Log

By default, trace output is displayed at the bottom of each Web page for which trac-ing is enabled. As mentioned, if the *<trace>* element's *PageOutput* attribute is set to *False* in the Web.config file, trace output is written instead to the Trace.axd file in your application's root directory. You can view this file by simply navigating to it in your browser. For example, you could use the following hyperlink to open the log:

```
<A href="Trace.axd">View trace log.</A>
```

By default, you can view Trace.axd only from the local server running the applica-tion. If you want to view the trace log from a remote machine, such as when debug-ging remotely, set the *<trace>* element's *LocalOnly* attribute to *False* in the Web.config file, as shown here:

```
<trace enabled="true" requestLimit="20" pageOutput="false"
    traceMode="SortByTime" localOnly="false" />
```

When you navigate to Trace.axd in a browser, the trace log appears as shown in Figure 6-8.

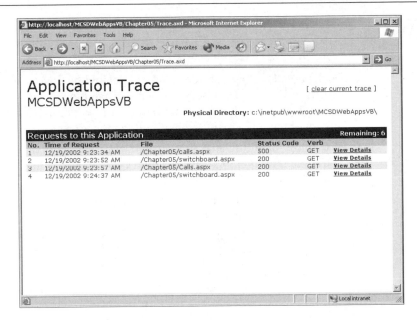

Figure 6-8   The Trace.axd log file

ASP.NET tracing stops after the server receives the number of HTTP requests entered in the *<trace>* element's *RequestLimit* attribute. To clear the list and start tracing again, click the Clear Current Trace link in the upper right corner of the Trace.axd page. The Clear Current Trace link redisplays Trace.axd and passes the query string *"clear=1"*, as shown in the following HTML:

```
<a href="Trace.axd?clear=1">Clear trace log.</a>
```

Summary

- Exception handling provides a way to deal with unusual occurrences in your program. Each of the different exception-handling techniques provides a way to set aside the complexity of dealing with these unusual occurrences so that they do not obscure the main logic of your application.

- Exception-handling structures use the *Try*, *Catch*, *Finally* (Visual Basic .NET) or *try*, *catch*, *finally* (Visual C#) keywords to handle exceptions within a procedure.

- Catch exceptions in order from most the most specific exception type to the most general exception type.

- Use the *Throw* (Visual Basic .NET) or *throw* (Visual C#) keyword to intentionally cause an exception.

- Error events handle exceptions in a separate event procedure. Use the *Server* object's *GetLastError* and *ClearError* methods to handle exceptions within error events.

- Use error pages to handle exceptions that occur outside of Web application code or as a backstop for presenting user-friendly error messages for unhandled errors in code.

- Monitor exceptions that are handled in your application by writing messages to the trace log using the *Trace* object's *Write* and *Warn* methods.

- Enable application-level tracing by setting the *<trace>* element's attributes in the Web.config file.

- Enable page-level tracing by setting the *Trace* attribute in a Web form's @ *Page* directive.

Lab: Adding Exception Handling to an Application

In this lab, you'll add exception-handling features to the preexisting Contact Management data application. When the Contact Management application was introduced in Chapter 5, "Storing and Retrieving Data with ADO.NET," it used some simple exception-handling blocks to deal with problems that might occur while updating records in a database. This lab extends those exception-handling structures to deal with specific types of data errors and implements tracing to view how errors are handled.

Estimated lesson time: 30 minutes

Exercise 1: Extend Exception Handling

The Contact Management application deals with database exceptions in a very simple way: if an exception is encountered, the application displays the error and then lets the user cancel the operation. The following code fragment shows this approach as implemented in the butAdd_Click event procedure of the AddContact Web form:

Visual Basic .NET

```
Try
    ' Modify the database.
    adptContacts.Update(dsContacts)
    ' Show success.
    litStatus.Text = rowNew.FirstName & " " & rowNew.LastName & _
        " added successfully.<br>"
    ' Clear fields.
    ClearTextBoxes()
    ' Occurs if ContactID is not unique.
Catch ex As Exception
    litStatus.Text = "The following database error occurred:<br>" & _
        ex.Message & "<br>" & _
        "Correct the error and click Add to add the contact " & _
        "or click Cancel to abort.<br>"
End Try
```

Visual C#

```
try
{
    // Modify the database.
    adptContacts.Update(dsContacts);
    // Show success.
    litStatus.Text = rowNew.FirstName + " " + rowNew.LastName +
```

```
            " added successfully.<br>";
        // Redisplay page to clear fields.
        ClearTextBoxes();
    }
    catch(Exception ex)
    {
        litStatus.Text = "The following database error occurred:<br>" +
            ex.Message + "<br>" +
            "Correct the error and click Add to add the contact " +
            "or click Cancel to abort.<br>";
    }
```

To create more detailed handling for data exceptions, edit the *Catch/catch* statements in the application to handle the following possible exceptions:

- *ConstraintException*   This exception occurs if the data set's unique key field constraint is violated. In practice, this can happen if two users are adding a contact at nearly the same time and they both get the same ContactID. When the second user tries to update the database, the *ConstraintException* exception occurs because the first user has already added a contact with that ContactID. To handle this situation, get another ContactID and try the update again, as shown in the following code:

Visual Basic .NET

```
Catch ex As ConstraintException
' Get another contact ID.
rowNew.ContactID = GetNewID(dsContacts.Tables("Contacts"))
' Try again.
Try
    adptContacts.Update(dsContacts)
    ' Show success.
    litStatus.Text = rowNew.FirstName & " " & rowNew.LastName & _
        " added successfully.<br>"
Catch
    litStatus.Text = "The record could not be added. " & _
        "Click Add to try again or click Cancel to abort."
End Try
```

Visual C#

```
catch (ConstraintException)
{
    // Get another contact ID.
    rowNew.ContactID = GetNewID(dsContacts.Tables["Contacts"]);
    // Try again.
    try
    {
        adptContacts.Update(dsContacts);
        // Show success.
        litStatus.Text = rowNew.FirstName + " " + rowNew.LastName +
            " added successfully.<br>";
```

```
    }
    catch
    {
        litStatus.Text = "The record could not be added. " +
            "Click Add to try again or click Cancel to abort.";
    }
}
```

- **DBConcurrencyException**   This exception can occur if a user tries to update the database while another user has exclusive access. In this case, it's best to notify the first user that the update was not made and allow that user to resubmit the change, as shown in the following code:

Visual Basic .NET

```
Catch ex As DBConcurrencyException
    ' The database may be locked by another session, so let the user try
    'again.
    litStatus.Text = "The database is currently locked. Wait a few " & _
        " seconds and then click Add again."
```

Visual C#

```
// The database may be locked by another session,
// so let the user try again.
catch (DBConcurrencyException )
{
    litStatus.Text = "The database is currently locked. Wait " +
        "a few seconds and then click Add again.";
}
```

- **DataException**   This is the general exception for data-related tasks. Handle this exception as a way to intercept problems you might not have thought of. The following code displays a message to the user and then records the exception for viewing in the trace log as a diagnostic tool:

Visual Basic .NET

```
Catch ex As DataException
    litStatus.Text = "The following database error occurred:<br>" & _
        ex.Message & "<br>" & _
        "Correct the error and click Add to add the contact " & _
        "or click Cancel to abort.<br>"
    Trace.Warn("Error", "Data exception", ex)
End Try
```

Visual C#

```
// General data exception, so report it.
catch(DataException ex)
{
    litStatus.Text = "The following database error occurred:<br>" +
```

```
        ex.Message + "<br>" +
        "Correct the error and click Add to add the contact " +
        "or click Cancel to abort.<br>";
    Trace.Warn("Error", "Data exception", ex);
}
```

The preceding changes to the *butAdd_Click* event procedure leave non-data-related exceptions unhandled. For the purpose of this lab, we'll handle those possible exceptions in Error event procedures in the following exercise.

Exercise 2: Add an Error Event Procedure

After handling the possible data exceptions in the *butAdd_Click* event procedure of the Contacts Web form, you should provide a way to handle and record unanticipated exceptions through the form's Error event procedure. This serves two purposes:

- It prevents the user from seeing technical error messages and replaces the error messages with more helpful information.
- It keeps information about unanticipated errors in a trace log that you can use as a diagnostic tool to help determine whether you need to handle other exceptions.

▶ **To handle unanticipated exceptions using the Error event procedure of the AddContact Web form**

1. Add a *Page_Error* event procedure to the Web form to deal with all other exceptions on the page. The following code saves information about the exception to the trace log, creates an error message to display, and clears the error so that the application can continue:

Visual Basic .NET

```
Private Sub Page_Error(ByVal sender As Object, _
    ByVal e As System.EventArgs) Handles MyBase.Error
    ' Write the error to the trace log.
    Trace.Warn("Error", "Error event", Server.GetLastError())
    ' Save a message to display as a Session state variable.
    Session("Error") = "An unexpected error occurred." + _
    'Try your task again."
    ' Clear the error.
    Server.ClearError()
    ' Clear text fields on this page.
    ClearTextBoxes()
End Sub
```

Visual C#

```
private void Page_Error(object sender, System.EventArgs e)
{
    // Write the error to the trace log.
```

```
Trace.Warn("Error", "Error event", Server.GetLastError());
// Save a message to display as a Session state variable.
Session["Error"] = "<p>An unexpected error occurred. " +
    "Try your task again.</p>";
// Clear the error.
Server.ClearError();
}
```

2. Modify the *Page_Load* event procedure to display the error message that was saved as a *Session* state variable in step 1. The following code shows the modified *Page_Load* procedure, with the additions in boldface:

Visual Basic .NET

```
Private Sub Page_Load(ByVal sender As System.Object, _
    ByVal e As System.EventArgs) Handles MyBase.Load
    ' Get the Cached variables.
    adptContacts = Cache("adptContacts")
    dsContacts = Cache("dsContacts")
    dsContactTypes = Cache("dsContactTypes")
    If Not IsPostBack Then
        ' Bind to data --
        'populates the drpContactTypes and drpState lists.
        drpContactTypes.DataBind()
        drpStates.DataBind()
    End If
    ' If there was an unhandled error, display it.
    If Session("Error") <> "" Then
        litStatus.Text = Session("Error")
        ' Reset the error message.
        Session("Error") = Nothing
    End If
End Sub
```

Visual C#

```
private void Page_Load(object sender, System.EventArgs e)
{
    // Get the Cached variables.
    adptContacts = (SqlDataAdapter) Cache["adptContacts"];
    dsContacts = (MCSDWebAppsCS.Chapter05.dsContacts) Cache["dsContacts"];
    dsContactTypes = (MCSDWebAppsCS.Chapter05.dsContactTypes)
        Cache["dsContactTypes"];
    if (!IsPostBack)
    {
        // Bind to data -- populates drpContactTypes and drpState.
        drpContactTypes.DataBind();
        drpStates.DataBind();
    }
    // If there was an unhandled error, display it.
    if(Session["Error"] != null)
```

```
      {
          litStatus.Text = Session["Error"].ToString();
          // Reset the error message.
          Session["Error"] = null;
      }
  }
```

Exercise 3: Create and View the Trace Log

Exercises 1 and 2 wrote messages to the trace log to help you catch unanticipated errors when people start using your application. To make these messages viewable, enable tracing and add a link within the application to display the trace log, as described in the following procedure.

▶ **To create viewable messages**

1. Modify the Web.config file to enable tracing. The following *<trace>* element enables tracing, saves the output as Trace.axd, increases the number of requests recorded to 20, and enables the trace log to be viewed remotely:

```
<trace enabled="true" requestLimit="20" pageOutput="false"
    traceMode="SortByTime" localOnly="false" />
```

2. Add a link to the SwitchBoard Web form to conditionally display the trace log. The following HTML creates the link as a Hyperlink server control so that you can make the link visible or invisible at run time, depending on the *<trace>* element setting:

```
<asp:HyperLink NavigateUrl="Trace.axd" ID="hypTrace" runat="server"
    text="View trace log." Visible="false"></asp:HyperLink>
```

3. Add the following (boldface) code to the SwitchBoard Web form's *Page_Load* event procedure to control the display of the trace log link:

Visual Basic .NET

```
Private Sub Page_Load(ByVal sender As System.Object, _
    ByVal e As System.EventArgs) Handles MyBase.Load
    ' Display the trace link if tracing is enabled.
    If Trace.IsEnabled Then
        hypTrace.Visible = True
    End If
    ' The first time this page is displayed...
    If Not IsPostBack Then
        AddToCache("adptCalls", SqlDataAdapter1)
        AddToCache("adptContactTypes", SqlDataAdapter2)
        AddToCache("adptContacts", SqlDataAdapter3)
        ' Fill data sets and add them to Cache.
        SqlDataAdapter1.Fill(DsCalls1)
        AddToCache("dsCalls", DsCalls1)
        SqlDataAdapter2.Fill(DsContactTypes1)
        AddToCache("dsContactTypes", DsContactTypes1)
```

```
            SqlDataAdapter3.Fill(DsContacts1)
            AddToCache("dsContacts", DsContacts1)
        End If
End Sub
```

Visual C#

```csharp
private void Page_Load(object sender, System.EventArgs e)
{
    // Display the trace link if tracing is enabled.
    if (Trace.IsEnabled)
        hypTrace.Visible = true;
    // The first time this page is displayed...
    if (!IsPostBack)
    {
        AddToCache("adptCalls", sqlDataAdapter1);
        AddToCache("adptContactTypes", sqlDataAdapter2);
        AddToCache("adptContacts", sqlDataAdapter3);
        // Fill data sets and add them to Cache.
        sqlDataAdapter1.Fill(dsCalls1);
        AddToCache("dsCalls", dsCalls1);
        sqlDataAdapter2.Fill(dsContactTypes1);
        AddToCache("dsContactTypes", dsContactTypes1);
        sqlDataAdapter3.Fill(dsContacts1);
        AddToCache("dsContacts", dsContacts1);
    }
}
```

Exercise 4: Extend Exception Handling to Other Web Forms

So far, this lab has shown you how to add exception handling in a step-by-step fashion. Now it's time to strike out on your own! Extend the exception handling on the Calls, DeleteContact, and ContactTypes Web forms by yourself. These Web forms should perform the following tasks:

- Handle possible data exceptions using exception-handling structures, as demonstrated in Exercise 1.

- Add Error event procedures to capture and record unanticipated exceptions, as demonstrated in Exercise 2.

When you have finished, compare your results to the Contact Management application included on the companion CD. Good luck!

Review

The following questions are intended to reinforce key information presented in this chapter. If you are unable to answer a question, review the appropriate lesson and then try the question again. Answers to the questions can be found in the appendix.

1. Explain why exception handling is important to a completed application.

2. List two different exception-handling approaches in ASP.NET Web applications.

3. Describe the purpose of error pages and why they are needed.

4. Explain why tracing helps with exception handling.

C H A P T E R   7

Advanced Web Forms Programming

About This Chapter

In this chapter, you'll learn how to perform some advanced programming tasks that don't fit neatly into any other category. Although you can successfully create Web applications without knowing the topics covered in this chapter, the lessons found here are an important part of mainstream Web programming, and they will help complete your skill set.

Before You Begin

To complete the lessons in this chapter, you must:

- Be comfortable creating Web applications using server controls and server-side code.
- Be somewhat familiar with using Microsoft Windows dynamic-link libraries (DLLs) and Component Object Model (COM) objects in an earlier programming language such as Microsoft Visual Basic version 6.0.
- Have some experience with a scripting language, such as Microsoft Visual Basic, Scripting Edition (VBScript) or Microsoft JScript. If you've never used a scripting language, you should review the VBScript User's Guide or JScript User's Guide topics in the Microsoft Visual Studio online Help before beginning Lesson 4.

Lesson 1: Saving and Retrieving User Information

Web applications that require users to register information can retrieve that information whenever a particular user revisits the Web site. For example, a shopping Web site might record the user's shipping and billing information and then retrieve that information to fill in address fields whenever that user places a new order.

After this lesson, you will be able to

- Explain how cookies make it possible to identify users and to store user information

- Store simple or complex information on a user's computer through a cookie

- Remove a cookie from a user's computer

- Create a unique identifier for a user and store it on his or her computer

- Use an XML file to store and retrieve information about a user based on that user's unique identifier

Estimated lesson time: 35 minutes

Identifying Web Application Users

Web applications can identify users by requiring them to enter a user name and password whenever they visit the Web site. Web applications can also identify users through information stored on their computers in the form of cookies. **Cookies** are small files that a Web application can write to the client's computer.

The advantage of using cookies is that the interaction happens invisibly to the user: users don't have to log on every time they visit your Web site; their information just appears automatically when needed.

The disadvantage of using cookies is that users can set their browsers not to accept cookies. Some users don't like the idea of Web sites storing information on their computers and possibly using that information to track their movements on the Internet. Therefore, you should always check to see whether a client accepts cookies before attempting to use them.

You can use two approaches when storing and retrieving user information through cookies:

- **Store all the user information as a cookie on the client's machine.** This approach is useful when the user information is simple and is not required on the server for any other tasks.

- **Store an identification key on the client's machine, and then retrieve user information from a data source on the server using that identification key.**   This is the best approach for storing more extensive information.

The following sections describe how to save and retrieve user information using each of these approaches.

Storing User Information on the Client

To store a cookie on the client's machine, follow these steps:

1. Check whether the client supports cookies by using the *Browser* object's *Cookies* property.
2. If the client supports cookies, check whether the cookie already exists by using the *Request* object's *Cookies* collection.
3. If the cookie does not already exist, create a new cookie object using the *HttpCookie* class.
4. Set the cookie object's *Value* and *Expiration* properties.
5. Add the cookie object to the *Response* object's *Cookies* collection.

The following *Page_Load* event procedure demonstrates the preceding steps by creating a cookie that tracks the last time a user viewed a Web page. The code checks whether the user accepts cookies and either adds a cookie if this is the user's first visit to the page or updates the cookie if the user has visited the page before.

Visual Basic .NET

```
Private Sub Page_Load(ByVal sender As System.Object, _
    ByVal e As System.EventArgs) Handles MyBase.Load
    ' (1) Check if browser accepts cookies.
    If Request.Browser.Cookies Then
        ' (2) If the cookie does not exist...
        If Request.Cookies("LastVisit") Is Nothing Then
            ' (3) Create the cookie.
            Dim cookLastVisit As New HttpCookie("LastVisit", _
                DateTime.Now.ToString())
            ' (4) Set the expiration to tommorrow.
            cookLastVisit.Expires = DateTime.Now.AddDays(1)
            ' (5) Add to cookies collection.
            Response.Cookies.Add(cookLastVisit)
            ' Display message.
            litMessage.Text = "This is your first visit."
        Else
            ' Get the cookie.
            Dim cookLastVisit As HttpCookie = Request.Cookies("LastVisit")
            ' Display a message showing time of last visit.
            litMessage.Text = "You last visited this page: " & _
                cookLastVisit.Value
            ' Update the cookie on the client.
```

```
            Response.Cookies("LastVisit").Value = Now.ToString()
            Response.Cookies("LastVisit").Expires = DateTime.Now.AddDays(1)
        End If
    Else
        litMessage.Text = "Your browser does not accept cookies."
    End If
End Sub
```

Visual C#

```
private void Page_Load(object sender, System.EventArgs e)
{
    // (1) Check if browser accepts cookies.
    if (Request.Browser.Cookies)
    {
        // (2) If the cookie does not exist...
        if (Request.Cookies["LastVisit"] == null)
        {
            // (3) Create the cookie.
            HttpCookie cookLastVisit = new HttpCookie("LastVisit",
                DateTime.Now.ToString());
            // (4) Set the expiration to tommorrow.
            cookLastVisit.Expires = DateTime.Now.AddDays(1);
            // (5) Add to cookies collection.
            Response.Cookies.Add(cookLastVisit);
            // Display message.
            litMessage.Text = "This is your first visit.";
        }
        else
        {
            // Get the cookie.
            HttpCookie cookLastVisit = Request.Cookies["LastVisit"];
            // Display a message showing time of last visit.
            litMessage.Text = "You last visited this page: " +
                cookLastVisit.Value;
            // Update the cookie on the client.
            Response.Cookies["LastVisit"].Value =
                DateTime.Now.ToString();
            Response.Cookies["LastVisit"].Expires =
                DateTime.Now.AddDays(1);
        }
    }
    else
    {
        litMessage.Text = "Your browser does not accept cookies.";
    }
}
```

Facts About Cookies

Cookies are case sensitive. For example, *LastVisit* is not the same cookie as *Lastvisit*. The *Expires* property specifies when the client's machine can discard the cookie. By default, cookies expire when the user's session ends. Setting *Expires* to the *DateTime.MaxValue* means that the cookie never expires.

You can remove the cookie from the client's machine by resetting the *Expires* property to the current time. For example, the following code removes the *LastVisit* cookie from the client's machine:

Visual Basic .NET

```
Private Sub butRemoveCookie_Click(ByVal sender As System.Object, _
    ByVal e As System.EventArgs) Handles butRemoveCookie.Click
    ' Set cookie to expire immediately.
    Response.Cookies("LastVisit").Expires = DateTime.Now
End Sub
```

Visual C#

```
private void butRemoveCookie_Click(object sender, System.EventArgs e)
{
    // Set cookie to expire immediately.
    Response.Cookies["LastVisit"].Expires = DateTime.Now;
}
```

Using Keys Within Cookies

You can save up to 4096 bytes of information in a single cookie, and you can identify information within a cookie using keys. For example, the following code saves the user's name and address information as a cookie with individual keys:

Visual Basic .NET

```
Private Sub butOK_Click(ByVal sender As System.Object, _
    ByVal e As System.EventArgs) Handles butOK.Click
    ' Create a cookie.
    Dim cookUserInfo As New HttpCookie("UserInfo")
    ' Fill in the keys from the form data.
    cookUserInfo("FirstName") = txtFirstName.Text
    cookUserInfo("LastName") = txtLastName.Text
    cookUserInfo("Street") = txtStreet.Text
    cookUserInfo("City") = txtStreet.Text
    cookUserInfo("State") = drpState.SelectedItem.Value
    cookUserInfo("ZIP") = txtZIP.Text
    ' Set the expiration.
    cookUserInfo.Expires = DateTime.Now.AddDays(30)
    ' Add the cookie.
    Response.Cookies.Add(cookUserInfo)
End Sub
```

Visual C#

```csharp
private void butOK_Click(object sender, System.EventArgs e)
{
    // Create a cookie.
    HttpCookie cookUserInfo = new HttpCookie("UserInfo");
    // Fill in the keys from the form data.
    cookUserInfo["FirstName"] = txtFirstName.Text;
    cookUserInfo["LastName"] = txtLastName.Text;
    cookUserInfo["Street"] = txtStreet.Text;
    cookUserInfo["City"] = txtStreet.Text;
    cookUserInfo["State"] = drpState.SelectedItem.Value;
    cookUserInfo["ZIP"] = txtZIP.Text;
    // Set the expiration.
    cookUserInfo.Expires = DateTime.Now.AddDays(30);
    // Add the cookie.
    Response.Cookies.Add(cookUserInfo);
}
```

To get the values from keys stored in a cookie, simply use the key's name, as shown in the following code:

Visual Basic .NET

```vbnet
Private Sub butGetData_Click(ByVal sender As System.Object, _
  ByVal e As System.EventArgs) Handles butGetData.Click
    ' Get the cookie.
    Dim cookUserInfo As HttpCookie = Request.Cookies("UserInfo")
    ' Fill in the fields.
    txtFirstName.Text = cookUserInfo("FirstName")
    txtLastName.Text = cookUserInfo("LastName")
    txtStreet.Text = cookUserInfo("Street")
    txtCity.Text = cookUserInfo("City")
    drpState.SelectedItem.Value = cookUserInfo("State")
    txtZIP.Text = cookUserInfo("ZIP")
End Sub
```

Visual C#

```csharp
private void butGetData_Click(object sender, System.EventArgs e)
{
    // Get the cookie.
    HttpCookie cookUserInfo = Request.Cookies["UserInfo"];
    // Fill in the fields.
    txtFirstName.Text = cookUserInfo["FirstName"];
    txtLastName.Text = cookUserInfo["LastName"];
    txtStreet.Text = cookUserInfo["Street"];
    txtCity.Text = cookUserInfo["City"];
    drpState.SelectedItem.Value = cookUserInfo["State"];
    txtZIP.Text = cookUserInfo["ZIP"];
}
```

Storing User Information on the Server

To store user information on the server instead of on the client's machine, simply use cookies as an identification device to store and retrieve user information on the server. You can store user information on the server using a database, an XML file, or some other type of data store.

To store user information on the server, follow these steps:

1. Create a unique key to identify the user.
2. Save the unique key as a cookie on the user's computer.
3. Create a file on the server to store user information.
4. Save the user information on the server using the unique key as an index.

The follow sections describe these steps in greater detail.

Creating Unique Keys to Identify Users

The Microsoft .NET Framework provides the *System.Guid* namespace for creating **globally unique identifiers (GUIDs)**. A GUID is a 128-bit integer that serves as a unique identifier across networks. You can use GUIDs as unique keys to identify all sorts of things, including users.

The following code creates a GUID and stores it as a cookie on the client's machine to later identify the user:

Visual Basic .NET

```
Private Sub butOK_Click(ByVal sender As System.Object, _
    ByVal e As System.EventArgs) Handles butOK.Click
    ' Get the request cookie.
    Dim cookUserID As HttpCookie = Request.Cookies("UserID")
    ' If it doesn't exist, create it.
    If cookUserID Is Nothing Then
        ' Create a new cookie with a new GUID.
        cookUserID = New HttpCookie("UserID", _
            System.Guid.NewGuid().ToString())
        cookUserID.Name = "UserID"
    End If
    ' Set the expiration.
    cookUserID.Expires = DateTime.Now.AddDays(30)
    ' Add the cookie to the response.
    Response.Cookies.Add(cookUserID)
    ' Save the user info from the form data.
    SetUserInfo(cookUserID.Value)
End Sub
```

Visual C#

```csharp
private void butOK_Click(object sender, System.EventArgs e)
{
    // Get the request cookie.
    HttpCookie cookUserID = Request.Cookies["UserID"];
    // If it doesn't exist, create it.
    if (cookUserID == null)
        // Create a new cookie with a new GUID.
        cookUserID = new HttpCookie("UserID",
            System.Guid.NewGuid().ToString());
    // Set the expiration.
    cookUserID.Expires = DateTime.Now.AddDays(30);
    // Add the cookie to the response.
    Response.Cookies.Add(cookUserID);
    // Save the user info from the form data.
    SetUserInfo(cookUserID.Value);
}
```

Creating a File to Store User Information

Part of the point of storing user information is to be able to retrieve that information quickly the next time the user visits your Web application. Because these users are already identified by a unique key (the GUID created in the preceding section), it makes sense that you will want to access their data through a data set. Data sets provide the *Find* method to retrieve rows of data by unique keys.

Using a data set means that the file you create on the server must be either a database or an XML file. XML provides a way to record structured data to a file without the complexity or overhead of a database, so for something as simple as user name and address information you'll probably want to use XML.

To create an XML file to store user information, follow these steps:

1. Create an XML file in Visual Studio containing test data for each of the data fields you want to record about the user.
2. Generate an XML schema from the XML file. The XML schema enables the data set to refer to data in the XML file by name.
3. Specify a key field within the XML schema. This will let you find records using that field with the data set's *Find* method.
4. Read the XML schema and XML file into a data set.

The following sections describe these steps in more detail.

Creating an XML File

To create an XML file in Visual Studio, choose Add New Item from the Project menu and then select XML File from the Templates list.

XML files look a lot like HTML files; however, XML elements and attributes are case sensitive and use a strict syntax. You use *<element>* and *</element>* tags to identify the data elements in an XML file. The following sample shows an XML file for storing user name and address information:

```
<?xml version="1.0" standalone="yes"?>
<USERS xmlns="http://tempuri.org/UserPrefs.xsd">
  <USER>
    <FIRSTNAME>Joan</FIRSTNAME>
    <LASTNAME>Reddington</LASTNAME>
    <STREET>436 Atlantic Ave.</STREET>
    <CITY>Melbourne Beach</CITY>
    <STATE>FL</STATE>
    <ZIP>32401</ZIP>
    <ID>79844302-6d86-4520-ac64-c8c3240e21a9</ID>
  </USER>
</USERS>
```

Creating an XML Schema

To use an XML file with a data set, you must first create an XML schema for the data set. An **XML schema** is a description of the data elements contained in the XML file. It provides the names of the elements and their types, indicates whether they are key fields, and provides other information.

To create an XML schema from an XML file, select Create Schema from the XML menu while the XML file is displayed in the Design view. Visual Studio creates a schema file describing the XML file, as shown in Figure 7-1.

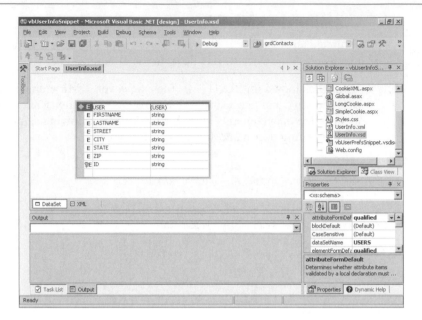

Figure 7-1   An XML schema

Specifying a Key Field

You add a primary key to the XML schema to enable searching. The schema shown in Figure 7-1 includes a key field that enables the data set to search for users by UserID.

To add a key field to the XML schema, follow these steps:

1. Right-click the element to create a key, point to Add, and then select New Key from the shortcut menu. Visual Studio displays the Edit Key dialog box, as shown in Figure 7-2.

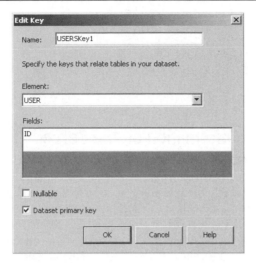

Figure 7-2   The Edit Key dialog box

2. Select the Dataset Primary Key check box and click OK to make the element a primary key within the data set. This enables you to use the *Dataset* object's *Find* method to retrieve rows from the data set using values for the element.

Reading the XML into a Data Set

When you've created an XML file and an XML schema, you can read those files into a data set using the *ReadXmlSchema* and *ReadXml* methods, respectively. The following code shows a helper function that returns a data set created from the UserInfo XML file:

Visual Basic .NET

```
Function GetUserData() As DataSet
    ' Set the path of the XML file and XML schema.
    Dim strPath As String = Server.MapPath(".")
    ' Declare a data set.
    Dim dsUsers As New DataSet()
    ' Apply the XML schema to the data set.
    dsUsers.ReadXmlSchema(strPath & "\UserInfo.xsd")
    ' Read the XML into the data set.
    dsUsers.ReadXml(strPath & "\UserInfo.xml")
    Return dsUsers
End Function
```

Visual C#

```
private DataSet GetUserData()
{
    // Set the path of the XML file and XML schema.
    string strPath  = Server.MapPath(".");
    // Declare a data set.
```

```
DataSet dsUsers = new DataSet();
// Apply the XML schema to the data set.
dsUsers.ReadXmlSchema(strPath + "\\UserInfo.xsd");
// Read the XML into the data set.
dsUsers.ReadXml(strPath + "\\UserInfo.xml");
return dsUsers;
}
```

Saving User Information on the Server

To save user information on the server as an XML file, use the *Dataset* object's *SaveXML* method. The following *SetUserInfo* procedure uses the *GetUserData* procedure described in the preceding section to get a data set from the XML file and then uses the *Find* method to check whether the UserID exists within that data set. If the UserID is not found, *SetUserInfo* adds a row for the user before setting the values for the fields in that row from server controls on a Web form. Finally, *SetUserInfo* writes the whole data set back to the server.

Visual Basic .NET

```
Sub SetUserInfo(ByVal UserID As String)
    ' Set the path of the XML file and XML schema.
    Dim strPath As String = Server.MapPath(".")
    ' Get the User's data set.
    Dim dsUsers As DataSet = GetUserData()
    ' Find the row in the data set.
    Dim rowUser As DataRow = dsUsers.Tables("User").Rows.Find(UserID)
    ' If the row is not found, then create a new row.
    If rowUser Is Nothing Then
        rowUser = dsUsers.Tables("User").NewRow
        dsUsers.Tables("User").Rows.Add(rowUser)
    End If
    ' Save data from form fields.
    rowUser("FirstName") = txtFirstName.Text
    rowUser("LastName") = txtLastName.Text
    rowUser("Street") = txtStreet.Text
    rowUser("City") = txtCity.Text
    rowUser("State") = drpState.SelectedItem.Text
    rowUser("ZIP") = txtZIP.Text
    rowUser("ID") = UserID
    ' Write the XML from the data set.
    dsUsers.WriteXml(strPath & "\UserInfo.xml")
End Sub
```

Visual C#

```
private void SetUserInfo(string UserID)
{
    // Set the path of the XML file and XML schema.
    string strPath  = Server.MapPath(".");
    // Get the User's data set.
```

```
DataSet dsUsers  = GetUserData();
// Find the row in the data set.
DataRow rowUser = dsUsers.Tables["User"].Rows.Find(UserID);
// If the row is not found, then create a new row.
if (rowUser == null)
{
    rowUser = dsUsers.Tables["User"].NewRow();
    dsUsers.Tables["User"].Rows.Add(rowUser);
}
// Save data from form fields.
rowUser["FirstName"] = txtFirstName.Text;
rowUser["LastName"] = txtLastName.Text;
rowUser["Street"] = txtStreet.Text;
rowUser["City"] = txtCity.Text;
rowUser["State"] = drpState.SelectedItem.Text;
rowUser["ZIP"] = txtZIP.Text;
rowUser["ID"] = UserID;
// Write the XML from the data set.
dsUsers.WriteXml(strPath + "\\UserInfo.xml");
}
```

Retrieving User Information from the Data Set

To retrieve user information from the XML file, use the *GetUserData* procedure to create a data set from the XML file, and then use the *Find* method to retrieve the row that corresponds to the UserID. The following *GetUserInfo* procedure retrieves user information from the data set and uses it to fill in server controls on a Web form:

Visual Basic .NET

```
Sub GetUserInfo(ByVal UserID As String)
    ' Get the User's data set.
    Dim dsUsers As Data.DataSet = GetUserData()
    ' Find the row in the data set.
    Dim rowUser As Data.DataRow = dsUsers.Tables("User").Rows.Find(UserID)
    ' If user wasn't found, exit.
    If rowUser Is Nothing Then Exit Sub
    ' Add data to form fields.
    txtFirstName.Text = rowUser.Item("FirstName")
    txtLastName.Text = rowUser.Item("LastName")
    txtStreet.Text = rowUser.Item("Street")
    txtCity.Text = rowUser.Item("City")
    drpState.SelectedItem.Text = rowUser.Item("State")
    txtZIP.Text = rowUser.Item("ZIP")
End Sub
```

Visual C#

```csharp
void GetUserInfo(string UserID)
{
    // Get the User's data set.
    DataSet dsUsers  = GetUserData();
    // Find the row in the data set.
    DataRow rowUser  = dsUsers.Tables["User"].Rows.Find(UserID);
    // If user wasn't found, exit.
    if (rowUser == null) return;
    // Add data to form fields.
    txtFirstName.Text = rowUser["FirstName"].ToString();
    txtLastName.Text = rowUser["LastName"].ToString();
    txtStreet.Text = rowUser["Street"].ToString();
    txtCity.Text = rowUser["City"].ToString();
    drpState.SelectedItem.Text = rowUser["State"].ToString();
    txtZIP.Text = rowUser["ZIP"].ToString();
}
```

Lesson 2: Using Unmanaged Code

Microsoft ASP.NET Web applications run under the control of the common language runtime (CLR). The CLR controls how the application's assembly executes, allocates, and recovers memory; therefore, ASP.NET applications are said to use **managed code**. In contrast, most other Windows executables use **unmanaged code** because the executable itself determines how memory is used.

Examples of unmanaged code include the Microsoft Win32 API, legacy DLLs and EXEs created for Windows applications prior to the Microsoft .NET Framework, and COM objects. In this lesson, you'll learn how to declare and call unmanaged code at the procedure level from a .NET assembly. For information about calling COM objects from .NET, see Lesson 3.

After this lesson, you will be able to

- Declare an unmanaged procedure for use in a .NET assembly
- Call an unmanaged procedure with scalar parameter types
- Convert structure and object parameters between.NET and unmanaged types
- Catch and handle errors from unmanaged code within a .NET assembly
- Understand the limitations of using unmanaged code within a .NET assembly

Estimated lesson time: 30 minutes

Using Platform Invoke

The process of executing native code from within a .NET assembly is called **platform invoke**, or **pinvoke** for short. You use platform invoke to call the Win32 API directly, to access existing (legacy) DLLs your company uses, or to access procedures compiled to native code for performance reasons. To use platform invoke, follow these steps:

1. Import the *System.Runtime.InteropServices* namespace.
2. Declare the unmanaged procedure using the *DllImport* attribute or the *Declare* statement.
3. Map the data types of the procedures parameters to the equivalent .NET types.
4. Call the unmanaged procedure and test its return value for success.
5. If the procedure did not succeed, retrieve and handle the exception code using the *Marshal* object's *GetLastWin32Error* method.

For example, the following code declares the Win32 API's *GetSystemInfo* procedure and then calls the unmanaged procedure to display information about the server's processor on a Web form:

Visual Basic .NET

```vb
' (1) Import InteropServices namespace.
Imports System.Runtime.InteropServices

Public Class Win32API
Inherits System.Web.UI.Page

' (2) Use a Declare statement to identify an unmanaged procedure to call.
Declare Auto Sub GetSystemInfo Lib "kernel32.dll" (ByRef Info As SYSTEM_INFO)

' (3) Define Structs or other types for unmanaged procedure parameters.
Structure SYSTEM_INFO
    Dim ProcessorArchitecture As Int16
    Dim Reserved As Int16
    Dim PageSize As Int32
    Dim MinAppAddress As Int32
    Dim MaxAppAddress As Int32
    Dim ActiveProcMask As Int32
    Dim NumberOfProcessors As Int32
    Dim ProcessorType As Int32
    Dim AllocGranularity As Int32
    Dim ProcessorLevel As Int32
    Dim ProcessorRevision As Int32
End Structure

Private Sub Page_Load(ByVal sender As System.Object, _
    ByVal e As System.EventArgs) Handles MyBase.Load
    ' Declare the parameter to pass in.
    Dim CurrentSystem As SYSTEM_INFO
    ' (4) Call the unmanaged procedure.
    GetSystemInfo(CurrentSystem)
    ' Display results.
    litSystemInfo.Text = "Number of processors: " + _
        CurrentSystem.NumberOfProcessors.ToString() + "<br>"
    litSystemInfo.Text += "Type of processor: " + _
        CurrentSystem.ProcessorType.ToString() + "<br>"
    litSystemInfo.Text += "Page size: " + _
        CurrentSystem.PageSize.ToString() + "<br>"
End Sub

End Class
```

Visual C#

```csharp
// (1) Use InteropServices namespace.
using System.Runtime.InteropServices;

public class Win32API : System.Web.UI.Page
{
    protected System.Web.UI.WebControls.Literal litSystemInfo;
```

```
// (2) Identify an unmanaged procedure to call.
[DllImport("KERNEL32.DLL", EntryPoint="GetSystemInfo",
SetLastError=true,CharSet=CharSet.Unicode, ExactSpelling=true,
    CallingConvention=CallingConvention.StdCall)]
 public static extern void GetSystemInfo(ref SYSTEM_INFO Info);

// (3) Define types for unmanaged procedure parameters.
[StructLayout(LayoutKind.Sequential)] public struct SYSTEM_INFO
{
    public Int16 ProcessorArchitecture ;
    public Int16 Reserved ;
    public Int32 PageSize ;
    public Int32 MinAppAddress;
    public Int32 MaxAppAddress ;
    public Int32 ActiveProcMask ;
    public Int32 NumberOfProcessors ;
    public Int32 ProcessorType ;
    public Int32 AllocGranularity ;
    public Int32 ProcessorLevel ;
    public Int32 ProcessorRevision ;
}

private void Page_Load(object sender, System.EventArgs e)
{
    // Declare the parameter to pass in.
    SYSTEM_INFO CurrentSystem;
    // (4) Call unmanaged procedure.
    GetSystemInfo(ref CurrentSystem);
    litSystemInfo.Text = "Number of processors: " +
        CurrentSystem.NumberOfProcessors.ToString() + "<br>";
    litSystemInfo.Text += "Type of processor: " +
        CurrentSystem.ProcessorType.ToString() + "<br>";
    litSystemInfo.Text += "Page size: " +
        CurrentSystem.PageSize.ToString() + "<br>";
}
}
```

In the preceding code, the Visual Basic .NET sample uses the *Declare* statement instead of the *DllImport* attribute. The *Declare* statement provides a simplified syntax for declaring unmanaged procedures, and it is converted to the following equivalent *DllImport* attribute code when compiled:

Visual Basic .NET

```
<DllImport("KERNEL32.DLL", EntryPoint:="GetSystemInfo", SetLastError:=True, _
CharSet:=CharSet.Unicode, ExactSpelling:=True, _
CallingConvention:=CallingConvention.StdCall)> _
Public Shared Sub GetSystemInfo(ByRef Info As SYSTEM_INFO)
    ' Leave procedure body empty
End Sub
```

You can use either form in your Visual Basic .NET code. Microsoft Visual C# supports only the *DllImport* form.

Converting Data Types

The .NET Framework uses a unified type system that is different from the types defined in the Win32 API. When you call an unmanaged procedure from a .NET assembly, the CLR collects the parameters and converts their types in a process called **marshaling**.

Scalar numeric types map between the two type systems based on their size in memory. So, for instance, a *dword* maps to an *Int32*, a *word* maps to an *Int16*, and so on. *String* data types in .NET are the equivalent of *BSTRS* in Win32. Strings are automatically converted between Unicode and ANSI formats if the *DllImport* attribute's *CharSet* field is set to *CharSet.Ansi*.

Structures in .NET are defined in much the same way that they are for the Win32 API. By default, .NET structures are arranged sequentially in memory in the order in which they are defined within the structure declaration. You can also explicitly define how structures are ordered in memory using the *StructLayout* attribute. The following code shows two equivalent declarations of the *SYSTEM_INFO* structure using sequential and explicit layouts:

Visual Basic .NET

```
' Sequential (default) layout
<StructLayout(LayoutKind.Sequential)> Structure SYSTEM_INFO
    Dim ProcessorArchitecture As Int16
    Dim Reserved As Int16
    Dim PageSize As Int32
    Dim MinAppAddress As Int32
    Dim MaxAppAddress As Int32
    Dim ActiveProcMask As Int32
    Dim NumberOfProcessors As Int32
    Dim ProcessorType As Int32
    Dim AllocGranularity As Int32
    Dim ProcessorLevel As Int32
    Dim ProcessorRevision As Int32
End Structure

' Equivalent explicit layout
<StructLayout(LayoutKind.Explicit)> Structure SYSTEM_INFO
    <FieldOffset(0)> Dim ProcessorArchitecture As Int16
    <FieldOffset(2)> Dim Reserved As Int16
    <FieldOffset(4)> Dim PageSize As Int32
    <FieldOffset(8)> Dim MinAppAddress As Int32
    <FieldOffset(12)> Dim MaxAppAddress As Int32
    <FieldOffset(16)> Dim ActiveProcMask As Int32
    <FieldOffset(20)> Dim NumberOfProcessors As Int32
    <FieldOffset(24)> Dim ProcessorType As Int32
```

```
    <FieldOffset(28)> Dim AllocGranularity As Int32
    <FieldOffset(32)> Dim ProcessorLevel As Int32
    <FieldOffset(36)> Dim ProcessorRevision As Int32
End Structure
```

Visual C#

```
// Sequential (default) layout
[StructLayout(LayoutKind.Sequential)] public struct SYSTEM_INFO
{
    public Int16 ProcessorArchitecture ;
    public Int16 Reserved ;
    public Int32 PageSize ;
    public Int32 MinAppAddress;
    public Int32 MaxAppAddress ;
    public Int32 ActiveProcMask ;
    public Int32 NumberOfProcessors ;
    public Int32 ProcessorType ;
    public Int32 AllocGranularity ;
    public Int32 ProcessorLevel ;
    public Int32 ProcessorRevision ;
}


// Equivalent explicit layout
[StructLayout(LayoutKind.Explicit)] public struct SYSTEM_INFO
{
    [FieldOffset(0)]public Int16 ProcessorArchitecture ;
    [FieldOffset(2)]public Int16 Reserved ;
    [FieldOffset(4)]public Int32 PageSize ;
    [FieldOffset(8)]public Int32 MinAppAddress;
    [FieldOffset(12)]public Int32 MaxAppAddress ;
    [FieldOffset(16)]public Int32 ActiveProcMask ;
    [FieldOffset(20)]public Int32 NumberOfProcessors ;
    [FieldOffset(24)]public Int32 ProcessorType ;
    [FieldOffset(28)]public Int32 AllocGranularity ;
    [FieldOffset(32)]public Int32 ProcessorLevel ;
    [FieldOffset(36)]public Int32 ProcessorRevision ;
}
```

Declaring a layout is required when you're passing objects to unmanaged code, because objects might be moved around in memory after they are created. The preceding code passed the *SYSTEM_INFO* structure by reference. Passing a structure by reference is equivalent to passing an object by value. The following code performs the same task, but passes an object by value rather than a structure by reference:

Visual Basic .NET

```
Public Class Win32API
    Inherits System.Web.UI.Page

    ' Pass an object by value.
```

```vb
                Declare Auto Sub GetSystemInfo Lib "kernel32.dll" _
                    (ByVal Info As SYSTEM_INFO)

                Private Sub Page_Load(ByVal sender As System.Object, _
                    ByVal e As System.EventArgs) Handles MyBase.Load
                    ' Create the object parameter to pass in.
                    Dim CurrentSystem As New SYSTEM_INFO
                    ' Call the unmanaged procedure with a parameter by value.
                    GetSystemInfo(CurrentSystem)
                    ' Display results.
                    litSystemInfo.Text = "Number of processors: " + _
                        CurrentSystem.NumberOfProcessors.ToString() + "<br>"
                    litSystemInfo.Text += "Type of processor: " + _
                        CurrentSystem.ProcessorType.ToString() + "<br>"
                    litSystemInfo.Text += "Page size: " + _
                        CurrentSystem.PageSize.ToString() + "<br>"
                End Sub
            End Class


        ' Define a class with a sequential layout.
        <StructLayout(LayoutKind.Sequential)> Public Class SYSTEM_INFO
            Dim ProcessorArchitecture As Int16
            Dim Reserved As Int16
            Public PageSize As Int32
            Dim MinAppAddress As Int32
            Dim MaxAppAddress As Int32
            Dim ActiveProcMask As Int32
            Public NumberOfProcessors As Int32
            Public ProcessorType As Int32
            Dim AllocGranularity As Int32
            Dim ProcessorLevel As Int32
            Dim ProcessorRevision As Int32
        End Class
```

Visual C#

```csharp
public class Win32API : System.Web.UI.Page
{
    protected System.Web.UI.WebControls.Literal litSystemInfo;


    // Pass an object by value.
    [DllImport("KERNEL32.DLL", EntryPoint="GetSystemInfo",
        SetLastError=true,CharSet=CharSet.Unicode, ExactSpelling=true,
        CallingConvention=CallingConvention.StdCall)]
    public static extern void GetSystemInfo(SYSTEM_INFO Info);

    private void Page_Load(object sender, System.EventArgs e)
    {
        // Create the object to pass in.
        SYSTEM_INFO CurrentSystem = new SYSTEM_INFO();
```

```
        // Call an unmanaged procedure with a parameter by value.
        GetSystemInfo(CurrentSystem);
        litSystemInfo.Text = "Number of processors: " +
            CurrentSystem.NumberOfProcessors.ToString() + "<br>";
        litSystemInfo.Text += "Type of processor: " +
            CurrentSystem.ProcessorType.ToString() + "<br>";
        litSystemInfo.Text += "Page size: " +
            CurrentSystem.PageSize.ToString() + "<br>";
    }
}

// Define a class with a sequential layout.
[StructLayout(LayoutKind.Sequential)] public class SYSTEM_INFO
{
    public Int16 ProcessorArchitecture ;
    public Int16 Reserved ;
    public Int32 PageSize ;
    public Int32 MinAppAddress;
    public Int32 MaxAppAddress ;
    public Int32 ActiveProcMask ;
    public Int32 NumberOfProcessors ;
    public Int32 ProcessorType ;
    public Int32 AllocGranularity ;
    public Int32 ProcessorLevel ;
    public Int32 ProcessorRevision ;
}
```

This section covered passing only the most common types of parameters to unmanaged procedures. An exhaustive list of the different possible types along with samples of how to pass them can be found in the Visual Studio .NET Help topic "Marshaling Data with Platform Invoke."

Handling Exceptions from Unmanaged Procedures

Unmanaged procedures typically return a value that indicates whether an exception occurred during their execution. Nonzero return values usually indicate success, and a zero return value usually indicates that an exception occurred. To handle exceptions from unmanaged code, follow these steps:

1. Declare the unmanaged procedure with the *SetLastError* field set to *True/true*. This is the default used by the Visual Basic .NET *Declare* statement.
2. Check the returned value from the unmanaged procedure.
3. If the procedure returned 0, get the unmanaged exception code using the *Marshal* object's *GetLastWin32Error* method.
4. Compare the exception code to a list of possible values.

For example, the following code uses the Win32 API *MoveFile* method and displays an appropriate error message for some of the possible exceptions:

Visual Basic .NET

```vbnet
' Declare an unmanaged procedure.
Declare Auto Function MoveFile Lib "kernel32.dll" (ByVal src As String, _
    ByVal dst As String) As Boolean

Private Sub Page_Load(ByVal sender As System.Object, _
    ByVal e As System.EventArgs) Handles MyBase.Load
    ' Call MoveFile on a read-only file to cause an error.
    If MoveFile(Server.MapPath(".\") + "protected.txt", _
        "newfile.txt") = True Then
        litStatus.Text = "File moved."
    Else
        ' MoveTo returns False if there is an error.
        Dim msg As String
        ' Set a message depending on error code returned.
        Select Case Marshal.GetLastWin32Error
            Case 2
                msg = "File not found."
            Case 3
                msg = "Path not found."
            Case 5
                msg = "Access denied."
            Case 15
                msg = "Drive not found."
            Case Else
                msg = "Unlisted error."
        End Select
        ' Display error.
        litStatus.Text = "The following error occurred: <br>" + msg
    End If
End Sub
```

Visual C#

```csharp
[DllImport("KERNEL32.DLL", EntryPoint="MoveFile",
SetLastError=true,CharSet=CharSet.Unicode, ExactSpelling=false,
    CallingConvention=CallingConvention.StdCall)]
public static extern bool MoveFile(string src, string dest);

private void Page_Load(object sender, System.EventArgs e)
{
    // Call MoveFile on a read-only file to cause an error.
    if (MoveFile(Server.MapPath(".\\") + "protected.txt", "newfile.txt"))
    {
        litStatus.Text = "File moved.";
    }
    else
    {
```

```
// MoveTo returns False if there is an error.
string msg ;
// Set a message depending on error code returned.
switch (Marshal.GetLastWin32Error())
{
    case 2:
        msg = "File not found.";
        break;
    case 3:
        msg = "Path not found.";
        break;
    case 5:
        msg = "Access denied.";
        break;
    case 15:
        msg = "Drive not found.";

        break;
    default:
        msg = "Unlisted error.";
        break;
}
// Display error.
litStatus.Text = "The following error occurred: <br>" + msg;
}
}
```

Limitations of Unmanaged Code

The .NET Framework adds many features that are either not available or implemented differently in unmanaged procedures. You should be aware of the following limitations whenever you start using unmanaged code from within a .NET assembly:

- **Performance**   Although native-code DLLs can perform some operations more quickly than equivalent code managed by the CLR, these benefits might be offset by the time it takes to marshal the data to pass between the unmanaged procedure and the .NET assembly.

- **Type safety**   Unlike .NET assemblies, unmanaged procedures might not be type-safe. This can affect the reliability of your .NET application. In general, reliability is a paramount concern with ASP.NET Web applications.

- **Code security**   Unmanaged procedures do not use the .NET Framework's model for code security.

- **Versioning**   Unmanaged code does not support .NET versioning; therefore, assemblies that call unmanaged procedures might lose the benefit of being able to coexist with other versions of the same assembly.

Lesson 3: Interoperating with COM

COM objects are another type of unmanaged code that you can use from .NET assemblies. Because COM is widely used, Visual Studio includes built-in tools for importing and using COM objects within .NET assemblies. Visual Studio also includes the option of automatically registering .NET class library assemblies for use from COM.

In this lesson, you'll learn both sides of the equation: how to use COM objects from .NET, and how to create .NET objects for use from COM. Together, these techniques allow you to integrate ASP.NET Web applications into existing software architecture.

After this lesson, you will be able to

- Create references to COM objects and use them from .NET code
- Register .NET class libraries for use from COM
- Selectively hide or expose public members of a .NET assembly for use with COM
- Handle exceptions that occur between .NET and COM objects
- Understand the limitations of using .NET objects from COM and of using COM objects from .NET

Estimated lesson time: 20 minutes

Using COM Objects from .NET

To use a COM object from a .NET assembly in Visual Studio, follow these steps:

1. Install and register the COM object on your system.
2. Open the .NET project in Visual Studio, and add a reference to the COM object, as shown in Figure 7-3. If the COM object does not appear on the COM tab of the Add Reference dialog box, you can add a reference directly to the executable by clicking Browse.

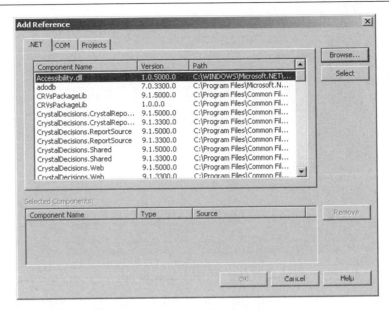

Figure 7-3   Adding a reference to a COM object

3. Create an instance of the COM object in code, and use it as you would any other object.

When you add a reference to a COM object, Visual Studio automatically generates an interop assembly for the object and places it in the project's /bin folder. The interop assembly is created from the COM object's type information and contains the metadata that the CLR uses to call the unmanaged code in the COM object.

You can view this interop assembly using the Microsoft Intermediate Language Disassembler (Ildasm.exe) included in the .NET Framework. Figure 7-4 shows the interop assembly generated for a simple COM object named *ShapesCOM*.

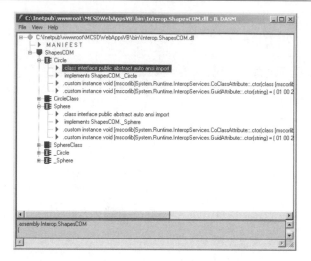

Figure 7-4   Viewing the interop assembly

You use COM objects from within .NET code the same way that you use .NET classes. For example, the following code creates instances of the *Circle* and *Sphere* COM objects and uses some of their members:

Visual Basic .NET

```
Private Sub butCalc_Click(ByVal sender As System.Object, _
    ByVal e As System.EventArgs) Handles butCalc.Click
    ' Create a Circle COM object.
    Dim Circle As New ShapesCOM.Circle
    ' Set the property.
    Circle.Radius = CSng(txtRadius.Text)
    ' Call the method.
    lblArea.Text = Circle.Area.ToString()
    ' Create a Sphere COM object.
    Dim Sphere As New ShapesCOM.Sphere
    ' Set the property.
    Sphere.Radius = CSng(txtRadius.Text)
        ' Call method.
        lblVolume.Text = Sphere.Volume.ToString()
    End Sub
```

Visual C#

```
private void butCalc_Click(object sender, System.EventArgs e)
{
    // Create a Circle COM object.
    ShapesCOM.Circle Circle = new ShapesCOM.Circle();
    // Set the property.
    float fRadius = System.Convert.ToSingle(txtRadius.Text);
    Circle.Radius = fRadius;
    // Call the method.
```

```
lblArea.Text = Circle.Area().ToString();
// Create a Sphere COM object.
ShapesCOM.Sphere Sphere = new ShapesCOM.Sphere();
// Set the property.
Sphere.Radius = fRadius;
// Call the method.
lblVolume.Text = Sphere.Volume().ToString();
}
```

Note   Visual Basic 6.0 allowed you to create COM properties (*Property Let* procedures) that were assigned by reference. Visual C# won't recognize those properties.
To use COM properties from Visual C#, they must be assigned by value.

Building .NET Objects for Use from COM

Visual Studio can automatically generate type library information and register a
.NET class library assembly for use from COM. These automatic tools do not work
for ASP.NET Web applications, so you must isolate the code you want to use from
COM in its own Class Library project.

To create .NET objects for use with COM, follow these steps:

1. Create a .NET class library project containing the objects you want to use from
   COM.
2. In the project's Build options, select the Register For COM Interop check box,
   as shown in Figures 7-5 and 7-6.

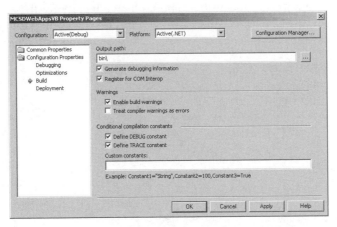

Figure 7-5   Registering a Visual Basic .NET project for COM interop

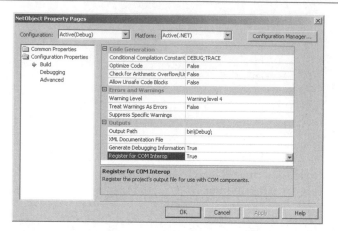

Figure 7-6   Registering a Visual C# project for COM interop

3. Build the project.

When you register a project for COM interop, Visual Studio automatically creates a type library for the public classes and members in the .NET assembly and registers those classes with the system registry.

Hiding Public .NET Classes from COM

In some cases, you might want to hide selected .NET classes from COM but keep them public for use from other .NET assemblies. The *ComVisible* attribute allows you to select which public .NET classes and members are included in the generated type library. This attribute applies hierarchically for the assembly, class, and member levels. For example, the following code hides all public classes in the assembly, exposes the *Circle* and *Sphere* classes, and hides the *Sphere* class's *Center* method:

Visual Basic .NET

```
' From AssemblyInfo.vb
' Hide public members from COM by default.
<Assembly: ComVisible(False)>

' From Shapes.vb
Imports System.Runtime.InteropServices

' Interface for all shapes.
Public Interface IFigure
    Property Top() As Single
    Property Left() As Single
    Function Area() As Single
    Function Perimeter() As Single
End Interface

' Definition of abstract class.
```

```vb
<ComVisible(True)> Public MustInherit Class Shape
    Implements IFigure
    Public MustOverride Property Top() As Single Implements IFigure.Top
    Public MustOverride Property Left() As Single Implements IFigure.Left
    Public MustOverride Function Area() As Single Implements IFigure.Area
    Public MustOverride Function Perimeter() As Single
    Implements IFigure.Perimeter
End Class

<ComVisible(True)> Public Class Circle
    Inherits Shape
    Private sxCenter, syCenter As Single
    Private sRadius As Single

    Public Overrides Property Top() As Single
        Get
            Top = sxCenter - sRadius
        End Get
        Set(ByVal Value As Single)
            sxCenter = Value + sRadius
        End Set
    End Property

    Public Overrides Property Left() As Single
        Get
            Left = syCenter - sRadius
        End Get
        Set(ByVal Value As Single)
            syCenter = Value + sRadius
        End Set
    End Property

    Public Overrides Function Area() As Single
        Area = 2 * System.Math.PI * (sRadius ^ 2)
    End Function

    Public Overrides Function Perimeter() As Single
        Perimeter = 2 * sRadius * System.Math.PI
    End Function

    Public Property Radius() As Single
        Get
            Radius = sRadius
        End Get
        Set(ByVal Value As Single)
            sRadius = Value
        End Set
    End Property

    Public Overridable Sub Center(ByVal X As Single, ByVal Y As Single)
```

```
                    sxCenter = X
                    syCenter = Y
            End Sub
    End Class


    <ComVisible(True)> Public Class Sphere
        Inherits Circle
        Private sCenter As Single

        Public Overrides Function Area() As Single
            Area = 4 * System.Math.PI * (MyBase.Radius ^ 2)
        End Function

        <ComVisible(False)> Public Shadows Sub Center(ByVal X As Single, _
          ByVal Y As Single, ByVal Z As Single)
            MyBase.Center(X, Y)
            sCenter = Z
        End Sub

        Public Function Volume() As Single
            Volume = (4 / 3) * System.Math.PI * (Radius ^ 3)
        End Function

        Public Property Front() As Single
            Get
                Return sCenter - Radius
            End Get
            Set(ByVal Value As Single)
                sCenter = Value + MyBase.Radius
            End Set
        End Property
    End Class
```

Visual C#

```
// From AssemblyInfo.cs
// Hide public members from COM by default.
[assembly: ComVisible(false)]

// From Shapes.cs
[ComVisible(true)]public class Sphere : Circle
{
    float fCenter;

    // Constructor.
    public Sphere()
    {
        // Initialize internal variable.
        fCenter = 0;
    }
```

```csharp
public override float Area()
{
    return (float)(4 * Math.PI * Math.Pow((double)base.Radius, 2));
}

[ComVisible(false)]public new void Center(float X, float Y)
{
    this.Center(X, Y, 0);
}

 [ComVisible(false)]public void Center(float X, float Y, float Z)
{
    base.Center(X, Y);
    fCenter = Z;
}

public float Volume()
{
    return (float)((4 / 3) * System.Math.PI *
        Math.Pow((double)base.Radius, 3));
}

public float Depth
{
    get
    {
        return fCenter - base.Radius;
    }
    set
    {
        fCenter = value + base.Radius;
    }
}
}

[ComVisible(true)] public class Circle : Shape
{
    float fxCenter, fyCenter, fRadius;

    // Constructor.
    public Circle()
    {
        // Initialize internal variables.
        fxCenter = 0;
        fyCenter = 0;
        fRadius = 0;
    }

    public override float Top
    {
```

```csharp
        get
        {
            return fxCenter - fRadius;
        }
        set
        {
            fxCenter = value + fRadius;
        }
    }

    public override float Left
    {
        get
        {
            return fyCenter - fRadius;
        }
        set
        {
            fyCenter = value + fRadius;
        }
    }

    public override float Area()
    {
        return (float)(2 * System.Math.PI *
            Math.Pow((double)fRadius, 2));
    }

    public override float Perimeter()
    {
        return 2 * fRadius * (float)System.Math.PI;
    }

    public float Radius
    {
        get
        {
            return fRadius;
        }
        set
        {
            fRadius = value;
        }
    }

    public virtual void Center(float X, float Y)
    {
        fxCenter = X;
        fyCenter = Y;
    }
```

```
}

[ComVisible(true)] public abstract class Shape : IFigure
{

    // Constructor.
    public Shape()
    {
    }

    public abstract float Top
    {
        get;
        set;
    }

    public abstract float Left
    {
        get;
        set;
    }

    public abstract float Area();

    public abstract float Perimeter();

}

public interface IFigure
{
    float Top
    {
        get;
        set;
    }

    float Left
    {
        get;
        set;
    }

    float Area();

    float Perimeter();
}
```

Notice that the *Shape* abstract class in the preceding code is visible to COM. Although *Shape* is not a creatable class and thus can't be used from COM, it must be visible to enable the use of its derived classes (*Circle* and *Sphere*) from COM.

Tools Used by COM Interop

Visual Studio automatically generates the interop assembly, type libraries, and other information for .NET to COM interoperation. Alternatively, you can use the command-line tools included with the .NET Framework and described in Table 7-1.

Table 7-1   COM Interop Tools

Tool	File name	Use to
Type Library Importer	Tlbimp.exe	Generate a .NET interop assembly for a COM object
Type Library Exporter	Tlbexp.exe	Generate a COM type library from a .NET assembly
Intermediate Language Disassembler	Ildasm.exe	View the generated interop assembly or other .NET assemblies
Assembly Registration Tool	Regasm.exe	Add or remove system registration database entries for a .NET assembly
Registry Editor	Regedit.exe	View system registry database entries for COM objects installed on a system, including .NET objects registered for COM interop

Handling Exceptions Between .NET and COM

.NET handles errors through exception classes. COM handles errors through 32-bit data types called *HRESULT*s. All of the .NET exception classes include *HResult* properties that map to COM *HRESULT* codes.

If an exception occurs in a .NET object, the exception is automatically mapped to the appropriate *HRESULT* and returned to COM. Similarly, if an exception occurs in a COM object, the COM *HRESULT* is mapped to the appropriate exception class, which is returned to .NET, where it can be handled just like any other exception.

If you are creating your own .NET exception classes for use with COM, be sure to set the class's *HResult* property so that the exception can be handled within COM.

Limitations of COM Interop

The .NET Framework was developed to address the limitations of COM. Because of this evolution, there are limits to the .NET features that you can use from COM. The following list describes these limits:

- *Shared/static* **members**   COM requires objects to be created before use, so it does not support .NET *Shared/static* members.

- *Shadows/new* **members**   COM flattens the inheritance tree of .NET objects, so members in a derived class that shadow members inherited from a base class are not callable.
- **Constructors with parameters**   COM can't pass parameters to an object's constructor.

In addition to these technical limitations, you should also be aware of these practical limitations when using COM objects from .NET:

- **Shared solutions might not allow COM objects.**   ASP.NET host service providers that use nondedicated servers can limit or prohibit the installation of COM objects on their servers.
- **COM objects are prone to memory leaks.**   COM uses reference counting to determine when to destroy objects and free memory. It is possible for this reference count to become incorrect, leaving objects in memory indefinitely.
- **Type libraries might be inaccurate.**   Because COM separates the object's description from its implementation, it's possible for this description to not accurately reflect the object. In this case, the generated interop assembly will also include those inaccuracies.
- **COM is unmanaged code.**   The limitations cited for unmanaged procedures in Lesson 2 apply to COM objects as well.

Lesson 4: Using Client-Side Scripts

ASP.NET provides a full set of programming tools for creating Web applications that run on servers, so why should you worry about adding scripts to run on the client's computer? Because scripts have direct access to the client's browser, they make it possible to do many things you can't do from server-side code. For example, you can use client-side scripts to perform the following tasks:

- **Control the browser window.**   You can't control the browser from server-side code. To open new windows, set focus within a window, navigate between frames, navigate within history, and perform other browser-related tasks, you must use client-side scripts.

- **Respond immediately to mouse-over events.**   Server-side code can respond to events only after the page is posted back to the server; client-side code can respond to page events as they occur.

- **Start the client's mail system.**   You can send mail from the client using the Mailto protocol. Additionally, you can send mail from the server using the *SmtpMail* class.

In this lesson, you'll learn how to add scripts to Web forms and HTML pages in Visual Studio to create code that executes on the client's computer.

After this lesson, you will be able to

- Test a browser to see whether it can run scripts
- Choose a scripting language that suits your needs
- Use objects provided by the Document Object Model (DOM) to control the browser window and the documents it contains
- Create scripts that run inline as the page is interpreted by the browser
- Create scripts that respond to events in the browser, such as mouse clicks and mouse-move events
- Get input from the user and display a response using scripts
- Send mail from either the client or server

Estimated lesson time: 30 minutes

Before You Use Scripts

Client-side scripts pose three issues you should be aware of:

- Not all browsers support scripting.
- Only Microsoft Internet Explorer supports VBScript.
- Scripting poses security concerns.

Because not all browsers support scripts, you should check the browser capabilities before displaying pages that contain client-side scripts. The following *Page_Load* event procedure checks whether a browser supports scripts and redirects users to a page recommending they download a new version if their browser does not support scripts:

Visual Basic .NET

```
Private Sub Page_Load(ByVal sender As System.Object, _
    ByVal e As System.EventArgs) Handles MyBase.Load
    If Request.Browser.VBScript Then
        Response.Redirect("VBScripts.htm")
        Exit Sub
    ElseIf Request.Browser.JavaScript Then
        Response.Redirect ("JScripts.htm")
    Else
        Response.Redirect("NoScripts.htm")
    End If
End Sub
```

Visual C#

```
private void Page_Load(object sender, System.EventArgs e)
{
    if (Request.Browser.VBScript)
        Response.Redirect("VBScripts.htm");
    else if (Request.Browser.JavaScript)
        Response.Redirect("JScripts.htm");
    else
        Response.Redirect("NoScripts.htm");
}
```

Another concern with client-side scripts is security. There are two aspects to this issue. First, your scripts are not secure—they can be viewed or copied by anyone visiting your application. Second, scripts can potentially spread viruses; therefore, some users set their browser security settings to disable scripts.

The *Browser* object's *VBScript* and *JavaScript* properties will return *True*, even if scripting has been disabled. To check whether scripting is enabled, you need to be a little clever. The following HTML tests whether scripting is enabled by trying to run a script. If scripting is enabled, the user is redirected to another page and he or she never sees the message that follows the script.

```
<html>
  <script>
    window.navigate("scripts.aspx")
  </script>
  <!-- If scripting is enabled, the following is never displayed -->
  <head>
    <title>Scripts</title>
```

```
</head>
<body MS_POSITIONING="FlowLayout">
<h2>Scripting is turned off.</h2>
<p>Your Internet security options specify that your browser will not run
scripts, and therefore you cannot view the page you requested. To turn
scripting on, reset your browser's Internet security options to Medium, or
enable active scripting in the custom security settings.</p>
<p><a href="CheckBrowser.htm">Click here</a> to try again.</p>
</body>
</html>
```

Choosing a Scripting Language

Client-side scripts can be written in either VBScript or JScript. Scripting languages have the following differences from compiled languages, such as Visual Basic .NET or Visual C#:

- **Script languages are not compiled.** Instead, they are interpreted by the browser at run time.
- **Script keywords are a "safe subset" of their parent languages.** Scripts don't allow you to create or delete files on the user's disk or to perform tasks that obviously risk crashing the user's computer.

Both VBScript and JScript are functionally equivalent—they differ only in syntax and keywords. In general, Visual C# programmers are more comfortable using JScript because it follows the C conventions; Visual Basic programmers are more comfortable using VBScript because it is closely related to Visual Basic. However, only Internet Explorer supports VBScript, so if your application needs to run on other browsers, you should use JScript.

If you are a Visual Basic programmer, you will probably not like the fact that JScript is case sensitive. In JScript, all keywords, variables, object references, methods, and properties must be correctly capitalized in order to work.

For more information about the scripting languages, see the following Visual Studio online Help topics:

- JScript User's Guide
- JScript Language Reference
- VBScript User's Guide
- VBScript Language Reference

Understanding the DOM

The Document Object Model (DOM) is made up of the objects that the browser provides for scripting. These objects let you control the browser window, the current page (or document), and objects on the page. Figure 7-7 shows the objects provided by the DOM.

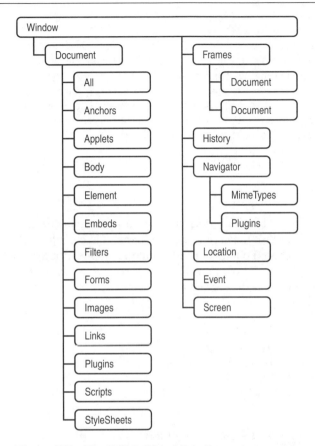

Figure 7-7 The DOM object hierarchy

Explaining all the objects in the DOM is outside the scope of this book. However, a great deal of information is available in the Visual Studio online Help in the "DHTML References" topic. That topic and the references it links to are part of the Web Workshop online Help.

Adding Inline Scripts

Web pages can include scripts inline as part of their content or as procedures that run in response to events. Inline scripts run the moment the browser encounters them. The example in the preceding section shows how this works by redirecting the browser to a new page if the browser allows scripting:

```
<html>
<script>
  window.navigate("scripts.aspx")
</script>
    <!-- If scripting is enabled, the markup that follows
       this code is never displayed -->
```

```
<head>
  <title>Scripts</title>
</head>
<body MS_POSITIONING="FlowLayout" onunload="return window_onunload()">
  <h2>Scripting is turned off.</h2>
  <p>Your Internet security options specify that your browser will
    not run scripts, and therefore you cannot view the page you requested.
    To turn scripting on, reset your browser's Internet security
    options to Medium, or enable active scripting in the custom security
    settings.</p>
  <p><a href="CheckBrowser.htm">Click here</a> to try again.</p>
</body>
</html>
```

If this script successfully runs, the user never sees the message that scripting is
turned off because the script runs before any page content. If an inline script refers
to an element on the page, that element must appear before the script refers to it.
For example, the following HTML displays two text boxes and uses a script to
move the cursor to the second text box:

VBScript

```
<HTML>
  <body language="vbscript">
    <form id="Form1" method="post" runat="server">
      <P>
        <asp:TextBox id="txtFirstName" Runat="server"></asp:TextBox>
      </P>
      <P>
        <asp:TextBox id="txtLastName" Runat="server"></asp:TextBox>
      </P>
      <script>window.document.all("txtLastName").focus()</script>
    </form>
  </body>
</HTML>
```

JScript

```
<HTML>
  <body language="javascript">
    <form id="Form1" method="post" runat="server">
      <P>
        <asp:TextBox id="txtFirstName" Runat="server"></asp:TextBox>
      </P>
      <P>
        <asp:TextBox id="txtLastName" Runat="server"></asp:TextBox>
      </P>
      <script>window.document.all["txtLastName"].focus()</script>
    </form>
  </body>
</HTML>
```

Inline scripts can also be used as attributes of HTML elements that perform actions, such as the HTML Button control. For example, the following HTML creates a button that opens a Help page in a new window:

```
<button id="butHelp" onclick="window.open('help.aspx', 'help',
  'height=200,width=300')">Help</button>
```

Notice that the preceding inline script is language-neutral—in other words, it will work whether the *language* attribute of the *<body>* element is set to VBScript or JScript. To use a scripting language other that the one set in the *<body>* element, you need to set the *<script>* element's *language* attribute. For example, the following scripts display a list of heading levels:

VBScript

```
<HTML>
  <script language="vbscript">
  For i = 1 to 6
    document.write("<h" & i & ">")
    document.write("H" & i)
    document.write("</h" & i & "><br>")
  Next
  </script>
</HTML>
```

JScript

```
<HTML>
  <script language="javascript">
  for (i = 1; i <= 6; i++)
  {
    document.write("<h" + i + ">");
    document.write("H" + i);
    document.write("</h" + i + "><br>");
  }
  </script>
</HTML>
```

The preceding code displays the six HTML heading levels, as shown in Figure 7-8.

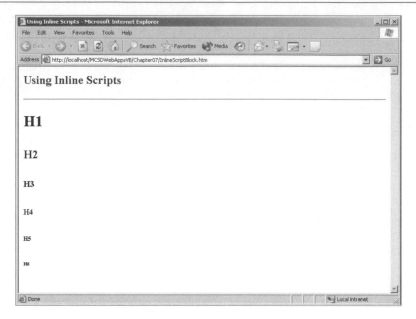

Figure 7-8   Inline scripts

Responding to Events with Script Procedures

Scripts also define procedures that respond to page events, such as the window loading, the buttons being clicked, and the mouse passing over objects.

To create a script event procedure, follow these steps:

1. Using Visual Studio, create or open the page for which you want to include the client-side scripts. The page can be a Web form (.aspx) or an HTML page (.htm).
2. Switch to the HTML view of the page.
3. From the drop-down list at the top left of the page, select the object for which you want to add the event procedure, as shown in Figure 7-9.

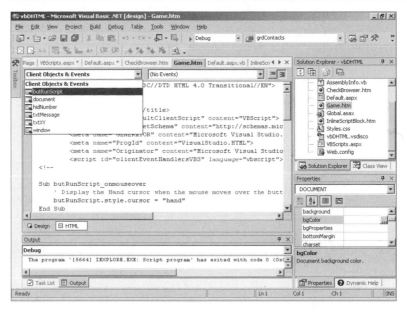

Figure 7-9   Selecting the object

4. From the drop-down list at the top right of the page, select the event that you want the code to respond to, as shown in Figure 7-10.

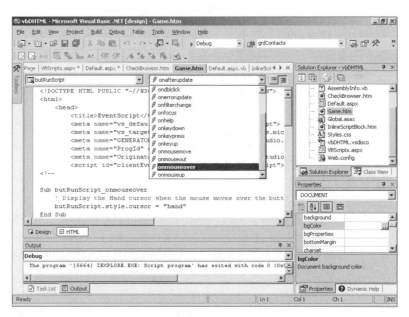

Figure 7-10   Selecting the event

Visual Studio creates a script block containing an empty event procedure, as shown in the following code:

VBScript

```
<script id=clientEventHandlersVBS language=vbscript>
<!--

Sub butRunScript_onmouseover

End Sub

-->
</script>
```

JScript

```
<script id=clientEventHandlersJS language=javascript>
<!--

function butRunScript_onmouseover() {

}

//-->
</script>
```

Any code you add to the event procedure will run when that page event occurs. For example, the following code switches the mouse cursor to the hand symbol when the user moves the mouse over the button:

VBScript

```
Sub butRunScript_onmouseover
  butRunScript.style.cursor = "hand"
End Sub
```

JScript

```
function butRunScript_onmouseover() {
  // Display the Hand cursor when the mouse moves over the button.
  butRunScript.style.cursor = "hand";
}
```

Client-side event procedures can detect a wide variety of events, including key-presses, mouse-over events, clicks, loads, and unloads. Unlike server-side events, client-side events do not provide arguments directly. Instead, you use the *window* object's *event* method to get values. For example, the following *mousemove* event procedure displays the coordinates of the cursor in the browser's status bar:

VBScript

```
Sub document_onmousemove
  ' Display X, Y coordinates as the mouse moves across the browser window.
  window.status = window.event.clientX & ", " & window.event.clientY
End Sub
```

JScript

```jscript
function window_onmousemove() {
  // Display X, Y coordinates as the mouse moves across the browser window.
  window.status = window.event.clientX + ", " + window.event.clientY;
}
```

The code in client-side event procedures can get and set the values displayed in server and HTML controls on the page. This means that you can get values from the user and provide responses without posting the page back to the server. For example, the following HTML code defines a page that plays a simple game with the user—all without posting back to the server:

VBScript

```vbscript
<!DOCTYPE HTML PUBLIC "-//W3C//DTD HTML 4.0 Transitional//EN">
<html>
  <head>
  <title>EventScript</title>
    <meta name="vs_defaultClientScript" content="VBScript">
    <meta name="vs_targetSchema"
      content="http://schemas.microsoft.com/intellisense/ie5">
    <meta name="GENERATOR" content="Microsoft Visual Studio.NET 7.0">
    <meta name="ProgId" content="VisualStudio.HTML">
    <meta name="Originator" content="Microsoft Visual Studio.NET 7.0">
<script id="clientEventHandlersVBS" language="vbscript">

Sub butRunScript_onclick
  ' Display a message in a text area.
  sMessage = "I am thinking of a number between 0 and 9. "
  sMessage = sMessage & "Press a number key to take a guess."
  txtMessage.value = sMessage
  ' Initialize the random number generator.
  Randomize
  ' Get a random number and store it in a hidden field.
  hidNumber.value = Int(9 * Rnd)
End Sub

Sub document_onkeypress
  ' If the keypress matches the number, display a success message.
  if (window.event.keyCode - 48) = CInt(hidNumber.value) then
    txtMessage.value = "You guessed it!"
  ' Otherwise tell the correct answer.
  else
    txtMessage.value = "You didn't guess it. It was: " & hidNumber.value
  end if
End Sub

</script>
  </head>
  <body MS_POSITIONING="FlowLayout">
```

```html
<p>
  <textarea id="txtMessage"></textarea>
</p>
<P>
  <INPUT type="button" id="butRunScript" value="Run Script"
    NAME="butRunScript">
</P>
<INPUT id="hidNumber" type="hidden" name="Hidden1">
</body>
</html>
```

JScript

```html
<!DOCTYPE HTML PUBLIC "-//W3C//DTD HTML 4.0 Transitional//EN" >
<HTML>
  <HEAD>
    <META NAME="GENERATOR" Content="Microsoft Visual Studio 7.0">
    <TITLE></TITLE>
    <meta name="vs_defaultClientScript" content="JavaScript">
    <meta name="vs_targetSchema"
      content="http://schemas.microsoft.com/intellisense/ie5">
    <meta name="GENERATOR" content="Microsoft Visual Studio.NET 7.0">
    <meta name="ProgId" content="VisualStudio.HTML">
    <meta name="Originator" content="Microsoft Visual Studio.NET 7.0">
<script id=clientEventHandlersJS language=javascript>
<!--

function window_onkeypress() {
  // If the keypress matches the number, display a success message.
  if ((window.event.keyCode - 48) == parseInt(hidNumber.value))
    txtMessage.value = "You guessed it!";
  // Otherwise tell the correct answer.
  else
    txtMessage.value = "You didn't guess it. It was: "
      + hidNumber.value;
}

function butRunScript_onclick() {
  // Display a message in a text area.
  sMessage = "I am thinking of a number between 0 and 9. "
    + "Press a number key to take a guess.";
  txtMessage.value = sMessage;
  // Get a random integer.
  hidNumber.value = Math.round(9 * Math.random());
}

//-->
</script>
</HEAD>
<BODY language=javascript onmousemove="return window_onmousemove()"
  onkeypress="return window_onkeypress()">
```

```
<p>
  <textarea id="txtMessage" style="WIDTH: 200px; HEIGHT: 88px"
    rows="5" cols="22" NAME="txtMessage"></textarea>
</p>
<P>
  <INPUT type="button" id="butRunScript" value="Run Script"
    NAME="butRunScript" language=javascript onmouseover="return
    butRunScript_onmouseover()" onclick="return
    butRunScript_onclick()">
</P>
<P><INPUT id="hidNumber" type="hidden" name="Hidden1"></P>
</BODY>
</HTML>
```

At run time, the preceding code displays a page that plays a guessing game, as shown in Figure 7-11.

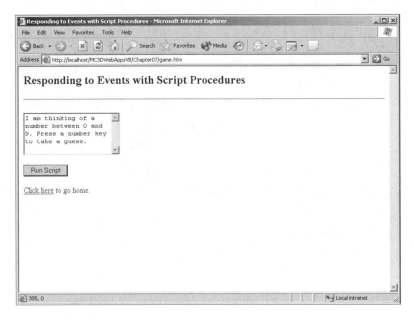

Figure 7-11   The guessing game

Sending Mail

To send mail using the client's mail system, create a hyperlink using the Mailto protocol. For example, the following HTML shows a hyperlink that creates a new message with a subject line and a short message body:

```
<A href="mailto:someone@microsoft.com?SUBJECT=Sending from a client&BODY=Some
 message text.">
```

When the user clicks this hyperlink, the client's browser starts the client's mail application and creates a message. You can use the Mailto protocol in place of any destination URL in a server control or an HTML control. For instance, the following HTML defines a Hyperlink server control that sends a mail message:

```
<asp:HyperLink ID="hypMail" NavigateUrl="mailto:someone@microsoft.com?
SUBJECT=Mailing a Webform&amp;BODY=Some message text."
Runat="server">Send mail.</ asp:HyperLink>
```

To send mail from the server, use the *SmtpMail* class from server-side code. The *SmtpMail* class does not start the client's mail system to allow the user to compose the message to send, to add attachments, or to validate addresses. Instead, you compose the message in code and send it one of two ways:

- You can send a simple message using the *SmtpMail* class's *Send* method.
- You can create a more complex message using the *MailMessage* class and then send that message using the *SmtpMail* class's *Send* method.

Both the *SmtpMail* class and the *MailMessage* class are part of the *System.Web.Mail* namespace in the .NET Framework, so add the following statement at the beginning of your module to simplify references to those classes in code:

Visual Basic .NET

```
Imports System.Web.Mail
```

Visual C#

```
using System.Web.Mail;
```

You don't need to create an instance of the *SmtpMail* class before using it. To send a simple message, just use the *Send* method, as shown here:

Visual Basic .NET

```
SmtpMail.Send ("someone@microsoft.com", "jesse@contoso.com",
               "Subject line", _
               "Message text.")
```

Visual C#

```
SmtpMail.Send("someone@microsoft.com", "jesse@contoso.com", "Subject line",
            "Message text.");
```

The preceding line of code immediately sends a message from some-one@microsoft.com to jesse@contoso.com. Both the from and to addresses are required, although they are not validated by the *Send* method. The *SmtpMail* class sends mail using your local SMTP server by default. To use a different server, set the *SmtpServer* property.

Using the *Send* method alone is fine for simple text messages, but to send a formatted message or a message containing an attachment, you need to create an object based on the *MailMessage* class and then use the *SmtpMail* class's *Send* method to send the message, as shown in the following code:

Visual Basic .NET

```
Private Sub butMail_Click(ByVal sender As System.Object, _
    ByVal e As System.EventArgs) Handles butMail.Click
    ' Create the message.
    Dim mailNew As New MailMessage()
    ' Set the message properties.
    mailNew.From = "someone@microsoft.com"
    mailNew.To = "jesse@contoso.com"
    mailNew.Subject = "This is the subject text."
    mailNew.Body = "This is the message text."
    ' Create an attachment.
    Dim atcItem As New _
    MailAttachment(Server.MapPath(".") & "\joey.jpg")
    ' Attach it to the message.
    mailNew.Attachments.Add(atcItem)
    ' Send the message.
    SmtpMail.Send(mailNew)
End Sub
```

Visual C#

```
private void butSendMail_Click(object sender, System.EventArgs e)
{
    // Create the message.
    MailMessage mailNew = new MailMessage();
    // Set the message properties.
    mailNew.From = "someone@microsoft.com";
    mailNew.To = "jesse@contoso.com";
    mailNew.Subject = "This is the subject text.";
    mailNew.Body = "This is the message text.";
    // Create an attachment.
    MailAttachment atcItem = new MailAttachment
        (Server.MapPath(".") +
        "\\joey.jpg");
```

```
        // Attach it to the message.
        mailNew.Attachments.Add(atcItem);
        // Send the message.
        SmtpMail.Send(mailNew);
}
```

This code creates a message, sets the message properties, attaches a file to the message, and sends the message. As with the previous *Send* method example, the *From* and *To* properties are required but are not validated.

Lesson 5: Consuming XML Web Services

XML Web services are business logic components that can be accessed over the Internet. *Consuming* a Web service simply means using that service from within your application. In this lesson, you'll learn how to locate, reference, and use XML Web services from a Web application.

After this lesson, you will be able to

- Search for XML Web services by company name
- Add a reference to an XML Web service from a Visual Studio .NET project
- Use an XML Web service from within a Web application
- Use an XML Web service from client-side scripts
- Use a licensed XML Web service

Estimated lesson time: 15 minutes

Finding XML Web Services

XML Web services are made public over the Web using a Universal Description, Discovery, and Integration (UDDI) registry. Currently, Microsoft and IBM manage two UDDI registry nodes available for locating XML Web services. Businesses register their Web services on these nodes so that customers (you and I) can locate the Web services they want to use.

There are many different ways to search for XML Web services on the Internet. The easiest way is just to select XML Web Services from the Start Page in Visual Studio .NET, as shown in Figure 7-12.

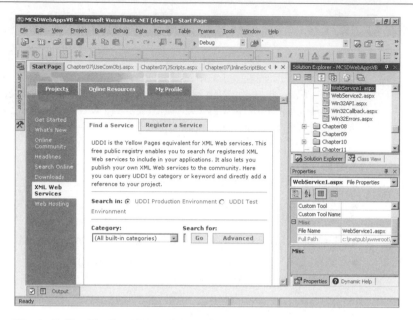

Figure 7-12   Finding XML Web services

The XML Web Services item on the Start Page lets you locate XML Web services by general category of task that the service performs, such as calendar, financial, math, or weather. The Search In option buttons above the Category box let you search for XML Web services that have been put into production (presumably these have been debugged and tested) or are still under development.

In some cases, a Web service might be available to the public but not listed in the UDDI registry. In these cases, you must know the address of the Web service. This information is often listed on the Web site of the company that offers the service, usually under a heading such as Developer Tools.

Using an XML Web Service

Using an XML Web service is much the same as using a .NET or COM component: you establish a reference to the class, create an instance of an object from the class, and then use the object's properties and methods within your code. There are several ways to establish a reference to an XML Web service from within Visual Studio .NET; perhaps the easiest is to do so from the Start Page.

To reference XML Web services from the Visual Studio .NET Start Page, follow these steps:

1. Find the XML Web service you want to use by clicking the XML Web Services link on the Online Resources tab on the Start Page in Visual Studio .NET.

2. Click the Add As Web Reference To Your Current Project hyperlink underneath the XML Web service description. Visual Studio adds a Web reference to the Web References section of Solution Explorer, as shown in Figure 7-13.

Figure 7-13   Web references

To use the reference in code, follow these steps:

1. Create a new object from the XML Web service class. The XML Web service class name is displayed in the Web References folder of Solution Explorer.
2. Use the XML Web service's properties and methods from the new object. XML Web service classes work with Visual Studio's autocomplete and Object Browser features, so using XML Web service properties and methods is the same as for any other object.

Note   The following example depends on the availability of a third-party Web site. At the time this book was written, this Web site was available. However, its future availability can't be guaranteed.

For example, the following code uses the CDYNE Credit Card Checker Web service to validate a credit card number entered in a text box:

Visual Basic .NET

```
Private Sub butCheck_Click(ByVal sender As System.Object, _
    ByVal e As System.EventArgs) Handles butCheck.Click
    Dim wsCheck As New com.cdyne.secure.LUHNChecker()
    Dim wsValid As com.cdyne.secure.ReturnIndicator
    wsValid = wsCheck.CheckCC(txtNumber.Text)
    lblMsg.Text = wsValid.CardType & " " & wsValid.CardValid.ToString()
End Sub
```

Visual C#

```
private void butCheck_Click(object sender, System.EventArgs e)
{
    com.cdyne.secure.LUHNChecker wsCheck = new com.cdyne.secure.LUHNChecker()
;
    com.cdyne.secure.ReturnIndicator wsValid;
```

```
        wsValid = wsCheck.CheckCC(txtNumber.Text);
        lblMsg.Text = wsValid.CardType + " " + wsValid.CardValid.ToString();
}
```

Using XML Web Services from Client-Side Scripts

In some cases, it makes more sense to call an XML Web service from client-side scripts than from server code. An XML Web service might take a long time to respond—there's no point in making the server wait for the response when the server is just going to pass that response on to the client anyway.

To use an XML Web service from client-side scripts, follow these steps:

1. Create a style class for the *WebService* behavior (Webservice.htc).
2. Add an HTML element to the page that uses the class you created in step 1.
3. Write script procedures to initialize and call methods on the XML Web service using the XML Web service behavior.

The following HTML creates a *webservice* style class and then initializes and calls a Web service to display a daily quote when the user clicks Show Quote:

VBScript

```
<HTML>
  <HEAD>
    <title>WebForm2</title>
    <style>
      .webservice { BEHAVIOR:url(webservice.htc) }
    </style>
<script language="VBScript">
Dim iCallID

Sub init(control, wsAddress, name)
  control.useService wsAddress, name
End Sub

Function getResult()
  if window.event.result.error And (iCallID = window.event.result.id) Then
    Dim xfaultcode, xfaultstring, xfaultsoap
    xfaultcode = window.event.result.errorDetail.code
    xfaultstring = window.event.result.errorDetail.string
    xfaultsoap = window.event.result.errorDetail.raw
    ' Display error information.
    alert("Error " & xfautlcode & " | " & xfaultstring & " | " & xfaultSoap)
  Else
    getResult = window.event.result.value
  End If
End Function

Sub getQuote()
```

```
' Initialize Web service on the selected control.
 init ws, "http://webservice.effective-web.net/globalself/
globalselfDailyThought.WSDL", "DailyQuote"
 ' Call a method within the Web service.
 iCallID = ws.DailyQuote.callService("getTodaysQuote")
 ' Result is displayed in the ws div element by onresult.
End Sub
</script>
  </HEAD>
  <body>
    <form id="WebForm2" method="post" runat="server">
      <h2>Using Web Services from Client-Side Code</h2>
      <div id="ws" class="webservice"
        onresult="ws.innerText = getResult()"></div>
      <br>
      <input type="button" onclick="getQuote()" value="Get Quote">
    </form>
  </body>
</HTML>
```

JScript

```
<HTML>
  <HEAD>
    <title>WebForm2</title>
    <style>
      .webservice { BEHAVIOR:url(webservice.htc) }
    </style>
<script language="JScript">
var iCallID;

function init(control, wsAddress, name)
{
  control.useService(wsAddress, name);
}

function getResult()
{
  if((event.result.error)&&(iCallID==event.result.id))
  {
    var xfaultcode = event.result.errorDetail.code;
    var xfaultstring = event.result.errorDetail.string;
    var xfaultsoap = event.result.errorDetail.raw;
    // Display error information.
    alert("Error " + xfautlcode + " | " + xfaultstring + " | " + xfaultSoap);
  }
  else
  {
    return event.result.value;
  }
}
```

```
function getQuote()
{
  // Initialize Web service on the selected control.
  init(ws, "http://webservice.effective-web.net/globalself/
globalselfGlobalSelf.WSDL", "DailyQuote");
  // Call a method within the Web service.
  iCallID = ws.DailyQuote.callService("getTodaysQuote");
  // Result is displayed in the ws div element by onresult.
}
</script>
  </HEAD>
  <body>
    <form id="WebForm2" method="post" runat="server">
      <h2>Using Web Services from Client-Side Code</h2>
      <div id="ws" class="webservice"
        onresult="ws.innerText = getResult();"></div>
      <br>
      <input type="button" onclick="getQuote()" value="Get Quote">
    </form>
    </DIV>
  </body>
</HTML>
```

For more information about using XML Web services from client-side scripts, search for "Web Service Behavior" in the Visual Studio online Help.

Using Licensed XML Web Services

The preceding XML Web service examples are available on the Internet for free as demonstrations. Other services might require a license in order to charge a fee for their use or to control and track who is using their services.

The XML Web services provided by Amazon.com and Google are good examples of XML Web services that require a license. Neither XML Web service charges for use at this time—in fact, Amazon.com actually credits users through their associates program. Instead, these companies use licensing to establish rules of use and to keep in touch with the developers using their services.

To use a licensed Web service, follow these steps:

1. Visit the Web service developer's Web site, and complete the requested license information.
2. Reference the XML Web service using the address of the Web Services Description Language (WSDL) file. Licensed XML Web services are often not listed in the UDDI.
3. Use the XML Web service methods.

For example, you can get the Amazon XML Web service information from the following address: *http://www.amazon.com/webservices*. You can download the XML Web service documentation from that address and apply for a developer's token that allows you to use the service. Once you have a developer's token, you use it in code to call the XML Web service methods. The Amazon.com XML Web service is available from this address: *http://soap.amazon.com/schemas2/AmazonWebServices.wsdl*.

Once you establish a Web reference to the preceding address, you can use the Web service, as shown in the following code:

Visual Basic .NET

```
Private Sub Page_Load(ByVal sender As System.Object, _
    ByVal e As System.EventArgs) Handles MyBase.Load
    ' Declare an object to represent the Web Service.
    Dim wsAmazon As New com.amazon.soap.AmazonSearchService
    ' Declare a structure to pass search criteria in.
    Dim Search As New com.amazon.soap.KeywordRequest
    ' Set the search criteria.
    Search.keyword = "ASP.NET"
    ' This is the special license number issued to developers.
    ' Get your own from Amazon.
    Search.devtag = "DT7Y0UZAPK4PI"
    ' This is the associates ID for Amazon partners. Get your
    ' own number from Amazon if you wish to get credit for sales.
    Search.tag = "webservices-20"
    ' This property determines how much detail is returned.
    Search.type = "heavy"
    ' Which version of the Web Service to use.
    Search.mode = "books"
    ' Get the ProductInfo from the Web Service.
    Dim Info As com.amazon.soap.ProductInfo = _
        wsAmazon.KeywordSearchRequest(Search)
    ' Declare a variable to use with For Each iteration.
    Dim Book
    ' Go through the returned ProductInfo array.
    For Each Book In Info.Details
        'Insert an image of the cover.
        litResult.Text += "<h4>Amazon Sales Rank: " & Book.SalesRank &_
        litResult.Text += "</h4><img src='" & Book.ImageUrlMedium & "'>"
    Next
End Sub
```

Visual C#

```
private void Page_Load(object sender, System.EventArgs e)
{
    // Declare an object to represent the Web Service.
    com.amazon.soap.AmazonSearchService wsAmazon =
```

```
      new com.amazon.soap.AmazonSearchService();
// Declare a structure to pass search criteria in.
com.amazon.soap.KeywordRequest Search =
      new com.amazon.soap.KeywordRequest();
// Set the search criteria.
Search.keyword = "ASP.NET";
// This is the special license number issued to developers.
// Get your own from Amazon.
Search.devtag = "DT7Y0UZAPK4PI";
// This is the associates ID for Amazon partners. Get your
// own number from Amazon if you wish to get credit for sales.
Search.tag = "webservices-20";
// This property determines how much detail is returned.
Search.type = "heavy";
// Which version of the Web Service to use.
Search.mode = "books";
// Get the ProductInfo from the Web Service.
com.amazon.soap.ProductInfo Info  =
      wsAmazon.KeywordSearchRequest(Search);
// Go through the returned ProductInfo array.
foreach(com.amazon.soap.Details Book in Info.Details)
{
    //Insert an image of the cover.
    litResult.Text += "<h4>Amazon Sales Rank: " +
        Book.SalesRank + "</h4>";
    litResult.Text += "<img src='" + Book.ImageUrlMedium + "'>";
}
}
```

The Amazon.com Web service documentation provides a practical guide to using their Web service in different ways and in a variety of languages.

Summary

- Cookies enable you to invisibly save information about a particular user. Cookies can be used to save the information directly on the user's computer or indirectly through a unique identifier, which is then referenced to retrieve user information from a data set stored on the server.

- Use the *Request* object's *Cookies* collection to retrieve a cookie from the user. Use the *Response* object's *Cookies* collection to create or modify a cookie on the user's computer.

- Set the *Cookie* object's *Expires* property to *Now* to delete a cookie from the user's computer.

- Use the *DllImport* attribute to declare unmanaged procedures for use within .NET assemblies.

- Create a reference to a COM object in Visual Studio to automatically create an interop assembly that allows you to use the COM object within .NET code.

- To hide public .NET members from COM, use the *ComVisible* attribute.

- Select a .NET class library project's Register For COM Interop build check box to automatically create a type library for the project and register the assembly with the system registry.

- Client-side scripts let you control the browser window, respond immediately to non-postback events, and perform other tasks that are not possible from server-side code.

- Use the *Browser* object's *VBScript* or *JavaScript* properties to test whether the browser can run scripts. Use an inline test script that redirects the users to another page to test whether a user has disabled scripting through his or her browser security settings.

- Add script event procedures to a page's HTML to respond to events that occur on the client side rather than the server side.

- Use the Mailto protocol to create a message that will be sent from the user's mail system. The Mailto protocol is used as part of a hyperlink.

- Use the *MailMessage* and *SmtpMail* classes to compose and send messages from the server's mail system.

- Create a Web reference to use an XML Web service from server-side code.

- Use the *WebService* behavior to use an XML Web service from client-side code.

Lab: Using Advanced Features

In this lab, you'll create an application that displays multiple pages using frames. This application lets users choose a background color for the application, compose and send mail from the server, and play a simple game. The Advanced Features application demonstrates these key features:

- Testing browser capabilities to make sure a user's browser supports frames, cookies, and scripts
- Saving cookies on the user's computer and then retrieving those cookies to set the background color for the application
- Sending mail from the server using the *MailMessage* and *SmtpMail* objects
- Displaying pages in frames and controlling the display of those frames from a Contents page
- Optionally including Web forms that use the Win32 API, COM objects, and XML Web services

When complete, the Advanced Features application will appear as shown in Figure 7-14.

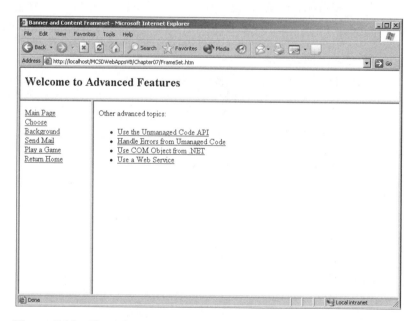

Figure 7-14   The Advanced Features application

Estimated lesson time: 45 minutes

Exercise 1: Check Advanced Feature Support

In this exercise, you'll create a default page for an application that checks to see whether the user's browser accepts cookies, can display frames, and runs scripts. If any of these features are not available, an appropriate message is displayed.

A **default page** is a page that Internet Information Services (IIS) displays if the user navigates to the Web application directory without specifying a particular page to view. IIS uses the names Default.htm and Default.aspx for the default page unless you change them for the application through IIS.

▶ **To create a default page that checks the user's browser for advanced feature support**

1. Add a Web form to your application named Default.aspx, and make that page the start page for your application.
2. Add the following *Page_Load* event procedure to the Web form:

Visual Basic .NET

```
Private Sub Page_Load(ByVal sender As System.Object, _
    ByVal e As System.EventArgs) Handles MyBase.Load
    ' Create a flag to track if any advanced features are disabled.
    Dim bProceed As Boolean = True
    ' Check if browser accepts cookies.
    If Request.Browser.Cookies = False Then
        Response.Write("Your browser does not accept cookies.<br>" & _
            "Change your browser's security settings allow cookies." & _
            "<br><br>")
        bProceed = False
    End If
    ' Check if browser supports scripting.
    If Request.Browser.JavaScript = False Then
        Response.Write("Your browser does not support scripts.<br>" & _
        "Update your browser software to the latest version.<br><br>")
        bProceed = False
    End If
    ' Check if browser supports VBScript.
    If Request.Browser.VBScript = False Then
        Response.Write("Your browser does not support VBScript.<br>" & _
            "Install the latest version of Internet Explorer.<br><br>")
        bProceed = False
    End If
    ' If browser passes other tests, see if scripting is enabled by
    ' trying a script.
    If bProceed Then
            ' If scripts are disabled, the following line is ignored.
            ' Otherwise, it displays the frameset.
```

```
        Response.Write("<script>window.navigate('frameset.htm')</script>")
        Response.Write("Scripting is disabled due to your browser " & _
            "security settings.<br> Change your browser's security " & _
            "settings allow scripting.<br><br>")
    End If
End Sub
```

Visual C#

```csharp
private void Page_Load(object sender, System.EventArgs e)
{
    // Create a flag to track if any advanced features are disabled.
    bool bProceed = true;
    // Check if browser accepts cookies.
    if (!Request.Browser.Cookies)
    {
        Response.Write("Your browser does not accept cookies.<br>" +
            "Change your browser's security settings allow cookies." +
            "<br><br>");
        bProceed = false;
    }
    // Check if browser supports scripting.
    if (!Request.Browser.JavaScript)
    {
        Response.Write("Your browser does not support scripts.<br>" +
            "Update your browser software to the latest " +
            "version.<br><br>");
        bProceed = false;
    }
    // Check if browser supports VBScript.
    if (!Request.Browser.VBScript)
    {
        Response.Write("Your browser does not support VBScript.<br>" +
            "Install the latest version of Internet Explorer.<br><br>");
        bProceed = false;
    }
    // If browser passes other tests, see if scripting is enabled by
    // trying a script.
    if (bProceed)
    {
        // If scripts are disabled, the following line is ignored.
        // Otherwise, it displays the frameset.
        Response.Write("<script>window.navigate('frameset.htm')" +
            "</script>");
        Response.Write("Scripting is disabled due to your browser " +
            "security settings.<br> Change your browser's security " +
            "settings to allow scripting.<br><br>");
    }
}
```

3. Add the following HTML content to the Web form:

```
<p>This Web application uses features that are either not available in
your browser or are disabled through your browser's security settings.
You cannot run this application until you update your browser as described
above. Then click <a href="default.aspx">here</a> to try again.</p>
```

When the default page you created with the preceding steps loads, it checks each of the advanced features that a browser might or might not support. If there are problems using any of those features, the page displays a warning message, as shown in Figure 7-15.

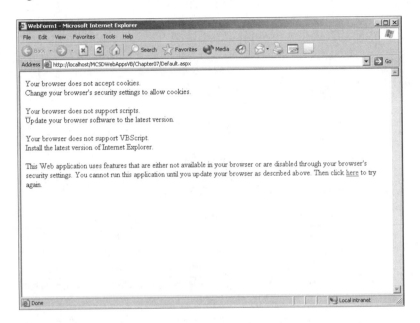

Figure 7-15   Warning message

If no problems are encountered, the user never sees the default page. Instead, he or she is redirected immediately to frameset.htm, which displays the other pages in the application.

Exercise 2: Store User Information

In this exercise, you'll create a Web form that allows the user to select a background color. The form "remembers" the user's choice between sessions by saving the background in a cookie on the user's machine. When complete, the Web form will appear as shown in Figure 7-16.

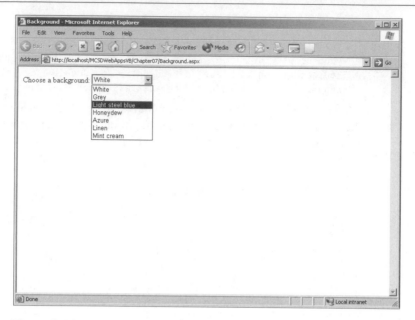

Figure 7-16   The Background.aspx Web form

▶   **To create the Background Web form**

1. Create a new Web form named Background.aspx.

2. Add a DropDownList server control to the Web form containing list items for some different background colors. This step is probably easier to do in HTML than in Design mode, because you can use cut and paste to create the list items quickly in HTML. The following HTML shows the definition for the Drop-DownList and its list items:

```
<asp:dropdownlist id="drpBackground" AutoPostBack="True" Runat="server"
Width="128px">
  <asp:ListItem Value="White">White</asp:ListItem>
  <asp:ListItem Value="Silver">Grey</asp:ListItem>
  <asp:ListItem Value="LightSteelBlue">Light steel blue</asp:ListItem>
  <asp:ListItem Value="Honeydew">Honeydew</asp:ListItem>
  <asp:ListItem Value="Azure">Azure</asp:ListItem>
  <asp:ListItem Value="Linen">Linen</asp:ListItem>
  <asp:ListItem Value="MintCream">Mint cream</asp:ListItem>
</asp:dropdownlist>
```

3. Modify the Web form's *<body>* element to specify a background color using data binding from the DropDownList. The following HTML shows the changes to the *<body>* element:

```
<body bgColor="<%# drpBackground.SelectedItem.Value %>">
```

4. Add the following code to the *Page_Load* event procedure to check for a cookie, create the cookie if it does not exist, or set the background color from the cookie if it does exist. The *Page_Load* event procedure also performs data binding for the page to update the background color.

Visual Basic .NET

```
Private Sub Page_Load(ByVal sender As System.Object, _
    ByVal e As System.EventArgs) Handles MyBase.Load
    ' On first display
    If IsPostBack = False Then
        ' Check if cookie doesn't exist...
        If Request.Cookies("BackgroundColor") Is Nothing Then
            ' Create a cookie with the default background color.
            Dim cookBackground As New HttpCookie("BackgroundColor", "0")
            ' Set the cookie to expire in one day.
            cookBackground.Expires = DateTime.Now.AddDays(1)
            ' Add the cookie to the response object.
            Response.Cookies.Add(cookBackground)
        Else
            ' Get the user's background color from the cookie.
            drpBackground.SelectedIndex = _
                CInt(Request.Cookies("BackgroundColor").Value)
        End If
    End If
    ' Update bound field to set background color
    Page.DataBind()
End Sub
```

Visual C#

```
private void Page_Load(object sender, System.EventArgs e)
{
    // On first display
    if (!IsPostBack)
    {
        //  If cookie doesn't exist...
        if (Request.Cookies["BackgroundColor"] == null)
        {
            // Create a cookie with the default background color.
            HttpCookie cookBackground = new
            HttpCookie("BackgroundColor", "0");
            // Set the cookie to expire in one day.
            cookBackground.Expires = DateTime.Now.AddDays(1);
            // Add the cookie to the response object.
            Response.Cookies.Add(cookBackground);
        }
        else
        {
            // Get the user's background color from the cookie.
            drpBackground.SelectedIndex =
```

```
                Convert.ToInt16(Request.Cookies["BackgroundColor"]
                    .Value);
        }
    }
    // Update bound field to set background color
    Page.DataBind();
}
```

5. Add the following code to update the cookie through the *Response* object when the user selects a background color from the DropDownList:

Visual Basic .NET

```
Private Sub drpBackground_SelectedIndexChanged(ByVal sender As _
    System.Object, ByVal e As System.EventArgs) Handles _
    drpBackground.SelectedIndexChanged
    ' Record color selection in a cookie.
    Dim cookBackground As New HttpCookie("BackgroundColor")
    ' Set the cookie's value.
    cookBackground.Value = drpBackground.SelectedIndex
    ' Set the cookie's expiration.
    cookBackground.Expires = DateTime.Now.AddDays(1)
    ' Add the cookie to the Response object.
    Response.Cookies.Add(cookBackground)
End Sub
```

Visual C#

```
private void drpBackground_SelectedIndexChanged(object sender,
    System.EventArgs e)
{
    // Record color selection in a cookie.
    HttpCookie cookBackground = new HttpCookie("BackgroundColor");
    // Set the cookie's value.
    cookBackground.Value = drpBackground.SelectedIndex.ToString();
    // Set the cookie's expiration.
    cookBackground.Expires = DateTime.Now.AddDays(1);
    // Add the cookie to the Response object.
    Response.Cookies.Add(cookBackground);

}
```

Exercise 3: Create a Mail Web Form

In this exercise, you'll create a Web form that allows you to compose and send a mail message from the server. When complete, the Mail Web form will appear as shown in Figure 7-17.

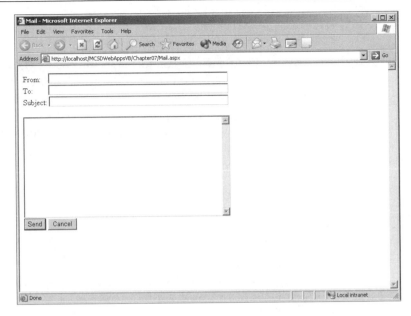

Figure 7-17   The Mail.aspx Web form

▶ **To create the Mail Web form**

1. Create a new Web form named Mail.aspx.

2. Add text and server controls to the Web form, as shown in the following HTML:

```
<P>
  From:   
  <asp:TextBox ID="txtFrom" Runat="server" Width="376px"></asp:TextBox>
  <asp:RequiredFieldValidator ID="vldtxtFrom" ControlToValidate="txtFrom"
    Runat="server" ErrorMessage="Required field.">
  </asp:RequiredFieldValidator>
  <br>
  To:       
  <asp:TextBox ID="txtTo" Runat="server" Width="377px"></asp:TextBox>
  <asp:RequiredFieldValidator ID="vldTo" ControlToValidate="txtTo"
    Runat="server" ErrorMessage="Required field.">
  </asp:RequiredFieldValidator>
  <br>
  Subject:
  <asp:TextBox ID="txtSubject" Runat="server" Width="376px"></asp:TextBox>
</P>
<asp:TextBox ID="txtMessage" Runat="server" TextMode="MultiLine"
Width="432px"
  Height="208px"></asp:TextBox>
<br>
<asp:Button ID="butSend" Runat="server" Text="Send"></asp:Button>
```

```
<input type="reset" id="butReset" value="Cancel">
<br>
<asp:literal id="litStatus" runat="server"></asp:literal>
```

The RequiredFieldValidator controls in the preceding HTML are needed because the *From* and *To* properties of the *MailMessage* object must be set before the message can be sent.

3. Add the following *Imports* or *using* statement to the beginning of the Web form's code module so that you can use short names for members of the *System.Web.Mail* namespace:

Visual Basic .NET

```
Imports System.Web.Mail
```

Visual C#

```
using System.Web.Mail;
```

4. Add the following code to the *butSend_Click* event procedure to create a *MailMessage* object and to send the message from the server:

Visual Basic .NET

```
Private Sub butSend_Click(ByVal sender As System.Object, _
    ByVal e As System.EventArgs) Handles butSend.Click
    ' Create message.
    Dim msgMail As New MailMessage()
    ' Set message properties.
    msgMail.From = txtFrom.Text
    msgMail.To = txtTo.Text
    msgMail.Subject = txtSubject.Text
    msgMail.Body = txtMessage.Text
    ' Send message.
    SmtpMail.Send(msgMail)
    ' Clear To, Subject, and Message fields.
    txtTo.Text = ""
    txtSubject.Text = ""
    txtMessage.Text = ""
    ' Show success.
    litStatus.Text = "<p>Message sent.</p>"
End Sub
```

Visual C#

```
private void butSend_Click(object sender, System.EventArgs e)
{
    // Create message.
    MailMessage msgMail = new MailMessage();
    // Set message properties.
    msgMail.From = txtFrom.Text;
    msgMail.To = txtTo.Text;
    msgMail.Subject = txtSubject.Text;
```

```
msgMail.Body = txtMessage.Text;
// Send message.
SmtpMail.Send(msgMail);
// Clear To, Subject, and Message fields.
txtTo.Text = "";
txtSubject.Text = "";
txtMessage.Text = "";
// Show success.
litStatus.Text = "<p>Message sent.</p>";
}
```

5. Add the following code to the *Page_Load* event procedure to clear the status message if the user cancels sending a message after successfully sending an earlier message:

Visual Basic .NET

```
Private Sub Page_Load(ByVal sender As System.Object, _
    ByVal e As System.EventArgs) Handles MyBase.Load
    ' Clear status message.
    litStatus.Text = ""
End Sub
```

Visual C#

```
private void Page_Load(object sender, System.EventArgs e)
{
    // Clear status message.
    litStatus.Text = "";
}
```

Exercise 4: Create a Frame-Based User Interface

In this exercise, you'll create a frameset containing regions for a table of contents, a banner, and a body. You'll create a table of contents page that displays selected pages in the body frame and updates the banner frame using a script. When complete, the frameset will appear as shown in Figure 7-18.

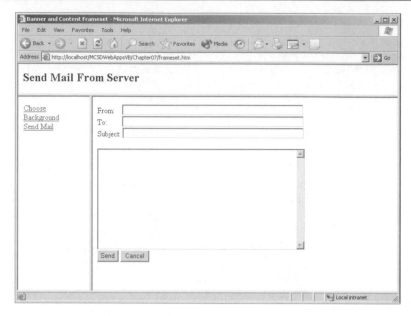

Figure 7-18   The completed frameset at run time

▶ **To create the frame-based user interface**

1. Create a new HTML page named Contents.htm.

2. Add the following hyperlinks to the Contents page:

```
<a href="Background.aspx" target="main"
  onclick="ShowBanner('Choose Background')">Choose Background</a>
<br>
<a href="Mail.aspx" target="main"
  onclick="ShowBanner('Send Mail From Server')">Send Mail</a>
<br>
```

The hyperlinks shown in the preceding HTML provide a way to navigate to the other pages in the application and will display those pages in the main frame of the frameset you will create in the following steps.

3. Add the following script procedure to the Contents page:

VBScript

```
<script language="vbscript">
' Updates the text in the banner frame.
Sub ShowBanner(Message)
  ' Write text to banner frame.
  parent.frames("banner").document.write("<h2>" & Message & "</h2>")
  ' Close document so next write replaces the current text.
  parent.frames("banner").document.close
End Sub
</script>
```

JScript

```
<script language="javascript">
// Updates the text in the banner frame.
function ShowBanner(Message)
{
  // Write text to banner frame.
  parent.frames["banner"].document.write("<h2>" + Message + "</h2>");
  // Close document so next write replaces the current text.
  parent.frames["banner"].document.close();
}
</script>
```

This ShowBanner script displays a title in the banner frame of the frameset from each of the hyperlinks created in step 2.

4. Create a frameset in which to display the project pages. From the Project menu, choose Add New Item, and then select Frameset from the Templates list and name the file Frameset.htm. When you click Open, Visual Studio displays the Select A Frameset Template dialog box.

5. Select the Banner And Content frameset template and click OK. Visual Studio displays a new, empty frameset in the Design window.

6. Right-click in the leftmost frame, and select Set Page For Frame from the shortcut menu. Visual Studio displays the Select Page dialog box.

7. Select Contents.htm in the Select Page dialog box, and click OK to display the Contents page in the frame.

8. Make the frameset the start page for the application. In Solution Explorer, right-click the Frameset.htm file, and select Set As Start Page from the shortcut menu.

Exercise 5: Extra Practice Using Advanced Features

Exercises 1 through 4 walked you through some of the tasks you explored in this chapter. Now strike out on your own by attempting to complete the following tasks that extend the Advanced Features application:

■ Add a Web form that displays information using a COM object from your system or the *ShapesCOM* object included on the companion CD.

■ Add a Web form that uses the *SystemInfo* Win32 API to display system information or select another unmanaged procedure to call through platform invoke.

■ Add a *Window_OnLoad* script to the Contents page to display a welcome message in the banner frame the first time the page is displayed.

■ Add the Guess A Number Web form created at the end of Lesson 4 to the Advanced Features application.

- Create a cookie within the Mail Web form to remember the From address entered by the user.
- Use the background color set on the Background Web form to change the background color displayed on each page in the frameset.

When you have finished, compare your results to the Advanced Features application included on the companion CD. Good luck!

Review

The following questions are intended to reinforce key information presented in this chapter. If you are unable to answer a question, review the appropriate lesson and then try the question again. Answers to the questions can be found in the appendix.

1. Write the HTML for a hyperlink that will send mail when the user clicks the link.

2. Write the code that creates a cookie containing the user name *Rob Young* and the current date to the user's computer. Set the cookie to remain on the user's computer for 30 days.

3. What attribute do you use to hide a public .NET class from COM?

4. Why can't you open a new browser window using server-side code? How would you display a page in a new window with a client-side script?

5. How do you declare an unmanaged procedure within .NET?

C H A P T E R   8

Maintaining Security

About This Chapter

In this chapter, you'll learn how to control access to your Web application using the three techniques that Microsoft ASP.NET provides for identifying users and allowing them to have access to your application. You'll also learn how to secure data transmitted across the Internet so that others can't read it.

This chapter does not provide a comprehensive guide to server or network security. That is truly a broad subject involving a great deal of conceptual and system-specific information. What this chapter does provide is a practical guide to implementing Web application security through ASP.NET.

Before You Begin

To complete the lessons in this chapter, you must:

- Have access to two computers in a Microsoft Windows network. This can be a simple workgroup-based network such as you might set up at home, but a domain-based network is best.
- Have Administrator privileges on a computer that functions as a server on the network.

If you don't have access to a Windows network, you can perform most of the tasks in this chapter using a single computer and running the applications locally, as you do in Microsoft Visual Studio's Debug mode. However, you will not be able to easily test authentication of multiple users.

Lesson 1: Authenticating and Authorizing Users

Authentication is the process of identifying users. **Authorization** is the process of granting access to those users based on identity. Together, authentication and authorization provide the means to keeping your Web application secure from intruders.

In this lesson, you'll learn how ASP.NET handles anonymous users, and you'll get an overview of the different ways you can identify and authorize users. This information will help you choose an authentication strategy based on the type of application you are creating.

After this lesson, you will be able to

- Describe how ASP.NET grants access to users who are not authenticated and how those users appear within Windows security tools
- Choose an authentication method based on your application's needs
- Add HTML pages to the list of file types that will be included with your application's authentication and authorization settings

Estimated lesson time: 10 minutes

Access by Anonymous Users

Anonymous access is the way most public Web sites work—sites containing public information allow anyone to see that information, so they don't authenticate users. ASP.NET Web applications provide anonymous access to resources on the server by impersonation. **Impersonation** is the process of assigning a user account to an unknown user.

By default, the anonymous access account is named IUSER_*machinename*. You use that account to control anonymous users' access to resources on the server.

To see or change the access privileges to the anonymous access account, use the Windows Computer Management snap-in as described in the following steps:

1. Log on to the server as the computer administrator.
2. From the Start menu, choose Administrative Tools, and then choose Computer Management to run the Computer Management console, as shown in Figure 8-1.

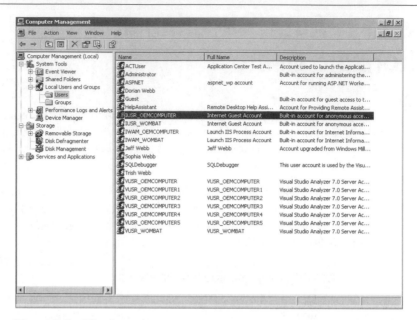

Figure 8-1   Viewing users

3. From the list on the left, choose Local Users And Groups, and then select the Users folder to display the list of authorized users for this computer.

4. From the user list on the right, double-click the anonymous user account named IUSR_*computername*. The Computer Management console displays the account's properties, as shown in Figure 8-2.

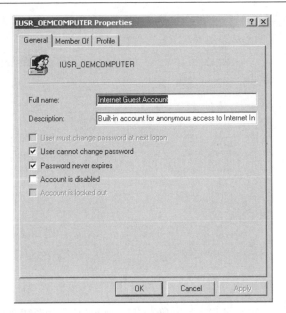

Figure 8-2   Properties of the anonymous access account

5. Click the Member Of tab to view the user groups the account belongs to.
   By default, anonymous users belong to the Guests group, which has limited
   privileges.

Under the default settings, ASP.NET uses the ASPNET account to run the Web
application. This means that if the application attempts to perform any tasks that
are not included in the ASPNET account's privileges, a security exception will
occur and access will be denied. The account name will also show up in the security event log of the event viewer, as shown in Figure 8-3.

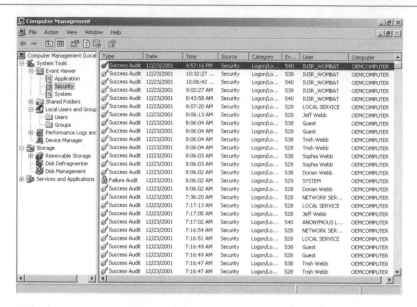

Figure 8-3   The security event log in the Computer Management console

You restrict the access of anonymous users by setting Windows file permissions. To be secure, your server must use the Microsoft Windows NT file system (NTFS). The earlier FAT or FAT32 file systems do not provide file-level security. For more information about setting Windows file permissions, see the Windows security Help topics.

Access by Authenticated Users

As stated earlier, anonymous access is fine for public information. But if your application contains private information or performs restricted tasks such as placing orders, you will want to authenticate and authorize individual users.

There are three major ways to authenticate and authorize users within an ASP.NET Web application:

- **Windows authentication**   Identifies and authorizes users based on the server's user list. Access to resources on the server is then granted or denied based on the user account's privileges. This works the same way as regular Windows network security.
- **Forms authentication**   Directs users to a logon Web form that collects user name and password information, and then authenticates the user against a user list or database that the application maintains.
- **Passport authentication**   Directs new users to a site hosted by Microsoft so that they can register a single user name and password that will authorize their access to multiple Web sites. Existing users are prompted for their Microsoft Passport user name and password, which the application then authenticates from the Passport user list.

Each of these approaches, along with anonymous access, has different advantages. These authentication methods are best suited for different types of Web applications, as summarized in Table 8-1.

Table 8-1   Web Application Types and Authentication Techniques

Application type	Use this type of authentication	Description
Public Internet Web application	Anonymous	This is the common access method for most Web sites. No logon is required, and you secure restricted resources using NTFS file permissions.
Intranet Web application	Windows authentication	Windows authentication authenticates network users through the domain controller. Network users have access to Web application resources as determined by their user privileges on the server.
Private corporate Web application	Windows authentication	Corporate users can access the Web application using their corporate network user names and passwords. User accounts are administered using the Windows network security tools.
Commercial Web application	Forms	Applications that need to collect shipping and billing information should implement Forms authentication to gather and store customer information.
Multiple commercial Web applications	Passport	Passport authentication allows users to sign in once through a central authority. The user's identity is then available to any application using the Passport SDK. Customer information is maintained in a Passport profile, rather than in a local database.

Windows, Forms, and Passport authentication uses the classes found in the *System.Web.Security* namespace. To use these classes in your code, you should add an *Imports* statement (Visual Basic .NET) or a *using* statement (Visual C#) at the beginning of each module that performs authentication, as shown here:

Visual Basic .NET

```
Imports System.Web.Security
```

Visual C#

```
using System.Web.Security
```

The following sections describe how to authenticate and authorize users using each of the three techniques.

Using Authentication with HTM and HTML Files

The three ASP.NET authentication modes apply to files that are part of the Web application. That includes Web forms (.aspx), modules (.asax), and other resources that are processed through the Web application's executable. It does not automatically include HTML pages (.htm or .html). Those pages are handled by Internet Information Services (IIS), rather than ASP.NET. If you want to authenticate users who access HTML pages from within your Web application using Windows, Forms, or Passport authentication modes, you must map those files to the ASP.NET executable.

To map .htm and .html files to the ASP.NET executable using the IIS snap-in, follow these steps:

1. In the IIS snap-in, select the folder containing your Web application, and then choose Properties from the Action menu. IIS displays the Properties dialog box.

2. Click the Home Directory or Virtual Directory tab, and then click Configuration. IIS displays the Application Configuration dialog box, as shown in Figure 8-4.

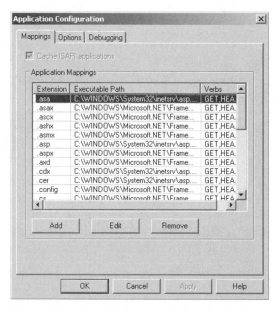

Figure 8-4   The Application Configuration dialog box

3. Click Add. IIS displays the Add/Edit Application Extension Mapping dialog box, as shown in Figure 8-5.

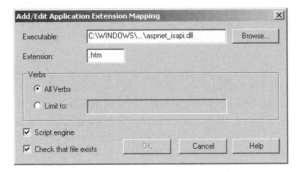

Figure 8-5   The Add/Edit Application Extension Mapping dialog box

4. Click Browse, and select the aspnet_isapi.dll file. That file is stored in the Windows Microsoft .NET Framework directory; the path will be something like C:\Windows\Microsoft.NET\Framework*versionnumber*\aspnet_isapi.dll.

5. Type **.htm** in the File Extension box, and click OK.

6. Repeat steps 3 through 5 for the .html file extension. Click OK to close the IIS dialog boxes when you've finished.

Lesson 2: Using Windows Authentication

Windows authentication uses the security features integrated into the Windows NT and Windows XP operating systems to authenticate and authorize Web application users. The advantage of Windows authentication is that your Web application can use the exact same security scheme that applies to your corporate network—user names, passwords, and permissions are the same for network resources and Web applications.

After this lesson, you will be able to

- Activate Windows authentication in your Web application
- Allow or deny access to your application based on the user's name or role in your organization
- Identify users within your application once they have logged on
- Use IIS settings to provide other forms of authentication
- Run code under the identity of the Web application user
- Run code under a specific identity

Estimated lesson time: 20 minutes

Enabling Windows Authentication

Windows authentication is the default authentication method when you create a new Web application project.

To see how Windows authentication works, follow these steps:

1. Create a new Web application project. For a Microsoft Visual Basic .NET project, change the *<authorization>* element in the Web.config file to appear as follows. For a Microsoft Visual C# project, add the following *<authorization>* element:

   ```
   <authorization>
       <deny users="?"  />
   </authorization>
   ```

2. Add the following HTML table definition to the project's startup Web form:

   ```
   <TABLE id="tblUser">
   <TR>
   <TD>Authenticated</TD>
   <TD><SPAN id="spnAuthenticated" runat="server"></SPAN></TD>
   </TR>
   <TR>
   <TD>User name</TD>
   <TD><SPAN id="spnUserName" runat="server"></SPAN></TD>
   ```

```
</TR>
<TR>
<TD>Authentication type</TD>
<TD><SPAN id="spnAuthenticationType" runat="server"></SPAN></TD>
</TR>
</TABLE>
```

3. Switch the Web form to Design view, and add the following code to the startup Web form's code-behind module:

Visual Basic .NET

```vb
' Add at module-level.
Imports System.Web.Security

Private Sub Page_Load(ByVal sender As System.Object, _
    ByVal e As System.EventArgs) Handles MyBase.Load
    spnAuthenticated.InnerText = User.Identity.IsAuthenticated
    spnUserName.InnerText = User.Identity.Name
    spnAuthenticationType.InnerText = User.Identity.AuthenticationType
End Sub
```

Visual C#

```csharp
// Add at module-level.
using System.Web.Security;

private void Page_Load(object sender, System.EventArgs e)
{
    spnAuthenticated.InnerText = User.Identity.IsAuthenticated.ToString();
    spnUserName.InnerText = User.Identity.Name;
    spnAuthenticationType.InnerText = User.Identity.AuthenticationType;
}
```

4. Run the project.

When the project runs locally, ASP.NET will authenticate you using the name that you used to log on to Windows, as shown in Figure 8-6.

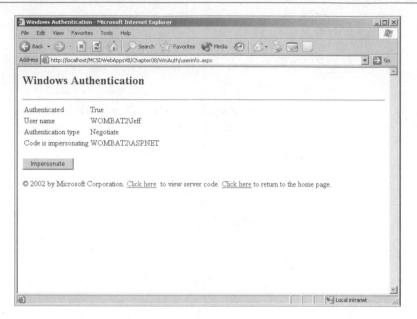

Figure 8-6   Windows authentication running locally

When you run the project remotely (as across the Internet), ASP.NET displays a dialog box in the browser to collect your user name and password, as shown in Figure 8-7.

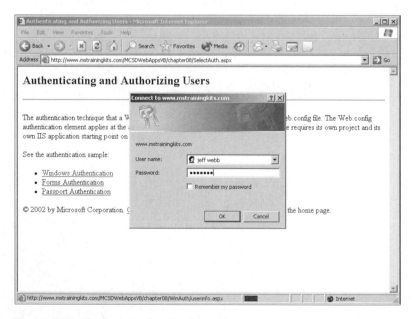

Figure 8-7   Windows authentication running remotely

If the user name and password you enter match those authorized for the network domain, ASP.NET authenticates you and authorizes you to use the application. If impersonation is enabled, the application executes using the permissions found in your user account. Otherwise, the application executes using the limited ASPNET user account.

When a user is authorized, ASP.NET issues an authorization certificate in the form of a cookie that persists for the duration of the user's session. The user's session ends when the browser closes or when the session times out.

Windows authentication works best in a domain-based network. Networks that use workgroups rather than domains have more limited use of network security features. Domain-based networks use a domain controller to identify and authorize network users, as shown in Figure 8-8.

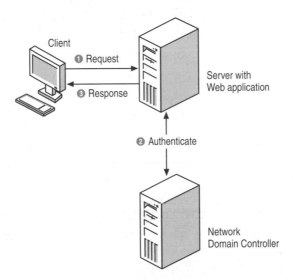

Figure 8-8   Domain-based network authentication

One of the key advantages of Windows authentication is that users who are logged on to the network don't have to log on again to access the Web application. They are automatically authenticated. Another advantage is that corporate users can use their same network user names and passwords when accessing the Web site remotely from home or while on business trips.

Windows authentication also lets you establish another layer of security by permitting or prohibiting specific users or groups of users. Also, Windows authentication overlaps similar features found in IIS. The following sections describe these topics in more detail.

Allowing or Denying Access to Specific Users

When the application uses Windows authentication, ASP.NET checks the project's
Web.config authorization list to see which network users are allowed to access the
application. The asterisk (*) and question mark (?) characters have special meaning
in the authorization list: the * character indicates all users; the ? character indicates
unauthenticated users. For example, the following authorization list from Web.config requires all users to be authenticated:

```
<authorization>
  <deny users="?"  />    <!-- Deny unauthenticated users -->
</authorization>
```

To restrict access to specific users, list their names separated by commas in an
<allow> element. When ASP.NET checks the authorization list in Web.config, it
accepts the first match that it finds. Be to sure to end the authorization list with a
<deny> element to deny access to any nonapproved users, as shown here:

```
<authorization>
<allow users="contoso\DeannaMeyer, contoso\MichaelEmanuel" />
    <!-- Allow two users. -->
<deny users="*"  />                    <!-- Deny anyone else. -->
</authorization>
```

This authorization list allows only two users access to the Web application. Everyone else is denied. In addition, Deanna Meyer and Michael Emanuel must have
accounts on the contoso network domain.

Using Role-Based Authorization

Role-based authorization lets you identify groups of users to allow or deny based
on their role in your organization. In Windows NT and Windows XP, roles map to
names used to identify user groups. Windows defines several built-in groups,
including Administrators, Users, and Guests. You can view, modify, or add groups
using the Computer Management console, as shown in Figure 8-9.

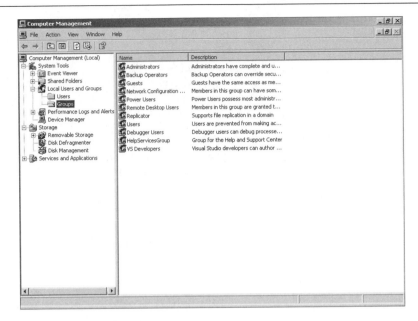

Figure 8-9   Viewing groups

To allow or deny access to certain groups of users, add the *<roles>* element to the authorization list in your Web application's Web.config file. For example, the following authorization list allows access only to users logged on to the contoso domain as system administrators:

```
<authorization>
    <allow roles="contoso\Administrators" />    <!-- Allow Administrators. -->
    <deny users="*"  />                          <!-- Deny anyone else. -->
</authorization>
```

Getting the User Identity

Once a user is authenticated and authorized, your application can get information about the user by using the *User* object's *Identity* property. The *Identity* property returns an object that includes the user name and role information, as shown in the following code:

Visual Basic .NET

```
Private Sub Page_Load(ByVal sender As System.Object, _
    ByVal e As System.EventArgs) Handles MyBase.Load
    spnAuthenticated.InnerText = User.Identity.IsAuthenticated
    spnUserName.InnerText = User.Identity.Name
    spnAuthenticationType.InnerText = User.Identity.AuthenticationType
End Sub
```

Visual C#

```
private void Page_Load(object sender, System.EventArgs e)
{
    spnAuthenticated.InnerText =
    User.Identity.IsAuthenticated.ToString();
    spnUserName.InnerText = User.Identity.Name;
    spnAuthenticationType.InnerText = User.Identity.AuthenticationType;
}
```

In addition, the *User* object provides an *IsInRole* method to determine the role of the current user, as in the following example:

Visual Basic .NET

```
If User.IsInRole("Administrators") Then
    ' Do something
End If
```

Visual C#

```
if(User.IsInRole("Administrators"))
    // Do something.
```

These methods and properties can be used in conjunction with the Global module's *AuthorizeRequest* event to customize the user authorization process. For example, you can use the *AuthorizeRequest* event to check user names against an external user file rather than use the list in Web.config.

Using IIS Settings with Windows Authentication

The authorization settings in Web.config overlap settings available in IIS. If authorization is set both in Web.config and in IIS, the IIS setting is evaluated first and then the setting in Web.config is evaluated. In general, this means that the most restrictive setting will be used.

To view authorization settings in IIS, follow these steps:

1. In the IIS snap-in, right-click the Web application's folder, and select Properties. IIS displays the folder's Properties dialog box.
2. Click the Directory Security tab, and then click Edit in the Anonymous Access And Authentication Control area. IIS displays the Authentication Methods dialog box, as shown in Figure 8-10.

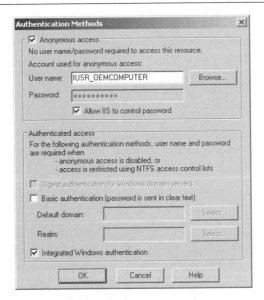

Figure 8-10   IIS authentication settings

The first group of settings in the dialog box controls anonymous access by unauthenticated users. Clearing the check box is the equivalent of specifying <*deny users="?"*> in Web.config. Allowing IIS to control the password for the anonymous account is highly recommended, but this setting might need to be overridden if your application is deployed over multiple servers.

The check boxes in the second group of dialog box controls allows your application to use Basic or Digest authentication in addition to Windows authentication. Those authentication methods provide less security than Windows authentication, Forms, or Passport authentication and are implemented through IIS rather than ASP.NET.

As you can see in Figure 8-10, you can enable multiple authentication methods through IIS. If multiple methods are enabled, you can detect which method was used to authenticate a user in code by using the *Identity* object's *Authentication-Type* method, as shown here:

Visual Basic .NET

```
Response.Write(User.Identity.AuthenticationType)
```

Visual C#

```
Response.Write(User.Identity.AuthenticationType);
```

For more information about Basic and Digest authentication, see the IIS Help.

Using Impersonation

The authentication and authorization settings in the Web.config file control access to your Web application from the outside world. However, once a user is authenticated, the application runs under the identity of the ASPNET user account by default. The ASPNET account is a limited user account created when you install the Microsoft .NET Framework.

Alternatively, you can set the application to run under the user's account by setting the application's *identity* element to enable impersonation, as shown here:

```
<configuration>
  <system.web>
    <!-- Impersonate the authenticated user in code -->
    <identity impersonate="true" />
  </system.web>
</configuration>
```

When the user requests a Web form from a folder containing the preceding Web.config settings, the Web form's code executes in the security context of the user's Windows account—not the default ASPNET user account. The code inherits the user's permissions (or lack of permissions), and access to resources is granted or denied based on those permissions.

To see the impersonated identity under which code is executing, use the *WindowsIdentity* class's *GetCurrent* method, as shown here:

Visual Basic .NET

```
Response.Write(System.Security.Principal.WindowsIdentity.GetCurrent().Name)
```

Visual C#

```
Response.Write(System.Security.Principal.WindowsIdentity.GetCurrent().Name);
```

The *identity* element can be used with any type of authentication; however, it is most useful with Windows authentication because Windows authentication users have accounts with specific permissions. Using the preceding Web.config settings with Forms or Passport authentication results in the ASP.NET code impersonating the generic IUSR_*machinename* account.

You can use the *identity* element to execute code using a specific Windows account. For example, the following Web.config setting causes code to run under the Administrator account:

```
<!-- Impersonate the Administrator account -->
<identity impersonate="true" username="Administrator" password="0#thip32x" />
```

You can combine this type of impersonation with folder-level authentication settings to grant authorized users administrative privileges by location. For example, the following Web.config settings allow the user Jane to execute code as the Administrator user in the /Admin folder. All other users are denied access.

```
<!-- From root-level Web.config file -->
<configuration>
  <system.web>
    <authentication mode="Windows" />
    <authorization>
      <deny users="?" />   <!-- Authenticate (but allow) all users. -->
    </authorization>
    <!-- Turn off impersonation (default). -->
    <identity impersonate="false" />
  </system.web>
</configuration>

<!-- From /Admin folder Web.config file -->
<configuration>
  <system.web>
    <authorization>
      <allow users="contoso\Jane" />   <!-- Allow only Jane. -->
      <deny users="*" />
    </authorization>
    <!-- Impersonate the Administrator account -->
    <identity impersonate="true" username="Administrator"
      password="0#thip32x" />
  </system.web>
</configuration>
```

This type of folder-level impersonation can also be used effectively with Forms or Passport authentication, because you are impersonating a specific user account instead of the generic IUSR_*machinename* account.

Lesson 3: Using Forms Authentication

Forms authentication automatically displays a designated Web form to collect user name and password information. Code associated with that Web form authenticates and authorizes users based on a user list stored in the application's Web.config file or in a separate user database.

The advantage of Forms authentication is that users do not have to be member of a domain-based network to have access to your application. Another advantage is that many Web applications—particularly commercial sites where customers order products—*want* to have access to user information. Forms authentication makes these types of applications easier to create.

After this lesson, you will be able to

- Activate Forms authentication for your Web application
- Create a Web form to collect user name and password information
- Authenticate users based on a user list stored in the application's Web.config file
- Add new users and authenticate existing ones from a database
- Limit access to specific locations

Estimated lesson time: 20 minutes

Enabling Forms Authentication

Forms authentication allows you to create your own database of users and validate the identity of those users when they visit your Web site.

To use Forms authentication to identify and authorize users, follow these steps:

1. Set the authentication mode in Web.config to Forms.
2. Create a Web form to collect logon information.
3. Create a file or database to store user names and passwords.
4. Write code to add new users to the user file or database.
5. Write code to authenticate users against the user file or database.

When someone accesses a Web application that uses Forms authentication, ASP.NET displays the logon Web form specified in Web.config. Once a user is authorized, ASP.NET issues an authorization certificate in the form of a cookie that persists for an amount of time specified by the authentication settings in Web.config. Figure 8-11 illustrates the authentication process.

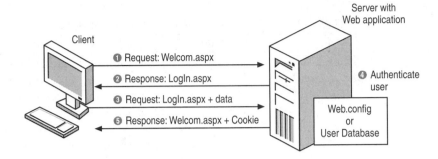

Figure 8-11   Forms authentication

The difference between Windows authentication and Forms authentication is that in Forms authentication your application performs all the authentication and authorization tasks. You must create Web forms and write code to collect user names and passwords and to check those items against a list of authorized users.

The following sections describe how to implement Forms authentication in your application based on the general steps listed earlier in this section.

Setting the Forms Authentication Mode

You set an application's authentication mode in the Web.config file's *<authorization>* element. To set your application to use Forms authentication, make the following changes to the Web.config file:

```
<authentication mode="Forms" >              <!-- Set authentication mode -->
  <forms loginUrl="LogIn.aspx" >            <!-- Specify a log on form -->
    <credentials passwordFormat="Clear">    <!-- Create a user list -->
      <user name="Jesse" password="JuneBug"/>
      <user name="Linda" password="Liste"/>
      <user name="Henry" password="Henry"/>
    </credentials>
  </forms>
</authentication>

<authorization>
  <deny users="?" />   <!--Deny all unauthenticated users -->
</authorization>
```

The preceding Web.config fragment shows a simplified example of Forms authentication using most of the default settings and including a user list as part of the Web.config file. Table 8-2 lists all the possible attributes for the elements that make up the Forms authentication settings.

Table 8-2   Forms Authentication Settings in Web.config

Element	Attribute	Description
<authentication>	*mode*	Set to *Forms* to enable Forms authentication.
<forms>	*name*	Use to set the name of the cookie in which to store the user's credential. The default is *.authaspx*. If more than one application on the server is using Forms authentication, you need to specify a unique cookie name for each application.
	loginUrl	Use to set the name of the Web form to display if the user has not already been authenticated. If omitted, the default is *Default.aspx*.
	protection	Use to set how ASP.NET protects the authentication cookie stored on the user's machine. The default is *All*, which performs encryption and data validation. Other possible settings are *Encryption*, *Validation*, and *None*.
	timeout	Use to set the number of minutes the authentication cookie persists on the user's machine. The default is *30*, indicating 30 minutes. ASP.NET renews the cookie automatically if it receives a request from the user and more than half of the allotted time has expired.
	path	Use to set the path used to store the cookie on the user's machine. The default is a backslash (\).
<credentials>	*passwordFormat*	Use to set the algorithm used to encrypt the user's password. The default is *SHA1*. Other possible settings are *MD5* and *Clear* (which prevents encryption).
<users>	*name*	Use to set the name of the user.
	password	Use to set the password for the user.

The *<credentials>* element allows you to store your user list in the Web.config file. That is convenient for simple authentication, where an administrator adds new users and sets their passwords, but it's not the best approach if you allow users to set up their own accounts or maintain their own passwords.

In those cases, you will want to create a users file or a users database to store user names and encrypted passwords. Using a database has the added benefit of allowing you to store all sorts of additional information about the user, such as shipping address and order history.

The following section shows how to authenticate users using credentials stored in Web.config. The subsequent sections show the more advanced (and more complicated) approach of using a user database.

Creating a LogIn Web Form

To authenticate users through Forms authentication, you need to create a Web form that allows users to log on. This Web form is identified by name in the *<forms>* element of Web.config.

The login Web form can be as simple as a pair of text boxes and a Button control, or it can appear on a page containing other, nonsecure content. For example, you can include logon fields on an application home page, as shown in Figure 8-12.

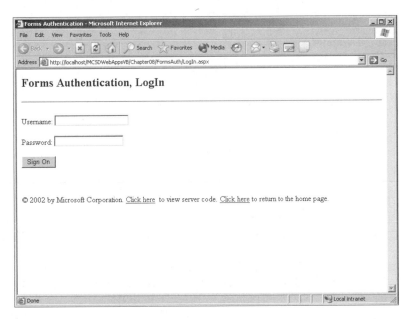

Figure 8-12   Login fields on an application home page

When the user clicks Sign On, the application authenticates the user name and password, issues an authentication certificate, and allows access to the rest of the application, as shown in the following code:

Visual Basic .NET

```
' Add at module-level.
Imports System.Web.Security

Private Sub butSignOn_Click(ByVal sender As System.Object, _
    ByVal e As System.EventArgs) Handles butSignOn.Click
    ' Authenticate username/password from <credentials>.
    If FormsAuthentication.Authenticate(txtUserName.Text, txtPassword.Text) _
```

```
            Then
                ' If found, display the application's Start page.
                FormsAuthentication.RedirectFromLoginPage(txtUserName.Text, True)
        Else
            ' Otherwise, clear the password.
            txtPassword.Text = ""
            ' If third try, display "Access Denied" page.
            If CInt(ViewState("Tries")) > 1 Then
                Response.Redirect("Denied.htm")
            Else
                ' Otherwise, increment number of tries.
                ViewState("Tries") = CInt(ViewState("Tries")) + 1
            End If
        End If
End Sub
```

Visual C#

```
// Add at module-level.
using System.Web.Security;

private void butSignOn_Click(object sender, System.EventArgs e)
{
    // Authenticate username/password from <credentials>.
    if (FormsAuthentication.Authenticate(txtUserName.Text,
        txtPassword.Text))
        // If found, display the application's Start page.
        FormsAuthentication.RedirectFromLoginPage(txtUserName.Text, true);
    else
    {
        // Otherwise, clear the password.
        txtPassword.Text = "";
        // If third try, display "Access Denied" page.
        if (System.Convert.ToInt32(ViewState["Tries"]) > 1)
            Response.Redirect("Denied.htm");
        else
            // Otherwise, increment number of tries.
            ViewState["Tries"] = System.Convert.ToInt32(ViewState["Tries"])
                + 1;
    }
}
```

There are a few important things to note about the preceding code:

- The *FormsAuthentication* class is part of the *System.Web.Security* namespace, so you must include that namespace using the Visual Basic .NET *Imports* statement or the Visual C# *using* statement, or the fully qualified references to the class.

- The *FormsAuthentication* class's *Authenticate* method checks the user name and password against the user list found in the *<credentials>* element of Web.config.

- The *FormsAuthentication* class's *RedirectFromLoginPage* method displays the application's start page. If the logon fields appear on the application's start page, you should disable them or otherwise indicate a successful logon.

- If the user name and password aren't valid, the code lets the user have two more tries before displaying an Access Denied page. That page is an HTML page rather than a Web form, since access to any Web forms in the application is also denied. If you redirect users to another page in this way, make sure that the page is outside the scope of the application.

Use the *FormsAuthentication* class to sign out when the user has finished with the application or when you want to remove the authentication cookie from his or her machine. For example, the following code ends the user's access to an application and requires him or her to sign back in to regain access:

Visual Basic .NET

```
Imports System.Web.Security

Private Sub butSignOut_Click(ByVal sender As System.Object, _
    ByVal e As System.EventArgs) Handles butSignOut.Click
    ' Remove authentication cookie.
    FormsAuthentication.SignOut()
    ' Redirect back to this page (displays log in screen).
    Response.Redirect("UserInfo.aspx")
End Sub
```

Visual C#

```
using System.Web.Security;

private void butSignOut_Click(object sender, System.EventArgs e)
{
    // Remove authentication cookie.
    FormsAuthentication.SignOut();
    // Redirect back to this page (displays log in screen).
    Response.Redirect("UserInfo.aspx");
}
```

Authenticating Users with a Database

The preceding sections showed how to authenticate users based on a list in Web.config. The *FormsAuthentication* class's *Authenticate* method is set up to read from that file automatically. That's fine if user names and passwords are created and maintained by a system administrator, but if you allow users to create their own user names or change their passwords, you'll need to store that information outside the Web.config file. This is because changing Web.config at run time causes the

Web application to restart, which resets any *Application* state and *Session* state variables used by the application.

You can store user names and passwords in any type of file; however, using a database has the following significant advantages:

- User names can be used as primary keys to store other information about the user.

- Databases can provide high performance for accessing user names and passwords.

- Adding, modifying, and accessing records are standardized through SQL.

When storing user names and passwords in a file or database, you have the option of encrypting them using the *FormsAuthentication* class's *HashPasswordForStoringInConfigFile* method. This uses the SHA1 or MD5 algorithms to encrypt data, as shown here:

Visual Basic .NET

```
' Encrypt the password.
Password = FormsAuthentication.HashPasswordForStoringInConfigFile(Password, _
    "SHA1")
```

Visual C#

```
Password = FormsAuthentication.HashPasswordForStoringInConfigFile(Password,
    "SHA1");
```

The following sections show how to add new user names and passwords to a simple database and how to use that database to authenticate users.

Adding Users to a Database

To add users to a database, collect the user name and password from two TextBox controls and provide an event procedure to add the user that displays a message indicating whether the user was added. The following event procedure calls the helper function *AddUser* to add the user name and password to the database:

Visual Basic .NET

```
Private Sub butNewUser_Click(ByVal sender As System.Object, _
    ByVal e As System.EventArgs) Handles butNewUser.Click
    If AddUser(txtUserName.Text, txtPassword.Text) Then
        spnNote.InnerText = "User added."
    Else
        spnNote.InnerText = "User exists. Choose a different user name."
    End If
End Sub
```

Visual C#

```csharp
private void butNewUser_Click(object sender, System.EventArgs e)
{
    if (AddUser(txtUserName.Text, txtPassword.Text))
        spnNote.InnerText = "User added.";
    else
        spnNote.InnerText = "User exists. Choose a different user name.";
}
```

The *AddUser* helper function shown in the following code encrypts the password before storing the user name and password in a database using the SQL INSERT command. If the user name already exists in the database, the exception-handling block catches the error and returns *False* to indicate that the user was not added.

Visual Basic .NET

```vbnet
Private Function AddUser(ByVal UserName As String, ByVal Password_
As String)
    As Boolean
    ' Declare variable to track success/failure.
    Dim bSuccess As Boolean
    ' Encrypt the password.
    Password =
        FormsAuthentication.HashPasswordForStoringInConfigFile(Password, _
        "SHA1")
    ' Create command to insert user name and password.
    Dim oleCommand As New OleDbCommand("INSERT INTO Users" + _
        " VALUES('" + UserName + "', '" + Password + "')", oledbUsers)
    ' Catch errors in case record already exists.
    Try
        ' Open the database connection.
        oledbUsers.Open()
        ' If record added, set success to true.
        If oleCommand.ExecuteNonQuery() Then bSuccess = True
        ' Close connection.
        oledbUsers.Close()
    Catch
        ' Otherwise, success if false.
        bSuccess = False
        ' Close connection.
        oledbUsers.Close()
    End Try
    ' Return success/failure.
    Return bSuccess
End Function
```

Visual C#

```csharp
private bool AddUser(string UserName, string Password)
{
    // Declare variable to track success/failure.
    bool bSuccess = false;
    // Encrypt the password.
    Password = FormsAuthentication.HashPasswordForStoringInConfigFile
        (Password, "SHA1");
    // Create command to insert user name and password.
    OleDbCommand oleCommand = new OleDbCommand("INSERT INTO Users" +
        " VALUES('" + UserName + "', '" + Password + "')", oledbUsers);
    // Catch errors in case record already exists.
    try
    {
        // Open the database connection.
        oledbUsers.Open();
        // If record added, set success to true.
        if (oleCommand.ExecuteNonQuery() != 0)
        {
            bSuccess = true;
            // Close connection.
            oledbUsers.Close();
        }
    }
    catch
    {
        // Otherwise, success if false.
        bSuccess = false;
        // Close connection.
        oledbUsers.Close();
    }
    // Return success/failure.
    return bSuccess;
}
```

Authenticating Users from a Database

When you authenticate users from Web.config, you use the *Authenticate* method. When you authenticate users from a database, you must write your own code to find and compare user names and passwords. The following event procedure uses the *CheckPassword* helper function to validate the user name and password text boxes before authenticating the user and allowing access to the application:

Visual Basic .NET

```vb
Private Sub butSignOn_Click(ByVal sender As System.Object, _
    ByVal e As System.EventArgs) Handles butSignOn.Click
    ' If user name and password are found,
    ' authorize the user and show start page.
    If CheckPassword(txtUserName.Text, txtPassword.Text) Then
```

```
                    FormsAuthentication.RedirectFromLoginPage(txtUserName.Text, True)
            Else
                ' Display message.
                spnNote.InnerText = "User name or password not found. Try again."
                ' Allow three tries to log in.
                ViewState("tries") = ViewState("tries") + 1
                If ViewState("tries") > 3 Then
                    Response.Redirect("Denied.htm")
                End If
            End If
        End If
End Sub
```

Visual C#

```
private void butSignOn_Click(object sender, System.EventArgs e)
{
    // Authenticate username/password from <credentials>.
    if (CheckPassword(txtUserName.Text, txtPassword.Text))
        // If found, display the application's Start page.
        FormsAuthentication.RedirectFromLoginPage(txtUserName.Text, true);
    else
    {
        // Otherwise, clear the password.
        txtPassword.Text = "";
        // Display message.
        spnNote.InnerText = "User name or password not found. Try again.";
        // If third try, display "Access Denied" page.
        if (System.Convert.ToInt32(ViewState["Tries"]) > 1)
            Response.Redirect("Denied.htm");
        else
        {
            // Otherwise, increment number of tries.
            ViewState["Tries"] =
            System.Convert.ToInt32(ViewState["Tries"]) + 1;
            if (System.Convert.ToInt32(ViewState["Tries"]) > 3)
                Response.Redirect("Denied.htm");
        }
    }
}
```

The *CheckPassword* helper function shown in the following code encrypts the password, finds the database record based on the user name, and compares the encrypted password against the password found in the database. Access to the database is performed within an exception-handling block to prevent locking conflicts from displaying errors to the user.

Visual Basic .NET

```vb
Private Function CheckPassword(ByVal UserName As String, _
    ByVal Password As String) As Boolean
    ' Declare variable to track success/failure.
    Dim bSuccess As Boolean
    ' Encrypt the password.
    Password = _
        FormsAuthentication.HashPasswordForStoringInConfigFile(Password, _
        "SHA1")
    ' Create command to get row from users table based on UserName.
    Dim oleCommand As New OleDbCommand("SELECT * FROM Users" + _
        " WHERE UserName='" + txtUserName.Text + "'", oledbUsers)
    ' Check for errors using database
    Try
        ' Open the database connection.
        oledbUsers.Open()
        ' Get the author ID.
        Dim rdrUsers As OleDbDataReader = oleCommand.ExecuteReader()
        While rdrUsers.Read()
            If Password = rdrUsers.Item("Password") Then bSuccess = True
        End While
        ' Close connection.
        oledbUsers.Close()
    Catch
        ' Otherwise set failure.
        bSuccess = False
        ' Close connection.
        oledbUsers.Close()
    End Try
    Return bSuccess
End Function
```

Visual C#

```csharp
private bool CheckPassword(string UserName, string Password)
{
    // Declare variable to track success/failure.
    bool bSuccess = false;
    // Encrypt the password.
    Password =
        FormsAuthentication.HashPasswordForStoringInConfigFile(Password,
        "SHA1");
    // Create command to get row from users table based on UserName.
    OleDbCommand oleCommand = new OleDbCommand("SELECT * FROM Users" +
        " WHERE UserName='" + txtUserName.Text + "'", oledbUsers);
    // Check for errors using database
    try
    {
        // Open the database connection.
        oledbUsers.Open();
```

```
        // Get the author ID.
        OleDbDataReader rdrUsers = oleCommand.ExecuteReader();
        while (rdrUsers.Read())
        {
            if (Password == rdrUsers["Password"].ToString())
                bSuccess = true;
        }
        // Close connection.
        oledbUsers.Close();
    }
    catch
    {
        // Otherwise set failure.
        bSuccess = false;
        // Close connection.
        oledbUsers.Close();
    }
    return bSuccess;
}
```

Controlling Access to Specific Locations

The authorization settings in the Web.config file apply hierarchically within the folder structure of a Web application. For instance, you might want to allow all users access to the root folder of a Web application but restrict access to Web forms (and tasks) available from a subfolder. To do this, set the authentication type in the root folder's Web.config file, and then use the <*authorization*> element in the subfolder's Web.config file to restrict access.

In the following Web.config settings, the root folder settings allow all users access and the /Restricted folder's Web.config file allows access only to Henry:

```
<!-- From Web.config in application's root folder -->
<configuration>
  <system.web>
    <authentication mode="Forms" >          <!-- Set authentication mode -->
      <forms loginUrl="LogIn.aspx" >        <!-- Specify a log on form -->
        <credentials passwordFormat="Clear"><!-- Create a user list -->
          <user name="Jesse" password="JuneBug"/>
          <user name="Linda" password="Leste"/>
          <user name="Henry" password="Henry" />
        </credentials>
      </forms>
    </authentication>
    <authorization>
      <allow users="*" />  <!-- Allow all users -->
    </authorization>
  </system.web>
</configuration>
```

```
<!-- From Web.config in /Restricted folder -->
<configuration>
  <system.web>
    <authorization>
      <allow users="Henry" /> <!-- Allow Henry -->
      <deny users="*" />      <!-- Deny everyone else -->
    </authorization>
  </system.web>
</configuration>
```

When you run a Web application with the preceding Web.config settings, users are not authenticated until they request a resource from the /Restricted folder. When a user requests a Web form from the /Restricted folder, the LogIn.aspx Web form is displayed and the user is authenticated.

Note   Authentication type (Windows, Forms, or Passport) can be set only at the application's root folder. To change authentication type in a subfolder, you must create a new Web application project and application starting point for that subfolder.

Lesson 4: Using Passport Authentication

Passport authentication identifies users via Microsoft Passport's single sign-on service. Microsoft Passport is meant to provide Internet users with a single identity that they can use to visit a wide variety of Web sites that require authentication. Information about the user is available to your application through a profile that is stored with Microsoft.

The advantages of Passport authentication are that the user doesn't have to remember separate user names and passwords for various Web sites and that the user can maintain his or her profile information in a single location. Passport authentication also provides access to other Microsoft services, such as Passport Express Purchase.

After this lesson, you will be able to

- Install the Passport SDK
- Activate Passport authentication for your application
- Get information from the user's Passport profile
- Sign out the user from your Web application by deleting the Passport cookies

Estimated lesson time: 20 minutes

Enabling Passport Authentication

Passport authentication uses the Microsoft centralized authentication provider to identify users. Passport provides a way to for users to use a single identity across multiple Web applications. To use Passport authentication in your Web application, you must install the Passport SDK, which is available by searching the Downloads area of the Microsoft Developer Network (MSDN), at *http:// msdn.microsoft.com/ downloads*.

The Passport SDK is free for preproduction development and testing. To deploy a site for public use, you must obtain an annual license from Microsoft. You can obtain more information about licensing from *http://www.microsoft.com/netservices/passport/*.

When a user accesses an application that implements Passport authentication, ASP.NET checks the user's machine for a current passport authentication cookie. If none is found, ASP.NET directs the user to a Passport sign-on page. Once the user signs in, the Passport service authenticates the user, stores an authentication cookie on the user's computer, and directs the user back to the originally requested Web page. Figure 8-13 illustrates the Passport authentication process.

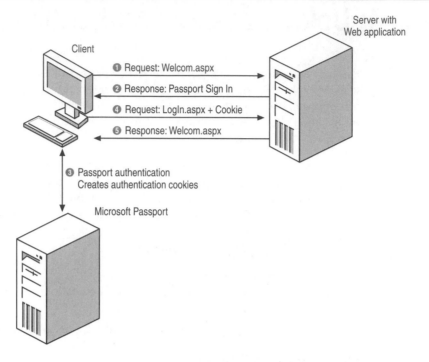

Figure 8-13   The Passport authentication process

To use Passport authentication, follow these steps:

1. Install the Passport SDK. Passport is not included with Visual Studio, although the .NET Framework does include classes for working with the Passport SDK once it is installed.

2. Set the application's authentication mode to Passport in Web.config. Set authorization to deny unauthenticated users.

3. Use the *PassportAuthentication_OnAuthenticate* event to access the user's Passport profile to identify and authorize the user.

4. Implement a sign-out procedure to remove Passport cookies from the user's machine.

For example, the following Web.config settings enable Passport authentication and require all users to be authenticated:

```
<authentication mode="Passport" />

<authorization>
  <deny users="?" /> <!-- Deny unauthenticated users -->
</authorization>
```

When you run an application locally with these settings, you are automatically redirected to the Passport sign-on page. If you've installed the preproduction (unlicensed) version of the Passport SDK, the sign-on page is not the same as the page displayed for a deployed site. Figure 8-14 shows the two Passport sign-on pages.

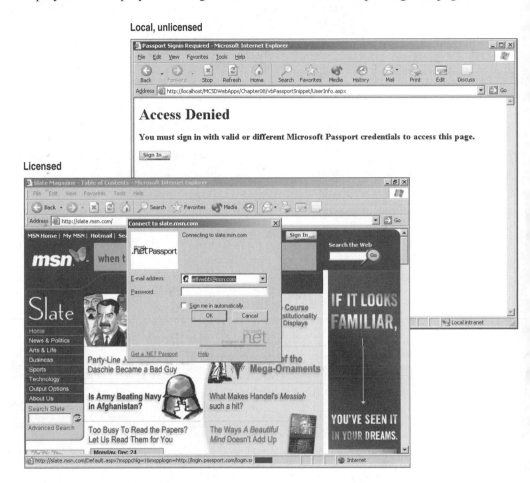

Figure 8-14   Passport sign-on pages

Once the user has signed in, Passport stores an authorization cookie on the user's machine and redirects the user back to his or her originally requested page. Passport stores a profile of information about the user. You can access that profile from the *PassportAuthentication_OnAuthenticate* event in the Global.asax module, as shown here:

Visual Basic .NET

```vbnet
' Add at module-level.
Imports System.Web.Security

Private Sub PassportAuthentication_OnAuthenticate(ByVal sender As Object, _
    ByVal e As PassportAuthenticationEventArgs)
    ' Get Session's passport identity if authenticated.
    If e.Identity.IsAuthenticated Then
        Response.Write("Name: " & e.Identity.Item("FirstName") & _
            " " & e.Identity.Item("LastName") & "<br>")
        Response.Write("Address: " & e.Identity.Item("City") & _
            "    " & e.Identity.Item("PostalCode") & "<br>")
        Response.Write("Email: " & e.Identity.Item("PreferredEmail") & _
            "<br>")
        Response.Write("Passport ID: " & e.Identity.Name & "<br>")
    End If
End Sub
```

Visual C#

```csharp
// Add at module-level.
using System.Web.Security;

protected void PassportAuthentication_OnAuthenticate(Object sender,
PassportAuthenticationEventArgs e)
{
    // Get Session's passport identity if authenticated.
    if (e.Identity.IsAuthenticated)
    {
        Response.Write("Name: " + e.Identity["FirstName"] +
            " " + e.Identity["LastName"] + "<br>");
        Response.Write("Address: " + e.Identity["City"] +
            "    " + e.Identity["PostalCode"] + "<br>");
        Response.Write("Email: " + e.Identity["PreferredEmail"] +
            "<br>");
        Response.Write("Passport ID: " + e.Identity.Name + "<br>");
    }
}
```

The preceding code displays the user's name, location, and identity information from his or her Passport profile. If you've installed the preproduction Passport SDK, that information reflects a test account rather than live data, as shown in Figure 8-15.

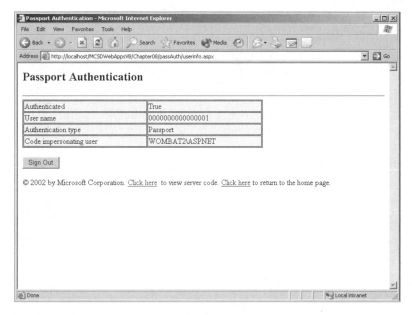

Figure 8-15   Passport identity information for the test account

The Passport authorization and profile information are stored in five separate cookies on the user's machine. The Passport SDK requires that you remove these cookies when the user signs out of your Web application. The following event procedure demonstrates how to sign out by deleting the Passport cookies:

Visual Basic .NET

```
Private Sub butSignOut_Click(ByVal sender As System.Object, _
    ByVal e As System.EventArgs) Handles butSignOut.Click
    ' Sign out by deleting Passport cookies.
    Response.Cookies("MSPProf").Expires = Now
    Response.Cookies("MSPAuth").Expires = Now
    Response.Cookies("MSPSecAuth").Expires = Now
    Response.Cookies("MSPProfC").Expires = Now
    Response.Cookies("MSPConsent").Expires = Now
    ' Redisplay this page (goes back to sign-on).
    Response.Redirect("UserInfo.aspx")
End Sub
```

Visual C#

```
private void butSignOut_Click(object sender, System.EventArgs e)
{
    // Sign out by deleting Passport cookies.
    Response.Cookies["MSPProf"].Expires = DateTime.Now;
    Response.Cookies["MSPAuth"].Expires = DateTime.Now;
```

```
        Response.Cookies["MSPSecAuth"].Expires = DateTime.Now;
        Response.Cookies["MSPProfC"].Expires = DateTime.Now;
        Response.Cookies["MSPConsent"].Expires = DateTime.Now;
        // Redisplay this page (goes back to sign-on).
        Response.Redirect("UserInfo.aspx");
}
```

Passport authentication also provides additional commercial and child-protection features that are explained in the Passport SDK.

Lesson 5: Providing Secure Communication

Up to now, we've discussed security as a matter of identifying users and preventing unauthorized users from accessing your Web applications, but it's just as important to ensure that sensitive data sent across the Internet can't be read by others.

To provide secure communication across the Internet, IIS supports a standardized means of encrypting and decrypting Web requests and responses. This cryptography requires that you request an encryption key called a **server certificate** from an independent third party called a **certificate authority**.

After this lesson, you will be able to

- Understand the process of using the Secure Sockets Layer (SSL) in IIS
- Get a server certificate to enable secure, encrypted communication between your Web application and users
- Begin secure communication between a user and your Web application
- End secure communication
- Require secure communication before users can access a Web form

Estimated lesson time: 20 minutes

Enabling Secure Communication

The **Secure Sockets Layer (SSL)** is the standard means of ensuring that data sent over the Internet can't be read by others. When a user requests a secure Web page, the server generates an encryption key for the user's session and then encrypts the page's data before sending a response. On the client side, the browser uses that same encryption key to decrypt the requested Web page and to encrypt new requests sent from that page. Figure 8-16 illustrates the process.

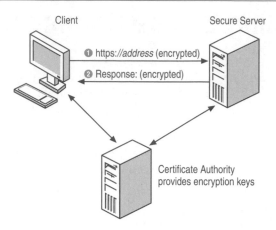

Figure 8-16   Secure communication using SSL

Using SSL in your application requires special authorization from a recognized certificate authority. This authorization comes in the form of a server certificate, which you install in IIS to identify your server. The certificate authority licenses server certificates (for a fee) and acts as a clearinghouse to verify your server's identity over the Internet.

When a user's browser begins secure communications, it requests the server certificate and checks it against a list of trusted sites provided by the certificate authority. If the server certificate does not match one of the sites already authorized by the user, or if the server certificate does not match the Web address for which it was registered, or if there are any other problems with the server certificate, the browser displays a warning, as shown in Figure 8-17.

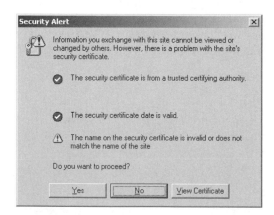

Figure 8-17   Problems with the server certificate

In this way, the certificate authority not only provides encryption for secure data transmission, but it also provides assurance to users that your Web site is authentic.

The largest certificate authority is VeriSign. At the time of this writing, in addition to their fee-based services, they also offer free trial certificates for testing and evaluation at *http:// www.verisign.com.*

To use SSL in your Web application, follow these steps:

1. Generate a certificate request from IIS.
2. Request a certificate from a certificate authority.
3. Install the certificate on the server using IIS.
4. Install the certificate on browsers if you are using a test certificate.
5. Use the Secure Hypertext Transfer Protocol (HTTPS) when accessing secure pages in your application.

The following sections describe these steps in greater detail.

Generating a Certificate Request

Before you can request a server certificate from a certificate authority, you must generate a certificate request from IIS. The certificate request contains encrypted information about your server that the certificate authority uses to identify your server over the Internet.

To generate a certificate request from the IIS snap-in:

1. Select Default Web Site in the console tree of the IIS snap-in, and then choose Properties from the Action menu. IIS displays the Default Web Site Properties dialog box.
2. Click the Directory Security tab in the Properties dialog box, and then click Server Certificate. IIS starts the Web Server Certificate Wizard, as shown in Figure 8-18.

Figure 8-18   The Web Server Certificate Wizard

3. Step through the wizard by reading each screen and clicking Next. The wizard instructions are straightforward.

4. When you click Finish at the end, the wizard creates an encrypted text file with the .cer file extension. That file is the certificate request that you send to the certificate authority.

IIS requires that a certificate be created at the server root before secure communications can be created or configured for subordinate sites on the server. That's why you have to select Default Web Site (or the root Web site if you have renamed it) in step 1. After you have installed a server certificate at the root, you can repeat the process for subordinate sites if you want separate certificates for those sites.

Requesting a Certificate

The process of requesting a server certificate from a certificate authority varies depending on the certificate authority you select. As mentioned earlier, VeriSign provides test certificates at no cost, which suits the purposes of this book very well!

To request a server certificate, follow these steps:

1. Visit the certificate authority's Web site, and request a server certificate for SSL. The various levels of security and support are typically based on an annual fee.

2. Select the type of server certificate you want to request, and complete the registration information for the request.

3. Copy or e-mail the certificate request you created in the preceding section to the certificate authority.

Once approved, the certificate authority will send you the server certificate, usually as part of an e-mail message. Save the certificate as a text file with the .cer file extension by cutting and pasting it into Notepad or some other editor, as shown in Figure 8-19.

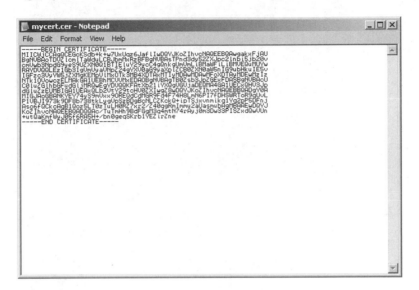

Figure 8-19   Saving the server certificate

Installing the Certificate

After you have saved your server certificate, you can install it in IIS to enable SSL for your Web applications.

To install a server certificate in IIS:

1. Select Default Web Site in the console tree of the IIS snap-in, and then choose Properties from the Action menu. IIS displays the Default Web Site Properties dialog box.
2. Click the Directory Security tab in the Properties dialog box, and then click Server Certificate. IIS starts the Web Server Certificate Wizard.
3. Click Next, and select Process The Pending Request And Install The Certificate, as shown in Figure 8-20.

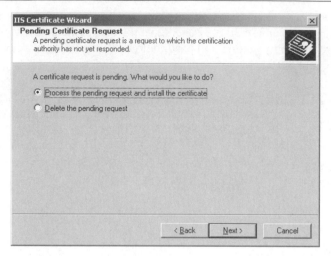

Figure 8-20   Installing the certificate with the IIS Web Server Certificate Wizard

4. Click Next, and enter the name of the certificate file, as shown in Figure 8-21. The certificate file is the file you created in the preceding section.

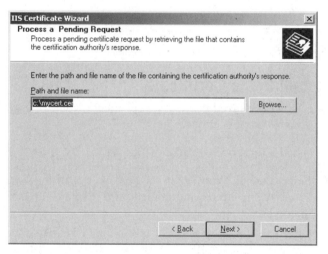

Figure 8-21   Entering the name of the server certificate file

5. Click Next, and then click Finish to complete the installation.

Using Secure Communications

After you have installed the server certificate, secure communication is enabled for any Web pages requested through HTTPS. For example, the following hyperlink displays a secure Web page, as shown in Figure 8-22.

```
<a href="https://www.contoso.com/mscdkit/Secure.aspx">Go to secure page.</a>
```

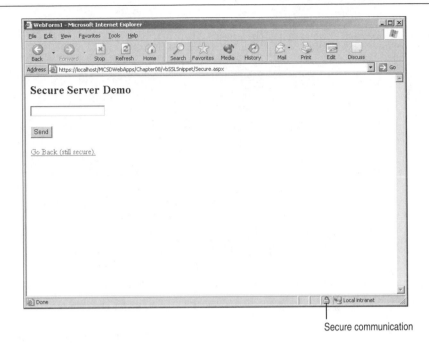

Secure communication

Figure 8-22   Secure Web page

The protocol HTTPS is what initializes the secure communication. When you've begun secure communication, it continues until you specify a nonsecure site. For example, clicking the Go Back link on the page shown in Figure 8-22 continues the secure communication because the link uses a relative address, as shown here:

```
<a href="Default.aspx">Go Back (still secure).</a>
```

To end secure communication, you need to include http in the URL, as in the following link:

```
<a href="http://www.contoso.com/mscdkit/Default.aspx">
Go Back (not secure).</a>
```

IIS lets you require secure communication for specific folders or files in your Web application. This prevents users from accidentally (or intentionally) viewing a secure page using nonsecure HTTP.

To require secure communication for a Web page using IIS, follow these steps:

1. Select the folder or file that requires secure communication, and then choose Properties from the Action menu. IIS displays the Properties dialog box.

2. Click the Directory Security tab, and then click Edit in the Secure Communications group. IIS displays the Secure Communications dialog box, as shown in Figure 8-23.

Figure 8-23   The Secure Communications dialog box

3. Select the Require Secure Channel (SSL) check box, and click OK.

When you require secure communication for a Web page, that page can't be viewed using HTTP. The user must type in or click a link using https; otherwise, access is denied, as shown in Figure 8-24.

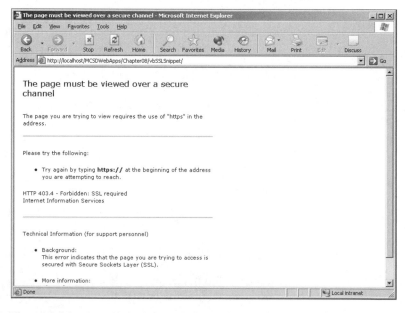

Figure 8-24   Access denied

Because the difference between using http and https is a somewhat obscure distinction for most users to remember, it's important to provide an http entry point for your application that links to the secure (HTTPS) pages. The http entry point can be simply a default page within the Web site that immediately redirects the user to the secure site. Requiring secure communication for an entire Web site is a sure way to cut traffic down to zero!

Summary

- Authentication is the process of identifying users. Authorization is the process of granting access to those users.

- The default method of access to a Web application is anonymous access. Anonymous users are granted access through the Windows IUSER_*machinename* user account, and the Web application's code runs using the ASPNET user account.

- Use the <*identity*> element in the Web.config file to run code using the permissions of a specific user.

- ASP.NET provides three authentication modes through the *System.Web.Security* namespace: Windows, Forms, and Passport.

- HTML pages aren't automatically included under ASP.NET authentication. To ensure that users are authenticated before they can view those types of files, use IIS to map the .htm and .html file extensions to the ASP.NET executable.

- To require authentication, add a <*deny users="?"*> element in the authorization section of Web.config. This applies to all three authentication types.

- Use the <*authorization*> element to allow or deny access to users under Windows authentication.

- To restrict access to a subfolder, add a Web.config file containing an <*authorization*> element specifying the users allowed to access the folder.

- Use the <*credentials*> element or an external user database to allow users under Forms authentication.

- Changing the Web.config file restarts the Web application, so it's not a good idea to add users to the Web.config <*credentials*> element at run time. Instead, use an external file or database to store user names and passwords.

- Install the Passport SDK to enable the Passport classes in the *System.Web.Security* namespace.

- To enable secure, encrypted communication over the Internet, install a server certificate and use HTTPS.

Lab: Creating a Secure Application

In this lab, you'll create a simple application that uses Forms authentication to identify and authorize users. The application allows new users to add their user name and password, allows existing users to sign in, and displays the user's identity once he or she has signed in. When complete, the Web application will appear as shown in Figure 8-25.

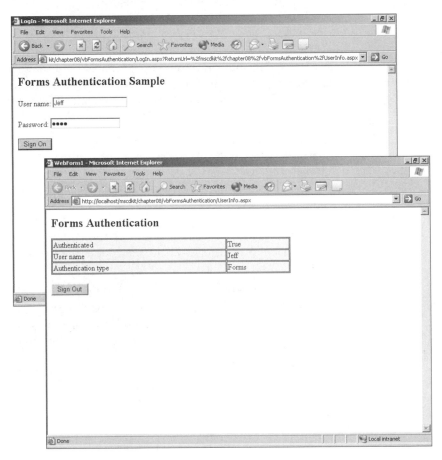

Figure 8-25   The LogIn and UserInfo Web forms

Estimated lesson time: 30 minutes

Exercise 1: Enable Forms Authentication

To enable Forms authentication:

1. Create a new ASP.NET Web Forms application, and open the Web.config file generated for the project.

2. Make the changes to the *<authentication>* element shown here:

```
<authentication mode="Forms">
  <forms loginUrl="LogIn.aspx">
    <credentials passwordFormat="SHA1">
    </credentials>
  </forms>
</authentication>
```

3. The preceding authentication settings enable Forms authentication, direct unauthenticated users to the LogIn.aspx Web form, and enable password encryption using the SHA1 algorithm. To require authentication using these settings, add the following *<authorization>* element to the Web.config file:

```
<authorization>
  <deny users="?" /> <!-- Deny unauthorized users -->
</authorization>
```

This authorization setting denies access to any unauthenticated users, thus forcing authentication.

When the changes to Web.config have been made, you can create the LogIn.aspx Web form that allows users to add new accounts and to log on to existing ones.

Exercise 2: Create the LogIn Web Form

In this exercise, you'll create a Web form named LogIn.aspx and a data file named Users.xml that are used to authenticate users. Because this is a simplified example, LogIn.aspx allows users to create a new account if their user name was not found.

In the real world, you might want to direct users to a separate Web form for creating new accounts or you might want an administrator to create their accounts and e-mail their passwords back to them. In either case, the basic concepts are the same.

To create the LogIn Web form and user data file:

1. Use Visual Studio or another text editor to create a text file containing the following line:

```
<users name="" password="" />
```

The sample will use this file to as a template to store user names and passwords. Because passwords will be encrypted, the first name and passwords are blank— you can delete this line later, after other user names and passwords have been added.

2. Create the LogIn.aspx Web form. This Web form contains text boxes, validation, and other controls, as shown in the following table.

Control type	Property	Value
Label	*Text*	*User name:*
TextBox	*ID*	*txtUserName*
RequiredFieldValidator	*ID*	*vldUserName*
	ControlToValidate	*txtUserName*
	ErrorMessage	*Name is required.*
Label	*Text*	*Password:*
TextBox	*ID*	*txtPassword*
	TextMode	*Password*
RequiredFieldValidator	*ID*	*vldPassword*
	ControlToValidate	*txtPassword*
	ErrorMessage	*Password is required.*
Button	*ID*	*butSignOn*
	Text	*Sign On*
Button	*ID*	*butAddUser*
	Text	*Add User*
	Visible	*False*
Label	*ID*	*lblStatus*

3. Begin writing the code for LogIn.aspx by adding the following line to beginning of the Login.aspx code module:

Visual Basic .NET

```
Imports System.Web.Security
```

Visual C#

```
using System.Web.Security;
```

4. Add the following code to the butSignOn control's Click event procedure to check the user name and password and to prompt the user if the user name is not found. The event procedure will use two helper functions: *UserExists* to check whether the user name exists in Users.xml, and *PasswordValid* to check whether the entered password is valid.

Visual Basic .NET

```
Private Sub butSignOn_Click(ByVal sender As System.Object, _
    ByVal e As System.EventArgs) Handles butSignOn.Click
    ' Check the user name.
    If UserExists(txtUserName.Text) Then
```

```
                            ' Check the password (encrypted).
                            If PasswordValid(txtUserName.Text, txtPassword.Text) Then
                                ' Sign the user on.
                                FormsAuthentication.RedirectFromLoginPage(txtUserName.Text, _
                                    True)
                            Else
                                ' Display an invalid password message.
                                lblStatus.Text = "Password does not match. Try again."
                            End If
                        Else
                            ' If user name not found, offer to add it.
                            lblStatus.Text =
                    "User name not found. Click Add User to add it now."
                            ' Make Add User button visible.
                            butAddUser.Visible = True
                        End If
                        ' Keep track of tries.
                        Session("Tries") = CInt(Session("Tries")) + 1
                        If Session("Tries") > 2 Then
                            ' After third try, deny access.
                            Response.Redirect("Denied.htm")
                        End If
                    End Sub
```

Visual C#

```
private void butSignOn_Click(object sender, System.EventArgs e)
{
    // Check the user name.
    if (UserExists(txtUserName.Text))
        // Check the password (encrypted).
        if (PasswordValid(txtUserName.Text, txtPassword.Text))
            // Sign the user on.
            FormsAuthentication.RedirectFromLoginPage(txtUserName.Text,
                true);
        else
            // Display an invalid password message.
            lblStatus.Text = "Password does not match. Try again.";
    else
    {
        // If user name not found, offer to add it.
        lblStatus.Text = "User not found. Click Add User to add it now.";
        // Make Add User button visible.
        butAddUser.Visible = true;
    }
    // Keep track of tries.
    ViewState["Tries"] = System.Convert.ToInt32(ViewState["Tries"]) + 1;
    if (System.Convert.ToInt32(ViewState["Tries"]) > 3)
        Response.Redirect("Denied.htm");
}
```

5. Add the *UserExists* and *PasswordValid* functions to load the Users.xml file into a data set and then search through the data set for a matching user name and password. If a match is found, the functions return *True*; otherwise, they return *False* as shown below:

Visual Basic .NET

```
Private Function UserExists(ByVal UserName As String) As Boolean
    ' Create a data set to read the XML file.
    Dim dsUsers As New DataSet()
    ' Use error handling in case is file missing.
    Try
        ' Build the Users.xml file path.
        Dim strXMLFile As String = Server.MapPath(".") & _
          "\Users.xml"
        ' Read the file
        dsUsers.ReadXml(strXMLFile, XmlReadMode.InferSchema)
        ' For each row in the Users table.
        Dim rowUser As DataRow
        For Each rowUser In dsUsers.Tables("Users").Rows
            ' Check for name match.
            If rowUser("name") = UserName Then
                Return True
                Exit For
            End If
        Next
    Catch
        ' In case of error return False.
        Return False
    Fnd Try
End Function


Private Function PasswordValid(ByVal UserName As String, _
    ByVal Password As String)
    ' Create a data set to read the XML file.
    Dim dsUsers As New DataSet()
    ' Use error handling in case is file missing.
    Try
        ' Build the Users.xml file path.
        Dim strXMLFile As String = Server.MapPath(".") & _
          "\Users.xml"
        ' Read the file
        dsUsers.ReadXml(strXMLFile, XmlReadMode.InferSchema)
        ' For each row in the Users table.
        Dim rowUser As DataRow
        For Each rowUser In dsUsers.Tables("Users").Rows
            ' Check for name match.
            If rowUser("name") = UserName Then
                If rowUser("password") = _
                    FormsAuthentication.HashPasswordForStoringInConfigFile_
```

```
                            (Password, "SHA1") Then
                            Return True
                            Exit For
                        End If
                    End If
            Next
        Catch
            ' In case of error return false.
            Return False
        End Try
End Function
```

Visual C#

```csharp
private bool UserExists(string UserName)
{
    // Create a data set to read the XML file.
    DataSet dsUsers = new DataSet();
    // Use error handling in case is file missing.
    try
    {
        // Build the Users.xml file path.
        string strXMLFile = Server.MapPath(".") +
            "\\Users.xml";
        // Read the file
        dsUsers.ReadXml(strXMLFile, XmlReadMode.InferSchema);
        // For each row in the Users table.
        foreach (DataRow rowUser in dsUsers.Tables["Users"].Rows)
            // Check for name match.
            if (rowUser["name"].ToString() == UserName)
                return true;
    }
    catch
    {
        // In case of error return False.
        return false;
    }
    // Otherwise, return false
    return false;
}

private bool PasswordValid(string UserName, string Password)
{
    // Create a data set to read the XML file.
    DataSet dsUsers = new DataSet();
    // Use error handling in case is file missing.
    try
    {
        // Build the Users.xml file path.
        string strXMLFile = Server.MapPath(".") +
```

```
                       "\\Users.xml";
                   // Read the file
                   dsUsers.ReadXml(strXMLFile, XmlReadMode.InferSchema);
                   // For each row in the Users table.
                   foreach (DataRow rowUser in dsUsers.Tables["Users"].Rows)
                       // Check for name match.
                       if (rowUser["name"].ToString() == UserName)
                           if (rowUser["password"].ToString() ==
                               FormsAuthentication.HashPasswordForStoringInConfigFile
                               (Password, "SHA1"))
                               return true;
               }
               catch
               {
                   // In case of error return False.
                   return false;
               }
               // Otherwise, return false.
               return false;
       }
```

6. The *PasswordValid* function in the preceding code uses the *HashPasswordFor-StoringInConfigFile* method because the passwords are stored using encryption. Create an *AddUser* function using the same method to store the password in Users.xml, as shown in the following code:

Visual Basic .NET

```
Private Sub butAddUser_Click(ByVal sender As System.Object, _
    ByVal e As System.EventArgs) Handles butAddUser.Click
    If AddUser(txtUserName.Text, txtPassword.Text) Then
        ' Display success.
        lblStatus.Text = "User added. Click Sign On to continue."
        ' Hide button.
        butAddUser.Visible = False
    Else
        ' Display failure.
        lblStatus.Text =_
        "User could not be added. Choose a different name."
    End If
End Sub

Private Function AddUser(ByVal UserName As String, ByVal Password _
    As String)
    ' If the user already exists, return False and exit.
    If UserExists(UserName) Then
        Return False
        Exit Function
    End If
    ' Otherwise, add user to XML file.
    Dim dsUsers As New DataSet()
```

```vb
' Use error handling in case is file missing.
Try
    ' Build the Users.xml file path.
    Dim strXMLFile As String = Server.MapPath(".") & _
      "\Users.xml"
    ' Read the file.
    dsUsers.ReadXml(strXMLFile, XmlReadMode.InferSchema)
    ' Add a new row.
    Dim rowUser As DataRow = dsUsers.Tables("users").NewRow()
    ' Set Username.
    rowUser("name") = UserName
    ' Set password (encrypted).
    rowUser("password") = _
      FormsAuthentication.HashPasswordForStoringInConfigFile _
      (Password, "SHA1")
    ' Add row.
    dsUsers.Tables("users").Rows.Add(rowUser)
    ' Write data set.
    dsUsers.WriteXml(strXMLFile)
    Return True
Catch
    ' In case of error return False.
    Return False
End Try
End Function
```

Visual C#

```csharp
private void butAddUser_Click(object sender, System.EventArgs e)
{
    if (AddUser(txtUserName.Text, txtPassword.Text))
    {
        // Display success.
        lblStatus.Text = "User added. Click Sign On to continue.";
        // Hide button.
        butAddUser.Visible = false;
    }
    else
        // Display failure.
        lblStatus.Text =
"User could not be added. Choose a different name.";
}

private bool AddUser(string UserName, string Password)
{
    // If the user already exists, return False and exit.
    if (UserExists(UserName))
    {
        return false;
    }
```

```
            // Otherwise, add user to XML file.
            DataSet dsUsers = new DataSet();
            // Use error handling in case is file missing.
            try
            {
                // Build the Users.xml file path.
                string strXMLFile  = Server.MapPath(".") +
                    "\\Users.xml";
                // Read the file.
                dsUsers.ReadXml(strXMLFile, XmlReadMode.InferSchema);
                // Add a new row.
                DataRow rowUser  = dsUsers.Tables["users"].NewRow();
                // Set Username.
                rowUser["name"] = UserName;
                // Set password (encrypted).
                rowUser["password"] =
                    FormsAuthentication.HashPasswordForStoringInConfigFile
                    (Password, "SHA1");
                // Add row.
                dsUsers.Tables["users"].Rows.Add(rowUser);
                // Write data set.
                dsUsers.WriteXml(strXMLFile);
                return truc;
            }
            catch
            {
                // In case of error return false.
                return false;
            }
        }
```

Exercise 3: Display User Information

In this exercise, you'll create the UserInfo.aspx Web form to display the user's name and authentication information using the *User* class's *Identity* object. You'll also create an HTML page to display if access is denied. Because HTML pages aren't automatically included in a Web application's authentication scheme, users can access that page even if they aren't authenticated.

To display user information:

1. Create the UserInfo.aspx Web form and make it the start page for the application. Unauthenticated users will actually be directed to the LogIn.aspx Web form first, because that's the login page specified in Web.config. After users are authenticated, they are directed to the application's start page by the *Redirect-FromLoginPage* method.

2. Add a table to the UserInfo.aspx page in which to display the user name and authentication information and a command button to allow the user to sign out from the application. The table includes named *<span>* elements as placeholders for the user data, as shown in the following HTML:

```html
<H2>Forms Authorization</H2>
<TABLE id="tblUser" borderColor="black" cellSpacing="1" cellPadding="1"
width="500" bgColor="aliceblue" border="1">
  <TR>
    <TD>Authenticated</TD>
    <TD><SPAN id="spnAuthenticated" runat="server"></SPAN></TD>
  </TR>
  <TR>
    <TD>User name</TD>
    <TD><SPAN id="spnUserName" runat="server"></SPAN></TD>
  </TR>
  <TR>
    <TD>Authentication type</TD>
    <TD><SPAN id="spnAuthenticationType" runat="server"></SPAN></TD>
  </TR>
  <TR>
    <TD>Code running as user</TD>
    <TD><SPAN id="spnImpUser" runat="server"></SPAN></TD>
  </TR></TABLE>
<P>
  <asp:Button id="butSignOut" runat="server" Text="Sign Out"></asp:Button>
</P>
```

3. Add the following code to the Web form's *Page_Load* event procedure to display user information:

Visual Basic .NET

```vbnet
Private Sub Page_Load(ByVal sender As System.Object, _
    ByVal e As System.EventArgs) Handles MyBase.Load
    ' Display user authentication information.
    spnAuthenticated.InnerText = User.Identity.IsAuthenticated()
    spnUserName.InnerText = User.Identity.Name()
    spnAuthenticationType.InnerText = User.Identity.AuthenticationType()
    spnImpUser.InnerText = _
        System.Security.Principal.WindowsIdentity.GetCurrent().Name
End Sub
```

Visual C#

```csharp
private void Page_Load(object sender, System.EventArgs e)
{
    // Display user authentication information.
    spnAuthenticated.InnerText = User.Identity.IsAuthenticated.ToString();
    spnUserName.InnerText = User.Identity.Name;
    spnAuthenticationType.InnerText = User.Identity.AuthenticationType;
    spnImpUser.InnerText =
        System.Security.Principal.WindowsIdentity.GetCurrent().Name;
}
```

4. Add the following code to the *butSignOut_Click* event procedure to sign the user out of the application using the *SignOut* method. This removes the authentication cookie that was stored on the user's computer and requires that the user sign in again to access the Web application.

Visual Basic .NET

```
Private Sub butSignOut_Click(ByVal sender As System.Object, _
    ByVal e As System.EventArgs) Handles butSignOut.Click
    ' Remove authentication cookie.
    FormsAuthentication.SignOut()
    ' Redirect back to this page (displays log in screen).
    Response.Redirect("UserInfo.aspx")
End Sub
```

Visual C#

```
private void butSignOut_Click(object sender, System.EventArgs e)
{
    // Remove authentication cookie.
    FormsAuthentication.SignOut();
    // Redirect back to this page (displays log in screen).
    Response.Redirect("UserInfo.aspx");
}
```

5. Add an HTML page to the application named Denied.htm. This is the page that the LogIn Web form displays if the user doesn't enter a correct user name and password after three tries. Denied.htm includes a message to the user, as shown in the following HTML:

```
<h2>Access Denied</h2>
<p>You must enter a valid user name and password to use this application.
</p>
```

Exercise 4: Advanced Topics

The preceding exercises show how to implement Forms authentication in a step-by-step fashion. To gain a thorough understanding of other types of authentication, you can experiment by changing the authentication mode in the preceding application's Web.config file.

■ To switch the application to Windows authentication, comment out the current *<authentication>* element in Web.config and add the element shown here:

```
<authentication mode="Windows" />
```

■ To switch the application to Passport authentication, install the Passport SDK and modify the *<authentication>* element in Web.config, as shown here:

```
<authentication mode="Passport" />
```

Finally, for extra credit, get a server certificate from a certificate authority, such as VeriSign, and implement secure communications for the application. Use HTTPS to activate secure communications, as shown in Lesson 5.

Review

The following questions are intended to reinforce key information presented in this chapter. If you are unable to answer a question, review the appropriate lesson and then try the question again. Answers to the questions can be found in the appendix.

1. Which ASP.NET authentication mode is best suited to identifying and authorizing users who belong to a corporate network?

2. What is the difference between Windows and Forms authentication user lists in Web.config?

3. How do you require authentication using the Web.config file? (The answer is the same for all ASP.NET authentication modes.)

4. How do you run a Web application using the permission set of an authenticated user?

5. How does the Secure Sockets Layer (SSL) provide security in a Web application?

6. How do you begin and end secure communication via SSL?

C H A P T E R   9

Building and Deploying Web Applications

About This Chapter

In this chapter, you'll learn how to publish your completed Web applications on a Web server for general use. You'll also learn how to monitor and maintain the application when it's in use so that it continues to perform well as the demands of your users change.

Before You Begin

To complete this chapter, you must:

- Have access to a Web server either through a Web hosting service or through your local area network.
- Have successfully completed one or more of the Web applications in this book.
- Be familiar with Microsoft Internet Information Services (IIS) and the Microsoft Management Console (MMC).
- Have installed Microsoft Visual Studio .NET Professional, Microsoft Visual Studio .NET Enterprise Developer, or Microsoft Visual Studio .NET Enterprise Architect. This requirement applies only to the last lesson in this chapter.

Lesson 1: Building a Web Application

At its simplest level, building an application in Visual Studio .NET requires almost no effort. In fact, the application is built automatically any time you click Run while developing or debugging the application.

However, when you are ready to deploy your application, you need to take these additional steps before building it:

1. Set the build options.
2. Identify the application.
3. Configure the application.

In this lesson, you'll learn how to perform these tasks to prepare your Web application before deployment.

After this lesson, you will be able to

- Build a release version of a Web application
- Add name, company, copyright, description, and version information to the application's assembly
- Set the application's configuration options in its Web.config file

Estimated lesson time: 10 minutes

Setting Build Options

Web applications have two build options: debug and release.

To change the build options, follow these steps:

1. Select the project in Solution Explorer, and then select the build option from the Solution Configurations drop-down list in the Visual Studio toolbar, as shown in Figure 9-1.

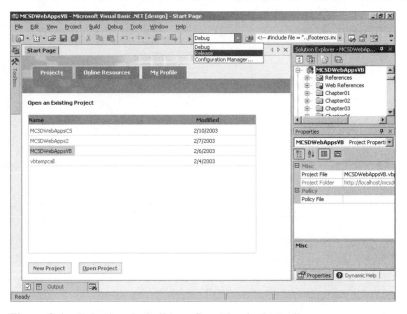

Figure 9-1   Selecting the build configuration in the toolbar

2. From the Project menu, select Properties. Visual Studio displays the project Properties Pages dialog box, as shown in Figures 9-2 and 9-3.

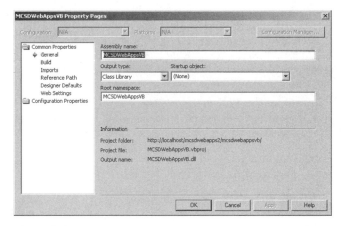

Figure 9-2   Project Property Pages dialog box (Visual Basic .NET)

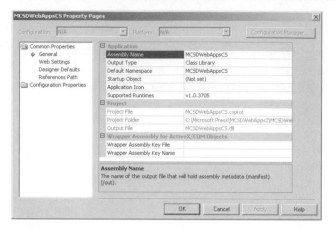

Figure 9-3   Project Property Pages dialog box (Visual C#)

The Common Properties and Configuration Properties folders in the project Property Pages dialog box allow you to set the build properties used when compiling the project. These options are found in different places for Microsoft Visual Basic .NET and Microsoft Visual C# projects, as described in Tables 9-1 and 9-2.

Table 9-1   Key Project Build Options (Visual Basic .NET)

Task	Folder and item	Set to
Make the project compatible with an earlier Microsoft .NET Framework version (Visual Studio version 1.1 and later).	Common Properties, Build, Supported Runtimes	On the Build page, click Change to open the .NET Framework Version dialog box, and select support for earlier versions of the .NET Framework, such as 1.0.3075.
Optimize the compiled code.	Configuration Properties, Optimizations	Select the Enable Optimizations check box to make the compiled code smaller, faster, and more efficient. Selecting this option makes debugging more difficult, however.
Disable integer overflow checks.	Configuration Properties, Optimizations	Select the Remove Integer Overflow Checks check box to perform integer calculations without checking for division by zero or overflow conditions. This is faster at run time but prevents these errors from being raised at run time.
Allow classes to be used from the Component Object Model (COM).	Configuration Properties, Build	Select the Register For COM Interop check box to generate a type library and register the application in the system registry. This option has an effect only on Class Library project types.

Table 9-2   Key Project Build Options (Visual C#)

Task	Folder and item	Set to
Make the project compatible with an earlier .NET Framework version (Visual Studio version 1.1 and later).	Common Properties, General, Applicaton, Supported Runtimes	Click the ellipsis (…) button to open the .NET Framework Version dialog box, and select support for earlier versions of the .NET Framework, such as 1.0.3075.
Optimize the compiled code.	Configuration Properties, Build, Code Generation, Optimize Code	Select True to make the compiled code smaller, faster, and more efficient. Selecting True makes debugging more difficult, however.
Disable integer overflow checks.	Configuration Properties, Build, Code Generation, Check For Arithmetic Overflow/Underflow	Select False to perform integer calculations without checking for division by zero or overflow conditions. This is faster but prevents these errors from being raised at run time.
Allow the use of the *unsafe* keyword.	Configuration Properties, Build, Code Generation, Allow Unsafe Code Blocks	Select True to allow the project to use pointers within procedures defined with the *unsafe* keyword.
Allow classes to be used from COM.	Configuration Properties, Build, Outputs, Register For COM Interop	Select True to generate a type library and register the application in the system registry. This option affects only Class Library project types. It is disabled for Web applications.

3. Open the project's Web.config file and set the *compilation* element to match the build setting you selected in step 1. For example, use the following setting for a release build:

```
<compilation defaultLanguage="vb" debug="false" />
```

Selecting the debug build option generates a program database file (.pdb) containing information about symbols used within the application when the project is compiled. Visual Studio .NET uses the program database to monitor the values of variables, set breakpoints, and evaluate *Debug* class members.

Selecting the release build option does not generate this file; this disables *Debug* class members and causes breakpoints to be ignored. Because release builds don't have to monitor this extra information, they execute faster than debug builds.

The application's build option and Web.config setting should agree. There is no advantage in having one set to debug and the other set to release; however, Visual Studio .NET does not automatically change one when you change the other.

Identifying the Application

Before you deploy an application, you should include information about the application such as the application's title, author, and version. This information is displayed when the user views the version properties of the application's assembly (.dll) from within Microsoft Windows, as shown in Figure 9-4.

Figure 9-4   Assembly properties

To identify your application, open the AssemblyInfo file and enter the application's information in the assembly attributes. For example, the following attributes set the product name and version information shown in Figure 9-4:

Visual Basic .NET

```
Imports System.Reflection
Imports System.Runtime.InteropServices

' General Information about an assembly is controlled through the following
' set of attributes. Change these attribute values to modify the information
' associated with an assembly.

' Review the values of the assembly attributes.

<Assembly: AssemblyTitle("Web Flyer Storefront")>
<Assembly: AssemblyDescription("Low-price reservation finder.")>
<Assembly: AssemblyCompany("Contoso Ltd. ")>
<Assembly: AssemblyProduct("Web Flyer")>
<Assembly: AssemblyCopyright("2002")>
<Assembly: AssemblyTrademark("Web Flyer is a trademark of Contoso Ltd.")>
<Assembly: CLSCompliant(True)>
```

```
' The following GUID is for the ID of the typelib if
' this project is exposed to COM
<Assembly: Guid("CE84F243-D7D9-4B7E-B43B-520A0D6B9B30")>

' Version information for an assembly consists of the following four values:
'
'       Major Version
'       Minor Version
'       Build Number
'       Revision
'
' You can specify all the values or you can default
' the Build and Revision Numbers  by using
' the '*' as shown below:

<Assembly: AssemblyVersion("2.1.*")>
```

Visual C#

```
using System.Reflection;
using System.Runtime.CompilerServices;

//
// General Information about an assembly is controlled through the following
// set of attributes. Change these attribute values to modify the information
// associated with an assembly.
//
[assembly: AssemblyTitle("Web Flyer Storefront")]
[assembly: AssemblyDescription("Low-price reservation finder.")]
[assembly: AssemblyConfiguration("")]
[assembly: AssemblyCompany("Contoso Ltd.")]
[assembly: AssemblyProduct("Web Flyer")]
[assembly: AssemblyCopyright("2002")]
[assembly: AssemblyTrademark("Web Flyer is a trademark of Contoso Ltd.")]
[assembly: AssemblyCulture("")]


//
// Version information for an assembly consists of the following four values:
//
//       Major Version
//       Minor Version
//       Build Number
//       Revision
//
// You can specify all the values or you can default the Revision and Build
// Numbers by using the '*' as shown below:

[assembly: AssemblyVersion("2.1.*")]
```

Two pieces of information are automatically generated for you in the Assembly-Info file:

- The *Guid* attribute is generated by Visual Studio .NET to identify the assembly to COM components. You need to change this number only if you break compatibility with earlier versions of the assembly by removing or significantly changing public objects and members that are used by COM components.
- The *AssemblyVersion* attribute automatically updates the build version number, indicated by the asterisk (*). You can add levels of versioning or remove the build number if you want.

Configuring the Application

Web applications use text configuration files (.config) to specify how they run. A Web application's configuration file (Web.config) resides in the Web application's root directory, but that file's function is really to override the settings inherited from the following locations:

- **The Machine.config file located in the Windows\Microsoft.NET\Framework*version*\config directory**   This sets the base configuration for all .NET assemblies running on the server.
- **The Web.config file located in the IIS root directory**   This sets the base configuration for all Web applications and overrides settings in Machine.config.
- **Any Web.config files in the current application's parent directories**   These settings are inherited from Web.config files along the application's path.

The Web.config file uses Extensible Markup Language (XML) elements to control different aspects of the Web application, as described in Table 9-3. Because these elements use XML syntax, they are case sensitive and must be typed exactly as shown.

Table 9-3   Web.config Attributes

Element	Use to	For more information, see
compilation	Set the build type to *debug* or *release*	"Setting Build Options," earlier in this lesson
customErrors	Display custom error pages in response to HTTP response codes	Chapter 6, "Catching and Correcting Errors"
authentication	Set the type of authentication to use to identify users	Chapter 8, "Maintaining Security"
authorization	List user names or user roles that are authorized to run the application	Chapter 8, "Maintaining Security"

Table 9-3   Web.config Attributes

Element	Use to	For more information, see
Trace	Enable tracing to help diagnose errors or tune performance	Chapter 6, "Catching and Correcting Errors"
sessionState	Determine how Microsoft ASP.NET stores *Session* state variables	Lesson 3 in this chapter, and Chapter 3, "Working with Web Objects"
globalization	Set cultural information for localized applications	Chapter 15, "Globalizing Web Applications"

When you make changes to an application's Web.config file, IIS automatically restarts the application and applies the changes. This has the side effect of resetting current *Application* or *Session* state variables, which can adversely affect users.

For security reasons, you can't access the Web.config file from a browser. If a user requests the Web.config file from your Web site, he or she will receive an access denied error message.

Lesson 2: Deploying a Web Application

Deploying a Web application means installing the application on the server where it will run. Because they run on servers, Web applications might not require an installation program. Instead, they can simply be uploaded to the Web server using the Visual Studio upload tools.

In this lesson, you'll learn how to deploy a completed Web application to a hosting service or to your own server. You'll also learn about IIS and security settings required by Web applications. This lesson does not cover creating an installation program for a Web application; for information about that task, see Lesson 3.

After this lesson, you will be able to

- Upload a completed Web application to a hosting service
- Create a virtual folder in IIS to host a Web application on your own server
- Copy a Web application to a virtual folder on your own server
- Install COM and .NET components used by your Web application
- Assign security privileges to the ASPNET user account

Estimated lesson time: 15 minutes

Using the Upload Tools

If you signed up with an ASP.NET host service, as described in Chapter 1, "Introduction to Web Programming," you can install your Web application on the host's servers directly from Visual Studio .NET.

To install your application on a hosting service from Visual Studio .NET, follow these steps:

1. Open the project you want to install using Visual Studio .NET.
2. On the Online Resources tab on the Visual Studio .NET Start Page, click Web Hosting.
3. On the Web Hosting page, click the Premier Providers or Additional Providers tab.
4. In the section of the providers page that lists your host, click Upload Directly To Your Account. Visual Studio .NET displays your host's upload page, as shown in Figure 9-5.

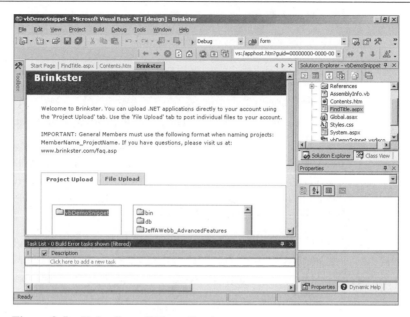

Figure 9-5   Uploading a Web application

5. Follow the upload instructions on the host's page. These instructions vary slightly among the different host services.

Hosting on Your Own Server

If your application is intended to run as part of a local network or if you have acccss to your own public Web server, install your application on the server by following these steps:

1. Use IIS to set up a virtual folder for the application.
2. Copy the Web application to the virtual directory.
3. Add any shared .NET components to the server's global assembly cache (GAC).
4. Set the security permissions on the server to allow the application to access required resources.

The following sections describe these steps in more detail.

Setting Up a Virtual Folder

ASP.NET Web applications run under IIS, so both IIS and the Microsoft .NET Framework must be installed on the server before that server can host Web applications. ASP.NET requires the following component versions:

- IIS version 5.0 or later.
- The .NET Framework using the same version number as you used to compile the Web application's assembly.

The Visual Studio .NET distribution disks include tools for setting up the required server components. When you have confirmed that the correct components are installed on the server, create a virtual folder for the application on the server by following these steps:

1. Using Windows Explorer, create a physical folder on the server to store the application.
2. Using IIS, start the Virtual Directory Creation Wizard to create the new virtual folder for the physical location created in step 1. Detailed instructions on using this wizard are covered in Chapter 2, "Creating Web Forms Applications."

Copying the Application

Web application boundaries are defined by the application's directory structure. That means that an application starts at its root folder and extends to all of its subordinate folders. This makes installing a Web application as easy as dragging the application's files and subfolders from its development directory to its physical location on the server.

In general, a Web application's content files can be organized into subfolders any way you want. However, you should follow a couple of conventions:

- The application's assembly (.dll) is stored in the /bin subfolder.
- The start page for the application is generally named Default.aspx or Default.htm.

Whether or not your application uses a default start page is determined by settings in IIS. A default page enables IIS to display a page if the user does not specify one in his or her request. For example, a user might make a request using only your domain name, such as *http://www.contoso.com*. If a default page is enabled, IIS will respond with *http:// www.contoso.com/default.aspx*.

Note Don't confuse IIS default pages with the Web Forms application start page in Visual Studio .NET. Visual Studio .NET requires that you set a start page for each project so that the development environment knows which page to display first during debugging. This setting has no effect on the IIS default page settings.

Installing Shared Components

If your application uses components that are shared with other applications on the server, such as custom server controls, those components must be installed on the server. There are three ways to do this, depending on the type of component:

- **For COM components**   Copy the component to the server and register the component using the COM registration tools.
- **For weak-named .NET components**   Copy the component to the application's /bin directory.
- **For strong-named .NET components**   Install the component in the server's GAC.

COM components generally provide a setup program to install or remove them from the system. If the component doesn't provide a setup program, you can copy it to the server and register it using the MFC RegSvr32.exe utility, as shown here:

```
RegSvr32 MyComp.dll
```

.NET component names come in two flavors: weak and strong. This distinction refers to how the names are stored within the assembly. Weak names are not guaranteed to be unique and thus cannot be shared without potentially causing conflicts. Strong names are digitally signed and provide a public key that ensures there are no conflicts. Furthermore, .NET components with strong names can't call unmanaged code (such as COM components) and thus avoid potential conflicts with dependencies.

Weak-named .NET components must be individually copied to the /bin directories of the Web applications where they are used. Strong-named .NET components can be copied into the server's GAC, as shown in Figure 9-6.

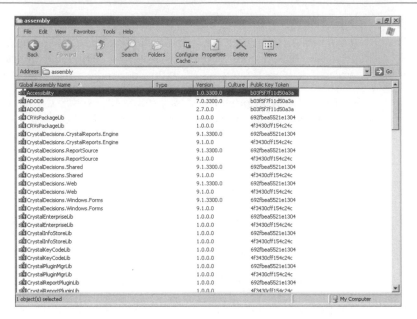

Figure 9-6   Viewing .NET components in the global assembly cache

The **global assembly cache (GAC)** is a special subfolder within the Windows folder that stores the shared .NET components. When you open the folder, Windows Explorer starts a Windows shell extension called the Assembly Cache Viewer (ShFusion.dll), as shown in Figure 9-6.

You can install strong-named .NET components by dragging them into the Assembly Cache Viewer, or by using the Global Assembly Cache tool (GacUtil.exe), as shown here:

```
GacUtil -i MyServeControls.dll
```

Assigning Security Privileges

By default, the ASP.NET worker process runs using the ASPNET account, which is created when you install the .NET Framework. This account has limited privileges, which can cause permission-denied errors if your application writes files or tries to read files outside the current Web application's boundaries.

If your application requires additional permissions, you have three options:

- Grant the ASPNET user access to the required files. To use this option, the server must be using the Windows NT file system (NTFS).
- Change the group the ASPNET user belongs to.
- Use impersonation to run the process as another user.

To grant the ASPNET user access to a file or folder, follow these steps:

1. In Windows Explorer, choose Folder Options from the Tools menu. Windows Explorer displays the Folder Options dialog box.

2. In the Folder Options dialog box, click the View tab, and clear the Use Simple File Sharing check box at the bottom of the Advanced Settings list, as shown in Figure 9-7. Click OK to make the change and close the dialog box.

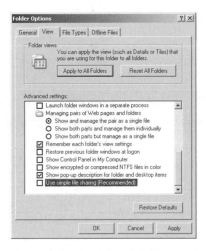

Figure 9-7   Enabling full file permissions

3. In Windows Explorer, right-click the file or folder you want to grant access to, and select Properties on the shortcut menu. Windows Explorer displays the Properties dialog box.

4. Click the Security tab, and then click Add to add the ASPNET user to the Group Or User Names list, as shown in Figure 9-8.

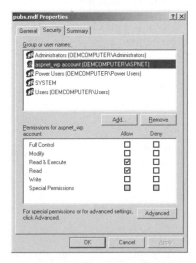

Figure 9-8   Adding the ASPNET user account

5. Select the check boxes in the permissions list to grant the required access. Click OK to make the changes and close the dialog box.

To change the group the ASPNET user account belongs to, follow these steps:

1. From the Start menu, point to All Programs, Administrative Tools, and then choose Computer Management. Windows displays the Computer Management console.

2. Expand Local Users And Groups in the console tree, and then select Users, as shown in Figure 9-9.

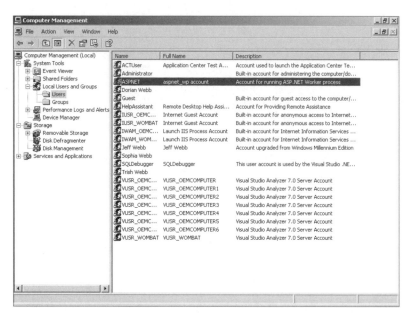

Figure 9-9   Modifying the ASPNET user account

3. Right-click the ASPNET user account, and select Properties on the shortcut menu. The Computer Management console displays the Properties dialog box for the ASPNET account, as shown in Figure 9-10.

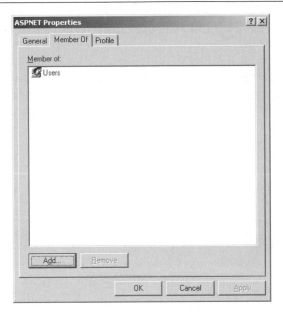

Figure 9-10   Adding a group to ASPNET

4. Click the Member Of tab, and then click Add to open the Select Groups dialog box to add the ASPNET user to a new group. Click OK to make the changes and close the dialog boxes.

Adding the ASPNET user to the Administrators group gives your Web application full privileges on the server; however, it also poses a potential security risk because outside users might be able to manipulate your application to hack your server.

To use impersonation to run the ASP.NET process as a user other than ASPNET, set the *identity* element's *impersonation* attribute in the application's Web.config file. For example, the following entry sets the application to run as the WebFlyr user account:

```
<identity impersonate="true" name="localhost\WebFlyr" password="hpB14dQi" />
```

If your application uses Windows authentication, you can also use impersonation to pass the identity of authenticated users through to the server. For example, the following Web.config fragment tells the application to use the permissions of the user who signed on to the application:

```
<identity impersonate="true" />          <!-- Use impersonation. -->

<authorization>
<deny users="?"  />                      <!-- Require authentication. -->
</authorization>
```

For more information about authenticating users, see Chapter 8, "Maintaining Security."

Lesson 3: Creating an Installation Program

If you're installing a Web application on multiple servers or if the servers are located on secure networks that do not allow you to deploy the application using Visual Studio's upload tools, you'll have to create an installation program for your application.

In this lesson, you'll learn how to create an installation program for a Web application that runs from the Web or from a CD-ROM. You'll also learn how to add shared components to that installation program through merge modules.

After this lesson, you will be able to

- Create a Setup and Deployment project for a Web application
- Add multiple IIS application folders to a project
- Create an installation program for use over the Web
- Create an installation program for use from a CD-ROM
- Add shared components to a Setup and Deployment project

Estimated lesson time: 30 minutes

Creating a Setup and Deployment Project

The easiest way to create an installation program for a Web application is to use the Setup And Deployment Projects' Setup Wizard template. To create a new Setup And Deployment project for a Web application, follow these steps:

1. Open the solution containing your Web application in Visual Studio.
2. From the File menu, point to Add Project, and then choose New Project. Visual Studio displays the Add New Project dialog box, as shown in Figure 9-11.

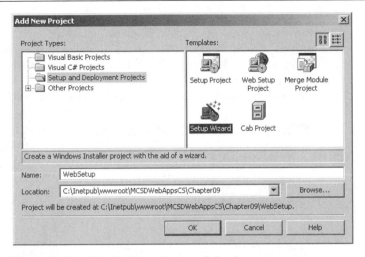

Figure 9-11   The Add New Project dialog box

3. Select Setup And Deployment Projects in the Project Types list, and select Setup Wizard from the Templates list. Type the name of the setup project to create, and click OK to begin the wizard. Visual Studio uses the project name as the name of the root virtual folder to create on the server.

4. Click Next on the wizard's Welcome page, select Create A Setup For A Web Application on the Choose A Project Type page, and click Next. Visual Studio displays the Choose Project Outputs To Include page, as shown in Figure 9-12.

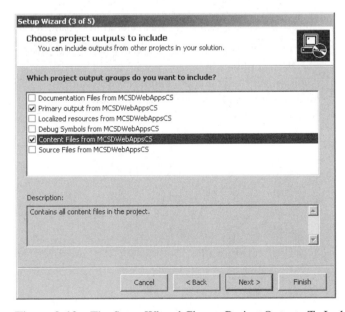

Figure 9-12   The Setup Wizard Choose Project Outputs To Include page

5. Select the project output that you want to install on the server. For a Web application, you must select at least the primary output and content files for your project. *Primary output* refers to the application's assembly; *content files* refers to the project's Web forms, HTML pages, user controls, configuration files, and other content used by a Web application. Click Next; Visual Studio displays the Choose Files To Include page, as shown in Figure 9-13.

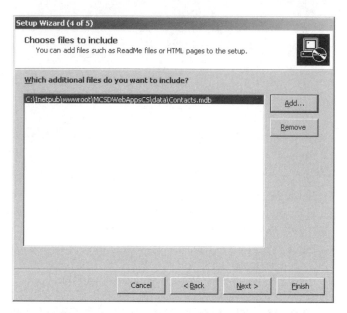

Figure 9-13   The Setup Wizard Choose Files To Include page

6. Click Add to open the Add Files dialog box, and select the files that are used by the Web application but are not included as part of the Web application project, such as Microsoft Access database files, text files, and so on. After adding the necessary files, click Next; Visual Studio displays the Create Project page, as shown in Figure 9-14.

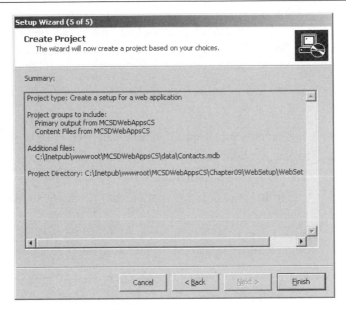

Figure 9-14   The Setup Wizard Create Project page

7. Click Finish to create the setup project and add it to the current solution. When complete, the setup project appears as shown in Figure 9-15.

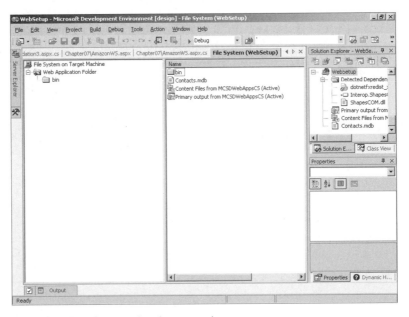

Figure 9-15   The completed setup project

By default, the Setup Wizard creates a project for installation from removable media, such as a CD-ROM. When built, this project writes the Windows Installer (Setup.exe), an initialization file (Setup.ini), and a content file (*projectname*.msi) to the /debug or /release folder of the setup project's folder.

In most cases, you'll need to take the following additional steps before building and deploying the setup project:

1. Change the setup project options to support Web deployment:
2. Review the setup project output and add needed files.
3. Rename the root virtual folder where your application will be installed.
4. Add virtual folders to create additional IIS application starting points on the target server.
5. Include shared .NET components to install in the server's GAC or shared COM components to install and register with the server's system registration database.

The following sections describe how to perform these steps.

Modifying the Setup Project for Web Deployment

The Visual Studio setup projects generate an installation program that uses the Windows Installer bootstrap executable (Setup.exe). This executable checks whether the target machine has the Windows Installer, prompts the user to download the Installer if it is not installed, and starts the Installer once it is available. By default, the Setup Wizard uses a bootstrap executable configured for local access to the setup resources, as when distributing the software on a CD-ROM.

To create a setup project that can be installed from an Internet address, follow these steps:

1. Select the setup project in Solution Explorer, and choose Properties from the Project menu. Visual Studio displays the setup project Property Pages dialog box, as shown in Figure 9-16.

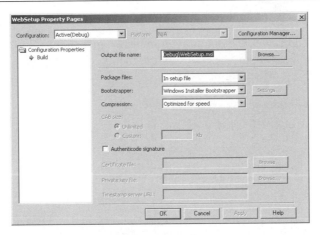

Figure 9-16   Setup project properties

2. Select Web Bootstrapper from the Bootstrapper drop-down list. Visual Studio displays the Web Boostrapper Settings dialog box, as shown in Figure 9-17.

Figure 9-17   Web Bootstrapper settings

3. In the Setup Folder box, type the Web address whcrc you will deploy the installation program and click OK. Then click OK to close the Property Pages dialog box.

4. Build the setup project, and copy the Setup.exe and projectname.msi files to the Web address specified in step 3.

5. Add a Web page with a link to the Setup.exe file specified in step 3. For example, the following link installs the Web application from the WebApps\Install folder:

```
<a href="http://www.contoso.com/WebApps/Install/Setup.exe">Install Web
Applicaton</a>
```

Reviewing the Setup Project's Contents and Adding Files

As mentioned, Web application setup projects must include at least the primary project output (the assembly) and the content files (Web forms and so on). Setup automatically creates the /bin folder and any subordinate folders for content files based on the source project's content.

To review the content before building a setup project, perform the following task:

- Right-click the output item in the setup project's File System window, and select Output from the shortcut menu. Visual Studio displays the content items, as shown in Figure 9-18.

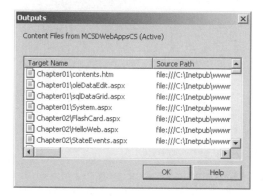

Figure 9-18   Viewing content output

The Outputs dialog box displays the source and destination locations of each item to install. Sometimes items in the source project don't appear in the Outputs list as you might expect. In those cases, select the item in the source project and verify that its Build Action property is set to Content.

Other times, you might want to include files in the setup project that aren't part of the source project. For example, you might want to install a Microsoft Access database in a data folder along with the rest of your Web application.

To add files to the setup project other than source files, follow these steps:

1. Right-click in the setup project's File System window, point to Add, and select File from the shortcut menu. Visual Studio displays the Add Files dialog box.
2. Select the files to add, and click OK to add them to the setup project's File System window.

Renaming and Adding Virtual Folders

The Setup Wizard creates one virtual folder to be installed as an application folder in IIS. This folder appears on the right side of the File System editor and is named Web Application Folder. The Setup Wizard gives this virtual folder the setup project's name. This will be the Web application's root folder when installed on the server, so you'll probably want to rename it.

To change the name of the root virtual folder to install, follow these steps:

1. Select the Web Application Folder in the File System editor.
2. In the Properties window, set the *VirtualDirectory* property.

Some Web applications include multiple application starting points within their folder structure. In Visual Studio, you create a new application starting point by adding a new Web application project. Each Web application project has its own root virtual folder containing Web.config and Global.asax files. To get Setup to create IIS application folders for these projects, you must add a custom Web folder to the setup project.

To add a custom Web folder to a setup project, follow these steps:

1. Right-click the File System On Target Machine item in the File System editor, point to Add Special Folder, and then select Web Custom Folder from the shortcut menu. Enter a name for the new folder.

2. Set the *VirtualDirectory* property of the Web folder to reflect the structure of your application. Use the relative address to create the folder within another application's domain. For example, MainApp/Restricted creates the folder Restricted within the MainApp virtual folder.

3. Add project output to the new Web folder as you did in the preceding section, "Reviewing the Setup Project's Contents and Adding Files."

Adding Shared Components

Components used by more than one application should have their own, separate setup projects called **merge modules**. Merge modules allow the server to manage the installation of shared components so that they're not unnecessarily overwritten and so that they can be safely removed when no longer used. Unlike regular setup projects, merge modules can't be installed by themselves—they can be installed only as part of an application installation.

To create a merge module, follow these steps:

1. From the Visual Studio File menu, point to New, select Project, and then select the Merge Module Project in the New Project dialog box.

2. In the setup File System editor, add the components to install. You can add special folders to the File System editor to add components to the server's System folder, GAC, or other shared locations.

3. Build the project. Visual Studio generates a merge module (*projectname*.msm) once the merge module is built.

To add a merge module to a setup project, follow these steps:

1. Open the setup project in Visual Studio.

2. From the Project menu, point to Add, and choose Merge Module. Visual Studio displays the Add Modules dialog box.

3. Select the merge module to add, and click OK.

Lesson 4: Maintaining a Deployed Application

After you have deployed a Web application, you need to monitor how it performs on the server. Many issues can crop up at this point because of the number of users accessing the application, the unpredictable nature of user interaction, and the possibility of malicious attack.

Maintaining a deployed application is an ongoing task that involves three major steps:

- Monitoring the application for error, performance, and security issues
- Repairing the application as issues are discovered
- Tuning the application to respond to user traffic

In this lesson, you'll learn how to perform these tasks, as well as learn about some optimization techniques.

After this lesson, you will be able to

- Use the Windows tools to monitor application errors, security, and performance on the server
- Create alerts to notify you when a problem occurs
- Chart performance and monitor activity using event logs
- Repair a deployed application by replacing the assembly or content files
- Use the server's configuration settings to control how ASP.NET applications maintain their processes
- Evaluate how programming techniques and ASP.NET features affect performance

Estimated lesson time: 20 minutes

Monitoring the Server

After your application is deployed, you need to monitor the server where it is running to help detect and correct problems related to security, performance, and unanticipated errors. Windows provides the following MMC snap-ins for monitoring security, performance, and error events:

- **The Event Viewer snap-in** Lists application, system, and security events as they occur on the system. Use this tool to see what is currently happening on the server and to get specific information about a particular event.
- **The Performance snap-in** Lets you create new events to display in the Event Viewer and allows you to track event counters over time for display graphically or in report form.

The following sections describe how to use these tools in more detail.

Viewing Events

Use the MMC Event Viewer snap-in to view application, system, and security events as they happen.

To run the Event Viewer, choose Event Viewer from the Administrative Tools submenu on the Windows Start menu. (You can show the Administrative Tools menu in Windows XP Professional by opening the Start button's Properties dialog box and clicking the Customize button on the Start Menu tab. The Administrative Tools option is located on the Advanced tab of the Customize Start Menu dialog box.) After clicking the Event Viewer shortcut, Windows displays the Event Viewer snap-in in the MMC, as shown in Figure 9-19.

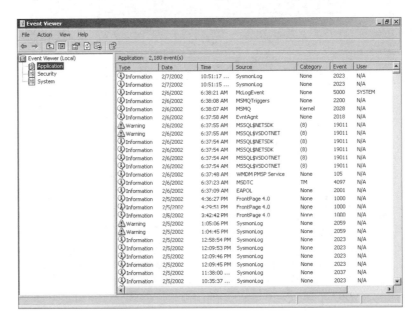

Figure 9-19   Viewing events

The Event Viewer snap-in displays general application, system, and security events at three levels: informational events, warning events, and error events.

To view information about a specific event, double-click the event. The snap-in displays the Event Properties dialog box, as shown in Figure 9-20.

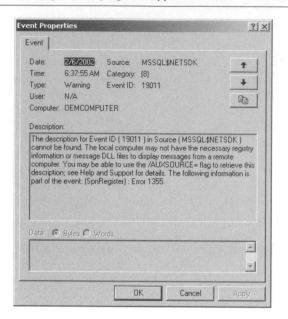

Figure 9-20   Viewing event details

You can use the Event Viewer to get a snapshot of what is happening on the server or to get details about a particular event. To create new events or to track events over time, you need to use the MMC Performance snap-in, as described in the following sections.

Defining New Events

In many cases, the standard system, application, and security events don't tell you what you really want to know. For example, you might want to know when the number of users connected to a Web application exceeds 1000 or when an unhandled exception occurs within the Web application. To add events such as these to your counter and trace logs, use the MMC Performance snap-in.

To run the Performance snap-in, choose Performance from the Administrative Tools submenu on the Windows Start menu. Windows displays the Performance snap-in, as shown in Figure 9-21.

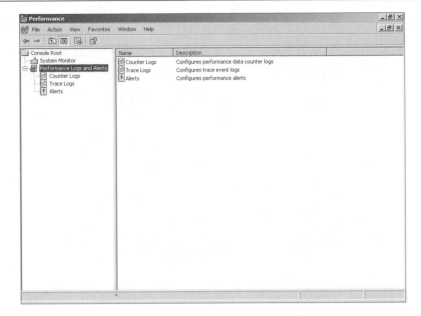

Figure 9-21   Adding events to monitor

The Performance snap-in allows you to create log files that record activity on the server and to create alerts that raise events in the Event Viewer. Using this tool, you can monitor a wide variety of information about the server, the applications it is hosting, and the users connected to it.

Perhaps the best way to understand how this works is to walk through adding an event to monitor on your own system, as described in the following steps:

1. From the Performance window, select Alerts from the Performance Logs And Alerts list in the left pane.

2. From the Action menu, choose New Alert Settings. The snap-in displays the New Alert Settings dialog box, as shown in Figure 9-22.

Figure 9-22   Naming a new alert

3. Type a name for identifying the alert, and click OK. The snap-in displays the new Alert dialog box, as shown in Figure 9-23.

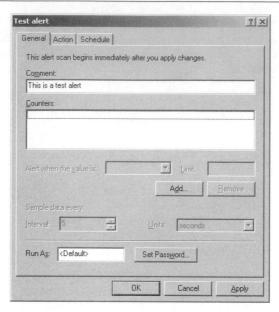

Figure 9-23   Setting alert properties

4. Add an event to monitor by clicking Add. The snap-in displays the Add
   Counters dialog box, as shown in Figure 9-24.

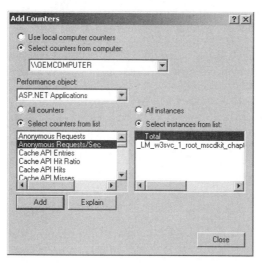

Figure 9-24   Adding counters to monitor ASP.NET users

5. Select the hardware item or application to monitor from the Performance
   Object drop- down list. The snap-in updates the counters list with items that
   apply to the selected Performance object. Click Add to add the selected counter
   to the alert. Click Close when you've finished.

6. Set the criterion that raises the alert in the new Alert dialog box by typing a number in the Limit box.

   For example, Figure 9-25 shows settings to raise the alert when the ASP.NET user count exceeds 1000.

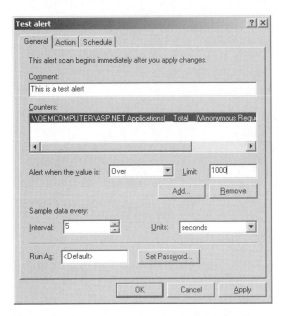

Figure 9-25   Setting a criterion to raise the alert

7. Click the Action tab to specify what the server should do when the alert is raised. By default, the server records the alert as an event that can be viewed from the Event Viewer. You can also send the alert as an e-mail or write the alert to a log file, as shown in Figure 9-26.

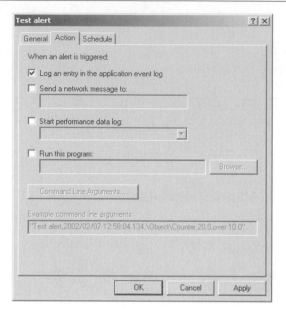

Figure 9-26   Specifying the action to take

8. When you have finished, click OK. The snap-in adds the alert to the Alerts list, as shown in Figure 9-27.

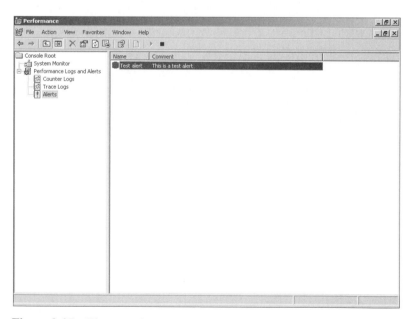

Figure 9-27   The new alert

By default, the snap-in starts monitoring the new alert immediately. You can stop or restart monitoring the alert by right-clicking the alert and choosing Stop or Start from the shortcut menu.

Windows raises the alert whenever the alert criterion is met. For some counters, such as error counts, this means that after the alert is raised the first time, it is raised after every interval. Because the error count is not automatically reset, it always exceeds the count limit when the limit is met. For these types of alerts, you should be careful what action you specify—sending an e-mail in response to an error count alert can result in a lot of redundant mail messages.

Creating Event Logs

Defining a new event by creating an alert is a good way to be notified the moment a problem occurs or when a performance has degraded, but to track errors and performance over time, you must create an event log. Event logs let you gather information about a wide variety of events over time and then display that information graphically or in text form.

To create an event log, follow these steps:

1. From the Performance window, select Counter Logs from the Performance Logs And Alerts list in the console tree.

2. From the Action menu, choose New Log Settings. The snap-in displays the New Log Settings dialog box, as shown in Figure 9-28.

Figure 9-28   Naming a new log file

3. Type the name of the log, and click OK. The snap-in displays the log file's properties dialog box, as shown in Figure 9-29.

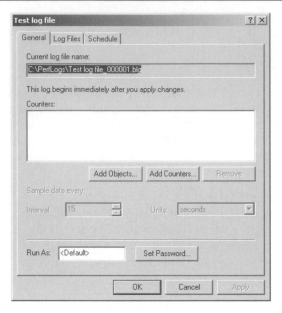

Figure 9-29   Setting log properties

4. Click Add Objects or Add Counters to add items to track within the log file.
   The snap-in displays the Add Counters dialog box, as shown in Figure 9-30.
   These counters work the same way they do for alerts.

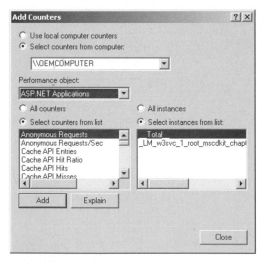

Figure 9-30   Adding counters to record

5. Click the Log Files tab to specify the format of the log file to create. The snap-
   in displays the Log Files properties, as shown in Figure 9-31.

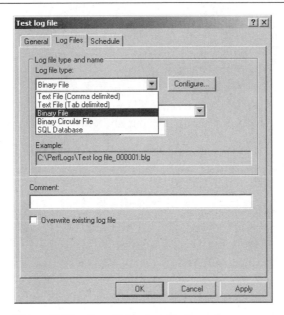

Figure 9-31   Specifying log file format

6. Log files can be saved in binary, text, or database formats. Click OK when you've finished. The snap-in adds the log to the Counter Logs list, as shown in Figure 9-32.

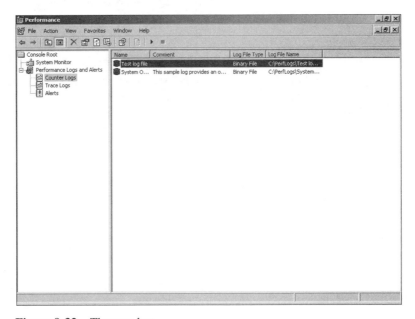

Figure 9-32   The new log

As with alerts, the snap-in starts monitoring the new log immediately. You can stop or restart monitoring the log by right-clicking the log and choosing Stop or Start from the shortcut menu.

Viewing Event Logs

By default, the Performance snap-in saves log files to the PerfLogs root folder. To view the log file from within the snap-in, follow these steps:

1. From the Performance window, select System Monitor from the console tree. The snap-in displays the system monitor with the current performance statistics, as shown in Figure 9-33.

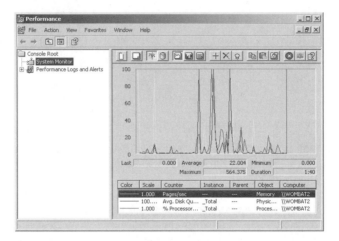

Figure 9-33   Current CPU, memory, and disk usage statistics

2. Click the View Log Data toolbar button. The snap-in displays the System Monitor Properties dialog box, as shown in Figure 9-34.

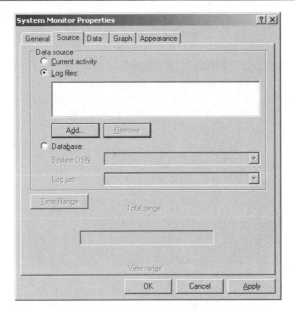

Figure 9-34   System Monitor Properties dialog box

3. Select Log Files, and click Add to specify a file to open. The snap-in displays the Select Log File dialog box, as shown in Figure 9-35.

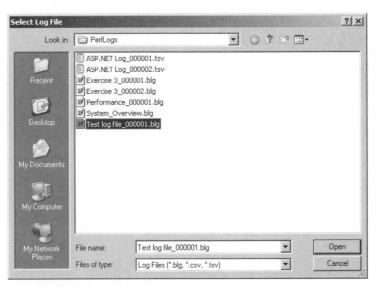

Figure 9-35   Opening a log file

4. Select a log file to open from the PerfLogs folder, and click Open to add it to the monitor.

5. Click the Data tab in the System Monitor Properties dialog box to add items from the log to the chart, as shown in Figure 9-36.

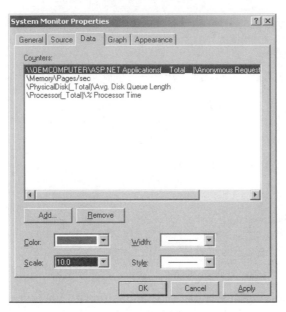

Figure 9-36   Adding items to chart

6. Click OK to close the System Monitor Properties dialog box. The snap-in displays the log file, as shown in Figure 9-37.

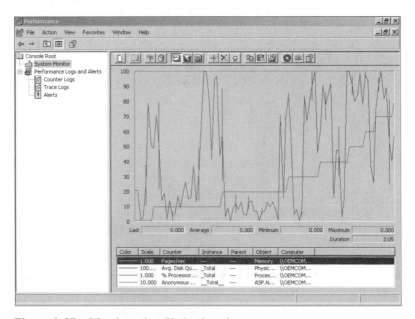

Figure 9-37   Viewing a log file in chart form

7. Click the View Report toolbar button to view the data as text rather than graphically. The System Monitor displays the text view, as shown in Figure 9-38.

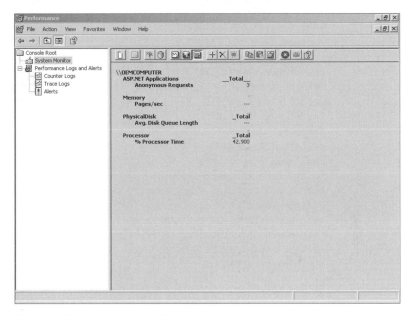

Figure 9-38   Viewing a log file in report form

More Info   The MMC Event Viewer and Performance snap-ins provide a way to monitor the health of a server, detect application errors, identify resource conflicts, and predict future hardware needs. For more information about performing these tasks, see the online Help provided with each of these snap-ins.

Repairing Deployed Applications

After a Web application is deployed, you can revise and repair it in place, without restarting the server or IIS.

To repair a deployed Web application, copy the new assembly (.dll) and/or content files (.aspx, .ascx, and so on) to the application folder on the server. ASP.NET automatically restarts the application when you replace the assembly; you do not need to install or register the assembly on the server.

ASP.NET Web applications also have a limited ability to repair themselves through process recycling. **Process recycling** is the technique of shutting down and restarting an ASP.NET worker process (aspnet_wp.exe) that has become inactive or is consuming excessive resources. You can control how ASP.NET processes are recycled through attributes in the *processModel* element in the Machine.config file, as shown in boldface here:

```
<processModel
  enable="true"
  timeout="Infinite"
  idleTimeout="Infinite"
  shutdownTimeout="0:00:05"
  requestLimit="Infinite"
  requestQueueLimit="5000"
  restartQueueLimit="10"
  memoryLimit="60"
  webGarden="false"
  cpuMask="0xffffffff"
  userName="machine"
  password="AutoGenerate"
  logLevel="Errors"
  clientConnectedCheck="0:00:05"
  comAuthenticationLevel="Connect"
  comImpersonationLevel="Impersonate"
  responseRestartDeadlockInterval="00:09:00"
  responseDeadlockInterval="00:03:00"
  maxWorkerThreads="25"
  maxIoThreads="25"
/>
```

Table 9-4 describes the *processModel* attributes that relate to process recycling.

Table 9-4   Process Recycling Attributes

Attribute	Specifies
timeout	The amount of time (hh:mm:ss) before the process is shut down and restarted. Use this setting to automatically recycle a process after a certain number of requests as a preventive measure.
shutDownTimeOut	How much time each process has to shut itself down. After this amount of time, the process is terminated by the system if it still running.
requestLimit	The number of queued requests to serve before the process is shut down and restarted. Use this setting the same way you use the *timeout* attribute.
restartQueueLimit	The number of queued requests to retain while the process is shut down and restarted.
memoryLimit	The percentage of physical memory the ASP.NET process is allowed to consume before that process is shut down and a new process is started. This setting helps prevent memory leaks from degrading the server.

Table 9-4   Process Recycling Attributes

Attribute	Specifies
responseRestart-DeadlockInterval	The amount of time to wait before restarting a process that was shut down because it was deadlocked. This setting is usually several minutes to prevent applications with serious errors from degrading the server.
responseDeadlock-Interval	The amount of time to wait before restarting a process that is deadlocked. The process is restarted if there are queued requests and the process has not responded within this time limit.

Tuning Deployed Applications

ASP.NET Web applications have a number of settings you can control to tune performance after the applications are deployed:

- Use the *processModel* element's attributes in the server's Machine.config file to control the number of threads and the time-out behavior that the server provides for Web applications.
- Use the *sessionState* element's attributes in the application's Web.config file to control how *Session* state information is saved.

The following sections discuss each of these techniques.

Adjusting *processModel* Attributes

The *processModel* element in the server's Machine.config file provides attributes that control certain performance aspects, such as the maximum number of requests to be queued, how long to wait before checking whether a client is connected, and how many threads to allow per processor, as shown here in boldface:

```
<processModel
  enable="true"
  timeout="Infinite"
  idleTimeout="Infinite"
  shutdownTimeout="0:00:05"
  requestLimit="Infinite"
  requestQueueLimit="5000"
  restartQueueLimit="10"
  memoryLimit="60"
  webGarden="false"
  cpuMask="0xffffffff"
  userName="machine"
  password="AutoGenerate"
  logLevel="Errors"
  clientConnectedCheck="0:00:05"
  comAuthenticationLevel="Connect"
```

```
comImpersonationLevel="Impersonate"
responseRestartDeadlockInterval="00:09:00"
responseDeadlockInterval="00:03:00"
maxWorkerThreads="25"
maxIoThreads="25"
/>
```

Table 9-5 describes the *processModel* attributes that relate to performance tuning.

Table 9-5   Performance Attributes

Attribute	Specifies
requestQueueLimit	The number of queued requests allowed before ASP.NET returns response code 503 (Server too busy) to new requests
clientConnectedCheck	The amount of time (hh:mm:ss) to wait before checking whether a client is still connected
maxWorkerThreads	The maximum number of threads per processor
maxIOThreads	The maximum number of I/O threads per processor

In general, lowering these settings allows your server to handle fewer clients more quickly. Increasing these settings permits more clients and more queued requests, but slows response times.

Adjusting *sessionState* Attributes

Storing state information for each client session takes time. If your Web application does not use *Session* state variables, you should turn off *Session* state tracking.

To turn off *Session* state, in the application's Web.config file, set the *sessionState* element's *mode* attribute to "*Off*", as shown here:

```
<sessionState
  mode="Off"
  stateConnectionString="tcpip=127.0.0.1:42424"
  sqlConnectionString="data source=127.0.0.1;user id=sa;password="
  cookieless="false"
  timeout="20"
/>
```

Turning off *Session* state means that you can't use *Session* state variables in code anywhere in the application.

Optimization Tips

Think of **tuning** as making adjustments to a deployed application that don't affect code. **Optimization** usually refers to writing code in a way that executes more quickly or consumes fewer resources. In general, optimizations simply reflect the good programming practices that you have learned so far in this book. Some of the most important points are summarized here:

- **Turn off debugging for deployed applications.**   Code that has been compiled with release options runs faster than code compiled with debug options.

- **Avoid round-trips between the client and server.**   ASP.NET uses postbacks to process server events on a page. Try to design Web forms so that the data on the Web form is complete before the user posts the data to the server. You can use the validation controls to ensure that data is complete on the client side before the page is submitted.

- **Turn off *Session* state if it isn't needed.**   In some cases, you can design your code to use other techniques, such as cookies, to store client data.

- **Turn off *ViewState* for server controls that do not need to retain their values.**   Saving *ViewState* information adds to the amount of data that must be transmitted back to the server with each request.

- **Use stored procedures with databases.**   Stored procedures execute more quickly than ad hoc queries.

- **Use *SqlDataReader* rather than data sets for read-forward data retrieval.**   Using *SqlDataReader* is faster and consumes less memory than creating a data set.

When applying these optimization tips, please be guided by good sense. For instance, if you need to retain data about a client session, go ahead and use *Session* state rather than write your own implementation to do the same thing.

Lesson 5: Deploying Across Multiple Servers

Web applications that serve a large number of users or that present large amounts of data need to able to add capacity as users' demands increase. The ability to add capacity to an application is called **scalability**. ASP.NET Web applications support this concept through their ability to run in multiple processes and to have those processes distributed across multiple CPUs and/or multiple servers.

A Web application running on a single server that has multiple CPUs is called a **Web garden** in the ASP.NET documentation. A Web application running on multiple servers is called a **Web farm**. In this lesson, you'll learn how to enable your Web application to use each of these server configurations.

After this lesson, you will be able to

- Configure a server with multiple processors to run a Web application on several or all of its CPUs
- Run a Web application on multiple servers
- Use a state server to share *Session* state information between multiple instances of the same Web application
- Share *Session* state information using a SQL database

Estimated lesson time: 10 minutes

Scaling Up with Multiple Processors

If your server has multiple processors, you can specify that ASP.NET runs on all or some of the CPUs by setting the *webGarden* attribute of the *processModel* element in the server's Machine.config file, as shown here in boldface:

```
<processModel
  enable="true"
  timeout="Infinite"
  idleTimeout="Infinite"
  shutdownTimeout="0:00:05"
  requestLimit="Infinite"
  requestQueueLimit="5000"
  restartQueueLimit="10"
  memoryLimit="60"
  webGarden="true"
  cpuMask="0xffffffff"
  userName="machine"
  password="AutoGenerate"
  logLevel="Errors"
  clientConnectedCheck="0:00:05"
  comAuthenticationLevel="Connect"
```

```
    comImpersonationLevel="Impersonate"
    responseRestartDeadlockInterval="00:09:00"
    responseDeadlockInterval="00:03:00"
    maxWorkerThreads="25"
    maxIoThreads="25"
/>
```

Table 9-6 describes the *processModel* attributes that relate to Web gardens.

Table 9-6   Web Garden Attributes

Attribute	Usage
webGarden	Set to *"true"* to run ASP.NET Web applications on more than one processor on this server.
cpuMask	Specifies which CPUs should run ASP.NET Web applications. The setting *"0xffffffff"* runs the applications on all CPUs.

The *cpuMask* attribute is a bit mask used to turn ASP.NET on (1) or off (0) for each CPU on the server. For example, binary 1101 turns ASP.NET on for CPUs 0, 2, and 3 on a four-CPU server, leaving CPU 1 free for other uses. Binary 1101 maps to the hexadecimal setting *"0x0000000d"*.

Running ASP.NET on multiple processors requires that you take special steps to handle *Application* and *Session* state information. See the section "Sharing State Information," later in this lesson, for more information.

Scaling Up with Multiple Servers

For multiple servers to handle requests for a single HTTP address, you need to install load balancing to your network. Load-balancing services can be provided by hardware or software solutions.

Microsoft Windows 2000 Advanced Server and Microsoft Windows 2000 Datacenter both include Network Load Balancing (NLB) software to distribute requests to multiple servers. See the Visual Studio .NET online Help topic "Network Load Balancing Provider" for more information about installing and using this tool.

When load balancing is enabled for your network, you can install your Web application on multiple servers and have client requests distributed automatically to the least busy server at any given time.

Running a Web application on multiple servers requires that you take special steps to handle *Application* and *Session* state information. See the following section for more information.

Sharing State Information

In both a Web garden and a Web farm, client requests are directed to the ASP.NET process that is currently least busy. That means that a single client can interact with different CPUs or servers over the course of his or her session. This has the following implications for *Application* and *Session* state variables:

- *Application* **state variables are unique to each separate instance of the Web application.** Clients can share information through *Application* state if the Web application is running on a Web garden or a Web farm.
- *Session* **state variables are stored in-process by default.** To enable *Session* state in a Web garden or Web farm, you need to specify a *Session* state provider.

The following sections explore these issues in more detail.

Sharing *Application* State

To share data across multiple sessions in a Web garden or Web farm, you must save and restore the information using a resource that is available to all the processes. This can be done through an XML file, a database, or some other resource using the standard file or database access methods.

Sharing *Session* State

ASP.NET provides two built-in ways to share *Session* state information across a Web garden or Web farm. You can share *Session* state using:

- **A state server, as specified by a network location**   This technique is simple to implement and doesn't require you to install Microsoft SQL Server.
- **A SQL database, as specified by a SQL connection**   This technique provides the best performance for storing and retrieving state information.

To share *Session* state information using a state server, follow these steps:

1. In the Web application's Web.config file, set the *sessionState* element's *mode* and *stateConnectionString* attributes. For example, the following settings use the state server located at the TCP/IP address 192.168.1.102 on port 42:

```
<sessionState
  mode="StateServer"
  stateConnectionString="tcpip=192.168.1.102:42"
  sqlConnectionString="data source=192.168.1.102;user id=sa;password="
  cookieless="false"
  timeout="20"
/>
```

2. Run the aspnet_state.exe utility on the *Session* state server. The aspnet_state.exe utility is installed in the \WINDOWS\Microsoft.NET \Framework*version* folder when you install Visual Studio .NET Professional or Visual Studio .NET Enterprise Architect editions.

To share *Session* state information using a SQL database, follow these steps:

1. In the Web application's Web.config file, set the *sessionState* element's *mode* and *sqlConnectionString* attributes. For example, the following settings use the SQL Server located at the TCP/IP address 192.168.1.102:

```
<sessionState
  mode="SQLServer"
  stateConnectionString="tcpip=192.168.1.102:42"
  sqlConnectionString="data source=192.168.1.102;user id=sa;password="
  cookieless="false"
  timeout="20"
/>
```

2. Run the InstallSqlState.sql utility on the *Session* state server. This utility installs the SQL database that shares *Session* state information across processes. The InstallSqlState.sql utility is installed in the \WINDOWS\Microsoft.NET \Framework*version* folder when you install Visual Studio .NET Professional, Visual Studio .NET Enterprise Developer, or Visual Studio .NET Enterprise Architect editions.

Summary

- Set the build option to Release and the *debug* attribute to *"false"* in Web.config before building your application for deployment.
- Use the AssemblyInfo.vb or AssemblyInfo.cs file to identify the application's assembly and provide versioning information.
- To deploy a Web application, use the Visual Studio .NET upload tools or simply copy the application's assembly and content files to the server.
- Set the security privileges on the ASPNET user account to enable your Web application to write files or access other security-restricted resources on the server.
- After deployment, monitor the Web application using the MMC Event Viewer and Performance Logs and Alerts snap-ins.
- You can repair Web applications by uploading new versions of the application's assembly or content files to the server.
- Web applications with memory leaks or other problems can repair themselves through ASP.NET process recycling.
- To enable a Web garden, use the *processModel* element attributes in the server's Machine.config file.
- To enable a Web farm, use a load balancer to distribute requests to multiple servers.
- For both Web gardens and Web farms, share *Session* state information by setting the *sessionState* element in the application's Web.config file.

Lab: Building and Deploying a Web Application

In this lab, you'll prepare a Web application for deployment, deploy the application to a server, and monitor and tune the application's performance. Before you begin, choose one of the applications you completed in an earlier chapter—or choose a Web application that you have completed on your own—to use for the exercises that follow.

This lab covers material that applies to all types of Web applications, so it will be more interesting if you choose an application you want to share with others or are interested in using yourself over the Internet.

Estimated lesson time: 30 minutes

Exercise 1: Prepare the Application

In this exercise, you'll build a release version of the Web application. Use the skills you learned in Lesson 1 to complete the following major tasks:

1. Identify the application and set its version number in the AssemblyInfo.vb or AssemblyInfo.cs file.
2. Set the compilation element's *debug* attribute to "*false*" in the application's Web.config file.
3. Set the application's build option to Release.
4. Build the application.

Exercise 2: Deploy the Application

How you deploy your application depends on the type of server you have available. If you are hosting your applications through a Web hosting service, as discussed in Chapter 1, "Introduction to Web Programming," use the Visual Studio .NET upload tools to deploy your application to the hosting service.

If you are hosting applications on your own server, use the skills you learned in Lesson 2 in this chapter to perform the following tasks:

1. Create a virtual folder for the application using IIS on the server.
2. Copy the Web application to the virtual folder.
3. View the security settings on the server to verify that the ASPNET user account has the permissions to perform the tasks required by your application.

4. If needed, grant access to resources used by your application.

5. Run the application from the server to verify that your security settings allow the application to run correctly.

Exercise 3: Chart Application Performance

In this exercise, you'll use the MMC Performance snap-in to keep a log of the number of requests processed by ASP.NET and chart those requests against processor activity on the server. When complete, the chart will appear similar to that shown in Figure 9-39.

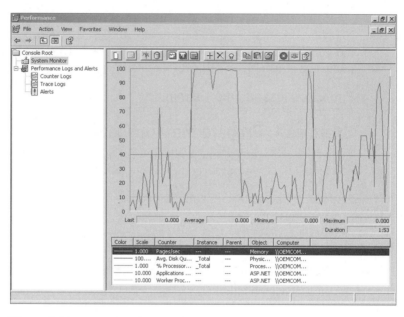

Figure 9-39   Charting Web application performance

Use the skills you learned in Lesson 3 to perform the following tasks:

1. Run the MMC Performance snap-in and connect to the server that's running the deployed Web application. If you deployed your application to a Web hosting service in Exercise 2, you won't be able to connect to that server. Instead, run the Web application locally on your development machine and connect to your local machine instead.

2. Create a new counter log named Exercise 3.

3. Add the counters to the log, as shown in the following table:

Performance object	Counter
Processor	%Processor time
ASP.NET applications	Anonymous requests
ASP.NET	Applications running
ASP.NET	Worker processes running

4. Start the counter log and then stop it after a few minutes to collect data about the server.

5. Select the System Monitor in the snap-in, and change the monitor's properties to view the log files:

   a. Right-click the System Monitor, and select Properties from the shortcut menu.

   b. Click the Properties Source tab, select Log Files, and then click Add to add the log files to the monitor.

   c. Click the Properties Data tab, and then click Add to add the ASP.NET counters to the monitor.

   d. On the Properties Data tab, set the scale of each of the ASP.NET counters to 10.

   e. Click OK to view the log as a chart.

   f. In the System Monitor, select Report to view the log data in text form.

   g. Experiment with other counters, such as ASP.NET application errors, cache hits, and so on.

Review

The following questions are intended to reinforce key information presented in this chapter. If you are unable to answer a question, review the appropriate lesson and then try the question again. Answers to the questions can be found in the appendix.

1. What permissions do Web applications run under by default?

2. Why is the Machine.config file important to deployed Web applications?

3. How do you configure a setup project to install an application over the Web?

4. How do you distribute shared components as part of an installation program?

5. How does deploying to a Web farm or a Web garden affect *Session* state in a Web application?

C H A P T E R   1   0

Testing Web Applications

About This Chapter

The goal of testing software is to ensure that the software meets product requirements. Two preconditions lurk in that simple statement:

- Without product requirements, you can't start testing.
- Without measurable goals, you don't know when to stop testing.

Product requirements and goals arc generally determined outside the development process—usually by customers or management. In this chapter, you'll learn how to apply product requirements to plan, create, run, and correct problems found by tests.

Before You Begin

To complete this chapter, you must:

- Have access to a Web server—either through a Web hosting service or through your local area network (LAN)—that you can use to test and debug Web applications.
- Have successfully completed and deployed one or more of the sample Web applications in this book.
- Be familiar with a Microsoft Windows scripting language, such as Microsoft VBScript or Microsoft JScript.
- Have installed Microsoft Application Center Test (ACT), included with Microsoft Visual Studio .NET Enterprise Architect Edition. This requirement applies only to the material in this chapter that discusses load testing Web applications.

Lesson 1: Creating Tests

All software intended for public consumption should receive some level of testing. The more complex or widely distributed a piece of software is, the more essential testing is to its success. Without testing, you have no assurance that software will behave as expected. The results in a public environment can be truly embarrassing.

For software, *testing* almost always means **automated testing**. Automated tests use a programming language to replay recorded user actions or to simulate the internal use of a component. Automated tests are *reproducible* (the same test can be run again and again) and *measurable* (the test either succeeds or fails). These two advantages are key to ensuring that software meets product requirements.

In this lesson, you'll learn how to write a test plan, how to ensure that the product is thoroughly tested using different types of tests, and how to create different types of tests using Visual Studio .NET.

After this lesson, you will be able to

- Understand a software test plan
- Identify different types of software testing
- Write unit tests for software components
- Create integration tests for completed components
- Explain how a test library can identify regressions
- Use ACT to create Web application load tests
- Test Web applications for different client configurations

Estimated lesson time: 30 minutes

Developing a Test Plan

The first step in testing is developing a test plan based on the product requirements. The test plan is usually a formal document that ensures that the product meets the following standards:

- **Is thoroughly tested**   Untested code adds an unknown element to the product and increases the risk of product failure.
- **Meets product requirements**   To meet customer needs, the product must provide the features and behavior described in the product specification. For this reason, product specifications should be clearly written and well understood.
- **Does not contain defects**   Features must work within established quality standards, and those standards should be clearly stated within the test plan.

Having a test plan helps you avoid **ad hoc testing**—the kind of testing that relies on the uncoordinated efforts of developers or testers to ensure that code works. The results of ad hoc testing are usually uneven and always unpredictable. A good test plan answers the following questions:

- **How are tests written?**   Describe the languages and tools used for testing.
- **Who is responsible for the testing?**   List the teams or individuals who write and perform the tests.
- **When are the tests performed?**   The testing schedule closely follows the development schedule.
- **Where are the tests and how are test results shared?**   Tests should be organized so that they can be rerun on a regular basis.
- **What is being tested?**   Measurable goals with concrete targets let you know when you have achieved success.

Some of these questions might have more than one answer, depending on the type of test. For instance, individual developers are often responsible for writing the first level of tests for their own code, while a separate testing team might be responsible for ensuring that all code works together. The following sections describe the different types of tests and the techniques used with Visual Studio .NET to perform these tests.

Types of Tests

The test plan specifies the different types of tests that will be performed to ensure the that product meets customer requirements and does not contain defects. Table 10-1 describes the most common test types.

Table 10-1   Types of Tests

Test type	Ensures that
Unit test	Each independent piece of code works correctly.
Integration test	All units work together without errors.
Regression test	Newly added features do not introduce errors to other features that are already working.
Load test (also called stress test)	The product continues to work under extreme usage.
Platform test	The product works on all of the target hardware and software platforms.

These test types build on each other, and the tests are usually performed in the order shown in Table 10-1. The testing process follows the flow diagram shown in Figure 10-1.

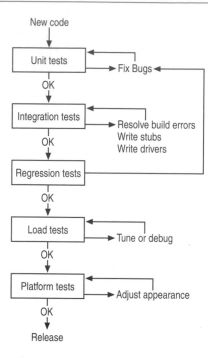

Figure 10-1   The testing cycle

The process shown in Figure 10-1 is based on a modular product design in which the product is developed as a set of components that can be programmed, tested, integrated, and released individually. This is the modern approach, and you should be wary of any project that proposes a monolithic design in which integration and testing are performed only at the end of the development cycle.

Unit Testing

A product *unit* is the smallest piece of code that can be independently tested. From an object-oriented programming perspective, classes, properties, methods, and events are all individual units. A unit should pass its unit test before it is checked into the project for integration.

Unit tests are commonly written by the developer who programmed the unit and are either written in the same programming language as the product unit being tested or in a similar scripting language, such as VBScript. The unit test itself can be as simple as getting and setting a property value, or it can be more complicated. For instance, a unit test might take sample data and calculate a result and then compare that result against the expected result to check for accuracy.

Group the unit tests together logically. Tests that check each property and method in a class can be included in a single procedure, which is then called from the *Sub Main* of a separate testing application. For example, the following test procedure creates an instance of the *FlashCardClass* created in Chapter 2, "Creating Web Forms Applications," and then tests each of its properties and methods:

Visual Basic .NET

```
Function TestFlashCard() As Boolean
    'Create class.
    Dim FlashCard As New MCSDWebAppsVB.FlashCardClass()
    'Test if class exists.
    If IsNothing(FlashCard) Then
        Console.WriteLine("FlashCardClass failed")
        'Return False and end here.
        Return False
    End If
    'Test shuffle method using maximum and minimum values.
    FlashCard.Shuffle(Integer.MinValue, Integer.MaxValue)
    'Test properties.
    Dim bResult As Boolean = True
    Dim intFirst As Integer = FlashCard.FirstNumber
    Dim intSecond As Integer = FlashCard.SecondNumber
    Dim dblAnswer As Double = intFirst + intSecond
    If dblAnswer <> FlashCard.Answer Then
        Console.WriteLine("Error: Numbers don't add up!")
        bResult = False
    End If
    'Shuffle again.
    FlashCard.Shuffle(Integer.MinValue, Integer.MaxValue)
    'Make sure the new values are unique.
    If intFirst = FlashCard.FirstNumber Then
        Console.WriteLine("Warning: FirstNumber not unique after shuffle")
    End If
    If intSecond = FlashCard.SecondNumber Then
        Console.WriteLine("Warning: SecondNumber not unique after shuffle")
    End If
    'Check different operators.
    FlashCard.Operation = "-"
    If FlashCard.FirstNumber -_
        FlashCard.SecondNumber <> FlashCard.Answer Then
        Console.WriteLine("Error: - operator doesn't substract.")
        bResult = False
    End If
    FlashCard.Operation = "x"
    If FlashCard.FirstNumber * FlashCard.SecondNumber <> FlashCard.Answer Then
        Console.WriteLine("Error: x operator doesn't multiply.")
        bResult = False
    End If
    FlashCard.Operation = "+"
```

```
        If FlashCard.FirstNumber + FlashCard.SecondNumber <> FlashCard.Answer Then
            Console.WriteLine("Error: + operator doesn't add.")
            bResult = False
        End If
        'Return success/failure.
        Return bResult
    End Function
```

Visual C#

```
static bool TestFlashCardClass()
{
    //Create class.
    csFlashCards.FlashCardClass FlashCard = new MCSDWebAppsCS.FlashCardClass(
);
    //Test is class exists.
    if (FlashCard == null)
    {
        Console.WriteLine("FlashCardClass failed");
        //Return false and end here.
        return false;
    }
    //Test shuffle method using maximum and minimum values.
    FlashCard.Shuffle(int.MinValue, int.MaxValue);
    //Test properties.
    bool bResult  = true;
    int intFirst = FlashCard.FirstNumber;
    int intSecond = FlashCard.SecondNumber;
    double dblAnswer = intFirst + intSecond;
    if (dblAnswer != (double)FlashCard.Answer())
    {
        Console.WriteLine("Error: Numbers don't add up!");
        bResult = false;
    }
    //Shuffle again.
    FlashCard.Shuffle(int.MinValue, int.MaxValue);
    //Make sure new values unique.
    if (intFirst == FlashCard.FirstNumber)
        Console.WriteLine("Warning: FirstNumber not unique after shuffle");
    if (intSecond == FlashCard.SecondNumber)
        Console.WriteLine("Warning: SecondNumber not unique after shuffle");
    //Check different operators.
    FlashCard.Operation = "-";
    if (FlashCard.FirstNumber - FlashCard.SecondNumber != FlashCard.Answer())
    {
        Console.WriteLine("Error: - operator doesn't substract.");
        bResult = false;
    }
    FlashCard.Operation = "x";
    if (FlashCard.FirstNumber * FlashCard.SecondNumber != FlashCard.Answer())
```

```
    {
        Console.WriteLine("Error: x operator doesn't multiply.");
        bResult = false;
    }
    FlashCard.Operation = "+";
    if (FlashCard.FirstNumber + FlashCard.SecondNumber != FlashCard.Answer())
    {
        Console.WriteLine("Error: + operator doesn't add.");
        bResult = false;
    }
    //Return success/failure.
    return bResult;
}
```

The most important factor in a unit test is *thoroughness*. Unit tests should exercise each piece of code in the application and use a range of possible values. The preceding sample demonstrates using a wide range by passing the integer *MinValue* and *MaxValue* properties to the *Shuffle* method.

The tests should report errors at the unit level so that locating and fixing problems is straightforward. The preceding sample does this by displaying a message in the Output window using *Console.WriteLine*. Alternatively, you can write errors to a testing log file using *Debug.WriteLine* or raise alerts using *Debug.Assert*.

Integration Testing

The first integration test always answers the question, "Does the application compile?" At this point, a compilation error in any of the components can keep the integration testing from moving forward. Some projects use nightly builds to ensure that the product will always compile. If the build fails, the problem can be quickly resolved the next morning.

The most common build problem occurs when one component tries to use another component that has not yet been written. This occurs with modular design because the components are often created out of sequence. You solve this problem by creating stubs. **Stubs** are nonfunctional components that provide the class, property, or method definition used by the other component. Stubs are a kind of outline of the code you will create later.

When all of the build problems are resolved, integration testing really becomes just an extension of unit testing, although the focus is now whether the units work together. At this point, it is possible to wind up with two components that need to work together through a third component that has not been written yet. To test these two components, you create a driver. **Drivers** are simply test components that make sure two or more components work together. Later in the project, testing performed by the driver can be performed by the actual component.

In addition to adding stubs and drivers to your application, you might need to add a testing interface to help automate the integration testing of some components. A **testing interface** is a set of public properties and methods or other tools that you can use to control a component from an external testing program. For example, the following testing interface generates a log of the results displayed by the FlashCard application's Web form:

Visual Basic .NET

```vbnet
' From FlashCards.aspx
Private Sub txtAnswer_TextChanged(ByVal sender As System.Object, _
    ByVal e As System.EventArgs) Handles txtAnswer.TextChanged
    If txtAnswer.Text = FlashCard.Answer Then
        lblFeedback.Text = "Correct!"
#If DEBUG Then
        LogResult()
#End If
        ' Get another set of numbers.
        FlashCard.Shuffle()
        ' Refresh display to show new numbers.
        RefreshDisplay()
    Else
        lblFeedback.Text = "Oops! Try Again."
#If DEBUG Then
        LogResult()
#End If
    End If
    ' Clear answer
    txtAnswer.Text = ""
End Sub

#If DEBUG Then
Public Sub TestUI()
    Dim strResult As String
    ' Check if correct.
    If lblFeedback.Text = "Correct!" Then
        strResult = lblFirst.Text + lblSecond.Text + "=" + txtAnswer.Text
    Else
        strResult = lblFirst.Text + lblSecond.Text + "!=" + txtAnswer.Text
    End If
    Dim filResult As StreamWriter = _
        File.AppendText(Server.MapPath(".\results.log"))
    filResult.Write(System.DateTime.Now.ToString() + ", ")
    filResult.WriteLine(strResult)
    filResult.Close()
End Sub
#End If
```

Visual C#

```
//From FlashCards.aspx
private void txtAnswer_TextChanged(object sender, System.EventArgs e)
{
    if(txtAnswer.Text == FlashCard.Answer().ToString())
    {
        lblFeedback.Text = "Correct!";
#if DEBUG
        TestUI();
#endif
        //Get another set of numbers.
        FlashCard.Shuffle();
        //Refresh display to show new numbers.
        RefreshDisplay();
        //Clear answer
        txtAnswer.Text = "";
    }
    else
    {
        lblFeedback.Text = "Oops! Try Again.";
#if DEBUG
        TestUI();
#endif
    }
}


#if DEBUG
public void TestUI()
{
    string strResult;
    //Check if correct.
    if (lblFeedback.Text == "Correct!")
        strResult = lblFirst.Text + lblSecond.Text + "=" + txtAnswer.Text;
    else
        strResult = lblFirst.Text + lblSecond.Text + "!=" + txtAnswer.Text;
    StreamWriter filResult =
        File.AppendText(Server.MapPath(".\\results.log"));
    filResult.Write(System.DateTime.Now.ToString() + ", ");
    filResult.WriteLine(strResult);
    filResult.Close();
}
#endif
```

The preceding code uses the *#If...#End If/#if...#endif* preprocessor directives to prevent the testing interface from being compiled into the release version of the product. This is important because a testing interface exposes the inner workings of the application, which you generally want to hide in the final version.

Regression Testing

Unit and integration tests form the basis of regression testing. As each test is written and passed, it gets checked into the test library for a regularly scheduled testing run. If a new component or a change to an existing component breaks one of the existing unit or integration tests, the error is called a **regression**.

If you design your test properly, the unit and integration tests report their errors in a way that makes it easy to locate the cause of the regression. If the test doesn't provide an easy way to locate the cause, you might need to improve those tests or you might need to write new tests to target the regression.

The key to success with both integration and regression testing is to run the full set of tests frequently—if possible, as part of the nightly build. Detecting problems early and resolving them as they occur prevents one error from hiding others.

Load Testing

When you deploy a Web application, it might be used by one or two clients at a time or it might get deluged by thousands of requests. To find out how well a Web application will work in these varying conditions, you need to perform load tests. Use the Microsoft ACT to create and run load tests on a Web application.

To use ACT, follow these steps:

1. Create a test by recording a user session with the Web application using ACT.
2. Set the load level and duration properties for the test.
3. Run the test.

In general, load tests are not created as early in the development process or run as frequently as unit, integration, or regression tests. The following sections describe how to create and run load tests in more detail.

Recording a Load Test

To record a load test in ACT, follow these steps:

1. From the ACT Actions menu, choose New Test. ACT displays the New Test Wizard.
2. Click Next. The wizard displays the Test Source page, as shown in Figure 10-2.

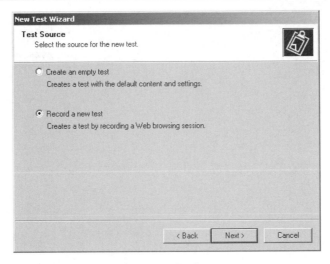

Figure 10-2   Recording a new load test

3. Select Record A New Test, and click Next. The wizard displays the Test Type page, as shown in Figure 10-3.

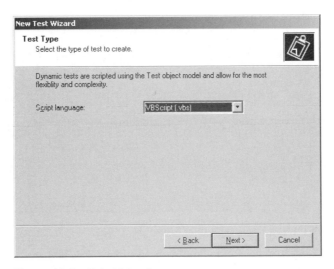

Figure 10-3   Selecting a language

4. Click Next. The wizard displays the Browser Record page, as shown in Figure 10-4.

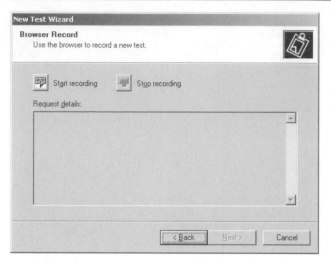

Figure 10-4   Starting and stopping recording

5. Click Start Recording. The wizard displays a browser window, as shown in Figure 10-5.

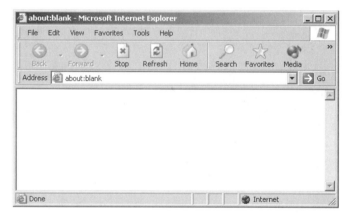

Figure 10-5   Performing actions to record

6. Perform the actions you want to record. For instance, you might walk through all the pages in your Web application, performing tasks on each page.

7. On the Browser Record page, click Stop Recording when you have finished recording actions, and then click Next. The wizard displays the Test Properties page, as shown in Figure 10-6.

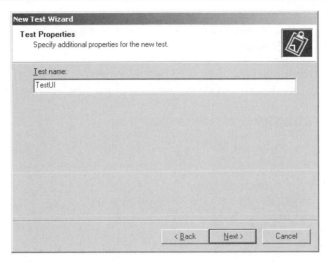

Figure 10-6   Naming the test

8. Enter a name for the test, and click Next. The wizard displays the Completing The New Test Wizard page. Click Finish to close the wizard.

Setting Test Properties

After you record a test, it is displayed in the Tests list in ACT, as shown in Figure 10-7.

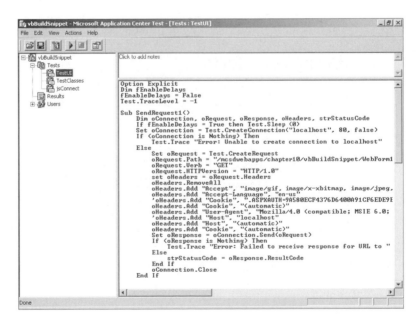

Figure 10-7   The recorded test

ACT tests can be written in the VBScript or JScript languages, but ACT records tests using VBScript only. After you record a test, set the load and duration of the test by following these steps:

1. Right-click your test, and choose Properties on the shortcut menu. ACT displays the test's load and duration properties, as shown in Figure 10-8.

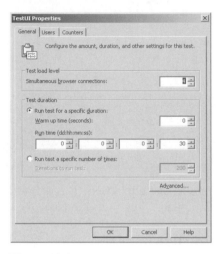

Figure 10-8   Test load and duration

2. Set the Test load level to increase the number of users accessing the Web application at the same time. Set the Test duration to run the test for a certain amount of time or for a certain number of requests. Click OK when you've finished.

Running Load Tests

To run a load test in ACT, select the test, and then choose Start Test from the Actions menu. ACT displays the Test Status dialog box, as shown in Figure 10-9.

Figure 10-9   The Test Status dialog box

Running tests with ACT and analyzing their results is covered in more detail in Lesson 2.

Platform Testing

For Web applications, platform testing usually means verifying four main conditions:

■ Web forms are displayed correctly on all supported browsers and supported versions of those browsers.

■ The Web application appropriately handles unsupported browser versions—for example, by displaying instructions for downloading the required version.

■ The client is prompted to install any required components, such as Microsoft ActiveX objects or plug-ins, if they are not already installed on his or her computer.

■ The Web application has acceptable performance over slower forms of network connections, such as modems.

To run platform tests, you need to set up a platform lab that contains computers representing the different hardware and software configurations that your application supports, as shown in Figure 10-10.

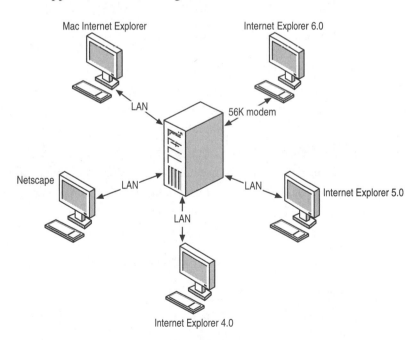

Figure 10-10 Platform testing lab

Verifying that each Web form is displayed correctly requires some human intervention. ASP.NET renders server controls differently on different browsers, so you should visually inspect your Web application as part of the final testing cycle.

Lesson 2: Running Tests

In the preceding lesson, you learned how to plan testing and how to create different types of tests using Visual Studio .NET. In this lesson, you'll learn how to run those tests and capture their results.

After this lesson, you will be able to

- Use ACT to run load tests on Web applications
- Record results and performance data from a load test
- Mimic different browser types with ACT and check browser responses for contained strings within test scripts
- Use the Windows Scripting Host to test .NET assemblies
- Create command files to build and test .NET assemblies
- Run command files at specified times using the Windows Task Manager to perform unattended nightly build and test runs

Estimated lesson time: 30 minutes

Running Tests with ACT

Lesson 1 briefly showed you how to create a load test and run it in ACT. This section describes how to configure and run ACT tests in more detail by describing how to perform the following tasks:

- Log test results.
- Configure the test to use multiple simultaneous connections.
- Run tests with different user name and password combinations.
- Add performance counters to a test.
- Mimic different browsers and different network connection types.

These tasks are explained in the following sections.

Logging Test Results

By default, ACT creates a log file for each test project in the /Perflogs folder on the drive where ACT is installed.

To change the location where ACT stores the log file, follow these steps:

1. Right-click the project item in the left pane of the ACT window, and choose Properties from the shortcut menu. ACT displays the test project's Properties dialog box, as shown in Figure 10-11.

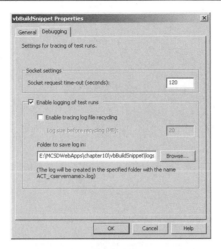

Figure 10-11   Setting log file location

2. Click the Debugging tab, and enter a location for storing test project logs in the Folder To Save Log In box. Click OK when you've finished.

ACT log files record different amounts of information, depending on the test's *TraceLevel* settings. To change the amount of information logged, set the *Test* object's *TraceLevel* property within a test script. For example, the following line of script tells ACT to log all messages:

VBScript
```
Test.TraceLevel = -1
```

JScript
```
Test.TraceLevel = -1;
```

The *TraceLevel* property has the settings shown in Table 10-2.

Table 10-2   *TraceLevel* Settings

Setting	Logs
-1	All information, including requests sent to the application, responses from the application, and messages written by *Trace* methods in the test script.
0	No information—turns off logging.
1	Requests sent to the application and responses from the application.
2	Messages written by *Trace* methods in the test script. This is the default setting.

Use the *Test* object's *Trace* method to write messages to the log from within the test script. For example, the following script writes a message to the log if ACT is not able to connect to the server:

VBScript

```
Dim g_oConnection

ConnnectToServer

Sub ConnectToServer()
Set g_oConnection = Test.CreateConnection("http://www.contoso.com, 80, false)
    If (g_oConnection is Nothing) Then
        Test.Trace "Error: Unable to create connection to contoso"
    End If
End Sub
```

JScript

```
var g_oConnection

ConnectToServer();

function ConnectToServer()
{
    g_oConnection = Test.CreateConnection
        ("http://www.contoso.com", 80, false);
    if (g_oConnection == null)
        Test.Trace("Error: Unable to create connection to contoso");
}
```

Using Multiple Connections

ACT can simulate different server load levels by adding simultaneous connections to use during the test. By default, ACT uses one connection to send requests to the Web application. Additional connections are the equivalent of additional simultaneous users.

To increase the number of connections used for a test, follow these steps:

1. Right-click the test item in the left pane of the ACT window, and choose Properties from the shortcut menu. ACT displays the test's Properties dialog box, as shown in Figure 10-12.

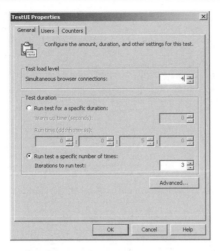

Figure 10-12   Test properties

2. Change the number in the Test Load Level section to set the number of simultaneous connections. Click OK when you've finished.

Adding Users and Passwords

ACT can supply user names and passwords to a Web application through the user's groups stored with the test project. This allows you to test how a Web application authenticates users and also permits you to test cookies.

To add user names and passwords to a user group, follow these steps:

1. Select Users in the left pane of the ACT window to expand the list of user groups.
2. Select a user group, and then enter user names and passwords in the table displayed in the right pane of the ACT window. Figure 10-13 shows changes to the Default Users Group.

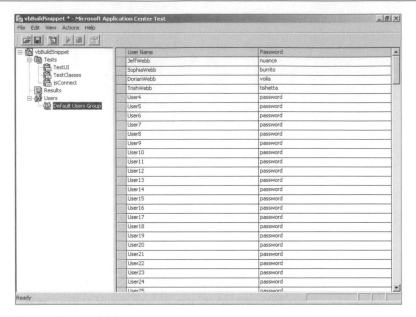

Figure 10-13   Adding users

3. Right-click the test item in the left pane of the ACT window, and select Properties. ACT displays the test's Properties dialog box, as shown in Figure 10-14.

Figure 10-14   Setting test properties to activate users

4. Click the Users tab, and select Specify Users. Click OK when you've finished.

ACT automatically changes users for each new iteration of a test and for each new connection it creates. You can also manually change users within a test using the *Test* object's *GetNextUser* method, as shown here:

VBScript

```
Sub ChangeUser()
    Test.GetNextUser
    Test.Trace("Next user name: " & Test.GetCurrentUser.Name)
End Sub
```

JScript

```
function ChangeUser()
{
    Test.GetNextUser();
    Test.Trace("Next user name: " + Test.GetCurrentUser.Name);
}
```

Adding Performance Counters

You can track a Web application's performance during a load test by adding performance counters to the test's properties. These performance counters are the same ones that you used to monitor server performance in Chapter 9, "Building and Deploying Web Applications," using the Microsoft Management Console (MMC) Performance Logs and Alerts snap-in.

To add performance counters to a load test, follow these steps:

1. Right-click the test item in the left pane of the ACT window, and choose Properties on the shortcut menu. ACT displays the test's Properties dialog box.

2. Click the Counters tab, and then click Add. ACT displays the Browse Performance Counters dialog box, as shown in Figure 10-15.

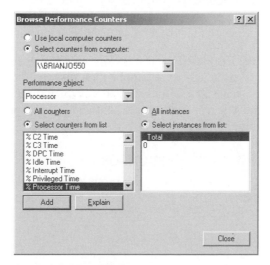

Figure 10-15   Adding counters

3. Select the counters you want to monitor, and click Add. Click Close when you have finished adding counters.

4. Click OK to close the test's Properties dialog box.

When a test runs, ACT saves performance statistics in an XML file that is listed in the test results pane of the ACT window, as shown in Figure 10-16.

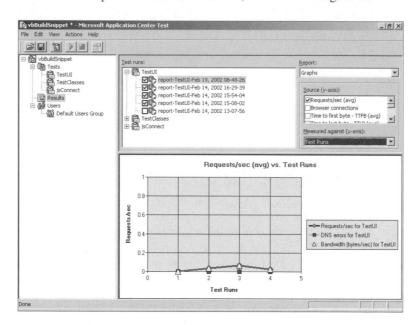

Figure 10-16   Viewing performance results

Mimicking Browser Types

ACT can mimic different types of browsers by modifying the user agent information included in the header it sends with each request. The Browser Type test in the ACTSamples project that is installed with ACT demonstrates how to do this.

You can copy the Browser Type test to your own test projects to test browser compatibility and to test whether your application responds correctly to unsupported browser types. Because ACT does not actually display the responses, however, you can't rely on this test to visually check that your Web application is displayed correctly on different browsers.

Getting Content of Responses

ACT returns the server's response to a request as the *Response* object's *Body* property. You can use the VBScript *Instr* function to test whether a response contains an expected result, as shown here:

VBScript
```
Set oResponse = oConnection.Send(oRequest)
If Instr(oResponse.Body, "Correct!") Then
    Test.Trace("Correct response.")
Else
    Test.Trace("Incorrect response.")
End If
```

JScript
```
oResponse = oConnection.Send(oRequest);
if (oResponse.Body.search"Correct!"))
    Test.Trace("Correct response.");
else
    Test.Trace("Incorrect response.");
```

The Body Search test in the ACTSamples project further demonstrates using *Instr* to locate items in a response.

More Info   The ACT online Help provides a complete reference to the testing object model and includes conceptual information about using ACT to load test Web applications.

Running Tests with .NET Assemblies

ACT was written primarily to interact with Web applications through requests and responses. This is great for testing the user interface aspects of a Web application, but it is limiting when you're trying to perform tests on the underlying classes used by the application.

For example, say that you want to use ACT to test the *FlashCardClass*, as shown in the section "Unit Testing," in Lesson 1. How would you do it? Probably by attempting something like this:

VBScript
```
Test.TraceLevel = -1

Dim FlashCard
Set FlashCard = CreateObject("vbFlashCards.FlashCardClass")

If (FlashCard Is Nothing) Then
    Test.Trace("Error: FlashCard not created.")
    Test.StopTest
End If
```

JScript

```
Test.TraceLevel = -1;

var FlashCard;
FlashCard = CreateObject("csFlashCards.FlashCardClass");

if (FlashCard == null)
{
    Test.Trace("Error: FlashCard not created.");
    Test.StopTest();
}
```

The only problem is that this doesn't work! Because Web applications are based on the Microsoft .NET Framework, you can't use their namespaces as an argument to the *CreateObject* method. *CreateObject* expects a Component Object Model (COM) object's programmatic identifier (progID), *not* a namespace.

To use scripting to test a .NET assembly, follow these steps:

1. In order to register a .NET assembly for use from COM, the assembly must be compiled as a separate class library. Web application assemblies can't be used from COM. Register the .NET assembly for use with COM.
2. Make sure that the COM application can find the .NET assembly.
3. Create the .NET object using the progID registered for the .NET assembly.

The following sections describe these steps in more detail.

Registering .NET Assemblies

Use the RegAsm.exe utility to register a .NET assembly with the system registration database. The RegAsm.exe utility is installed with the .NET Framework.

To use the RegAsm.exe utility, follow these steps:

1. Open a Visual Studio .NET command prompt. From the Start menu, point to All Programs, Microsoft Visual Studio .NET, Visual Studio .NET Tools, and then choose Visual Studio .NET Command Prompt.
2. Within the command prompt, navigate to the folder containing the assembly to register, and run the following command:

RegAsm.exe assembly.dll

The variable *assembly.dll* is the name of the assembly to register.

RegAsm.exe registers the public classes from the .NET assembly using their namespace and class names as their progIDs. For example, registering the Shapes assembly created for COM interoperation in Chapter 7, "Advanced Web Forms Programming," results in the registry entries shown in Figure 10-17.

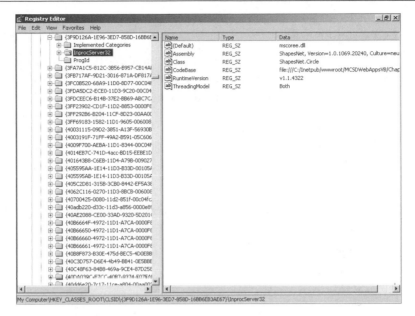

Figure 10-17   Shapes system registration database entries

Locating the .NET Assembly

After you register a .NET assembly, COM components need a way to find the assembly. There are a number of ways to do this, but the three simplest ways are:

- Install the assembly in the global assembly cache (GAC).
- Copy the assembly to the same folder as the COM component that will use it.
- Copy the COM component to the folder where the assembly resides.

Assemblies installed in the GAC are available to all applications on the computer. Assemblies must be configured to use strong names before they can be installed in the GAC. For complete instructions on configuring and installing assemblies in the GAC, see the Visual Studio .NET online Help.

For assemblies that are not intended for sharing with other applications, copying the assembly or the COM component to the same folder might be the easiest solution. This is particularly true for testing, when you might not want an assembly to be generally available.

Creating the .NET Object

After you have registered a .NET assembly and made sure that the COM components can find it, you can create an instance of the .NET object using the COM object creation methods, such as the VBScript *CreateObject* function.

To see how this works with a testing tool such as the Windows Scripting Host, follow these steps:

1. Register a Web application's assembly as described in the section "Registering .NET Assemblies," earlier in this chapter.
2. Copy CScript.exe from the \Windows\system32 or \WINNT\system32 folder to the Web application's \bin folder. This is the copy of CScript.exe that you will use to run your testing script; it must be in the same folder as the .NET assembly so that the COM and .NET objects can interoperate.
3. Create a VBScript or JScript file, and run it using the copy of CScript.exe stored in the \bin folder.

The following code demonstrates how to test *FlashCardClass* using the Windows Scripting Host:

VBScript

```
' TestFlash.vbs
' FlashCardClass unit test
Option Explicit

Dim FlashClass

Set FlashClass = CreateObject("vbFlashCards.FlashCardClass")
' Check if class created.
If (FlashClass is Nothing) Then
    WScript.Echo "Error: FlashCardClass not created."
    WScript.Quit
End If
' Test Shuffle
FlashClass.Shuffle 1, 1000
Dim X, Y
x = FlashClass.FirstNumber
y = FlashClass.SecondNumber
' Shuffle again
FlashClass.Shuffle 1, 1000
If (x = FlashClass.FirstNumber) or (y = FlashClass.SecondNumber) Then
    WScript.Echo "Warning: Number not unique."
End If
' Test Answer
If (FlashClass.FirstNumber + FlashClass.SecondNumber = FlashClass.Answer) The
n
    WScript.Echo "Success: Answer adds up!"
Else
    WScript.Echo "Error: Answer incorrect."
End If
```

JScript

```
//TestFlash.js
//FlashCardClass unit test
var FlashClass;

FlashClass = new ActiveXObject("vbFlashCards.FlashCardClass");
//Check if class created.
if (FlashClass == null)
{
    WScript.Echo("Error: FlashCardClass not created.");
    WScript.Quit();
}
//Test Shuffle
FlashClass.Shuffle(1, 1000);
var X, Y;
x = FlashClass.FirstNumber;
y = FlashClass.SecondNumber;
//Shuffle again
FlashClass.Shuffle(1, 1000);
if ((x == FlashClass.FirstNumber) || (y == FlashClass.SecondNumber))
    WScript.Echo("Warning: Number not unique.");
//Test Answer
if (FlashClass.FirstNumber + FlashClass.SecondNumber == FlashClass.Answer())
    WScript.Echo("Success: Answer adds up!");
else
    WScript.Echo("Error: Answer incorrect.");
```

To run the preceding script, use a command line similar to the following:

```
@rem VBScript
bin\cscript TestFlash.vbs > logs\FlashErr.log

@rem JScript
bin\cscript TestFlash.js > logs\FlashErr.log
```

Running Unattended Builds and Tests

Running unit, integration, and load tests on a regular basis provides constant quality assurance and checks for regressions. Most development teams run builds and a set of tests nightly. Running the tests at night prevents conflicts with check-ins and doesn't disrupt workflow while a machine is tied up doing a build. Because they run late at night, these builds are usually unattended, meaning that no one has to be there to start them or monitor their progress.

To run unattended builds and tests, follow these steps:

1. Create a command file to set the environment variables, build, and test commands you want to run.
2. Use the Windows Task Manager to schedule the command file to be run.

3. Monitor the log files written by the commands to ensure that the builds and tests are succeeding.

The following sections describe these steps in more detail.

Creating a Command File

You can create a command file (.bat) to execute any set of commands you want to run. In general, the command file has three main sections that perform the following tasks:

- Set environment variables, such as PATH and LIB, that are required to find the components used by the build
- Run the Visual Studio .NET development environment to build the assembly
- Run the test tools used to test the assembly

The environment variables used by Visual Studio .NET can be found in the VsVars32.bat command file that is installed in Visual Studio .NET's Command\Tools folder. You can cut and paste the settings from this file to your command file.

To run Visual Studio .NET from the command line, use the DevEnv.exe command with the project's solution file (.sln). For example, the following command line builds the FlashCards application using the Debug configuration and records any errors in the Logs folder:

```
DevEnv vbFlashCards.sln /build Debug > Logs\builders.log
```

You can put all of the steps together in a single command file. For example, the following command file sets the required environment variables, builds a Web application, and runs test scripts on the assembly:

```
@rem Build.bat
@rem ===================================================================
@rem Environment settings from vsvars32.bat
@rem ===================================================================
@SET VSINSTALLDIR=E:\Program Files\Microsoft Visual Studio .NET\Common7\IDE
@SET VCINSTALLDIR=E:\Program Files\Microsoft Visual Studio .NET
@SET FrameworkDir=C:\WINDOWS\Microsoft.NET\Framework
@SET FrameworkVersion=v1.0.3705
@SET FrameworkSDKDir=C:\Program Files\Microsoft Visual Studio
.NET\FrameworkSDK
@rem Root of Visual Studio common files.

@rem
@rem Root of Visual Studio ide installed files.
@rem
@set DevEnvDir=%VSINSTALLDIR%
```

```
@rem
@rem Root of Visual C++ installed files.
@rem
@set MSVCDir=%VCINSTALLDIR%\VC7

@set PATH=%DevEnvDir%;%MSVCDir%\BIN;%VCINSTALLDIR%\Common7\Tools;
%VCINSTALLDIR%\Common7\Tools\bin\prerelease;%VCINSTALLDIR%\Common7\Tools\bin;
%Framework SDKDir%\bin;%FrameworkDir%\%FrameworkVersion%;%PATH%;
@set INCLUDE=%MSVCDir%\ATLMFC\INCLUDE;%MSVCDir%\INCLUDE;
%MSVCDir%\PlatformSDK\include\prerelease;%MSVCDir%\PlatformSDK
\include;%FrameworkSDKDir%\include;%INCLUDE%
@set LIB=%MSVCDir%\ATLMFC\LIB;%MSVCDir%\LIB;
%MSVCDir%\PlatformSDK\lib\prerelease;
%MSVCDir%\PlatformSDK\lib;%FrameworkSDKDir%\lib;%LIB%

@rem =======================================================================
@rem End environment settings
@rem =======================================================================

@rem =======================================================================
@rem Development environment build commands
@rem =======================================================================
devenv vbBuildSnippet.sln /build debug > logs\builderrs.log
@rem =======================================================================
@rem End build commands
@rem =======================================================================

@rem =======================================================================
@rem Testing commands
@rem =======================================================================
bin\cscript RunTests.vbs > logs\testerrs.log
@rem =======================================================================
@rem End testing commands
@rem =======================================================================
```

Scheduling Tasks

To schedule a command file to run on a regular basis, use the Windows Task Manager.

To run the Task Manager, follow these steps:

1. From the Start Menu, point to All Programs, Accessories, System Tools, and then choose Scheduled Tasks. Windows displays the Scheduled Tasks folder.
2. Double-click Add Scheduled Task to run the Scheduled Task Wizard.
3. Click Next, and then click Browse and specify the command file to run. After you've selected the command file, the wizard displays the schedule page, as shown in Figure 10-18.

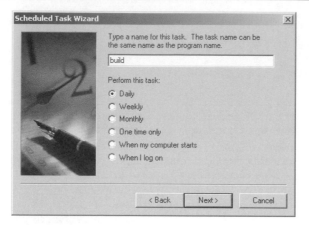

Figure 10-18   Choosing a schedule

4. Select an option indicating when to run the task, and click Next. The wizard displays the time page, as shown in Figure 10-19.

Figure 10-19   Choosing a time to run

5. Enter a time to run the task, and click Next. The wizard displays the password page, as shown in Figure 10-20.

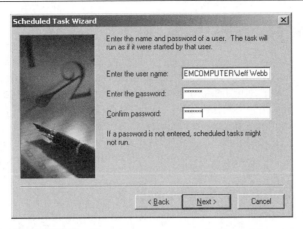

Figure 10-20   Entering user name and password

6. Enter the user name and password under which to run the command, click
    Next, and then click Finish to complete the wizard.

Viewing Log Files

Because builds and tests scheduled with the Task Manager run unattended, it is
important to monitor log files created by the commands in the build process. The
build and test commands shown earlier in this section used the redirect operator (>)
to write output from commands to log files stored in a Log folder.

Viewing log files in Notepad is easy, as shown in Figure 10-21.

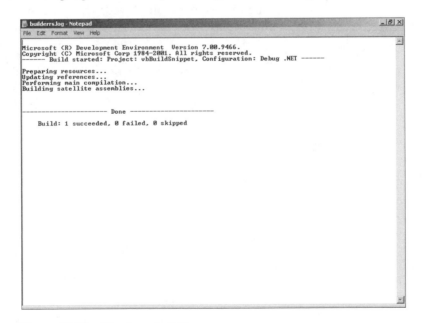

Figure 10-21   Viewing a build log

Lesson 3: Debugging

Testing is probably one of the few endeavors in which failure is a kind of success. In this lesson, you'll learn how to use those successes to fix problems in your code. The topics covered in this lesson build on the discussion of the Visual Studio debugging tools begun in Chapter 1, "Introduction to Web Programming." This includes fixing specific problems uncovered by testing, adding diagnostic code to an application, and debugging a Web application as it runs on a remote server.

After this lesson, you will be able to

- Apply the results of unit tests to fix common problems
- Use the *Debug* and *Trace* diagnostic classes to display alerts and generate logs during development
- Configure a Web server to allow remote workstations to debug Web applications
- Debug Web applications as they run on a remote server

Estimated lesson time: 30 minutes

Putting Test Results to Work

Something you probably noticed if you ran the unit tests for the FlashCards application shown in Lesson 1 is that FlashCards didn't pass the tests. That's because FlashCards is a simplified demonstration program, not a robust application intended for commercial use. Try that excuse at work sometime!

Seriously, though, the results are instructive. The first set of errors you encounter with the *FlashCardClass* unit tests are overflows, because you used integer *MinValue* and *MaxValue* properties to initialize the random numbers. Adding two values near the integer's maximum value results in a number larger than an integer. The related code is shown here:

Visual Basic .NET

```
' Test code
Function TestFlashCard() As Boolean
    'Create class
    Dim FlashCard As New vbFlashCards.FlashCardClass()
    'Test is class exists.
    If IsNothing(FlashCard) Then
        Console.WriteLine("FlashCardClass failed")
        ' Return false and end here.
        Return False
    End If
    'Test shuffle method.
```

```
        FlashCard.Shuffle(Integer.MinValue, Integer.MaxValue)
        'Test properties.
        If (FlashCard.Answer <> FlashCard.FirstNumber + FlashCard.SecondNumber) _
            Then
            Console.Write("Error: Answers don't match")
        End If
End Function


' FlashCardClass code with error.
' Calculates answer based on current operation.
Public Function Answer() As Integer
    Select Case mstrOp
        Case "+"
            Return mintFirstNumber + mintSecondNumber 'Overflow!!!!
        Case "x", "*"
            Return mintFirstNumber * mintSecondNumber
        Case "-"
            Return mintFirstNumber - mintSecondNumber
        Case Else
            Return 0
    End Select
End Function
```

Visual C#

```
//Test code.
static bool TestFlashCardClass()
{
    //Create class
    csFlashCards.FlashCardClass FlashCard = new csFlashCards.FlashCardClass()
;
    //Test is class exists.
    if (FlashCard == null)
    {
        Console.WriteLine("FlashCardClass failed");
        //Return false and end here.
        return false;
    }
    //Test shuffle method using maximum and minimum values.
    FlashCard.Shuffle(int.MinValue, int.MaxValue);
    //Test properties.
    int intFirst = FlashCard.FirstNumber;
    int intSecond = FlashCard.SecondNumber;
    double dblAnswer = intFirst + intSecond;
    if (dblAnswer != (double)FlashCard.Answer())
    {
        Console.WriteLine("Error: Numbers don't add up!");
    }
}

//FlashCardClass code with error.
```

```
//Calculates answer based on current operation.
public int Answer()
{
    switch(mstrOp)
    {
        case "+":
            return mintFirstNumber + mintSecondNumber;
        case "x":
            return mintFirstNumber * mintSecondNumber;
        case "*":
            return mintFirstNumber * mintSecondNumber;
        case "-":
            return mintFirstNumber - mintSecondNumber;
        default :
            return 0;
    }
}
```

You have two ways to tackle this problem: restrict the range of possible *FirstNumber* and *SecondNumber* property values, or change the return type for the *Answer* method. The second approach is more obvious from a user's standpoint because integers are a common input type and it would be hard to explain a new, smaller type for those properties.

The following code shows the changes to the *Answer* method that allow it to pass its unit test:

Visual Basic .NET

```
Public Function Answer() As Double
    Select Case mstrOp
        Case "+"
        Return CDbl(mintFirstNumber) + CDbl(mintSecondNumber)
        Case "x", "*"
        Return CDbl(mintFirstNumber) * CDbl(mintSecondNumber)
        Case "-"
        Return CDbl(mintFirstNumber) - CDbl(mintSecondNumber)
        Case "/"
        Return CDbl(mintFirstNumber) / CDbl(mintSecondNumber)
        Case Else
        Return 0
    End Select
End Function
```

Visual C#

```
public double Answer()
{
    switch(mstrOp)
    {
        case "+":
```

```
              return mintFirstNumber + mintSecondNumber;
         case "x":
              return mintFirstNumber * mintSecondNumber;
         case "*":
              return mintFirstNumber * mintSecondNumber;
         case "-":
              return mintFirstNumber - mintSecondNumber;
         default :
              return 0;
    }
}
```

Another problem arises with *FlashCardClass* if you specify an *Operation* property other than +, -, /, * or *x*. The *Operation* property simply returns 0, which is a little sloppy. The following changes ensure that only valid operations are used:

Visual Basic .NET

```
Public Property Operation() As String
    Get
        Operation = mstrOp
    End Get
    Set(ByVal Value As String)
        If InStr("+-/x*", Value) Then
            mstrOp = Value
        Else
            Throw New Exception("Unrecognized operator")
        End If
    End Set
End Property
```

Visual C#

```
public string Operation
{
    get
    {
        return mstrOp;
    }
    set
    {
        if (" +-/x*".IndexOf(value, 1) != 0)
            mstrOp = value;
        else
            throw(new Exception("Unrecognized operator"));
    }
}
```

These bug fixes illustrate how important it is to perform unit tests before checking new classes into a project. When a class is part of a larger project, it becomes much harder to locate the cause of an error.

Using the *Debug* and *Trace* Classes

The .NET Framework includes the *Debug* and *Trace* classes in the *System.Diagnostics* namespace as tools to help you ferret out errors and unexpected behaviors in your application. These classes let you display alerts or write messages based on results within your application.

The difference between the two classes is how they are handled in release builds. By default, *Debug* methods and properties are automatically stripped out of code compiled for release. *Trace* methods and properties are retained in release code by default. This gives you two levels of diagnostics: one for debugging errors prior to release, and one for diagnosing performance and problems in the field.

Because *Debug* and *Trace* are part of a .NET namespace, you need to add an *Imports* or *using* statement to code modules before using them:

Visual Basic .NET

```
Imports System.Diagnostics
```

Visual C#

```
using System.Diagnostics;
```

Displaying Alerts and Messages

The *Debug* and *Trace* classes' *Assert* method tests a value and displays an alert if the value is *False*. Use *Assert* to halt an application for an unexpected result. For example, the following code displays an alert if the numbers shown on the Flash-Cards form don't add up as expected:

Visual Basic .NET

```
Private Sub txtAnswer_TextChanged(ByVal sender As System.Object, _
    ByVal e As System.EventArgs) Handles txtAnswer.TextChanged
    If txtAnswer.Text = FlashCard.Answer Then
        lblFeedback.Text = "Correct!"
        Debug.Assert(CInt(txtAnswer.Text) = CInt(lblFirst.Text) + _
        CInt(lblSecond.Text), "Form values don't add up!")
        ' Get another set of numbers.
        FlashCard.Shuffle()
        ' Refresh display to show new numbers.
        RefreshDisplay()
        ' Clear answer
        txtAnswer.Text = ""
    Else
        lblFeedback.Text = "Oops! Try Again."
    End If
End Sub
```

Visual C#

```csharp
private void txtAnswer_TextChanged(object sender, System.EventArgs e)
{
    if(txtAnswer.Text == FlashCard.Answer().ToString())
    {
        lblFeedback.Text = "Correct!";
        Debug.Assert(Convert.ToInt32(txtAnswer.Text) ==
            Convert.ToInt32(lblFirst.Text) +
            Convert.ToInt32(lblSecond.Text),
            "Form values don't add up!");
        //Get another set of numbers.
        FlashCard.Shuffle();
        //Refresh display to show new numbers.
        RefreshDisplay();
        //Clear answer
        txtAnswer.Text = "";
    }
    else
    {
        lblFeedback.Text = "Oops! Try Again.";
    }
}
```

In a Web application, the alert is displayed on the server. If you're running the Web application's server on your local machine, this alert appears as expected, as shown in Figure 10-22. If you're running the Web application on a remote server, however, you won't see the alert if you're attached to the application's process running on the server only for remote debugging, as described later in this lesson.

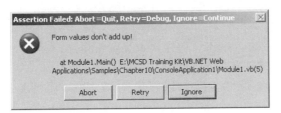

Figure 10-22   Displaying an alert (local server)

Use the *Write* or *WriteLine* methods to write a message without halting the application. By default, these messages are displayed in the Visual Studio .NET Output window during debugging.

Logging Debug and Trace Messages

To record debug and trace messages on a deployed application, create a *TextWriterTraceListener* class and add it to the *Debug* or *Trace* class's *Listeners* collection. For example, the following code directs debug messages to the server's console:

Visual Basic .NET

```
Debug.Listeners.Add(New TextWriterTraceListener(Console.Out))
Debug.WriteLine("Starting tests.")
```

Visual C#

```
Debug.Listeners.Add(new TextWriterTraceListener(Console.Out));
Debug.WriteLine("Starting tests.");
```

To write messages to a file rather than to the console, specify a file name and use the *Flush* method to write the output. For example, the following code writes a message to the Results.log file:

Visual Basic .NET

```
Debug.Listeners.Add(New TextWriterTraceListener("Results.log"))
Debug.WriteLine("Starting tests.")
Debug.Flush()
```

Visual C#

```
Debug.Listeners.Add(new TextWriterTraceListener("Results.log"));
Debug.WriteLine("Starting tests.");
Debug.Flush();
```

Remote Debugging

You usually debug a Web application by running the code locally on your development machine, but that's not the environment in which the application ultimately runs. To resolve problems with Web applications in real-world situations, you need to be able to debug them as they run on a remote server.

To debug an application on a remote server, follow these steps:

1. Install the Visual Studio .NET remote debugging server components on the Web application server.
2. Configure the server permissions to allow you to debug applications remotely.
3. Attach to the remote Web application process from your debug machine.

The following sections describe these steps in greater detail.

Installing Remote Components

The Visual Studio .NET Setup Wizard includes an option for installing remote components. Run Visual Studio .NET Setup on the server, and choose the Full Remote Debugging option during installation, as shown in Figure 10-23.

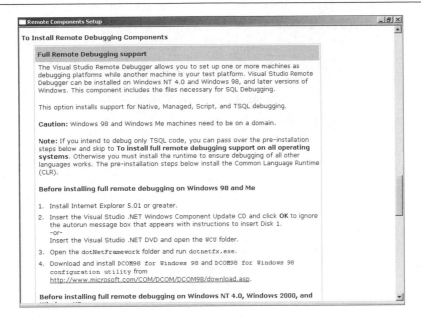

Figure 10-23   Installing remote debugging components

Setup installs the required components and configures the server to allow remote debugging.

Setting Server Permissions

To be able to debug processes running on a server, you must have a user account on the server and that account must belong to the Debugger Users group. The Visual Studio .NET Setup Wizard creates this group when you install the remote debugging components. You should make sure that all users who need debugging privileges on the server belong to this group.

Use the MMC to add users to this group, as shown in Figure 10-24.

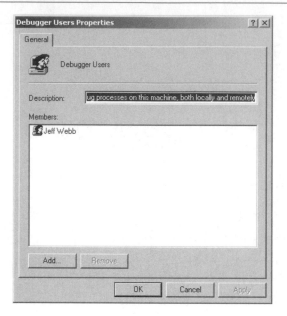

Figure 10-24   Adding remote debugger users

Attaching to a Remote Process

Visual Studio .NET can attach to processes running on a remote server. While attached to the process, Visual Studio .NET can receive Output window messages, display alerts from the *Assert* method, set breakpoints, view variables, and step through code running on the remote server.

To attach to a remote process, follow these steps:

1. From the Tools menu, choose Debug Processes. Visual Studio .NET displays the Processes dialog box, as shown in Figure 10-25.

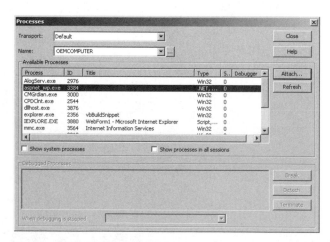

Figure 10-25   Attaching to a process

2. By default, Web applications run in the process named aspnet_wp.exe. Select the remote process you want to debug, click Attach, and then click Close.

When attached to a remote process, Visual Studio .NET can step into the code by setting breakpoints. The easiest way to do this with a Web application is to set a breakpoint for the *Page_Load* function to halt the application at the beginning of a Web form and then set breakpoints or watches within the remote code as desired.

To set a breakpoint in a remote process, follow these steps:

1. Click the Breakpoints tab in Visual Studio .NET, as shown in Figure 10-26.

Figure 10-26   Breakpoints window

2. Click the New button on the Breakpoints window toolbar. Visual Studio .NET displays the New Breakpoint dialog box, as shown in Figure 10-27.

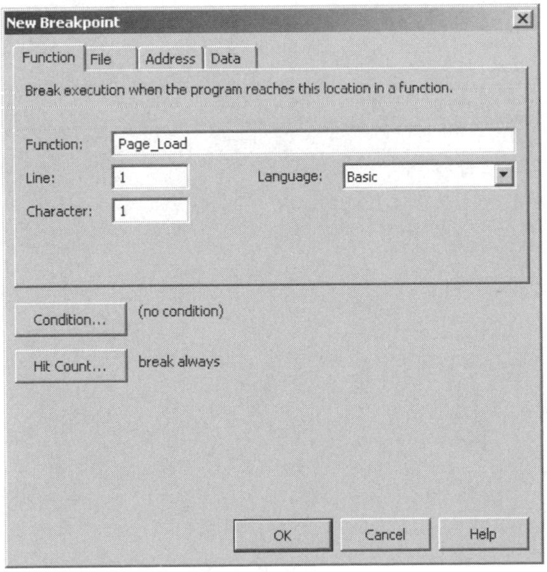

Figure 10-27   Adding a breakpoint

3. Enter a procedure name in the Function box, and click OK. For Web applications, it's easiest to stop the application at the *Page_Load* event procedure and then set additional breakpoints as required.

When a remote process is stopped at a breakpoint, you can use Visual Studio .NET's debugging tools to view variables, step through code, or execute commands as you would with a local process.

Summary

- Testing measures conformance to product requirements.
- Unit tests check that each piece of code works correctly.
- Integration tests verify that all components work together.
- Regression tests make sure that new code does not break existing code.
- Load tests check that the product works under extreme usage.
- Platform tests make sure that a Web application is displayed correctly and has reasonable performance using different browser and network connection configurations.
- Use ACT to record user interaction with a Web application in VBScript, and then replay that script to simulate multiple users and log application errors and server performance.
- To test a .NET assembly with the Windows Scripting Host, register the assembly for use with COM, and then copy the scripting host (CScript.exe) to the assembly's folder.
- To run attended builds and tests, create a command file containing the build commands to execute and test scripts to run, and then schedule the command file to run using the Windows Task Scheduler.
- Use the *Debug* and *Trace* diagnostic classes to display alerts and log error conditions during the development process.
- By default, code written with the *Debug* class is stripped out of release builds, and code using the *Trace* class is left in.
- Visual Studio .NET can attach to the process of a Web application running on a remote server to debug that application in a real-world setting.

Lab: Testing and Debugging

In this lab, you'll apply the lessons from this chapter to review a real-world testing plan, write unit tests for a sample application, load test a deployed application, and step through a Web application running on a remote server using the Visual Studio .NET debugging tools.

Estimated lesson time: 30 minutes

Exercise 1: Review a Test Plan

Testing strategies and terminology vary from company to company. In this exercise, you'll use a test plan from your own company to identify the concepts discussed in Lesson 1. If you don't work for a company that uses test plan documents, search the Internet using the phrase *software test plan*, and choose a test plan from the search results.

Using an actual test plan, highlight any mention of the following items:

- Unit testing
- Integration testing
- Ad hoc testing

See whether you can find answers to the questions posed in Lesson 1:

- How are tests written?
- Who is responsible for the testing?
- When are the tests performed?
- Where are the tests and test results stored?
- What is being tested?

Based on this information, does the plan give you a clear idea of how testing will verify that the product requirements are met?

Exercise 2: Write Unit Tests

In this exercise, you'll use VBScript or JScript to create unit tests for the *Circle* and *Sphere* classes that were derived from the *Shapes* abstract class in Chapter 3, "Working with Web Objects." The unit tests should verify that the following conditions are met:

- *Circle* and *Sphere* classes can be created.
- Classes can be passed to procedures accepting the *IFigure* interface.
- All properties work with minimum and maximum values.
- All methods return expected results for two or more test cases.

▶ **To create unit tests in VBScript or JScript**

1. Register the assembly for use with COM by running the RegAsm.exe utility from the Visual Studio .NET command prompt.
2. Copy the Windows Scripting Host (CScript.exe) to the folder containing the assembly to test.
3. Using Visual Studio .NET, Notepad, or some other editor, create the tests in VBScript or JScript.
4. Run the scripts from the Visual Studio .NET command prompt using the copy of CScript.exe in the assembly folder.

When you have finished, compare your results to those found in the sample files on the companion CD.

Exercise 3: Create a Load Test

If you have Visual Studio .NET Enterprise Architect, use ACT to create a load test for a Web application that has been deployed to a test server. Choose any deployed Web application that you want, but follow these test parameters:

1. Record at least five different requests to the server.
2. Add performance counters for the server's percentage of processor time, memory pages per second, and average disk read queue length.
3. Log the results to a Log folder within the Web application's folder structure.
4. Set the test properties to run for 30 seconds using four simultaneous connections.
5. Run the test.
6. View the performance counters for the server in chart form within ACT.

When you have finished, compare your results to the ACT sample recorded for the FlashCards sample application on the companion CD.

Exercise 4: Step Through a Remote Process

In this exercise, you'll use Visual Studio .NET to pause and step through a Web application running on a remote server. To complete this exercise, you must belong to the Debugger Users group on the server and the server must have the Visual Studio .NET remote components installed.

▶ **To step through a Web application running on a remote server**

1. From your workstation, access the Web application using Microsoft Internet Explorer. This ensures that the Web application is running on the server when you try to attach to its process.

2. From the Visual Studio .NET Tools menu, choose Debug Processes. Select the server where the application is running, select the application's process (named aspnet_wp.exe), and then click Attach.

3. Set a breakpoint on the *Page_Load* function.

4. Switch to Internet Explorer, and click Refresh.

5. Switch back to Visual Studio .NET. The remote application should be paused at *Page_Load*.

6. Set breakpoints at other locations in code.

7. In Visual Studio .NET, click Continue to run to the next breakpoint.

Review

The following questions are intended to reinforce key information presented in this chapter. If you are unable to answer a question, review the appropriate lesson and then try the question again. Answers to the questions can be found in the appendix.

1. How do unit, integration, and regression testing relate to each other?

2. Why is load testing likely to be more important for a Web application than for a standalone Windows application?

3. What is the difference between the *Debug* and *Trace* classes?

4. What are the two special steps you need to take to ensure that a COM component can use a component from a .NET assembly?

C H A P T E R   1   1

Creating Custom Web Controls

About This Chapter

Custom controls extend the tools available to Web developers. Using custom controls, you can encapsulate key aspects of the visual interface and program logic that you want to reuse throughout your application, or throughout your organization. Microsoft Visual Studio .NET provides three types of custom control for use on Web forms. In this chapter, you'll learn how to develop and use each of these controls:

- **Web user controls** These combine existing server and HTML controls by using the Visual Studio .NET Designer to create functional units that encapsulate some aspect of the user interface. User controls reside in content files, which must be included in the project in which the controls are used.

- **Composite custom controls** These create new controls from existing server and HTML controls. Although similar to user controls, composite controls are created in code rather than visually, and therefore they can be compiled into an assembly (.dll), which can be shared between multiple applications and used from the Toolbox in Visual Studio .NET.

- **Rendered custom controls** These create entirely new controls by rendering HTML directly rather than using composition. These controls are compiled and can be used from the Toolbox, just like composite controls, but you must write extra code to handle tasks that are performed automatically in composite controls.

Before You Begin

To complete this chapter, you must:

- Be familiar with the life cycle of Web applications.
- Understand object-oriented programming techniques, namespaces, and state information issues, as discussed in Chapter 3, "Working with Web Objects."
- Have experience developing Web applications with the standard server and HTML controls.

Lesson 1: Creating Web User Controls

Web user controls combine one or more server or HTML controls on a Web user control page, which can, in turn, be used on a Web form as a single control. User controls make it possible to create a single visual component that uses several controls to perform a specific task.

Once created, user controls can be used on Web forms throughout a project. However, because they are not compiled into assemblies, they have the following limitations not found with other types of controls:

- A copy of the control must exist in each Web application project in which the control is used.
- User controls can't be loaded in the Visual Studio .NET Toolbox; instead, you must create them by dragging the control from Solution Explorer to the Web form.
- User control code is initialized after the Web form loads, which means that user control property values are not updated until after the Web form's Load event.

In this lesson, you'll learn how to create user controls and how to use them on a Web form.

After this lesson, you will be able to

- Create a Web application that contains and uses user controls
- Add properties, methods, and events to a user control
- Include the user control on a Web form by editing the Web form's HTML
- Enable design-time settings, such as grid layout, for a user control

Estimated lesson time: 30 minutes

Creating and Using User Controls

There are five steps to creating and using a user control in a Web application:

1. Add a Web user control page (.ascx) to your project.
2. Draw the visual interface of the control in the designer.
3. Write code to create the control's properties, methods, and events.
4. Use the control on a Web form by dragging it from Solution Explorer to the Web form on which you want to include it.
5. Use the control from a Web form's code by declaring the control at the module level and then using the control's methods, properties, and events as needed within the Web form.

The following sections describe these steps in greater detail. The last section, "Enabling Grid Layout," describes special considerations you need to take into account when working with user controls.

Creating a User Control and Drawing Its Interface

You create user controls out of other server and HTML controls in the Visual Studio .NET Toolbox. You do this by drawing the controls on a **user control page**, which is simply another file type in a Web application project, just like a Web form or an HTML page. User controls are identified by their .ascx file extensions.

To create a user control and add it to a Web application, follow these steps:

1. From the Project menu, choose Add Web User Control. Visual Studio .NET displays the Add New Item dialog box.

2. Type the name of the user control in the Name box, and click OK. Visual Studio .NET creates a new, blank user control page and adds it to the project, as shown in Figure 11-1.

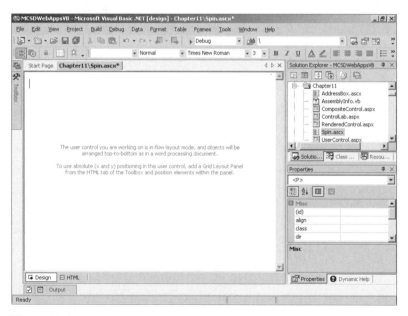

Figure 11-1   A new, blank user control page

After you've added a user control page to your project, create the visual interface of the control by adding server or HTML controls to it. User controls support flow layout only, so if you want to position controls on the page using grid layout, add an HTML Grid Layout Panel control to the user control as a container for the controls you want to position. Figure 11-2 shows a simple user control created by placing two Button server controls on an HTML Grid Layout Panel control.

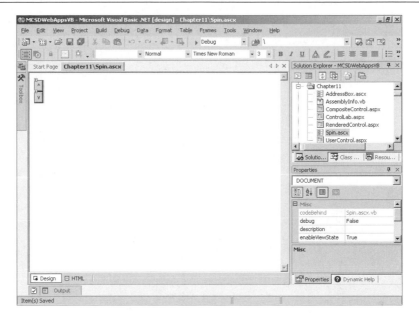

Figure 11-2   A simple user control

The control shown in Figure 11-2 is the Web form's equivalent of a Spin control. The control allows you to increment or decrement a value by clicking the up or down arrow. This example is used in the sections that follow; the HTML for the user control is shown here for reference:

```
<DIV id="pnlGrid" runat="server" style="WIDTH: 20px; POSITION: relative;
HEIGHT: 48px" ms_positioning="GridLayout">
  <asp:Button id="butUp" Text="^" runat="server" />
  <asp:Button id="butDown" Text="v" runat="server" />
</DIV>
```

Writing the Control's Properties, Methods, and Events

You manipulate the controls you add to the user control from the user control's code module. That allows you to hide the inner workings of the control and expose the tasks the control performs as properties, methods, and events.

To edit the user control's code module, simply double-click the user control. Visual Studio .NET automatically generates the code template shown in Figure 11-3 when you create a user control.

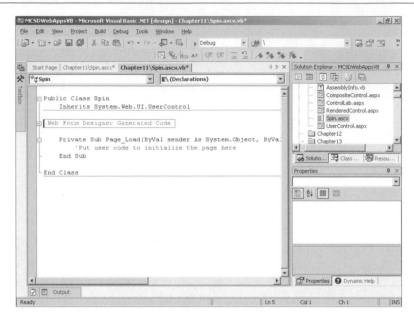

Figure 11-3   The user control code template (Visual Basic .NET)

The code in Figure 11-3 is similar to the generated code for a Web form, with these notable differences:

■ **The user control's class is based on the *System.Web.UI.UserControl* base class.**   This base class provides the base set of properties and methods you use to create the control and get the control's design-time settings from its HTML attributes on the Web form.

■ **The user control's Load event occurs when the control is loaded by the Web form that contains it.**   The control's Load event procedure runs *after* the Web form's Load event procedure, which is important to remember when you work with user controls on a Web form.

To create properties and methods for the user control that you can use from a Web form, follow these steps:

1. Create the public property or method that you want to make available on the containing Web form.
2. Write code to respond to events that occur for the controls contained within the user control. These event procedures do the bulk of the work for the user control.
3. If the property or method needs to retain a setting between page displays, write code to save and restore settings from the control's *ViewState*.

For example, the following code shows a *Value* property that returns the value of the Spin control created in the preceding section:

Visual Basic .NET

```
Public Property Value() As Integer
    Get
        ' Return the Value.
        Return ViewState("Value")
    End Get
    Set(ByVal Value As Integer)
        ' Set the Value.
        ViewState("Value") = Value
    End Set
End Property
```

Visual C#

```
public int Value
{
    get
    {
        // Return the Value.
        return Convert.ToInt32(ViewState["Value"]);
    }
    set
    {
        // Set the Value.
        ViewState["Value"] = value;
    }
}
```

The user changes the value of the Spin control by clicking the up and down buttons, so the following code increments or decrements the value, depending on which button the user clicks:

Visual Basic .NET

```
Private Sub butDown_Click(ByVal sender As System.Object, _
    ByVal e As System.EventArgs) Handles butDown.Click
    ' Decrement the Value.
    Me.Value -= 1
End Sub

Private Sub butUp_Click(ByVal sender As System.Object, _
    ByVal e As System.EventArgs) Handles butUp.Click
    ' Increment the Value.
    Me.Value += 1
End Sub
```

Visual C#

```
private void butDown_Click(object sender, System.EventArgs e)
{
    // Decrement the Value.
    this.Value -= 1;
}
```

```
private void butUp_Click(object sender, System.EventArgs e)
{
    // Increment the Value.
    this.Value += 1;
}
```

Adding the Control to a Web Form

User controls can be dragged directly from Solution Explorer onto a Web form.
When you add a user control to a Web form in this way, Visual Studio .NET generates a @*Register* directive and HTML tags to create the control on the Web form.

For example, the following sample shows the HTML generated when you drag the
Spin user control onto a Web form:

```
<%@ Register TagPrefix="uc1" TagName="Spin" Src="Spin.ascx" %>
<%@ Page Language="vb" AutoEventWireup="false"
Codebehind="UserControl.aspx.vb" Inherits="MCSDWebAppsVB.UserControl" %>
<HTML>
  <body>
    <form id="Form1" method="post" runat="server">
      <uc1:Spin id="Spin1" runat="server" Value="5"></uc1:Spin>
    </form>
  </body>
</HTML>
```

User controls can exist alongside and interact with other controls on a Web form.
For example, the following HTML shows the Spin user control next to a TextBox
control:

```
<%@ Register TagPrefix="uc1" TagName="Spin" Src="Spin.ascx" %>
<%@ Page Language="vb" AutoEventWireup="false"
Codebehind="UserControl.aspx.vb" Inherits="MCSDWebAppsVB.UserControl" %>
<HTML>
  <body>
    <form id="Form1" method="post" runat="server">
      <h2>Creating and Using User Controls</h2>
      <hr>
      <asp:TextBox id="TextBox1" runat="server"></asp:TextBox>
      <uc1:Spin id="Spin1" runat="server" Value="5"></uc1:Spin>
    </form>
  </body>
</HTML>
```

Notice that the user control includes an attribute for the *Value* property. When the
Spin control loads at run time, Microsoft ASP.NET will set the control's properties
based on the attributes in the HTML. The control's attributes provide a way to set
the control's properties from HTML.

When you view the preceding HTML in Visual Studio .NET's Design mode, it appears as shown in Figure 11-4.

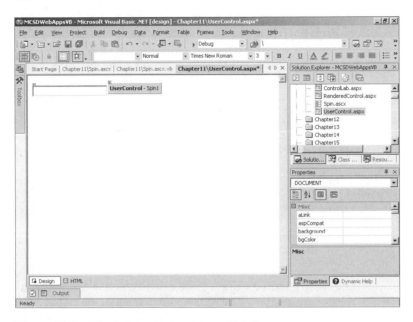

Figure 11-4   The Spin user control on a Web form

As you'll notice in Figure 11-4, the Web Forms Designer doesn't display the user control as it will appear at run time. Instead, it shows a sort of generic control. This is a limitation of Visual Studio .NET—it can't display user controls in Design mode.

Another thing you'll notice is that the Spin control supports only flow layout on the Web form. That is a limitation of the control itself. To support grid layout and absolute positioning on the Web form, you have to add code to support the *style* attribute. You'll see that technique later in this lesson.

Using the Control in Code

After you've created a user control and added it to a Web form, you can use it from the Web form's code module by following these steps:

1. Declare the user control at the module level. For example, the following line declares the Spin user control that was added to the Web form in the preceding section:

Visual Basic .NET

```
Protected WithEvents Spin1 As Spin
```

Visual C#

```
protected Spin Spin1;
```

2. Use the control's properties, methods, and events as you would any other control. For example, the following event procedure displays the Spin control's value in a text box:

Visual Basic .NET

```
Private Sub Page_PreRender(ByVal sender As System.Object, _
    ByVal e As System.EventArgs) Handles MyBase.PreRender
    ' Display the Spin control's value.
    TextBox1.Text = Spin1.Value
End Sub
```

Visual C#

```
private void Page_PreRender(object sender, System.EventArgs e)
{
    // Display the Spin control's value.
    TextBox1.Text = Spin1.Value.ToString();
}
```

One very important thing to notice here is that the preceding code uses the Web form's PreRender event, not its Load event. If you use the Load event, you'll see only the *Value* set in the user control's HTML *Value* attribute the first time you click the Spin control. (Try it!) That's because the user control's code doesn't run until after the Web form's Load event has finished. Any changes that were saved in the control's *ViewState* aren't loaded until the control's Load event procedure has run.

Adding Events to the User Control

In addition to properties and methods, user controls can provide events that can respond to user actions on the Web form.

To add an event to a user control, follow these steps:

1. Declare the event within the user control's code module. For example, the following code declares a Click event for the Spin user control:

Visual Basic .NET

```
' Declare event for Spin control.
Public Event Click(ByVal sender As System.Object, ByVal e As
System.EventArgs)
```

Visual C#

```
// Declare the event.
public event EventHandler Click;
```

2. Create a method to raise the event. This step makes it easier for other classes to derive from this class, because they can override this method.

Visual Basic .NET

```
' Method to raise event.
Protected Overridable Sub OnClick(ByVal e As EventArgs)
    RaiseEvent Click(Me, e)
End Sub
```

Visual C#

```
// Method to raise event.
protected virtual void OnClick(EventArgs e)
{
    if (Click != null)
    {
        Click(this, e);
    }
}
```

3. Raise the event from within the user control's code. For example, the following code raises the Click event whenever a user clicks the up or down buttons in the Spin user control:

Visual Basic .NET

```
Private Sub butDown_Click(ByVal sender As System.Object, _
    ByVal e As System.EventArgs) Handles butDown.Click
    ' Decrement the Value.
    Me.Value -= 1
    ' Call the OnClick method.
    OnClick(e)
End Sub

Private Sub butUp_Click(ByVal sender As System.Object, _
    ByVal e As System.EventArgs) Handles butUp.Click
    ' Increment the Value.
    Me.Value += 1
    ' Call the OnClick method.
    OnClick(e)
End Sub
```

Visual C#

```
private void butDown_Click(object sender, System.EventArgs e)
{
    // Decrement the Value.
    this.Value -= 1;
    // Call the OnClick method.
    OnClick(e);
}
```

```
    private void butUp_Click(object sender, System.EventArgs e)
    {
        // Increment the Value.
        this.Value += 1;
        // Call the OnClick method.
    }
```

To use the user control event from a Web form, include the user control on a Web form, as shown in the preceding two sections, and then write an event procedure that responds to the event. For example, the following code updates a text box when the user clicks the Spin control:

Visual Basic .NET

```
Private Sub Spin1_Click(ByVal sender As Object, _
    ByVal e As System.EventArgs) Handles Spin1.Click
    ' Update info from the user control's event handler.
    TextBox1.Text = Spin1.Value
End Sub
```

Visual C#

```
    private void InitializeComponent()
    {
        // Add this line to wire the event.
        this.Spin1.Click += new System.EventHandler(this.Spin1_Click);
    }

private void Spin1_Click(object sender, System.EventArgs e)
{
    // Display the Spin control's value.
    TextBox1.Text = Spin1.Value.ToString();
}
```

Enabling Grid Layout

As mentioned, user controls don't have built-in support for the absolute positioning used by a Web form's grid layout. In ASP.NET, controls support absolute positioning through the *style* attribute. You can simply add a *style* attribute to your user control's HTML on the Web form to get design-time support for absolute positioning. For example, the following HTML creates a Spin user control that you can drag to different locations on a Web form in Design mode:

```
<UserControl:Spin id="Spin1" runat="server" Value="5"
  style="Z-INDEX: 101; LEFT: 248px; POSITION: absolute; TOP: 88px">
  </UserControl:Spin>
```

You'll see the problem with this solution as soon as you run the Web application, however. At run time, ASP.NET ignores the *style* attribute and displays the Spin user control using flow layout.

To make the *style* attribute work, you have to add a *Style* property to the user control to set the control's position and size based on the attribute settings. If your control uses a container, such as the Grid Layout Panel used by the Spin user control, you can simply pass the user control's *style* attribute to the Panel control, as shown in the following code:

Visual Basic .NET

```
Public Property Style() As String
    Get
        ' Return the containing Panel control's style attribute.
        Return pnlGrid.Attributes("style")
    End Get
    Set(ByVal Value As String)
        ' Set the containing Panel control's style attribute.
        pnlGrid.Attributes("style") = Value
    End Set
End Property
```

Visual C#

```
public string Style
{
    get
    {
        // Return the containing Panel control's style attribute.
        return pnlGrid.Attributes["style"];
    }
    set
    {
        // Set the containing Panel control's style attribute.
        pnlGrid.Attributes["style"] = value;
    }
}
```

You can use this same programming technique—sometimes called **delegation**—to implement other standard control attributes such as *Visible*, *Enabled*, or *BackColor*. Simply add a property to the user control that passes the attribute value to a containing control using the *Attributes* property, as shown in the preceding code.

Lesson 2: Creating Composite Custom Controls

Composite custom controls combine one or more server or HTML controls within a single control class, which can be compiled along with other control classes to create an assembly (.dll) that contains a custom control library. Once created, the custom control library can be loaded into Visual Studio .NET and used in the same way as the standard server and HTML controls.

Composite custom controls are functionally similar to user controls, but they reside in their own assemblies, so you can share the same control among multiple projects without having to copy the control to each project, as you must do with user controls. However, composite controls are somewhat more difficult to create because you can't draw them visually using the Visual Studio .NET Designer. You have many more options for defining their behavior, however, so composite controls are more complex than user controls.

After this lesson, you will be able to

- Create a two-project solution that you can use to develop and debug composite custom controls
- Add a composite custom control to a Web form in a test project by manually using the *@Register* directive and HTML tags
- Create a composite custom control's appearance by adding controls to it using the *CreateChildControls* method
- Create properties, methods, and events for a composite custom control
- Handle design-time changes to the control, such as resizing or repositioning on a Web form using grid layout
- Create new controls by deriving directly from a single server control

Estimated lesson time: 35 minutes

Creating and Using Composite Custom Controls

There are six steps to creating and using a custom control in a Web application:

1. Create a solution containing a custom control project.
2. Add a Web application project to the solution, and set it as the startup project. You will use the Web application project to test the custom control during development.

3. Add a project reference from the Web application to the custom control project, and add an HTML *@Register* directive and control element to use the custom control on a Web form.

4. Create the custom control's visual interface by adding existing controls to it through the custom control's *CreateChildControls* method.

5. Add the properties, methods, and events that the custom control provides.

6. Build and test the custom control.

The following sections describe these steps in greater detail.

Creating the Custom Control Project

Custom controls are simply classes that are built into an assembly. These custom control classes inherit much of their behavior from the *WebControl* class, and they implement various interfaces, depending on the type of control you're creating.

The easiest way to get started is to use the Web Control Library project template provided by Visual Studio .NET. To create a custom control using the project template, follow these steps:

1. From the File menu, point to New, and then select Project. Visual Studio .NET displays the New Project dialog box, as shown in Figure 11-5.

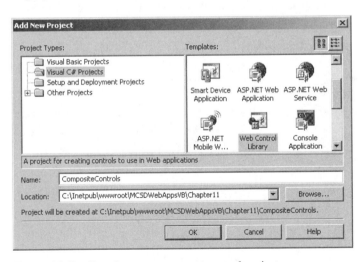

Figure 11-5   Creating a new custom control project

2. Select the Web Control Library template icon from the Templates list, type the name of the project in the Name box, and click OK. Visual Studio .NET creates a project containing code for a single custom control named WebControl1, as shown in Figure 11-6.

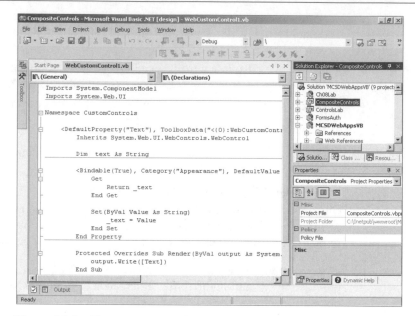

Figure 11-6   The custom control code template (Visual Basic .NET)

The code shown in Figure 11-6 serves as a template for creating a new custom control. The template includes a class named WebControl1 that contains one property, which is named Text as shown in the following code.

Visual Basic .NET

```
Imports System.ComponentModel
Imports System.Web.UI

<DefaultProperty("Text"), ToolboxData("<{0}:WebCustomControl1 _
runat=server></{0}:WebCustomControl1>")>
Public Class WebCustomControl1
    Inherits System.Web.UI.WebControls.WebControl

    Dim _text As String

    <Bindable(True), Category("Appearance"), DefaultValue("")> _
      Property [Text]() As String
        Get
            Return _text
        End Get

        Set(ByVal Value As String)
            _text = Value
        End Set
End Property

    Protected Overrides Sub Render(ByVal output As _
```

```
              System.Web.UI.HtmlTextWriter)
          output.Write([Text])
      End Sub

  End Class
```

Visual C#

```csharp
using System;
using System.Web.UI;
using System.Web.UI.WebControls;
using System.ComponentModel;

namespace CompositeControls
{
    /// <summary>
    /// Summary description for WebCustomControl1.
    /// </summary>
[DefaultProperty("Text"),
    ToolboxData("<{0}:WebCustomControl1
    runat=server></{0}:WebCustomControl1>")]
    public class WebCustomControl1 : System.Web.UI.WebControls.WebControl
    {
        private string text;

        [Bindable(true),
            Category("Appearance"),
            DefaultValue("")]
        public string Text
        {
            get
            {
                return text;
            }

            set
            {
                text = value;
            }
        }

        /// <summary>
        /// Render this control to the output parameter specified.
        /// </summary>
        /// <param name="output"> The HTML writer to write out to </param>
        protected override void Render(HtmlTextWriter output)
        {
            output.Write(Text);
        }
    }
}
```

The preceding code contains some elements you might not have seen before. Table 11-1 describes each of these items in turn.

Table 11-1   The Custom Control Template

Part	Name	Description

`<DefaultProperty("Text"), ToolboxData("<{0}: WebCustomControl1 runat=server></{0}: WebCustomControl1>")>`
 	
`[DefaultProperty("Text"), ToolboxData("<{0}: WebCustomControl1 runat=server></{0}: WebCustomControl1>")]`
	Class attributes	Class attributes determine the design-time settings for the control. These values help determine what appears in the Visual Studio .NET Properties window when the custom control is selected on a Web form.

`Inherits System.Web.UI. WebControls.WebControl`
 	
`: System.Web.UI.WebControls.WebContro l`
	Base class	Custom controls are derived from one of the base control classes.

`<Bindable(True), Category("Appearance"), DefaultValue("")>`
 	
`[Bindable(true), Category("Appearance"), DefaultValue("")]`
	Property attributes	Like class attributes, property attributes specify the design-time settings of a property.

`Property [Text]() As String`
 	
`public string Text`
	Property definition	The property definition specifies what the property does at run time. The square brackets ([]) indicate that the property name can be a keyword (although in this case, it is not).

`Protected Overrides Sub Render(ByVal output As System.Web.UI.HtmlTextWriter)`
 	
`protected override void Render(HtmlTextWriter output)`
	Render method	The *Render* method displays the custom control. This overrides the base class's *Render* method.

The following sections describe how to add to and modify these parts to create a composite custom control, but for more complete information about attributes, see the Visual Studio .NET Help topic "Design-Time Attributes for Components."

Creating the Test Project

The custom control project created in the preceding section has the output type of Class Library. This means that the project can be used only from another application—it can't run as a stand-alone application. To run and debug a custom control in Visual Studio .NET, you must add a second project to the current solution.

To create a custom control test project and add it to the current solution, follow these steps:

1. With the custom control project open, point to Add Project on the File menu, and then choose New Project. Visual Studio .NET displays the New Project dialog box.

2. Select ASP.NET Web Application from the Templates list, type the name of the project in the Location box, and click OK. Visual Studio .NET creates a new Web application project and adds it to the current solution.

3. In Solution Explorer, right-click the Web application project, and select Set As StartUp Project from the shortcut menu. Visual Studio .NET indicates that the Web application is the startup project by displaying the project name in bold-face.

4. In Solution Explorer, right-click the Web application's References item, and select Add Reference from the shortcut menu. Visual Studio .NET displays the Add Reference dialog box, as shown in Figure 11-7.

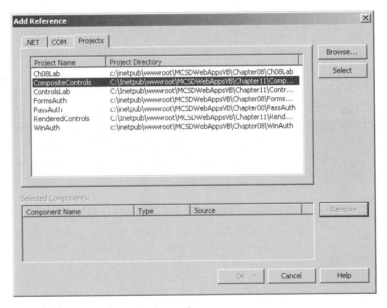

Figure 11-7   Adding a project reference

5. Click the Projects tab, click Select to add a reference from the custom control project to the Web application project, and then click OK. Visual Studio .NET adds the reference, as shown in Solution Explorer in Figure 11-8.

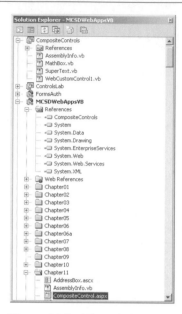

Figure 11-8   The solution

Establishing a project reference as described in the preceding steps copies the custom control assembly (.dll) to the /bin directory of the Web application. This makes the custom control available to the Web application. Any changes to the custom control assembly are automatically copied to the Web application's /bin directory.

As you develop your custom control, remember that changes aren't updated in the test Web application until you rebuild the custom control. That happens automatically when you run the application, but not when you switch between the custom control and the test Web application in Design mode. To see changes to the control in Design mode, you must rebuild the custom control before switching to the test application.

Adding the Custom Control to the Test Project

To test and debug the custom control during development, you must add an instance of the control to a Web form in the test Web application created in the preceding section.

To add a custom control to a Web form, follow these steps:

1. In the test Web application, display a Web form, and switch to HTML mode by clicking the HTML tab at the bottom left corner of the Design window.

2. Add a *Register* directive to the top of the Web form. For example, the following directive registers the custom control assembly named CompositeControls:

```
<%@ Register TagPrefix="Custom" Namespace="CompositeControls"
Assembly="CompositeControls" %>
```

3. Create an instance of the custom control on the Web form using HTML syntax. For example, the following HTML creates an instance of WebCustomControl1 created in the preceding section:

```
<Custom:WebCustomControl1 id="custTest" runat="server" />
```

For custom controls, the *Register* directive's three attributes have the meanings described in Table 11-2.

Table 11-2   The *Register* Directive's Attributes

Attribute	Description
TagPrefix	This name identifies the group that the user control belongs to. For example, the tag prefix for ASP.NET server controls is "*asp*". You use this prefix to create a naming convention to organize your custom controls.
Namespace	This is the project name and namespace within the custom control assembly that contains the controls to register. Microsoft Visual Basic .NET uses the project name as an implicit namespace, so for controls written in Visual Basic .NET, use the project name.
Assembly	This is the name of the assembly (.dll) containing the custom controls. The control assembly must be referenced by the Web application. As mentioned, referencing the assembly maintains a copy of it in the Web application's /bin directory.

The *@Register* directive's *TagPrefix* makes up the first part of the name you use in the custom control's HTML element. The second part is the project name and class name of the control within the assembly. *TagPrefix="Custom"* and the class name WebCustomControl1 mean that you create the custom control using an HTML *<Custom:WebCustomControl1 .../>* element.

Custom controls can exist alongside and interact with other controls on a Web form. For example, the following HTML shows the WebControl1 custom control next to a Button control:

```
<%@ Page Language="vb" AutoEventWireup="false" Codebehind="Default.aspx.vb"
Inherits="MCSDWebAppsVB.CustomControl"%>
<%@ Register TagPrefix="Custom" NameSpace="CompositeControls "
Assembly="CompositeControls" %>
<HTML>
<body>
<form id="Form1" method="post" runat="server">
  <asp:button id="butCount" runat="server" />
  <Custom:WebCustomControl1 id="custTest" runat="server"
    Text="This is a custom control" />
</form>
</body>
</HTML>
```

Notice that the custom control includes an attribute for the *Text* property. The control's HTML attributes provide a way to set the control's properties from HTML. Unlike user controls, custom controls are displayed correctly in the Visual Studio .NET Designer, as shown in Figure 11-9.

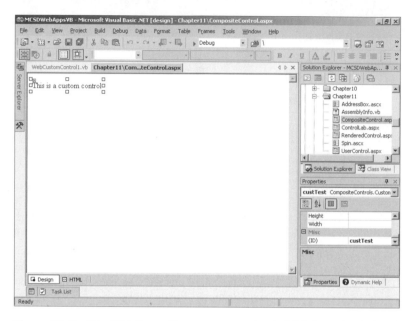

Figure 11-9   The WebControl1 custom control on a Web form (at design time)

Another thing you should notice about custom controls is that when they are selected in the Visual Studio .NET Designer, their properties appear in the Properties window. Again, unlike user controls, custom controls are fully supported by Visual Studio .NET.

To use the custom control in code, simply refer to it as you would any other control. For example, the following Button Click event procedure increments the value shown in the WebCustomControl1 custom control:

Visual Basic .NET

```
Private Sub butAdd_Click(ByVal sender As System.Object, _
    ByVal e As System.EventArgs) Handles butAdd.Click
    ' Increment the Text property of the custom control.
    custTest.Text = Val(custTest.Text) + 1
End Sub
```

Visual C#

```
private void butAdd_Click(object sender, System.EventArgs e)
{
    // Convert the string to a number.
    int intText = 0;
```

```
try
{
    intText = int.Parse(custTest.Text);
}
catch
{
    intText = 0;
}
// Increment the number.
intText ++;
// Display result in control
custTest.Text = intText.ToString();
}
```

When you run the preceding code as part of a test Web application, ASP.NET displays the Web form with the custom control and the Button server control, as shown in Figure 11-10.

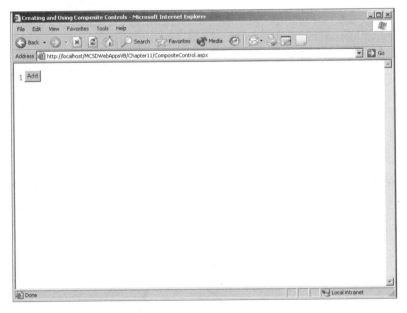

Figure 11-10   The WebControl1 custom control on a Web form (at run time)

If you click the Button control in this example more than once, the displayed value never gets past 1. Whoa! What gives? The custom control template that Visual Studio .NET creates doesn't take steps to save properties between page displays. To do that, you'll need to add code, as described in the following sections.

Creating the Composite Control's Appearance

You create the visual interface of composite custom controls by adding existing server or HTML controls to the *Controls* collection in the *CreateChildControls* method. The custom control's *CreateChildControls* method overrides the method in the base class.

The following code shows how to create a composite custom control's appearance. The code creates a composite custom control named MathBox. The MathBox control contains TextBox, Button, and Label controls, which are declared at the class level so that they are available to all procedures in the class. The *CreateChildControls* procedure adds these controls and some Literal controls to the custom control's *Controls* collection to create the custom control's appearance.

Visual Basic .NET

```
Public Class MathBox
    Inherits System.Web.UI.WebControls.WebControl

    Dim txtMath As New TextBox()
    Dim butSum As New Button()
    Dim lblResult As New Label()

    ' Create control's appearance.
    Protected Overrides Sub CreateChildControls()
        ' Add the sub controls to this composite control.
        ' Set the TextMode property and add textbox.
        txtMath.TextMode = TextBoxMode.MultiLine
        Controls.Add(txtMath)
        ' Start a new line
        Controls.Add(New LiteralControl("<br>"))
        ' Set the Text property and add the Button control.
        butSum.Text = "Sum"
        Controls.Add(butSum)
        ' Add Label and Literals to display result.
        Controls.Add(New LiteralControl("  Result: <b>"))
        Controls.Add(lblResult)
        Controls.Add(New LiteralControl("</b>"))
    End Sub
End Class
```

Visual C#

```
public class MathBox : System.Web.UI.WebControls.WebControl
{
    TextBox txtMath = new TextBox();
    Button butSum = new Button();
    Label lblResult = new Label();
```

```
private string text;

protected override void CreateChildControls()
{
    // Add the sub controls to this composite control.
    // Set the TextMode property and add textbox.
    txtMath.TextMode = TextBoxMode.MultiLine;
    Controls.Add(txtMath);
    // Start a new line
    Controls.Add(new LiteralControl("<br>"));
    // Set the Text property and add the Button control.
    butSum.Text = "Sum";
    Controls.Add(butSum);
    // Add Label and Literals to display result.
    Controls.Add(new LiteralControl("  Result: <b>"));
    Controls.Add(lblResult);
    Controls.Add(new LiteralControl("</b>"));

}
}
```

The *MathBox* class shown in the preceding code is used as the basis for the rest of this lesson. If you add it to the composite control project created in the preceding sections, you can add it to the test Web application using the same *@Register* directive you added for the WebCustomControl1, and you'll create an instance of the control with the following HTML:

```
<Custom:MathBox id="mathTest" runat="server" />
```

If you add the MathBox custom control to a Web form at this point, you'll notice it appears as only a small green box at design time. At run time, however, the control will appear as shown in Figure 11-11.

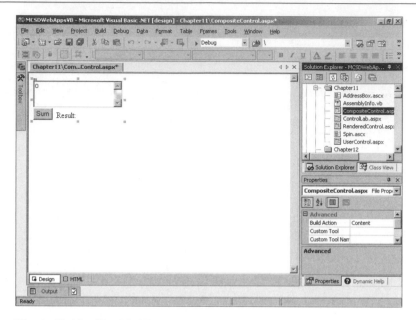

Figure 11-11   The MathBox custom control (at run time)

The MathBox custom control doesn't have a design-time appearance at this point because it does not yet expose any design-time properties. That problem is remedied in the next section.

You don't need to override the *Render* method when creating a composite custom control. The custom control code template that Visual Studio .NET generates overrides this method. Therefore, if you're using the template, you must delete the generated *Render* method or change it to delegate back to the base class (making it a null operation), as shown here:

Visual Basic .NET

```
' Delegate back since not needed in composite control.
Protected Overrides Sub Render(ByVal writer As HtmlTextWriter)
    MyBase.Render(writer)
End Sub
```

Visual C#

```
// Delegate back since not needed in composite control.
protected override void Render(HtmlTextWriter output)
{
    base.Render(output);
}
```

Creating Properties and Methods

The MathBox custom control will add a list of numbers entered in its text box and return the result. From a design standpoint, that requires two properties: *Values*, which contains an array of numbers; and *Result*, which contains the sum of those numbers. It also implies a *Sum* method to perform the calculation.

The following code shows the *Values* and *Result* properties and the *Sum* method used by MathBox. It also includes a *Text* property for consistency with the ASP.NET server controls and to simplify setting default text from HTML attributes.

Visual Basic .NET

```vb
' MathBox Properties and Methods.
<DefaultValue("")> Property Text() As String
    Get
        ' Make sure child controls exist.
        EnsureChildControls()
        ' Return the text in the TextBox control.
        Return txtMath.Text
    End Get
    Set(ByVal Value As String)
        ' Make sure child controls exist.
        EnsureChildControls()
        ' Set the text in the TextBox control.
        txtMath.Text = Value
    End Set
End Property

Property Values() As String()
    Get
        EnsureChildControls()
        ' Return an array of strings from the TextBox.
        Return txtMath.Text.Split(Chr(13))
    End Get
    Set(ByVal Value() As String)
        EnsureChildControls()
        ' Set the text in the TextBox from an array.
        txtMath.Text = String.Join(Chr(13), Value)
    End Set
End Property

ReadOnly Property Result() As String
    Get
        EnsureChildcontrols()
        ' Return the result from the Label.
        Return lblResult.Text
    End Get
End Property
```

```vb
Sub Sum()
    EnsureChildcontrols()
    ' If there is text in the TextBox.
    If txtMath.Text.Length Then
        ' Break the text into an array, line by line.
        Dim arrNums As String()
        arrNums = txtMath.Text.Split(Chr(13))
        Dim strCount As String, dblSum As Double
        ' Add each element in the array together.
        For Each strCount In arrNums
            ' Use error handling to ignore non-number entries.
            Try
                dblSum += Convert.ToDouble(strCount)
            Catch
            End Try
        Next
        ' Display the result in the label.
        lblResult.Text = dblSum.ToString
    Else
        lblResult.Text = "0"
    End If
End Sub
```

Visual C#

```csharp
// MathBox properties and methods.
[DefaultValue("0")]
public string Text
{
    get
    {
        // Make sure child controls exist.
        EnsureChildControls();
        // Return the text in the TextBox control.
        return txtMath.Text;
    }

    set
    {
        // Make sure child controls exist.
        EnsureChildControls();
        // Set the text in the TextBox control.
        txtMath.Text = value;
    }
}

char[] strSep = {'\r'};

public string[] Values
{
```

```
        get
        {
            EnsureChildControls();
            // Return an array of strings from the TextBox.
            return txtMath.Text.Split(strSep);
        }
        set
        {
            EnsureChildControls();
            // Set the text in the TextBox from an array.
            txtMath.Text = String.Join(" ", value);
        }
    }

    public string Result
    {
        get
        {
            EnsureChildControls();
            // Return the result from the Label.
            return lblResult.Text;
        }
    }

    public void Sum()
    {
        EnsureChildControls();
        // If there is text in the TextBox.
        if (txtMath.Text.Length != 0)
        {
            // Break the text into an array, line by line.
            string[] arrNums;
            arrNums = txtMath.Text.Split(strSep);
            double dblSum = 0;
            // Add each element in the array together.
            foreach (string strCount in arrNums)
            {
                // Use error handling to
                // ignore non-number entries.
                try
                {
                    dblSum += Convert.ToDouble(strCount);
                }
                catch
                {
                }
            }
            // Display the result in the label.
            lblResult.Text = dblSum.ToString();
        }
```

```
        else
            lblResult.Text = "0";
        }
    }
}
```

The *EnsureChildControls* statement in the preceding code ensures that the child controls have been instantiated. You use this in a composite control before referring to any contained controls.

After you add properties and methods to the composite control, rebuild the control to update the control's assembly. At that point, the composite control should appear in Design mode as well as at run time, as shown in Figure 11-12.

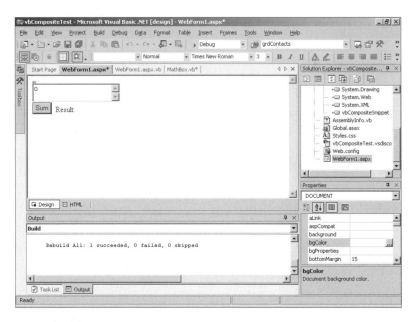

Figure 11-12   The MathBox custom control (at design time)

In Visual Studio .NET, version 1.0, custom controls may not always appear at design time. If this happens, you can usually cause them to appear by setting one of the custom control's properties, as shown by the following HTML:

```
<Custom:MathBox id="mthTest" runat="server" Text="0" />
```

Because composite controls use their base class's *Render* method, they automatically support absolute positioning with grid layout. In other words, you can drag composite controls to various positions on a Web form, and they will be displayed there at run time.

Handling Events

So far, the MathBox control can accept values, perform calculations, and display a result, but if you click the Sum button, it doesn't do any of that.

To enable the Sum button, follow these steps:

1. Add an event handler for the button's Click event to the *CreateChildControls* procedure using the *AddHandler* method.
2. Create a procedure to handle the event. This procedure has to have the same arguments and return type as the button's Click event.

The following code shows the additions to the MathBox control in boldface. Notice that the event procedure simply calls the *Sum* method created earlier to perform the calculation and display the result.

Visual Basic .NET

```
Protected Overrides Sub CreateChildControls()
    ' Add the sub controls to this composite control.
    ' Set the TextMode property and add textbox.
    txtMath.TextMode = TextBoxMode.MultiLine
    Controls.Add(txtMath)
    ' Start a new line
    Controls.Add(New LiteralControl("<br>"))
    ' Set the Text property and add the Button control.
    butSum.Text = "Sum"
    Controls.Add(butSum)
    ' Add Label and Literals to display result.
    Controls.Add(New LiteralControl("  Result: <b>"))
    Controls.Add(lblResult)
    Controls.Add(New LiteralControl("</b>"))
    ' Add a handler for the Button's Click event.
    AddHandler butSum.Click, AddressOf Me.butSumClicked
End Sub


' Event procedure for Button Click
Sub butSumClicked(ByVal source As Object, ByVal e As EventArgs)
    ' Call the Sum method.
    Sum()
End Sub
```

Visual C#

```
protected override void CreateChildControls()
{
    // Add the sub controls to this composite control.
    // Set the TextMode property and add textbox.
    txtMath.TextMode = TextBoxMode.MultiLine;
    Controls.Add(txtMath);
    // Start a new line
```

```
        Controls.Add(new LiteralControl("<br>"));
        // Set the Text property and add the Button control.
        butSum.Text = "Sum";
        Controls.Add(butSum);
        // Add Label and Literals to display result.
        Controls.Add(new LiteralControl("  Result: <b>"));
        Controls.Add(lblResult);
        Controls.Add(new LiteralControl("</b>"));
        // Add event handler.
        butSum.Click += new EventHandler(butSumClicked);
}

void butSumClicked(object sender, EventArgs e)
{
        // Call the Sum method.
        Sum();
}
```

Raising Events

In addition to handling the Sum button's Click event, you might want to raise an event that can be handled from the Web form containing the custom control.

To raise an event from a custom control, follow these steps:

1. Add a public event declaration to the custom control's class.
2. Raise the event from code within the custom control using the control's event method.

The following code shows how to declare and raise an event from within the Math-Box control class:

Visual Basic .NET

```
' Declare an event
Event Click(ByVal sender As Object, ByVal e As EventArgs)

' Event procedure for Button Click
Sub butSumClicked(ByVal source As Object, ByVal e As EventArgs)
    ' Call the Sum method.
    Sum()
    ' Call method to raise event.
    OnClick(EventArgs.Empty)
End Sub

Protected Overridable Sub OnClick(ByVal e As EventArgs)
    ' Raise the event.
    RaiseEvent Click(Me, e)
End Sub
```

Visual C#

```
// Declare the event.
public event EventHandler Click;

 void butSumClicked(object sender, EventArgs e)
{
    // Call the Sum method.
    Sum();
    // Call the event method.
    OnClick(EventArgs.Empty);
}

protected virtual void OnClick(EventArgs e)
{
    if (Click != null)
        // Raise the event.
        Click(this, e);
}
```

To make the Click event the default event for the control, add a *DefaultEvent* attribute to the class declaration. A default event is the event that Visual Studio .NET automatically creates when you double-click the control within the Web form. The following code shows the addition in boldface:

Visual Basic .NET

```
<DefaultEvent("Click")> Public Class MathBox
```

Visual C#

```
[DefaultEvent("Click")]
    public class MathBox : System.Web.UI.WebControls.WebControl
```

To use the MathBox control's event from a Web form, double-click the control in the test Web form and use the following event procedure:

Visual Basic .NET

```
Private Sub mathTest_Click(ByVal sender As System.Object, _
    ByVal e As System.EventArgs) Handles mathTest.Click
    Response.Write(mathTest.Result)
End Sub
```

Visual C#

```
private void mthTest_Click(object sender, System.EventArgs e)
{
    Response.Write(mthTest.Result.ToString());
}
```

Handling Control Resizing

Composite controls handle a lot of design-time and run-time display features automatically through their base class's *Render* method. However, they can't automatically resize their child controls because there is no reasonable way to tell what type of resizing behavior is appropriate.

To handle resizing composite controls, follow these steps:

1. Override the base class's *Render* method.
2. Add code to resize the child controls as appropriate.
3. Call the base class's *Render* method to display the control.

The following code resizes a TextBox child control based on the width and height of the MathBox control:

Visual Basic .NET

```
Protected Overrides Sub Render(ByVal writer As _
    System.Web.UI.HtmlTextWriter)
    EnsureChildcontrols()
    ' Resize text box to match control width.
    txtMath.Width = Me.Width
    ' Resize text box to match control height.
    txtMath.Height = Unit.Parse(Me.Height.Value  butSum.Height.Value)
    ' Render the control.
    MyBase.Render(writer)
End Sub
```

Visual C#

```
protected override void Render(HtmlTextWriter output)
{
    EnsureChildControls();
    // Resize text box to match control width.
    txtMath.Width = this.Width;
    // Resize text box to match control height.
    double dHeight = this.Height.Value - butSum.Height.Value;
    txtMath.Height = Unit.Parse(dHeight.ToString());
    // Render the control.
    base.Render(output);
}
```

Superclassing Server Controls

The preceding sections showed you how to create a composite control from multiple existing controls. You can use the same techniques to create new controls from an existing single control to add properties, methods, or events for that control or to change the behavior of that control.

Because that type of custom control is based on only one control, you can derive directly from that control's class rather than using the more general class of *WebControl*. Custom controls of this type aren't really composite controls—they're sometimes referred to as **superclassed** controls.

For example, the following *SuperText* class creates a custom control based on the TextBox server control and adds a method to sort the contents of the text box:

Visual Basic .NET

```
Public Class SuperText
    Inherits System.Web.UI.WebControls.TextBox

    ' New method for the text box.
    Public Sub Sort()
        ' Create an array.
        Dim arrText As String()
        ' Put the words in the text box into the array.
        arrText = Me.Text.Split(" ")
        ' Sort the array.
        Array.Sort(arrText)
        ' Join the string and put it back in the text box.
        Me.Text = String.Join(" ", arrText)
    End Sub

End Class
```

Visual C#

```
public class SuperText : System.Web.UI.WebControls.TextBox
{

    public void Sort()
    {
        // Create an array.
        string[] arrText;
        // Put the words in the text box into the array.
        char[] strSep = {' '};
        arrText = this.Text.Split(strSep);
        // Sort the array.
        Array.Sort(arrText);
        // Join the string and put it back in the text box.
        this.Text = String.Join(" ", arrText);
    }
}
```

To use the control from a Web form, register the control's assembly as shown in the preceding examples, and include the following HTML on a Web form:

```
<Custom:SuperText id="superTest" runat="server"  />
<asp:Button ID="butSort" Runat="server" Text="Sort"  />
```

To test the *Sort* method, add the following code to the Web form's code module:

Visual Basic .NET

```
Private Sub butSort_Click(ByVal sender As System.Object, _
    ByVal e As System.EventArgs) Handles butSort.Click
    superTest.Sort()
End Sub
```

Visual C#

```
private void butSort_Click(object sender, System.EventArgs e)
{
    superTest.Sort();
}
```

At either run time or design time, the SuperText control behaves just like a normal TextBox, as shown in Figure 11-13.

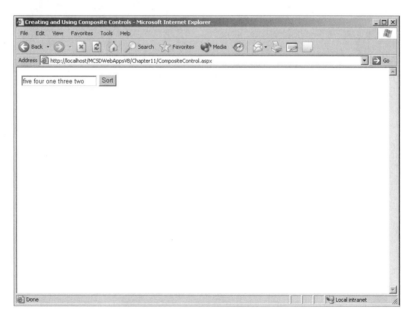

Figure 11-13   SuperText in action

Lesson 3: Creating Rendered Custom Controls

Rendered custom controls are created almost entirely from scratch, which means that you have complete control over how they appear and act. However, because they are not composed of child controls, the way composite controls are, you have to write code to perform the tasks that you could otherwise delegate to child controls.

Composite and rendered controls are closely related, and this lesson extends the skills you developed in Lesson 2. Some of the topics here apply equally to composite and rendered controls—you should consider this lesson to be advanced topics for Web custom control development. That said, there's still a lot more that could be taught on the subject. For a comprehensive guide to developing Web custom controls, see *Developing ASP.NET Server Controls and Components*, by Nikhil Kothari and Vandana Datye (Microsoft Press, 2002).

After this lesson, you will be able to

- Create a custom control's appearance using the *Render* method and the *HtmlTextWriter* utility methods
- Save and restore property values through the control's *ViewState*
- Get text and controls contained between a custom control's begin and end HTML tags
- Respond to user actions on a control by raising cached or postback events
- Get data that was entered on the control by the user
- Add custom controls to the Visual Studio .NET Toolbox
- Change the Toolbox icon and HTML *TagPrefix* used for the control by Visual Studio .NET

Estimated lesson time: 40 minutes

Creating and Using Rendered Controls

If you walked through the procedures described in Lesson 2, you've already created a rendered custom control. The code template that Visual Studio .NET generates when you create a Web Control Library project is, in fact, a rendered control, but it's a simple control that doesn't do much. You can create more interesting controls more quickly using composition, which is why we looked at creating composite controls before creating rendered controls.

Because rendered custom controls are very similar to composite custom controls, the techniques you learned in Lesson 2 apply throughout this lesson as well, with one exception: instead of creating the control's visual interface from other controls, rendered controls create their visual interfaces exclusively from HTML elements.

This means that you don't have built-in properties, methods, or events you can use to get or display data; instead, you must create them yourself.

Creating rendered custom controls is similar to creating composite custom controls. To create rendered custom controls, follow these steps:

1. Create a solution containing a custom control project.
2. Add a Web application project to the solution, and set it as the startup project. You'll use the Web application project to test the custom control during development.
3. Add a project reference from the Web application to the custom control project, and then add an HTML @*Register* directive and control element to use the custom control on a Web form.
4. Create the custom control's visual interface by overriding the base class's *Render* method.
5. Write code to store property values, respond to user actions, and get data from the user as needed.

The following sections describe the last two steps in greater detail. The last two sections in this lesson show how to add completed custom controls to the Toolbox and how to set the icons and generated tags used by Visual Studio .NET for the controls. These last two sections apply equally to composite controls.

Creating the Rendered Control's Appearance

You create a rendered custom control's appearance by overriding the base class's *Render* method and writing to the method's output argument using the *HtmlTextWriter* utility methods. The *HtmlTextWriter* methods summarized in Table 11-3 let you add HTML to the output argument.

Table 11-3   *HtmlTextWriter* **Utility Methods**

Method	Description
AddAttribute	Adds an HTML attribute to the next HTML element to be rendered.
RenderBeginTag	Renders the begin tag of an HTML element for later writing by the *WriteLine* method.
RenderEndTag	Renders the end tag of an HTML element and writes the element and any rendered attributes that are pending. All rendered attributes are cleared after *RenderEndTag*.
Write	Immediately writes a string.
WriteAttribute	Immediately writes an HTML attribute.
WriteBeginTag	Immediately writes the begin tag of an HTML element.
WriteEndTag	Immediately writes the end tag of an HTML element.

Table 11-3 *HtmlTextWriter* **Utility Methods**

Method	Description
WriteFullBeginTag	Immediately writes the begin tag along with the closing bracket (>) for the HTML element.
WriteLine	Immediately writes a line of content. This is equivalent to the *Write* method, but *WriteLine* adds a newline character as well.

As you can probably tell from Table 11-3, there are two approaches to writing HTML elements to the output argument. The most direct approach is to use the *Write* methods to add the HTML directly to *HtmlTextWriter*. For example, the following code creates a button that displays a message box when the user clicks it:

Visual Basic .NET

```
Imports System.ComponentModel
Imports System.Web.UI

Public Class AlertButton
    Inherits System.Web.UI.WebControls.WebControl

    Protected Overrides Sub Render(ByVal output As _
        System.Web.UI.HtmlTextWriter)
        ' Write a title
        output.Write("<h3>Rendered Control</h3>")
        ' Opens an Input HTML tag (inserts "<INPUT").
        output.WriteBeginTag("INPUT")
        ' Write some attributes.
        output.WriteAttribute("value", "Custom Button")
        output.WriteAttribute("type", "button")
        output.WriteAttribute("onclick", "javascript:alert('Howdy!')")
        ' Close the Input HTML tag (inserts ">").
        output.WriteEndTag("INPUT")
    End Sub

End Class
```

Visual C#

```
using System;
using System.Web.UI;
using System.Web.UI.WebControls;
using System.ComponentModel;

namespace csRenderedSnippet
{
    public class AlertButton : System.Web.UI.WebControls.WebControl
    {
        protected override void Render(HtmlTextWriter output)
        {
            // Write a title
```

```
                          output.Write("<h3>Rendered Control</h3>");
                          // Opens an Input HTML tag (inserts "<INPUT").
                          output.WriteBeginTag("INPUT");
                          // Write some attributes.
                          output.WriteAttribute("value", "Custom Button");
                          output.WriteAttribute("type", "button");
                          output.WriteAttribute("onclick", "javascript:alert('Howdy!')");
                          // Close the Input HTML tag (inserts ">").
                          output.WriteEndTag("INPUT");
                     }
                }
          }
```

If you add this code to a custom control project, build the control, and then add the resulting custom control to a Web form, at run time the control will appear as shown in Figure 11-14.

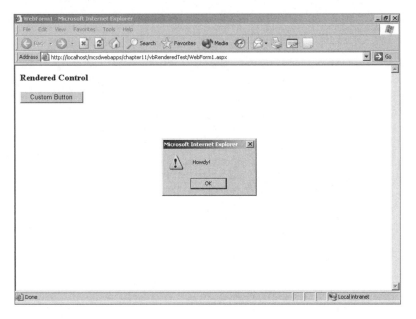

Figure 11-14   The AlertButton rendered custom control in action

As an alternative to writing directly to *HtmlTextWriter*, you can render tags and attributes and then write them as a unit using the *RenderEndTag* method. The following code shows the AlertButton custom control *Render* method written using this alternative approach:

Visual Basic .NET

```
Protected Overrides Sub Render(ByVal output As _
    System.Web.UI.HtmlTextWriter)
    ' Write a title
```

```
    output.Write("<h3>Rendered Control</h3>")
        ' Add some attributes.
        output.AddAttribute("value", "Custom Button")
        output.AddAttribute("type", "button")
        output.AddAttribute("onclick", "javascript:alert('Howdy!')")
        ' Opens an Input HTML tag (inserts "<INPUT").
        output.RenderBeginTag("INPUT")
        ' Close the Input HTML tag (inserts ">").
        output.RenderEndTag()
    End Sub
```

Visual C#

```
protected override void Render(HtmlTextWriter output)
{
    // Write a title
    output.Write("<h3>Rendered Control</h3>");
    // Add some attributes.
    output.AddAttribute("value", "Custom Button");
    output.AddAttribute("type", "button");
    output.AddAttribute("onclick", "javascript:alert('Howdy!')");
    // Opens an Input HTML tag (inserts "<INPUT").
    output.RenderBeginTag("INPUT");
    // Close the Input HTML tag (inserts ">").
    output.RenderEndTag();
}
```

The advantage of rendering the HTML elements in this way is that you can create the HTML attributes in any sequence.

Storing Property Settings

The composite custom control samples shown in Lesson 2 stored property settings using the properties from their contained controls. Because rendered controls don't have contained controls, you must use the rendered control's *ViewState* to store any property settings you want to retain between page displays.

The following code shows a *Text* property that retains its value between page displays:

Visual Basic .NET

```
Property Text() As String
    Get
        ' If the property has been set
        If Not IsNothing(ViewState("Text")) Then
            ' Return the settng.
            Return ViewState("Text")
        Else
            ' Otherwise return "".
            Return ""
        End If
```

```
        End Get
        Set(ByVal Value As String)
            ' Store the property setting.
            ViewState("Text") = Value
        End Set
End Property
```

Visual C#

```
public string Text
{
    get
    {
        // If the property has been set
        if (ViewState["Text"] != null)
            // Return the settng.
            return ViewState["Text"].ToString();
        else
            // Otherwise return "".
            return null;
    }

    set
    {
        // Store the property setting.
        ViewState["Text"] = value;
    }
}
```

Setting *ViewState* serializes data and stores it in a hidden field on the Web form. When the page is posted back to the server, returning a value from *ViewState* retrieves and deserializes the data from the hidden field.

ViewState is optimized for *String*, *ArrayList*, and *HashTable* data types, but it can save any data that can be serialized or that provides a *TypeConverter*. For other types of data, you can create your own code to save and restore *ViewState* by overriding the *SaveViewState* and *LoadViewState* methods.

Getting Contained Text

HTML elements often enclose literal text that they modify in some way, as shown by the following HTML tags used to create boldface text:

```
<b>Bold me</b>
```

To get contained text from within a custom control, follow these steps:

1. Add a *ParseChildren* attribute to the control's class definition.
2. Implement the *INamingContainer* interface in the custom control class.
3. Retrieve the contained text using the *Controls* collection.

The following custom control class shows how to retrieve the text between a custom control's begin and end tags to display the contained text in red:

Visual Basic .NET

```
' ParseChildren attribute enables contained controls.
<ParseChildren(False)> Public Class Red
    Inherits WebControls.WebControl
    ' This interface makes it possible to get the Controls array.
    Implements INamingContainer

    Protected Overrides Sub Render(ByVal output As _
        System.Web.UI.HtmlTextWriter)
        ' Contained text is returned as a Literal control.
        Dim litText As LiteralControl
        ' Get the contained text from the Controls collection.
        litText = Controls(0)
        ' Make it red using the <font> element.
        output.Write("<font color='red'>" & litText.Text & "</font>")
    End Sub

End Class
```

Visual C#

```
[ParseChildren(false)]
 public class Red : System.Web.UI.WebControls.WebControl, INamingContainer
{
    //
 INamingContainer interface makes it possible to get the Controls array.

    protected override void Render(HtmlTextWriter output)
    {
        // Contained text is returned as a Literal control.
        LiteralControl litText ;
        // Get the contained text from the Controls collection.
        litText = (LiteralControl)Controls[0];
        // Make it red using the <font> element.
        output.Write("<font color='red'>" + litText.Text + "</font>");
    }
}
```

On a Web form, you would use the preceding custom control through the following HTML:

```
<custom:red id="Red1" runat="server">Some red text</custom:red>
```

You can use the *Controls* collection to get any items that exist between the custom control's begin and end tags, including other controls. For example, the following custom control class groups contained controls in a panel, centers the controls on the page, and displays them on a red background:

Visual Basic .NET

```vb
' ParseChildren attribute enables contained controls.
<ParseChildren(False)> Public Class Center
    Inherits WebControls.WebControl
    ' This interface makes it possible to get the Controls array.
    Implements INamingContainer

    Protected Overrides Sub Render(ByVal output As _
        System.Web.UI.HtmlTextWriter)
        ' Add some attributes for the panel.
        output.AddAttribute("align", "center")
        output.AddStyleAttribute("BACKGROUND-COLOR", "red")
        ' Start a panel
        output.RenderBeginTag("div")
        ' Declare a variable to get contained controls.
        Dim ctrItem As Control
        ' For each contained control.
        For Each ctrItem In Controls
            ' Render the control
            ctrItem.RenderControl(output)
        Next
        output.RenderEndTag()
    End Sub

End Class
```

Visual C#

```csharp
[ParseChildren(false)]
public class Center : System.Web.UI.WebControls.WebControl,
    INamingContainer
{
    //
  INamingContainer interface makes it possible to get the Controls array.

    protected override void Render(HtmlTextWriter output)
    {
        // Add some attributes for the panel.
        output.AddAttribute("align", "center");
        output.AddStyleAttribute("BACKGROUND-COLOR", "red");
        // Start a panel
        output.RenderBeginTag("div");
        // For each contained control.
        foreach (Control ctrItem in Controls)
        {
            // Render the control
            ctrItem.RenderControl(output);
        }
        output.RenderEndTag();
    }
}
```

Responding to User Actions

Composite custom controls can use their contained controls' events to respond to user actions, as shown in Lesson 2. Rendered controls, however, need to take special steps to respond to user actions. How you deal with user actions depends on the type of event:

- Cached events can be raised from the custom control's code.
- Postback events must be raised from the client side using a script rendered by the custom control.

The following sections show how to raise each of these types of events.

Raising Cached Events

Cached events are handled by the Web form's server-side code when the Web form is posted back to the server and after the Load and postback events have been handled. Raising a cached event involves two steps:

1. Declare an event to raise.
2. Raise the event from somewhere within the custom control's code.

For example, the following custom control class defines an OnChange event that is raised whenever the *Text* property changes:

Visual Basic .NET

```vb
<DefaultEvent("OnChange")>Public Class RenderText
    Inherits WebControls.WebControl

    Event Change(ByVal sender As Object, ByVal e As EventArgs)

    Property Text() As String
        Get
            ' If the property has been set
            If Not IsNothing(ViewState("Text")) Then
                ' Return the settng.
                Return ViewState("Text")
            Else
                ' Otherwise return "".
                Return ""
            End If
        End Get
        Set(ByVal Value As String)
            ' Store the property setting.
            ViewState("Text") = Value
            OnChange(EventArgs.Empty)
        End Set
    End Property
```

```vb
' Event method.
Protected Overridable Sub OnChange(ByVal e As EventArgs)
    ' Raise event.
    RaiseEvent Change(Me, EventArgs.Empty)
End Sub

Protected Overrides Sub Render(ByVal output As _
    System.Web.UI.HtmlTextWriter)
    ' Set the Input control's attributes.
    output.AddAttribute("value", Me.Text)
    ' Create an Input control element using above.
    output.RenderBeginTag("Input")
    ' Close the Input control element (inserts />).
    output.RenderEndTag()
End Sub

End Class
```

Visual C#

```csharp
[DefaultEvent("Change")]
public class RenderText : System.Web.UI.WebControls.WebControl
{
    // Declare event.
    public event EventHandler Change;

    public string Text
    {
        get
        {
            // If the property has been set
            if (ViewState["Text"] != null)
                // Return the settng.
                return ViewState["Text"].ToString();
            else
                // Otherwise return "".
                return null;
        }
        set
        {
            // Store the property setting.
            ViewState["Text"] = value;
            // Call event method.
            OnChange(EventArgs.Empty);
        }
    }

    protected virtual void OnChange(EventArgs e)
    {
        if (Change != null)
            // Raise event.
```

```
            Change(this, e);
    }

    protected override void Render(HtmlTextWriter output)
    {
        // Set the Input control's attributes.
        output.AddAttribute("value", this.Text);
        // Create an Input control element using above.
        output.RenderBeginTag("Input");
        // Close the Input control element (inserts />).
        output.RenderEndTag();
    }
}
```

Notice that the class definition above sets Change as the default event for the control. That means that Visual Studio .NET will generate the event procedure if you double-click the custom control in the Web Forms Designer.

Use the following code to handle the Change event from the Web form:

Visual Basic .NET

```
Private Sub txtTest_OnChange(ByVal sender As System.Object, _
    ByVal e As System.EventArgs) Handles txtTest.OnChange
    Response.Write("Text changed!")
End Sub
```

Visual C#

```
private void txtTest_Change(object sender, System.EventArgs e)
{
    Response.Write("Text changed!");
}
```

Raising Postback Events

Postback events cause the Web form to be posted back to the server for immediate processing. They are handled immediately after the Web form's Load event. To raise a postback event from a custom control, follow these steps:

1. Implement the *IPostBackEventHandler* interface in the custom control.
2. Declare an event to raise.
3. Render an HTML element that can respond to client-side events, such as OnClick.
4. Add an attribute to the HTML element containing a script to post the page back to the server.
5. Raise the event from the *RaisePostBackEvent* method, which is part of the *IPostBackEventHandler* interface.

The following code shows how to use these steps to raise the Click postback event from a custom control:

Visual Basic .NET

```
' Raises PostBack event.
<DefaultEvent("Click")> Public Class AlertButton
    Inherits System.Web.UI.WebControls.WebControl
    ' (1) Interface that allows PostBack event processing.
    Implements IPostBackEventHandler

    ' (2) Declare postback event
    Event Click(ByVal sender As Object, ByVal e As EventArgs)


    ' (3) Render an HTML element that can detect user events.
    Protected Overrides Sub Render(ByVal output As _
        System.Web.UI.HtmlTextWriter)
        ' Add some attributes.
        output.AddAttribute("value", "Postback Button")
        output.AddAttribute("type", "button")
        ' (4) Add attribute to raise Postback event on client.
        output.AddAttribute("onclick", "javascript:alert('Howdy!');" & _
            Page.GetPostBackEventReference(Me))
        ' Opens an Input HTML tag (inserts "<INPUT").
        output.RenderBeginTag("INPUT")
        ' Close the Input HTML tag (inserts ">" and writes attributes).
        output.RenderEndTag()
    End Sub

    ' Part of the IPostBackEventHandler interface.
    ' you must create this method.
    Public Sub RaisePostBackEvent(ByVal eventArgument As String) _
        Implements System.Web.UI.IPostBackEventHandler.RaisePostBackEvent
        ' (5) Raise the event.
        OnClick(EventArgs.Empty)
    End Sub

    Protected Overridable Sub OnClick(ByVal e As EventArgs)
        ' Raise the event.
        RaiseEvent Click(Me, EventArgs.Empty)
    End Sub

End Class
```

Visual C#

```csharp
// (1) IPostBackEventHandler interface  allows PostBack event processing.
[DefaultEvent("Click")] public class AlertButtonThree :
  System.Web.UI.WebControls.WebControl, IPostBackEventHandler
{
    // (2) Declare postback event
    public event EventHandler Click;

    // (3) Render an HTML element that can detect user events.
    protected override void Render(HtmlTextWriter output)
    {
        // Write a title
        output.Write("<h3>Rendered Control</h3>");
        // Add some attributes.
        output.AddAttribute("value", "Custom Button");
        output.AddAttribute("type", "button");
        // (4) Add attribute to raise Postback event on client.
        output.AddAttribute("onclick", "javascript:alert('Howdy!');" +
            Page.GetPostBackEventReference(this));
        // Opens an Input HTML tag (inserts "<INPUT").
        output.RenderBeginTag("INPUT");
        // Close the Input HTML tag (inserts ">").
        output.RenderEndTag();
    }

    // Part of the IPostBackEventHandler interface.
    // you must create this method.
    public void RaisePostBackEvent(string eventArgument)
    {
        // (5) Call the event method to raise event.
        OnClick(EventArgs.Empty);
    }

    protected virtual void OnClick(EventArgs e)
    {
        // Raise the event.
        if (Click != null)
            Click(this, e);
    }

}
```

When the user clicks the preceding custom control at run time, the button's OnClick event runs the following script:

```
alert('Howdy!');              //Displays a message box.
__doPostBack('winTest','');  //
Generated by Page.GetPostBackEventReference(Me);
```

The *__doPostBack* method posts the page back to the server, where it is intercepted by the *IPostBackEventHandler* interface's *RaisePostBackEvent* method, which in turn raises the Click event from within the control.

Use the following code to handle the Click event from the Web form:

Visual Basic .NET

```
Private Sub altTest_Click(ByVal sender As System.Object, _
    ByVal e As System.EventArgs) Handles altTest.Click
    Response.Write("Button clicked!")
End Sub
```

Visual C#

```
private void altTest(object sender, System.EventArgs e)
{
    Response.Write("Button clicked!");
}
```

Getting Data from the User

Rendered controls don't automatically retain the data entered by the user. You can see this if you create a TextBox custom control by rendering an HTML *Input* element: you can type in the *Input* element, but as soon as the page is posted back to the server, whatever you typed is gone.

To get data from the user, follow these steps:

1. Implement the *IPostBackDataHandler* interface.
2. Add a *name* attribute to uniquely identify the HTML element to get data from.
3. Override the *LoadPostBackData* method from the *IPostBackDataHandler* interface. Use this method to get the data from the user.
4. Override the *RaisePostDataChangedEvent* method from the *IPostBackData-Handler* interface. You don't have to write code for this method, but you must override it because it is part of the interface.
5. Raise an event to indicate that the data has changed. This step is optional—if you don't want to provide a change event for the control, you don't have to.

The following custom control shows how to use these steps to retain data entered by a user in a custom TextBox control rendered from an HTML *Input* element:

Visual Basic .NET

```
<DefaultEvent("Change")> Public Class RenderText
    Inherits WebControls.WebControl
    ' (1) Interface that allows you to get PostBack data.
    Implements IPostBackDataHandler

    Event Change(ByVal sender As Object, ByVal e As EventArgs)
```

```
Property Text() As String
    Get
        ' If the property has been set
        If Not IsNothing(ViewState("Text")) Then
            ' Return the settng.
            Return ViewState("Text")
        Else
            ' Otherwise return "".
            Return ""
        End If
    End Get
    Set(ByVal Value As String)
        ' Store the property setting.
        ViewState("Text") = Value
        ' Call event method.
        OnChange(EventArgs.Empty)
    End Set
End Property

Protected Overrides Sub Render(ByVal output As _
    System.Web.UI.HtmlTextWriter)
    ' Set the Input control's attributes.
    output.AddAttribute("value", Me.Text)
    ' (2) You must define this attribute to enable PostBack data.
    output.AddAttribute("name", Me.UniqueID)
    ' Create an Input control element using above.
    output.RenderBeginTag("Input")
    ' Close the Input control element.
    output.RenderEndTag()
    ' Write the element to the HtmlTextWriter.
    output.WriteLine()
End Sub

' (3) Get data from the user.
' You must create this method.
Public Function LoadPostData(ByVal postDataKey As String, _
    ByVal postCollection As _
    System.Collections.Specialized.NameValueCollection) As Boolean _
    Implements System.Web.UI.IPostBackDataHandler.LoadPostData
    ' If the user changes Input value, update the text property.
    If Me.Text <> postCollection(postDataKey) Then
        Me.Text = postCollection(postDataKey)
        ' Returning True invokes RaisePostDataChangedEvent below.
        Return True
    Else
        ' Returning False does not invoke RaisePostDataChangedEvent.
        Return False
    End If
End Function
```

```
' (4) Override RaisePostDataChangedEvent method.
' You must create this method.
Public Sub RaisePostDataChangedEvent() Implements _
    System.Web.UI.IPostBackDataHandler.RaisePostDataChangedEvent
    ' (5) Call the event method. This is optional.
    OnChange(EventArgs.Empty)
End Sub

' Event method.
Protected Overridable Sub OnChange(ByVal e As EventArgs)
    ' Raise event
    RaiseEvent Change(Me, EventArgs.Empty)
End Sub
End Class
```

Visual C#

```csharp
// (1) IPostBackDataHandler interface allows you to get PostBack data.
[DefaultProperty("Text"), DefaultEvent("Change")] public class RenderText :
    System.Web.UI.WebControls.WebControl, IPostBackDataHandler
{
    // Declare event.
    public event EventHandler Change;

    [DefaultValue("")]
    public string Text
    {
        get
        {
            // If the property has been set
            if (ViewState["Text"] != null)
                // Return the settng.
                return ViewState["Text"].ToString();
            else
                // Otherwise return "".
                return null;
        }

        set
        {
            // Store the property setting.
            ViewState["Text"] = value;
            // Call event method.
            OnChange(EventArgs.Empty);
        }
    }

    protected override void Render(HtmlTextWriter output)
    {
        // Set the Input control's attributes.
```

```
            output.AddAttribute("value", this.Text);
            // (2) You must define this attribute to enable PostBack data.
            output.AddAttribute("name", this.UniqueID);
            // Create an Input control element using above.
            output.RenderBeginTag("Input");
            // Close the Input control element (inserts />).
            output.RenderEndTag();
    }


    // (3) Get data from the user.
    // You must create this method.
    public bool LoadPostData(string postDataKey,
        System.Collections.Specialized.NameValueCollection postCollection)
    {
        // If the user changes Input value, update the text property.
        if (this.Text != postCollection[postDataKey])
        {
            this.Text = postCollection[postDataKey];
            // Returning true invokes RaisePostDataChangedEvent.
            return true;
        }
        else
            // Returning False does not invoke RaisePostDataChangedEvent.
            return false;
    }


    // (4) Override RaisePostDataChangedEvent method.
    // You must create this method.
    public void RaisePostDataChangedEvent()
    {
        // (5) Call the event method. This is optional.
        OnChange(EventArgs.Empty);
    }

    protected virtual void OnChange(EventArgs e)
    {
        if (Change != null)
            // Raise event.
            Change(this, e);
    }
}
```

Adding Custom Controls to the Toolbox

After you've created and debugged a set of custom controls, you can add them to
the Visual Studio .NET Toolbox by following these steps:

1. Choose Customize Toolbox from the Tools menu. Visual Studio .NET displays
   the Customize Toolbox dialog box, as shown in Figure 11-15.

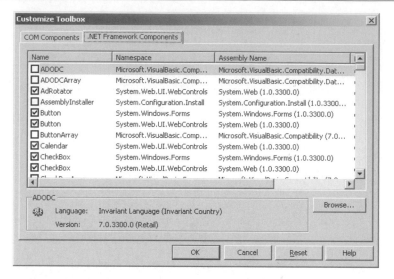

Figure 11-15   Adding items to the Toolbox

2. Click the .NET Framework Components tab, and then click Browse. Visual Studio .NET displays the Open dialog box.

3. Use the Open dialog box to locate and select the assembly (.dll) containing the custom controls to add to the Toolbox, and then click Open. Visual Studio .NET opens the assembly and adds the contained controls to the list of controls in the Customize Toolbox dialog box.

4. Click OK to close the Customize Toolbox dialog box.

After you've added custom controls to the Toolbox, they appear under the General category when Visual Studio .NET is in Design mode, as shown in Figure 11-16.

Figure 11-16   Custom controls in the Toolbox

To add a custom control to a Web form, simply double-click the control or drag the control from the Toolbox to the Web form. When you add a custom control from the Toolbox, Visual Studio .NET automatically adds the *@Register* directive for the control to the Web form and inserts the HTML for the custom control, as shown in boldface in the following HTML:

```
<%@ Page Language="vb" AutoEventWireup="false"
Codebehind="CustomControl.aspx.vb" Inherits=" MCSDWebAppsVB.CustomControl"%>
<%@ Register TagPrefix="Custom" Namespace="RenderedControls"
Assembly="RenderedControls" %>
<HTML>
  <body>
  <form id="Form1" method="post" runat="server">
    <Custom:Chart id="Chart1" runat="server"></cc1:Chart>
  </form>
  </body>
</HTML>
```

The icons that appear for the custom control in the Toolbox and the *TagPrefix* used in the HTML for the control can be changed using attributes in the custom control's assembly, as described in the following section.

Setting the Toolbox Icon and *TagPrefix* for Custom Controls

You can customize your controls to display unique icons in the Toolbox and use their own *TagPrefix* attributes in HTML. If you've already added the custom controls to your Toolbox, you must unload them and then add them back to the Toolbox before any of these changes take effect.

To add a Toolbox icon to a custom control, follow these steps:

1. Create a 16-by-16 bitmap file containing the icon to display in the Toolbox.
2. Name the bitmap file using the same base name as the class name for the custom control it represents. For example, Red.bmp is the icon for the custom control with the class name Red.
3. Set the bitmap file's *Build Action* property to *Embedded Resource* in Solution Explorer.
4. Rebuild the control.

To change the *TagPrefix* used by a custom control in HTML, follow these steps:

1. Add the following lines to the custom control project's AssemblyInfo file:

Visual Basic .NET

```
Imports System.Web.UI

<Assembly: TagPrefix("project.namespace", "prefix")>
```

Visual C#

```
using System.Web.UI

[assembly: TagPrefix("namespace", "prefix")]
```

2. Rebuild the project.

In the preceding procedure, *project.namespace* is the project name and namespace for the custom control, and *prefix* is the prefix to use for the custom controls from that namespace.

Summary

- Create user controls by drawing server and HTML controls on a user control page (.ascx).

- Add a user control to a Web form by dragging the control from Solution Explorer, instead of from the Toolbox.

- User controls must be part of the project in which they are used and are initialized after their containing Web form's Load event.

- Create composite custom controls by defining a class derived from the *WebControl* base class.

- Composite controls are made up of server and HTML controls added through the *CreateChildControls* method.

- To add features to an existing server control, superclass that control by deriving a new custom control from the existing control's class.

- Rendered custom controls provide more control over the appearance and behavior of the control, but they require more programming to handle the tasks that composite custom controls usually handle through their child controls.

- Use the *Render* method and the *HtmlTextWriter* utility methods to create the appearance of a rendered custom control.

- Use the *IPostBackEventHandler* interface to enable a rendered control to trigger postback events.

- Use the *IPostBackDataHandler* interface to enable a rendered control to get data that the user enters in a control at run time.

Lab: Creating Custom Controls

In this lab, you'll create a test Web application project to contain the three different controls you create in each of the exercises. When complete, the controls will appear on the Web form, as shown in Figure 11-17.

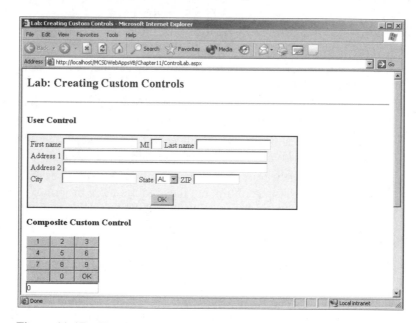

Figure 11-17   The completed test application with user and custom controls

Estimated lesson time: 60 minutes

Exercise 1: Create an AddressBox User Control

In this exercise, you'll create a Web application containing a user control that gathers name and address information. Use the skills you developed in Lesson 1 to create and test a user control by completing the following major tasks:

1. Create a Web application project.

2. Add a user control page (.ascx) that contains text and controls for collecting name, address, city, state, and ZIP code information.

3. Use validation controls within the user control to ensure that required fields are completed.

4. Use a Grid Layout Panel HTML control to format and position the text and controls within the user control.

5. Provide a Click event that is fired from the user control after the data entries are validated.

6. Provide public read-only properties to return address information from the user control.

7. Provide a public read/write *Style* property to support absolute positioning in grid layout.

8. Test the user control by adding it to a Web form and accessing its event and properties from code.

When you have finished (or if you get stuck), compare your results to the Address-Box user control included on the companion CD.

Exercise 2: Create the DigitPad Composite Custom Control

In this exercise, you'll create a Web Control Library containing a custom control that allows the user to enter numbers by clicking buttons. Use the skills you developed in Lesson 2 to create and test the custom control by completing the following major tasks:

1. Add a Web Control Library project to the solution you created in the previous exercise.

2. Add a reference from the user control project to the Web Control Library project so that you can test the custom control from Web forms within that project.

3. Create a composite custom control that uses InputButton HTML controls to accept numeric input.

4. Provide a postback event that is fired from the custom control once the numeric data is complete.

5. Provide a public read-only property to return the number entered in the control.

6. Test the user control by adding it to a Web form and accessing its events and properties from code.

When you have finished, compare your results to the DigitPad custom control included on the companion CD.

Exercise 3: Create the BarChart Rendered Custom Control

In this exercise, you'll add a rendered custom control to the Web Control Library you created in Exercise 2. The custom control will create a simple bar chart from numbers entered between the HTML begin and end tags of the custom control. Use the skills you developed in Lesson 3 to create and test the custom control by completing the following major tasks:

1. Add a new Web custom control class to the Web Control Library project you created in the previous exercise.
2. Create a *Values* property that gets an array of data from text entered between the begin and end tags of the custom control.
3. Create a *ChartTitle* property that sets or returns a heading displayed at the top of the chart.
4. Override the control's *Render* method to create a bar chart from the data in the *Values* property. To simplify the charting, use Horizontal Rule HTML controls (<HR>) to create the chart.
5. Test the user control by adding it to a Web form and accessing its events and properties from code.

Compare your results to the BarChart custom control included on the companion CD.

Review

The following questions are intended to reinforce key information presented in this chapter. If you are unable to answer a question, review the appropriate lesson and then try the question again. Answers to the questions can be found in the appendix.

1. Briefly describe the best uses for each of the three types of Web controls by completing the following sentences:

   - Create a Web user control when you want to...

   - Create a composite custom control when you want to...

   - Create a rendered custom control when you want to...

2. How is deriving important to creating custom Web controls?

3. What is the most important method to override when you're creating a composite custom control?

4. What is the most important method to override when you're creating a rendered control?

5. How is raising a postback event in a composite control different from raising a postback event in a rendered control?

C H A P T E R   1 2

Optimizing Web Applications with Caching

About This Chapter

High-performance Web applications should be designed with caching in mind. **Caching** is the technique of storing frequently used items in memory so that they can be accessed more quickly. Caching is important to Web applications because cach time a Wcb form is requested, the host server must process the Web form's HTML and run Web form code to create a response. By caching the response, all that work is bypassed. Instead, the request is served from the reponse already stored in memory.

In this chapter, you'll learn how to store Web forms, parts of Web forms, and application data in the cache. You'll also learn how to monitor the items stored in the cache to determine whether you're using caching effectively.

Before You Begin

To complete this chapter, you must:

- Know how to create and deploy a Web application.
- Understand the life cycle of a Web form and be familiar with the *Application* and *Session* objects.

Optionally, you might also need know how to use Microsoft Application Center Test (ACT) to load-test a Web application.

Lesson 1: Caching Web Forms

Caching an item incurs considerable overhead, so it's important to choose the items to cache wisely. A Web form is a good candidate for caching if it is frequently used and does not contain data that frequently changes. By storing a Web form in memory, you are effectively freezing that form's server-side content so that changes to that content do not appear until the cache is refreshed.

In this lesson, you'll learn how to cache Web forms and how to control how long they are stored in memory. You'll also learn about caching multiple responses from a single Web form.

After this lesson, you will be able to

- Cache a Web form response and control how long it is stored in memory
- Store multiple responses for a single Web form
- Use custom strings to cache multiple responses for a single Web form
- Cache a response from within code
- Control whether the cached response is stored on the server, on the client, or elsewhere

Estimated lesson time: 20 minutes

Using the *OutputCache* Directive

Use the *@OutputCache* page directive to cache a Web form in the server's memory. The *@OutputCache* directive's *Duration* attribute controls how long the page is cached. For example, the following Web form is cached for 60 seconds:

```
<%@ Page Language="vb" AutoEventWireup="false"
Codebehind="WebFormCaching.aspx.vb" Inherits="MCSDWebAppsVB.WebFormCaching"%>
<%@ OutputCache Duration="60" VaryByParam="None" %>
<!DOCTYPE HTML PUBLIC "-//W3C//DTD HTML 4.0 Transitional//EN">
<HTML>
  <body>
    <form id="Form1" method="post" runat="server">
      <h2>Caching Web Forms</h2>
      <hr>
      <p>Click Refresh to see how server-side information is cached.</p>
      <p>Time this page was cached (server-side code):
        <% Response.Write(Now.ToString()) %>
      </p>
      <p>Current time (client-side code):
        <script>document.write(Date());</script>
      </p>
    </form>
  </body>
</HTML>
```

The first time any user requests this Web form, the server loads the response in memory and retains that response for 60 seconds. Any subsequent requests during that time receive the cached response.

After the cache duration has expired, the next request for the Web form generates a new response, which is then cached for another 60 seconds. Thus the server processes the preceding Web form once every 60 seconds—at most.

Caching Multiple Responses from a Single Web Form

When used on a Web form, the *OutputCache* directive has two required attributes: *Duration* and *VaryByParam*. The *VaryByParam* attribute lets you cache multiple responses from a single Web form based on varying HTTP POST or query string parameters. Setting *VaryByParam* to *None* caches only one response for the Web form, regardless of the parameters sent.

For example, the following Web form caches a different response for each different selection from the drpTimeZone control:

```
<%@ OutputCache Duration="60" VaryByParam="drpTimeZone" %>
<%@ Page Language="vb" AutoEventWireup="false"
Codebehind="WebFormCache2.aspx.vb" Inherits="MCSDWebAppsVB.WebFormCache2"%>
<HTML>
  <body>
    <form id="Form1" method="post" runat="server">
      <h2>Caching Multiple Versions of a Web Form</h2>
      <hr>
      <p>Select a time zone and click Submit to see how server-side
        information is cached.</p>
      <asp:DropDownList id="drpTimeZone" runat="server">
        <asp:ListItem Value="1">GMT+1</asp:ListItem>
        <asp:ListItem Value="2">GMT+2</asp:ListItem>
        <asp:ListItem Value="0" Selected="True">GMT</asp:ListItem>
        <asp:ListItem Value="-1">GMT-1</asp:ListItem>
        <asp:ListItem Value="-2">GMT-2</asp:ListItem>
      </asp:DropDownList><INPUT type="submit" value="Submit">
        <p>Time this page was cached (server-side code):
  <% Response.Write(DateTime.Now.AddHours(Val(drpTimeZone.SelectedItem.Value)
)) %>
      </p>
      <p>Current time (client-side code):
        <script>document.write(Date());</script>
      </p>
    </form>
  </body>
</HTML>
```

At run time, up to five different responses will be cached for this Web form—one for each possible selection from the drpTimeZone control.

You can also cache multiple responses from a single Web form using the *VaryBy-Headers* or *VaryByCustom* attribute. For example, the following *OutputCache* directive caches different responses based on the requested language:

```
<%@ OutputCache Duration="120" VaryByParam="None" VaryByHeader="Accept-
Language" %>
<%@ Page Language="vb" AutoEventWireup="false"
Codebehind="WebFormCache3.aspx.vb" Inherits="MCSDWebAppsVB.WebFormCache3"%>
<HTML>
  <body>
    <form id="Form1" method="post" runat="server">
      <h2>Caching Multiple Versions of a Web Form by Header</h2>
      <hr>
      <p>Change your regional settings in the Windows Control panel then
        click Submit below to see how different versions of this page
        are cached.</p>
      <INPUT type="submit" value="Submit" id="Submit">
      <p>Request language:
    <% Response.Write(Request.Headers.GetValues("Accept-Language")(0)) %>
      </p>
      <p>Time this page was cached (server-side code):
        <% Response.Write(DateTime.Now) %>
      </p>
      <p>Current time (client-side code):
        <script>document.write(Date());</script>
      </p>
    </form>
  </body>
</HTML>
```

This Web form caches a different response for each request that has a different Accept-Language header.

The *VaryByCustom* attribute lets you cache different responses based on a custom string. To use *VaryByCustom*, override the *GetVaryByCustomString* method in the Web application's Global.asax file. For example, the following code creates a custom string (*appName*) that allows different responses to be cached for different client browsers:

Visual Basic .NET

```
' From Global.asax
Public Overrides Function GetVaryByCustomString(ByVal context As
    HttpContext, _
    ByVal arg As String) As String
    If (arg = "appName") Then
        Return "appName=" & context.Request.Browser.Browser
    End If
End Function
```

Visual C#

```csharp
// From Global.asax
public override string GetVaryByCustomString(HttpContext context,
string arg )
{
    if (arg == "appName")
        return "appName=" + context.Request.Browser.Browser;
    else
        return "";
}
```

The following Web form caches different responses based on the client's browser using the *appName* custom string created in the preceding code:

```
<%@ OutputCache Duration="120" VaryByParam="None" VaryByCustom="appName" %>
<%@ Page Language="vb" AutoEventWireup="false"
Codebehind="WebFormCache4.aspx.vb" Inherits="MCSDWebAppsVB.WebFormCache4"%>
  <body>
    <form id="Form1" method="post" runat="server">
      <h2>Caching Multiple Versions of a Web Form by Custom String</h2>
      <hr>
      <p>View this page from different browsers and click Submit below
         to see how different versions of this page are cached.</p>
      <INPUT type="submit" value="Submit" id="Submit" lang="en-uk">
      <p>Client browser:
         <script>document.write(navigator.appName)</script>
      </p>
      <p>Time this page was cached (server-side code):
         <% Response.Write(DateTime.Now) %>
      </p>
      <p>Current time (client-side code):
         <script>document.write(Date());</script>
      </p>
    </form>
  </body>
</html>
```

Controlling Caching in Code

The preceding sections show how to control caching within a Web form's HTML using the *OutputCache* directive. You can also control Web form caching within code using the *Response* object's *Cache* property, which returns an *HttpCachePolicy* object for the response. The *HttpCachePolicy* object provides members that are similar to the *OutputCache* directive's attributes. Table 12-1 compares the key *HttpCachePolicy* members and the *OutputCache* attributes.

Table 12-1   *HttpCacheObject* members vs. *OutputCache* attributes

HttpCachePolicy member	*OutputCache* attribute	Use to
VaryByParams	*VaryByParam*	Cache multiple responses for a single Web form based on an HTTP POST parameter or query string.
VaryByHeaders	*VaryByHeader*	Cache multiple responses for a single Web form based on the HTTP request header sent from the client.
SetVaryByCustom	*VaryByCustom*	Cache multiple responses for a single Web form based on a custom string.
SetExpires	*Duration*	Set the amount of time a response is cached.
SetSlidingExpiration	N/A	Change between an absolute expiration and sliding expiration.
SetCacheability	*Location*	Specify where the response is cached.
SetAllowResponseIn-BrowserHistory	N/A	Cache the response in the client browser's history regardless of the *SetCacheability* setting.
AddValidationCallback	N/A	Register a callback function to validate the cached response before returning the response to the client.
SetRevalidation	N/A	Set a flag to revalidate the cached response stored on the proxy server, host server, or at all locations.
SetValidUntilExpires	N/A (*True* by default)	Cause ASP.NET to ignore cache invalidation headers sent by some client browsers when the user clicks Refresh.

For example, the following code caches the Web form's response for 5 seconds:

Visual Basic .NET

```
Private Sub Page_Load(ByVal sender As System.Object, _
    ByVal e As System.EventArgs) Handles MyBase.Load
    ' Display time page was cached.
    lblTime.Text = Now
    ' Set OutputCache Duration.
    Response.Cache.SetExpires(Now.AddSeconds(5))
    ' Set OutputCache VaryByParams.
    Response.Cache.VaryByParams("None") = True
    ' Set OutputCache Location.
    Response.Cache.SetCacheability(HttpCacheability.Public)
End Sub
```

Visual C#

```csharp
private void Page_Load(object sender, System.EventArgs e)
{
    // Display time page was cached.
    lblTime.Text = System.DateTime.Now.ToString();
    // Set OutputCache Duration.
    Response.Cache.SetExpires(System.DateTime.Now.AddSeconds(5));
    // Set OutputCache VaryByParams.
    Response.Cache.VaryByParams["None"] = true;
    // Set OutputCache Location.
    Response.Cache.SetCacheability(HttpCacheability.Public);
}
```

The preceding code is equivalent to the following *OutputCache* directive:

```
<%@ OutputCache Duration="5" VaryByParam="None" Location="Any" %>
```

Controlling Where Items Are Cached

The *OutputCache* directive's *Location* attribute and the *HttpCachePolicy* object's *SetCacheability* property determine where Microsoft ASP.NET stores cached responses. By default, ASP.NET caches responses at any available location that accepts cache items—the client, proxy servers, or the host server. In practice, those locations might or might not allow caching, so you can think of the *Location/Set-Cacheability* setting as more of a request than a command. Table 12-2 describes the *Location/SetCacheability* settings.

Table 12-2   *OutputCache Location* and *HttpCachePolicy SetCacheability* **Settings**

Location setting	*SetCacheability* setting	Caches response at
Any	*HttpCacheability.Server*	Any available location: client, proxy server, or host server.
Client	*HttpCacheability.Private*	Client on which the request originated.
Downstream	*HttpCacheability.Public*	Client or proxy server.
None	*HttpCacheability.NoCache*	No location. This setting disables caching.
Server	*HttpCacheability.ServerAndNo-Cache*	Host server on which request is processed.
ServerAndClient	*HttpCacheability.ServerAndPrivate*	Host server on which request is processed and client on which request originated.

In Microsoft .NET Framework version 1.1 and later, you can override the cache location settings using the *HttpCachePolicy* object's *SetAllowResponseInBrowser-History* method. Setting that method to *True* allows the response to be stored in the client's history folder even if the location setting is *None* or *Server*.

Lesson 2: Caching Parts of Web Forms

Sometimes you want to cache only part of a Web form response. For instance, a Web form might contain many pieces of variable information plus a single large table that almost never changes. In this case, you might place that table in a Web user control and store the response for that control in cache. This technique is sometimes called **fragment caching**.

In this lesson, you'll learn how to use fragment caching and how the cache settings are different between Web form and fragment caching. You'll also learn about combining these two caching techniques.

After this lesson, you will be able to

- Store part of a Web form response in memory by caching a user control
- Cache multiple responses for a single user control
- Set user control caching from within code
- Combine Web form caching with user control caching

Estimated lesson time: 15 minutes

Caching Parts of a Web Form with User Controls

To cache part of a Web form, follow these steps:

1. Place the controls and content that you want to cache in a Web user control.
2. Set the caching attributes for that Web user control.
3. Create an instance of the Web user control on the Web form.

For example, the following simple user control is cached for 60 seconds:

```
<%@ Control Language="vb" AutoEventWireup="false"
  Codebehind="CachedControl1.ascx.vb" Inherits="MCSDWebAppsVB.CachedControl1"
  TargetSchema="http://schemas.microsoft.com/intellisense/ie5" %>
<%@ OutputCache Duration="60" VaryByParam="None" %>
<asp:Panel BorderWidth="1" BackColor="LemonChiffon" Runat="server"
  ID="pnlControl" Width="50%">
  <P><% Response.Write(Me.id) %></P>
  <P>Time this control was cached:
    <% Response.Write(Now) %>
  </P>
</asp:Panel>
```

The preceding HTML uses the *OutputCache* directive to cache the control. Alternatively, you can include the *PartialCaching* attribute in the control's class declaration. For example, the following code is equivalent to the *OutputCache* directive shown in the preceding code:

Visual Basic .NET

```
Imports System.Web.UI

<PartialCaching(60)> Public Class CachedControl1
```

Visual C#

```
using System.Web.UI;

[PartialCaching(60)] public class CachedControl1 : System.Web.UI.UserControl
```

The *OutputCache* directive has several attributes that apply only to user controls; these attributes are described in Table 12-3.

Table 12-3   Special *OutputCache* Attributes for User Controls

Attribute	Use to
Shared	Cache a single response from a user control for use on multiple Web forms. By default, ASP.NET caches a separate response for each Web form that uses a cached user control. This attribute is only available in the .NET Framework version 1.1 or later.
VaryByControl	Cache multiple responses for a single user control based on the value of one or more controls contained in the user control.

For example, the following *OutputCache* directive causes any Web form that includes the user control to share a single cached response:

```
<%@ OutputCache Duration="60" VaryByParam="None" Shared="True" %>
```

Caching Multiple Versions of a User Control

You can cache multiple versions of a user control based on the value of controls contained in a user control (*VaryByControl*) or based on a custom string (*VaryByCustom*). For example, the following user control caches a different response for each different selection from the drpTimeZone control:

```
<%@ Control Language="vb" AutoEventWireup="false"
  Codebehind="CachedControl2.ascx.vb" Inherits="MCSDWebAppsVB.CachedControl2"
  TargetSchema="http://schemas.microsoft.com/intellisense/ie5" %>
<%@ OutputCache Duration="60" VaryByControl="drpTimeZone" Shared="True" %>
<asp:Panel BorderWidth="1" BackColor="LemonChiffon" Runat="server"
  ID="pnlControl" Width="50%">
  <P><% Response.Write(Me.id) %></P>
  <P>Select a time zone and click Submit to see how server-
side information is cached.</P>
```

```
        <asp:DropDownList id="drpTimeZone" runat="server">
          <asp:ListItem Value="1">GMT+1</asp:ListItem>
          <asp:ListItem Value="2">GMT+2</asp:ListItem>
          <asp:ListItem Value="0" Selected="True">GMT</asp:ListItem>
          <asp:ListItem Value="-1">GMT-1</asp:ListItem>
          <asp:ListItem Value="-2">GMT-2</asp:ListItem>
        </asp:DropDownList>
        <P>Time this control was cached:
          <% Response.Write(Now.AddHours(Val(drpTimeZone.SelectedItem.Value))) %>
        </P>
      </asp:Panel>
```

The *VaryByCustom* attribute works the same way for user controls as it does for Web forms. For example, the following user control caches different responses for each different browser:

```
<%@ OutputCache Duration="60" VaryByParam="None" VaryByCustom="appName"
  Shared="True" %>
<%@ Control Language="vb" AutoEventWireup="false"
  Codebehind="CachedControl3.ascx.vb" Inherits="MCSDWebAppsVB.CachedControl3"
  TargetSchema="http://schemas.microsoft.com/intellisense/ie5" %>
<asp:Panel BorderWidth="1" BackColor="LemonChiffon" Runat="server"
  ID="pnlControl" Width="50%">
  <P><% Response.Write(Me.id) %></P>
  <P>Browser name:
    <% Response.Write(Request.Browser.Browser) %>
  </P>
  <P>Time this control was cached:
    <% Response.Write(Now) %>
  </P>
</asp:Panel>
```

As with Web form caching, the *VaryByCustom* attribute uses the overridden *GetVaryByCustomString* method from Global.asax to get the custom string. See the section "Caching Multiple Responses from a Single Web Form" in Lesson 1 for an example of how to override *GetVaryByCustomString*.

Using Cached User Controls in Code

In general, cached controls are used to present data such as queries from a database, rather than as interactive components. However, if you do need to access a cached control from code, you must first check that the control exists. If the control is read from the cache, you can't access its members from code. Control members are available only when the control is not read from the cache, such as when the control is first instantiated and when it is reloaded after its cache duration has expired.

For example, the following code checks to see whether a cached control exists before accessing a public property:

Visual Basic .NET

```
Public Class UserControlCache
    Inherits System.Web.UI.Page
    Protected VaryByParam_None As CachedControl1

    Private Sub Page_PreRender(ByVal sender As Object, _
        ByVal e As System.EventArgs) Handles MyBase.PreRender
        If Not IsNothing(VaryByParam_None) Then
            ' Use a cached user control in code.
            Dim x As String
            x = VaryByParam_None.Time
        End If
    End Sub
End Class
```

Visual C#

```
public class UserControlCache : System.Web.UI.Page
{
    protected CachedControl1 VaryByParam_None;

    private void UserControlCache_PreRender(object sender, EventArgs e)
    {
        string x = "";
        if (VaryByParam_None != null)
            // Use a cached user control in code.
            x = VaryByParam_None.Time;
    }
}
```

Combining Web Form Caching and User Control Caching

When caching is set at both the Web form and user control levels, the cache settings interact as follows:

- The cache location is determined by the Web form setting. Location settings on a user control have no affect.

- If the Web form's cache duration is longer than the user control's, both the Web form response and the user control response will expire using the Web form setting.

Lesson 3: Caching Application Data

In addition to Web form and fragment caching, you can also cache any frequently used application data. In general, cached application data is considered read-only, because it reflects a copy of information stored elsewhere. However, you can use the *CacheItemRemovedCallback* delegate to store changes to cached data before they are unloaded from memory.

After this lesson, you will be able to

- Use the *Cache* object to store and retrieve application data
- Specify how long an item remains in the cache
- Remove an item from the cache
- Detect when a cached item is about to be removed from memory
- Establish a dependency between a cached item and an external source, such as a data file

Estimated lesson time: 15 minutes

Using the *Cache* Object

Use the intrinsic *Cache* object to store frequently used items in the server's memory for quick retrieval. The *Cache* object is global—that is, data stored in the *Cache* object is available anywhere within a Web application. In this way, the *Cache* object is very similar to the intrinsic *Application* object.

There are several ways to store data in the *Cache* object:

- **Use assignment.**   Assigning a value to an unused key in the *Cache* object automatically creates that key and assigns the value to that key. Assigning a value to a key that already exists replaces the cached value with the assigned value.
- **Use the *Insert* method.**   The *Insert* method uses parameters rather than assignment to create or change cached data. *Insert* optionally accepts parameters to establish dependencies and set expiration policy.
- **Use the *Add* method.**   The *Add* method is similar to *Insert*; however, it requires all parameters and returns an object reference to the cached data.

For example, the following *Cache* statements all add the same item to the cache:

Visual Basic .NET

```
' At module-level:
Imports System.Web.Caching

Private Sub Page_Load(ByVal sender As System.Object, _
```

```
            ByVal e As System.EventArgs) Handles MyBase.Load
        If Not IsPostBack Then
            Cache("NewItem") = "Some string data"
            Cache.Add("NewItem", "Some string data", Nothing, _
                Cache.NoAbsoluteExpiration, System.TimeSpan.FromMinutes(1), _
                Caching.CacheItemPriority.Default, Nothing)
            Cache.Insert("NewItem", "Some string data")
        End If
End Sub
```

Visual C#

```csharp
// At module-level
using System.Web.Caching;

private void Page_Load(object sender, System.EventArgs e)
{
    if(!IsPostBack)
    {
        Cache["NewItem"] = "Some string data";
        Cache.Add("NewItem", "Some string data", null,
            Cache.NoAbsoluteExpiration, System.TimeSpan.FromMinutes(1),
            CacheItemPriority.Default, null);
        Cache.Insert("NewItem", "Some string data");
    }
}
```

Table 12-4 describes the parameters used by the *Cache* object's *Insert* and *Add* methods.

Table 12-4   Parameters for the *Cache* Object's *Insert* and *Add* methods

Parameter	Description
key	The identifier used to access the cached data.
value	The data to cache.
dependencies	A *CacheDependency* object that references a file used to track changes to data outside of the cache. Use dependencies to synchronize data in the cache with data stored elsewhere.
absoluteExpiration	A *DateTime* object that identifies when the data should be removed from the cache. If you're using sliding expiration, specify *Cache.NoAbsoluteExpiration* for this parameter.
slidingExpiration	A *TimeSpan* object that identifies how long the data should remain in the cache after the data was last accessed. If you're using absolute expiration, specify *Cache.NoSlidingExpiration* for this parameter.

Table 12-4   Parameters for the *Cache* Object's *Insert* and *Add* methods   *(continued)*

Parameter	Description
priority	A *CacheItemPriority* enumeration value identifying the relative priority of the cached data.
onRemoveCallback	A delegate to call when the data is removed from the cache. Use *onRemoveCallback* to notify the application when items are removed from the cache.

You access cached data through the item's key, just as you did with the *Application* and *Session* objects. Because cached items might be removed from memory, you should always check for their existence before attempting to retrieve their value, as shown in the following code:

Visual Basic .NET

```
Private Sub Page_PreRender(ByVal sender As Object, _
    ByVal e As System.EventArgs) Handles MyBase.PreRender
    ' Display value:
    If IsNothing(Cache("NewItem")) Then
        lblNewItem.Text = "NewItem not found."
    Else
        lblNewItem.Text = Cache("NewItem")
    End If
End Sub
```

Visual C#

```
private void DataCache1_PreRender(object sender, EventArgs e)
{
    // Display value:
    if (Cache["NewItem"] == null)
        lblNewItem.Text = "NewItem not found.";
    else
        lblNewItem.Text = Cache["NewItem"].ToString();
}
```

To remove data from the cache, use the *Cache* object's *Remove* method. For example, the following code removes the cache item used in the preceding code:

Visual Basic .NET

```
Private Sub butRemove_Click(ByVal sender As System.Object, _
    ByVal e As System.EventArgs) Handles butRemove.Click
    Cache.Remove("NewItem")
End Sub
```

Visual C#

```
private void butRemove_Click(object sender, System.EventArgs e)
{
    Cache.Remove("NewItem");
}
```

Controlling How Long Data Is Cached

The *Cache* object's *Add* and *Insert* method parameters allow you to control how long an item is stored in the server's memory. In practice, these parameter settings provide only indirect control of how long data remains in memory. If your server runs low on available memory, ASP.NET recovers as much memory as possible from expired cache items. If that's not enough, ASP.NET will unload unexpired items from the cache based on their priority and when they were last accessed.

Use the *Add* or *Insert* method's *priority* parameter to set the relative importance of cached items. Table 12-5 lists the priority settings in order from highest to lowest.

Table 12-5   Cache Priority Settings

Setting	Comment
CacheItemPriority.NotRemoveable	Highest priority.
CacheItemPriority.High	
CacheItemPriority.AboveNormal	
CacheItemPriority.Normal, *CacheItemPriority.Default*	*Normal* and *Default* are the same.
CacheItemPriority.BelowNormal	
CacheItemPriority.Low	Lowest priority; item is likely to be removed.

Responding to Cache Events

The *Add* and *Insert* methods' *onRemoveCallback* parameter allows you to associate a callback function to run when the item is removed from the cache. This is the only "event" that the *Cache* object provides.

The following code uses the *CacheItemRemovedCallback* delegate to display information about a cache item before it is removed. The code associated with the callback is shown in boldface for clarity.

Visual Basic .NET

```
Imports System.Web.Caching

Public Class DataCache1
    Inherits System.Web.UI.Page
    Dim onRemove As CacheItemRemovedCallback

    Private Sub Page_Load(ByVal sender As System.Object, _
        ByVal e As System.EventArgs) Handles MyBase.Load
        If Not IsPostBack Then
            onRemove = New CacheItemRemovedCallback(AddressOf RemovedCallback)
            Cache.Add("NewItem", "Some string data", Nothing, _
                Cache.NoAbsoluteExpiration, System.TimeSpan.FromMinutes(1), _
                Caching.CacheItemPriority.Default, onRemove)
```

```vb
        End If
    End Sub

    Private Sub butRemove_Click(ByVal sender As System.Object, _
      ByVal e As System.EventArgs) Handles butRemove.Click
        Cache.Remove("NewItem")
    End Sub

    Public Sub RemovedCallback(ByVal key As String, ByVal value As Object, _
      ByVal reason As System.Web.Caching.CacheItemRemovedReason)
        Cache("Status") = "Cache item: " + key + " value: "_
            + value.ToString() + " was " + reason.ToString
    End Sub

    Private Sub Page_PreRender(ByVal sender As Object, _
      ByVal e As System.EventArgs) Handles MyBase.PreRender
        ' Display status.
        If Not IsNothing(Cache("Status")) Then _
            lblStatus.Text = Cache("Status").ToString
    End Sub
End Class
```

Visual C#

```csharp
using System.Web.Caching;

namespace MCSDWebAppsCS
{
    public class DataCache1 : System.Web.UI.Page
    {
        CacheItemRemovedCallback onRemove;

        private void Page_Load(object sender, System.EventArgs e)
        {
            if(!IsPostBack)
            {
                onRemove = new CacheItemRemovedCallback(this.RemovedCallback);
                Cache.Add("NewItem", "Some string data", null,
                    Cache.NoAbsoluteExpiration, System.TimeSpan.FromMinutes(1),
                    CacheItemPriority.Default, onRemove);
            }
        }

        void RemovedCallback(string key, Object value ,
            CacheItemRemovedReason reason)
        {
```

```
                    Cache["Status"] = "Cache item: " + key + " value: " +
                        value.ToString() + " was " + reason.ToString();
                }

            private void butRemove_Click(object sender, System.EventArgs e)
            {
                Cache.Remove("NewItem");
            }

            private void DataCache1_PreRender(object sender, EventArgs e)
            {
                // Display status.
                if (Cache["Status"] != null)
                    lblStatus.Text = Cache["Status"].ToString();
            }
        }
    }
```

Updating the Cache When Data Changes

Items stored in the cache are often copies of data that is stored and maintained elsewhere, such as records in a database. Use the *Add* and *Insert* methods' *dependency* parameter to establish a relationship between a cached data item and an external source, such as a file, a folder, or a group of files.

The *dependency* parameter accepts a *CacheDependency* object, which in turn identifies the file, folder, or set of files to watch for changes. ASP.NET checks the time stamp of the items in the *CacheDependency* object—if one of those time stamps is later than the *DateTime* entered for the cached item, ASP.NET unloads that item from the cache.

For example, the following code creates a cache item with a dependency. When the user clicks the Change button, the time stamp on the Newitem.txt file is changed, causing ASP.NET to remove *NewItem* from the cache.

Visual Basic .NET

```
Imports System.Web.Caching

Public Class DataCache2
    Inherits System.Web.UI.Page
    Dim strFile As String = Server.MapPath(".") + "\NewItem.txt"

    Private Sub Page_Load(ByVal sender As System.Object, _
        ByVal e As System.EventArgs) Handles MyBase.Load
        If Not IsPostBack Then
            Cache.Add("NewItem", "Some cached data with a dependency.", _
            New CacheDependency(strFile, Now()), Cache.NoAbsoluteExpiration, _
```

```vb
                    System.TimeSpan.FromMinutes(1), _
                    Caching.CacheItemPriority.Default, null)
        End If
    End Sub

    Private Sub butChange_Click(ByVal sender As System.Object, _
        ByVal e As System.EventArgs) Handles butChange.Click
        System.IO.File.SetLastWriteTime(strFile, Now)
    End Sub

    Private Sub Page_PreRender(ByVal sender As Object, _
        ByVal e As System.EventArgs) Handles MyBase.PreRender
        ' Display value:
        If IsNothing("NewItem") Then
            lblNewItem.Text = "NewItem not found."
        Else
            lblNewItem.Text = Cache("NewItem")
        End If
    End Sub

End Class
```

Visual C#

```csharp
using System.Web.Caching;

namespace MCSDWebAppsCS
{
    {
        string strFile  = "";

        private void Page_Load(object sender, System.EventArgs e)
        {
            strFile = Server.MapPath(".") + "\\NewItem.txt";
            if(!IsPostBack)
            {
                Cache.Add("NewItem", "Some string data",
                    new CacheDependency(strFile, System.DateTime.Now),
                    Cache.NoAbsoluteExpiration,
                    System.TimeSpan.FromMinutes(1),
                    CacheItemPriority.Default, onRemove);
            }
        }

        private void butChange_Click(object sender, System.EventArgs e)
        {
            System.IO.File.SetLastWriteTime(strFile, System.DateTime.Now);
        }
```

```
private void DataCache2_PreRender(object sender, EventArgs e)
{
    // Display value:
    if (Cache["NewItem"] == null)
        lblNewItem.Text = "NewItem not found.";
    else
        lblNewItem.Text = Cache["NewItem"].ToString();
}
}
}
```

Lesson 4: Monitoring Cache Performance

To use caching effectively, you must balance three factors:

- Available memory
- Frequency of requests for specific items
- Volatility of those requested items

To enable you to weigh these factors, ASP.NET provides caching performance counters that you can use to monitor how items are served from the cache. In this lesson, you'll learn how to use the Microsoft Management Console (MMC) Performance Logs and Alerts snap-in to monitor how effectively caching is used within your application.

After this lesson, you will be able to

- Monitor an application's use of caching for Web forms and user controls
- Monitor an application's use of caching for application data
- Use the Turnover Rate counter to flag inefficient use of caching

Estimated lesson time: 5 minutes

Using the Performance Monitor

You can use the Performance Logs and Alerts snap-in to view the number of cache entries, the number of cache hits, and the ratio of requests served from the cache at the application level. These performance counters can help you evaluate the effectiveness of your caching policy.

For information about starting and using the Performance Logs and Alerts snap-in, see Lesson 3 in Chapter 9, "Building and Deploying Web Applications." ASP.NET provides cache performance counters for individual Web applications. To monitor the cache performance counters for a Web application:

1. From the Performance Logs and Alerts snap-in, click the + (Add) button. The snap-in displays the Add Counters dialog box, as shown in Figure 12-1.

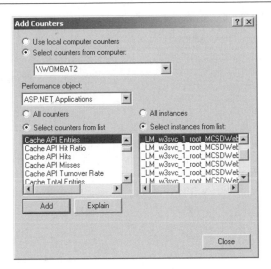

Figure 12-1   Adding cache performance counters for an application

2. From the Performance Object list, select ASP.NET Applications, and then select the cache counters from the counters list and the application to monitor from the instances list.

3. Click Add to add the selected cache counters to the monitor.

4. Click Close when you have finished adding counters to the snap-in.

Choosing Cache Performance Counters

ASP.NET provides three categories of cache performance counters:

- **Cache Total counters**   Return statistics that combine cached Web forms, user controls, application data, and internal use of the cache by ASP.NET.

- **Cache API counters**   Return statistics representing application data stored in the *Cache* object.

- **Output Cache counters**   Return statistics representing Web forms and user controls stored in the cache.

Table 12-6 describes the individual performance counters available for each of these three categories.

Table 12-6   Cache Counters

Counter	Description
Entries	Number of items that are currently cached
Hits	Number of requests served from the cache
Misses	Number of requests for cached items that could not be served from the cache

Table 12-6   Cache Counters   *(continued)*

Counter	Description
Hit Ratio	Number of hits divided by the number of misses
Turnover Rate	Number of new entries plus the number of removed entries per second

You can use the preceding counters to determine whether an application uses caching effectively. For example, if there are a lot of entries in the output cache, but the hit ratio is very small, your application might be caching Web forms that are not frequently used. If the turnover rate is very high, your server might want to reduce the number of items you store in the cache, make the period they are stored in the cache longer, or increase the memory available on your server.

Summary

- Caching improves Web application performance by storing responses to frequent requests in memory rather than processing each request separately.
- Cached responses should not contain data that changes frequently, because the response is "frozen" in memory for the duration of the cache.
- Use the *VaryByParam* attribute to cache multiple responses for a Web form based on different control selections.
- To cache part of a Web form, create that portion of the Web form as a user control and add an *OutputCache* directive to that control.
- Before using a cached user control in code, test to make sure it exists. Cached controls are available in code only when they are instantiated or when they are reloaded into the cache.
- Cache application data using the *Cache* object.
- Use the *onRemoveCallback* delegate to detect when cached data is about to be unloaded from memory.
- Set a dependency to cause cached data to expire when an external data source has changed.
- Monitor an application's use of the cache through the MMC Performance Logs and Alerts snap-in.

Lab: Combining Caching at Multiple Levels

In this lab, you'll optimize a Web application by using caching to:

- Store multiple responses from a single Web form in the server's memory
- Save an application-wide customer list generated from a query to a SQL database
- Save customer order information in a cached data set

You'll also use the Performance Logs and Alerts snap-in to monitor caching within the deployed application. When complete, the application will appear as shown in Figure 12-2.

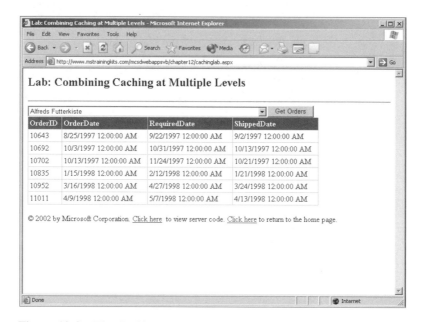

Figure 12-2   The CachingLab.aspx Web Form

Estimated lesson time: 20 minutes

Exercise 1: Cache Multiple Versions of the Web Form

In this exercise, you'll create a Web form that displays a list of customers from the Northwind Traders database. Users can select a customer from a drop-down list and click a button to view a list of orders in a data grid.

To minimize the number of times each request must be processed on the server, you will cache the Web form for 1 minute. Because the drop-down list can vary the response, you will use the *VaryByParam* attribute to store multiple responses from the Web form.

▶ **To create the Web form**

1. Add a Web form named CachingLab.aspx to your application, and make that page the start page for your application.

2. Create DropDownList, DataGrid, and Button controls on the Web form, as shown in the following HTML:

```
<HTML>
  <body>
    <form id="Form1" method="post" runat="server">
      <h2>Lab: Combining Caching at Multiple Levels</h2>
      <hr>
      <asp:dropdownlist id="drpCustList" runat="server"
        Width="496px"></asp:dropdownlist>
      <asp:button id="butGetOrders" runat="server"
        Text="Get Orders"></asp:button>
      <asp:datagrid id=grdOrders runat="server" Width="80%"
        DataSource="<%# dsOrders %>" Height="160px" BorderColor="#CCCCCC"
        BorderStyle="None" BorderWidth="1px" BackColor="White"
        CellPadding="3">
        <SelectedItemStyle Font-Bold="True" ForeColor="White"
          BackColor="#669999"></SelectedItemStyle>
        <ItemStyle ForeColor="#000066"></ItemStyle>
        <HeaderStyle Font-Bold="True" ForeColor="White"
          BackColor="#006699"></HeaderStyle>
        <FooterStyle ForeColor="#000066"
          BackColor="White"></FooterStyle>
        <PagerStyle HorizontalAlign="Left" ForeColor="#000066"
          BackColor="White" Mode="NumericPages"></PagerStyle>
      </asp:datagrid>
    </form>
  </body>
</HTML>
```

3. Add the following *OutputCache* directive to the top of the Web form:

```
<%@ OutputCache Duration="60" VaryByParam="drpCustList" Location="Any" %>
```

The preceding directive caches a separate response for each different selection from the drop-down list. Responses are cached for 60 seconds each and can be stored at any location that accepts caching.

Exercise 2: Cache a Customer List

In this exercise, you'll populate the Web form's drop-down list of customers and store the resulting list in the *Cache* object. Even though the customer list is already cached as part of the Web form in the preceding exercise, caching the customer list separately makes the data available to other parts of the application that might require it. Also, because the customer list changes infrequently, that item can have a longer expiration time than the Web form.

▶ **To populate the customer list and store the data in the cache**

1. Add the following code to the CachingLab Web form's Load event procedure to check whether the customer list exists in the cache and to populate the drop-down list from the cached list:

Visual Basic .NET

```
Protected CustList As New ListItemCollection
Protected NWindDSN As String = "data source=(local); " + _
   "initial catalog=Northwind;integrated security=SSPI;" + _
   "persist security info=True;workstation id=WOMBAT2;packet size=4096"

Private Sub Page_Load(ByVal sender As System.Object, _
    ByVal e As System.EventArgs) Handles MyBase.Load
    ' The first time the page is displayed...
    If Not IsPostBack Then
        ' If the customer list isn't already cached...
        If IsNothing(Cache("CustList")) Then
            ' Cache the customer list.
            CacheCustList()
        Else
            ' Otherwise, get the list from cache.
            CustList = Cache("CustList")
        End If
        ' Add items to the drop-down list.
        Dim itmCustList As ListItem
        For Each itmCustList In CustList
            drpCustList.Items.Add(itmCustList)
        Next
    End If
End Sub
```

Visual C#

```
protected ListItemCollection CustList = new ListItemCollection();
protected string NWindDSN  =
"data source=(local); initial catalog=Northwind;integrated security=SSPI;
persist security info=True;workstation id=WOMBAT2;packet size=4096";

private void Page_Load(object sender, System.EventArgs e)
```

```
        {
            // The first time the page is displayed...
            if (!IsPostBack)
            {
                // If the customer list isn't already cached...
                if (Cache["CustList"]==null)
                    // Cache the customer list.
                    CacheCustList();
                else
                    // Otherwise, get the list from cache.
                    CustList = (ListItemCollection)Cache["CustList"];
                // Add items to the drop-down list.
                foreach (ListItem itmCustList in CustList)
                    drpCustList.Items.Add(itmCustList);
            }
        }
```

2. Add the following code to get the customer list from the Northwind Traders database and add the list to the cache:

Visual Basic .NET

```
Sub CacheCustList()
    ' Create a SQL database connection.
    Dim connNWind As New SqlConnection(NWindDSN))
    ' Command to get customer names and IDs.
    Dim cmdCustList As New SqlCommand("Select CustomerID, " + _
        "CompanyName From Customers Order By CompanyName", connNWind)
    Dim drCustList As SqlDataReader
    ' Open connection.
    connNWind.Open()
    Try
        drCustList = cmdCustList.ExecuteReader
        Do While drCustList.Read
            CustList.Add(New ListItem(drCustList.GetValue(1), _
                drCustList.GetValue(0)))
        Loop
        ' Cache the item for 5 minutes with sliding expiration and a high
        ' priority.
        Cache.Add("CustList", CustList, Nothing,_
Cache.NoAbsoluteExpiration, _
            System.TimeSpan.FromMinutes(5),_
Caching.CacheItemPriority.High, _
            Nothing)
    Catch ex As Exception
        Response.Write("An error occurred: " + ex.Message)
    Finally
        connNWind.Close()
    End Try
End Sub
```

Visual C#

```csharp
void CacheCustList()
{
    // Create a SQL database connection.
    SqlConnection connNWind = new SqlConnection(NWindDSN);
    // Command to get customer names and IDs.
    SqlCommand cmdCustList = new SqlCommand("Select CustomerID, " +
        "CompanyName From Customers Order By CompanyName", connNWind);
    SqlDataReader drCustList;
    // Open connection.
    connNWind.Open();
    try
    {
        drCustList = cmdCustList.ExecuteReader();
        while( drCustList.Read())
        {
            CustList.Add(new ListItem(drCustList.GetValue(1).ToString(),
                drCustList.GetValue(0).ToString()));
        }
        // Cache the item for 5 minutes with sliding expiration
        //and high priority.
        Cache.Add("CustList", CustList, null, Cache.NoAbsoluteExpiration,
            System.TimeSpan.FromMinutes(5), CacheItemPriority.High, null);
    }
    catch(Exception ex)
    {
        Response.Write("An error occurred: " + ex.Message);
    }
    finally
    {
        connNWind.Close();
    }
}
```

The preceding *Cache* object *Add* method adds the customer list using sliding expiration and a high priority. Those settings help ensure that the customer list remains cached practically indefinitely if the item is frequently accessed.

Exercise 3: Cache Data from a Stored Procedure

In this exercise, you'll cache data sets containing lists of customer orders. Again, you could rely on the Web form cache settings to store this data, but caching the data sets separately makes them available for other uses within the application, and using sliding expiration means that frequently used customer order lists are more likely to be served from the cache than from the database.

► **To cache the customer order data sets**

1. Add the following code to the CachingLab Web form's *butGetOrders_Click* event procedure to check whether the customer order data set exists in the cache, to retrieve the data set from the cache, and to display the data set in the DataGrid control:

Visual Basic .NET

```
' Public variable for databinding to DataGrid.
Public disorders As DataSet

Private Sub butGetOrders_Click(ByVal sender As System.Object, _
    ByVal e As System.EventArgs) Handles butGetOrders.Click
    dsOrders = New DataSet
    ' If the customer list isn't already cached...
    If IsNothing(Cache(drpCustList.SelectedItem.Value)) Then
        ' Cache the customer list.
        CacheOrders()
    Else
        ' Otherwise, get the list from cache.
        dsOrders = Cache(drpCustList.SelectedItem.Value)
    End If
    ' Bind the grid to display the orders.
    grdOrders.DataBind()
End Sub
```

Visual C#

```
// Public variable for databinding to DataGrid.
public DataSet dsOrders = new DataSet();
    private void butGetOrders_Click(object sender, System.EventArgs e)
{
    DataSet dsOrders = new DataSet();
    // If the customer list isn't already cached...
    if (Cache[drpCustList.SelectedItem.Value]==null)
        // Cache the customer list.
        CacheOrders();
    else
        // Otherwise, get the list from cache.
        dsOrders = (DataSet)Cache[drpCustList.SelectedItem.Value];
    // Bind the grid to display the orders.
    grdOrders.DataBind();
}
```

2. Add the following code to get the data set from the Northwind Traders database and to add the data set to the cache:

Visual Basic .NET

```vb
Sub CacheOrders()
    ' Connection string for database.
    Dim connNWind As New SqlConnection(NWindDSN)
    ' Command for stored procedure.
    Dim cmdOrders As New SqlCommand("CustOrdersOrders", connNWind)
    cmdOrders.Parameters.Add(New SqlParameter("@CustomerID", _
      drpCustList.SelectedItem.Value))
    ' Set the command properties.
    cmdOrders.CommandType = CommandType.StoredProcedure
    Dim adptOrders As New SqlDataAdapter(cmdOrders)
    Try
        ' Excecute the stored procedure.
        adptOrders.Fill(dsOrders)
    Catch ex As Exception
        Response.Write("An error occurred: " + ex.Message)
    End Try
    ' Cache the item for 1 minute with sliding expiration
    and default priority.
    Cache.Add(drpCustList.SelectedItem.Value, dsOrders, Nothing, _
      Cache.NoAbsoluteExpiration, System.TimeSpan.FromMinutes(1), _
      Caching.CacheItemPriority.Default, Nothing)
End Sub
```

Visual C#

```csharp
void CacheOrders()
{
    // Connection string for database.
    SqlConnection connNWind = new SqlConnection(NWindDSN);
    // Command for stored procedure.
    SqlCommand cmdOrders = new SqlCommand("CustOrdersOrders", connNWind);
    cmdOrders.Parameters.Add(new SqlParameter("@CustomerID",
        drpCustList.SelectedItem.Value));
    // Set the command properties.
    cmdOrders.CommandType = CommandType.StoredProcedure;
    SqlDataAdapter adptOrders = new SqlDataAdapter(cmdOrders);
    try
    {
        // Excecute the stored procedure.
        adptOrders.Fill(dsOrders);
    }
    catch (Exception ex )
    {
        Response.Write("An error occurred: " + ex.Message);
    }
    // Cache the item for 1 minute with sliding expiration and default
```

```
        // priority.
        Cache.Add(drpCustList.SelectedItem.Value, dsOrders, null,
            Cache.NoAbsoluteExpiration, System.TimeSpan.FromMinutes(1),
            CacheItemPriority.Default, null);
    }
```

The preceding code creates the data set using a stored procedure for greater efficiency. You can play with the cache duration of the orders data set to see the effect on performance.

Exercise 4: Test Cache Performance

In this exercise, you'll use the Performance Logs and Alerts snap-in to monitor the performance of the application you created in the preceding exercises.

▶ **To test the application's performance**

1. Build and deploy the CachingLab application. You can deploy the application to your local machine or to a test server for convenience.

2. Start the MMC Performance Logs and Alerts snap-in.

3. Add the following performance counters for the application at its deployed location:

   - Requests/Sec.
   - Cache API Entries
   - Cache API Hit Ratio
   - Cache Total Turnover Rate
   - OutputCache Entries
   - OutputCache Hit Ratio

4. Use ACT to load-test the application. See Chapter 10, "Testing Web Applications," for instructions on using ACT.

   Figure 12-3 shows the results from the snap-in after load testing.

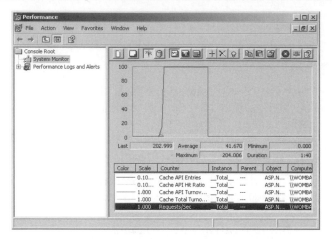

Figure 12-3   CachingLab Performance

5. Optionally, adjust the duration settings for the cached Web form, customer list, and order data set to see their effect on performance.

Review

The following questions are intended to reinforce key information presented in this chapter. If you are unable to answer a question, review the appropriate lesson and then try the question again. Answers to the questions can be found in the appendix.

1. Write a directive to cache responses for a Web form for 30 seconds, storing different cache responses based on the value of the lstNames control.

2. A Web form uses fragment caching to store a frequently used user control. At run time, an *Object not found* error occurs whenever the page is refreshed. What is a likely cause of the error?

3. How can you detect when application data is about to be removed from the cache?

4. Which ASP.NET performance counter is the best indicator of inefficient caching?

C H A P T E R   1 3

Formatting Web Application Output

About This Chapter

ASP.NET provides two complementary ways for you to format output in a Web application:

- **Use cascading style sheets (CSS) to control the appearance of elements on a Web form.**   These styles can set the color, size, font, and behavior of the HTML elements on a Web page.
- **Use Extensible Stylesheet Language Transformations (XSLT) to convert information from an Extensible Markup Language (XML) file to HTML output and position that information on a Web form.**   XSLT puts data from the XML file into HTML elements and applies styles to those elements.

In this chapter, you'll learn when and how to use each of these formatting techniques within a Web application.

Before You Begin

To complete this chapter, you must:

- Know how to create Web forms using HTML mode within Microsoft Visual Studio .NET.
- Be familiar with the HTML elements used to create Web forms and HTML pages.

Lesson 1: Using Cascading Style Sheets

Cascading style sheets (CSS) collect and organize all of the formatting information applied to HTML elements on a Web form. Because they keep this information in a single location, style sheets make it easy to adjust the appearance of Web applications.

Visual Studio .NET includes style-editing tools, along with a default style sheet that is created as part of new Web application projects. In this lesson, you'll learn how to use the Visual Studio .NET tools to modify the default style sheet, attach the sheet to Web forms, and switch between style sheets at run time.

After this lesson, you will be able to

- Explain how Microsoft ASP.NET applies styles defined at different levels within a Web form
- Attach a style sheet to a Web form
- Modify styles within a style sheet
- Create new styles and add them to a style sheet
- Create style classes that can be applied to different types of HTML elements
- Change style sheets at run time to provide an enlarged-type version of a Web form or to format a Web form for printing
- Use behaviors to control dynamic elements on a Web form

Estimated lesson time: 35 minutes

How Styles Work

As mentioned in the opening of this lesson, style sheets store formatting in a single location: the CSS file. However, formatting can be applied at three different levels within a Web application. Before you start working with style sheets, you should understand how styles defined at different levels affect formatting. Table 13-1 describes these levels and how they apply to the elements on a Web form.

Table 13-1   Levels of Style

Level	Defined in	Applies to
Global	The style sheet file	All pages referencing the style sheet
Page	The page's *head* element	All elements on the current page
Inline	The HTML element itself	Only the current element

These three levels follow precedence rules that are similar to the levels of scoping you're already familiar with as a programmer. Inline formatting takes precedence over local formatting, which, in turn, takes precedence over global formatting. These precedence rules are the reason style sheets are referred to as **cascading**. Figure 13-1 illustrates how styles defined at different levels are applied to a paragraph element.

Figure 13-1   Style precedence

The following HTML shows the style definitions used to create the output shown in Figure 13-1:

```
<HTML>
  <HEAD>
    <title>WebForm1</title>
    <!-- (1) Style sheet reference. -->
    <LINK REL="stylesheet" TYPE="text/css" HREF="Styles.css">
    <!-- (2) Page-level style definition. -->
    <style>
      p {
      font-family: 'Comic Sans MS', Lucida Sans, sans-serif;
      font-size: medium;
      }
    </style>
  </HEAD>
  <body>
    <p>The alignment is from the style sheet.</p>
    <p>The font is from the style in the page's head element.</p>
    <!-- (3) Inline style definition -->
```

```
    <p style="FONT-SIZE: large; FONT-STYLE: italic">The italic is from
      the inline style.</p>
  </body>
</HTML>

<!-- (1) From Styles.css style sheet referenced in HEAD element. -->
p
{
  font-size: small;
  text-align: center;
}
```

The preceding example shows how style attributes can be applied to a single element at different levels. The *font-size* attribute is applied at all three levels, but you see only the effects of the page level and inline settings because the page setting takes precedence over the style sheet setting. The *text-align*, *font-family*, and *font-style* attributes are each defined only once, so their effects are additive.

There are a couple of advantages to storing style definitions in a style sheet file (.css) rather than locally in each Web form or inline with each HTML element:

- Formatting can be maintained in one location so that you make changes only once for an entire application.
- Several sets of parallel formatting rules can be maintained in separate style sheets for formatting output on different devices or for different user needs. For example, an application might provide standard, enlarged-type, and printer-friendly style sheets that the user can select at run time.

Tip   In general, you should use page and inline styles only when you have a really good reason to override the global styles. Relying heavily on page and inline styles can make it difficult to maintain the formatting in a Web application.

Using Style Sheets with Web Forms

When you create a new Visual Basic .NET Web application, Visual Studio .NET automatically creates a style sheet named Styles.css for the application. However, Visual Studio .NET does not automatically use that style sheet in any of the Web forms or HTML pages you create.

To use that style sheet, you must add a link element to the page's *head* element, as shown here in boldface:

```
<HEAD>
<title>WebForm1</title>
<meta name="GENERATOR" content="Microsoft Visual Studio.NET 7.0">
<meta name="CODE_LANGUAGE" content="Visual Basic 7.0">
```

```
<meta name="vs_defaultClientScript" content="JavaScript">
<meta name="vs_targetSchema" content="http://schemas.microsoft.com/
intellisense/ie5">
<LINK REL="stylesheet" TYPE="text/css" HREF="Styles.css">
</HEAD>
```

Important   Only Microsoft Visual Basic .NET projects are created with a new default style sheet. For Microsoft Visual C# projects, you must create a new style sheet from scratch or cut and paste the contents of a default style sheet from a Visual Basic .NET project to get started.

Modifying Styles

Use the Style Builder to change the appearance of any of the styles in a style sheet. Changes to the style sheet change the appearance of all Web forms that reference that style sheet.

To modify a style, follow these steps:

1. Open the style sheet in Visual Studio. Visual Studio .NET displays the style definitions in the Document window and an outline of the style sheet in the Tool window, as shown in Figure 13-2.

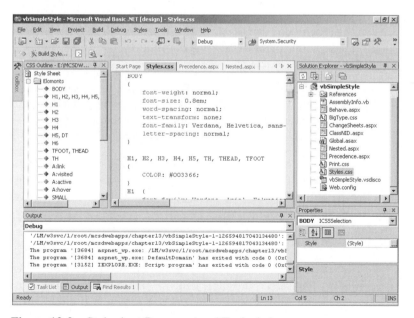

Figure 13-2   Style sheet Document and Tool windows

2. Select the style to modify from the Tool window. Visual Studio .NET displays the definition for that style in the Document window.

3. Right-click in the style definition or right-click the style in the Tool window, and select Build Style from the shortcut menu. Visual Studio .NET displays the Style Builder Wizard, as shown in Figure 13-3.

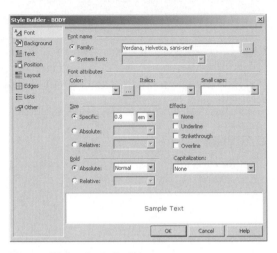

Figure 13-3   Style Builder

4. Use the Style Builder to compose the formatting that you want to add or modify in the selected style, and then click OK.

When you have finished, you'll see that the Style Builder adds the new or modified style attributes to the style definition.

Adding Styles

So far, we have created applied styles using HTML element names. CSS uses the element name to locate the default formatting to apply to each element. However, you can also apply styles using class names or element IDs.

Using class names allows you to apply a single style to a number of different elements or to style the same element differently, depending on how the element is used. Using element IDs allows you to apply a style to a unique element on one or more Web forms.

To add a style, follow these steps:

1. Open the style sheet. Right-click the style sheet's Document or Tool window, and select Add Style Rule from the shortcut menu. Visual Studio .NET displays the Add Style Rule Wizard, as shown in Figure 13-4.

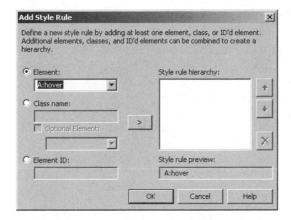

Figure 13-4   Add a style

2. Select the type of style you want to create. You can create styles that apply to HTML elements, classes, or specific element IDs. Type the name of the item to create the style for and click the > (Add) button to add the item to the style rule.

3. Repeat step 2 for each item you want the style to apply to.

Using Style Classes

Style classes allow you to apply the same formatting to different HTML elements on a Web form. When you create a style rule for a class, Visual Studio .NET adds a style definition to the style sheet using a *.classname* identifier, as shown here:

```
.emphasis
{
  font-style: italic;
}
```

The preceding *.emphasis* style class formats all elements that use the class in italic, as shown in Figure 13-5.

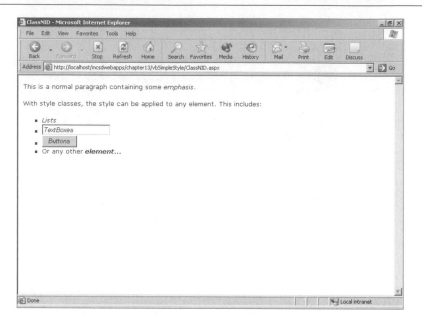

Figure 13-5   Applying a style class

You apply the style class to HTML elements by using the *class* attribute. You apply the style to server controls by using the *CssClass* attribute. The following HTML shows this difference in boldface:

```
<p>This is a paragraph containing <span class="emphasis">emphasis</span>.</p>
<asp:TextBox ID="Text1" Runat="server" CssClass="emphasis">Some text
</asp:TextBox>
```

Creating Styles for Specific Elements

You can also create styles for specific elements on a Web form based on their element IDs. Element IDs must be unique for each element on a page, so formatting set by element ID can apply to only one element on each page. When you create a style rule for an element ID, Visual Studio .NET adds a style definition to the style sheet using a *#elementID* identifier, as shown here:

```
#inserted
{
    text-decoration: underline;
}

#deleted
{
    text-decoration: line-through;
}
```

The preceding style definitions format elements with the ID *inserted* as underlined text and elements with the ID *deleted* with strikethrough, as shown in Figure 13-6.

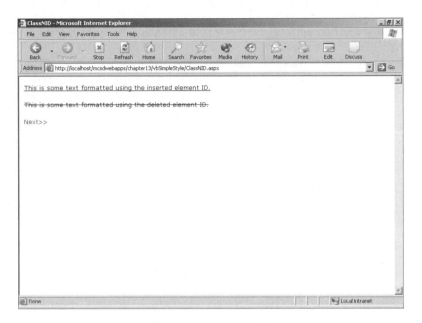

Figure 13-6   Applying a style by element ID

Styles applied in Visual Studio .NET don't always show up right away in the Web Forms Designer. If you're not seeing the formatting applied through a particular style, try the following:

- Make sure the style sheet has been saved.
- Switch the Web form between HTML view and the Design view.
- Right-click the Web form, and select View In Browser from the shortcut menu.

Creating Nested Styles

If you look at the style definitions in the default style sheet, Styles.css, you'll notice that some style definitions list multiple element names. These definitions establish which formatting to use for nested elements. For example, the following styles specify different bullet types for nested, unnumbered lists:

```
UL LI    {
  list-style-type:  square ;
  }

UL LI LI {
  list-style-type:  disc;
  }
```

```
UL LI LI LI    {
  list-style-type:  circle;
  }
```

The preceding nested files format the nested list items, as shown in Figure 13-7.

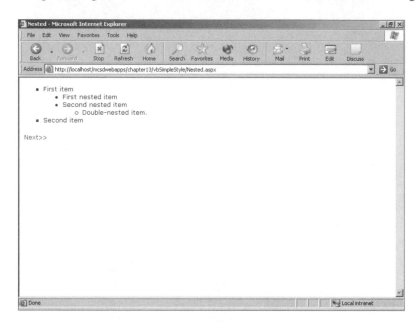

Figure 13-7   Nested list

To create your own nested styles, add multiple items to the Style rule hierarchy in the Add Style Rule dialog box, as shown in Figure 13-8.

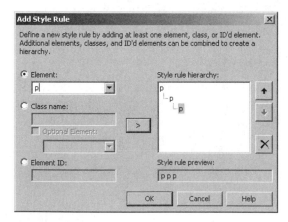

Figure 13-8   Creating nested styles

Changing Style Sheets at Run Time

As mentioned, you can create multiple style sheets and then allow the user to select the styles to use at run time to format the Web form for printing or to provide features such as enlarged-type versions of Web forms.

To switch style sheets automatically when printing a Web form, use the *media* attribute of the style sheet *link* element to specify the style sheet to use for printing and screen display. For example, the following *link* elements apply formatting from the default style sheet when the Web form is displayed on screen, but they use the Print.css style sheet when the user prints the Web form:

```
<LINK REL="stylesheet" TYPE="text/css" HREF="Styles.css" media="screen">
<LINK REL="stylesheet" TYPE="text/css" HREF="Print.css" media="print">
```

To switch between style sheets at run time, create a client-side script to change the *href* element of the style sheet *link* element. For example, the following HTML creates a Web form that switches between the style sheets Styles.css and BigType.css when the user clicks a hyperlink in text:

VBScript

```
<HTML>
<HEAD id="myhead">
<title>ChangeSheets</title>
<LINK ID="ScreenStyle" REL="stylesheet" TYPE="text/css" HREF="Styles.css">
<script language="vbscript">
' VBScript
' Switch between default and large-type style sheets.
Sub SwitchSheets()
    If document.all("ScreenStyle").GetAttribute("HREF") = "Styles.css" then
        document.all("ScreenStyle").SetAttribute "HREF", "BigType.css", 0
    else
        document.all("ScreenStyle").SetAttribute "HREF", "Styles.css", 0
    end if
End Sub
</script>
</HEAD>
  <body>
    <form id="Form1" method="post" runat="server">
      <h2>Changing Style Sheets at Run-Time</h2>
      <p>This page first appears using the default style sheet.</p>
      <p><a onclick="SwitchSheets" href="#">Click here
        </a> to switch between the standard and the enlarged-type version.</
p>
    </form>
  </body>
</HTML>
```

JScript

```
<HTML>
  <HEAD>
    <title>ChangeSheets</title>
    <LINK ID="ScreenStyle" REL="stylesheet" TYPE="text/css"
      HREF="Styles.css" media="screen">
    <LINK ID="PrintStyle" REL="stylesheet" TYPE="text/css"
      HREF="Print.css" media="print">
    <script id=clientEventHandlersJS language=jscript>
      function SwitchSheets()
    {
      // Switch between default and large-type style sheets.
      if (document.all["ScreenStyle"].getAttribute("HREF") == "Styles.css")
          document.all["ScreenStyle"].setAttribute ("HREF",
            "BigType.css", 0);
      else
          document.all["ScreenStyle"].setAttribute ("HREF", "Styles.css", 0);
    }
    </script>
  </HEAD>
  <body MS_POSITIONING="FlowLayout">
    <FORM id="Form1" method="post" runat="server">
      <H2>Changing Style Sheets at Run-Time</H2>
      <P>This page first appears using the default style sheet.</P>
      <P><A onclick="SwitchSheets();" href="#">Click here</A>
        to switch between the standard and
        the enlarged-type version.</P>
      <A href="Behave.aspx">Next&gt;&gt;</A>
    </FORM>
  </body>
</HTML>
```

Figure 13-9 shows the how the Web form changes at run time when the user changes the style sheets by clicking the link.

Figure 13-9   Changing style sheets at run time

Using Behaviors

In addition to formatting, styles can also define behaviors that HTML elements exhibit at run time. **Behaviors** are a sort of dynamic formatting: because Web content isn't always static, style sheets use behaviors to describe dynamic changes.

For example, HTML+TIME animations use the *time* class to apply animations to HTML elements on a page, as shown here:

```
<style>
  .time {behavior: url(#default#time2);}
</style>
```

The *behavior* property imports behavior files that contain Microsoft JScript or Microsoft Visual Basic Scripting Edition (VBScript) code that controls what the behavior does. The Behaviors Library topic in the Visual Studio .NET online Help provides a number of sample behaviors that you can download and use in your own code.

For example, the following HTML imports the Movable.htc sample behavior file and uses it to create a paragraph that the user can drag to a new location on the Web form at run time:

```
<HEAD>
  <title>Behave</title>
  <style>
    .movable {behavior: url(behaviors/movable.htc); CURSOR: move;
    mv--boundary: 0 800 600 0}
  </style>
</HEAD>
<body>
  <form id="Form1" method="post" runat="server">
    <p class="movable">You can drag this text around the screen.</p>
  </form>
</body>
</HTML>
```

In the preceding HTML, the style definition for the *movable* class includes the URL of the behavior file, the cursor style to use, and the boundaries the elements are confined to. The style is applied by the *p* element's *class* attribute. At run time, the user can drag the paragraph around the screen, as shown in Figure 13-10.

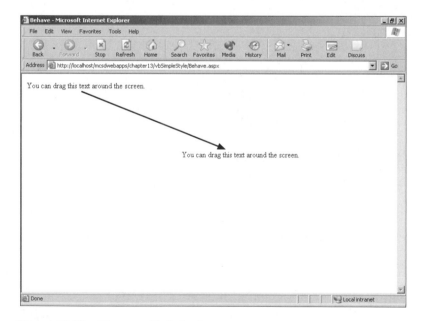

Figure 13-10   The movable behavior

The *movable* behavior can be applied to any element on a Web form, including server controls. Some behaviors, however, can be applied only to certain types of controls. For instance, the *ColorPick* behavior shown in the following code can be applied only to HTML Text Field controls (input elements of type *text*):

```
<HTML xmlns:control>
<HEAD>
  <title>Behave</title>
  <style>
    .color { BEHAVIOR: url(behaviors/ColorPick.htc) }
  </style>
</HEAD>
<body>
  <form id="Form1" method="post" runat="server">
    <p>Use the color picker below to change the background color:</p>
    <input ID="ColorPic" type="text" class="color" value="#fFFf00"
      onchange="document.bgColor=ColorPic.value;" style="cp--grid-size:2">
  </form>
</body>
</HTML>
```

The preceding HTML displays a color palette that the user can click to change the background color at run time, as shown in Figure 13-11.

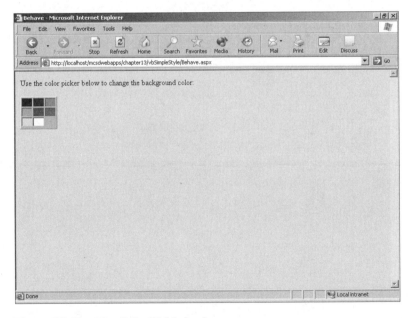

Figure 13-11   The *ColorPick* behavior

Finally, some behaviors create their own types of elements that you can use on a Web form. For example, the *Slider* sample behavior creates a *slider* element that you can use to get input from a user. To use the Slider control, you must first add an *xmlns* attribute to the Web form's *html* element to declare the name for the control, as shown here:

```
<HTML xmlns:control>
  <HEAD>
    <title>Behave</title>
    <style>
      control\:slider { BEHAVIOR: url(behaviors/slider.htc) }
    </style>
  </HEAD>
  <body>
    <form id="Form1" method="post" runat="server">
      <control:slider ID="Slider" onchange="alert(Slider.value)"
        STYLE="sl--orientation:horizontal"></control:slider>
    </form>
  </body>
</HTML>
```

The preceding HTML creates a Slider control that displays the control's value when the user slides the control on a Web form, as shown in Figure 13-12.

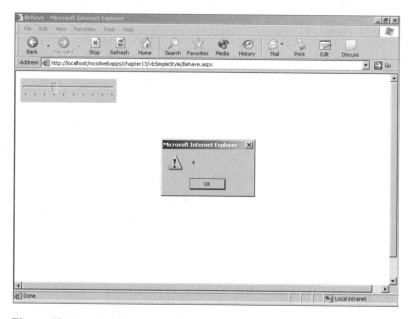

Figure 13-12   The *Slider* behavior

Important   Although you can use behaviors that create controls on Web forms, it's usually a better idea to create and use custom controls for tasks that aren't handled by the standard server and HTML controls. Controls created by behaviors are not displayed correctly in the Visual Studio .NET Designer window and don't provide properties and methods that are readily available from server-side code. Custom controls provide both of these advantages.

Lesson 2: Using XSL Transformations

In this lesson, you'll learn about using XSL to transform XML files, using expressions written in XML path language (XPath).

After this lesson, you will be able to

- Use the XML control to transform an XML data file into formatted HTML on a Web form
- Explain the differences between XML and HTML
- Create an XML file
- Create XSL templates to control how the XML file is transformed into HTML
- Use the XSL elements to repeat tasks, perform conditional operations, insert HTML elements, and sort output
- Evaluate expressions using XPath

Estimated lesson time: 40 minutes

How XSL Transformations Work

XSL transformations use the XML server control to generate formatted output from an XML input file using a set of rules stored in an XSL description file. The XSL file is similar to the CSS file you learned about in the preceding lesson—it provides the formatting rules that are applied to the output displayed on the Web form. Unlike CSS files, however, XSL files can position elements anywhere on the Web form and can perform logical operations, such as repeating and conditional operations.

You can think of XSL files as an intelligent formatting layer that complements—rather than replaces—CSS. Use XSL to place structured data on a Web form, and then use CSS to set the appearance of the elements within that layout.

To perform an XSL transformation on a Web form, follow these steps:

1. Add an XML server control to a Web form.
2. Set the control's *DocumentSource* property to the XML file to format.
3. Set the *TransformSource* property to the XSL file to use to format the output.

At run time, the XML server control processes the XML input using the XSL description to provide formatted output, as shown in Figure 13-13.

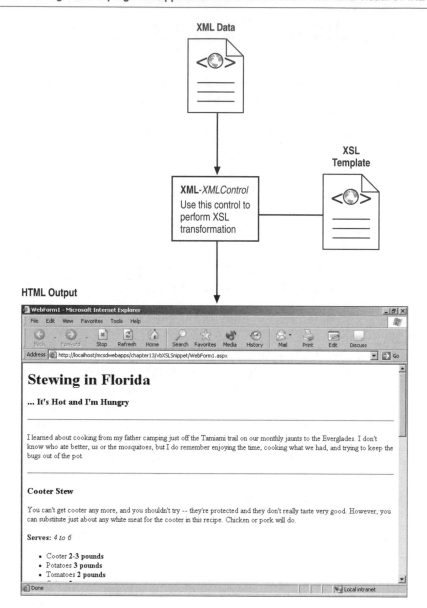

Figure 13-13   Performing XSL transformation

Creating an XML File

XML files are a way to describe structured data in text format. XML identifies data items using *<element>...</element>* tags much the same as HTML. Unlike HTML, however, the rules of XML are strict:

- **Each item must have a begin tag and an end tag.**   In HTML, *<li>*, *
*, and other tags can exist without equivalent *</li>* or *</br>* tags. That is not allowed in XML.

- **Item tag names are case sensitive.**   In HTML, *<P>* and *<p>* are equivalent. In XML, they constitute different tags.

- **Attribute values must always be enclosed in double quotation marks.**   In HTML, you can omit quotation marks for numeric attributes such as *<table cols=3>*. In XML, you must always include the quotation marks: *<table cols="3">*.

- **The nested items must be terminated before the containing item is terminated.**   For example, the following is OK in HTML: *Bold text<i>italic bold regular italic</i>*. However, in XML it must be written like this: *Bold text<i>italic bold</i> <i>regular italic</i>*

These strict rules allow XML to have an important capability that HTML does not have: in XML, you can define your own tags, and you can assign those tags any meaning you choose.

To create an XML file in Visual Studio .NET, choose Add New Item from the Project menu, choose XML file from the Templates list, and then click Open.

When you create a new XML file, it's a good idea to first write out the tags and structure that you'll use throughout the document. This saves you the trouble of trying to retag elements if you discover that you missed something. For example, the following XML describes cookbook data that we'll be using as a sample in this lesson:

```
<cookbook>
  <title></title>
  <subtitle></subtitle>
  <description></description>
  <recipe>
    <title></title>
    <subtitle></subtitle>
    <description></description>
    <servings></servings>
    <ingredients>
      <ingredient>
        <name></name>
        <quantity></quantity>
      </ingredient>
      <ingredient>
```

```
      <name></name>
      <quantity></quantity>
    </ingredient>
  </ingredients>
  <instructions>
    <introduction></introduction>
    <step></step>
    <step></step>
    <step></step>
    <summary></summary>
  </instructions>
  </recipe>
</cookbook>
```

The data for each of these items will go between each of the begin and end tags. What's important to notice at this point is the structure of the file and that the element names describe the *content* of the element, rather than its *formatting*. By labeling the content, you can apply content-based formatting using XSL.

The XML structure is strictly hierarchical. XML refers to the items in this hierarchy as **XML nodes**. Nodes have parent-child relationships that are identified using the XPath, as shown in Figure 13-14.

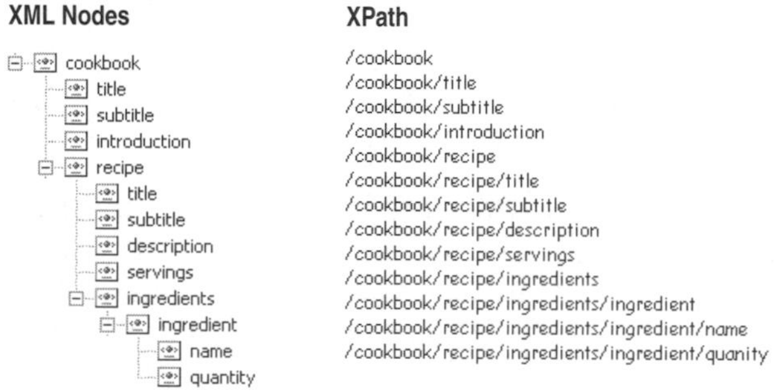

XML Nodes	XPath
⊟ cookbook	/cookbook
title	/cookbook/title
subtitle	/cookbook/subtitle
introduction	/cookbook/introduction
⊟ recipe	/cookbook/recipe
title	/cookbook/recipe/title
subtitle	/cookbook/recipe/subtitle
description	/cookbook/recipe/description
servings	/cookbook/recipe/servings
⊟ ingredients	/cookbook/recipe/ingredients
⊟ ingredient	/cookbook/recipe/ingredients/ingredient
name	/cookbook/recipe/ingredients/ingredient/name
quantity	/cookbook/recipe/ingredients/ingredient/quanity

Figure 13-14   XML nodes

XML is well suited for structured data such as stock quotes, employee information, product inventory, order status, and other data that we're used to dealing with in an organized fashion. XML is not as well suited for information that uses creative or ad hoc organization.

Creating an XSL File

The XSL file provides the layout and logic that transforms data stored in the XML file into the output you see on the Web form. To create an XSL file in Visual Studio, choose Add New Item from the Project menu, choose XSLT File from the Templates list, and then click Open.

The XSL file contains template statements that select the items to import from the XML file. Each template includes standard HTML elements to apply formatting to the elements imported from the XML file. For example, the following XSL template converts cookbook title, subtitle, and introduction elements from an XML file to *h1*, *h2*, and *p* elements in HTML:

```
<?xml version="1.0" encoding="UTF-8" ?>
<xsl:stylesheet version="1.0" xmlns:xsl="http://www.w3.org/1999/XSL/
Transform">
  <xsl:template match="/cookbook">
    <xsl:apply-templates select="cookbook" />
    <h1><xsl:value-of select="title" /></h1>
    <h3><xsl:value-of select="subtitle" /></h3>
    <hr />
    <p><xsl:value-of select="introduction" /></p>
    <hr />
    <h2><xsl:text>Recipes</xsl:text></h2>
    <xsl:apply-templates select="recipe" />
  </xsl:template>
</xsl:stylesheet>
```

The preceding example uses the XSL elements and attributes summarized in Table 13-2.

Table 13-2   Basic XSL Elements

Element	Attributes	Use to
xsl:stylesheet	*version*	Identify the version of XSL being used. Version 1.0 is the current version at the time of this writing.
	xmlns:xsl	Specify the prefixes for elements in the XSL file.
xsl:template	*match*	Define a template for an XML node.
xsl:apply-templates	*select*	Apply a template to the selected node.
xsl:value-of	*select*	Retrieve the value of an XML node or evaluate an XPath expression.
xsl:text		Include literal text or white space characters in the output.

Figure 13-15 shows how these elements work to transform cookbook XML data through the XML server control.

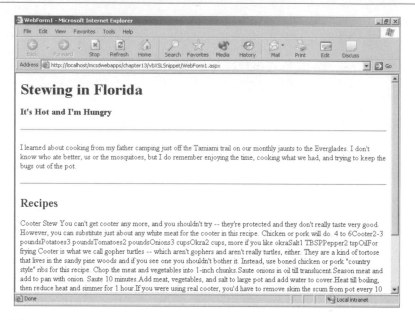

Figure 13-15   Basic XSL elements in action

The XSL elements demonstrated in Figure 13-15 perform the minimum tasks for displaying data with XSL: they define a template, import data into that template, display values from the XML, and insert literal text. Those are all tasks that are more easily performed simply by using regular HTML and style sheets. However, using XSL offers two advantages:

- You can change the position of the element (page layout) in the XSL file without having to change your data.
- You can perform logical operations on data, such as looping and conditional processing.

These advantages are discussed in the following sections.

Changing Layout

You change page layout in XSL by moving elements in the XSL file. For example, the following XSL displays the cookbook XML in a two-column format and displays the subtitle before the title:

```
<?xml version="1.0" encoding="UTF-8" ?>
<xsl:stylesheet version="1.0" xmlns:xsl="http://www.w3.org/1999/XSL/
Transform">
  <xsl:template match="/cookbook">
    <xsl:apply-templates select="cookbook" />
      <table>
        <tr>
```

```
        <td width="300">
          <h3><xsl:value-of select="subtitle" />
          <xsl:text>...</xsl:text></h3>
          <h1><xsl:value-of select="title" /></h1>
        </td>
        <td width="500">
          <xsl:text>recipe text goes here..</xsl:text>
        </td>
      </tr>
      <tr>
        <td width="300">
          <hr />
          <xsl:value-of select="introduction" />
          <hr />
        </td>
        <td width="500">
        </td>
      </tr>
    </table>
  </xsl:template>
</xsl:stylesheet>
```

Figure 13-16 shows the changes to the output on the Web form.

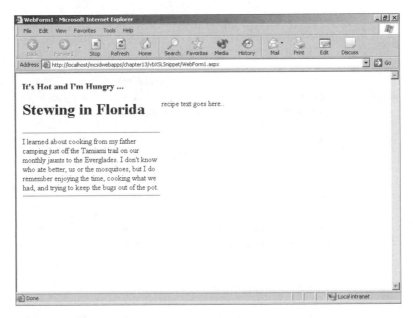

Figure 13-16   Changing layout with XSL

Including Other Templates

An XSL file can contain multiple templates. You define an XSL template for each XML node that is uniquely formatted. For example, the cookbook XML shown earlier in this lesson could be organized into four templates:

- The main template formats the title and description of the book and provides a starting point. XSL execution starts with this template because it selects the root node (match="/ cookbook").
- The recipe template formats the recipes included in the book.
- The ingredients template formats the list of ingredients.
- The instructions template formats the steps that follow the list of ingredients.

Use the *xsl:apply-templates* element to apply a template to a node. For example, the following XSL applies the ingredient and instruction templates from the recipe template, which is in turn applied from the main template. The links between the templates are shown in boldface:

```xml
<?xml version="1.0" encoding="UTF-8" ?>
<xsl:stylesheet version="1.0" xmlns:xsl="http://www.w3.org/1999/XSL/
Transform">

  <xsl:template match="/cookbook">
    <xsl:apply-templates select="cookbook" />
    <h1><xsl:value-of select="title" /></h1>
    <h3><xsl:text>...</xsl:text><xsl:value-of select="subtitle" /></h3>
    <hr />
    <p><xsl:value-of select="introduction" /></p>
    <hr />
    <xsl:apply-templates select="recipe" />
  </xsl:template>

  <xsl:template match="recipe">
    <h3><xsl:value-of select="title" /></h3>
    <p><xsl:value-of select="description" /></p>
    <p><b><xsl:text>Serves: </xsl:text></b>
    <i><xsl:value-of select="servings" /></i></p>
    <xsl:apply-templates select="ingredients" />
    <xsl:apply-templates select="instructions" />
  </xsl:template>

  <xsl:template match="ingredients">
    <ul>
      <li><xsl:value-of select="ingredient/name" />
      <xsl:text>    </xsl:text>
      <b><xsl:value-of select="ingredient/quantity" /></b></li>
    </ul>
  </xsl:template>
```

```
<xsl:template match="instructions">
  <p><xsl:value-of select="introduction" /></p>
  <ol>
    <li><xsl:value-of select="step" /></li>
  </ol>
  <p><xsl:value-of select="summary" /></p>
</xsl:template>

</xsl:stylesheet>
```

At run time, the preceding XSL template creates HTML output, as shown in Figure 13-17.

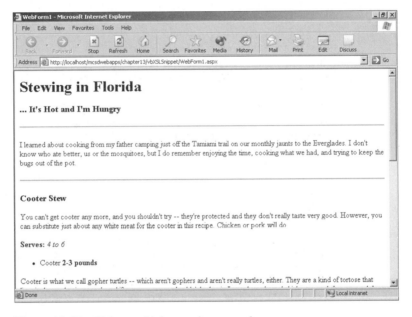

Figure 13-17   Using multiple templates together

But wait! There's only one ingredient (cooter) and one instruction (cut it up). As the templates are written, they process only one node each. To repeat tasks, you need to use the XSL looping elements, as described in the following section.

Repeating Tasks

To format repeating elements in an XML file, such as list or table items, use the *xsl:for-each* XSL element. The *xls:for-each* element selects the repeated node, and then the contained XSL is applied to each occurrence of that node, as shown here:

```
<xsl:for-each select="ingredient">
  <xsl:value-of select="name" /><br />
</xsl:for-each>
```

The preceding XSL outputs the name of each repeated ingredient node. To refer to the repeated node itself, use the *"."* XPath identifier. For example, the following XSL outputs the text of each repeated step node in the XML:

```
<xsl:for-each select="step">
  <xsl:value-of select="." /><br />
</xsl:for-each>
```

The following XSL uses the *xsl:for-each* element (shown in boldface) to display all of the recipes, ingredients, and steps in the cookbook:

```
<?xml version="1.0" encoding="UTF-8" ?>
<xsl:stylesheet version="1.0" xmlns:xsl="http://www.w3.org/1999/XSL/
Transform">

  <xsl:template match="/cookbook">
    <xsl:apply-templates select="cookbook" />
    <h1><xsl:value-of select="title" /></h1>
    <h3><xsl:text>...</xsl:text><xsl:value-of select="subtitle" /></h3>
    <hr />
    <p><xsl:value-of select="introduction" /></p>
    <hr />
    <xsl:for-each select="recipe">
      <xsl:apply-templates select="." />
    </xsl:for-each>
  </xsl:template>

  <xsl:template match="recipe">
    <h3><xsl:value-of select="title" /></h3>
    <p><xsl:value-of select="description" /></p>
    <p><b><xsl:text>Serves: </xsl:text></b>
    <i><xsl:value-of select="servings" /></i></p>
    <xsl:apply-templates select="ingredients" />
    <xsl:apply-templates select="instructions" />
  </xsl:template>

  <xsl:template match="ingredients">
    <ul>
      <xsl:for-each select="ingredient">
        <li><xsl:value-of select="name" />
        <xsl:text> </xsl:text>
        <b><xsl:value-of select="quantity" /></b></li>
      </xsl:for-each>
    </ul>
  </xsl:template>

  <xsl:template match="instructions">
    <p><xsl:value-of select="introduction" /></p>
    <ol>
```

```
      <xsl:for-each select="step">
        <li><xsl:value-of select="." /></li>
      </xsl:for-each>
    </ol>
    <p><xsl:value-of select="summary" /></p>
  </xsl:template>

</xsl:stylesheet>
```

At run time, the preceding XSL formats the cookbook XML, as shown in Figure 13-18.

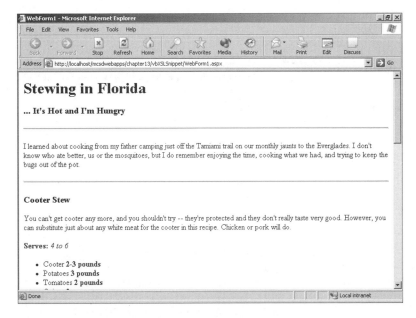

Figure 13-18   Formatting repeated elements

Inserting Hyperlinks and Other HTML Elements

Use *xsl:element* to compose HTML elements that contain attributes, such as hyperlinks, server controls, or HTML controls. For example, the following XSL creates a hyperlink that returns the user to the top of the page:

```
<xsl:element name="a">
  <xsl:attribute name="name">
    <xsl:text>#top</xsl:text>
  </xsl:attribute>
  <xsl:text>Return to top.</xsl:text>
</xsl:element>
```

At run time, the preceding XSL generates the following output:

```
<a href="#top">Return to top.</a>
```

You can couple this XSL with the XPath *generate-id* function to automatically create a table of contents for your document that links to locations within a document, as shown in boldface in the following XSL:

```
<xsl:template match="/cookbook">
  <h1><xsl:value-of select="title" /></h1>
  <h3><xsl:text>...</xsl:text><xsl:value-of select="subtitle" /></h3>
  <hr />
  <p><xsl:value-of select="introduction" /></p>
  <hr />
  <!-- Display table of contents -->
  <h4>Contents</h4>
  <xsl:apply-templates mode="contents" select="recipe" />
  <xsl:for-each select="recipe">
    <xsl:apply-templates select="." />
  </xsl:for-each>
</xsl:template>

<xsl:template match="recipe">
  <!-- Create location links -->
  <xsl:element name="a">
    <xsl:attribute name="name">
      <xsl:value-of select="generate-id(title)" />
    </xsl:attribute>
    <h3><xsl:value-of select="title" /></h3>
  </xsl:element>
  <p><xsl:value-of select="description" /></p>
  <p><b><xsl:text>Serves: </xsl:text></b>
  <i><xsl:value-of select="servings" /></i></p>
  <xsl:apply-templates select="ingredients" />
  <xsl:apply-templates select="instructions" />
</xsl:template>

<xsl:template mode="contents" match="recipe">
  <!-- Create table of contents links -->
  <xsl:element name="a">
    <xsl:attribute name="href">
      <xsl:text>#</xsl:text>
      <xsl:value-of select="generate-id(title)" />
    </xsl:attribute>
    <xsl:value-of select="title" />
  </xsl:element>
  <br />
</xsl:template>
```

At run time, the preceding XSL generates the output shown in Figure 13-19.

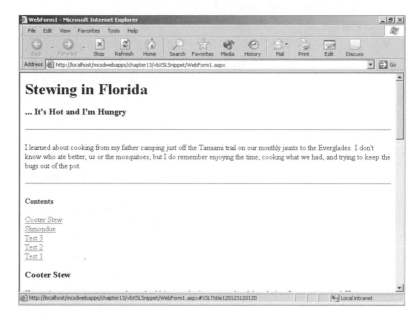

Figure 13-19   Generating a table of contents

The *generate-id* XPath function generates a unique ID for the XML node passed to it as an argument. The ID takes the form *XSLTnodename#*, where # is a 12-digit integer, as in this example: XSLTtitle120123120120.

Sorting Items

Use the *xsl:sort* element to sort items within another XSL element. For example, the following XSL sorts the table of contents created in the preceding section:

```
<h4>Contents</h4>
<xsl:apply-templates mode="contents" select="recipe">
  <xsl:sort select="title" order="ascending" />
</xsl:apply-templates>
```

The *xsl:sort* element can be included in *xsl:apply-templates* elements, as shown in the preceding code, or in *xsl:for-each* elements.

Performing Conditional Tasks

XSL includes two sets of elements for performing conditional tasks: use *xsl:if* to evaluate a single condition; use *xsl:choose* with contained *xsl:when* and *xsl:other-wise* elements to evaluate multiple conditions. Table 13-3 summarizes these conditional elements.

Table 13-3   Conditional XSL Elements

Element	Attribute	Use to
xsl:if	*test*	Test a Boolean expression and process the contained elements if the result is *true*.
xsl:choose		Test multiple conditions using contained *xsl:when* and *xsl:otherwise* elements. This is the equivalent of a *Select Case* (Visual Basic .NET) or *switch* (Visual C#) statement.
xsl:when	*test*	Test one Boolean expression within an *xsl:choose* element, and then process the contained item and exit the *xsl:choose* element if the result is *true*. This is the equivalent of the *Case* (Visual Basic .NET) or *case* (Visual C#) statement.
xsl:otherwise		Process the contained item if none of the *xsl:when* elements within an *xsl:choose* element are *true*. This is the equivalent of the *Case Else* (Visual Basic .NET) or *default* (Visual C#) statement.

The conditional elements' *test* attribute evaluates an XPath expression to determine whether the XSL contained in the conditional element should be processed. For example, the following XSL creates a table of contents if there are more than four recipes in the cookbook:

```
<xsl:if test="count(recipe) > 4">
  <h4>Contents</h4>
  <xsl:apply-templates mode="contents" select="recipe" />
</xsl:if>
```

The preceding XSL uses the XPath *count* function to return the number of recipe nodes in the cookbook. If the count is greater than 4, the *Contents* heading is output and the *contents* template is processed; otherwise, the contents are omitted.

Similarly, you can use XPath functions within *xsl:choose* elements to change output based on several conditions. For example, the following XSL inserts a line break after every four contents items; otherwise, it separates items with a tab space:

```
<xsl:template mode="contents" match="recipe">
  <xsl:element name="a">
    <xsl:attribute name="href">
      <xsl:text>#</xsl:text>
      <xsl:value-of select="generate-id(title)" />
    </xsl:attribute>
    <xsl:value-of select="title" />
  </xsl:element>
  <xsl:choose>
    <xsl:when test="position() mod 4 = 0">
```

```
        <br />
      </xsl:when>
      <xsl:otherwise>
        <xsl:text>  </xsl:text>
      </xsl:otherwise>
    </xsl:choose>
</xsl:template>
```

The preceding XSL uses the XPath *position* function to return the position of the current node within the node's collection. It also uses the XPath *mod* operator to determine whether the current position is evenly divisible by four.

More Info   We've only scratched the surface of what you can do with XSL here. XML, XSL, and XPath are all languages in their own right. This lesson gives you enough information to get started, but for a complete education, see the Microsoft XML SDK documentation included in the Visual Studio .NET online Help. Microsoft Press books that cover this subject include *XML Step by Step, Second Edition*, by Michael J. Young, and *XML Programming (Core Reference)*, by R. Allen Wyke, Sultan Rehman, and Brad Leupen.

Summary

- Styles follow this order of precedence based on where they are applied: local (applied to an element), page (applied within a page's *head* element), and global (applied through a style sheet).

- Use the *link* element within a Web form's *head* element to attach a style sheet.

- Use the Visual Studio .NET Style Builder Wizard to modify existing styles.

- Use the Visual Studio .NET Add Style Rule Wizard to create a new style.

- Create a style class to apply the same formatting to different types of elements.

- Use the *CssStyle* attribute to apply a style class to a server control. Use the *class* attribute to apply a style class to an HTML element.

- XSL transformations convert XML input files to HTML through the XML server control.

- XML organizes data into a hierarchical set of nodes.

- XSL templates apply formatting to nodes within an XML file.

- Use the *xsl:value-of* element to retrieve data from an XML node.

- Use the *xsl:text* element to include literal text and white-space characters in XSL output.

- Use the *xsl:for-each* element to repeat tasks for lists, tables, and other repeated nodes within an XML file.

- Use the *xsl:if*, *xsl:choose*, *xsl:when*, and *xsl:otherwise* elements to perform conditional processing within XSL.

Lab: Creating the Cookbook

In this lab, you'll build a single Web form that uses a customized style sheet, provides an enlarged-type style sheet for visually impaired users, and uses XML with XSL transformations to format information. You'll also be encouraged to apply your knowledge of XML to real-world data you're already familiar with.

Estimated lesson time: 30 minutes

Exercise 1: Create and Attach a Style Sheet

Use the skills you learned in Lesson 1 to create your own style sheet based on the default style sheet Visual Studio .NET creates. Because style (and taste) are personal matters, you can make the changes suggested in the following steps, or you can develop your own unique look. When you have finished, your result might look similar to Figure 13-20.

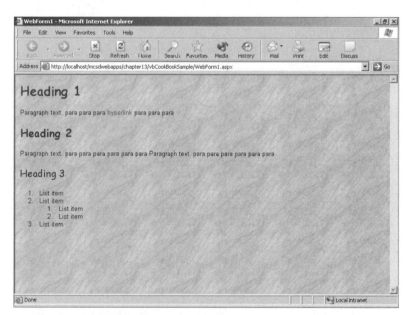

Figure 13-20   Test Web form with styles

▶ **To create a custom style sheet and attach it to a Web form**

1. Make the following suggested changes to the default style sheet (Styles.css), or choose your own changes:

   - Change the default font for all headings to Comic Sans MS.
   - Change the default font for body text to Lucida Sans-Serif.

- Add a background image to the page from within the style sheet.
- Change the color of the headings and rule lines to stand out against your chosen background image.

2. When you have finished modifying the style sheet, attach it to a Web form by adding a *link* element in the Web form's *head* element, as shown here in bold-face:

```
<HEAD>
    <meta name="GENERATOR" content="Microsoft Visual Studio.NET 7.0">
    <meta name="CODE_LANGUAGE" content="Visual Basic 7.0">
    <meta name="vs_defaultClientScript" content="JavaScript">
    <meta name="vs_targetSchema"
        content="http://schemas.microsoft.com/intellisense/ie5">
    <LINK REL="stylesheet" TYPE="text/css" HREF="Styles.css">
</HEAD>
```

3. Add some sample text and headings to the Web form to test the appearance of your style sheet.

4. View the Web form in the browser, and adjust the style sheet until you're happy with the Web form's appearance.

Exercise 2: Provide Alternative Style Sheets

In this exercise, you'll create an alternative style sheet that displays headings and text in a larger font size, making your Web form readable for users with impaired vision. You'll also add a client-side control that enables the user to switch to the large-type style sheet at run time. When you have finished, your result should look similar to Figure 13-21.

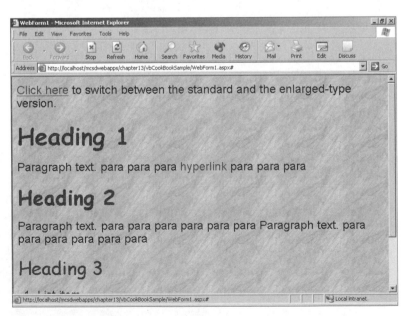

Figure 13-21   Enlarged-type sample

▶ **To create the enlarged-type style sample**

1. Add a new, empty style sheet to your project. Name the file BigType.css.

2. Cut and paste the contents of the default style sheet (Styles.css) into BigType.css. If you're using Visual C#, you'll have to get the default style sheet from a Visual Basic .NET project and add it to your Visual C# project.

3. In BigType.css, change the *body* element's font size to large.

4. On the Web form created in Exercise 1, add an *ID* and a *media* attribute to the *link* element that attaches the default style sheet to the Web form, as shown here in boldface:

```
<LINK ID="ScreenStyle" REL="stylesheet" TYPE="text/css" HREF="Styles.css"
media="screen">
```

5. Add another *link* element to use the default style sheet for printing, as shown here:

```
<LINK ID="PrintStyle" REL="stylesheet" TYPE="text/css" HREF="Styles.css"
media="print">
```

6. Add a hyperlink with an *onclick* event to switch between the default style sheet and BigType.css, as shown here:

```
<a onclick="SwitchSheets()" href="#">Click here
</a> to switch between the standard and the enlarged-type version.
```

7. Add the following client-side script to switch between style sheets:

VBScript

```
<script language="vbscript"> ' Switch
 between default and large-type style sheets.
Sub SwitchSheets()
    If document.all("ScreenStyle").GetAttribute("HREF", 0) = "Styles.css"
then
        document.all("ScreenStyle").SetAttribute "HREF", "BigType.css", 0
    else
        document.all("ScreenStyle").SetAttribute "HREF", "Styles.css", 0
    end if
End Sub
</script>
```

JScript

```
<script id="clientEventHandlersJS" language="jscript">
function SwitchSheets()
{
    // Switch between default and large-type style sheets.
    if (document.all["ScreenStyle"].getAttribute("HREF") == "Styles.css")
        document.all["ScreenStyle"].setAttribute ("HREF",
        "BigType.css", 0);
    else
```

```
                        document.all["ScreenStyle"].setAttribute ("HREF",
                        "Styles.css", 0);
                   }
                   </script>
```

8. Display the Web form in the browser and test switching back and forth between the BigType.css and the default style sheets. Make adjustments to BigType.css to create the best appearance.

Exercise 3: Perform XSL Transformation

In this exercise, you'll add an XML server control to the Web form you created in Exercise 1 and modified in Exercise 2. You'll set the XML control's *Document-Source* and *TransformSource* properties to the sample XML and XSL files used in Lesson 2, which are included on the companion CD. When you have finished, your result should appear as shown in Figure 13-22.

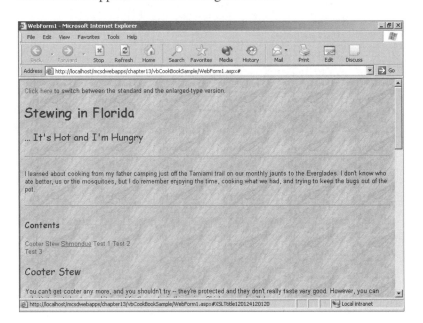

Figure 13-22   The cookbook sample

▶ **To perform the sample XSL transformation**

1. Using the same Web form from Exercises 1 and 2, delete the sample text you used to test style sheets. Retain the hyperlink and client-side script you created in Exercise 2.

2. Add an XML server control after the hyperlink, as shown in the following HTML:

```
<a onclick="SwitchSheets" href="#">Click here</a> to switch between the
standard and the enlarged-type version.
<asp:Xml id="XmlTransform" runat="server" DocumentSource=""
TransformSource="" />
```

3. Copy the cook.xml and cook.xsl sample files to your project directory.

4. Set the XML control's *DocumentSource* property to cook.xml and *Transform-Source* property to cook6.xsl.

5. Display the Web form in the browser to confirm that the XML transformation works correctly.

Exercise 4: On Your Own

Think about ways to apply XML with XSL transformations to data that you currently present on the Web with HTML. Using XML to label content is a much more conceptual task than using HTML directly to format content, and it takes some getting used to. Perhaps the best way to learn is to try it on your own, using real-world data that you're familiar with, as described in the following steps:

1. Choose a simple project, such as an order form or an address list, and then create a sample XML file based on that data.

2. Create an XSL file that contains templates to transform the XML file into HTML.

3. Create a Web form that uses an XML control to perform the transformation.

4. As you work, think about the following questions:

   - How do you determine the node hierarchy?
   - What are the advantages of creating collections within the hierarchy? For example:

     ```
     <items>
       <item>Item 1</item>
       <item>Item 2</item>
     </items>
     ```

   - How does writing XML leverage your database and object-oriented programming skills?

Review

The following questions are intended to reinforce key information presented in this chapter. If you are unable to answer a question, review the appropriate lesson and then try the question again. Answers to the questions can be found in the appendix.

1. What is the advantage of using CSS rather than in-line styles for formatting a Web application?

2. Why would you create a style for a class rather than for an HTML element?

3. How do CSS and XSL relate to each other when it comes to formatting a Web application?

4. What are the differences between HTML and XML?

C H A P T E R   1 4

Providing Help

About This Chapter

In this chapter, you'll learn about the different ways that you can display user assistance (Help) from within a Web application. You'll learn how to use the HTML Help Workshop to create compiled Help files and how to display those files from a Web application interactively.

Before You Begin

To complete this chapter, you must:

■ Be familiar with HTML
■ Be comfortable creating Web forms in HTML mode

Lesson 1: Adding Help to Web Applications

Web applications can display help in several ways: as ToolTips for controls, as Web forms or HTML pages, or as compiled HTML Help files. In this lesson, you'll learn to use these different techniques from within Web forms.

After this lesson, you will be able to

- Add ToolTips to server controls and HTML controls on a Web form
- Display Help as a Web form or an HTML page in a browser window
- Control the size and focus of the browser window displaying Help
- Display Help using the HTML Help Viewer

Estimated lesson time: 15 minutes

Displaying ToolTips

A **ToolTip** is a short, descriptive message that's displayed when the user places the mouse pointer over a control and leaves it there for a couple of seconds. These messages are used throughout Microsoft Windows applications to provide helpful information about toolbar buttons and other graphical controls whose meaning might not otherwise be obvious. In a sense, ToolTips are subtitles for the icon-impaired. Figure 14-1 shows a ToolTip in action.

Figure 14-1   A ToolTip

Most server controls include a *ToolTip* property that you can set to the message you want to display. At run time, Microsoft ASP.NET outputs the *ToolTip* property as the control's *title* attribute, which Microsoft Internet Explorer displays as a Tool-Tip. Only Internet Explorer displays the *title* attributes as ToolTips. Other browsers do not display ToolTips.

HTML controls do not include a *ToolTip* property. Instead, you can use the *title* attribute directly. The following HTML shows the difference between setting a ToolTip for a server control and setting one for an HTML control:

```
<asp:Button id="butOK" runat="server" Text="OK"
  ToolTip="Submits purchase."></asp:Button>
<INPUT type="reset" value="Cancel" title="Cancels purchase.">
```

Not all controls include a *ToolTip* property or *title* attribute. In particular, the Drop-DownList and ListBox server controls do not provide a *ToolTip* property or a *title* attribute.

Displaying Help as Web Forms or HTML

Creating your Help content as Web forms or HTML pages is probably the simplest approach to providing user assistance. The Help files can reside in either the same project folder as your Web application or in a subordinate folder.

You use hyperlinks or other controls to display the Help in the browser, just as you would any other page, with one important difference: you usually want to display Help in a new window or in a separate frame from the rest of the Web application, as shown in Figure 14-2.

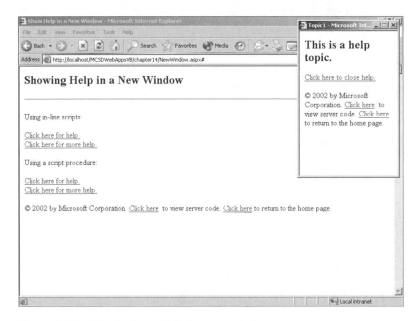

Figure 14-2   Displaying a Help browser window

Displaying Help in a separate browser window preserves the user's place in the Web application and allows him or her to compare the Help to the current task being performed.

To display Help in a separate window, use the client-side window object's *open* method, as shown in the following hyperlink:

```
<a href="#" onclick="window.open('topic1.aspx', 'helpwin').focus()">
  Click here for help.</a>
```

The preceding HTML uses the *onclick* event to display the Help topic in a new browser window on top of the Web application's window. Setting the *href* attribute to "#" simply links to the current location in the Web application, rather than direct- ing the user to a new location. The first argument to the *open* method specifies the Help topic to display; the second argument names the new window so that subse- quent Help topics are directed to the same window. Finally, the *focus* method ensures that the Help window is displayed on top of the Web application.

Other Help hyperlinks within the Web application can use the same onclick script to display different topics in the same window. If your application includes more than one Help hyperlink per Web form, it's a good idea to place the script in a pro- cedure and call it from the onclick procedure, as shown here:

VBScript

```
<HTML>
  <HEAD>
  <title>WebForm1</title>
<script language="vbscript">
' Shows a Web form or HTML page in a small browser window
' and switches the focus to that window.
Sub ShowHelp(topicName)
  Dim HelpWindow
  ' Display topic in named window.
  Set HelpWindow = window.open(topicName,
     "helpwin","left=600,height=300,width=200")
  ' Displays the window on top.
  HelpWindow.focus
End Sub
</script>
  </HEAD>
  <body>
    <h2>Show Help in a New window</h2>
    <A onclick="ShowHelp('topic1.aspx')" href="#">Click here
      for help.</A>
    <BR>
    <A onclick="ShowHelp('topic2.aspx')" href="#">Click here
      for more help.</A>
  </body>
</HTML>
```

JScript

```
<HTML>
  <HEAD>
<script language=jscript>
// Shows a Web form or HTML page in a small browser window
// and switches the focus to that window.
function ShowHelp(topicName)
{
  var HelpWindow;
```

```
  // Display topic in named window.
  HelpWindow = window.open(topicName,
     "helpwin","left=600,height=300,width=200");
  // Displays the window on top.
  HelpWindow.focus();
}
</script>
  </HEAD>
  <body>
    <h2>Show Help in a New window</h2>
    <a href="#" onclick="ShowHelp('topic1.aspx')">Click here for
      help.</a>
    <br>
    <a href="#" onclick="ShowHelp('topic2.aspx')">Click here for
      more help.</a>
  </body>
</HTML>
```

Within the Help topic, you can use the *window* object's *close* method to provide a link to close the Help window within the Help topic, as shown here:

```
<a href="#" onclick="window.close()">Click here to close help.</a>
```

There are other ways to display a topic in a named window, such as using the target attribute of a hyperlink. However, those techniques make it more difficult to ensure that the Help window is displayed on top of the Web application.

Displaying HTML Help

You can use the *window* object's *showHelp* method to display HTML Help files, regular HTML files, or Web forms using the HTML Help Viewer (hh.exe). An HTML Help file consists of topic files written in HTML that have been compiled into a single, compressed file that provides additional Help features.

The *showHelp* method displays topics in the HTML Help Viewer, which by default is displayed on top of the Web application's browser window, as shown in Figure 14-3.

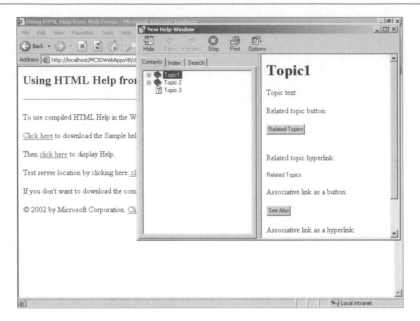

Figure 14-3   The HTML Help Viewer

To display a Web form or an HTML page using *showHelp,* specify the Web form or HTML page file name as the first argument of the method, as shown here:

```
<a href="#" onclick="window.showHelp('Topic1.aspx')">Show Help</a>
```

The preceding HTML displays the Web form Topic1.aspx when the user clicks the Show Help hyperlink. The Topic1.aspx file in not a compiled Help file—it is simply a Help topic written using ASP.NET. Using *showHelp* in this way gives you the advantage of the window always being on top of the Web application—even when the Web application has the focus.

The *showHelp* method can also display topics from compiled Help files. These files are made up of HTML pages that are compiled into a single file (.chm) using the HTML Help Workshop. When you work with compiled Help files, *showHelp* identifies the topic to display using a context ID that is mapped to a topic file name during compilation.

To display a topic from a compiled HTML Help file, specify the compiled file name and topic file name as the first argument of the *showHelp* method, as shown here:

```
<a href="#" onclick="window.showHelp('c:\\Help\\HelpSample.chm')">
  Show Help</a><br>
```

The preceding HTML displays the compiled file named HelpSample.chm. Note that the compiled Help file must be downloaded and stored on the user's machine. Using compiled Help files has the following advantages over storing and displaying Help files as separate Web forms or HTML pages:

■ **Reduced size**   Compiling Help compresses the topics so that their total size is much less than the total of the individual source topics.

■ **Contents, Index, and Search tools**   The HTML Help Workshop includes tools for creating these features and adding them to your Help system.

■ **Embedded display**   The HTML Help Microsoft ActiveX control and Java applet allow you to display your Help within the browser window rather than as a separate window.

■ **Ease of localization**   Because HTML Help maps topic file names to context IDs, it's possible to have multiple compiled Help files written in different natural languages that all use the same set of context IDs.

Compiling HTML Help has a couple of limitations that you should be aware of as well:

■ **Source files must be in HTML format**   Web forms can't be compiled into .chm files.

■ **The entire compiled file must be downloaded to the user's machine**   If you have a large Help file and your users are connected via modem, it can take a long time to load Help the first time. Once the Help file is downloaded, however, it can be accessed quickly.

The following lessons discuss creating compiled HTML Help files and using those files from Web applications in more detail.

Lesson 2: Using the HTML Help Workshop

Microsoft Visual Studio .NET includes the HTML Help Workshop, which is installed in a separate location on the developer's machine. In this lesson, you'll learn how to use the HTML Help Workshop to create a compiled Help file that includes a table of contents, an index, and full-text search capabilities.

After this lesson, you will be able to

- Create a new Help project
- Add topics to a Help project and compile those topics into a single Help file
- Build a table of contents automatically during compilation
- Modify an automatically generated table of contents
- Add index keywords to Help topics
- Create different types of cross-references between topics within a Help file
- Add special features such as associative links and Related Topics links to Help topics
- Enable full-text searches within a Help file
- Compile and preview Help from the HTML Help Workshop or from the command line

Estimated lesson time: 30 minutes

Creating HTML Help

An HTML Help file is made up of individual HTML pages, each representing a single Help topic. Each Help topic can include keywords that are included in the index and cross-references to other topics. HTML Help projects include the types of files described in Table 14-1.

Table 14-1   HTML Help Project Files

File type	Use to
Help topic (.htm)	Create content to display in Help
Project (.hhp)	Define how the project is compiled and which Help topic, contents, and index files to include
Contents (.hhc)	Create a table of contents for the Help file
Index (.hhk)	Create an index for the Help file
Search stop list (.stp)	Exclude specific words from searches
Compiled (.chm)	Deploy the completed Help file

The HTML Help Workshop provides tools to organize, edit, and compile these files. By default, Visual Studio .NET installs the HTML Help Workshop in the Program Files\HTML Help Workshop folder during setup.

To create a new HTML Help project, follow these steps:

1. From the HTML Help Workshop File menu, choose New. The New dialog box opens.
2. In the New dialog box, select Project and click OK. The New Project Wizard opens. The wizard lets you convert an existing WinHelp project or create a new HTML Help project.
3. Click Next to create a new project. The wizard displays the Destination page.
4. Type the location and name of the Help project file you want to create, and then click Next. The wizard displays the Existing Files page.
5. Select the check boxes for any contents, index, or topic files you've already created, and click Next. If you select any of these existing files, the wizard prompts you for the location of each of the selected file types. Otherwise, the wizard creates a new, empty Help project, as shown in Figure 14-4.

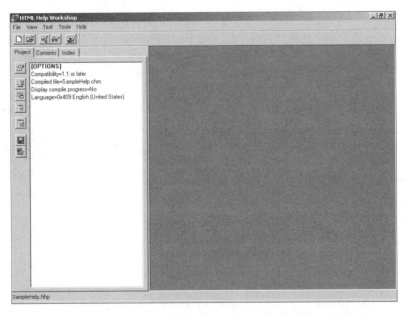

Figure 14-4 A new, empty Help project

Using HTML Help Workshop is fairly simple. You use the Project, Contents, and Index tabs on the left pane to edit the contents of the project, contents, and index files. The buttons at the top of the pane create new files, open existing files, compile the project, display the compiled project, and display HTML Workshop Help.

To add topic files to the Help project, follow these steps:

1. Click the New button on the toolbar, select HTML File in the New dialog box, and then specify a title for the topic. The Workshop creates a new Help topic file, as shown in Figure 14-5.

Figure 14-5   Creating topic files

2. Save the HTML file, and then click Add/Remove Topic Files on the Project tab. The Topic Files dialog box opens.

3. Click Add, and then select the files to add to the project. Click Open.

4. Click OK to close the Topic Files dialog box. The Workshop adds the file to the project.

The HTML Help Workshop provides only basic text-editing capabilities. In general, you author your Help topic files in a full-featured HTML editor, such as Microsoft FrontPage, and then use the Workshop to create the project file and compile the Help.

Setting Project Options

Help project options are displayed on the Project tab of the HTML Help Workshop. These options are stored in the Help project file (.hhp) in plain text and can be modified using the HTML Help Workshop or a text editor such as Notepad.

To set project options in the HTML Help Workshop, on the Project tab, click Change Project Options. The Workshop displays the Options dialog box, as shown in Figure 14-6.

Figure 14-6   Setting options

The project options let you specify a title for the Help project, locale information about the project, how the contents and index files are created, whether to support searching, and other features. These items are placed in the OPTIONS section of the project file. For example, the following project options create index and contents files automatically when compiling a Help file named HelpSample.chm, which displays the title "HTML Help Sample" in the Help window:

```
[OPTIONS]
Auto Index=Yes
Auto TOC=9
Compatibility=1.1 or later
Compiled file=HelpSample.chm
Contents file= Contents.hhc
Default topic=topic1.htm
Display compile progress=No
Full text search stop list file=Search.stp
Index file=Index.hhk
Language=0x409 English (United States)
Title=HTML Help Sample
```

The project file also includes a FILES section that lists the Help topic files to compile. The order of the files in this section determines the order of items in the contents file when Auto TOC is selected in the OPTIONS section. For example, the following topic files appear in sequential order in contents:

```
[FILES]
topic1.htm
topic1a.htm
topic1b.htm
topic2.htm
topic3.htm
```

Building Tables of Contents

When building the table of contents automatically, the HTML Help Workshop uses the heading level of the topic and its order in the *FILES* section of the project file to determine how the table of contents is organized.

The Workshop puts *<h1>* headings at the top level, *<h2>* headings under those, and so on until a new *<h1>* heading is encountered. If you have multiple heading levels within a single topic, the Workshop creates subordinate contents items for each of those headings—even though they all represent the same Help topic. For this reason, it's best to use only one HTML heading element per Help topic when generating contents automatically.

For example, the following *FILES* section includes topic files with three heading levels, as indicated by their file names:

```
[FILES]
topic1.htm
topic1a.htm
topic1b.htm
topic2.htm
topic2a.htm
topic2b.htm
topic2bi.htm
topic2bii.htm
topic3.htm
```

At run time, the generated contents files appear as shown in Figure 14-7.

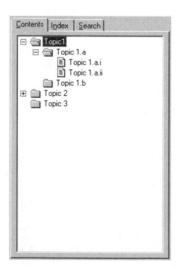

Figure 14-7   Automatic table of contents

The Workshop stores the generated table of contents in an HTML file. You can generate an automatic table of contents, turn off Auto TOC in the project file, and then edit the generated contents file to customize the table of contents.

To edit a contents file, click the Contents tab in the HTML Help Workshop. The Workshop displays the contents, as shown in Figure 14-8.

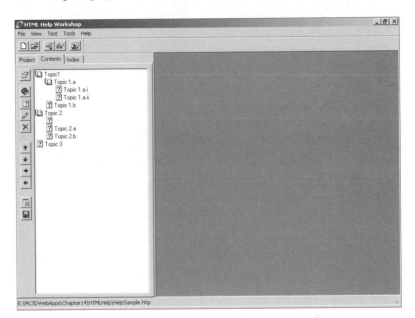

Figure 14-8   Editing the contents file

One thing you might have noticed in the automatic contents shown in Figure 14-8 is that the icons for top-level topics aren't consistent. For instance, Topic 3 shows a page icon rather than a book icon.

To change the icon displayed for a topic, follow these steps:

1. On the Contents tab, select the contents topic, click Edit Selection, and then in the Table Of Contents Entry dialog box, click the Advanced tab, as shown in Figure 14-9.

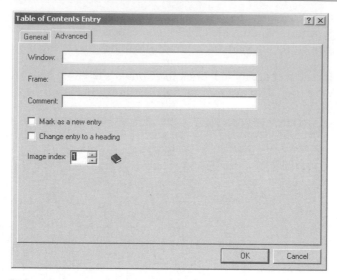

Figure 14-9   Changing the contents entry icon

2. Select the image to use for the entry in the Image Index list box, and then click OK.

The contents file is stored as an HTML file that uses object elements to specify the contents items, as shown by the following HTML:

```
<!DOCTYPE HTML PUBLIC "-//IETF//DTD HTML//EN">
<HTML>
<HEAD>
<meta name="GENERATOR" content="Microsoft&reg; HTML Help Workshop 4.1">
<!-- Sitemap 1.0 -->
</HEAD><BODY>
<UL>
  <LI> <OBJECT type="text/sitemap">
    <param name="Name" value="Topic1">
    <param name="Local" value="topic1.htm">
  </OBJECT>
  <UL>
    <LI> <OBJECT type="text/sitemap">
      <param name="Name" value="Topic 1.a">
      <param name="Local" value="topic1a.htm">
    </OBJECT>
    <UL>
      <LI> <OBJECT type="text/sitemap">
        <param name="Name" value="Topic 1.a.i">
        <param name="Local" value="topic1ai.htm">
      </OBJECT>
      <LI> <OBJECT type="text/sitemap">
        <param name="Name" value="Topic 1.a.ii">
        <param name="Local" value="topic1aii.htm">
```

```
      </OBJECT>
    </UL>
    <LI> <OBJECT type="text/sitemap">
      <param name="Name" value="Topic 1.b">
      <param name="Local" value="topic1b.htm">
      <param name="ImageNumber" value="1">
    </OBJECT>
  </UL>
  <LI> <OBJECT type="text/sitemap">
    <param name="Name" value="Topic 2">
    <param name="Local" value="topic2.htm">
  </OBJECT>
  <UL>
    <LI> <OBJECT type="text/sitemap">
      <param name="Name" value="">
      <param name="Local" value="topic2.htm">
     </OBJECT>
    <LI> <OBJECT type="text/sitemap">
      <param name="Name" value="Topic 2.a">
      <param name="Local" value="topic2a.htm">
    </OBJECT>
    <LI> <OBJECT type="text/sitemap">
      <param name="Name" value="Topic 2.b">
      <param name="Local" value="topic2b.htm">
    </OBJECT>
  </UL>
  <LI> <OBJECT type="text/sitemap">
    <param name="Name" value="Topic 3">
    <param name="Local" value="topic3.htm">
    <param name="ImageNumber" value="1">
  </OBJECT>
</UL>
</BODY></HTML>
```

The HTML list elements specify the hierarchy of the items in the table of contents. The object elements specify the title, icon, location, and other information about the link. For example, the following contents item links to a company's New Products page and opens the page in a new window when the user clicks it:

```
<OBJECT type="text/sitemap">
  <param name="Name" value="New Products">
  <param name="Local" value="http://www.mycompany.com/newproducts.htm">
  <param name="WindowName" value="NewWindow">
  <param name="Comment" value="Sample of text/sitemap params">
  <param name="New" value="1">
  <param name="ImageNumber" value="7">
</OBJECT>
```

Adding Index Entries

The HTML Help Workshop can automatically build an index file from object elements entered in the topic files. Within a topic file, an index entry is created as an ActiveX object with a specific *classID*, as shown in the following HTML:

```
<Object type="application/x-oleobject"
  classid="clsid:1e2a7bd0-dab9-11d0-b93a- 00c04fc99f9e">
  <param name="Keyword" value="Index Item 1">
  <param name="Keyword" value="Index Item 1, Subitem a">
  <param name="Keyword" value="Index Item 1, Subitem b">
</OBJECT>
```

The preceding HTML creates three index entries for that link to the topic file, as shown in Figure 14-10.

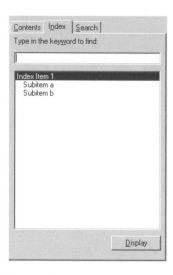

Figure 14-10   Automatic index entries at run time

The HTML Help Workshop does not automatically store index entries from topic files in the index file; however, you can add index entries to the index file to help organize or to supplement the automatic entries. The index file (.hhk) and the topic index entries are added together to create the index displayed in the compiled Help file. For example, the following index file (.hhk) is combined with the automatic entries to create the results shown in Figure 14-11:

```
<!DOCTYPE HTML PUBLIC "-//IETF//DTD HTML//EN">
<HTML>
<HEAD>
<meta name="GENERATOR" content="Microsoft&reg; HTML Help Workshop 4.1">
<!-- Sitemap 1.0 -->
</HEAD><BODY>
<UL>
```

```
<LI> <OBJECT type="text/sitemap">
  <param name="Name" value="Index Item 1">
  <param name="Name" value="Topic 1.b">
  <param name="Local" value="topic1b.htm">
</OBJECT>
<LI> <OBJECT type="text/sitemap">
  <param name="Name" value="Index Item 2">
  <param name="Name" value="Topic 2.a">
  <param name="Local" value="topic2a.htm">
</OBJECT>
</UL>
</BODY></HTML>
```

Figure 14-11   Combined index entries

Adding Cross-References

There are three ways to cross-reference Help topics within HTML Help:

- Use standard HTML hyperlinks to create a link from one Help topic to another. Hyperlinks allow one-to-one relationships.

- Use the Related Topics command to create a link from one topic to a list of other specific topics files.

- Use associative links (*ALinks*) to create links from one topic to a list of other topics based on keywords entered in those topic files.

Because you already know how to create hyperlinks (by now, you'd better), the following sections discuss how to add related topics and create associative links.

Adding Related Topics

You can add related topics as a cross-reference or a hyperlink.

- To add a related topics cross-reference to a Help topic, insert an HTML Help ActiveX control in the topic file. For example, the following object element displays a button that lists two related topics as pop-up menu choices:

```
<OBJECT id=hhctrl type="application/x-oleobject"
  classid="clsid:adb880a6-d8ff-11cf-9377-00aa003b7a11"
  codebase="hhctrl.ocx#Version=4,74,9273,0"
  width=100
  height=100>
  <PARAM name="Command" value="Related Topics, MENU">
  <PARAM name="Button" value="Text:Related Topics">
  <PARAM name="Item1" value="Topic 2;Topic2.htm">
  <PARAM name="Item2" value="Topic 3;Topic3.htm">
</OBJECT>
```

At run time, the preceding HTML appears as shown in Figure 14-12.

Figure 14-12   Related topics

- To display related topics as a hyperlink instead of as a button control, specify a *Text* parameter rather than a *Button* parameter in the object element. For example, the following HTML displays the preceding Related Topics as a hyperlink:

```
<OBJECT id= hhctrl type="application/x-oleobject"
  classid="clsid:adb880a6-d8ff-11cf-9377-00aa003b7a11"
  codebase="hhctrl.ocx#Version=4,74,9273,0"
  width=100
  height=100>
  <PARAM name="Command" value="Related Topics, MENU">
  <PARAM name="Text" value="Text:Related Topics">
  <PARAM name="Item1" value="Topic 2;Topic2.htm">
  <PARAM name="Item2" value="Topic 3;Topic3.htm">
</OBJECT>
```

Creating Associative Links

Associative links reference keywords rather than specific file names. For this reason, they are useful for cross-referencing between HTML Help files—you don't have to know how the topics within a compiled file are named, you just need to know which keywords were used. Associative links are useful within a single Help file as well—file names can change during development, and it's easier to maintain a keyword list than it is to update file names within cross-references.

There are two parts to an associative cross-reference:

- The keywords entered in the target topic files provide the destinations that cross-references link to.
- The link entered in the referencing topic file provides the source from which the cross- reference links.

To create associative link keywords, insert an object element in the target topic. For example, the following object element creates the associative link keyword *"Link1"*:

```
<Object type="application/x-oleobject"
  classid="clsid:1e2a7bd0-dab9-11d0-b93a- 00c04fc99f9e">
  <param name="ALink Name" value="Link1">
</OBJECT>
```

Associative links are very similar to keywords used in indexing HTML Help. However, they do not appear in the index. The reason for this is to allow cross-referencing and indexing to be maintained separately.

To create a link to topics with a specific keyword, insert an HTML Help control ActiveX object in the topic file making the cross-reference. For example, the following object element displays a list of cross-references in a pop-up menu when the user clicks the control:

```
<OBJECT id=hhctrl type="application/x-oleobject"
  classid="clsid:adb880a6-d8ff-11cf-9377-00aa003b7a11"
  codebase="hhctrl.ocx#Version=4,74,9273,0"
  width=100
  height=100>
  <PARAM name="Command" value="ALink, menu">
  <PARAM name="Button" value="Text:See Also">
  <PARAM name="Flags" value=",,1">
  <PARAM name="Item1" value="">
  <PARAM name="Item2" value="Link1">
</OBJECT>
```

At run time, the preceding HTML displays a list of topic titles that contain the associative link keyword *"Link1"*, as shown in Figure 14-13.

Figure 14-13   Associative links

To display associative links as a hyperlink rather than as a button control, omit the *Button* parameter from the object element, and call the object's Click event from the hyperlink. For example, the following HTML displays the links when the user clicks the See Also hyperlink:

```
<OBJECT id=hhctrl type="application/x-oleobject"
  classid="clsid:adb880a6-d8ff-11cf-9377-00aa003b7a11"
  codebase="hhctrl.ocx#Version=4,74,9273,0"
  width=100
  height=100>
  <PARAM name="Command" value="ALink, menu">
  <PARAM name="Flags" value=",,1">
  <PARAM name="Item1" value="">
  <PARAM name="Item2" value="Link1">
</OBJECT>

<a href="#" onclick="hhctrl.Click()">See also</a>
```

Enabling Searches

To enable full-text searches within a Help file, select Compile Full-Text Search Information from the Compiler tab of the Project Options dialog box.

When full-text searching is enabled, the HTML Help Workshop builds a concordance table of all the words in your topic files and includes that table in the compiled Help file. Because this table references all words in the topic files, it can become quite large. To help control the size of this table, you can omit words that are not useful for searching. For example, you might want to omit articles, conjunctions, personal pronouns, and numbers from full-text searching.

To omit words from full-text searching, follow these steps:

1. Create a text file listing the words to omit.
2. On the Project tab in HTML Help Workshop, click Change Project Options.
3. On the Files tab of the Options dialog box, type the file name of the list of words to omit in the Full Text Search Stop List File box.

When a user tries to search on a word that you include in the stop list, HTML Help displays a message box stating that the phrase can't be searched on.

Compiling and Previewing Help

To compile an HTML Help project, choose one of the following methods:

- On the Project tab of the HTML Help Workshop, click Save All Files And Compile.
- Use the HTML Help Compiler (hhc.exe) from the command line. For example, the following command line compiles the HelpSample.hhp Help project:

```
hhc.exe HelpSample.hhp
```

To preview a compiled HTML Help project, choose one of the following methods:

- Click the View Compiled File toolbar button, and then select the file name of the compiled file.
- Double-click the compiled Help file (.chm) in Windows.

Important   You can't recompile a Help file while the compiled Help file is open for viewing. You must close the compiled Help file before recompiling.

Lesson 3: Linking HTML Help to Web Forms

In this lesson, you'll learn how to display HTML Help from within a Web form. This lesson expands on the techniques introduced in Lesson 1 by showing the different ways you can display HTML Help, describing the differences between compiled and noncompiled Help, and explaining how to make Help respond to user actions in a Web application.

After this lesson, you will be able to

- Display compiled and noncompiled HTML Help using the HTML Help Viewer
- Display HTML Help in an ordinary browser window
- Cause different Help topics to be displayed, depending on which controls in a Web form have the focus

Estimated lesson time: 10 minutes

Displaying the HTML Help Viewer

As shown in Lesson 1, HTML Help is displayed in the HTML Help Viewer using the *showHelp* method. How you use *showHelp* depends on whether your HTML Help is compiled:

- Noncompiled Help can be displayed using the address of the Help topic via the Internet, as shown here:

  ```
  <a href="#" onclick="window.showHelp('Topic1.htm')">Help!</a>
  ```

- Compiled Help must be copied locally before you can display topics using *showHelp*, as shown here:

  ```
  <a href="#" onclick="window.showHelp('c:\\Help\\HelpSample.chm')">Help!</a>
  ```

The HTML Help Viewer is displayed differently depending on whether the Help file is compiled, as shown in Figure 14-14.

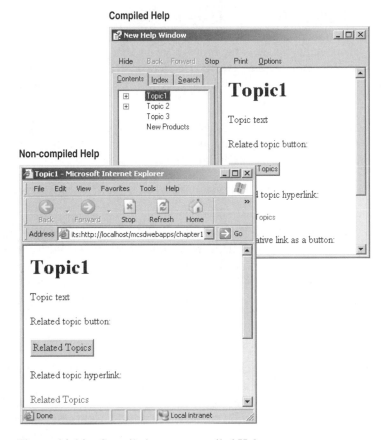

Figure 14-14   Compiled vs. noncompiled Help

As you can see in Figure 14-14, compiled Help displays Contents, Index, and Search features, while noncompiled Help displays only the requested Help topic file. By using compiled Help, you get the full features of the HTML Help system; however, the user must first download the compiled Help file.

To download a compiled Help file to the user's machine, create a hyperlink to the compiled Help file and provide the user with instructions on where to save the Help file. For example, the following HTML creates a hyperlink that downloads the HelpSample.chm file and instructs the user to save the file to a specific folder:

```
<a href="HelpSample.chm">Click here</a> to download the sample Help file and
then save the file to the C:\Help folder on your computer.</p>
```

When the user clicks the preceding hyperlink, the browser asks the user whether he or she wants to open or save the Help file. When the user saves the file to the specified directory, the *showHelp* method can display topics from the file.

Displaying HTML Help in the Browser

The *showHelp* method isn't the only way to display compiled Help files. You can also display topics in the browser using URLs from within the Help file itself. The browser can't display HTML Help's Contents, Index, or Search features, but it can open topics from the compiled file across the Internet, which is something *showHelp* can't do!

To display a compiled Help file in the browser, create a hyperlink using the topic file's URL within the compiled file. For example, the following hyperlink displays Topic1.htm in a new browser window:

```
<a href="ms-its:http://www.mycompany.com/Help/HelpSample.chm::/topic1.htm"
  target="HelpWin">Show Help</a>
```

The preceding hyperlink uses the *ms-its:* pluggable protocol and the Help path syntax to display a topic file from within a compiled Help file stored on the Web. The *ms-its:* protocol is provided in Internet Explorer versions 4.0 and later. The HTML Help path syntax has the form *compiledfile::/topicfile*, where *compiledfile* is the URL for the compiled Help file and *topicfile* is the HTML topic file name within the compiled Help file.

Displaying Context-Sensitive Help

If you're displaying compiled HTML Help in the HTML Help Viewer, you can use context IDs to identify topics within the Help file and associate those topics with tasks in your Web application. This type of Help is called **context-sensitive Help** because the topic displayed depends on the current context (or task) within the application.

Trying to display context-sensitive Help within a Web application presents a couple of challenges:

- Although you can capture the Help key (F1) using the onkeydown event and the *window.event.keyCode* property, you can't cancel the default action for F1 within Internet Explorer. The default action is to display Internet Explorer Help.
- The *contextID* argument for the *showHelp* method doesn't work from within a Web form or an HTML page.

To solve these problems, you must choose a mechanism other than F1 to display Help within your Web application, and you must use the HTML Help path syntax to display the appropriate Help topic. The following HTML uses the onfocus event to display different Help topics as the user moves between controls on a Web form:

VBScript

```
<HTML>
  <HEAD>
  <title>Context Help</title>
<script language="vbscript">
Dim LastTopic

Sub ShowContextHelp(Topic)
    If (document.all("chkHelp").checked And LastTopic <> Topic) Then
        ' Display Help for this context.
        window.showHelp "c:\help\HelpSample.chm::/" & Topic
        ' Store topic name.
        LastTopic = Topic
    End If
End Sub
</script>
  </HEAD>
  <body onfocus="ShowContextHelp('Topic1.htm')">
    <form id="WebForm2" method="post" runat="server">
      <H2>Context Sensitive Help</H2>
      <INPUT onfocus="ShowContextHelp('Topic2.htm')" type="text">
      <BR>
      <INPUT onfocus="ShowContextHelp('Topic3.htm')" type="button"
        value="Button">
      <BR>
      <INPUT id="chkHelp" type="checkbox" name="chkHelp">Show user
        assistance.
    </form>
  </body>
</HTML>
```

JScript

```
<HTML>
  <HEAD>
    <title>Context Help</title>
  <script language="jscript">
    var LastTopic;

    function ShowContextHelp(Topic)
    {
        if ((document.all("chkHelp").checked) && (LastTopic != Topic))
        {
            // Display Help for this context.
            window.showHelp("c:\\help\\HelpSample.chm::/" + Topic);
            // Store topic name.
            LastTopic = Topic;
        }
    }
  </script>
```

(continued)

```
        </HEAD>
        <body onfocus="ShowContextHelp('Topic1.htm')">
          <form id="WebForm2" method="post" runat="server">
            <h2>Context Sensitive Help</h2>
            <INPUT type="text" onfocus="ShowContextHelp('Topic2.htm')">
            <br>
            <INPUT type="button" value="Button"
              onfocus="ShowContextHelp('Topic3.htm')">
            <br>
            <INPUT id="chkHelp" type="checkbox">Show user assistance.
          </form>
        </body>
</HTML>
```

The CheckBox control allows the user to turn on context-sensitive Help. At run time, the *ShowContextHelp* procedure displays the Help topic for each item on the page when the focus changes to a new item, as shown in Figure 14-15.

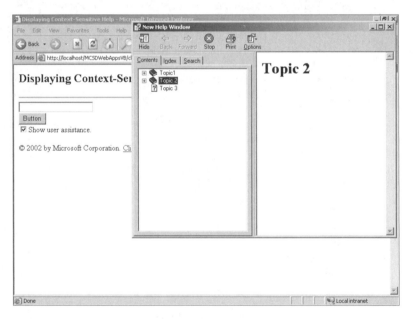

Figure 14-15   Context-sensitive Help

Summary

- You can provide user assistance within Web applications by using ToolTips, Web forms or HTML pages, or HTML Help.
- HTML Help provides built-in Contents, Index, and Search capabilities.
- Use the window object's *showHelp* method in client-side scripts to display the HTML Help Viewer.
- Use the HTML Help Workshop to create HTML Help projects and to compile HTML Help.
- Use the HTML Help ActiveX object to add index keywords, related topics, and associative links to Help topics.
- To display compiled Help files from a Web application, you must first download the file to the user's machine.

Lab: Building and Using an HTML Help File

In this lab, you'll create a compiled HTML Help file containing several topics and contents, Index, and Search features. You'll then link the Help file to a Web application.

Estimated lesson time: 30 minutes

Exercise 1: Create a Help Project

In this exercise, you'll use the skills you learned in Lesson 2 to create a new HTML Workshop Help project, create five Help topic files, and add those files to the Help project. To keep this exercise simple, the content of the Help topic files is minimal, although you can supply any additional content you feel like creating.

▶ **To create a new HTML Help project**

1. Start the HTML Help Workshop. Choose New from the File menu, select Project from the New dialog box, and then follow the New Project Wizard pages to create an empty project in a folder named HelpDemo on your computer.

2. Create five new HTML files titled Topic1 through Topic5. Add headings and save the files as shown in the following table:

Title	Heading	Save as
`<title>Topic1</title>`	`<h1>Topic1</h1>`	Topic1.htm
`<title>Topic2</title>`	`<h2>Topic2</h2>`	Topic2.htm
`<title>Topic3</title>`	`<h3>Topic3</h3>`	Topic3.htm
`<title>Topic4</title>`	`<h3>Topic4</h3>`	Topic4.htm
`<title>Topic5</title>`	`<h2>Topic5</h2>`	Topic5.htm

3. Add each of the topic files to the Help project. When complete, the HTML Help Workshop should appear as shown in Figure 14-16.

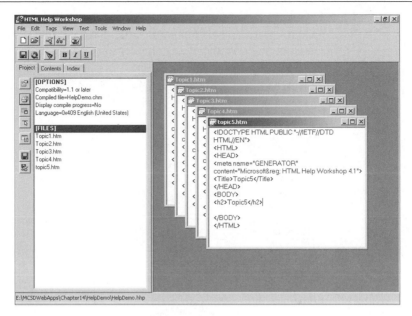

Figure 14-16   Creating a Help project

Exercise 2: Enable Contents, Index, and Search

In this exercise, you'll continue to use the skills you learned in Lesson 2 to automatically generate Contents, Index, and Search features when the Help project is compiled.

▶ **To enable Contents, Index, and Search features**

1. In the Help project's Options dialog box, click the Files tab, select check boxes to automatically create a contents file and to include keywords in the index, and then type names for the contents and index files, as shown in Figure 14-17.

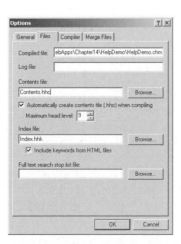

Figure 14-17   Creating contents and index files automatically

2. Click the New button on the HTML Help Workshop toolbar, and select Index file to create a new, empty index file. Save the file as Index.hhk. This file must exist in order for the Help compiler to build the index entries.

3. Click the Compiler tab, and select the Compile Full-Text Search Information check box, as shown in Figure 14-18. Click OK to close the dialog box.

Figure 14-18   Enabling full-text searches

4. On the Project tab of the HTML Help Workshop, click Save All Files And Compile. The Workshop builds the contents, index, and search information and then compiles the file and displays a log of the results, as shown in Figure 14-19.

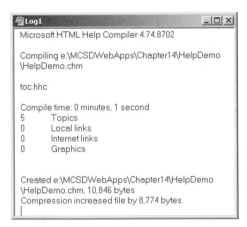

Figure 14-19   Compiler log

5. Click View Compiled File on the HTML Help Workshop toolbar, enter the location and name of the HelpDemo.chm file in the View Compiled File dialog box, and then click View. The Workshop displays the compiled Help file, as shown in Figure 14-20.

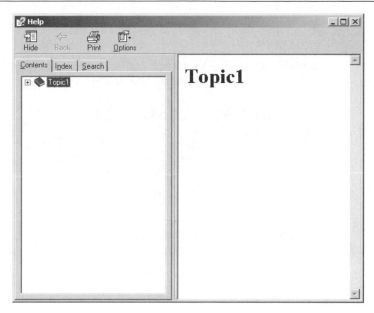

Figure 14-20   Compiled Help

Exercise 3: Add Index Keywords

In this exercise, you'll add indexed keywords to the Help topic files and then recompile the Help file to create automatic index entries.

▶ **To add index keywords to topic files**

1. In the HTML Help Workshop, open the Topic2.htm topic file, and insert a new line between the *<body> </body>* tags.

2. From the Edit menu, choose Compiler Information. The Workshop displays the Compiler Information dialog box.

3. Click Add, type "**Item1**" as the name of the index keyword to add to the topic, and then click OK. Click OK again to close the Compiler Information dialog box and add the index entry to Topic2.htm. The following HTML shows the generated text that's added to Topic2.htm:

```
<Object type="application/x-oleobject"
  classid="clsid:1e2a7bd0-dab9-11d0-b93a-00c04fc99f9e">
  <param name="Keyword" value="Item1">
</OBJECT>
```

4. Copy the preceding HTML to each of the other topic files. Add or change the keyword parameters to create different keywords. For example, the following HTML inserts three index keywords in a topic file:

```
<Object type="application/x-oleobject"
  classid="clsid:1e2a7bd0-dab9-11d0-b93a-00c04fc99f9e">
  <param name="Keyword" value="Item1">
```

```
<param name="Keyword" value="new">
<param name="Keyword" value="improved">
</OBJECT>
```

5. If the Help file from Exercise 2 is open, close it. Recompile the Help project, and view the resulting index. It should appear similar to Figure 14-21.

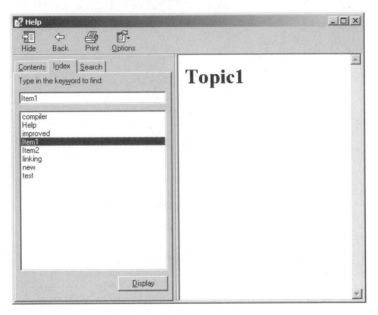

Figure 14-21   Keywords in the index

Exercise 4: Link Help to a Web Form

In this exercise, you'll use the skills you learned in Lesson 3 to link the compiled Help you created in the preceding exercises to a simple Web form.

▶ **To link compiled Help to a Web form**

1. Create a new, empty Web application project named vbHelpDemo or csHelpDemo.

2. Add the following HTML to Webform1 to instruct the user how to download the Help file and to provide a way to display Help on the Web form:

```
<p>To use Help with this Web form:</p>
<ol>
    <li><a href="HelpDemo.chm">Click here</a> to download Help.</li>
    <li>Save the file to the c:/help folder on your computer.</li>
    <li>Then use the buttons below to display Help topics.</li>
</ol>
<INPUT type="button" value="Show Help"
onclick="window.showHelp('c:\\help\\HelpDemo.chm')">
<br>
```

```
<INPUT type="button" value="Show Topic3"
onclick="window.showHelp('c:\\help\\HelpDemo.chm::/Topic3.htm')">
<br>
<INPUT type="button" value="Show Topic5"
onclick="window.showHelp('c:\\help\\HelpDemo.chm::/Topic5.htm')">
```

3. Copy the compiled Help file created in the preceding exercises to the Web application project directory.

4. Run the Web application. After you download the Help file, clicking the HTML Button controls display Help, as shown in Figure 14-22.

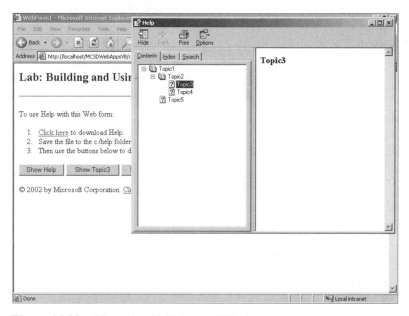

Figure 14-22   Displaying Help from a Web form

Review

The following questions are intended to reinforce key information presented in this chapter. If you are unable to answer a question, review the appropriate lesson and then try the question again. Answers to the questions can be found in the appendix.

1. Which HTML attribute does the server control's *ToolTip* property map to in the HTML rendered by ASP.NET?

2. How does displaying HTML Help using the *window* object's *showHelp* method differ from displaying HTML Help using a browser window?

3. How do you add index keywords to a Help topic?

C H A P T E R 1 5

Globalizing Web Applications

About This Chapter

Globalization is the process of creating an application that meets the needs of users from multiple cultures. This process involves more than just translating the user interface elements of an application into multiple languages—it also includes using the correct currency, date and time format, calendar, writing direction, sorting rules, and other issues. Accommodating these cultural differences in an application is called **localization**.

Fortunately, the Microsoft .NET Framework simplifies localization tasks substantially by making its formatting, date/time, sorting, and other classes culturally aware. Using classes from the *System.Globalization* namespace, you can set your application's current culture, and much of the work is done for you automatically!

In this chapter, you'll learn how to detect a user's culture and create appropriate responses, ranging from redirecting the user to a separate, localized Web application to handing cultural differences within code and displaying a localized user interface.

Before You Begin

To complete this chapter, you must:

- Be familiar with HTML
- Be comfortable creating Web forms in HTML mode

Lesson 1: Choosing an Approach

Before you begin the process of localization, you need to understand the advantages and disadvantages of the different approaches to globalizing Web applications. In this lesson, you'll learn about three different ways to structure your application for globalization. These approaches are organized from simplest to most complex. The last approach is covered in more detail in Lesson 2.

After this lesson, you will be able to

- Choose a globalization approach that best meets your needs
- Detect and respond to a user's culture
- Create a culture-specific Web application using settings in Web.config
- Change the culture used within your application to evaluate dates, format currencies, and handle other culture-dependent tasks
- Detect the culture currently in use by the application
- Explain the difference between the *CurrentCulture* and *CurrentUICulture* properties

Estimated lesson time: 30 minutes

Ways to Globalize Web Applications

There are several different approaches to creating Web applications that support multiple cultures. Each approach is based on the globalization tools that the .NET Framework provides. Choose a single approach or a combination of approaches based on your applications needs, as described in Table 15-1.

All three of the approaches depend on detecting the user's culture at run time and then forming a response based on that information. The following sections show in greater detail how to detect the user's culture and respond by using each of these approaches. These sections also provide more detail on the relative advantages of each approach.

Table 15-1   Globalization Approaches

Approach	Description	Best for
Detect and redirect	Create a separate Web application for each supported culture, and then detect the user's culture and redirect the request to the appropriate application.	Applications with lots of text content that requires translation and few executable components.
Run-time adjustment	Create a single Web application that detects the user's culture and adjusts output at run time using format specifiers and other tools.	Simple applications that present limited amounts of content.
Satellite assemblies	Create a single Web application that stores culture-dependent strings in resource files that are compiled into satellite assemblies. At run time, detect the user's culture and load strings from the appropriate assembly.	Applications that generate content at run time or that have large executable components.

Detecting the User's Culture

The .NET Framework provides components for supporting multiple cultures and language in the *System.Globalization* namespace. The *CultureInfo*, *Calendar*, and comparison classes that you use throughout this chapter are all part of that namespace. Use the following line to import that namespace so that you can use its classes without qualifying the references:

Visual Basic .NET

```
Imports System.Globalization
```

Visual C#

```
using System.Globalization;
```

Microsoft ASP.NET uses the *Request* object's *UserLanguages* property to return a list of the user's language preferences. The first element of the array returned by *UserLanguages* is the user's current language. You can use that value to create an instance of the *CultureInfo* class representing the user's current culture.

To get the user's culture at run time, follow these steps:

1. Get the *Request* object's *UserLanguages* property.

2. Use the returned value with the *CultureInfo* class to create an object representing the user's current culture.

For example, the following code gets the user's culture and displays the English name and the abbreviated name of the culture in a label the first time the page is displayed:

Visual Basic .NET

```
Private Sub Page_Load(ByVal sender As System.Object, _
   ByVal e As System.EventArgs) Handles MyBase.Load
   ' Run the first time the page is displayed
   If Not IsPostBack Then
      Dim sLang As String
      ' Get the user's preferred language.
      sLang = Request.UserLanguages(0)
      ' Create a CultureInfo object from it.
      Dim CurrentCulture As New CultureInfo(sLang)
      lblCulture.Text = CurrentCulture.EnglishName & ": " & _
         CurrentCulture.Name
   End If
End Sub
```

Visual C#

```
private void Page_Load(object sender, System.EventArgs e)
{
    // Run the first time the page is displayed
    if (!IsPostBack)
    {
        // Get the user's preferred language.
        string sLang = Request.UserLanguages[0];
        // Create a CultureInfo object from it.
        CultureInfo CurrentCulture = new CultureInfo(sLang);
        lblCulture.Text = CurrentCulture.EnglishName + ": " +
            CurrentCulture.Name;
    }
}
```

Tip   The *CultureInfo* class's *Name* property and the *Request* object's *UserLanguages* array values use different capitalization schemes. If you're comparing the two values, be sure to convert the *Name* property to lowercase.

Redirecting to Culture-Specific Web Applications

Conceptually, redirecting is the simplest way of dealing with multiple cultures. When a user requests the default page for your application, you detect his or her culture and then redirect the response to the appropriate Web application, as shown in Figure 15-1.

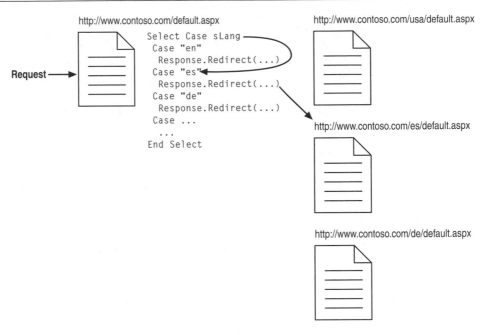

Figure 15-1   Detect and redirect

This approach has some advantages in addition to conceptual simplicity:

- Content is maintained separately, so this approach allows the different applications to present very different information, if needed.
- Users can be automatically directed to sites that are likely to be geographically close, and so can better meet their needs.
- Content files (Web forms and HTML pages, for example) can be authored in the appropriate natural language without the complexity of including resource strings.

Maintaining content separately is best suited for Web applications that present large amounts of content that must be translated or otherwise changed for other cultures. Using this approach requires that the executable portion of the Web application be compiled and deployed separately to each culture-specific Web site. This requires more effort to maintain consistency and to debug problems across Web sites.

Redirecting Based on Primary Language

Both the *Request* object's *UserLanguages* array and the *CultureInfo* class's *Name* property return culture information in two parts: the first two letters are the language code; the last two letters contain a region code. For example, English US (en-US) and English United Kingdom (en-GB) both use English, but they display different currencies and date order.

To redirect requests based on language alone, follow these steps:

1. Get the user's preferred language or *CurrentCulture*, as shown previously.
2. Get the first two letters of the returned value.
3. Compare those letters to the list of language codes.

For example, the following code detects the user's language and then redirects the user to one of several different language-specific Web sites:

Visual Basic .NET

```vbnet
Private Sub Page_Load(ByVal sender As System.Object, _
    ByVal e As System.EventArgs) Handles MyBase.Load
    Dim sLang As String
    ' Get the user's preferred language.
    sLang = Request.UserLanguages(0)
    ' Get the first two characters of language.
    sLang = sLang.Substring(0, 2)
    ' Redirect user based on his/her culture.
    Select Case sLang
        Case "en"
            ' Use US site.
            Response.Redirect("http://www.contoso.com/usa")
        Case "es"
            ' Use Spanish site.
            Response.Redirect("http://www.contoso.com/es")
        Case "de"
            ' Use German site.
            Response.Redirect("http://www.contoso.com/de")
        Case "zh"
            ' Use Chinese site.
            Response.Redirect("http://www.contoso.com/zh")
        Case Else
            ' Use US site.
            Response.Redirect("http://www.contoso.com/usa")
    End Select
End Sub
```

Visual C#

```csharp
private void Page_Load(object sender, System.EventArgs e)
{
    // Get the user's preferred language.
    string sLang = Request.UserLanguages[0];
    // Get the first two characters of language.
    sLang = sLang.Substring(0, 2);
    // Redirect user based on his/her culture.
    switch (sLang)
    {
        case "en":
            // Use US site.
```

```
            Response.Redirect("http://www.contoso.com/usa");
            break;
        case "es":
            // Use Spanish site.
            Response.Redirect("http://www.contoso.com/es");
            break;
        case "de":
            // Use German site.
            Response.Redirect("http://www.contoso.com/de");
            break;
        case "zh":
            // Use Chinese site.
            Response.Redirect("http://www.contoso.com/zh");
            break;
        default:
            // Use US site.
            Response.Redirect("http://www.contoso.com/usa");
            break;
        }
    }
}
```

See the *"CultureInfo* Class" topic in the Microsoft Visual Studio .NET online Help for a listing of the language and culture codes.

Setting Culture in Web.config

Use the Web.config file's *globalization* element to create a culture-specific Web application. The *culture* attribute of the *globalization* element specifies how the Web application deals with various culture-dependent issues, such as dates, currency, and number formatting.

Web.config *globalization* settings in subordinate folders override the *globalization* settings in the application's root Web.config file. You can store content for various cultures in subfolders within your application, add Web.config files with the *globalization* settings for each culture, then direct users to the appropriate folder based on the user's *CurrentCulture*. For example, the following Web.config entry handles the Web application's requests and responses using the Arabic (Saudi Arabia) [ar-SA] culture:

```
<globalization requestEncoding="utf-8" responseEncoding="utf-8"
  culture="ar-SA" />
```

At run time, the Web application displays dates, currency, and number formats according to the *culture* attribute setting in the Web.config's *globalization* element, as shown in Figure 15-2.

Figure 15-2   A culture-specific response

In Figure 15-2, the dates, times, numbers, and currencies are displayed using the Arabic (Saudi Arabia) settings. However, the entire page is not displayed in right-to-left formatting, as you might expect for Arabic. To display the page correctly, you must set the HTML *dir* attribute for the page's *body* element, as shown here:

```
<body dir="rtl">
```

You can use the *dir* attribute individually in panels, text boxes, or other controls as well. Setting the *dir* attribute on the *body* element applies right-to-left formatting to the entire page, as shown in Figure 15-3.

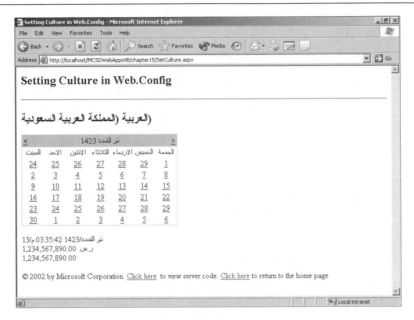

Figure 15-3   Right-to-left formatting

Adjusting to Current Culture at Run Time

By default, Web applications run on the server using a neutral culture. **Neutral cultures** represent general languages, such as English or Spanish, rather than a specific language and region. When you set the *culture* attribute for a Web application in Web.config, ASP.NET assigns that culture to all the threads running for that Web application. **Threads** are the basic unit to which the server allocates processor time—ASP.NET maintains multiple threads for a Web application within the aspnet_wp.exe worker process.

Using Web.config to set the culture creates a static association between the application and a specific culture. Alternatively, you can set the culture dynamically at run time using the *Thread* class's *CurrentCulture* property, as shown here:

Visual Basic .NET

```
Imports System.Globalization
Imports System.Threading

Private Sub Page_Load(ByVal sender As System.Object, _
    ByVal e As System.EventArgs) Handles MyBase.Load
    Dim sLang As String
    ' Get the user's preferred language.
    sLang = Request.UserLanguages(0)
    ' Set the thread's culture to match the user culture.
    Thread.CurrentThread.CurrentCulture = New CultureInfo(sLang)
End Sub
```

Visual C#

```
using System.Globalization;
using System.Threading;

private void Page_Load(object sender, System.EventArgs e)
{
    // Get the user's preferred language.
    sLang = Request.UserLanguages[0];
    // Set the thread's culture to match the user culture.
    Thread.CurrentThread.CurrentCulture = new CultureInfo(sLang);
}
```

The preceding code detects the user's culture and then sets the culture of the current thread to match. ASP.NET will then format date, currency, and numeric strings using the user's culture.

Setting the culture dynamically at the thread level has the following advantages over creating separate Web applications for each culture:

- All cultures share the same application code, so the application doesn't have to be compiled and deployed for each culture.
- The application resides at a single Web address—you don't need to redirect users to other Web applications.
- The user can choose from a full array of available cultures.

Setting the culture dynamically is best suited for simple Web applications that don't contain large amounts of text that must be translated into different languages. To provide large amounts of translated content through a single Web application, use the technique described in the section "Using Satellite Assemblies," later in the chapter.

Setting the Current Culture

The following code illustrates the main advantages of setting the culture dynamically at the thread level. The first time the page loads, the code builds a list of all available cultures and stores them in a drop-down list box. When the user chooses a culture from the drop-down list, the code assigns that culture to the current thread, and ASP.NET displays the Web form using the selected culture.

Visual Basic .NET

```
Imports System.Globalization
Imports System.Threading

Private Sub Page_Load(ByVal sender As System.Object, _
    ByVal e As System.EventArgs) Handles MyBase.Load
    ' Add cultures to drop-down
    ' list box the first time the page is displayed.
    If Not IsPostBack Then
```

```vbnet
        ' Create an array of specific cultures.
        Dim arrCultures() As CultureInfo = _
            CultureInfo.GetCultures(CultureTypes.SpecificCultures)
        Dim item As CultureInfo
        ' For each specific culture
        For Each item In arrCultures
            ' Add the name of the culture as an item in the list box.
            drpCulture.Items.Add(New ListItem(item.EnglishName, item.Name))
            ' If the item is the thread's current culture, select it.
            If item.Name = Thread.CurrentThread.CurrentCulture.Name Then
                ' Select this list item
                drpCulture.SelectedIndex = drpCulture.Items.Count - 1
            End If
        Next
    End If
End Sub

Private Sub drpCulture_SelectedIndexChanged(ByVal sender As System.Object, _
    ByVal e As System.EventArgs) Handles drpCulture.SelectedIndexChanged
    ' Change the culture of the current thread to match selection.
    Thread.CurrentThread.CurrentCulture = New _
        CultureInfo(drpCulture.SelectedItem.Value)
    ' Get the culture for the selected item.
    Dim SelectedCulture As New CultureInfo(drpCulture.SelectedItem.Value)
End Sub

Private Sub Page_PreRender(ByVal sender As Object, _
    ByVal e As System.EventArgs) Handles MyBase.PreRender
    ' Display the culture's native name in the heading.
    head1.InnerHtml = Thread.CurrentThread.CurrentCulture.NativeName
    ' Display Date, Currency, and Numeric strings formatted for the culture.
    Label1.Text = DateTime.Now.ToString("F")
    Label2.Text = 1234567890.ToString("C")
    Label3.Text = 1234567890.ToString("N")
End Sub
```

Visual C#

```csharp
using System.Globalization;
using System.Threading;

private void Page_Load(object sender, System.EventArgs e)
{
    // Add cultures to drop-down
    // list box the first time the page is displayed.
    if (!IsPostBack)
    {
        // Create an array of specific cultures.
        CultureInfo[] arrCultures =
            CultureInfo.GetCultures(CultureTypes.SpecificCultures);
        // For each specific culture
```

(continued)

```csharp
        foreach (CultureInfo item in arrCultures)
        {
            // Add the name of the culture as an item in the list box.
            drpCulture.Items.Add(new ListItem(item.EnglishName,
                item.Name));
            // If the item is the thread's current culture, select it.
            if (item.Name == Thread.CurrentThread.CurrentCulture.Name)
                // Select this list item
                drpCulture.SelectedIndex = drpCulture.Items.Count - 1;
        }
    }
}

private void drpCulture_SelectedIndexChanged(object sender,
    System.EventArgs e)
{
    // Change the culture of the current thread to match selection.
    Thread.CurrentThread.CurrentCulture = new
        CultureInfo(drpCulture.SelectedItem.Value);
    // Get the culture for the selected item.
    CultureInfo SelectedCulture = new
        CultureInfo(drpCulture.SelectedItem.Value);
}

private void Page_PreRender(object sender, System.EventArgs e)
{
    // Display the culture's native name in the heading.
    head1.InnerHtml = Thread.CurrentThread.CurrentCulture.NativeName;
    // Display Date, Currency, and Numeric strings formatted for the culture.
    Label1.Text = DateTime.Now.ToString("F");
    Label2.Text = 1234567890.ToString("C");
    Label3.Text = 1234567890.ToString("N");
}
```

The preceding code sets the heading and label text in the *PreRender* event so that the culture change takes place before the text is stored in those controls. The *ToString* method uses format specifiers to format each string according to the current culture. For more information about format specifiers, see the "Formatting Types" topic in the Visual Studio .NET online Help. Figure 15-4 shows the preceding code in action on a Web form.

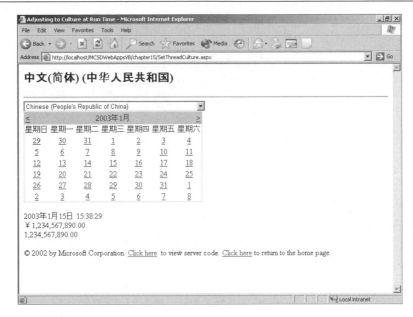

Figure 15-4   Setting the culture at the thread level

When the user selects a new culture from the drop-down list in Figure 15-4, the heading, calendar, date, currency, and numeric strings are translated automatically.

Responding to the Thread's Culture

You can also get the culture that a Web application is running under by using the thread's *CurrentCulture* property. For example, the following code displays a panel on a Web form using right-to-left formatting if the current culture is Arabic or Hebrew:

Visual Basic .NET

```
Private Sub Page_Load(ByVal sender As System.Object, _
    ByVal e As System.EventArgs) Handles MyBase.Load
    ' Get culture of current thread.
    Dim CurrentCulture As CultureInfo = Thread.CurrentThread.CurrentCulture
    ' Get the primary language.
    Dim sLang As String = CurrentCulture.Name.Substring(0, 2)
    ' If it's Arabic or Hebrew, display right-to-left.
    If sLang = "ar" or sLang = "he" Then
        panel1.Attributes.Add("dir", "rtl")
    End If
End Sub
```

Visual C#

```csharp
private void Page_Load(object sender, System.EventArgs e)
{
    // Get culture of current thread.
    CultureInfo CurrentCulture = Thread.CurrentThread.CurrentCulture;
    // If culture is Arabic or Hebrew, use right-to-left layout.
    string sLang  = CurrentCulture.Name.Substring(0, 2);
    if ((sLang == "ar") ||(sLang == "he"))
    {
        Panel1.Attributes.Add("dir", "rtl");
    }
}
```

Using Satellite Assemblies

The preceding section showed you how to handle cultural differences within a single Web application, but it omitted one important detail: how do you handle translated content? That's a job for satellite assemblies.

Satellite assemblies allow you to store the translated strings for each culture in a separate, resource-only assembly file that you can load automatically based on the setting of the *CurrentUICulture* property. Using satellite assemblies provides the same advantages as adjusting to the culture at run time, plus satellite assemblies simplify displaying content from multiple translated sources. The next lesson describes how to create and use satellite assemblies in detail.

Lesson 2: Creating and Using Satellite Assemblies

Satellite assemblies are assembly files (.dll) that contain localized resources for an application. Each satellite assembly file contains the resources for one culture. An application can have many satellite assemblies, depending on how many cultures the application supports.

In this lesson, you'll learn how to prepare a Web application to use satellite assemblies, how to store localized user-interface elements within a satellite assembly, and how to load and display elements from the satellite assembly at run time.

After this lesson, you will be able to

■ Create localized resources and add them to satellite assemblies

■ Enable HTML elements within your application to display localized strings from satellite assemblies

■ Load resources into a *ResourceManager* object

■ Understand how ASP.NET selects the resources to load based on the *CurrentUICulture* property

■ Get strings from the *ResourceManager* object and display them in the user interface

Estimated lesson time: 30 minutes

How Satellite Assemblies Work

Web application projects use satellite assemblies to store the translated strings, graphics, and other culture-dependent aspects of an application's user interface. To create the assemblies themselves, you use the Resource Manager. At run time, the Web application loads the translated strings into the Web form based on the current thread's *CurrentUICulture* property, as shown in Figure 15-5.

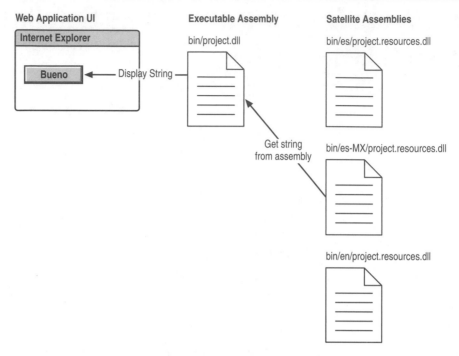

Figure 15-5   Satellite assemblies at work

To use satellite assemblies, follow these steps:

1. Set the *id* and *runat* attributes for all of the user-interface elements of your application that require translation. Server controls have these attributes by default, but you will need to add them to HTML elements such as *heading*, *paragraph*, and *span* so that you can load translated strings into those elements.

2. Create a fallback resource file containing the default strings to display in the user interface if the user's culture is not specified or not recognized. Name the fallback resource file *filename*.resx—for example, strings.resx.

3. Create resource files containing the translated strings to display for each general language that your Web application supports. Name the translated resource files *filename.languagecode*.resx—for example, strings.es.resx.

4. Optionally, create resource files containing the translated strings to display for each specific culture that your Web application supports. Name the resource file *filename.languagecode-regioncode*.resx—for example, strings.ex-MX.resx.

5. Write code to load the resources for the Web form using the *ResourceManager* class.

6. Write code to detect the user's culture and set the *Thread* class's *CurrentCulture* and *CurrentUICulture* properties to match. ASP.NET uses the *CurrentCulture* property to determine formatting for dates, currency, and numbers;

ASP.NET uses the *CurrentUICulture* property to determine which satellite assembly is used when loading translated strings.

7. Write code to get strings from the resource files and display them in elements on the Web form.

The following sections describe these steps in more detail.

Enabling HTML Elements for Resources

Resources from satellite assemblies are loaded into Web form elements on the server side. Therefore, you need to make sure that all the elements on your Web form have *id* and *runat* attributes that make them available from server-side code. By default, ASP.NET server controls have these elements; however, HMTL elements do not.

For example, the following HTML shows a simple Web form with a heading, some text, and some controls:

```
<HTML>
  <HEAD>
    <title>Using Satellite Assemblies</title>   </HEAD>
  <body>
    <form id="Form1" method="post" runat="server">
      <h1>Sample heading</h1>
      <p>Some introductory text.</p>
      <span>Enter a number: </span>
      <asp:TextBox ID="txtCurrency" Runat="server" />
      <br>
      <span>Amount in local currency: </span>
      <asp:Label ID="lblCurrency" Runat="server" />
      <br>
      <br>
      <asp:Button ID="butOK" Text="OK" Runat="server" />
      <input type="button" onclick="txtCurrencty.value=''"
        value="Cancel">
    </form>
  </body>
</HTML>
```

To enable the preceding Web form for using resources, you need to change the HTML elements, as shown in the following code in boldface:

```
<%@ Page Language="vb" AutoEventWireup="false" Codebehind="Satellite.aspx.vb"
Inherits="vbSatelliteSnippet.WebForm1"%>
<!DOCTYPE HTML PUBLIC "-//W3C//DTD HTML 4.0 Transitional//EN">
<HTML>
  <HEAD>
    <title>Using Satellite Assemblies</title>   </HEAD>
  <body>
```

(continued)

```
<form id="Form1" method="post" runat="server">
  <h1 id="head1" runat="server">Sample heading</h1>
  <p id="p1" runat="server">Some introductory text.</p>
  <span id="sp1" runat="server">Enter a number: </span>
  <asp:TextBox ID="txtCurrency" Runat="server" />
  <br>
  <span id="sp2" runat="server">Amount in local currency: </span>
  <asp:Label ID="lblCurrency" Runat="server" />
  <br>
  <br>
  <asp:Button ID="butOK" Text="OK" Runat="server" />
  <input id="butCancel" runat="server" type="button"
    onclick="txtCurrencty.value=''" value="Cancel">
  </form>
  </body>
</HTML>
```

The preceding *id* and *runat* attributes cause Visual Studio .NET to handle those elements as server controls. When you switch from HTML view to Design view, Visual Studio .NET adds the following declarations to the Web form's code file:

Visual Basic .NET

```
Protected WithEvents head1 As System.Web.UI.HtmlControls.HtmlGenericControl
Protected WithEvents p1 As System.Web.UI.HtmlControls.HtmlGenericControl
Protected WithEvents sp1 As System.Web.UI.HtmlControls.HtmlGenericControl
Protected WithEvents sp2 As System.Web.UI.HtmlControls.HtmlGenericControl
Protected WithEvents butCancel As System.Web.UI.HtmlControls.HtmlInputButton
```

Visual C#

```
protected System.Web.UI.HtmlControls.HtmlGenericControl head1;
protected System.Web.UI.HtmlControls.HtmlGenericControl p1;
protected System.Web.UI.HtmlControls.HtmlGenericControl sp1;
protected System.Web.UI.HtmlControls.HtmlGenericControl sp2;
protected System.Web.UI.HtmlControls.HtmlInputButton butCancel;
```

These declarations allow you to set the value and *innerHTML* attributes of these HTML elements at run time.

Creating Resource Files

You can create three types of resource files when using satellite assemblies to provide translated strings within a Web application, as described in Table 15-2.

Table 15.2.   Resource File Types for Satellite Assemblies

Type	Named	Compiled into	Provides
Fallback	*file*.resx—for example, strings.resx	The executable assembly	User-interface strings when culture is not specified or not recognized by the Web application
Language-specific	*file.langcode*.resx—for example, strings.es.resx	Resource-only assembly stored in a subfolder of the bin folder identified by language code—for example, bin\es\	Translated strings for cultures using a particular language
Culture-specific	*file.langcode-regioncode*.resx—for example, strings.es-MX.resx	Resource-only assembly stored in a subfolder of the bin folder identified by the language and region code—for example, bin\es-MX\	Translated strings for cultures using a specific dialect of a language

The culture codes used to identify language and culture-specific resource files are listed in the "*CultureInfo* Class" online Help topic. Those codes are also used in the *Name* property of the *CultureInfo* class and the *Request* object's *UserLanguages* array.

To add resource files to a Web application project in Visual Studio .NET, follow these steps:

1. From the Project menu, choose Add New Item, and then select Assembly Resource File from the Templates list.

2. Type the name of the resource file you want to create, and then click Open. Visual Studio .NET creates a new resource file and adds it to the project, as shown in Figure 15-6.

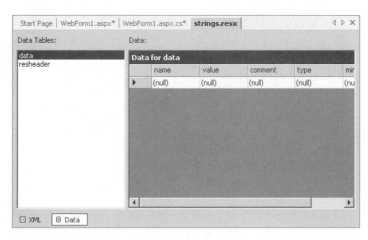

Figure 15-6   A new resource file

To enter translated strings for the Web form's user interface into a resource file, follow these steps:

1. Type an identifier for the Web form element in the Name field of the resource file. The identifier must be unique within the scope of the application, so a convention such as *formname.elementname* works well—for example, webform1.butOK.

2. Type the translated string for that element in the Value field of the resource file.

Figure 15-7 shows translated strings entered for the server control and HTML elements created in the preceding section.

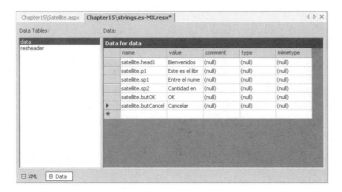

Figure 15-7   Translated strings in a resource file

Tip   The Name field within a resource file is case sensitive by default. To avoid errors locating resources at run time, use a consistent capitalization scheme when naming resource elements.

Loading Resource Files

The .NET Framework provides resource management as part of the *System.Resources* namespace. To use classes from that namespace without fully qualifying their names, include an *Imports/using* statement at the beginning of your Web form, as shown here:

Visual Basic .NET

```
Imports System.Resources
```

Visual C#

```
using System.Resources;
```

To load resources into a Web form, create an instance of the *ResourceManager* class. For example, the following line loads the resource file for the Web application:

Visual Basic .NET

```
' Load resources.
Protected gStrings As New ResourceManager("MCSDWebAppsVB.strings", _
    GetType(Satellite).Assembly)
```

Visual C#

```
// Load resources.
protected ResourceManager gStrings = new
    ResourceManager("MCSDWebAppsCS.strings", typeof(Satellite).Assembly);
```

The preceding example loads the resources stored in the Strings assembly file associated with the Satellite Web form's parent assembly and stores the returned object in the *gStrings* variable. The arguments for the *ResourceManager* class's constructor are described in Table 15-3.

Table 15-3   *ResourceManager* **Arguments**

Argument	Description
baseName	The namespace of the resource within the project. For Visual Basic .NET projects, this is *projectname.resourcebasename*. For Visual C# projects, this is *rootnamespace.resourcebasename*. The *resourcebasename* part omits culture codes, so *MyProj.strings* includes Strings.resx, Strings.en.resx, Strings.es.rex, and so on.
assembly	The object representing the current executable assembly. Use the *Type* class's *Assembly* property to get the value to pass to this argument—for example, GetType("Webform1").Assembly.

Getting and Setting User-Interface Culture

As shown in Lesson 1, you get the user's culture from the *Request* object's *UserLanguages* array, and you set the current thread's culture using the *Thread* class's *CurrentCulture* property. When working with satellite assemblies, you need to add one more step: setting the *CurrentUICulture* property. This property specifies which satellite assembly is used when loading strings from the *ResourceManager* object.

To set the current user-interface culture for a thread, set the *Thread* object's *CurrentUICulture* property. For example, the following code gets the user's preferred language and then sets both the culture and user-interface culture for the current thread:

Visual Basic .NET

```
Private Sub Page_Load(ByVal sender As System.Object, _
    ByVal e As System.EventArgs) Handles MyBase.Load
    If Not IsPostBack Then
        ' Get the user's perferred language.
        Dim sLang As String = Request.UserLanguages(0)
```

(continued)

```
                      ' Set the thread's culture for formatting, comparisons, etc.
                      Thread.CurrentThread.CurrentCulture = _
                          CultureInfo.CreateSpecificCulture(slang)
                      ' Set the thread's UICulture to load resources
                      ' from satellite assembly.
                      Thread.CurrentThread.CurrentUICulture = New CultureInfo(slang)
              End If
      End Sub
```

Visual C#

```csharp
private void Page_Load(object sender, System.EventArgs e)
{
    if (!IsPostBack)
    {
        // Get the user's perferred language.
        string sLang = Request.UserLanguages[0];
        // Set the thread's culture for formatting, comparisons, etc.
        Thread.CurrentThread.CurrentCulture =
            CultureInfo.CreateSpecificCulture(sLang);
        // Set the thread's UICulture to load resources
        // from satellite assembly.
        Thread.CurrentThread.CurrentUICulture = new CultureInfo(sLang);
    }
}
```

In the preceding code, the *CurrentCulture* and *CurrentUICulture* properties are set differently. *CurrentCulture* uses the *CreateSpecificCulture* method to ensure that the returned object is not a neutral culture. Neutral cultures represent general languages rather than a specific language and region. The *CurrentCulture* property can't be set to a neutral culture because it uses region information to format currencies, among other things.

When you have set the thread's *CurrentUICulture*, ASP.NET automatically selects the resources that match, in the following order:

1. If a satellite assembly is found with an exactly matching culture, the resources from that assembly are used.
2. If a satellite assembly is found with a neutral culture that matches the *CurrentUICulture*, resources from that assembly are used.
3. If a match is not found for the *CurrentUICulture*, the fallback resources stored in the executable assembly are used.

Displaying Resource Strings

After you have completed all of the preceding tasks, displaying strings from a resource file on the Web form is straightforward.

To display strings from the resource file on a Web form, use the *ResourceManager* object's *GetString* method to retrieve strings and assign them to the *Text*, *value*, or *innerHTML* properties of the Web form's elements.

The following code brings the preceding steps together to load a resource file, get the user's culture, set the current thread's culture, and display strings from the resource file in the Web form server control and HTML elements:

Visual Basic .NET

```
Imports System.Resources
Imports System.Globalization
Imports System.Threading

' Load resources.
Protected gStrings As New ResourceManager("MCSDWebAppsVB.strings", _
    GetType(Satellite).Assembly)

Private Sub Page_Load(ByVal sender As System.Object, _
    ByVal e As System.EventArgs) Handles MyBase.Load
    If Not IsPostBack Then
        ' Get the user's preferred language.
        Dim sLang As String = Request.UserLanguages(0)
        ' Set the thread's culture for formatting, comparisons, etc.
        Thread.CurrentThread.CurrentCulture = _
            CultureInfo.CreateSpecificCulture(sLang)
        ' Set the thread's UICulture to load resources from
        ' satellite assembly.
        Thread.CurrentThread.CurrentUICulture = New CultureInfo(sLang)
        ' Get strings from resource file.
        head1.InnerHtml = gStrings.GetString("satellite.head1")
        p1.InnerHtml = gStrings.GetString("satellite.p1")
        sp1.InnerHtml = gStrings.GetString("satellite.sp1")
        sp2.InnerHtml = gStrings.GetString("satellite.sp2")
        butOK.Text = gStrings.GetString("satellite.butOK")
        butCancel.Value = gStrings.GetString("satellite.butCancel")
    End If
End Sub
```

Visual C#

```
using System.Globalization;
using System.Threading;
using System.Resources;

// Load resources.
protected ResourceManager gStrings = new ResourceManager
 "MCSDWebAppsCS.strings",
    typeof(Satellite).Assembly);
```

(continued)

```
private void Page_Load(object sender, System.EventArgs e)
{
    if (!IsPostBack)
    {
        // Get the user's perferred language.
        string sLang = Request.UserLanguages[0];
        // Set the thread's culture for formatting, comparisons, etc.
        Thread.CurrentThread.CurrentCulture =
            CultureInfo.CreateSpecificCulture(sLang);
        // Set the thread's UICulture to load resources
        // from satellite assembly.
        Thread.CurrentThread.CurrentUICulture = new CultureInfo(sLang);
        // Get strings from resource file.
        head1.InnerHtml = gStrings.GetString("satellite.head1");
        p1.InnerHtml = gStrings.GetString("satellite.p1");
        sp1.InnerHtml = gStrings.GetString("satellite.sp1");
        sp2.InnerHtml = gStrings.GetString("satellite.sp2");
        butOK.Text = gStrings.GetString("satellite.butOK");
        butCancel.Value = gStrings.GetString("satellite.butCancel");
    }
}
```

At run time, the preceding code displays the translated strings from the resource files based on the user's preferred language, as shown in Figure 15-8.

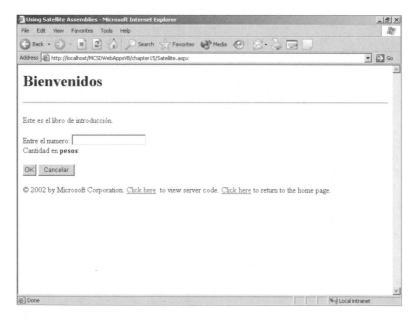

Figure 15-8   Displaying strings from a resource file

Lesson 3: Globalization Issues

The .NET Framework handles many globalization issues automatically, based on the setting in the *CurrentCulture* property. However, globalization issues also affect some basic programming techniques. In this lesson, you'll learn about some general programming issues you need to think about when developing global applications. You'll also learn about issues that arise when storing and presenting the extended character sets used by some languages.

After this lesson, you will be able to

- Discuss some of the general programming issues affected by globalization
- Save Web forms containing special characters from other languages
- Use Web forms stored in different character encodings
- Detect the user's requested character encoding
- Create responses using different character encodings

Estimated lesson time: 10 minutes

General Programming Issues

The "Best Practices for Developing World-Ready Applications" topic in the Visual Studio .NET online Help provides a helpful list of items that you should consider when developing Web applications that will be translated into different languages. The following sections provide more detail on points from that topic that are relevant to Web applications.

Sorting and Comparing Strings

Sorting and string comparison you perform using the .NET Framework classes give the correct result based on the current culture. You need to worry about globalization issues only when implementing your own techniques for those tasks, such as when you are implementing custom sorting procedures. In those cases, use the *System.Globalization* namespace's *CompareInfo* class to perform culturally aware string comparisons.

Custom Validation Controls

ASP.NET server controls acquire specific properties based on the current culture. This includes the validation controls. You do need to consider globalization issues when creating custom validation controls, however.

For example, if you are writing a custom validation procedure that verifies that input is numeric, don't rely on the numeric value of the input characters. Instead, use a culturally aware test such as using the *Convert* class within an exception-handling structure to test whether the value is numeric.

Building Strings

Because some languages read from right to left, and because some words change meaning when in proximity to other words, it's difficult to build strings using concatenation in a way that works for all cultures. Instead, you store completed strings in a resource file and retrieve the strings as needed by using the Resource Manager.

Getting Substrings

In some languages, character symbols (called *glyphs*) are composed of two characters. In those cases, you might need to adjust how you get substrings. For example, getting the first character of a user's response would be meaningless in those cases.

Character Encoding

Characters within strings can be represented many different ways within a computer. These different ways of representing characters are called **character encodings** because they encode characters into numbers that the computer can understand.

The common language runtime (CLR) uses the UTF-16 character encoding, which maps characters to 16-bit numbers. These 16-bit numbers provide enough room to accommodate the characters for almost all written languages. Unfortunately, that's about double the size that other character encoding schemes use, which makes the UTF-16 character encoding less than optimal for transmitting text over the Internet.

Therefore, ASP.NET uses the UTF-8 character encoding by default when interpreting requests and composing responses. UTF-8 is optimized for the lower 127 ASCII characters, which means it provides an efficient way to encode languages that use the Latin alphabet. UTF-8 is also backward-compatible with the ASCII character encoding, meaning that UTF- 8 readers can interpret ASCII files.

The CLR handles the conversion between encodings by using classes from the *System.Text* namespace. You usually don't need to be aware that any of this is going on, with the following exceptions:

- If you go to save a Web form or an HTML file that includes extended characters from the UTF-8 encoding
- If you need to support specific encodings other than UTF-8

Saving Encoded Files

When you create a Web form that contains characters other than the first 127 ASCII characters, Visual Studio .NET prompts you to save the file using encoding, as shown in Figure 15-9.

Figure 15-9   Saving files with character encoding

To save a file with encodings, follow these steps:

1. From the File menu, choose Save As, click the Save drop-down arrow, and then select Save With Encoding. Visual Studio .NET displays the Advanced Save Options dialog box, as shown in Figure 15-10.

Figure 15-10   Specifying encoding while saving a file

2. Choose the encoding you want use for saving the file. Click OK.

Saving the file using the UTF-8 character encoding with signature allows ASP.NET to automatically detect the encoding of the file. If you don't choose to include the signature, or if you use another encoding, you must specify the *fileEncoding* attribute in the Web.config file, as shown here:

```
<globalization requestEncoding="utf-8" responseEncoding="utf-8"
  fileEncoding="utf-8" />
```

Using Other Encodings

By default, Web applications interpret requests and compose responses using the UTF-8 character encoding. These defaults are set in the *globalization* element of the Web.config file, as shown in the preceding section.

If a Web application receives a request for an encoding other than UTF-8, ASP.NET interprets that request using the request's encoding. However, ASP.NET does not automatically generate the response in that encoding.

To detect when a request has a specific encoding, get the *Request* object's *ContentEncoding* property. For example, the following code displays the encoding of a request on a Web form:

Visual Basic .NET

```
Response.Write(Request.ContentEncoding.WebName)
```

Visual C#

```
Response.Write(Request.ContentEncoding.WebName);
```

To specify a specific encoding for a response, set the *Response* object's *ContentEncoding* property using the *System.Text* namespace's *Encoding* class, or use the value returned from the *Request* object's *ContentEncoding* property. For example, the following code creates a response using the *shift_JIS* character encoding:

Visual Basic .NET

```
Imports System.Text
Private Sub Page_Load(ByVal sender As System.Object, _
    ByVal e As System.EventArgs) Handles MyBase.Load
    Response.ContentEncoding = Encoding.GetEncoding("shift_JIS")
    Response.Write("This response uses the character encoding: ")
    Response.Write(Response.ContentEncoding.WebName)
End Sub
```

Visual C#

```
using System.Text;
private void Page_Load(object sender, System.EventArgs e)
{
    Response.ContentEncoding = Encoding.GetEncoding("shift_JIS");
    Response.Write("This response uses the character encoding: ");
    Response.Write(Response.ContentEncoding.WebName);
}
```

For more information about character encoding, see the following online Help topics:

- "Unicode in the .NET Framework"
- "Encoding Base Types"
- "System.Text Namespace"

You can also find information about character encoding on the following Web sites:

- *http://www.unicode.org*
- *http://www.w3.org/TR/REC-html40/charset.html*

Summary

- Use the *Request* object's *UserLanguages* array to detect the user's culture.
- Set the *culture* and *uiCulture* attributes of the *globalization* element in Web.config to create culture-specific Web applications.
- The .NET Framework identifies cultures using the language and region codes listed in the "*CultureInfo* Class" online Help topic.
- Set the culture used by the application for formatting dates, currencies, numbers, and determining sort order using the *Thread* class's *CurrentCulture* property.
- Use the *Thread* class's *CurrentUICulture* to determine which satellite assembly is used to load localized resources.
- Add *id* and *runat* attributes to HTML elements to be able to display localized strings from resource files in those elements at run time.
- Elements within a resource file are case sensitive and must be uniquely named within the scope of the application, so use a naming convention such as *web-form.id*.
- When creating Web forms that use non-ASCII characters, save the file using the UTF-8 character encoding with a signature. Including the signature allows ASP.NET to automatically detect the file's encoding.

Lab: Creating a Currency Converter

In this lab, you'll create a simple currency converter Web application that uses the user's culture to determine the type of conversion to perform:

- An unrecognized culture converts euros to dollars and pesos, and displays text in English as the fallback interface.
- An English-US culture converts dollars to euros and pesos and displays an English-language interface.
- A Spanish-Mexican culture converts pesos to dollars and euros and displays a Spanish-language interface.

When complete, the Web application will appear as shown in Figure 15-11.

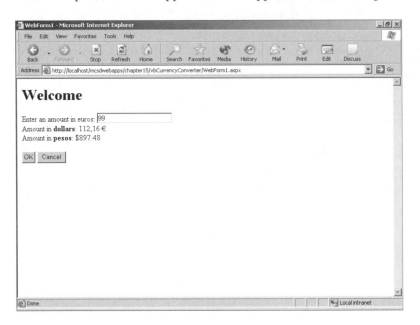

Figure 15-11   Currency converter (fallback interface)

Estimated lesson time: 20 minutes

Exercise 1: Create the Currency Converter Web Form

The currency converter Web application contains a single Web form that receives input from a text box and displays output in two labels when the user clicks OK. The Web form also includes a Cancel HTML button that clears the text box.

Because the application will be localized, the HTML elements on the Web form must have *id* and *runat* attributes so that the localized resource strings can be loaded into those controls from server-side code.

▶ **To create the Currency Converter Web form**

1. Create a new Web form named **Converter**.
2. Switch to HTML view, and enter the following HTML between the *<form>* and *</form>* tags of the Web form:

```
<h1 id="head1" runat="server">Head1</h1>
<span id="sp1" runat="server">Enter an amount: </span>
<asp:TextBox ID="txtCurrency" Runat="server" />
<br>
<span id="sp2" runat="server">Amount in: </span>
<asp:Label ID="lblCurrency1" Runat="server" />
<br>
<span id="sp3" runat="server">Amount in: </span>
<asp:Label ID="lblCurrency2" Runat="server" />
<br><br>
<asp:Button ID="butOK" Text="OK" Runat="server" />
<input id="butCancel" runat="server" type="button"
  onclick="txtCurrency.Text=''" value="Cancel">
```

3. When you have finished, switch the Web form back to Design view. This is an important step because it generates the correct control declarations in the code file.

Exercise 2: Create the User-Interface Resource Files

The Web form created in the preceding exercise contains only dummy entries for the text that will actually be displayed in the user interface. For instance, the Web form's heading is "Head1." In this exercise, you'll create the strings that are displayed in place of those dummy entries at run time.

▶ **To create the user-interface resource files**

1. From the Project menu, choose Add New Item, and then select Assembly Resource File from the list of templates. Name the resource file **strings.resx**.
2. Add the entries shown in Figure 15-12 to the resource file to create the fallback values for the user interface.

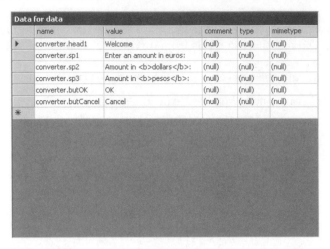

Figure 15-12   Fallback values for the user interface

3. Create a new resource file named **strings.en-US.resx**, and add the entries shown in Figure 15-13 to create the interface for users with the English-US culture:

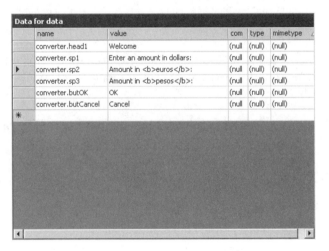

Figure 15-13   English-US culture values

4. Create another new resource file named **strings.es-MX.resx**, and add the entries shown in Figure 15-14 for the Spanish-Mexican culture:

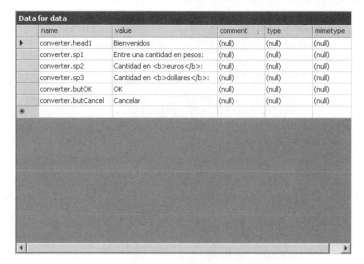

name	value	comment	type	mimetype
converter.head1	Bienvenidos	(null)	(null)	(null)
converter.sp1	Entre una cantidad en pesos:	(null)	(null)	(null)
converter.sp2	Cantidad en euros:	(null)	(null)	(null)
converter.sp3	Cantidad en dollares:	(null)	(null)	(null)
converter.butOK	OK	(null)	(null)	(null)
converter.butCancel	Cancelar	(null)	(null)	(null)

Figure 15-14   Spanish-Mexican culture values

5. When you have finished, click Save All to save your work.

You can create additional resource files for other cultures if you want. Just include the culture code in the resource file name, as shown in the preceding steps. Visual Studio .NET will automatically compile the resources as satellite assemblies and store them in the appropriate subfolder when you build the application.

Exercise 3: Load Resources Based on User Culture

In this exercise, you'll detect the user's culture, load resources, and display the resources matching the user's culture.

▶   **To load resources based on the user's culture**

1. Add the following *Imports* or *using* statements to the beginning of the Web form's code file:

Visual Basic .NET

```
Imports System.Resources
Imports System.Globalization
Imports System.Threading
```

Visual C#

```
using System.Resources;
using System.Globalization;
using System.Threading;
```

2. Add the following code at the class level of the Web form to load the resources into the *ResourceManager* object. Replace the projectName placeholder in the following code with the name of your application's root namespace.

Visual Basic .NET

```
Protected gStrings As New ResourceManager("projectName.strings", _
    GetType(Converter).Assembly)
```

Visual C#

```
protected ResourceManager gStrings = new
    ResourceManager("projectName.strings", typeof(Converter).Assembly);
```

3. Add the following code to the *Page_Load* event procedure to detect the user's culture, set the application thread's user interface culture to match, and display the localized resource strings in the user interface:

Visual Basic .NET

```
Private Sub Page_Load(ByVal sender As System.Object, _
    ByVal e As System.EventArgs) Handles MyBase.Load
    If Not IsPostBack Then
        ' Get the user's preferred language.
        Dim sLang As String = Request.UserLanguages(0)
        ' Set the thread's UICulture to load resources.
        Thread.CurrentThread.CurrentUICulture = New CultureInfo(sLang)
        ' Set the thread's culture for date/string/currency formats.
        Thread.CurrentThread.CurrentCulture = _
            CultureInfo.CreateSpecificCulture(sLang)
        ' Get strings from resource file.
        head1.InnerHtml = gStrings.GetString("converter.head1")
        sp1.InnerHtml = gStrings.GetString("converter.sp1")
        sp2.InnerHtml = gStrings.GetString("converter.sp2")
        sp3.InnerHtml = gStrings.GetString("converter.sp3")
        butOK.Text = gStrings.GetString("converter.butOK")
        butCancel.Value = gStrings.GetString("converter.butCancel")
    End If
End Sub
```

Visual C#

```
private void Page_Load(object sender, System.EventArgs e)
{
    if (!IsPostBack)
    {
        // Get the user's preferred language.
        string sLang = Request.UserLanguages[0];
        // Set the thread's UICulture to load resources
        //from satellite assembly.
        Thread.CurrentThread.CurrentUICulture = new CultureInfo(sLang);
        // Set the thread's culture for date/string/currency formats.
```

```
Thread.CurrentThread.CurrentCulture =
    CultureInfo.CreateSpecificCulture(sLang);
// Get strings from resource file.
head1.InnerHtml = gStrings.GetString("converter.head1");
sp1.InnerHtml = gStrings.GetString("converter.sp1");
sp2.InnerHtml = gStrings.GetString("v.sp2");
sp3.InnerHtml = gStrings.GetString("v.sp3");
butOK.Text = gStrings.GetString("v.butOK");
butCancel.Value = gStrings.GetString("v.butCancel");
    }
}
```

You have to load the localized user-interface strings only the first time the page is displayed, as shown in the preceding code. ASP.NET retains the value of the controls between page displays automatically.

Exercise 4: Perform Culture-Dependent Conversion

Just as the currency converter application displays a different interface for different cultures, it also performs different conversions based on the current culture. In this exercise, you'll write the code that performs the culture-dependent conversions.

▶ **To perform the culture-dependent conversions**

Add the following code to the *butOK_Click* event procedure to detect the current culture and perform different conversions based on that information:

Visual Basic .NET

```
Private Sub butOK_Click(ByVal sender As System.Object, _
    ByVal e As System.EventArgs) Handles butOK.Click
    ' Get the amount.
    Dim SrcAmount As Double = Convert.ToDouble(txtCurrency.Text)
    Dim DestAmount As Double
    ' Culture variables for currency formatting.
    Dim Europe As New CultureInfo("fr-FR")
    Dim USA As New CultureInfo("en-US")
    Dim Mexico As New CultureInfo("es-MX")
    ' Perform conversions based on current user-interface culture.
    Select Case Thread.CurrentThread.CurrentCulture.Name
        Case "en-US"
            ' Convert from dollars.
            DestAmount = SrcAmount * 1.1329
            lblCurrency1.Text = DestAmount.ToString("C", Europe)
            DestAmount = SrcAmount * 9.0655
            lblCurrency2.Text = DestAmount.ToString("C", Mexico)
        Case "es-MX"
            ' Convert from pesos.
            DestAmount = SrcAmount * 0.125
            lblCurrency1.Text = DestAmount.ToString("C", Europe)
```

(continued)

```
            DestAmount = SrcAmount * 0.1103
            lblCurrency2.Text = DestAmount.ToString("C", USA)
        Case Else
            ' Convert from euros.
            DestAmount = SrcAmount * 8.0021
            lblCurrency1.Text = DestAmount.ToString("C", USA)
            DestAmount = SrcAmount * 0.1103
            lblCurrency2.Text = DestAmount.ToString("C", Mexico)
    End Select
End Sub
```

Visual C#

```csharp
private void butOK_Click(object sender, System.EventArgs e)
{
    // Get the amount.
    double SrcAmount = Convert.ToDouble(txtCurrency.Text);
    double DestAmount;
    // Culture variables for currency formatting.
    CultureInfo Europe = new CultureInfo("fr-FR");
    CultureInfo USA = new CultureInfo("en-US");
    CultureInfo Mexico = new CultureInfo("es-MX");
    // Perform conversions based on current user-interface culture.
    switch (Thread.CurrentThread.CurrentCulture.Name)
    {
        case "en-US":
            // Convert from dollars.
            DestAmount = SrcAmount * 1.1329;
            lblCurrency1.Text = DestAmount.ToString("C", Europe);
            DestAmount = SrcAmount * 9.0655;
            lblCurrency2.Text = DestAmount.ToString("C", Mexico);
            break;
        case "es-MX":
            // Convert from pesos.
            DestAmount = SrcAmount * 0.125;
            lblCurrency1.Text = DestAmount.ToString("C", Europe);
            DestAmount = SrcAmount * 0.1103;
            lblCurrency2.Text = DestAmount.ToString("C", USA);
            break;
        default:
            // Convert from euros.
            DestAmount = SrcAmount * 8.0021;
            lblCurrency1.Text = DestAmount.ToString("C", USA);
            DestAmount = SrcAmount * 0.1103;
            lblCurrency2.Text = DestAmount.ToString("C", Mexico);
            break;
    }
}
```

The preceding code creates *CultureInfo* objects (Europe, United States, and Mexico) for each cultural conversion. These objects provide the appropriate currency formatting in the *ToString* methods. The *Europe* object uses the culture code for France, because France uses the euro as currency. There isn't a culture code for the European Union.

The preceding example also hard-codes the exchange rates into the procedure. You wouldn't do that in a real-world situation, of course. Getting current exchange rates is an appropriate task for Web Services. See Chapter 7, "Advanced Web Forms Programming," for a lesson on how to use XML Web Services.

Review

The following questions are intended to reinforce key information presented in this chapter. If you are unable to answer a question, review the appropriate lesson and then try the question again. Answers to the questions can be found in the appendix.

1. What is the difference between the *CurrentCulture* property and the *Current-UICulture* property?

2. How do you detect the user's culture?

3. What is a neutral culture?

4. How does character encoding affect file formats?

A P P E N D I X   A

Questions and Answers

Chapter 1: Introduction to Web Programming

Page 49

1. Give two examples of how an ASP.NET Web application is different from a traditional Windows application.

   Web applications and traditional Windows applications have the following differences:

Feature	ASP.NET Web application	Unmanaged Windows application
Architecture	Client/server	Local user
Execution	Runs under common language runtime using managed code	Runs under Windows using unmanaged code

2. What are the two main parts of the .NET Framework?

   The common language runtime (CLR).

   The .NET Framework class library.

3. How do you restore the default window settings in Visual Studio .NET?

   From the Tools menu, choose Options, and then click Reset Window Layout.

4. Why doesn't the Visual Studio .NET Code Editor automatically complete the following partial line of code (Visual C# users only)?

   ```
   int intX = system.math
   ```

   The namespace *System.Math* must be capitalized in Visual C# for IntelliSense to recognize the namespace.

5. When can't you use ASP.NET to create a Web application?

   When you are developing for non–Microsoft Windows Web servers, such as Linux/Apache.

Chapter 2: Creating Web Forms Applications

Page 87

1. Explain where Visual Studio .NET stores Web application projects.

   Web application projects are stored in a new virtual folder for each project. The properties of that virtual folder determine where the files are physically stored. These properties can be viewed in IIS.

2. List the four major differences between Web and Windows applications.

   - **Web forms cannot use the standard Windows controls. Instead, they use server controls, HTML controls, user controls, or custom controls created specially for Web forms.**

   - **Web applications are displayed in a browser. Windows applications display their own windows and have more control over how those windows are displayed.**

   - **Web forms are instantiated on the server, sent to the browser, and destroyed immediately. Windows forms are instantiated, exist for as long as needed, and are destroyed.**

   - **Web applications run on a server and are displayed remotely on clients. Windows applications run on the same machine they are displayed on.**

3. Describe the life cycle of a Web application: When are Web forms instantiated and how long do they exist?

   A Web application starts with the first request for a resource within the application's boundaries. Web forms are instantiated when they are requested. They are processed by the server and are abandoned immediately after the server sends its response to the client. A Web application ends after all client sessions end.

4. How do you preserve persistent data, such as simple variables, in a Web application?

   You can preserve data in state variables, such as ApplicationState, SessionState, or ViewState.

5. What determines the boundaries of a Web application?

   IIS determines Web application boundaries by the structure of the application's virtual folders. A Web application boundary starts in the folder containing the start page of the application, and it ends at the last subordinate folder or when it encounters another start page in a subordinate folder.

Chapter 3: Working with Web Objects

Page 151

1. How does the .NET Framework organize its classes?

   The .NET Framework uses namespaces to organize its classes.

2. In Visual Basic .NET, what is the difference between a class module and a code module?

   Class modules are instantiated at run time to create objects that provide separate storage for variables and properties in each instance. Code modules do not have instances, so any module-level variables they use are shared among calls to the module's procedures.

3. In Visual C#, how do you declare a method to make it available without having to first instantiate an object from the class?

   To create a method that can be called without instantiating an object, declare that method as *static*.

4. How do you call a member of a base class from within a derived class?

   To refer to a member of a base class in Visual Basic .NET, use the *MyBase* **keyword. To refer to a member of a base class in Visual C#, use the base keyword.**

5. Where would you save the following data items so that they persist between requests to a Web form?

   - A control created at run time
   - An object that provides services to all users
   - User preferences

   Save controls created at run time in the Page object's *ViewState*.

   Save objects that provide services to all users in the *Application* **state.**

   Save user preferences in *SessionState*.

Chapter 4: Creating a User Interface

Page 223

1. What is the main difference between the Button server control and the Button HTML control?

   When clicked, the Button server control triggers an ASP.NET *Click* **event procedure on the server. The Button HTML control triggers the event procedure indicated in the button's** *onclick* **attribute, which runs on the client.**

2. How do you get several RadioButton controls to interoperate on a Web form so that only one of the RadioButton controls can have a value of *True/true* at any given time?

   Set the *GroupName* **property of each RadioButton to the same name.**

3. Why does ASP.NET perform validation on both the client and the server?

Client-side validation helps avoid round-trips to the server. Validating on the client ensures that the data is valid before it is submitted, in most cases. However, because validation might be turned off (or maliciously hacked) on the client, data must be revalidated on the server side. This provides full assurance that the data is valid while avoiding as many round-trips as possible.

4. What types of validation would you use to verify that a user entered a valid customer number?

You would use a RequiredFieldValidator and a RegularExpressionValidator. If you have access to a list of expected customer numbers, you could replace the RegularExpressionValidator with a CustomValidator that checked the list.

5. What is wrong with the following line of code?

Visual Basic .NET

```
Server.Transfer("Default.htm")
```

Visual C#

```
Server.Transfer("Default.htm");
```

You can't use the *Transfer* method with HTML pages. It works only with .aspx pages.

6. Why can't you open a new browser window from within server code?

Server code executes on the server, whereas the new window is created on the client. You need to use client-side code to do things that affect the client, such as upload files, display new windows, or navigate back in history.

Chapter 5: Storing and Retrieving Data with ADO.NET

Page 304

1. What steps would you follow and what objects would you use to quickly find the number of records in a database table?

There are two ways to accomplish this task:

- **Use a database connection and a command object to execute a SQL command that re-turns the number of rows in the table.**

- **Use a database connection and data adapter object to create a data set for the table, and then get the number rows in the data set.**

2. How do typed data sets differ from untyped data sets, and what are the advantages of typed data sets?

Typed data sets use explicit names and data types for their members, whereas untyped data sets use collections to refer to their members. The following examples show a typed reference vs. an untyped reference to a data item:

Visual Basic .NET

```
' Typed reference to the Contacts table's HomePhone column.
DataSet1.Contacts.HomePhoneColumn.Caption = "@Home"
' Untyped reference to the Contacts table's HomePhone column.
DataSet1.Tables("Contacts").Columns("HomePhone").Caption = "@Home"
```

Visual C#

```
// Typed reference to the Contacts table's HomePhone column.
DataSet1.Contacts.HomePhoneColumn.Caption = "@Home";
// Untyped reference to the Contacts table's HomePhone column.
DataSet1.Tables["Contacts"].Columns["HomePhone"].Caption = "@Home";
```

Typed data sets do error checking at design time. This error checking helps catch typos and type mismatch errors, which would be detected only at run time with untyped data sets.

3. How do you call a stored procedure?

Create a command object, set the object's *CommandText* property to the name of the stored procedure, and set the *CommandType* property to *StoredProcedure*. To execute the stored procedure, use the command object's *ExecuteNonQuery*, *ExcecuteScalar*, *ExecuteReader*, or *ExecuteIXmlReader* method. For example, the following code calls the Ten Most Expensive Products stored procedure on the Northwind Traders database:

Visual Basic .NET

```
' Create a command object to execute.
Dim cmdTopTen As New SqlCommand(connNWind)
' Set command text.
cmdTopTen.CommandText = "Ten Most Expensive Products"
' Set the command properties.
cmdTopTen.CommandType = CommandType.StoredProcedure
' Create a data reader object to get the results.
Dim drdTopTen As SqlDataReader
' Open the connection.
connNWind.Open()
' Excecute the stored procedure.
drdTopTen = cmdTopTen.ExecuteReader()
```

Visual C#

```
// Create a connection for NorthWind Trader's database.
SqlConnection connNWind = new SqlConnection("integrated security=SSPI;" +
  "data source=(local);initial catalog=Northwind");
// Create a command object to execute.
SqlCommand cmdTopTen = new SqlCommand(connNWind);
cmdTopTen.CommandText = "Ten Most Expensive Products";
// Set the command properties.
cmdTopTen.CommandType = CommandType.StoredProcedure;
// Create a data reader object to get the results.
```

```
SqlDataReader drdTopTen;
// Open the connection.
connNWind.Open();
// Excecute the stored procedure.
drdTopTen = cmdTopTen.ExecuteReader();
```

4. Explain the difference between handling transactions at the data set level and at the database level.

Data sets provide implicit transactions, because changes to the data set aren't made permanent in the database until you call the *Update* method. To handle transactions in a data set, process the *Update* method and check for errors. If errors occur during an update, none of the changes from the data set is made in the database. You can try to correct the error and resubmit the update, or you can roll back the changes to the data set using the *RejectChanges* method.

Databases provide explicit transactions through the *Transaction* object. You create a *Transaction* object from a database connection and then assign that *Transaction* object to the commands you want to include in the transaction through the command object's *Transaction* property. As you perform the commands on the database, you check for errors. If errors occur, you can either try to correct them and resubmit the command, or you can restore the state of the database using the *Transaction* object's *RollBack* method. If no errors occur, you can make the changes permanent by calling the transaction object's *Commit* method.

Chapter 6: Catching and Correcting Errors

Page 338

1. Explain why exception handling is important to a completed application.

When an unhandled exception occurs in an application, the application stops—the user can't proceed, and any work he or she did immediately prior to the exception is lost. Exception handling provides a way to intercept and correct unusual occurrences that would otherwise cause these problems.

2. List two different exception-handling approaches in ASP.NET Web applications.

Exceptions can be handled in exception-handling blocks using the *Try*, *Catch*, and *Finally* keywords in Visual Basic .NET or the *try*, *catch*, and *finally* keywords in Visual C#. They can also be handled using Error event procedures at the Global, Application, or Page levels using the Server object's *GetLastError* and *ClearError* methods.

3. Describe the purpose of error pages and why they are needed.

Because Web applications run over the Internet, some exceptions occur outside the scope of the application. This means that your application can't respond directly to these exceptions. These types of exceptions are identified by HTTP response codes, which IIS can respond to by displaying custom error pages listed in your application's Web.config file.

4. Explain why tracing helps with exception handling.

Tracing allows you to record unusual events while your application is running, without users being aware of it. If an unanticipated exception occurs, your application can write a message to the trace log, which helps you diagnose problems during testing and after deployment.

Chapter 7: Advanced Web Forms Programming

Page 411

1. Write the HTML for a hyperlink that will send mail when the user clicks the link.

```
<a href="mailto:you@microsoft.com?SUBJECT=Sending from a client&BODY=Some
message text.">Send mail</a>
```

2. Write the code that creates a cookie containing the user name *Rob Young* and the current date to the user's computer. Set the cookie to remain on the user's computer for 30 days.

Visual Basic .NET

```
Dim cookUserInfo As New HttpCookie("UserInfo")
cookUserInfo("Name") = "Rob Young"
cookUserInfo("Time") = DateTime.Now.ToString()
cookUserInfo.Expires = DateTime.Now.AddDays(30)
Response.Cookies.Add(cookUserInfo)
```

Visual C#

```
HttpCookie cookUserInfo = new HttpCookie("UserInfo")
CookUserInfo["Name"] = "Rob Young"
CookUserInfo["Time"] = DateTime.Now.ToString()
cookUserInfo.Expires = DateTime.Now.AddDays(30)
Response.Cookies.Add(cookUserInfo)
```

3. What attribute do you use to hide a public .NET class from COM?

Use the *ComVisible* attribute to select which public .NET classes and members are visible to COM. This attribute applies hierarchically for the assembly, class, and member levels.

4. Why can't you open a new browser window using server-side code? How would you display a page in a new window with a client-side script?

Server-side code can execute tasks only on the server. To perform a task on the client's computer, such as opening a new browser window, the code needs to run on the client.

You can open a new window using the DOM *window* object. For example, the following HTML Button control opens a Help page in a new window:

```
<button id="butHelp"
onclick="window.open('help.aspx', 'help', 'height=200,width=300')">Help</
button>
```

5. How do you declare an unmanaged procedure within .NET?

Use the *DllImport* attribute or a Visual Basic .NET *Declare* statement to declare an unmanaged procedure for use with a .NET assembly. The *DllImport* attribute is found in the *System.Runtime.InteropServices* namespace.

Chapter 8: Maintaining Security

Page 472

1. Which ASP.NET authentication mode is best suited to identifying and authorizing users who belong to a corporate network?

Windows authentication is best suited to authenticating users of a corporate network because it uses the accounts and permissions that already exist for network users.

2. What is the difference between Windows and Forms authentication user lists in Web.config?

User lists for Windows authentication are included in the <authorization> element of Web.config.

User lists for Forms authentications are included in the <credentials> element of Web.config or as part of an external users database or file.

3. How do you require authentication using the Web.config file? (The answer is the same for all ASP.NET authentication modes.)

Include the following <authorization> element to require authentication:

```
<authorization>
   <deny users="?" />
</authorization>
```

4. How do you run a Web application using the permission set of an authenticated user?

Use the *identity* element in Web.config to execute code using the authenticated user's account. For example:

```
<!-- Impersonate the authenticated user -->
<identity impersonate="true" />
```

5. How does the Secure Sockets Layer (SSL) provide security in a Web application?

SSL protects data exchanged between a client and a Web application by encrypting the data before it is sent across the Internet.

6. How do you begin and end secure communication via SSL?

To begin secure communication, specify https in an address. For example:

```
<a href="https://www.contoso.com/secure.htm">Secure page.</a>
```

To end secure communication, specify http. For example:

```
<a href="http://www.contoso.com/Default.htm">Not secure.</a>
```

Chapter 9: Building and Deploying Web Applications

Page 524

1. What permissions do Web applications run under by default?

   By default, Web applications run as the ASPNET user, which has limited permissions equivalent to the Users group.

2. Why is the Machine.config file important to deployed Web applications?

   The Machine.config file controls many aspects of how Web applications run, including how processes are recycled, what types of request queue limits are imposed, and what interval is used when checking if users are still connected.

3. How do you configure a setup project to install an application over the Web?

   To configure a setup project to install an application over the Web, select the Web Bootstrapper option from the setup project's properties. This setting allows the Windows Installer to be downloaded and installed over the Web.

4. How do you distribute shared components as part of an installation program?

   Shared components should be included as a merge module within the setup project. Merge modules manage the installation of shared components so that they're not unnecessarily overwritten and so that they can be safely removed when no longer used. Unlike regular setup projects, merge modules can't be installed by themselves—they can be installed only as part of an application installation.

5. How does deploying to a Web farm or a Web garden affect *Session* state in a Web application?

   Web applications that are deploycd to a Web farm or a Web garden need to identify a *Session* state provider in their Web.config file. This is because a single client's requests can be directed to different processes over the course of his or her session. The *Session* state provider allows each different process to access the client's *Session* state.

Chapter 10: Testing Web Applications

Page 571

1. How do unit, integration, and regression testing relate to each other?

   Unit testing is the foundation that ensures that each piece of code works correctly. Integration testing extends this concept by verifying that pieces work together without errors. Regression tests are made up of the existing unit and integration tests, which are run on a regular schedule to assure that new code did not break previously working code.

2. Why is load testing likely to be more important for a Web application than for a stand-alone Windows application?

   Because Web applications can be public on the Internet, they can have hundreds, thousands, or even millions of users. Load tests let you simulate the expected demand to locate resource conflicts, performance bottlenecks, and other problems that aren't apparent in single-user tests.

3. What is the difference between the *Debug* and *Trace* classes?

   Under the default environment settings, code using the *Debug* class is stripped out of release builds, while code using the *Trace* class is left in. The classes are otherwise equivalent.

4. What are the two special steps you need to take to ensure that a COM component can use a component from a .NET assembly?

   To use a .NET component from a COM tool, such as VBScript, you must:

   - **Register the .NET assembly in the system registry using RegAsm.exe.**
   - **Make sure that the COM component can find the .NET assembly, either by placing the .NET assembly in the global assembly cache, by placing the two components in the same folder, or by following the other assembly-probing rules.**

Chapter 11: Creating Custom Web Controls

Page 633

1. Briefly describe the best uses for each of the three types of Web controls by completing the following sentences:

   - Create a Web user control when you want to…
   - Create a composite custom control when you want to…
   - Create a rendered custom control when you want to…

   Create a Web user control when you want to…

   …quickly create a group of controls that can be reused throughout a project to perform some logical unit of work.

   Create a composite custom control when you want to…

   …combine one or more existing controls into a compiled assembly that can be easily reused in many different projects.

   Create a rendered control when you want to…

   …build an entirely new control that can be compiled into an assembly for use in multiple projects.

2. How is deriving important to creating custom Web controls?

   Both composite and rendered custom controls are derived from the *Web-Control* base class. That class provides the methods that you override to create the appearance of the custom control.

3. What is the most important method to override when you're creating a composite custom control?

You override the *CreateChildControls* method to add existing controls to a composite custom control.

4. What is the most important method to override when you're creating a rendered control?

You override the *Render* method when creating a rendered custom control.

5. How is raising a post-back event in a composite control different from raising a post-back event in a rendered control?

In a composite control, you can use one of the contained controls to raise a post-back event. In a rendered control, you must implement the *IPostBackEventHandler* interface and write a client-side script to raise a post-back event.

Chapter 12: Optimizing Web Applications with Caching

Page 667

1. Write a directive to cache responses for a Web form for 30 seconds, storing different cache responses based on the value of the lstNames control.

```
<%@ OutputCache Duration="30" VaryByParam="lstNames" %>
```

2. A Web form uses fragment caching to store a frequently used user control. At run time, an *Object not found* error occurs whenever the page is refreshed. What is a likely cause of the error?

The most likely cause is that the user control is referenced in code after it has been cached. Once cached, a user control's properties and methods are no longer available.

3. How can you detect when application data is about to be removed from the cache?

Use the *onRemoveCallback* delegate.

4. Which ASP.NET performance counter is the best indicator of inefficient caching?

The Turnover Rate performance counter.

Chapter 13: Formatting Web Application Output

Page 706

1. What is the advantage of using CSS rather than in-line styles for formatting a Web application?

Using CSS allows you to maintain formatting separately from the content of your Web forms, so changes are easier to make and consistency is easier to maintain.

2. Why would you create a style for a class rather than for an HTML element?

You create *style* classes when you want to apply the same formatting to different types of elements within an application. For example, you might want to create an emphasis *style* class that applies the same formatting to any text, control, heading, or image that you want to draw the user's attention to.

3. How do CSS and XSL relate to each other when it comes to formatting a Web application?

CSS and XSL are complementary techniques for formatting. CSS determines the font, color, size, background, and other appearance aspects of HTML elements on a Web page. XSL is used to transform XML files into HTML output. In this way, XSL controls the position and appearance of items based on their content. Used together, XSL performs the high-level tasks of composition and layout while CSS performs the low-level tasks of applying fonts, colors, and other appearance features.

4. What are the differences between HTML and XML?

1.   HTML uses predefined element names, such as <p> and <br>. In XML, you create your own element names to identify hierarchical nodes of data.

2.   XML syntax is much stricter than HTML: elements must always have end-tags, element names are case sensitive, attribute values must always be enclosed in quotation marks, and nested elements must be terminated within their parent elements.

3.   XML identifies data conceptually based on the data's content, rather than based on the type of formatting to apply.

Chapter 14: Providing Help

Page 740

1. Which HTML attribute does the server control's *ToolTip* property map to in the HTML rendered by ASP.NET?

The *ToolTip* property is rendered as the title attribute at run time.

2. How does displaying HTML Help using the *window* object's *showHelp* method differ from displaying HTML Help using a browser window?

The *showHelp* method cannot open compiled HTML Help from a network address; the compiled file must first be downloaded to the user's machine.

You can display HTML Help from a network address within a browser window, provided you use the *ms-its:* protocol. However, the HTML Help Contents, Index, and Search features are not automatically available from a browser window.

3. How do you add index keywords to a Help topic?

   Insert an object element in the Help topic using the HTML Help ActiveX control. For example, the following object element adds the "numbers" index keyword:

```
<Object type="application/x-oleobject"
  classid="clsid:1e2a7bd0-dab9-11d0- b93a-00c04fc99f9e">
  <param name="Keyword" value="numbers">
</OBJECT>
```

Chapter 15: Globalizing Web Applications

Page 778

1. What is the difference between the *CurrentCulture* property and the *CurrentUICulture* property?

   The *CurrentCulture* property affects how the .NET Framework handles dates, currencies, sorting, and formatting issues. The *CurrentUICulture* property determines which satellite assembly is used when loading resources.

2. How do you detect the user's culture?

   Use the *Request* object's *UserLanguages* array. The value at element 0 corresponds to one of the culture codes used by the *CultureInfo* class. For example:

```
SLang = Request.UserLanguages(0)
```

3. What is a neutral culture?

   Neutral cultures represent general languages without region-specific differences, such as currency. For example, the "es" culture code represents Spanish.

4. How does character encoding affect file formats?

   When using non-ASCII characters in a Web form, you must save the file with a specific character encoding, such as UTF-8. ASP.NET can automatically detect UTF-8 file encoding if the file is saved with a signature; otherwise, you need to specify the file encoding used in the *fileEncoding* attribute of the *globalization* element in Web.config.

Glossary

A

abstract class A class that can't be instantiated but that is used as a base from which other classes can be derived. In Microsoft Visual Basic .NET, abstract classes are declared using the *MustInherit* keyword. In Microsoft Visual C#, abstract classes are declared using the *abstract* keyword.

abstract member A member of a base class that can't be invoked, but instead provides a template for members of a derived class. In Microsoft Visual Basic .NET, abstract members are declared using the *MustOverride* keyword. In Visual C#, abstract members are declared using the *abstract* keyword.

ad hoc testing Testing that relies on the uncoordinated efforts of developers or testers to ensure that code works. This type of testing contrasts with automated testing, which uses test scripts or programs to systematically check that all parts of an application work correctly.

addition The process of combining two or more things.

alias The name you use to identify resources on the Web. Aliases represent physical resources on the Web server, such as a Web form, an HTML page, or a graphic.

application domain The process space within which an ASP.NET Web Forms application runs.

ASP.NET The portion of the Microsoft .NET Framework used to create Web applications and XML Web services. ASP.NET is an evolution of Microsoft Active Server Pages (ASP).

assembly The executable component of an application created using the Microsoft .NET Framework. Web applications, as well as other types of .NET applications, compile their executable code into an assembly file with a .dll file extension. The compiled code consists of IL assembly language (ILAsm), which is then compiled into its final state at run time by the common language runtime (CLR).

authentication The process of determining the identity of a user. In effect, authentication validates that the user is who he or she claims to be.

authorization The process of granting access privileges to resources or tasks within an application. Applications typically authenticate users and then authorize them based on their identities or roles within an organization.

automated testing A type of testing that uses tests written in a scripting or programming language to systematically check that all parts of an application work as expected. Automated testing checks that an application's components work separately (called *unit testing*), that all components work together (called *integration testing*), and that changes haven't broken existing features (called *regression testing*).

B

base class A class that provides properties and methods as a foundation for a derived class. In object-oriented programming, one class can be based on another through inheritance. Using this technique, the base class provides characteristics (such as properties and methods) to a derived class. The derived class can reuse, modify, or add to the base class's members.

behaviors Components that encapsulate specific functionality or actions on a Web form or an HTML page. When applied to a standard HTML element on a page, a behavior modifies that element's default behavior. Behaviors are implemented as styles.

C

caching The technique of storing frequently used items in memory so that they can be accessed more quickly.

cascading   *See* cascading style sheets (CSS).

cascading style sheets (CSS)   Web application project files (.css) that collect and organize all of the formatting information applied to elements on a Web form or an HTML page. Because they keep this information in a single location, cascading style sheets make it easy to adjust the appearance of Web applications. Web applications can have multiple style sheets and can switch style sheets at run time to dynamically change the appearance of a Web application.

certificate authority   An independent third party that provides server certificates to enable secure communications across the Web through the Secure Sockets Layer (SSL). These server certificates must be purchased and installed on your Web server to use SSL and the HTTPS protocol.

character encoding   The method of representing alphanumeric characters as numbers so that a computer can handle strings.

class   A data structure that groups properties and methods used to perform tasks in programs. Classes are the fundamental building blocks of object-oriented programs. Objects are instances of classes.

context-sensitive Help   A type of Help system in which the topic displayed depends on the current context (or task) within the application.

cookie   A small file that a Web application can write to the client's computer. Cookies are used to identify a user in a future session or to store and retrieve information about the user's current session.

CSS   *See* cascading style sheets (CSS).

D

data binding   A way to link data (such as a data set) in your application to the properties of a control.

default page   A page that Internet Information Services (IIS) displays if the user navigates to the Web application directory without specifying a page to view. IIS uses the name Default.htm or Default.aspx as the default page unless you change it using the IIS property settings for the application.

delegation   A programming technique by which a member of one class uses a member from another class to perform some task. Delegation differs from inheritance in that the first class implements a property or method and then calls (or *delegates to*) the other class's property or method. The two classes do not have to be related to each other—in other words, the first class does not have to be derived from the second class.

delegates   Types used to invoke one or more methods in which the actual method invoked is determined at run time.

deploying   Installing an application on the computer where it will run.

derived class   A class that is based on another class (called a *base class*) through inheritance. A derived class inherits the members of its base class and can override or shadow those members.

DHTML behaviors   *See* behaviors.

dirty read   The process of reading database records without locking the records being read. This means that an uncommitted change can be read and then rolled back by another client, resulting in a local copy of a record that is not consistent with what is stored in the database.

drivers   In the context of testing, drivers are test components that make sure two or more components work together. Drivers are necessary to test components during development when an application is being developed from the bottom up.

E

error   *See* exceptions.

exception handling The process of dealing with unusual occurrences within code so that they do not cause the program to crash or lose data.

exception log A record of exceptions that occurred while an application was running.

exceptions Unusual occurrences that happen within the logic of an application.

F

fragment caching The technique of caching part of a Web form or placing controls or other response items in a user control.

frames Regions of a Web page that you can use to display other Web pages. You use frames to display multiple regions that scroll and behave independently.

G

GAC *See* global assembly cache (GAC).

global assembly cache (GAC) A special subfolder within the Microsoft Windows folder that stores the shared .NET assemblies. Assemblies stored in the GAC are shared with all other applications installed on the computer.

globalization The process of creating an application that meets the needs of users from multiple cultures.

globally unique identifier (GUID) A 128-bit integer that serves as a unique identifier across networks. GUIDs are used throughout Windows and the .NET Framework to identify components.

GUID *See* globally unique identifier (GUID).

I

image map A graphic containing multiple regions that the user can click to cause different actions to occur.

impersonation The process of assigning one user identity to another user. ASP.NET uses impersonation to authorize anonymous users to access resources on the Web server. By default, anonymous users impersonate the ASPNET user account.

inheritance The process of basing one class on another. In this process, a base class provides class members to a derived class. The advantage of inheritance is that you can write and maintain code once in the base class and reuse it multiple times in the derived classes.

interfaces In the context of object-oriented programming, an interface is a contract that defines the members that a group of classes provides. Once you implement a particular interface in a class, instances of that class can be used for any argument or variable declared as that interface.

L

localization The process of accommodating cultural differences within an application. Localized applications can support multiple languages, currencies, writing direction, and calendars based on the cultures that they support.

M

managed code Code that runs under the common language runtime (CLR). The CLR takes care of many tasks that would have formerly been handled in the application's executable. Managed code solves the Windows programming problems of component registration and versioning (sometimes called DLL hell) because managed code contains all the versioning and type information that the CLR needs to run the application. The CLR handles registration dynamically at run time, rather than statically through the system registry, as is done with applications based on the Component Object Model (COM).

marshaling The process by which the CLR collects parameters and converts their types whenever a .NET assembly calls an unmanaged procedure.

merge modules Deployment projects for shared components that allow a server to manage the installation of those components so that they're not unnecessarily overwritten and so that they can be safely removed when no longer used.

multiple inheritance The programming technique of deriving a class from two or more base classes. Visual Basic .NET and Visual C# do not support multiple inheritance.

N

namespace collisions The problem that occurs when two items use the same name at a single level of the namespace hierarchy.

neutral cultures Cultures that map to a specific language but not to a specific region.

nodes *See* XML nodes.

O

One-Click Hosting A feature ASP.NET Web service providers offer that allows developers to upload completed Web applications directly from the Microsoft Visual Studio .NET Start Page's Web Hosting pane.

optimization Writing code in a way that executes more quickly or consumes fewer resources.

overloading In the context of object-oriented programming, the programming technique of providing versions of a method that takes different types of arguments. The *ToString* method is a good example of an overloaded method.

overriding In the context of object-oriented programming, the programming technique of replacing a member inherited from a base class with a different member in the derived class.

P

platform invoke (pinvoke) The process of executing native code from within a .NET assembly.

process recycling The technique of shutting down and restarting an ASP.NET worker process (aspnet_wp.exe) that has become inactive or is consuming excessive resources.

project The collection of Visual Studio .NET source files that make up an application.

R

regression A problem in which a new or modified component breaks some previously working component. Regression is uncovered during testing.

reproducibility The ability to produce the same result again and again.

S

satellite assembly An assembly file (.dll) that contains localized resources for an application. Each satellite assembly file contains the resources for one culture. An application can have many satellite assemblies, depending on how many cultures the application supports.

save point A point within a database transaction from which you can restore the database state.

scalability The ability to add capacity to an application as user demand increases.

Secure Sockets Layer (SSL) The standard means of ensuring that data sent over the Internet can't be read by others. When a user requests a secure Web page, the server generates an encryption key for the user's session and then encrypts the page's data before sending a response. On the client side, the browser uses that same encryption key to decrypt the requested Web page and to encrypt new requests sent from that page.

SEH *See* structured exception handling (SEH).

server certificate A file installed through IIS that provides an encryption key for use with the Secure Sockets Layer (SSL). Server certificates are obtained from a certificate authority, which licenses server certificates for a fee and acts as a clearinghouse to verify your server's identity over the Internet.

server controls Visual components used on a Web form to create the user interface of a Web application.

session The sum of interaction between an instance of a client browser and a Web application. A session begins when the browser first requests a resource from within the application. A session ends either when the browser closes on the client's machine or when the session times out after a period of inactivity. (The default is 20 minutes.)

shadowing The programming technique of replacing a member of a basc class with a new member in a derived class. Shadowing differs from overriding in that the base class's shadowed member is no longer available from the derived class.

shared members Methods that can be called directly without first creating an instance of a class. These members are called *static* members in Visual C#.

signature The name, parameter list, parameter types, and return type of a member.

solution A group of Visual Studio .NET projects that make up a single functional unit.

SSL *See* Secure Sockets Layer (SSL).

Start Page The first Web form displayed when you run a Web application project from within Visual Studio .NET. The Start Page is also the first page the Visual Studio .NET development environment displays in the Document window. This Visual Studio .NET Start Page contains various panes to help simplify some common tasks, such as opening a recent file and making information easier to find.

start-up project The first project Visual Studio .NET starts when you run a multiple-project solution. The start-up project is shown in boldface within the Solution Explorer window.

static members Methods that you can call directly without first creating an instance of a class. These members are called *shared* members in Visual Basic .NET.

step in Moving from a calling procedure to a called procedure during debugging. Also used in reference to setting breakpoints to stop execution in a specific procedure during debugging.

step over Executing a procedure call as a single statement during debugging.

structured exception handling (SEH) The programming technique of using exception-handling blocks or exception events to handle unusual occurrences in an application.

stubs Nonfunctional components that provide the class, property, or method definition used by another component during testing. Stubs are necessary to test components during development when an application is being developed from the top down.

subweb A virtual folder that contains a Web site.

superclassing The programming technique of deriving a new class from an existing class using inheritance. Superclassing generally refers to a situation in which most of the derived class's behavior and members come directly from the base class.

T

template *See* XSL template.

testing interface A set of public properties and methods that you can use to control a component from an external testing program.

thread The basic unit to which the server allocates processor time. A single process can have multiple threads.

ToolTip A short, descriptive message that is displayed when a user places the mouse pointer over a control and leaves it there for a couple of seconds. These messages are used throughout Windows applications to provide helpful information about toolbar buttons and other graphical controls whose meaning might not otherwise be obvious.

tracing A programming technique for recording events, such as exceptions, in an application. Tracing is used during debugging and in the testing phase of application deployment.

transaction A group of commands (treated as a single unit) that change the data stored in a database. The transaction ensures that the commands are handled in an all-or-nothing fashion—if one of the commands fails, all of the commands fail, and any data that was written to the database by the commands is backed out. In this way, transactions maintain the integrity of data in a database.

tuning The process of making adjustments to a deployed application that don't affect code.

U

unhandled exceptions Exceptions that have not been dealt with in code. Unhandled exceptions cause applications to stop executing and appear to the user as errors in the application.

unmanaged code Code in which the executable itself determines how memory is used. Unmanaged code contrasts with managed code, where memory is allocated and recovered by the CLR.

user control page A Web application project file with the .ascx file extension that combines one or more server controls into a single, visual component that can be used on Web forms.

V

view state The current property settings of server controls on a Web form. By default, ASP.NET automatically maintains view state between postback events.

virtual folder A shared resource identified by an alias that represents a physical location on a server.

W

Web farm A Web application running on multiple servers.

Web form The central user-interface component within a Web application.

Web garden A Web application running on a single server using multiple processors.

wiring an event The process of creating a connection between an object's event and the event procedure that responds to the event.

X

XML nodes Uniquely named elements within an XML file. XML nodes are organized hierarchically with parent-child relationships.

XML schema A description of the data elements contained in the XML file. The XML schema provides the names of the elements, their types, whether they are key fields, and other information.

XSL template An element within an XSL file that provides the information used to format an XML node during an XSL transformation.

Index

Symbols

A

C

Cantilever Clamp

Stronger than human hands, clamps are mechanical hands that can hold practically anything. The **cantilever clamp** features a wide jaw opening, and it floating jaws can grip parallel to the work piece. The cantilever design eliminates twisting and minimizes deflection of the clamped parts. Cantilever clamps often come with hard pads that can rotate to grip flat or serrated surfaces, or soft pads that are ideal for delicate or rounded surfaces.

At Microsoft Press, we use tools to illustrate our books for software developers and IT professionals. Tools very simply and powerfully symbolize human inventiveness. They're a metaphor for people extending their capabilities, precision, and reach. From simple calipers and pliers to digital micrometers and lasers, these stylized illustrations give each book a visual identity, and a personality to the series. With tools and knowledge, there's no limit to creativity and innovation. Our tagline says it all: *the tools you need to put technology to work*.

MICROSOFT LICENSE AGREEMENT
Book Companion CD

IMPORTANT—READ CAREFULLY: This Microsoft End-User License Agreement ("EULA") is a legal agreement between you (either an individual or an entity) and Microsoft Corporation for the Microsoft product identified above, which includes computer software and may include associated media, printed materials, and "online" or electronic documentation ("SOFTWARE PRODUCT"). Any component included within the SOFTWARE PRODUCT that is accompanied by a separate End-User License Agreement shall be governed by such agreement and not the terms set forth below. By installing, copying, or otherwise using the SOFTWARE PRODUCT, you agree to be bound by the terms of this EULA. If you do not agree to the terms of this EULA, you are not authorized to install, copy, or otherwise use the SOFTWARE PRODUCT; you may, however, return the SOFTWARE PRODUCT, along with all printed materials and other items that form a part of the Microsoft product that includes the SOFTWARE PRODUCT, to the place you obtained them for a full refund.

SOFTWARE PRODUCT LICENSE

The SOFTWARE PRODUCT is protected by United States copyright laws and international copyright treaties, as well as other intellectual property laws and treaties. The SOFTWARE PRODUCT is licensed, not sold.

1. **GRANT OF LICENSE.** This EULA grants you the following rights:

   a. **Software Product.** You may install and use one copy of the SOFTWARE PRODUCT on a single computer. The primary user of the computer on which the SOFTWARE PRODUCT is installed may make a second copy for his or her exclusive use on a portable computer.

   b. **Storage/Network Use.** You may also store or install a copy of the SOFTWARE PRODUCT on a storage device, such as a network server, used only to install or run the SOFTWARE PRODUCT on your other computers over an internal network; however, you must acquire and dedicate a license for each separate computer on which the SOFTWARE PRODUCT is installed or run from the storage device. A license for the SOFTWARE PRODUCT may not be shared or used concurrently on different computers.

   c. **License Pak.** If you have acquired this EULA in a Microsoft License Pak, you may make the number of additional copies of the computer software portion of the SOFTWARE PRODUCT authorized on the printed copy of this EULA, and you may use each copy in the manner specified above. You are also entitled to make a corresponding number of secondary copies for portable computer use as specified above.

   d. **Sample Code.** Solely with respect to portions, if any, of the SOFTWARE PRODUCT that are identified within the SOFTWARE PRODUCT as sample code (the "SAMPLE CODE"):

      i. **Use and Modification.** Microsoft grants you the right to use and modify the source code version of the SAMPLE CODE, *provided* you comply with subsection (d)(iii) below. You may not distribute the SAMPLE CODE, or any modified version of the SAMPLE CODE, in source code form.

      ii. **Redistributable Files.** Provided you comply with subsection (d)(iii) below, Microsoft grants you a nonexclusive, royalty-free right to reproduce and distribute the object code version of the SAMPLE CODE and of any modified SAMPLE CODE, other than SAMPLE CODE, or any modified version thereof, designated as not redistributable in the Readme file that forms a part of the SOFTWARE PRODUCT (the "Non-Redistributable Sample Code"). All SAMPLE CODE other than the Non-Redistributable Sample Code is collectively referred to as the "REDISTRIBUTABLES."

      iii. **Redistribution Requirements.** If you redistribute the REDISTRIBUTABLES, you agree to: (i) distribute the REDISTRIBUTABLES in object code form only in conjunction with and as a part of your software application product; (ii) not use Microsoft's name, logo, or trademarks to market your software application product; (iii) include a valid copyright notice on your software application product; (iv) indemnify, hold harmless, and defend Microsoft from and against any claims or lawsuits, including attorney's fees, that arise or result from the use or distribution of your software application product; and (v) not permit further distribution of the REDISTRIBUTABLES by your end user. Contact Microsoft for the applicable royalties due and other licensing terms for all other uses and/or distribution of the REDISTRIBUTABLES.

2. **DESCRIPTION OF OTHER RIGHTS AND LIMITATIONS.**

   - **Limitations on Reverse Engineering, Decompilation, and Disassembly.** You may not reverse engineer, decompile, or disassemble the SOFTWARE PRODUCT, except and only to the extent that such activity is expressly permitted by applicable law notwithstanding this limitation.

   - **Separation of Components.** The SOFTWARE PRODUCT is licensed as a single product. Its component parts may not be separated for use on more than one computer.

   - **Rental.** You may not rent, lease, or lend the SOFTWARE PRODUCT.

- **Support Services.** Microsoft may, but is not obligated to, provide you with support services related to the SOFTWARE PRODUCT ("Support Services"). Use of Support Services is governed by the Microsoft policies and programs described in the user manual, in "online" documentation, and/or in other Microsoft-provided materials. Any supplemental software code provided to you as part of the Support Services shall be considered part of the SOFTWARE PRODUCT and subject to the terms and conditions of this EULA. With respect to technical information you provide to Microsoft as part of the Support Services, Microsoft may use such information for its business purposes, including for product support and development. Microsoft will not utilize such technical information in a form that personally identifies you.

- **Software Transfer.** You may permanently transfer all of your rights under this EULA, provided you retain no copies, you transfer all of the SOFTWARE PRODUCT (including all component parts, the media and printed materials, any upgrades, this EULA, and, if applicable, the Certificate of Authenticity), **and** the recipient agrees to the terms of this EULA.

- **Termination.** Without prejudice to any other rights, Microsoft may terminate this EULA if you fail to comply with the terms and conditions of this EULA. In such event, you must destroy all copies of the SOFTWARE PRODUCT and all of its component parts.

3. **COPYRIGHT.** All title and copyrights in and to the SOFTWARE PRODUCT (including but not limited to any images, photographs, animations, video, audio, music, text, SAMPLE CODE, REDISTRIBUTABLES, and "applets" incorporated into the SOFTWARE PRODUCT) and any copies of the SOFTWARE PRODUCT are owned by Microsoft or its suppliers. The SOFT-WARE PRODUCT is protected by copyright laws and international treaty provisions. Therefore, you must treat the SOFTWARE PRODUCT like any other copyrighted material **except** that you may install the SOFTWARE PRODUCT on a single computer provided you keep the original solely for backup or archival purposes. You may not copy the printed materials accompanying the SOFTWARE PRODUCT.

4. **U.S. GOVERNMENT RESTRICTED RIGHTS.** The SOFTWARE PRODUCT and documentation are provided with RESTRICTED RIGHTS. Use, duplication, or disclosure by the Government is subject to restrictions as set forth in subparagraph (c)(1)(ii) of the Rights in Technical Data and Computer Software clause at DFARS 252.227-7013 or subparagraphs (c)(1) and (2) of the Commercial Computer Software—Restricted Rights at 48 CFR 52.227-19, as applicable. Manufacturer is Microsoft Corporation/One Microsoft Way/Redmond, WA 98052-6399.

5. **EXPORT RESTRICTIONS.** You agree that you will not export or re-export the SOFTWARE PRODUCT, any part thereof, or any process or service that is the direct product of the SOFTWARE PRODUCT (the foregoing collectively referred to as the "Restricted Components"), to any country, person, entity, or end user subject to U.S. export restrictions. You specifically agree not to export or re-export any of the Restricted Components (i) to any country to which the U.S. has embargoed or restricted the export of goods or services, which currently include, but are not necessarily limited to, Cuba, Iran, Iraq, Libya, North Korea, Sudan, and Syria, or to any national of any such country, wherever located, who intends to transmit or transport the Restricted Components back to such country; (ii) to any end user who you know or have reason to know will utilize the Restricted Components in the design, development, or production of nuclear, chemical, or biological weapons; or (iii) to any end user who has been prohibited from participating in U.S. export transactions by any federal agency of the U.S. government. You warrant and represent that neither the BXA nor any other U.S. federal agency has suspended, revoked, or denied your export privileges.

DISCLAIMER OF WARRANTY

NO WARRANTIES OR CONDITIONS. MICROSOFT EXPRESSLY DISCLAIMS ANY WARRANTY OR CONDITION FOR THE SOFTWARE PRODUCT. THE SOFTWARE PRODUCT AND ANY RELATED DOCUMENTATION ARE PROVIDED "AS IS" WITHOUT WARRANTY OR CONDITION OF ANY KIND, EITHER EXPRESS OR IMPLIED, INCLUDING, WITHOUT LIMITA-TION, THE IMPLIED WARRANTIES OF MERCHANTABILITY, FITNESS FOR A PARTICULAR PURPOSE, OR NONINFRINGEMENT. THE ENTIRE RISK ARISING OUT OF USE OR PERFORMANCE OF THE SOFTWARE PRODUCT REMAINS WITH YOU.

LIMITATION OF LIABILITY. TO THE MAXIMUM EXTENT PERMITTED BY APPLICABLE LAW, IN NO EVENT SHALL MICROSOFT OR ITS SUPPLIERS BE LIABLE FOR ANY SPECIAL, INCIDENTAL, INDIRECT, OR CONSEQUENTIAL DAM-AGES WHATSOEVER (INCLUDING, WITHOUT LIMITATION, DAMAGES FOR LOSS OF BUSINESS PROFITS, BUSINESS INTERRUPTION, LOSS OF BUSINESS INFORMATION, OR ANY OTHER PECUNIARY LOSS) ARISING OUT OF THE USE OF OR INABILITY TO USE THE SOFTWARE PRODUCT OR THE PROVISION OF OR FAILURE TO PROVIDE SUPPORT SERVICES, EVEN IF MICROSOFT HAS BEEN ADVISED OF THE POSSIBILITY OF SUCH DAMAGES. IN ANY CASE, MICROSOFT'S ENTIRE LIABILITY UNDER ANY PROVISION OF THIS EULA SHALL BE LIMITED TO THE GREATER OF THE AMOUNT ACTUALLY PAID BY YOU FOR THE SOFTWARE PRODUCT OR US$5.00; PROVIDED, HOWEVER, IF YOU HAVE ENTERED INTO A MICROSOFT SUPPORT SERVICES AGREEMENT, MICROSOFT'S ENTIRE LIABILITY REGARDING SUPPORT SERVICES SHALL BE GOVERNED BY THE TERMS OF THAT AGREEMENT. BECAUSE SOME STATES AND JURISDICTIONS DO NOT ALLOW THE EXCLUSION OR LIMITATION OF LIABILITY, THE ABOVE LIMITATION MAY NOT APPLY TO YOU.

MISCELLANEOUS

This EULA is governed by the laws of the State of Washington USA, except and only to the extent that applicable law mandates governing law of a different jurisdiction.

Should you have any questions concerning this EULA, or if you desire to contact Microsoft for any reason, please contact the Microsoft subsidiary serving your country, or write: Microsoft Sales Information Center/One Microsoft Way/Redmond, WA 98052-6399.